D1569291

Four Years With
THE IRON BRIGADE

The Civil War Journals of William R. Ray,
Co. F., Seventh Wisconsin Infantry

Four Years With
THE IRON BRIGADE

The Civil War Journals of William R. Ray,
Co. F., Seventh Wisconsin Infantry

Edited by
Lance Herdegen & Sherry Murphy

Da Capo Press

Cataloging-in-Publication Data is available from the Library of Congress.
First Da Capo Press edition 2002

ISBN 0-306-81119-7

Published by Da Capo Press
A Member of the Perseus Books Group
http://www.dacapopress.com

Da Capo Press books are available at special discounts for bulk purchases in the U.S. by corporations, institutions, and other organizations. For more information, please contact the Special Markets Department at the Perseus Books Group, 11 Cambridge Center, Cambridge, MA 02142, or call (800) 255-1514 or (617) 252-5298.

1 2 3 4 5 6 7 8 9--06 05 04 03 02

*For Shirley, who still dances with such grace
to the drums of her grandmothers*

— Lance Herdegen

*For William R. Ray, who had no idea what a fascinating
legacy he provided future generations*

— Sherry Murphy

William R. Ray, circa 1864
Company F., Seventh Wisconsin Volunteer Infantry

Courtesy of Sherry Murphy

CONTENTS

continued . . .

CONTENTS (continued)

Maps

Photos and Illustrations

Foreword

I t is with great pleasure and excitement for me that, at long last, a book on the glorious Seventh Wisconsin Volunteers has been written. The Seventh Wisconsin, or "Huckleberries," were part of the famed Iron Brigade, an outfit consisting of volunteers from Wisconsin, Michigan, and Indiana. The brigade fought in virtually every major battle of the Army of the Potomac from the beginning of the war through Appomattox.

The enlisted men of the Seventh, like the officers who led them, were a proud and courageous group of individuals who hailed from nearly every walk of life. Their service ranged from the daily boredom and grind of camp life to the deadly and horrendous Civil War combat experience. Days were long and arduous, disease was rampant, and food and clothing often scarce. Yet, somehow these volunteers found the determination to stay the course through to the end of the war.

The story of William Ray epitomizes the life and trying times of the common soldier of the Seventh Wisconsin, and captures the essence of those who served.

Steve Victor
August 2000
Great-Great-Great Grandson of Colonel William Wallace Robinson,
and Great-Great Grandson of Colonel Hollon Richardson

Preface

These journals detail the day-to-day life of a Wisconsin Volunteer in the Civil War from his enlistment through the end of the war and return home. According to their author and Iron Brigade member William Royal Ray, the journals represent "small sketches and gatherings of the times & things that is transpiring around me." And there was a lot "transpiring" around him.

William Ray enlisted August 19, 1861, as a member of Company F, Seventh Wisconsin Volunteers. Although he had no way of knowing it then, his outfit would be brigaded with several other Western regiments and eventually earn the sobriquet "Iron Brigade." By the middle of the war the brigade was recognized as one of the finest in service. Unfortunately, its members were often called upon to perform heroic deeds, and the horrendous casualties that came as a result of their actions tore away the core of the brigade. Ray was one of the handful of men who served throughout the brigade's tenure. He was wounded three times: at Gainesville (or Brawner's Farm) on August 28, 1862, on the first day of Gettysburg in 1863, and again at the Wilderness on May 5, 1864. And yet he continued to return to his regiment and offer his efforts to put down the rebellion.

As is the case with many soldier journal and diaries, it took decades and luck to bring his story to light. Ray was my grandmother's foster mother's father. His daughter, Emma Charlotte Ray, married George Thomas Ellis. Although they wanted a daughter, their union produced four boys. My grandmother was Winnifred Mae Poston. Winnifred's mother died when she was about five years old, and the George Ellis family decided to take her in and raise her. For reasons that are still unclear, they never adopted

Winnifred. When her last foster brother, Clyde Ellis, died, Winnifred inherited his house and its contents. Ray's journals were found in the back of a closet, where they had been hidden away collecting dust for decades. They were given to me about 1984. According to my mother, other items belonging to Ray and relating to his Civil War experience were also found in the home, including his distinctive wartime black hat and a sword, but they were sold in a yard sale for a few dollars by the tenants who were renting the house at the time.

Ray's writings comprise nineteen journals of all different sizes and shapes. The first fourteen are entirely about his Civil War experiences (August 1861 through April 1865). The fifteenth details the end of the war, his mustering out, and return home. The balance comprise his observations about his life and experiences in Wisconsin and his move to Iowa and beyond. They end in November 1871.

I have attempted to transcribe the diaries faithfully in order to retain their unique color and perspective. Ray did not employ an abundance of punctuation and it was not always consistently applied. I have therefore added some for the sake of readability. Many people wrote phonetically in the middle of the nineteenth century, and Ray was no different. I have left his spelling intact.

Sherry Murphy
Foster Great-Great Granddaughter
Vancouver, WA, November 2000

* * *

I would like to thank my husband, Courtney, for his patience and encouragement during the ten-plus years it took to transcribe these journals; my mother, Florence Carpenter, for rescuing the diaries and giving them to me; my sister, Erni Stivison, for her assistance with the epilogue and research; and my children, Tracy Spencer, Holly Sullivan and Sean Murphy for their loving support.

S.M.

Introduction

William R. Ray, the Seventh Wisconsin,

and the Iron Brigade

Williiam R. Ray was caught up in the great sectional conflict between North and South from the very first days of the war. He left hearth and family in 1861 to help put down what he called the "Rebellion in this once Glorious Union." He traveled from his home at Cassville, Wisconsin, on the Mississippi River to nearby Lancaster, where he "signed the muster roll of the Union Guards." Within a few weeks, the "greenhorn patriots" (as one soldier called them in those days) were called to Camp Randall in Madison to become Company F of the Seventh Wisconsin Volunteer Infantry. The company clerks recorded of Ray that he was a blacksmith, 5-foot-9, unmarried, with hazel eyes and light hair. He was just 23.

It was on September 19, 1861, two days before his regiment left Wisconsin for the war front, that Ray began a journal to "keep account of everything that transpires" in his life as a soldier. "If lost and found by any person," he wrote on its first page, "make known or bring to Capt Callis Company 7th Regt Wis Volunteers and oblige friend." For the next four years he carefully and extensively recorded his experiences. It was fortunate that he did so. His regiment soon became part of the "Iron Brigade of the West," one of the most celebrated military organizations of the American Civil War, equaled in reputation—but not in service—only by the Stonewall Brigade of the Confederate Army of Northern Virginia.

Composed originally of the Second, Sixth, and Seventh Wisconsin, Nineteenth Indiana, and Battery B of the Fourth U.S. Artillery, the brigade was organized October 1, 1861, at Washington. It was attached to the city defenses. The organization first attracted attention those days because it was the only Western organization in the Eastern armies and because the men were issued the regular army's Model 1858 black felt dress hat. But despite all the drill, training, and soldierly bearing, the men of the "Black Hat Brigade" were left behind in 1862 when the Army of the Potomac moved on Richmond from the east up the Virginia peninsula. They spent May, June, and July in a reserve position at Fredericksburg, Virginia.

In August 1862, the four regiments were assigned to the new Army of Virginia and sent in pursuit of the forces of Confederate General Thomas "Stonewall" Jackson. In a three week period beginning late on the afternoon of August 28, 1862, the Westerners fought in four of the bloodiest battles of the Civil War—Gainesville (Brawner's Farm), Second Bull Run, South Mountain, and Antietam. After those weeks, the tough Westerners were forever known as "the Iron Brigade of the West." General George B. McClellan said he gave them the fighting name after watching the brigade fight its way up the National Road at South Mountain.

In October 1862, much reduced by hard fighting, the brigade was reenforced by another Western regiment—the Twenty-fourth Michigan. Little used at Fredericksburg and Chancellorsville, it was at Gettysburg on July 1, 1863, that the five regiments earned a distinguished place in American military history. The recognition came at a terrible cost. Of the 1,883 men engaged in Pennsylvania, 1,153 were killed, wounded, or missing. The Black Hats fought on in 1864 through the bloody Overland Campaign, the Petersburg siege, and Appomattox Court House. It was determined sometime after Appomattox that the Iron Brigade had suffered a higher proportion of battle deaths than any such unit in the Federal armies.

Despite that grim statistic, however, the Iron Brigade is probably more celebrated today than a century ago. The reason for being overlooked is more one of distance than deliberate slight. The Wisconsin, Indiana, and Michigan men were far from the major veteran reunions and old soldier gatherings in Eastern cities, where the early attention was given to such fighting organizations as the Irish Brigade, First Jersey Brigade, Vermont Brigade, and New York's Excelsior Brigade. Rufus Dawes published his *Service with the Sixth Wisconsin Volunteers* in 1890, and O. B. Curtis added his *History of the Twenty-fourth Michigan* the following year. Augustus Buell of Battery B saw *The Cannoneer* printed in 1897. Philip Cheek and Mair Pointon added their history of Company A of the Sixth Wisconsin in 1909. But the books and other lesser works received little attention outside of Wisconsin, Indiana, and Michigan.

The spotlight has shifted in recent years, however. The Iron Brigade's compelling story and rich historical record has made it a popular subject for present-day writers and editors. Even a casual search of current Civil War titles in print relating to Iron Brigade topics turns up more than two dozen books. Also significant in the revival of the Iron Brigade's reputation has been the quality of recent publications.

Two books are credited for creating the current interest. Bruce Catton brought the brigade to popular attention just before the Civil War centennial when he wrote extensively about the Black Hats in his *Mr. Lincoln's Army* and *Glory Road*. In 1961, Alan T. Nolan's powerful unit history, *The Iron Brigade*, expanded its reputation among modern readers. The Second and Sixth Wisconsin, and Twenty-fourth Michigan, and even two companies of the regiments, have had book-length histories.

Overlooked in the flurry of modern publications (except for two collections of letters from individual soldiers) has been the Seventh Wisconsin. Little has been printed on the regiment, a fact that is not surprising given that the veterans left only a few scattered memoirs or written accounts of their war service and none ever penned a formal history. Also adding to the obscurity is the fact that in battle, the Seventh Wisconsin often acted within the structure of the brigade. It never had the opportunity to win individual distinction like the Sixth Wisconsin did when it charged the Railroad Cut at Gettysburg, or the Second Wisconsin did when it was led by General John Reynolds to McPherson's Woods during the opening phase of the same battle.

Yet, the Seventh Wisconsin's record may be the most exceptional of the five Iron Brigade regiments. The Second Wisconsin and Nineteenth Indiana went off the army rolls in 1864 after three years of service. The Twenty-fourth Michigan left the front for duty in the North in the months before Appomattox Court House. Only the hard survivors of the Sixth and Seventh Wisconsin regiments, "veteranized" in January 1864, saw the war through from the bright days of the Washington camps of 1861 to march in the glorious Grand Review of 1865.

Often highlighted in modern Civil War scholarship is the grim statistic reported by Colonel William F. Fox in his *Regimental Losses in the*

American Civil War, first published in 1889, that the Second Wisconsin lost the highest percentage of killed in battle of any regiment in the Union army in proportion to the number enlisted. Alan Nolan, in his investigation of the data, concluded the Seventh Wisconsin is sixth on that list. The others were not far behind, with the Nineteenth Indiana coming in at 11th, the Twenty-fourth Michigan at 20th, and the Sixth Wisconsin at 30th. Fox notes correctly, however, the percentage for the Seventh should be higher because the total enrollment includes 256 conscripts, very few of whom actually reported for duty.

Less attention is given to Fox's report that the casualty records of the War Department demonstrate the Seventh Wisconsin is first on the list of regiments that lost the most men killed in actual battle. The Seventh had 280 men killed outright or mortally wounded, compared with 278 for the Eighty-third Pennsylvania, and 277 for the Fifth New Hampshire. The records were later revised by the various states. Soldiers originally listed as missing in the official reports were determined to belong properly among the killed in action. New Hampshire, said Fox,

> published a supplement to its printed muster-out rolls, in which it accounts definitely for most of its missing. . . . But the War Department declines—and very properly—to account for missing men as killed until they receive official information to that effect. The official channels, through which such information must come, are the original records of the muster-out rolls; the final statements, as they are technically termed; and the affidavits which may accompany a pension claim.

As a result of the revision, Fox moved the Fifth New Hampshire to the top of his list with 296 killed or died of wounds, compared with 282 for the Eighty-third Pennsylvania, and 281 for the Seventh Wisconsin.

The Seventh Wisconsin's rankings are only one indication of the regiment's record of service. More significant is the Seventh's distinction of serving at critical places in important battles. The Iron Brigade spearheaded the opening attack at Antietam and was with the first infantry to reach the field at Gettysburg. From the time of its organization in late 1861 until the last day at Appomattox, the brigade was present with the army, ready to serve whenever and wherever called for duty. A partial listing shows the regiment lost 42 killed, wounded, or missing at Gainesville (Brawner's Farm), 22 at South Mountain, 15 at Antietam, 37 at Gettysburg, 55 at the Wilderness, 20 at Spotsylvania, 17 at Petersburg, and 6 at Five Forks.

This splendid record of service adds to the significance of William Ray's journals. Outside of the official papers and returns of the regiments, his account may be the most important primary source discovered on soldier life in the Iron Brigade. No other collection of letters or diary or journal written during 1861-1865 comes close to it. He was an eyewitness to some of the most important events of the war and keenly aware he was marching to history's drum. He wrote of the life of the enlisted man—of soldier joy and soldier hardship, of battles and guard mounts, of church meetings and soldier sins. He was wounded at Gainesville and again at Gettysburg and a third time at the Wilderness. Almost every day he wrote in his journal books, often just a line or two, but sometimes many hundreds of words on a single day. And unlike some heavily edited published accounts, Ray's journals reflect exactly how the soldiers lived (with weeks and even months of tedium and hardship) and died (when suddenly and without much warning the men were ordered to march and fight).

In the final tally, the account of William Ray, the Grant County blacksmith boy turned Union volunteer, provides a deep insight into those perilous days, and a sense of what it was like to be a soldier in the ranks of the most celebrated fighting brigade of the Civil War.

Lance J. Herdegen
Milwaukee, WI, December 2000

*   *   *

In addition to my family, at the Institute for Civil War Studies at Carroll College, I would like to thank Librarian Becky Steffes and students Andy Ackeret, Mary Benecke, Jesse Gant, and Scott Gutzke for their patience and assistance. I also would like to thank John Heiser and Major Mark Johnson for their excellent maps.

Finally, both Sherry and I would both like to thank our editor, Theodore P. Savas, for his recognition of the importance of this manuscript, for his intuition in having us work together, and for his valuable contributions to the book. His guidance and input during our work was invaluable.

L.H.

1861

The volunteer companies of the Seventh Wisconsin were called to Madison in September 1861 amid the great panic over the shocking Federal defeat at Bull Run on July 21, 1861. Unlike the first six regiments sent from Camp Randall, the Seventh was mustered company by company. On September 21, in new state uniforms of militia gray, it was sent to the war front in Washington and assigned to a new brigade commanded by Brigadier General Rufus King.

King was a familiar figure from back home. A native of New York and an 1833 graduate of the U.S. Military Academy, he arrived in Wisconsin in 1845 to take the editor's chair of *The Milwaukee Sentinel*. An experienced officer and a personal friend of Federal commander Irvin McDowell, King was given a general's star and a new infantry brigade made up of the Second, Fifth, and Sixth Wisconsin, and the Nineteenth Indiana. Attached was Battery B of the Fourth U.S. Artillery, famous in the "old" army for its service at Buena Vista in the Mexican War.

There was talk at first of an all-Wisconsin brigade, but military officials and Lincoln administration power brokers, always fearful of giving any governor too much authority, kept the Nineteenth Indiana in King's brigade and moved the Fifth Wisconsin to another organization. King and other Wisconsin officials voiced their outrage, however, and when the Seventh Wisconsin arrived from "Badgerdom" it found orders attaching it to King's Western brigade.

The welcome for the Seventh was a joyous one. "Our boys and those of the 2d [Wisconsin] made extravagant demonstrations of delight when they saw the grey uniforms and blue flags coming up the road from towards Washington," said a Sixth Wisconsin man. "The men are not only of good size and hardy look," said a brigade officer, "but they have an intelligent and smart look, which is assurance that they bring brain as well as muscle to the work."

The colonel of the Seventh Wisconsin was Joseph Vandor (sometimes spelled Van Dor) of Milwaukee. He was an old Hungarian campaigner, stiff and stubborn, and recommended to Wisconsin Governor Alexander Randall as "a brave man and thorough disciplinarian." The fact Vandor was still trying to master English became apparent at an early drill in firing by front and rear ranks. Vandor, mounted and at his proper place behind the regiment, ordered, "Rear rank, about face! Read, aim . . ." The order "brought the long line of file closers and officers to their knees, while the gallant lieutenant colonel and major were seen charging toward some friendly trees."

The adjutant shouted, "Colonel, that is not correct, you will shoot the file closers."

But the stubborn Hungarian straightened up. "I don't car a tam. If your colonel ish te mark, fire anyway," he said, and a thousand muskets emptied their blanks cartridges at the noble colonel.

Vandor was soon "promoted to a foreign consulship, a polite way Mr. Lincoln had of banishing general officers not wanted in the field."

William W. Robinson of Sparta, a Mexican War veteran and the lieutenant colonel of the regiment, was promoted to colonel in Vandor's place, and one of the most interesting of Wisconsin's soldiers, Charles A. Hamilton of Milwaukee, the grandson of Alexander Hamilton, advanced to lieutenant colonel. George Bill of Lodi, the captain of Company A, became major. The regiment and the rest of the brigade were ordered to Arlington Heights, Virginia, where they—including Private William Ray—went into winter quarters and were employed drilling and performing outpost duty near Falls Church for the next several months.

Unlike some of its sister regiments, little has been written about the Seventh Wisconsin, and even less is known about the daily routines of its citizen soldiers during the first months of the war. Ray's early journals thus fill valuable gaps in our knowledge.

Volume 1

To Put Down
Rebellion

Wm R. Ray Book

If lost and found by any person make known or bring to Capt Callis Company 7th Regt, Wis Volunteers, and oblige friend[1]

Read this book although it will truble you some to do it. And put it in safe keeping as well as the contents of the pocket. [*Ed. Note*: Pocket is empty.]

September 19, 1861

And I commence this book to keep account of evrything that transpires. I should have commenced it just one month since to do justice to the campaign I have started on that is to put down Rebellion in this once Glorious Union.

I am not able to drill nor havnt been for over a week or more but I am getting better. The cause of it is we were on Battalion drill. That is the whole of the Regiment were out togather and the order was given to carry arms at will and so they was carried in evry shape and form. And then the order was given to double quick march. And we started on it which is in a pretty good run.

The Seventh Wisconsin Volunteer Infantry

Company A: Lodi Guards
Company B: Columbia County Cadets
Company C: Platteville Guards
Company D: Stoughton Light Guard
Company E: Marquette County Sharpshooters
Company F: Lancaster Union Guards
Company G: Grand Rapids Union Guards
Company H: Badger State Guards
Company I: Northwestern Tigers
Company K: Badger Rifles

LAKE SUPERIOR

Superior City

MICHIGAN

St. Paul, MN

Mississippi River

Green Bay

Oshkosh

Manitowoc

Sheboygan

La Crosse

MINNESOTA

Fond du Lac

LAKE MICHIGAN

IOWA

Prairie du Chien

Lodi

West Bend

Madison

Ray's Lancaster Union Guards (Co. F)

Lancaster

Janesville

MILWAUKEE

Mississippi River

Galena

ILLINOIS

Wisconsin was organized as a territory on July 4, 1836, and originally included much of what would eventually become Iowa, Minnesota, and the Dakotas. The first Europeans to reach Wisconsin were probably the French, who came over the lakes and down the rivers from Canada seeking fur. They found thick woods, rich soil and water, and cold winters good for producing prime pelts. Their trading posts developed into towns and villages with a rich legacy of French names that still remain today. Other Europeans arrived and discovered that Wisconsin, in many ways, was similar in climate and geography to their native lands.

By the time Southern guns fired on Fort Sumter in April 1861, Wisconsin census takers counted 775,881 residents, up from 470,490 of 10 years earlier. Two million acres were under plow and Wisconsin ranked second in the nation in wheat production. Mining was well established in the southwest corner of the state and lumbermen were beginning to harvest the vast timber resources.

In the first year of the war Wisconsin furnished 11 infantry regiments, three of which (2nd, 6th, and 7th) served in what would be known as the Iron Brigade. Wisconsin provided some 91,300 men to the Union cause, and Badger state regiments served in every theater of the war. Some 11,600 died of battle wounds or disease.

Theodore P. Savas

September 21, 1861

Past Macfarlin [MacFarland] we are at Stoten [Stoughton]. There is a Company from this place. The name is Stoten [Stoughton] Light Guards. And it causes a great deal of excitement. We have just left Janesville and the citizens fetched our dinner into the camp. Well, we are at Harvard Station in Illinois. I guess they will not treat us here from the appearances. We are sixty miles from Chicago. We expect meet with a great reception. We are at Woodstock now. Just stopped.

September 22, 1861

And we are at Plymoth, Indiana [Plymouth, Indiana] so they say. We are now at Warsaw. We are at Fort Wayne now. I guess we are. We are near some upper Sandusky [Ohio] it is considerable town. We are at Busyrus[?], it is quite a place. We are just leaving Chrisiline and having a great time of it. We were promised some coffee and got some except about eighteen of our Company and the Captain didnt look after us and the guards wouldnt let us out when all the rest got out. We are at Mansfield [Ohio] now. We are at Pittsburg [Pittsburgh] and in the cars for Harrisburg [Pennsylvania] and the citizens of this place gave us our breakfast as soon as we came off the other cars.

We are off for Harrisburg. We have just past the Iron works and the Iron Mountain also. It is quite a place but the houses are the common class as they are all the working class. The name of the town is Johnstown. It is so much truble to find out the name of a town.

September 24, 1861

And I am on top of the Capital of the state of Pennsylvania and it is a grand sight. It is as good a building as our own at Madison. I must quit writing and go back to the depot where we have been ever since nine oclock, and it is about two. And are going to start at three oclock for Washington. The secretary of war [Simon Cameron of Pennsylvania] is here and says we are a good regiment. He looked at us. We are started for Baltimore and are crossing a bridge about one mile and a quarter long. Now the train is stopped because they could not pull us. The train is so long. There is so much drunkeness hollowing [hollering] that we cant hear ourselves think. They put us in the cattle and all kinds of cars. Verry dirty. We have loaded our guns to go through Baltimore.

September 25, 1861

We are at Goldsborough. That far from Harrisburg. We stayed at Harrisburg all night and slept in the cattle cars all night. But we are at Little York, it a manufacturing town, carworks and other things. We are twenty five miles from the line between Maryland and Pennsylvania.

September 26, 1861

We have passed through Baltimore. We slept in the station or depot house in Baltimore. We were received there the warmest of any place that we have passed through yet. It was delightful sight but I saw one woman that shook her fist at us. We are at Washington Junction now. The fourth Wisconsin Regiment is here as guards for the road and a magnificent bridge that is right here. The other goes to Harpers Ferry. Ever since we struck the line of Maryland there is troops stationed to guard the roads to keep secessionist of [off].[2]

Washington, September 26, 1861

And we are in Washington and nobody killed nor hurt but a good many sick. We are on north Capitol street, sitting on large blocks of marble which has been hauled for building I suppose as there is a building right in front us that is built of it. It a verry large building. We are waiting for something to eat. No telling what we will get or when. We have to keep our knapsacks on so as to be ready. We can see soldiers evry place we look. There is lots of encampments around here.

We are now at the soldiers rest. I try to give a detail of evry thing that transpires. It is as follows. Well, were put into double file and marched into the soldiers rest which holds all the regiment and we stacked our arms, pulled knapsacks and marched into the Soldiers retreat and got dinner. I must fall into rank. (now I have went in to fall in but found out it was false. There is so [much] hollowing. So I have come back on the steps again to return) which was as follows. Good coffee, better bread than we had at Camp Randall[3] but awful poor meat and this is [what] we had. We have fared hard on the way coming here.

There is a bathing place in soldiers retreat and I went and washed my feet and come outside and to big wooden washpans or troughs rather and washed my hands and face. A man can wash all over in the bathing tubs. They say they are fighting at Chain Bridge.[4] I guess we will have to stay here all night.

September 27, 1861

(Well, well the above that I have written proved not to be true) but I cant help that for we are in one of the city halls. There is a large building here and it is divided into halls and each Company occupys a hall and plenty of room to. Well last night when we got our beds fixed and laid down. Then the officers hollowed up Co F and fix knapsacks so & we rolled up things again and fell into ranks and marched here. We did not know where we was going until we marched in here. Some said we were going to Chain Bridge and some said one place and another. We are on the second floor and have a balcony to walk out on and the only balcony there is on the house so we have a good situation.

I am sitting in the window as I write. The windows is large and raise up so as to make a doorway to go on to the balcony. I understand that we are likely to go to

Chain Bridge and General Heinz [Samuel P. Heintzelman], he wants us. He says if he had a brigade of Wisconsin boys, he would have the best in the field. We have a great name or at least the Wisconsin boys does. They do not notice us in this city as at other citys heretofore because there is so many here. There is in and about this city two hundred and sixty thousand troops. Well you may imagine what is going on here. It would take a large volume to note evrything for just in our Company there is not any doing things alike hardly. We are strongly guarded.

Well I must mention about Baltimore again. We were greeted in evry way, lots of young ladies running along the streets, waving the flags. Hurrah here comes Capt Mackee [David McKee, Lancaster, Wisconsin] of the Grant Co grays [Grant County Grays], second regiment of Wisconsin Volunteers. His Company is the colored [color] Company.[5] I have just heard a letter read from the same regiment just sent to Loren Parsons. We are going to Chain Bridge I guess. Olie Foot [Orey J. Foot] of our company has had the delerium tremens. He is better now.[6]

Well we are in our tent. We struck our tents in a hurry to keep our things dry. But we will have to take them down to sett them over square. They are sett in evry shape.

September 28, 1861

We struck our tents to pitch them in uniform style. It is a verry pretty day but we had a cold a night, about as cold as Wisconsin. The Vermont regiment left and we go on the same ground. We have to wait until we have orders to do anything. We are on confiscated property. We were marched out to this place yesterday. It is about one mile & a half from the city. It is a pretty place and good water. It is a better place than camp Randall. I have seen Arlington Heights[7] from the top of a high building in the city. And now we can see encampments in evry direction. We have had only about half enough to eat yet but I don't know who is to blame. They say when we get things fixed up square, they will give us all the law allows us which is eighteen ounces of bread, three quarters of a pound of pork or one pound and a quarter of beef when we don't get pork and I forget how much coffee—but there is a great plenty of evrything and good to but the Vermont regiment said they had about half rotten mean for two days & then about seaven hundred of them raised and wouldnt stand it so they got the best kind of evry thing ever after.

September 29, 1861

We are all fixed up right. Our rations will be divided equal today by weight and measurement according to law. I was lucky as to get a chair yesterday. When the Vermont Regiment left, they left it so we have something to write on. Our meat was so salty last night we could not eat it. It was salt beef and the cooks didnt think of its being so salt. We had fresh beef before of the first quality. We have good cooks, I believe one of them is Phillipp [Phillip] Brother & James Thorp.[8]

September 30, 1861

And it is a pretty day. Just had dinner. It consisted of soup and bread. The soup was verry poor but we do not have enough bread, but have it promised as usual. We commenced to drill this morning for the first since we left Wisconsin.

October 2, 1861

October and I am well but awful hungry. We have the poorest to eat of any and the poorest management. We are at Chain Bridge now at this end. And encamped in stones throw of the second and sixth regiment of Wisconsin Volunteers. Evry Company has got their Breakfast but ours.

I am sitting on the ground on an old rag, detailed as an extra guard which makes one hundred & twenty eight on guard and then they will go out. They put guards around the second regiment but they will go out any how. So we do it also. They will quit trying to keep us in. The second regiment was guarded just the same.

October 4, 1861

It is a verry pretty day or morning. I have been mending my pants and scouring my gun. It keeps us pretty busy. Get up when the drum beats, fall in, answer to roll call, get breakfast, scour guns, black shoes, comb head to keep tangles out, keep lice out, wash socks, wash shirts and writing and various things to numerous to mention. Well it is about Drill time.

Tis evening and a balloon [observation balloon] is up but it is going down. It is the second one I have seen since we come south. The other one went up when we was up to Camp Randall near washing [Washington]. It went up in the night and had a light in it but the supposition is that on the side of the rebels it was dark. We are going to Arlington Heights tomorrow morning. It is said that the whole of the Brigade is going. It is about five miles. I will write some tomorrow if can.

October 6, 1861

And I want my Breakfast but I expect it be an hour yet before we get it. We are at Arlington Heights this morning. We slept out last night on our tents for they didnt come until after dark. It was verry hard march. Our regiment passed I should think half of the second regiment and a great many of the sixth also. The second said that it was harder than any other march they had ever performed. I will quit until after breakfast as this Sunday we ought to rest but we shall have to work about all day as the ground is verry dirty.

October 7, 1861

And it is nearly eight oclock and we have not had our breakfast. Our officers neglects us in some way for we only had two meals yesterday and verry poor ones too. But I will kick up a smudge pretty soon if I have to report to headquarters. There is something fetched to light yesterday for all the rations was not cooked that we drawed. It was the cooks fault for if they could save it and sell it they would put in their own pockets. There some in this Company that wants to cook in messes, me for and about half of the Company but the big wigs they don't see it. They are mounting guard now and our men has to go without their breakfast.

October 8, 1861

And it is muddy and cloudy for it rained verry hard last night and we got a little wet but it didnt hurt us any for we are getting used to it. We don't drill any since we came here. I am writing a letter for Jesse Shipton[9] as he cant. I wrote one for him before but he is one of the two detailed to carry water for the cooks. And he has just gone for some and will wait until he comes back to tell me what to say.

October 10, 1861

And it is raining again. I guess it is setting in for a good rain as it is near the rainy season and if it is we will have a muddy time of it. There is all kinds of games going on to take money and kill time but I take no part in them and will spend my time writing. I have just written to my nephew Richard Lander [son of older sister Thurza Ann Ray (born 1820) and Isaac C. Lander]. It is the first letter I have written to relatives except Henry [older brother, born 1822] and Mother.

We went to be examined yesterday, well the whole brigade went which consists of the second, sixth and seaventh Wis regiments and the nineteenth Indiania [Indiana] Regiment.[10] We fixed up as good as we could, that is blacked our shoes and sewed on buttons & rip in pants & coats and brush them and pack our knapsacks as neatly as we could in have things as neat as possible. We were marched about one mile & a half and drawn up in line with the second Regt and in the rear of the nineteenth Indiana Regt and they were in a line with the sixth. And then we wheeled by Company which brought us just the length of each Company apart. Then the inspection began which lasted about three hours. The inspectors had sharp eyes. They could see when there was a button off or a bit of rust on the guns. They would cock the gun and if there was any rust about the tube [firing cone] they would stick it in your face and it would make them feel a little ashamed. They notice our hair also any that had not short hair, they would show it to the officers & say it must be cut of. Also those with beards verry long beard had had to have it cut of some. They must have their hair cut once a month.

Sunday, October 13, 1861

And I am well this morning and packed up to start for the Battlefield for what we know it is as follows. Yesterday after we had been on dress parade we marched to our street and were dismissed as usual. In about three minutes we were called into ranks in great excitement and it started from the officers. Then they said we must get ready to march in ten minutes and didnt tell us what to pack up. So some packed one thing and some another. And commands were given and then countermanded which made great confusion. We got our suppers in a hurry. I rolled up my blanket in a small roll as I could to put around my neck and under my arm and to tie the ends togather with a string and put on my overcoat. Then we fooled around an hour or so and were called into ranks again and were ordered to put our blank catridges in the lower chamber of our boxes and put our nine rounds or old catridges in the upper chambers and we received ten rounds more which made nineteen rounds. I couldnt believe we would go until this happened then I begun to think some little about it.

We were dismissed again and called into ranks again to form battallion. Our guns were examined by our officers and asked us if we had got our catridges, if we had blowed through the tube of our gun. We went in our place in the battalion and then were doubled up before the Lieutanant Colonel [William W. Robinson of Sparta] and he spoke verry good to us. Told us we had orders to march or hold ourselves in readiness to march at ten minutes notice and we were to have one days provision in our haversacks, our canteens filled with water, coffee or tea. Take evrything out of our knapsacks and put our blankets and oilcloths in it and nothing else. And we were to be up and have our breakfast before light in the morning &c. He told how to act and not do anything without we had command. He talked to us quite cheeringly.

O how the wind does blow this morning and we have not marched yet. We are likely to any minute. It is near nine Oclock now. We followed the orders as I have stated before precisely. We were also ordered to fix things and at the tap of the drum to put out lights and keep still and go to sleep which we did but I had rather a poor bed but slept tolerable well. I will wait a little while before writing any more.

October 14, 1861

And I am well but didnt get enough to eat for dinner. But this company cooking is done for after supper tonight and then we go to messing, that is two tents togather which is twelve men. We had a great fuss today at dinner time for we only got about half a ration of meat and meat and bread was all we had. And we had it so much that it wouldnt do any longer. So Jesse Shipton took his piece of meat and went to the Colonel [Joseph Vandor of Milwaukee] and the Lieutanant Colonel [Robinson] and they talked quite a while, ask questions about it and was wonderstruck about it so they told him to go to the Captain [John R. Callis of Lancaster].[11] They asked him if there had been complaint made to the officers and he said there had been. Then he asked what Company he belonged to. He said Co F. What Captain said, said the Colonel. He said Capt Callis. The Colonel said it was bad and he didnt know the reason of it and no more was said.

I and Frank Boyantan and Whitney, [Francis A. Boynton and Warren W. Whitney][12] one of the Corporals was talking about me and Frank having to go to other Companys on battallion drill to fill them up and Frank said that was played out and captain heard him and called him into his tent and said to him—I believe you want to go into Co H and Frank said—I beg your pardon, Capt, it is not so, then the Capt jumped up and said—don't call me a liar and shook his fist in franks face. But Frank didnt flinch and says I know what I am about. They had a little talk. Then the Capt come out to us and says boys do you get enough to eat. There was several spoke up, I with them, said we didnt get enough to eat so the [captain] said William Ray, you may go to Co H and I said I was going as I had calculated to ever since he had promised me I might. So that took him down and he said no more and just then Jesse Shipton came up and the Capt wanted to know if that was all he got. He said it was. He looked at him and said you have ate some off that have you not. No said Shipton. At any rate it was not to exceed one inch & half square. He said that he had been to the Colonels, thats to bad. But I mentioned it before. So Frank Boyantan, James Garner & I are going into Co H.

October 15, 1861

And we had a little larger piece of meat but is verry fat pork boiled. Hurrah, it is noised about the Camp that the South wants to come to a settlement. And appears to free all the negros and pay two thirds of the expenses but I do not credit it. We have a police, it is for cleaning up the streets that is Co police. Then there is General police to clean off the parade ground. They is four out of each Company for each buisness. Well I must clean my gun.

October 17, 1861

I am on guard today. I was on the second relief and came on at ten oclock and off at twelve and go on at four Oclock again and it is two Oclock now and I can write a little now. I am well and get plenty to eat now. I had plenty of rice, molasses & bread. It is said there is one case of the smallpox in the Regiment and they are Vaccinnating on double quick time today but as I am on guard I cant get it today.

October 19,1861

And it is verry cloudy this morning and foggy. I have just returned from police duty for I being on guard day before yesterday and rested yesterday forenoon and drilled in the afternoon and had to be on police today. And it is said drill also but I don't think so. At any rate they have gone on Battalion drill and I am not. And some tell me that I will have to go on guard tomorrow to pay for it but I guess not. At any rate, we were released in time to go on drill but some of us didnt go and some said we didnt have to go but I will see the Orderly sergeant when they come back and know for certain. Stating this occurance puts me in mind of giving our officers names, the

Captain name is J.B. Callis, first Lieutenant S Woodhouse [Samuel Woodhouse], second Lieutenant H F Young [Henry F. Young], the next in rank in office is the Sergeants. Orderly Sergeant or first Sergeant is J. W. Mackinzie [John W. McKenzie], second A. R. Macartney [Alexander R. McCartney], third L. Parsons [Loren G. Parsons], Fourth G. W. Cowin [George W. Cowan], fifth Ugene Sloat [William E. Sloat]. The next and last officers is Corporals, G. Henderson [George H. Henderson], P. Runnion [John Runion], F. Kidd [Fletcher S. Kidd], F.A. Kidd [Alphonzo A. Kidd], Simon Woodhouse, J. Bradley [John C. Bradley], W. Whitney [Warren W. Whitney], G. Holbert [George G. Halbert]. This is all the officers.[13]

J. Clark [James A. Clark][14] has just fetched a pack of cards and evry man in the tent at Camp Randall took a vow that they wouldnt have a game of cards played in it if it could be helped so they have broke their vow. But there has one come in since then and he is one of that kind. We are the worst tent in the Company. There is seaven in it and about the largest that is average the largest and it the most Blackguard tent.

October 20, 1861

It is a verry pretty day and it is Sabbath day. Our parson [Samuel L. Brown of Beaver Dam] has moved his tent up by our street where most all the notable things are because it is the right wing of the Regiment or some call it the head but the latter is not proper. We didnt go to be vaccinated.

October 22, 1861

And it raining this morning and verry disagreeable. And are on marching orders. We received new marching orders last night to go and reinforce our troops at Leesburg which it is said was having a hard battle yesterday. So the Orderly came around last night after we went to bed and told us to be ready to march with five minutes notice so there was a great excitement but not so great as on twelfth. For we fixed our things and got eighteen rounds of catriges and went to bed. But the cooks were up all night cooking three days rations and we eat our breakfast as usual. And we will have nothing but fat pork to eat. But I take my meat and fry my bread with it and that makes a verry good meal. It appears like hard living but I am fleshier now than ever I was so I am not doing verry bad. We are just waiting for the order to march to fight.

But to march for anything else we do not like to because we have got such a good Camp ground and have done a great deal of work on it and it is nice as any dooryard. This ground here holds water as good as mamas washtub. It is a yellow clay verry sticky and on the road where there is a mudhole, it stinks verry in places. The cause I suppose is on account of the young timber which is verry thick, the prettyiest young timber I ever saw. But there has been a great many thousand acres cut down in fact nearly all the timber twixt here and Bullsrun [Bull Run]. A great deal or probably all of it has been under cultivation once. And most of the timber is pine but considerable cedar intermixed therewith. There is a few trees standing and they are verry pretty which goes to show it was one of the prettyiest kind of groves once but it had to be cut down for the good of the country so that the rebels wouldnt have such as chance on our forts which are situated on the Arlington Heights all along for about fifteen miles. They are from a quarter to a mile apart. I have been in one that lays a few rods to the south of us which is Tillinghurst [Tillinghast] and there is one on the north a few rods which is Fort Cass. I will say more about the Forts when I get acquainted. They have just mounted the guard.

I am glad I am not on guard for it is rainy and muddy but no worse than when I stood on guard last week. Hurrah, the news boys are hollowing out. Here is the latest news, morning paper. Another Battle. Battle at boker [?] Leesburg. Colonel killed.[15] So we have news pretty quick but often when the boys hollows out such & such things happened in their papers and when the boys pays for it, then they cant find anything in worth notice. Then I laugh at them for letting the little boy fool them so but they don't come it on me for I get papers from home which gives me more pleasure than anything else for they come from Mother, the Northwestern Christian Advocate. I like to read them for there is nothing going in our tent but rowdyism and card playing and ever since James Clark fetched a deck of cards into the tent, there is always some visiters and a tent full and this muddy weather, it is bad. I like visitors but not to play cards but when I get into the other Co I hope it will be better.

Oh how it rains and the water is running through our tent. And I may do evrything. I have carried half of the water since we came to this Camp but I do it and hope it will not last long. The boys is drawing to a close. I have just been into the next tent to see a man that got his leg and ankle jamed verry bad but neither broke or unjointed. It happened last week. He is getting better fast. Well it is getting dark. The mail has just come but no letters for me but a great many for Co.

October 24, 1861

It has cleared of again and is a pretty morning. There has a great fight at Leesburg day [Dranesville skirmish] before yesterday and the news came this morning that we got badly whiped out. They are getting the better of us lately and I expect we will have to fight pretty soon. Well the drum beats for drill and it is knapsacks drill to. It be hard but we must do it so as to get used to carrying them. We will verry soon get our new uniform. It is pretty cold now for the last day or two but I do not suffer much. I have warmer clothes than I had at home. My shoes are good, stockings are whole yet, but some of them have worn out their shoes already.

October 25, 1861

A pretty morning. We are not out of the sound of the cars yet. We can hear them at Georgetown this morning. I was down oppisite Washington on this side of the

Potomac yesterday on Brigade drill. That is twenty four out of evry Co in the Brigade and the Brigade is the four Regiments I mentioned. And Brigadier Gen King [Rufus King] drilled us and he did not get there until late and he gave us a hard drill.

Well it is afternoon and we had a hard drill of it this forenoon. It was another knapsacker. Lieutanant Colonel [Robinson] has had command of us for about a week. Our old Colonel has no patience but he is a good military man but he cant do anything with us volunteers. He is a German. He cant talk right good English and that trubled some and he had been used to regulars in the old Country and when he talked us as he did there, it made us all a little Gruffy and we did not try to do so good. There is talk of him resigning. I like him verry well myself for I think he is in the right of some things concerning the Co officers. That is if they would study their book more and not run to the city so much and eat so many Oyster dinners, they could drill better. That is they could command their companys better. For volunteers has to be coaxed and not drove as the regulars are for that will not do. There was a verry hard frost last night here. It is the first frost I have seen this year.

Well about that fight at Leesburg, there was four hundred of our men killed, wounded & missing.[16] It was a hard fight but our men routed them it is said. But we didnt go up there as we expected that night when we were ordered to pack our knappsacks. That fellow that I spoke of getting hurt last week is getting better. He walks out on his crutches a little. There is the least sickness in Company of any Company in the Regiment. For the last two or three days they have drilled us hard and I still have to go into other companies to drill. But I shall not have to do it when I go into the other Co for good. I believe I have never told the names of my tentmates. Well there is Jesse Shipton, Olie Foot, Frank Boyanton, James Clark, James Garner [William J. Garner] , Richard Pierce [Richmond B. Pierce], the one is a verry steady man.[17] That is six besides myself. And the tents are about ten feet square so you may guess how much room there is left. There several that leaves their things laying abut the tent instead of putting them in their knappsack. But that happens in all crowds. Olie Foot had to stand on guard two hours extra yesterday for not saluting General McDowel [Irvin McDowell]. The officers are particular about it. Mcdowel came along the road where Olie was on guard and he did not think of presenting arms so Mcdowel called the officer of the guard and gave him two hours extra to punish him.

October 26, 1861

I am just ready to go on Battalion Drill with knapsacks again and if they don't quit drilling us so hard with our knapsacks on, there will be half of us on the sick list. We were never drilled so hard before as we have been for three or four days.

October 27, 1861

And I am sitting by a fire on the hillside near the Arlington house. I was chosen this morning as Brigade guard around Headquarters which is the Arlington House and I was on the first relief and have just come off. My number is the third and that number comes on the Porch (or Piazza I suppose) and it is a verry pretty place, as I have a view of the city of Washington & Georgetown both. It is and old house at least has that appearance but fireproof in evry respect. It is built of some stone material I suppose. It is plastered all over with cement so I cant tell what the material consists of. There is considerable iron about it. There is or has been a verry nice garden as there is a great many kinds of flowers in it amongst the weeds and some of most all kinds of trees and shrubs. It has all appearance of being an old garden. The house is built of rather old style. The Potomac is full view of us also tide water it is said for we are right opposite the long Bridge in sight of the capitol and white house (I was past both once). Well I must eat my dinner. We are about one mile from camp and are not allowed to go home so we have to bring rations for twenty four hours.

The Potomac river is about half a mile from here and there is a gradual rise to within about forty rods of the house of about one foot in ten I should think. And from that to the top of the hill it is about double that I should think. At any rate I want to give you some idea and you may imagine the rest. And it is about as pretty as you can imagine. Betwixt the river and the house there is various kinds of trees such a cedars, verry pretty ones, prettier than the Wisconsin cedars. The limbs begin to put out from them at about three to six feet from the ground. And keep getting shorter to the top which is a verry small twig and on top of that twig there is a single leaf. You know the kind of leaves of cedars and that finishes the height of the tree. The foliage is verry thick on them. Upon the whole they put me in mind of the cedars of Lebanon that we read about in the Scriptures. Those cedars constitute about half of the forest twixt here and the river. Then there is the walnuts, oaks and quakenasps & maples and various trees such as there is in the Badger State. And there is some chestnuts. Then there is the Persimon. That I shall ever recollect at any rate the fruit that grows on them. For some of the boys brought some into camp soon after we came to where we are now and I got hold of one and it looked ripe but I didnt take a second taste of it as evrybody may know that has ever tasted a green Persimon but I came down here afterwards and got some that was good for they are the nicest kind of fruit when ripe but they are all gone or I would have some for there is a tree right before me. And there is some pine such as the Badger pine. There is no underbrush and it is quite clean. All this is in front of the house that you can see, for back of the house it is a thick woods of small timber but no underbrush for all about here the trees are trimmed up the same as on orchards.

October 28,1861

And all is right this morning. And I am waiting for the new Pickets guards to come. But it will be about one hour first. I can hear the Drums at camp. It is for guards. I want my breakfast although I went up to camp last night and got a good supper, all I could eat. We have plenty of beef now a days but I am afraid we wont have it verry long. Well it is evening or after dinner and I do not feel verry well but eat a little dinner. And I guess I will get along verry well if I kind of starve myself. And don't eat verry well. Payday will soon come and then I will fix evrything aright.

October 31,1861

And the last day of the second Autumn month and I am well. And sitting on my knapsack on the river bottom or our Brigade drill ground. And have been inspected and are resting until the mustering officer comes to us to call the roll and then we have to support arms and when he calls our name we must shoulder arms and then order arms. Well here he comes and we must get into ranks.

Well we have got home for as soon as soon as we all answered to our names we were fetched home. That is by company to fix up our quarters for Inspection. And we have fixed our tent up pretty good and clean but three of us had to do it. We expect some to get our pay today but it may not come for a week yet. But this is general Inspection & payday and yesterday was General muster day. Yesterday forenoon we fixed up, brushed our clothes & shoes, buttons, cleaned our guns &c. At one Oclock afternoon we fell in and formed Battalion. Marched about three miles down to the river bottom near long Bridge. It is a verry pretty place to drill a brigade which there was our whole Brigade and a Regiment of cavelry. They are formed into companies and ten companys makes a regiment. They work about the same way as we do except them being on horseback and having swords. They went through some queer gestures. It looked rather wild when they charged, their horses running at full speed and swords flying in all directions. I was taken out as guard and stationed on the road to keep the civillians back. The road runs right along the river bank and the meadow run one mile back where timber set in. And this was confiscated property. It had been a fine meadow some day but is turned out now for drill ground. It was about two miles long. After the Cavelry had done manuevering they left.

And the Infantry took the field and performed until near sunset. And then came home and had Dress parade which was after dark. And General McDowel said the Co F knappsacks were packed the best of any Co in the Brigade. And I think if we had of had our blue suit on we would have looked as well as any but we have only drawed one pair of pants, two pair of drawers & our cap which is deep blue. Pants sky blue, drawers cotton flannel. They are verry good cloth. We will be dressed the same as the sixth Regt but the second is dressed in deep blue clothes all around except their hats which is black. They have brass mountings on their hats and a large black Ostrich feather on the right side and they have white gloves also. Oh they look pretty and they go by the name of the Bloody second and the sixth goes by the name of Baby sixth and sometimes by the name of Bragging Sixth. They are not liked verry well by either of the other regiments. They call us the bully seaventh and we are in size of men and the most of them also for I had a good chance to see all of the Brigade when they performed yesterday from where I was on guard along the road.

Our regiment is not so well drilled as the others but we have not been in more than half so long. I am writing by candle light tonight for the first time. The tent is pretty still tonight although there is two playing cards to my left within three feet. But they are good fellows except that. But they are gaining on bad habits now verry fast since the sutler came and they got his tickets and could buy cards and gamble with the tickets instead of money. As they will buy anything at the sutler[18] as well as money and now payday is coming. Then the sutler will bring his accounts into the Captains and they will keep it back in their hands.

November 1 and it is after noon and I am sitting in the tent door. Well I must go and wash some—my haversack and some socks and wash my feet and head and ears and take a general clean up as we are not going to drill this evening.[19]

November 2, 1861

And it is raining verry hard and a verry nasty time all around but we must put up with it. Our tent is full of visitors but there is no card playing today. Frank Boyantan is playing the flute instead of playing and we have a fife to so we enjoy ourselves pretty well today. And there is not much chance to write but I have read some. I am getting so that I can read if there is a noise. I must quit and try to read some as nothing has transpired worthy of note except our meals comes verry slim. Only coffee for breakfast & meat for dinner but plenty of bread.

November 4, 1861

And it verry pleasant and it is three Oclock and we have worked verry hard today. We have moved on to our new Camp Ground. We have worked all day at the street and have got it fixed up verry pretty all around our tent. The best of any in town. It is verry pretty day. Verry. Our camp is not more than two hundred yards from the old one.

November 5, 1861

And it is cloudy today. We have not drilled any today yet but I guess we will in an hour or so. We have been fixing the street and are building a cook house. We elected another cook last night which makes three now. There has been several cooks since we left Madison. They cook a little while and get tired. D. Rector & L. Day [Danforth Rector and Leicester Day][20] has been cooking about one month and it is to hard work so we elected Wm Miles[21] [William Horton Miles] last night. So there is three after this and it is work enough too. We have got cedar and pine boughs in our tent for a bed. Mostly cedar, they are about three inches deep. We only cut the verry finest limbs of the trees and covered with they make a fine bed and warm too. I must fix for Brigade drill. This is taking twenty four men out of a Company and the rest stays at home. I have been down on that drill three times.

November 6, 1861

And it is raining this morning. Just about such a rain as we have in Wisconsin in the month of May but it is not cold. We sleep warm since we moved our tents for we have fixed it better than ever it was. The wind cant get in at all around the bottom. And the cloth is naturaly so thick that it will not let rain or wind in either.

Last night about eight Oclock we received orders to get ready to march by tomorrow morning at eight or this morning it is now. For we don't know where we are going but suppose going to get our pay. Well I will lay by until after breakfast

Well it is nearly noon and we didnt go to the review as it was to be. We were to be reviewed by McClelen [Army Commander George B. McClellan] and he has been put in to scoots [General Winfield Scott] office or the office that Scott held but has resigned and I understand that there was to be a great gathering there. I also understand that we were going down on the ground where we drill and if that is the case we would not have to travel more than a mile. The news comes in the morning papers that the Federals were bombarding Charlston [Charleston, South Carolina] and had taken Fort Sumpter [Fort Sumter] but I think it is not so. I hope so. They say that the Rebels are drawing away from Bullsrun [Bull Run] to go South to protect their homes.

November 7, 1861

And I am on guard today and the wind blows cold from the Northwest but the sun shines warm. It put me verry much in mind of the many days that I have followed the plow in old Wisconsin. But we have a fire by the guardhouse but one side is cold all the time and keeps us turning around. Well it is afternoon. I was on the first relief as usual. It is the best relief too for we are off guard so as to get our meals at the right time.

I think a good deal about home today. I suppose the cause of it is such a chilly day that sets me to thinking. We all wear our overcoats today. It is the first time I have. I guess it will not rain this time while I am on guard as it happens to about evry time. Evry two men has fires on the ends of their beats so it is not hard standing guard. There is such a report as having another battle at Hatteras inlet. It is in the morning papers.

November 8, 1861

And it is a verry pretty morning and I am very well. And feel well considering that I stood on guard yesterday. And did not get to sleep more than two hours in the twenty four. But there was considerable excitement in camp last night when the news came that [Confederate General John B.] Floyd and his command consisting of fifteen thousand men were taken prisoners, also that Ft Sumpter was taken and Charleston was burned by our troops. We could hear cheering in camps all around as distant as one mile & a half from our Camp. And there was hearty cheering here also. But the morning papers do not mention anything about it.[22]

Well I have been to see a sick man in his tent by the name of [Henry] Hudson[23] and done all I could for him. He has the inflamitory Rheumatism and I told him about my mothers remedy which consisted of Sulphur and wax. About one tablespoonful of sulpher to each foot and the wax must be made into a cake and the sulphur put into the middle of the cake and the edges stuck fast to the foot with sulphur in the hollow of the foot.

November 10, 1861

And it has been several days since I wrote any and I shall have to correct some things especially about Floyd being taken prisinor. It has been proved to be false but he must surrender in a few days. For Rosencranz [Union General William Rosecrans] has surrounded him and he intends to starve him out and I hope he will do it.

Well it is sabbath day and a verry pretty one too and I have been to work a most all day. I am sorry to say it but you not blame me reader when you know how we are situated. There is two men sick in our tent and we had a rain yesterday and last night and it was verry damp so I thought I wouldnt put off building a fire place in the tent any longer as it is pretty chilly of nights now. There was three of the boys went and got some brick. They brought them about two miles. It was a hard job. James Garner & I built it. Richard Pierce was writing, James Clark was sick & the others carried the brick so they done enough.

November 11, 1861

And it looks like rain this morning and warm south wind. There getting to be considerable sickness in Camp. Frank Boyantan went to the Doctors this morning. For the last week there has been one on the sick list from this tent evry day. I was vaccinated last Sunday a week ago and it didnt work. I think of getting it done again and then if it don't work then I think I will be safe from smallpox.

November 12, 1861

And it is a verry pretty day and there was some frost last night. It is a little chilly to stand still where the wind blows in the shade. I being down on brigade drill yesterday, I didnt have to go today and have this evening to myself. This brigade drill I will explain. It is twelve files out of evry Co in the Brigade and those that stay at home do not drill this afternoon and I improved the time by washing my shirt and writing in this sketch. I received two letters last night after going to bed. The mail came in verry late. The Chaplain carries it and is postmaster also. The fireworks played verry brisk all around last night. It is called in the morning serenadeing Mclellen [McCellan] on account of his promotion to a higher office. That is taking

Scotts place. The rockets were of the different colors. The colors were red, white & blue. We could see the rockets. Some of them went to a great height in the air, we did not know what it meant last night. It is said the germans turned out enmass.

November 13, 1861

And it is a verry pretty day. As pretty as it can be. It is similar to Indian summer in Wisconsin. And I have signed the payroll and receipt roll also. They are going to pay and are paying the regiment of today. They make us sign all the papers first. Well it is nearly dinner time or is (dinner time but we havent got dinner). Well we have got our dinner which consisted of beans and bread and the beans was well cook today. Well I guess we will get our pay which is twenty six dollars and forty one cents and I think I will send about twenty dollars home and payday causes considerable excitement.

November 16, 1861

And it is morning and a verry cold one to. I was carrying water for the cooks yesterday and it was rainy and verry muddy. We got our pay on the 14 instead of the 13 as I heretofore said. And I gave 15 dollars to the captain to express home. Oh but the ground is frooze where it is muddy but we have a fire in the fireplace. I spent my time yesterday in writing home to Henry when I was not carrying water. Well I must eat my breakfast.

November 17, 1861

And it is a little warmer today although the wind blows verry hard. It dries up the mud verry fast. We had another Inspection this morning. And were called out again on dress parade form to receive Govenor Randal [Wisconsin Governor Alexander Randall] and present arms to him which is the highest respect that can be shown to a person in this vicinity. The privates when using arms does have to present arms to a field Officer and all higher in office and all lower in office. That is commissioned officers. We have to bring our left arm up across our breast and touch the gun with our fingers. We carry the gun in our right hand by the guard and the cock of the lock at shoulder arms. Then to present arms we bring the gun up before us.

November 19, 1861

And it is a pretty day and we have to march at eight Oclock. We have our dinners in our haversack & all we have to carry is haversack, canteen and maybe our overcoats. We are going someplace, we don't know where. We was out about five miles yesterday on a grand review of about 16 thousand infantry and two thousand Cavelry. And a great deal of Artillery. I don't know how much. And after marching around about three hours, we halted, the sun about one hour high. For there was a messenger come to Mcdowel with the news that the 14th N.Y. regiment was surrounded by the rebels. We halted and Mcdowel put off at post haste. And we stayed there until after sundown and started home which we reached about 7 Oclock which was long after dark and we was verry tired and soon went to bed. But got the order to march just as we got in bed. Well we are at the same place as yesterday which is near Munson Hill a place of great note. There is a verry strong fort on it. It is quite a large mound rising above the surrounding country. Well I sitting on the whilst I write.

Well when we reach this place which was about half past ten Oclock and was formed by the Colonel into mass by division. There was ten men detailed out of evry Company and Co F being the largest. And the Companys having to be equalized when in Battalion and I being on the left wing of the Co was taken of as usual and put into Co E. So I was one of the ten that went off from Co E on extra duty and were marched out and stacked our arms and taken of to a wagon and got axes and were taken to a piece of timber and set to chopping. Our squad from this Regt was 104 men and I with a great many of them went to chopping and those that had not an ax had to drag brush. The timber consists of pines & cedars of different sizes from eight inches in diameter down to small switches. There is about 7 acres of it. Well we worked about two hours then there was some men came from Co E to take our place for our Captains found it out. That is, there was some from Co H as well as our Co so that made it that Co E didnt furnish but 4 men. That is but 4 of their own men. And our Captains thought that wouldnt do.

There has not been any drilling today yet. And therefore I think that we were brought out here to get used to marching. And seeing so many folks & things for there is as many here today as yesterday and they are clearing the rubbish and trees of the ground. And that piece of timber that I spoke of when cleared off will be an inroad to another large field. I do not know how large but this field we are in now contains as near as I can guess about one section or 1000 acres. And if all comes that is talked of there will be sixty thousand men.

November 20, 1861

And it is rather a cool day but still a pretty sunshiny day. And the wind blows cold but still I am comfortably warm with only one light woolen shirt on and a pretty heavy jacket such as I have worn all the time heretofore. I have not had much to do today but fix up things about the tent and write. I have wrote a letter to Otice Way. And have sent a paper to George Ray [son of brother Henry]. The cause of me not having much to do is this. That there is a great review today. I spoke about it yesterday. Well instead of sixty thousand, there will be eighty thousand so it is said this morning. We got home last night about dark. It was two of the tufest works I had done for a long time. But to return: Well the order came this morning that there was only twenty four files or forty eight men out of a Co to go so I being on the left flank of the Co and they took them from the right flank so that let me out with a great many others. But we got orders to carry water for the cook. But that is not much. I have only carried four pails of water today and if they all carry half that much there will be plenty.

The camp is quite still today. I was glad when they left me but I would like to be there now to see the sight. I can hear the cannon roar verry plain. This morning the country seemed to be alive. There was so many going evry way, we got up long before daylight, had our breakfast just at daybreak. I think the object is to ascertain their real strength and how they are drilled. It will be an awful hard day on the men. There is so much standing as well as marching. It is the hardest work I ever done and what would make it worse, it frooze considerable last night and then it thawing out today. The ground would be slippery but god be thanked I have been free from it. And got to attend to some buisness. I sent home a pretty picture called the rose of washington. There was a great many small pictures therein on the same paper. Well my book is nearly full and I will try to buy another. Well I have got another book, it is as near the size as could be of the old one and I got a pencil with the book or at the same time and it is as near the same size as could be. So I have as good a fit out as while writing this book to write the other and will have to begin in the new book. Well I put some potatoes in the fire to roast and I must look at them.

November 21, 1861

Well the sun has again and it is a verry pretty morning and my potatoes was cooked and they tasted good to. Well about the review. I cannot acertain for certain what the number of men was. Some say 15,000 men, some says more and some less. But when the official report comes out in the papers I will note it down. Well it was long after dark when the Co came in last night but the Boys says it was not any harder work than the days before and the day that they wouldnt have missed going for anything, some says for five dollars. At any rate I would like to have been there with my pen in hand. I could have noted down the most important movements. I understand that we do not drill today. And if that is so I will have a good chance to write as well as doctor a little for my cold which got a little worse last night. I send the other day to Washington by a teamster for a box of Graffenbar [Graefenberg][24] pills and twenty five cents worth of Czane paper and I fix some paper tea for my cold. The ground frooze a little last night and the fire feels good this morning. Our fireplace warms up the tent pretty well. Well I must say goodby to this old companion in the shape of a little black covered book for it full.

Goodby, I have the war fever as we say.

Volume 2

November 22, 1861 to December 30, 1861

A Soldiering in Dixie

Wm. R. Ray
Place of Nativity
Cassville Grant Co [County], Wisconsin
United States of America
And hope to God it may continue so
Henry when this you see — remember me
A Soldiering in Dixie

Wm. R. Rays notebook. He being a member of Capt Callis Co [Company] which is F or the Lancaster Union Guards and If found by any person please notify the owner or give it to Capt Callis and oblige the owner and receive a reward. Wm. R. Ray

November 22, 1861

Camp Arlington near Washington in Virginia. Well here goes for filling up another notebook with small sketches and gatherings of the times and things that is transpiring around me. I have just sent home a book that I filled since I enlisted. Well the drums are beating and I suppose for drill. I will be ready at any rate. Well we have been out and drilled two hours and I have cleaned my gun and brasses and now the cooks are hollowing for us to get our dinners and my tentmates elected me to draw the victuals and I must go. And there the drummers are beating the dinner call. Well our dinner consisted of hominy. We tented pretty good.

Well about the review. The papers state that there was seaventy thousand soldiers and twenty five thousand civillians. It is said to be the largest review that ever was in the United States.[25] I will read the paper and then note down accordingly. We did not drill yesterday. But I was detailed to help one of the teamsters to haul wood and so that I did not get to rest. But it was not hard work that I done. I sent my other book home and a Frank Leslie newspaper *[Frank Leslie's Illustrated Newspaper]* that had an engraving of the fleet off Port Royal [Port Royal Sounds, South Carolina) and the bombardment of the fort. I sent it home on account of the picture. Well I must quit writing in this book and begin to write a letter.

November 23, 1861

And it is raining this morning and rained most of the night. It was not verry cold last night. It is just about such weather as an April rain in Wisconsin. It is verry disagreeable weather. Hello, here it comes harder and more water and a great wind.

Well our Orderly was in Washington day before yesterday and he heard some of the big officers talking about the Kings Brigade as being the best drilled on the review and expically the Wis Regts as being the best and largest. That accounts for us staying at home the day of the review. That we couldnt march in the same space as the other Regts. And he also heard that Mcdowel had offered two Regts for the fifth Wisconsin to put in this brigade instead of the Indianna Regt that is in now.[26]

November 24, 1861

And it is a pretty day but the wind blows some. It is Sunday evening and we are expecting to go to the funeral of A.W. Atwood [Olander W. Atwood], one of our Company boys.[27] He was a verry wild fellow but still good hearted. I loaned him some money after he came out of the hospital the first time and the rations didnt suit him and he wanted to buy something that suited his taste. And also some paper, envelopes & stamps to write to his wife and money was scarce then in the Co but I saved a little and then run out after all before payday and had'nt enough to post a letter to my own mother. But it is not the first favor that I have done for the sick. I do not have a verry good name amongst some of the well boys for not accommodating them but I do not care for that for my conscience is clear on that score. Then this Attwood exposed himself and I often told him so, but he was one of them kind that couldnt be still when there was anything going on but he must have a hand in it. He wouldnt get mad for me telling him to go into his tent. He has a brother in the sixth regiment and he has gone with four men that the Orderly detailed to pick out a place and dig the grave. And when they come back we will go or the Co will go to bury him. It is customary for the Co to go to the funeral of a comrade but there is nothing compulsary about it. So the Captain put it to vote and all with the exception of five or six voted to go. But it is most always the case that there is some don't care for nobody in a company like this.

The order was given to fix up our tents and clean them out this morning and it was dark. There was four, I with them, went about half a mile after cedar boughs and two stayed and cleaned out of the tent and washed the knifes & forks, tin cups & plates. And there was one out of the tent on Co police. And we put the fresh boughs in all over the floor which made it look verry nice. Then the weekly inspection of arms and knappsacks came next and we supposed that inspections was over for the day. And there was a man from the opposite tent across the street came in and I was reading the N. York Herald [New York Herald] and spoke something about the war and we got into quite a argument and I was blowing away like fury and who should open the tent but Capt and him and the Colonel stuck their heads in and looked and viewed the tent and fastened up the door and as they turned to go away I heard the Capt say to the Colonel — that tent looks well and the Colonel answered and said, it does look verry well.

John Harvil [John Harville][28] came into our tent a little while since and is here yet. He brought us the news that we had the name of having the best and cleanest quarters of any in the Co by the Colonels decision and he inspected evry tent. He could see how we had things fixed for there was only three in the tent but if he had come here a great many times he would found such a crowd here that he couldnt a seen anything else. For we have a great many visiters. Our tent being so comfortable and always having a fire. There is fireplaces in most of the tents but they are too lazy to get wood. One think that he has brought more wood than another and so it goes. We have some in here evry day that are kind a sick to sit by the fire. We have the name of having the best fireplace in the Co. There is somebody running here evry day to get a little paper or tobacco or to toast their bread and so on and the boys put me in to turn them of saying that I could do it with such a good face and I can the hearty ones but not the sick for I do evrything I can for them. But the hearty ones damn them, I say they had as much of a money as we had at payday and if they didnt use it right that is no reason that I should give to them. So the boys tell them that I own it and then I pound them roughshod for coming here to get it given them.

Well when we first come here there was plenty of old axes laying around so I picked up one and saved it and tried to get the boys to put a handle in it but they didnt do it. So I put one in and then they all had something to do so they couldnt help me to grind it. And I got a fellow to help me grind it. Then they was running here to get it until it got dull and then Frank Boyanton ground it again and we could not get it hardly long enough to chop our own wood. Now I have just refused it to a man that wanted it. I can refuse it easy because there is nice camp axes to sell and if we loose ours we shall have to buy one and they might as well do that as anybody. Then they will have one without the truble of borrowing.

Well Jesse Shipton & Richard Pierce have just got back from digging Attwoods grave. It is out just this side of Balls Cross Roads, a noted place but of no importance as I can see but there is a great deal said about it. I and J. D. Overton [John D. Overton][29] got the promise of a pass tomorrow to go to Alexandria which is about six miles from here. It is said to be a large place. Well it is snowing now for the first time and is likely to snow and if so I shall not go there tomorrow. We did not bury Attwood today as it was late when the men got home from digging the grave.

November 25, 1861

And it is a cold windy day. It did not snow much and I did not get to go to Alexandria neither. There is snow on the shady side of objects yet and it is likely to be. The ground frooze pretty hard last night and it will hardly thaw out today. The reason that I didnt go to Alexandria today is that Overton was put on guard and I was put on water guard which is to carry water for the cooks. So we calculate to go some day soon.

Well they have buryed Attwood and got home. I would of liked to a gone to the funeral but being on guard I couldnt. The following is an account of the funeral. It is the first one that this Co have had to go to. And I hope it will be the last. Well, the Co was called into ranks, that is all that wanted to go (there was some five or six that didnt go) and were marched to the hospital where the ambulance was ready to take the corpse to its final resting. And they started the regiment band before with muffled drums and playing a funeral tune, it was a malodious but verry solemn tune. Then the ambulance bearing the corpse and the driver and the big brother of the deceased. Then the boys marched after the ambulance in single file.

Well, the Co has just got to the parade ground and there is where the Regt forms before going on Battalion drill. I guess the boys will want to go on double quick today for the wind blows cold from the west. But I have not had to be out in it much today for the cooks does not use so much. And I having the same man as I had the last time to help me and he shirked and I carried ten pails full more than he did. And I shall watch him today for he has the name of shirking. His name is Isaac Raymer [Isaac C. Raemer].[30] I hadnt ought to have on guard today as I was on extra duty this time around but the Orderly being away, the second sargeant didnt mark it and I went to the Orderly and told him how it was and said he would like for me to do it as there was so many had a pass today and that he would mark it on the next round and if he does it will be a long time before I come on again. Well I must go and see if the cooks wants water.

November 27, 1861

And I didnt write any yesterday. The cause of it is that I was at Alexandria and six more on the same pass and it will be the last time that I going any place with so many on the same pass. And that kept me on the same run to keep pace with pass. Therefore I didnt get to write any as I would of a liked to. But I will give as good an account of what I seen as near possible. Well after getting the pass signed, it was near an hour before we all got ready to and had a hard time to get started but when we did, we went a good pace and got there about ten oclock. The distance is six miles from here. We rambled about until we got pretty well scattered but I stayed with the pass and the man that carried it got tight or verry near drunk. His name is George Atkinson.[31]

But we went first to the docks and they were in a verry bad state but they were repairing. The docks are all wood and they are verry rotten. Evrything indicates the neglect and a want of industry and enterprise. In fact it is so all over the city (for such it may be called). The streets are verry dirty and in some places there is a verry bad stench raises which must be verry unhealthy. The streets are filled with people, mostly soldiers. And at almost evry street corner there is a guard stationed. And there is no strong drinks sold that is stronger than beer and some places they are not allowed to sell that even. But George Atkinson found something stronger but it was in the suburbs of the city I guess. I went down several times to the docks and saw small crafts coming in and going out. And a good many fishing smacks as they are called. Those all go by sail that I have spoken of for the larger had only two masts. But there lay the Pensacola Man of War anchored out in the river, the river here being quite large. The Pensacola mounts 24 guns. She is pretty good size, that is I thought so but there was a sailor along with us and he said it was a ship but a small one. It had three masts. It had steam also, it is a steamship.

November 28, 1861

And it is Thanksgiving day and we are observing it to. This morning we had orders to fix for review after getting our dress coats. We have one uniform suit now. We fixed up with one new suit. Guns clean and evrything cleaned for Govenor [Alexander] Randall was a going to view us and make a speech. We formed on the parade ground and the Co was equalized and Co F was the right number for the first time so they did not take any off. We were marched to the front of the Arlington [House] and were formed into column by division and the other Regts of the Brigade also and we went through the performance of presenting arms to the Govenor and then General [Rufus] King gave the soldiers and officers an introduction to Randall and then he proceeded to speak and make a good speech. He addressed the Wisconsin boys first, then turned to the Indiania Regt. And at last to the whole Brigade and after he was done speaking, the Colonel of the Indiania Regt proposed three cheers for the Govenor. Then Gen King, then George which meant George B.

Mcllen then for three for the Union and then we were dismissed by King and marched home by our own officers. I understand that the Colonel or Lieutanant Col was invited to dine at the Arlington House on a Thanksgiving dinner which he excepted. There was a great many officers to hear the speech. It was short but to the point.

Well it is a pleasant day, that is pleasant over head and warm but not so pleasant among some of my tentmates. The cause of it is the stealing of a map. One of the boys stole a map from another but I am out of the muss. And I will watch him myself. I will not mention any name at present. Well we looked as well as any of the Regts today when we got our uniform on and I guess we will wear them now and I will send my old clothes home if I can. Well I will quit for a while and sew on a button on my coat.

November 29, 1861

And it is a pretty afternoon but the forenoon was a little misty and rainy. It is quite warm now, I could go without my coat verry well now for a couple of hours, but it will soon be cool enough. We did not drill any this forenoon but I guess we will drill in firing some this afternoon. I have spent the forenoon in reading and writing a letter for Wm Smith, [William A. Smith], a great cronie of mine.[32] Oh, but it is warm, we having a fire in the tent. And now the sun coming out it is too warm. I guess I will go and buy some popcorn as the pedlars is right here. It is done up in papers like tobacco.

Well it is candlelight and I got my corn. It was verry good but still verry dear eating. Well it is raining again and guess it will rain here instead of snow which we would have in Wisconsin. We were out on drill and fired blank catridges long enough to fire away ten rounds. Then we went to drilling and had the best drill that we ever had and came home tired but we did not have any dress parade and it wasnt such a hard drill although we double quicked considerable. I have got another Frank Leslie newspaper ready to send home which I gave eight cents for.

December 3, 1861

And it is a long time since I wrote any in my book. And I am water carrier today again and I am glad of it. I hope it will always come so. I would rather do it than to stand guard. It is verry cold this morning. It is so much so that the mud is dried up for once and I carried water enough to do the cooks awhile so therefore I to write.

The boys are going doublequick after forming on the parade and the orderly seargeants giving in their accounts which they have to do now evry morning. Then the major gave the command from the right of the company to the rear into Column which was performed then he gave the command to trail arms and doublequick which was done until they had a mind to stop which wasnt so soon as usual for it is so cold. And it being the coldest night we have had and I slept as comfortable as I ever slept in my life. But there has been one left our tent which is Jesse Shipton and we have more room and live more comfortable for we have fixed up things better. We have changed our bed so that we only take up about half of the tent floor. For we lay with our feet togather, that is three on one side and three on the other side and the blankets lap over each other so that it is double thickness over our feet. We spread the blankets crossways and the three can lay under them verry well so we have three over us instead of two when we laid two and two.

There was a bad affair happened in our Co yesterday which terminated in six of them being put in the guardhouse and there was a great many more that ought to went in for they done the same thing but didnt get catched at it. The cause of it is that we didnt drill yesterday morning and our boys with a great many others went to tearing down a house that an old man lived in. But I think that our boys wouldnt of done it, but it was begun the day before by some of the sixth Regt boys it is said. And our Captain told us that they was going to court martial them but I don't know as they will but will scare them a little. I guess there is from this time out to be a patrol around this vicinity and if they catch any body out they will [make] them prisinors.

The account of us not drilling yesterday morning was this. That the Capt wanted one of the Lieutenants to take a squad and the orderly to take the other squad and first one then the other didnt want to do it. And just for sport the Lieutanant Young ordered us to shoulder arms and right face and double quicked us to our quarters and told us to break ranks and do as we pleased. But the other officers didnt like it much. And after the boys got in the guardhouse, some of the field officers it is said, accused the Captain of dismissing his Co for the purpose of giving his boys a chance to get the things before the other Companies were dismissed. But that is not so, I feel quite certain.

And there is another thing that has transpired and it is shameful to mention and it all terminated from me refusing one of my tentmates a pipe of tobacco. He is a pretty good beggar and I got tired of furnishing him it so I told him that he might draw sutlers tickets and buy it. And it made him mad but he took the tobacco but this wasnt the only thing that he was deficient for. It was most evry thing such as butter. Well when he bought some butter he told me the same as I told him when he got the tobacco. But mind he hadnt bought any butter before. And I and all the rest had bought. I had bought two lbs and several more had done the same and he always ate a part of it. Well, this mans name is Boyanton [Boynton]. I hate to mention names but must this. And I have loaned money one time and another to evry one of my tentmates and always gave them a share of what I got. That is anything that they or I would divide. And then when Boyanton and I was talking about our trubles, first one then another pitched on to me, that is with their tongue, but I always dared them to prove their accusations against me and then that would stump them. And I done wrong, I must admit for getting vexed and saying so much. I tell you, I was into pretty for I could stop them at most anything. I talked with them as long as they would say a word to me. And then I had to stop as a matter of course and I told them to keep evrything to themselves and I would do the same but behold when I bought some onions and brought into the tent, Orley Foot thought that I might give him some but I refused to do it. He said he had given me some but I said if he would prove it. But it stumped him and shut up about things and matters.

Well I must carry some water then write some more and I have spilled my ink. Well I have carried six more pails of water which makes sixteen today. The cooks do not use so much as when I carried before for them. I carried forty pails full. There is brigade drill this evening and the boys that didnt go have to dig a ditch to carry the water off from our street when it rains. So that they do not get to play as usual. I hardly can tell what is the reason that I come on water guard unless that the orderly gives me a little lenity for I have been on three or four times. It is easier work than standing on guard around the camp and therefore I think he has shown me some lenity but it may not be so.

December 4, 1861

And it is a pretty day. It is quite warm. Congress has sitt now and we had the Presidents message here in camp last night.[33] I bought one of the papers, it an extra to the National Republican. The message fills just one side of it. I think much of the message, it is right to the point and he has left evrything to Congress that he could so as to not show to much authority, I suppose. And he thinks that it will be more satisfactory to the people at large to have congress have a voice in evrything that is passed now. There havnt been many newsboys around since it, the weather, has been cold until last night. The fellow came along in a buggy that I bought my paper of.

Well it night again and no mail for me. I do not see what is the reason. I write a great many. I have written upwards of twenty and have not received more than half that many. But I think that they are delayed on the road and the mail only running from Cassville twice a week. That may account for it some. But I must have patience although I laid in a good stock of that material when I got the last letter. But that has almost run out. And I do hope that I shall not have to lay in another stock before getting another letter. But probably the folks have'nt as much time to write as I have. And I have sent several valuables home that I would like to hear from.

December 5, 1861

And all is well with the exceptions of our chimney which was throwed over last night by somebody, I don't know who. But there was a man came into our tent this [morning] and I suppose he thought he was doing us a favor when he told us that he knew who done it. But he wouldnt tell us. So I guess we will never out who done it. But it is of little consequence for we have been talking about tearing it up but never got at it. And now we have it rebuilt better than it was. So I think that we didnt loose much by it, but gained. Frank and Olie has built it this time and they have gone to get more brick as they was excused from drill today by the Captain.

Well it is three Oclock and I have been after a cedar to sett at the corner of tent which I have done as well as most of the Co except those that went on Brigade drill which was twenty four. It helps the look of our quarters and I understand that we are going to stay here this winter. And there is such talk that the officers made an estimate of how many teams it would take to take this brigade on a twenty days march. Which was the calculation at time it is said but finding that there was not sufficient teams to take the most nessary things that had and must go, it was postponed. And we are to go into winter quarters here on this ground and the Colonel told the Orderly Sargeants to make out a requisition for what socks and blankets was needed by their respective Companys by tatoo which is eight Oclock. That it is beat by the drummer. But I sleep warm enough now, so warm that I sweat when laying in bed last night.

James Garner, one of my tentmates bought a fiddle last night. I was and the rest of the boys was against it but now I must admit that it seems nice to have a little music now since I got to hear it. Well it is night now, probably seaven Oclock and we did'nt have any dress parade tonight for the boys didnt get back until sundown or after and they just stopped out on the ground to hear the orders read. But it is said that we will have to go on picket the latter part of next week. The sixth Regt going first for three days, then us go three days. For they say that we do not begin to be as good men for fatiguing work as when we first. And it is said also that the cause of it is we do not work or travel enough. And I knew that I cant stand it to doublequick as well now as I could two months since. At any rate I would like to try picketing.

December 6, 1861

And another fine morning has made it appearance. And all is right for we now eat our rations and have for several days. The cause is we are all well in this tent and have better bread than we did for a while. Our fireplace works exceedingly well. It warms up the tent good, but we do not need it so much now for it is verry pleasant and warm enough to go without an overcoat, it bids fair for pleasant weather now. We do not have any drill today for we are fixing up and adorning the street with pines and cedars and making a large bower across the street. It looks verry pretty for there is from two to three and four trees to evry tent and all evergreen that it makes it look verry pretty. It looks like spring putting the trees and warm day togather.

December 7, 1861

And it is a pretty day. It is about three oclock. I am on guard. I am on the second relief and therefore I have to go on at half past four. I came off half past twelve and that made it late before I got my dinner.

December 8, 1861

And it is a murky morning and the night was so. No rain but fog so much so that I couldnt see more than a rod at times. I will give you a detail of what transpired yesterday and also what a guard has to do. The first thing as usual is a drummer comes out and beats the drummers call and then the pipers and drummers comes out and beat the revalie which brings us out of bed and into the ranks in the street to answer to roll call. This is at half past six Oclock. Then at seaven the drummer that beats the drummers call, he beats the breakfast call. Then at eight Oclock the Police call is beat by him then at quarter past eight, he beats the drummers call again. Then the drums and pipers come out on the parade and beat the guard call and then the guards begin to assemble on the left of them. And when they have all got there and the commissioned and non-commissioned officers also and then they examine our arms to see if they are clean and to be sure that they are not loaded. Then we are marched to the guardhouse by the officer of the guard and the Officer of the day look after the Camp and the Generals things. The officers are detailed by the field officers of the Regiment the day before they serve and the guards are at the same time.

It takes a captain to be officer of the day and Lieutanants to be officer of the guard. The orders day before yesterday were as follows. At dress parade Capt [Samuel J.] Nasmith, Officer of the day, Lieutanant [J. N. P.] Bird, Officer of the guard, Co A, 4 privates, B 4p, C 3p 1 corporal, D 4p, E 3p 1 corporal, F 4 p, G 3 p 1 corporal, H 4 p, I 4 p, and Co K 3 p 1 Sargeant and six extra guards which were used the day I was on. The above is for the day I was on and it is the same evry day as to numbers.

Well to return. And after we are marched to the guardhouse, the officer of the guard takes down the names of enough for the first relief and puts a [corporal] with them and him sends around to relieve the old guard, Then he takes the names of the rest and numbers them of for reliefs and puts a corporal with each relief. Then dismisses us until time for us to relieve the first relief which is evry two hours. I was on the second relief and my post was no [number] two. Well when the two hours was up, the Officer of the guard or the sargeant, the officer if there and if not there, the sargeant will hollow out, turn out such a relief, which ever may be due to go on. For instance when it was time for to relieve the first relief he hollowed out, turn out second relief, go and relieve first. And so it went until next morning and we were relieved by the new guard.

The orders in daytime were to let soldiers pass in and just as they pleased but keep out pedlars and civillians unless they have a pass signed by the colonel or some higher officer. But at night it is different. We got orders to let no one in unless they had the countersign which was Waterloo last night. And if we seen anybody trying to cross our beat we must hollow out, halt, and he halts. We ask him who goes there, but must never let anybody come nearer than six paces before saying halt and must hollow halt twice and he does not stop neither first nor second time, I must hollow for the corporal of the guard double quick and he tries to catch him so as to punish him for running the guard. But if he should stop the first time I hollowed to him and I ask who goes there and he says a friend with the countersign or says a friend, I say friend and if there is more than one I say advance one at a time and give the countersign. And if given right, I say it is right go your way. Well I must quit and finish this some other time.

December 9, 1861

Well it is the 9th and I am not verry well this evening. I am writing by candlelight and my head aches and I have a verry bad cold. For when I stood on guard it was a muddy beat and it was a foggy night. At times I could'nt see two rods [28 feet] but it was warm and I didnt get to sleep any. I have just received two papers, I guess from mother but no letters, but I shall not have much time to read them for we are going out on picket tomorrow. We start at eight Oclock in the morning. The sixth went Sunday morning and we have to go and relieve them. Well I must quit this evening.

December 10, 1861

And it is half past seaven and the boys are on their heels jumping for joy for they start at eight oclock to go on picket. There is twenty four files goes out of evry Co in the Regt and it did not take me therefore I have to stay in camp but probably will have something to do. I am glad I didnt have to go for I am quite unwell and have been for several days. It is the first time I have been sick since I enlisted. I have just hired Frank Boyanton to take down notes while they are on picket. He is a smart and well educated fellow and I give him fifty cents for it. It is paying pretty dear but as I could not go, I do not mind it so much. Well the boys are gone, I guess I will have all day to write as I have not been detailed to do anything.

Well, I will finish giving an account of guard duty that I commenced on the eighth inst. And if I see anybody coming on my beat I say to him when he gets within six paces, halt and if he halts I ask who goes there and he says a friend. I say advance friend and give the countersign. If right I let him go and if not right I hold him at the point of the bayonet and call for the corporal of the guard and the number of my post whatever it may be. And the corporal comes and I give him up to him.

And there is what they call the grand round. It is to try the sentinels to see if they are on the alert and to see if they can catch them in any way. The grand round consists of Officer of the Day, Officer of the Guard, a sargeant and sometimes the Colonel comes with them. And they all try the guard by going togather and when they come within six paces I halt them not knowing who it is. And I ask who goes there. The sargeant will say, the grand round. I say advance Sargent and give the countersign. When this is done they all advance and question the sentinel about his duty and if he does not know, they tell him. And besides this there is some officers tries to run the beats of different sentinels to see if he looking out as he ought to be. Well I must go and do company police duty.

December 11, 1861

Well the Corporal put me to carry water for the cooks and he also put me at the same today for it is not verry hard work. Well I must finish about the guard duty. And the officers of the regiment tried to run my beat several times but I always halted them. There was two officers run my beat at one end whilst I was on the other end and it was a little foggy that night but I saw two men come running and I run to see if they was going to run the beat and sure enough they did run it but I hollowed halt at the top of my voice. But they crossed my beat and I hollowed again and they stopped. By this I got pretty close and hollowed for the corporal of the guard No. 2 double quick and it was near the guard house. So in a minute the corporal was by the other officer and made him give the countersign and let them go again. Then after a while the officer of the guard tried to run the beat at the other end and I stopped him and made him give the countersign and the officer of the day said that there never had been as good sett of guards around this regiment before. For he couldnt run the guard at all without them seeing him. And ever since the Colonel told us that it was for to school us that he had a guard and not for to oppress, we have taken more interest in it and the officers instructs us more also than they used to. We cannot leave the guards house except to get our meals. When on guard, we must stay there the twenty four hours and receive the new guard in the morning. And then we are released from duty until two oclock drill in the afternoon. Then we have to go on dress parade and the next day we go on general police and then that releases the guard and they go to their respective Co and drill until their turn comes again. Then go through the same and so on to the end of the chapter. This finishes the account of guard duties.

The sixth regt got home last evening from picket duty about sundown and never seen a secesh while gone it is said. But our boys will have a harder time of it than they for the wind is blowing a hurricane and it is raining some.

December 13, 1861

And it is a pretty morning and I am on guard today. The cause of it is that yesterday the corporal come around to see who would volunteer to go on guard today so as any of the boys that was on picket wouldnt have to go on today. And James Garner and I volunteered to go out of this tent and I am on the third relief so I don't go on post until noon or after. Our boys got in from picket about sundown last evening and in good spirits. Nobody hurt, nobody killed and they don't drill this forenoon and I guess not any today. Some of the boys got one mule and two horses while on picket. Some of our regt done better than the sixth did and they told it about that our boys seen some of our own cavelry and got scared and run for life. There is a strong antipathy between the two regt and it is getting stronger all the time. And it all arose from a dispute about a few boards the day we came to this camp.

December 15, 1861

And it is a verry pretty day and I can sit in the tent comfortable without a fire, but have an overcoat on. I have just got dinner. It consisted of bean soup and a few beans therein and bread. And the beans were cooked good. Yesterday afternoon the regiment, at least twenty four files out of a Co and it did not take me, and went out to balls crossroads [Ball's Cross Roads] to go through a sham fight. There was five Brigades there and some Cavelry and Artillery also. We could hear them from here. They was firing about one hour but don't kill anybody as they fired blank catridges but it made the noise. The boys didnt get home until about dark. There I hadnt anything to do yesterday and I wrote an answer to a letter that I got from Henry the night before and have written one today to Mary Jane [Mary Jane Ray — older sister, born 1824] as an answer to one that I received at the same time. I received one from Otice Way [relative of Amos Way, husband of younger sister Evelina Ray, born 1841] at the same time which made three.

And when I was on my post, Olie Foot, one of my tentmates brought them to me. And it being about eight oclock at night I could not read them but I did read the one from Otice as it was written verry plain with black ink. And the moon was shining as pretty as I ever seen it and today being Sunday I didnt have to do police duty. I went up to the guards house when the others did that was on guard Friday and we were dismissed. And that being at eight Oclock we didnt have to go on the inspection as it was at the same hour. But heretofore inspection came off at ten oclock and then them that were dismissed from police duty on Sunday had to go on inspection. It does appear to me that I am lucky if there is such a thing but this all happened so because I volunteered to go on guard Friday so as the boys that was on picket wouldnt have to go. But it wasnt so in other Cos for they had to go that was on picket and there was no drill so they got to rest that day which they needed, that is our boys did.

December 16, 1861

And it is a verry pretty day and there is some excitement in camp which is caused by a report that the rebels have advanced as far as Falls Church in great numbers and were fortifying thereabouts. And I saw Mcdowel and his staff go out that way as fast as their horses could run and that has a great impression. And we have been examined to see how many catridges and caps we had and if they were good ones and if not we got them after dinner. And we had bean soup verry thin and poor it was too. We have just got orders to put on our blue clothes but I had them for that was the last order. But some of the boys wears their gray clothes any way but I have got so that I do nothing without orders.

December 17, 1861

And it is a pretty day and the cause of our putting on our new blue clothes is that we went on Brigade drill, twenty four files. Last night there was considerable excitement in camp last night by thirty four horse wagon loads of corn coming in from within a little distance of Fairfax Courthouse. It is as follows. There was night before last, a great many cavelry went westward and yesterday morning there was about eighty teams it said went by on a forageing expidition. And in an hour or so Mcdowel went by post haste and then last night about dark some of our boys said they seen thirty four horse wagon loads go by. And that the teamsters told them that there was forty more loads to come tomorrow and that there was a strong guard around the field of infantry and cavelry. And they said that the federal killed one sesech and that the secesh fired ten rounds on them and wounded one horse only a little. And once there was fifteen or twenty secesh cavelry come right on to them but as soon as they seen the federals they broke for the brush as fast as their horses would take them.

Well it will soon be drill time and I am ready for it. Well it is three oclock and we have been on review. We was reviewed by Mcdowel. We drilled in marching, firing blank catridges and a great many different moves.

December 19, 1861

And another pretty day. And we went to Manson [Munson's] Hill or Baileys crossroads either as it is right between the two and I suppose that all of Mcdowels was there at any rate. I think there was as many as fifteen Regts there and we all had twenty rounds of blank catridges. That is the infantry did. There was one regt of Cavelry and three or four Batteries of artillery, each battery containing from four to six cannon. We were the first regiment to fire and then advanced a little, then fired again and advanced again, fired again, then our catridges give out and we fell in the rear. We went through the whole as near as we could I suppose when we get into the battlefield. And I hope that wont be long. We had our knappsacks on our back all day and them packed. With heavy marching, it was pretty hard days work. But I have had harder at home some days. We are getting used to it and it don't tire us so. There was cannon and infantry firing, cavelry charging. We was about two hours fighting the battle and didnt kill a man. We got home about dark with keen appetites.

December 23, 1861

And it has been a few day since I wrote any but I couldnt do it any sooner verry well as I have been so busy at one thing and another. Yesterday I wrote a long letter to Newton [older brother, born 1819] and on Saturday I was detailed to carry wood for the cooks and in the afternoon three of my tentmates got excused from drill and they built up the tent or built up a pen the side of the tent with poles about 78 in and banked it and daubed it up and sett the tent on top of it and it makes a great deal more room for we can stand almost straight on the sides. Today we have built up bunks. We had a great time to get started at it for we couldnt agree on it, which to have it. And some wouldnt anyway. At last Olie and I went to work and built us one and they thought that we took too much room. Then James Clark & Garner went work and put one up and they put it so high that Frank and Richard could make theirs under it and they did it and have got the best of any of us. And we have more room in the tent than before and evrything is out of the way. And we have got the bottom of the tent tacked down to the poles and now winds cant get in except a little at the door and I sewed on some buttons and cut holes in my oilcloth and hung it up in front of the door. Well the weather is severe. Last night it rained considerable and it has rained and snowed a little alternately all day and the wind blows verry hard and it is cold and getting colder. I am writing by candlelight. The order read on dress parade last evening were to drill on double quick today and go on a grand review tomorrow. But we havnt drilled and I guess we will not do anything tomorrow.

December 25, 1861

And it is a verry pretty morning, verry. As well as being Christmas as evrybody knows. And there is no drill today in our Co. I don't know how it is with others. The camp was all alive last night. The officer of day had occasion several times to tell the boys to be still. Cap Callis being officer of the day, he wouldnt be verry hard on them.

We have got our tent fixed up first rate and clean and tidy and plenty of wood to keep it warm. We are going to have a great time I guess today. Everything is lively as can be. I wish I could be at home today for they are enjoying themselves, I hope, and I think so at any rate. Well we didnt drill any yesterday forenoon with the exceptions of going out on the parade ground and coming back and being dismissed. For it was verry cold. We drill in the afternoon. We don't drill as much as other Companies and have the name of doing as well and sometimes better. We have the best officers of any Co in the Regt for understanding drill. Our second Lieutenant [Henry Young of Lancaster] is the best drill master in the Regt I think. Some of the boys didnt like him at first because he was so strict but as they have more experience in what must be done, they like him verry well now and I like him better all the time.

Our tent works so well that a great many others are building theirs up in the same manner and having good bunks fixed up. We sleep better (but we have never suffered any) at least I sleep well. Well I went last evening and drew $2.50 cts worth of sutlers tickets but shouldnt of if some of them hadnt wanted something to spend today for I loaned $1.50 cts to two different tentmates that had drew all the tickets they could without an order from the Capt and they hated to do that. You see from this that the Capt has given orders to the sutlers not to let his boys have more than eight dollars apiece on their wages. And they having drawn that amount they had to stop until payday. It was James Garner and James Clark that I loaned the money to. I laid in a good supply of paper & envelopes & stamps & mother sent me 16 three cent stamps and there is never a day passes lately but I loan something.

Well we didnt go on review yesterday as was calculated and I guess and hope that that kind of work is done with. For I think that winter has set in in earnest although it is thawing some already. And it is only about nine oclock. Our street is verry dirty this morning. For it being such bad weather we did not clean it up and today there is as many building up their tents that there is no chance to clean it. But we have the name of having the best and prettiest camp of any regt in the service. This is the statement that several New York papers have made and some of the Washington papers also. That it is the cleanest and the streets are thrown up, that is the Cos streets. Then the General streets are thrown up and sidewalks made also and evergreen trees sett in evry appropriate place to make it look well and each Co vied with the other which should have the prettiest. And it got to be pretty nice.

Well it is candlelight and we have had a good oyster supper and two apples apiece. I never seen a livlier time, especially tonight. I never could eat oysters before but I ate those and ate about one quart.

December 26, 1861

And Christmas is over and we had a great time. Last night our band after roll call went out on the main street and began playing and after a large crowd had collected they went over and serenaded the second Regt and their Colonel and when we got home, the second came and done the same by us. But theirs was a splendid brass band and good players also and many were the hearty cheers that was given. And after the band had played a few national tunes, they went over to the sixth Regt and gave them a round. But their guards would'nt let the crowd in but let the band in and that made a harder feeling than ever existed before. And some of the boys run the guard and at that they called out the guard and that wouldnt suffice. And they called out a lot more from the regiment and came and charged on the crowd which was verry large by this time. And they dispersed it. Our orderly was a little tight I guess, and he went around and got all he could to turn out with guns and bayonets fixed, swearing that they could whip out the sixth Regt but they didnt do anything but talk as is generally the case. But if they hadnt charged on them, the whole of the second regt would have been over here. There was a great many got here as it was and no telling what would have been done. Probably a worse row.

December 29, 1861

And it is a cloudy day but warm. I think it will rain soon. Well we were out on another division drill yesterday and it went off well with the exceptions of a man in Co C. of the second Regt had his gun burst while in the act of firing it and it injured him some but two of his comrades a great deal more. Quite bad, I understand. The gun bursted from the but half way up the barrel. It is thought to be his fault. It is supposed he had overloaded it as a great many have in a way of seeing which can get rid of their catridges first and he has been known to do the same thing. And they would put in from four to six catridges. I suppose they think because it is blank catridges they can do as they please with them and not be in danger. I know of a great many of our boys doing the same thing but no accident be happened them. But after they heard of the gun bursting I saw a great many pulling catridges out and grass &c. They do it for fear of their gun. There was men all around me that had in from two to four but I mind they didnt shoot them out from fear. Well we were marched around for about four hours from one place to another and a great deal of the time it was doublequick march. Run to one place and fire a little until the unseen enemy would run then away we would go and fire again in another place where the enemy was likely to break the ranks.

December 30, 1861

And it has been a chilly day but thawed a little. We have not drilled any today. We have just been on dress parade and the order was read that there would be a general muster tomorrow morning by one of General King aids [aides], the second will be mustered in first at 7 oclock and us at half past nine oclock and the sixth regt right afterward. The mustering in consists of the regts forming on their respective parade grounds in heavy marching orders which means to have all our things packed in our knapsacks &c with haversack and knife, fork, spoon, tin cup and plate and evrything must be neat and which I have got. But verry few has them clean. My gun is bright as a silver dollar. My shoes is blacked, buttons and brass shining. In fact, I am ready for I have washed and dried evrything. We will be closely inspected, expically our guns. But I expect to be on guard and then I shall not have to fix for it much. Well after we are inspected they call our names and we answer here just as I used to do when at school. And after that we go to our quarters. Then in a few days we get our pay. The pay roll is made out now in our Co and the first of next month is payday but probably we will not get it for several days after. There one man in our Co by the name of Largeant [J. Wesley Largent][34] is getting his discharge and there is one in the second Regt also that has got his today, his name is Homer Wilcox [William Wilcox, Company D, Second Wisconsin]. He has been unable for duty for 4 months.

Well this book is full and I am not done [with] my story yet. I could have written another. I probably shall send it by Largeant to Henry if he can take it. Well good by old book and you are the second that I have filled.

What I received from the state in clothing.

1 pair of shoes
2 pair of socks

1 cotton coat
1 pair cotton pants
2 shirts
1 cap & cover
1 coat woolen
1 pair of pants
1 overcoat

What I rec from United states

1 overcoat
1 dress coat
1 pair of pants
1 cap
1 pair of socks
1 pair shoes
1 shirt

Written 20 letters
Written 30 letters
Received 15 letters only since I enlisted

1862

The new year brought new uniforms and rising hopes to the Wisconsin and Indiana volunteers of Rufus King's brigade. The improved morale was due to the steady round of drills, camps of instruction, parades, and inspections ordered by General George B. McClellan, who had replaced Irvin McDowell as overall army commander. With his encouragements and pronouncements, "Little Mac," as McClellan was affectionally called by his men, made the troops in his new regiments feel they were becoming real soldiers.

The volunteers were eager for action—especially with the threat of a Confederate army at the very gates of Washington. Thus McClellan's lack of offensive activity as the weeks wore on was viewed with no little frustration. Under political pressure and frustrated himself with McClellan's failure to engage the enemy, President Abraham Lincoln in early March ordered his leading general to move on the Confederate fortifications at Centreville, Virginia. The orders to "be held in readiness to march at a minutes warning with knapsacks packed, and three days rations cooked," were read to the assembled companies of the Seventh Wisconsin. "Boys, if them orders exactly suit you, you may cheer," said Colonel William Robinson. One of the Badger volunteers wrote home, "You had better believe we roused him up three times . . ."

The advance, however, proved a bust. The Federals discovered that the vaunted Confederate fortifications were empty, bristling with painted wooden logs in place of real artillery pieces. The Rebels under General Joseph Johnston had slipped away undetected. The newspapers were full of the embarrassment, and the soldiers marched sullenly back to their Washington camps.

Eventually, McClellan decided to launch his effort against Richmond from the east, up the Virginia peninsula. The Western Brigade, part of Irvin

McDowell's corps, was marched overland to Fredericksburg, Virginia, in support of the effort and as a means of protecting the Federal capital. And there it was unexpectedly halted while McClellan fought and lost the first large-scale engagements of the war in the Eastern Theater just a stone's throw from Richmond. "I cannot tell you how we all felt at being left behind . . . and we were left out of the ranks of McClellan, the idol of all the army," a young Wisconsin officer wrote home. Rufus King was promoted and Colonel Lysander Cutler of the Sixth Wisconsin became temporary brigade commander.

The grey militia uniforms provided by the states were just about played out (the Second Wisconsin, for example, was taunted as the "Ragged Ass Second"), and Cutler began a policy of issuing the new Federal uniforms of blue. The coat was the dark blue nine-button regulation wool frock, the dress garb of the regulars. But it was the Model 1858 hat of the U.S. Regulars—a showy black felt affair looped up on the side with a brass eagle crest, trimmed with an infantry-blue cord and black plume as well as regimental designations in brass—that brought attention to the Westerners.

In May 1862, West Pointer John Gibbon, who was appointed as the new commander of the brigade, determined to make the tall hat a consistent item for his Westerners. Soon soldiers in nearby regiments began talking of a "Black Hat Brigade." Born in Pennsylvania and growing up in North Carolina, Gibbon was an unlikely replacement as commander of a volunteer brigade. But the new general noted the "quick intelligence" of his frisky Western men and was determined to make them real soldiers. His arduous schedule of drills and camp duties made him one of the most cordially despised brigade commanders in the entire army. It was not until their first battle that the Western men came to appreciate what he had done for them.

The first serious fighting experienced by William Ray and his comrades came late on the afternoon of August 28, 1862, in the opening engagement of the Second Bull Run Campaign. As the "Black Hat Brigade" marched along the Warrenton Turnpike outside Groveton, it was attacked by a much larger Confederate force under the command of General Thomas "Stonewall" Jackson. Surprised, the Western men swung into line and plunged into their first battle. For 90 minutes they exchanged brutal volleys at ranges of 50 yards. When darkness finally brought the bloodshed to a halt, it was discovered two of every five men in the Seventh Wisconsin was dead, wounded, or missing.

One of the first to go down was Private William Ray.

Volume 3

January 28, 1862 to March 1, 1862

A Wounded Man

Wm R. Ray, Co F
7th Regt Wis Vols

[*Ed. Note*: no entries between December 30, 1861 and January 28, 1862]
Tuesday, January 28, 1862

Well it has been a long time since I have written any and there has some things worthy of note transpired, but to return. This is morning about eight oclock. It commenced raining and is still raining. After breakfast, I put my oilcloth on and went over to the second Regt to see Wm Gleason[35] to buy a notebook that he found in a secesh house. It being quite a large book and having some few old accounts in but of no use to me or him either. Well after he got it he commenced to keep a diary of his adventures which is well done and is verry interesting and is of considerable length as he has kept a full detail of the battle of Bull Run or at least what he passed through which makes it verry interesting. And there being a great many pages yet unfilled, I thought it worth $1.00 and gave it for the book and had to leave it with him for one week so that he could copy of what he had written therein to sent to his father and mother. What he wrote is done with a pencil and I shall have to run over it with the pen and ink so that it will not get defaced. There is some of it verry much so now but he will write it over where it is partly rubed out. But it is a large book, at least so much so that I cannot carry it in my pocket and I will be under the necessity of carrying it in my knappsack which I do not like.

Well it is dinner time but I am not much hungry as I have been eating a lunch consisting of bread and cheese and butter also. The two latter articles I buy with my own money and keep them on hand all the time for sometimes we get boiled fat pork and nothing else but bread and we have that anyhow at all times. So you see that is rather rough living and I think that all a man lives for is what he can eat and wear that is and not buy it therefore I spend some of my money in that way. I only sent ten dollars back home this last payday, therefore kept back sixteen dollars and was owing one dollar and thirty cents to different ones in the Co. And I got two dollars and a half worth of tickets from the sutlers but loaned one dollar and a half to two of my tentmates which made about three dollars that I had loaned amongst the Co including all small debts. We had to buy a stove and it cost three dollars and I had to pay one dollar and a half towards it myself before I could get the boys started. And we got the stove at last that we have needed so long and when they saw that I was going to pay so much, Frank Boyanton said he would pay me fifty cents back next payday so that will be coming next payday.

And it being the muddiest time I ever seen. The mud being knee deep in place and all over it was shoe top deep and had been so for some time and the right wing of the Regt having to go on picket and all that was able must go and that included me so I concluded to buy a pair of boots and did so. They cost five dollars and they proved to be to small by the time I got out to the advanced picket lines and I traded with a fellow and made a good trade and come home a little easier than I went out. And that was not verry easy I tell you for either or both pair of boots being new it made it hard walking and mud being so deep and sticky in places as to nearly pull ones boots off.

Last Wednesday which was the 22nd, we started for the picket lines which we reached about eleven oclock and were duly posted with from four to eight men on a post. Half of a regiment pickets the same length that the whole regt used to do and has a small reserve. But as soon as we started from Camp evry man picked his road and some walked faster than others and we got strung out to a mile in length along the Road. That is just our Co, for each Co, as soon as they got ready, they started and just as they got there they relieved the sixth Regiment boys and glad they was for us do so for they had been on duty three days. The reason of them being on the third day is as follows. We were to have gone the day before or 21st and it was raining in the morning and verry muddy and Gen. [Rufus] King sent word to the sixth to stay until the next morning. But the three days they were on duty it rained and snowed and stormy all the time.

We were posted on the left wing of the line on the most advanced posts. Our Co and Co C were on at the left wing and Cos A, D and I were on the right wing. I and five or six others were on post (as it is called) the full time or forty eight hours. There is only one man stands at a time and they are relieved and go back to where the others is. That is where the four (or more) have a fire. I was on what was called the first reserve which [consists] of as many men as the commander chooses to put on the first twenty four hours. There was fifteen of us. Then the commander which was our Captain in the absence of the Major had all but seaven called back to the reserve and our Co being large, there was enough on the reserve the first twenty four hours to relieve those that had been on and when that was done all but us first reserve went back to form the second reserve and had all taken away from our post but me and six others. And Lieutanant Woodhouse was relieved by Lieutanant Young and he chose the men he wanted to stay which being me and the other six I have spoken of before. We had one post to watch, it being right on the road but our fire was back a hundred yards or more from the post.

About three oclock in the morning of the second day there was a hog come up to within four rods of me. I made a jump towards it and it run off and in a few minutes a fox or something that barked like one came up to the opposite side of the road and barked. I strained my eye to see it but it being so verry dark I could see nothing. It was as dark a night as I ever stood on guard or done anything in fact. The pine trees are so thick and the dead branches interwoven so close that a man has no little labor to get through the forest.

We relieved each other evry hour. I do not know how the boys done on the other posts but we all wanted to be on post all the time. That is the second reserve would rather be out on the advanced lines than back where they were for evry one wants to see the Elephant (as the saying goes).[36]

Well it is dark and I begin to write by candlelight and behind me are two of my tentmates playing cards. That is bad but no so bad as long as they play peaceable. As when we have a tent full of visitors and they get to playing and get mad and make a terrible fuss. I cannot enjoy myself at all when there is so much fuss. And hard feelings it sours evrything. I have done all I could to keep cards out of the tent but a man must let the majority rule.

There was rather a bad affair happened in our Co this evening. It was as follows. Lieutanant Young, Orderly Sargeant and first Corporal got a pass to go to Washington yesterday morning and to come back this evening. And when they came back, the Orderly and Corporal were drunk but could just walk and that was all except that they commenced hollowing and the boys gathered around them and some way or another I don't know how, they got started about the affair of pulling the first Corporal out of the office of Comisary for the Company and that sett him raving to a high degree and the Orderly disappeared and I suppose went to the tent. But the Corporal made considerable noise, then James Garner came in and said he was going to carry the boys their supper that was on guard, he being on water guard.

And they have to carry the guards their meals, at least it is so in our Company. And I said help him take their supper to them and when we got up to the Cookhouse, Lieutenant hollowed to me wanting me to build him a fire. But he was as sober as I and I never drank a drop of liquor in my life but I often do little jobs for him. And he said for me to go on and take their suppers to them and when I came back I went to see if he had got a fire started yet which he had. And I sit down to have a chat but the Captain came in and wanted to know of Young how it was and he told Capt in a kind way how it was. He cleared himself of any foul and Capt said it was his duty to arrest the Orderly and Corporal. He said he was sitting eating his supper and a man came to the door and said there was a great noise in Co F and that he had better attend to it. So he started (but as I went to the Lieutanants tent I overheard the Captain in the Corporals quarters talking in this style - says he, you are drunk and it is my duty to arrest you) and ferreted it out and that it had played out, this getting drunk and making so much noise and that he would arrest the one that done so and Cap went out and that is the last I heard of the fracas. I didnt like the Captain verry well at first but I like him now as well as any officer in the Regt almost. The Lieutenant I have spoken of in the affair, I rather trust him with the care of the Co than any other man I know of. But he has his faults and so have I and so has evry man the world over. Well I will let this subject drop by the name of a ridiculous affair.

Well the drums are the roll call and I must dry up writing for this evening and call it a half a day (and go home I was going to say) and quit.

January 30, 1862

And raining again and has been all of this day which now two oclock and raining. O but the mud is deep, it being the worst I ever seen in any place in my life. Therefore we have done nothing in the way of work. I received a circular last evening from J. W. Yate of Syracuse New York to act as ageant for him in the sale of writing desks of an improved kind. And I addressed him a letter with one dollar therein for one of the desks or more just as the money would buy and have them sent by mail. And if they are what he represents them to be they are a great thing for a soldier. So handy and neat and he gave me great inducements to purchase. He will warrant me the sale of the order but I only sending a dollar. I thought if I get one for myself and nothing more, I cannot loose much. Therefore I risked it.

Oh, I am so tired of sitting around and doing nothing. But there is such a report that we make a move next Monday and it being Thursday now we will soon be on the move. The Ordinance Sargeant has just been in our tent. He says he thinks we get our new guns tomorrow. He has made out the requisition for them. They are the Austrian Rifle. They are a splendid gun. The Second Regt has got them and it leaves us the only regt in this brigade with the old musket and our officers are trying for them and they have the promise of the first that come.

February 6, 1862

And it has been a week since I wrote. I have had rather poor health in the time but it is improving and I begin to feel natural. I was on guard the first and caught cold and it settled all over me which caused evry bone in me to ache. Well the weather has been different evry day since I last wrote. It is raining now quite hard and has been since seaven oclock. And this morning came my turn to get wood and I have got some but not enough to do a day so I shall have to get some more. Rain or shine I never seen such bad weather as I have since I came to the sunny south as the poets calls it. And if it is all like this part I know they lie and it is verry bad weather for the sick ones and makes a great many hearty ones sick. But through all the little sickness I have had I never was excused from drill but once and never asked for it then. I can and do thank God for blessing me with good health which is the first and the best thing to take care of and pays the best of anything. Whew how hard it rains now, but our good faithful old tent turns all the water and we keep dry. And that is the greatest and best thing for good health. I believe my taking so good care of myself is the reason of me having so much better health than my comrades and some even laugh at me for acting so old womanish. But it soon turns so that I can twit them for their negligence and I sometimes make them bite their lips.

Well I hope and I also think that the war will soon end for there was a flag of truce come from secesh down on the fourth and the Congress cleaned out the house it is said. And proceeded to hold a secret session or meeting of some kind. We don't know yet nor neither will we know for a while what they are doing. It is also rumored that there was another flag came in yesterday and the talk is, but I guess nobody here in Camp knows, that their terms are verry reasonable. And I hope they are. The boys are in high spirits about getting to go home soon but I think we will have to stay here awhile yet. But I am tired of staying here in this Camp for it is mud shoe top high and has been for a month and is likely to be a month more. The [place] we are encamped on is a sticky clay soil with a little gravel intermixed and it holds water like a cistern almost. Ever since we have been here whenever and wherever there is a hole dug to the depth of two feet it would fill half full of water in a few minutes in the dryest time we had here. And if does not stop soon we may have to build boats to go out to roll call. Well wherever there a track it rains full and stays so. But to go one mile either way from here we might get ground for a camp where there is gravel and sand and stone and there the ground keeps in as good order as need be for the water soaks right through. We have drilled two or three times this week for as some mornings the ground has been frooze so as to bear up, but it soon thawed out.

Well we had a queer affair happen on the fourth inst. It is as follows. We had dress parade at nine oclock in the morning and after going through it which ended by the adjutant reading a great many orders and the resignations and promotions. The resignations were as follows. Col. Joseph Vandor and Corporals A. Clark and Philipps (forgot given name) all of the seventh Regt. Wis Volunteers. The promotions are Chester R. Garner and I forgot the other mans name as Corporals instead of the two that Resigned. Both resignations and promotions were in Co. H, seaventh Regt Wis volt but that leaves us without a Colonel and we are better off without one if we cannot have one better than Old Vandor. For he couldnt drill us to amount to anything for he hadnt patience to drive volunteers and one day soon after we came to this Camp he went out as usual and got so much vexed that we didnt drill more than an hour and came back and give up the Regt to Lieutanant Colonel [Robinson] to drill which he has done without any truble and Vandor never came near us but once afterward and then it was about two weeks after when we went on brigade. He came and took command and made a bad job of it and disgraced us all he could I believe and he never as much as come to see us afterward. The Lieutanant Colonel has had command for about four months and he drilled us without any swearing and scolding the officers as the old colonel used to do. I am expecting evry day to hear the promotion of Lieutanant Colonel W. W. Robinson read on dress parade as being Colonel of this Regt.

Well to return, well after the orders were finished the Colonel closed us in mass and examined us for we had laid still so long he wanted to see what condition we were in. And after he had examined all he steped out and said as follows. That he never seen the Regt in worse condition since he had command of it with the exceptions of Co. F and it was as usual all right, clean and tidy. He said that no other Co should have a pass to go anyplace but Co. F until they could come out in better condition. He said that included officers and all that couldnt have a pass. Then each Capt took their Cos and drilled Co drill awhile and come home. Evry Co in the Regt is our enemy now. We cant walk around without hearing denunciations of all kinds. It made us feel big as well as paid us for working to keep things clean.

February 8, 1862

And all is right this morning. And I am enjoying good health. But I feel rather bad from the affects of standing guard. Which I done yesterday. I was on the first relief which I like the best of the three reliefs. I went on post as follows, half past eight, half past two, half past eight, half past two, standing two hours each time. The guard is not allowed to leave the guards house more than ten minutes at a time. And this only in a case of nature. So we have to stay in that old guards house all the time when of post with no place to lie down to sleep except on the muddy floor. But there is a good fireplace which makes it more comfortable that it was in the forepart of winter. And we have to stay until half past eight in the morning to receive the new guard. And have to go without our breakfast until about nine oclock and upon the whole it is no fool of a job to stand guard. Especially when a man comes on once a week or more. But however it cannot be remedied as I can see for there is a good many sick and there are so many detailed for other duties.

The Regt has to chop its own wood now and there are five men detailed evry day from each Company for that purpose. But our guards around the Camp have been limited to a great extent. So much so that there are only ten around Camp and two to a house nearby which makes in all twelve on a relief. Which makes the total number of privates thirty six and I think that is as few as could be done with and have any guard around the Camp at all. Well, I had a good place for the number of my post was eleven which was by the aforesaid house and the weather was good but soon after I got home it began to snow but has quit. And I hope will stay quit as long as we stay in Virginia. The mud has dried up some but is verry bad yet.

Well I must soon quit writing in this book until I answer a letter I received from Newton on the evening of the sixth inst. Which brought news of himself and relatives being well. But I must mention about the great victory of the Federals in Tennessee where they took Fort Henry (a verry strong Fortress) and one hundred privates and officers prisoners. Also thirty five guns of heavy caliber. It is really a great victory. And the rumor is that the Cameron Dragoons took thirteen rebel prisoners last night out near Fairfax courthouse. There was a Captain and a Sargeant wounded and one of the rebels were killed. I will give a more detail account tomorrow of the victory of our troops when it comes official in the papers.

February 9, 1862

And it is Sunday evening and the mud is drying up verry fast yesterday and today. I have written one letter today. It was to my brother Newton. I answer to one I received from him last week. It brought the news of George [George Metcalf married Ray's older sister, Sarah Ray, in 1855] being verry bad and he had been called to see him die but he got over the bad spell. But I expect evry letter I get from home that it will bring the news of death which I should be verry sorry to hear. I got a paper this evening the title of which is the Missouri democrat and bore the name of A. A. Bennett written with a pencil. So I suppose that it came from him. He is my old schoolmaster. It is from his teachings that I learned or got most of my schooling such as reading, writing, spelling & arithmetic and that is all I ever studied except I studied Geography a verry little.

Well I am writing on a patent desk as it is called. It is the one I sent for to Syracuse N.Y. I have spoken of it heretofore. He sent me one and twenty seven cents in postage stamps. It cost forty three cents to bring it and it did not prove to be as good as I anticipated for it is all paper and got somewhat crushed up by coming by mail. It contained a lot of paper of different kinds. Also so many envelopes as there are sheets of paper, a bottle of ink, a pen and penholder and a silver pencil and a black led pencil. And there is a checker board marked on the desk and there are checkers to play with also but for all that it is not worth what it cost I think, which was seventy five cents. But I cannot lose much for there is so much paper &c in it which will come useful but it is paying dear for the whistle (as Franklin said when he bought a whistle).

Well the business of that flag of truce that came from the Rebels was to let Government know that if they hung the bridge burners of Missouri that they would kill evry prisoner they had got from us. And I have not heard yet what terms they settled it on. There was a man in our Co bet five dollars that we would be in Wisconsin in a months time. I hope it will be so but under the present circumstances I will term him a crazy fellow or some kind of a fellow and probably a good fellow if it turns out to be so but I would be verry glad.

Well James Garner has got a book from the Philadelphia book store. The title of it is the lives of highwaymen and robbers of different countries. It is a Novel or that is what I call it. It is a book that I don't care much about reading. Well it must be nearly roll call and I will quit.

February 11, 1862

And I am ready for drill which be verry soon but the drummers call has not beat yet and I thought that I would write a little. Well it is a pleasant morning with the ground frooze hard so as to bear the trains across the mudholes which are getting less for a few days past but the sky is clouded and as likely as not will rain before night but I hope not. We begun yesterday evening to drill the bayonet exercise for the first time. I like it verry much. There, there is the drummers call which tells us to get on our accoutriments for dress parade which we have in the morning instead of evening as it used to be.

Well it is afternoon and our dinner consisted of hominy and a little sugar to sweeten it with. We had a skirmish drill this morning after dress parade. It is verry pretty and exciting movements. And we are to drill two hours this afternoon in the bayonet excercise. It is most time to go to drill. I mailed a paper to A.A. Bennett. It was the national republican, a daily paper with some interesting news therein. The paper he sent me was an old one and quite large and I thought that a little daily would be worth as much to him as the old paper was to me. But if he had sent me a late paper instead of the one he did, why I should have sent him a better one.

February 13, 1862

And have just returned from the picket lines to the Regt reserve. Well yesterday morning the Regt took up its line of march for the picket lines which we reached half past ten oclock but about a mile back the left wing took the other road to the left and our Co & A went on to the lines, we taking the left and the other Co the right of the road. And relieved the Indianna boys. By this it got to be eleven oclock and we stood until eleven today. There was I and three other boys and a man acting as Corporal which made five. We stood two hours apiece until it went around then we stood an hour a piece. I said we but it was them for I was taken quite sick about dark and Julius

[Nickerman][37] warmed some water and I drank it until vomited. After that I felt better. It was caused from a foul stomach I think. I have felt rather bad for a week or more and I even went so far as to have my name put down to go to the doctors and when I went to the hospital there was so many to be doctored that it made me mad or kind a so for that morning there was eighteen from Co F on the list but the Doct didnt excuse half of them and if I had went and got medicine then probably I should have missed this sick spell. But however I am over it and feel a great deal better but havent a verry good appetite today. But I shall soon be able to eat my rations.

Well Co C came and relieved us and when we reached camp found hot Coffee, cold salt beef & pork and our regular loaf of bread. I have not ate as much as a days rations for two days. O but the weather is pretty and has been for several day. Whew how warm the sun shines on this the south side of our bough house. We had to bring our knappsacks out this time and our oilcloth and one blanket & overcoat. I suppose the Doct laid in complaint because we laid around on the ground shivering instead of taking our blankets.

February 16, 1862

And it is a verry pretty day after the snow storm of yesterday which was all day and the snow got to the depth of three inches and is going verry fast today and will be the cause of making it verry muddy (but to return).

Well we came home from picket on the fourteenth, the second Regt came and relieved us at noon. When we started home and came around by Munson Hill and Baileys crossroads which was as much as three miles farther than to have come the way we have always went and come. And what the Colonels reasons was for so doing I cannot tell unless he thought that it would be a dryer road but I am sure that it was not dryer and I guess he must have thought so to from the mud he seen and got on him and his horse. Oh but it was a hard jaunt for me and my boots hurt my feet verry bad. I tell you I guess all were glad when we reached camp which was nearly night. And then sit down and eat cold meat and bread and coffee.

But Our Regt was so fortunate as to get a prisinor or our scout from this Regt and a scout from a New York Regt took him prisinor. He being a secesh scout and they had watched him for several weeks but without success until this time when they took him and brought him into our Colonels quarters. And he sent him to Kings headquarters which was about half a mile distant back to a house while his Brigade is on picket duty. While on picket our Colonel dwells in the same kind of a house that we did and no better.

And when we reached home our new guns had come and yesterday morning we went on dress parade which we never did before after coming off picket the day before. But there was some important orders to be read. Also some promotions to be read. The first being the Lieutanant Colonel promoted to Colonel and the Major being promoted to Lieutanant Colonel and Captain Bills of Co A, it is said was promoted to Major and all of this being in the Seaventh Regt Wisconsin Volunteers. And as it was snowing the Colonel dismissed us and we went to our quarters and then we gave up our catridges and went and got our new guns from the Ordinance Sargeants. Then they were given out as the roll was called and the guns being numbered, we took guns accordingly.[38] Then we went to work and cleaned up our old guns in the best manner possible to return them. Then the order come to fall in without arms and form on the parade ground to receive orders from division headquarters. And then the Colonel ordered us back to get our guns and form again which we did.

Then Mcdowel [General Irvin McDowell] came by going to the Sixth Regt which were formed like us and the orders was read to them I suppose the same as ours. Which was as follows. That Mcdowels division had to furnish Co men to go on the western rivers to man gunboats which were laying idle for want of men to work them and this was a call for volunteers from Regts now in service. And they must be sailors or rafts men or boat men and men that are used to the water. There were a great many probably twenty or thirty out of the Sixth and as many out of our Regt I think. There was only one man went out of our Co. His name is [John] Johnson.[39] This speaks well for our officers. That is that the men are satisfied with them. But their names are not to be striken from the rolls as they are to return when they are done with them. I would of liked to went but didnt know anything about the business.

Well we come back to our quarters and cleaned guns. We got evrything pertaining to the new guns which are as follows. First a brass stopple, a verry pretty one, a good wormer and a good screwdriver and wrench. Those are in one piece. We went out on inspection this morning with new guns which are colored black except the lock guard and rammer which are bright. So we will not have to spend so much time cleaning guns as before. Those we have are rifles and four inches shorter than the muskets and half a pound heavier but they carry verry nice and much easier than the musket. So we are ready for the secesh now. But I don't think that we will have a chance to try them on secesh from the wagons boys or the Federals have taken the rebels. For we have taken 19,000 rebels in the last ten days. We have taken Roanoak [Roanoke] Island with two thousand prisinors and we have got Bowlingreen. I believe the enemy retreated from it. And we have got Fort Donaldson [Donelson] with 15,000 prisinors and some big officers which are Gen Floyd, Pillow and Backner [Confederate Generals John B. Floyd, Gideon J. Pillow and Simon B. Buckner]. Three of the most noted officers in the Rebel army. This will weaken them verry much.[40] We are taking them on all sides and I think we will never advance on Manassas from this side but probably from the other side or the rear in a military way of speaking.

Well the drums are beating for roll call and I shall have to quit writing for tonight. Oh, but I got three letters or found them awaiting my return from picket, for the mail was not brought out to us this time while on picket. There was two from

Newton, one from Henry. Henrys contained one sheet of foolscap and each of Newtons contained two sheets of foolscap which made four and it was for one letter only. The cause of him writing so much is this. What I told him in answer to what he said that was that he would quit writing or I would tire of reading in one of his letters. And I told him that I wouldnt tire of reading if he wrote a haversack full. Then I would take it on picket to read and have food for the mind as well as for the body. So that is the reason he wrote so long a letter. And I being almost on the sick list and feeling verry bad. So it took me two days to read them all.

February 17, 1862

And raining again this morning. Oh what weather we have. It makes me dissatisfied. I am getting tired of staying here in this mudhole as we call it. We have the worst Camp grounds of any Camp I have seen. That is for mud but we have advantages otherwise. Such as being near the City and not having to haul our provisions so far and getting our mail evry day and so on. All of which are the most prominent. Well I have got a verry sore ankle caused from my boot rubbing it whilst going out on picket and returning. And I expect to go on guard tomorrow. I must quit writing this book and answer some of them long letters.

February 20, 1862

And it is a verry pretty day. Our troops are in possession of Savannah [Tennessee]. It was a verry strong place but our boys did take it. I have stated that Floyd was taken prisinor at Fort Donelson but he escaped with five thousand men to Savannah but got taken there. Gen Johnson was taken prisinor also with a great many other southern leaders with 20,000 prisnors.[41] This is a hard blow for them and a good one for us. Well I have answered all my letters and now I must write one to Mother.

Well there is a hard wind blowing from the North which will dry up the ground verry fast. And I will be glad of that for the mud is as bad as ever. Well Richard Pierce has just come in from trying his gun and he says that it shoots verry well.

February 21, 1862

And it is a verry pretty day. Last night Jack frost dried up the mud so that empty wagons would go on the top but the sun is getting to have considerable power. Therefore it will soon be as muddy as ever. Well it is dinner time. I am not well yet but feel some better. I got six powders from the doctor this morning and have to take one evry two hours. They are a bitter thing.

Well the boys was out drilling this morning and now they are ordered to clean up brasses and buttons &c for to go down to the Arlington House to celebrate Washingtons birthday which evry true American knows comes tomorrow.

Oh, but what a pretty day. I understand that the forts are to fire five hundred guns tomorrow and I guess there will be a great time all around. Well after dinner I think I shall write a letter to Mother. Well I have concluded to not write to Mother until after the Celebration of tomorrow and postage stamps are scarce with me at present, and no money to buy more with. The reason of the scarceity of money with me is that I loaned it to Orley Foot one of my tentmates and he has not paid it back. And he was to pay it in a week but he has let one week after another pass and has not paid it. He is a great spend thrift but the more proper name for him would be a blackleg for he is a nuisance to the Co I think. For he gets drunk whenever he has a chance or can get the whiskey. Well I must take another of them nasty powders.

February 22—Washington's Birthday

And raining and likely to rain all day. I feel some better this morning so much so that I didnt go on the sick list and I wanted to go down to the Arlington House but I expect evry minute that the order will be countermanded. About sunrise the canons were booming and all was astir as usual on secesh boys. I expect we should have had a great time today if had not rained. There has been some more prominent places evacuated by the rebels. They have evacuated Columbia and Clarksville. The former was first place was calculated to be almost impregnable but the latter was not of much consequence.

Well there they go. Boom boom goes the cannon all around and on evry side. Well it is evening and we have been down to the Arlington House and heard an extract from George Washington's speech read that he delivered to Congress a short time before he died. The whole of Kings Brigade being formed in a half circle and closed in mass after the reading of the speech. Gen King proposed three cheers for it and the United States and the victories our troops have won such as Fort Henry, Donelson and so forth. They were hearty cheers I tell you. Then he proposed to have us fire a few rounds so he gave the orders and we were formed in line of battle, each Regt by itself. The Second Regt being in the rear of ours and the sixth on the Right, Indiana Regt on the left and so formed as to make like the letter Z as near as I can tell and firing begun. And after two or three volleys the drums sounded when we ceased firing.

And were ordered to fire by file and after a few rounds, there was ramrod shot from the second Regt which broke in three pieces, one piece going through the right leg of the man that stood behind me and another piece went through his bootleg. The other piece run into the ground within three inches of the mans foot that stood beside him. The but of the ramrod stuck in his leg until he pulled it out. The ramrod broke into three pieces about equal in length. The but piece run through his leg to the boot on the other side and there stoped. The middle piece it thought went through bootleg in another place. The other piece not touching anybody.

Well when I hear the fuss behind me, I looked around and saw Bill Atkinson [William Atkinson][42] had stept away from behind me and was kind a stooped over. Then I seen his gun laying on the ground and looked. Looked to see if it had bursted or what was the matter and could see nothing but a piece of round bright iron and I had kept loading all this time and was going to fire and thought I would look around. And I saw him throw down the but of the ramrod and it was bloody and I turned and shot and looked again and he was gone. And by this time the Colonel and Lieut Col, Adjutant and our Captain had got there and they picked up the pieces. It caused a great excitement but I didnt think much about it but kept on loading and shooting and this all occurred in less than a minute. Then the drums sounded. We ceased firing and the surgeons being there, they went to work fixing it up a little and sent word to Cap to send a man for the ambulance which didnt accompany us this time. Each regt has an ambulance and then we were ordered home and when we got home there was two ramrods missing out of the Co.

February 23, 1862

And I am on guard again which makes twice in this week and I don't like it much. But I am in great hopes that our stay in Virginia wont be long if the news is true about Nashville being surrendered up to our troops if they wouldnt burn it. It being the most prominent city in the southern states and if this is true, the war is virtually to an end now. And be that as it may they cannot hold out much longer. Well it is about half past ten, the time for the second relief to go on post but I am No two on the third relief today. There the second Regt band has commenced playing. How pretty it sounds. And this being Sunday, they are playing tunes to suit it.

Well about that wounded man. It proved to be only a flesh wound and not so bad as thought at first. I am sorry and also the whole Co for he was well liked by all. And was always at his post. Well I got a good first rate letter from home or two letters in one envelope. It was from Henry and Caroline [Henry Ray's wife]. Henry writing about half of the sheet and Caroline the other half. And it was a sheet of foolscap which as a matter of course made a good letter.

Well I don't feel so well today as yesterday but I wouldnt refuse to go on guard as there are so many in my own fix. But I fear that there are a great many that get off standing guard that nothing ails them but laziness. But it will not do to give way to despondence and I never have nor will I do it.

February 26, 1862

And it is now about five oclock and it is raining. Where there has been a great many things transpiring since I last wrote. Well I came off guard on Monday morning and that day about noon the wind commenced blowing and kept raising until it blew a perfect gale and the tents begun to weave and creak and our tent being on the west end of the row and the wind coming from that quarter, it gave it a hard strain which broke out one of the guy ropes and that gave it a double chance which terminated in the overthrow of our tent. Away she went. And away went papers, clothes and all such things. But lo, look, behold when we looked around there were many others in the same fix. Evry man is out holding to some part of his tent. There is one pulling on the ropes, one driving stakes, another propping it with poles &c and the wildest excitement prevails all over the camp. And all is in good humor & laughing and saying something about the poor soldiers, such as this is soldiering isnt it boys. Another says oh, who wouldnt be a soldier. Another anybody is a fool that wouldnt be a soldier. Another says this is another fine day and another says oh yes, but it is over the left. Ho, look at Toms cap, there it goes, there goes. Look boys, there is a fellow down in the mud. He gets up and sees his cap retreating and finds it in some ditch which is full of water. He puts it on his head, confiding himself with the thought that the mud and water that is in it will hold it on and as it happens, he is not deceived for the mud glues it fast to his hair.

And looking to the east I could see things going to destruction in a manner as I thought. But when the tents come to be raised and things changed around until they come to their owners, it terminated that the loss of this regt didnt exceed ten dollars I think. Well the gale still continued without abating. Well we piled up our things and weighted them down and got behind the promiscuous heap making it serve the purpose of a wind break. And there I sat watching others work for Dick was on general police and must go to work and the other boys sended into tents that were standing but I didnt chose to crowd myself into others tents if they were so fortunate as not to have them blown down and so I got new stakes and drove them well and got things fixed a little and looked up the boys and asked a few neighbors to the raising and we raised it in spite of the wind. And we kept fixing and got it quite comfortable by sundown and got our stove set up and got a fire started. And it felt like home once more and one helped another until we got them all up.

When we got our tent up we were not sorry that it blew over for those that held and proped theirs up got torn and whiped to pieces a great deal worse. But oh, how the boys did laugh at us when ours fell. But I soon seen we had the better of and some at least what I called the wise ones even took their tents down and thereby saved them from many a hard strain. Oh, but great was the destruction in the sixth Regt. For three fourths of theirs were blown down and a great many were torn all to pieces. And there was some trees in their camp and at the beginning of the blast some half a dozen fell right amongst the tents making great destruction. But I believe there was nobody hurt. I suppose the reason is that they were out looking at their tents going before the merciless blast. I think some of them must have suffered with the cold for the wind kept blowing and it frooze pretty hard that night and they couldnt raise theirs. The reason of their tents being torn so much is this, that they were not extra good when new and they had been in service two months longer than ours, thereby got more rotten. We had no roll call that night and I went to bed about eight oclock and the wind was still blowing and I went to sleep and didnt know how long it blew. But when I awoke in the morning it was a perfect calm.

Well through all the trubles, all was in good spirits and many were the cheers that went up from the soldiers and many were the hearty laughs. And many were the jokes that were cracked that day and a great many since. Well it will be a day long to be remembered amongst the soldiers and probably will be recorded on the pages of history for all time to come and I think I shall never forget it as long as I live. I think it is indelible on my mind but not on account of suffering or loss. Oh yes, I did loose one old sock in the affair. Oh, I tell you, this is a good old state away down in Virginia. Oh, sacred place. Oh, you have been the cause of me loosing my old sock. Oh well, it is no use of crying for spilt as the milk maid said when the pail of milk fell off her head.

It is raining yet and raining hard too. I often think of the guards that have to stand on their lonely beat through the storm. But we have built a new guard house and it is as comfortable in it as in our tents. When off the tour the guard can have a good fire and shelter. I answered the letter yesterday that I received from Caroline & Henry on Saturday last.

There has some important things transpired today. This afternoon we went down on brigade drill. When we got to or near Arlington House, Colonel halted us and the following orders were read as well as I could hear. That this Brigade should get ready and hold itself in readiness to march at a minutes warning and that the soldiers equipments should be reduced to the lowest extremity possible so as not to be loaded to heavy for we were to have small light tents and would have to carry them as no teams should accompany us but those to carry our provisions. This is as near it as I could hear it. But the sum and substance is we are going to start on a Campaign to someplace, we don't know where.

When the Adjutant finished reading the order, says the Colonel, now boys, cant you give three cheers. And I tell you, if we didnt make the woods ring, it was all right. Then we marched around in front of the Arlington house. Then we doubled column at half distance, one battalion after the other. Then we marched in review by the Verandah, went down the hill, taking a circle, come back to the same place. Then deployed columns, we being on the front and the second Indiana Regt on the Right flank and the sixth on the left Flank which made a hollow square in the rear of us. Then each battalion fired by battalions sixth first & then us then the second. Then the Indiana Regt. We fired three times around so, the sixth doing the best. Then we fired by file and I tell you we made some racket then for every man fires at will. And it is wonderful how often a man can load and fire in a minute but it is becoming second nature to us. We fired six or eight rounds and the drum sounded which put a stop to our boyish play. And so it ended and we marched home. And all are or I am glad that we are going to march verry soon. And I guess all the boys are. Well it is said that four goes togather as tentmates through the Campaign. Well it is after taps and I must quit writing and have the light extinguished.

February 28, 1862

And verry windy. I have just ate dinner which consisted only of bread & coffee. But we excuse the cooks this time for it is mustering day and we have been down to the Arlington house and were inspected and the roll called, each Co coming home as they were done. And our Co being the second we didnt have to stay long.

Well the capture of Nashville has been confirmed. The talk is that the rebels have made an attack on Harpers Ferry and thereabouts. And that there were a great many soldiers being moved there from about Washington. The Railroad was employed exclusively in working for Uncle Sam on yesterday and that the transportation of newspapers had been prohibited from coming into Washington. And I think it is so for I havent seen or heard a newsboy today. Evrything goes to show that there is or soon will be an important move made by the army of the Potomac.

We have or this Regt have got the new tents. They are said to weigh only seaven pounds and are so constructed as to be formed into a knappsack in which we are to put our overcoat, our oilcloth and one blanket. And the rest of our things are to be packed in our knappsacks and left in our tents so as to be ready to load into wagons and brought to us if we should not return. But this is only hearsay. But I hope that it will prove true and before many days pass and nobody is allowed to have a pass to go anyplace but must stay near Camp.

Well I got a Grant Co Herald last night and find some verry interesting news for it brings the news from home in a manner. I had ought to have them evry week for mother signed and paid for it and paid the postage for it to come to me. But I do not get more than two a month instead of four for they are a weekly paper. And they are one dollar and a half a year. And it costs at the rate of fifty cents a year for postage to this place which makes two dollars a year. And I think I ought to get them all.

Well there is a news boy crying out Philadelphia Enquirer. Our troops fly before the rebels but I don't believe but it may be so. But probably they done it to draw the rebels on to a harbor battle. Oh, but it is windy and likely to be until sundown and probably it will quit then.

Well we went out and drilled a little in our Co street. Lieutanant Young drills us lately and he wouldnt have done it but it was the order from the Colonel and he must do it but it was only short drill. He always favors us when he can. He is the best officer in our Co, so I think.

Well I have read the Herald and I don't feel much like writing for it is cold and last night it frooze up tight so we had good dry traveling this morning and it does not thaw much and will not today for it is three oclock now. Well we have a visitor from old Grant and the same town that I came from. It is Wm Mcartney, a brother to our second seargent. He came to camp late last evening and came to our tent to see us. But it was after roll call and we had just gone to bed. There we didnt chat much. I always thought that I would like to see somebody from home but I didnt care much about when it came to it. From home I said but it is not from exactly but from the same town. And is an old acquaintance. My Mother has been acquainted with the family for twenty five years or more.

March 1, 1862

And it is verry windy and was all night. Last night was the coldest night we have had. It frooze the ink in the tent but not solid. Well I went on the sick list this morning. Last night my head ached and I was chilly & had some fever so I thought it would be folly to put of going to the Doctor any longer. But if I had had a box of pills, I should have cured myself for it is nothing more than a foul stomach. And now I cant get the medicine until afternoon for the Stewards and most of the men that works in the hospital are sick and unwell but I sent for a box of pills this morning and will get them tonight.

Well I must get another book.

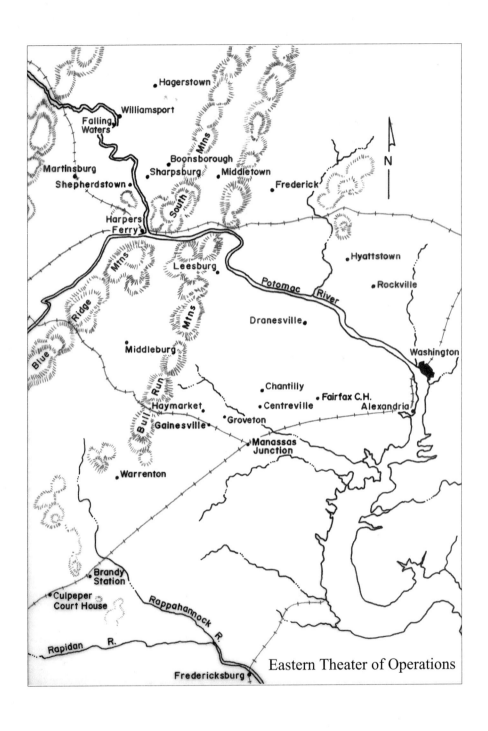

Eastern Theater of Operations

March 5, 1862 to May 14, 1862

Camp Starveout

Camp Arlington, March 5, 1862

And I now begin the fourth book having finished the third several days since or rather filled them with the news such as I could pick up around Camp or anyplace. When anything would occur worthy of note, I would scratch it down on my book.

It is a fine day and has been fine weather for several days past. But I being sick I cannot be out much to enjoy it. I am better than when I last wrote but was not able to go out on picket with the Regt which went yesterday morning and will not be back until tomorrow. All of my tentmates went. Therefore I am left alone which just suits me. I can sit and write and read without molestation except a few that call in a little while to sit and chat. But I being a poor hand to talk when unwell therefore they do not stay long. I went out after some wood since dinner and met [James] Clark the teamster just as I had got my load and he said if I could wait till he went out and got his load of wood and come back he would haul it for me and I would not have to wait but a few minutes. I done so gladly and I found by the time I got a little chopped that I was pretty weak. I now have plenty of wood to do over night. I got four powders from the doctors this morning and had to take one every three hours and there is three of them gone and the other I must take at six o'clock. I have not ate as much in five days as I would in one day when well and hearty.

There is a great deal of sickness in the regt at present. There [was] a funeral yesterday. There is two from this Co in the hospital that are verry sick and at one time were not expected to live. I got three papers from home last night and one was the Northwestern Christian Advocate. One Wisconsin Weekly State Journal and the other a Sunday School Advocate. This being sent by some of Henrys children I suppose. For I have sent some little papers and things and they send them in return for the others I suppose. I got a letter from my Nephew Isaac the night before stating that he was well and they had not been disbanded as yet as they once supposed they would be.

Well we don't get any news for several days concerning the war on account of the military authorities stopped it being sent on the wires except by permission of them. We expect to move every day. It may be tomorrow or next day and that is one thing I dislike a soldiers life for. For when we lay down at night we don't know but that we will have to get up and march before morning. But so it is and it cant be no other as the saying is. Well I am getting tired of writing. I have written that over which was written with a pencil in this book it being a description of the battle of bull run &c.

March 6, 1862

And a verry pretty morning and thawing out verry fast what frooze last night, it being a verry cold night. Nothing of importance this morning. I feel some better and eat pretty well so I guess I shall get along without any more medicine. We expect the boys in from picket today.

March 9, 1862

And Sunday morning and a verry pretty weather and the mud is most or in a great degree dried up which makes everything look better. Well we have just been out on our weekly inspection and the Capt says we were in the best order that he ever seen us. When through [with] the inspection Lieut Young read a lengthy article concerning guard & picket duty as laid down in the army regulations of 1862. Then we were dismissed, the Capt warning us about keeping our things packed and fixed so as to be ready to march in the shortest notice. We shall have to leave one blanket here and packed away in some shape. I don't know how.

Well the boys returned from picket as usual verry tired and hungry. And nothing uncommon transpired. We got no war news of any consequence lately since the military authorities have taken the telegraph and press into their hands. That is to a certain degree in as much as the war news except things that have transpired and got old and stale.

Well I have got well and hearty again and have been drilling for several days and I think I shall be able to carry my knappsack by the time we start on the expected Campaign. We have got our new tents and were out practicing pitching them yesterday. They are so fixed that as many as likes can pitch togather and never less than two. They button together in the middle and that is on the top where the ridge pole should or would be to any other kind of tents. But they have only two sticks for with joints. One at each end and there is a rope at each end which is staked down and stretches it tight endwise. And there is a stake at each corner. One man has to carry one end stick and three pegs, one rope and half of the cloth. The whole of it weighs about four pounds. It adds an considerable heft on our knappsacks but if I am hearty I can carry it. Well I got a letter from Newton two or three days since. He had had the rheumatism some. The folks were well with the exception of George Metcalf and he was as usual.

March 10, 1862

And here I am lying in my little tent one mile west of Fairfax [Virginia]. Last night at twelve o'clock the order came for us to be ready to march at four o'clock. Well I woke up as I thought about ten o'clock and heard them calling in the old guard and putting them that were not able to march on in their stead and heard the wagons rumbling. I thought that something was up. And then I overheard them talking about marching in Co etc. Then I gets up, builds a fire and went out to see about it. And saw a light in the third tent and went there and they told me about that we must pack up what things we couldn't take and leave them in our tents. And we must take one blanket, oilcloth, our coat and a change of clothes and as much more as we had a mind to. And then I packed my Knapsack adding my ink bottle, portfolio, testament and then Dick and I packed up our other blankets. Then the revilee was beat and we turned out 38 files [76 men], the most our Company has turned out for several weeks. Roll call over we got breakfast which consisted of cold fat pork boiled & coffee and bread. We went and got three days provision, 30 crackers being allowed and a chunk of raw ham. Then verry shortly we got in to ranks and the regt formed on the parade ground and started being a hour behind time.

Well we got along slow until daylight then I soon seen we were the tail end of the Brigade. Well we come by Baileys cross roads and kept coming and resting every two or three miles until we got here which was about two o'clock. And we closed column by division with first division in front, stacked arms and Wm Turnby [William Turnby][43] and I pitched tents together. But to return, McDowel came with us. Also King. It is said the whole army of the Potomac has moved within three days. We being the last to move. We expected to stop short of Fairfax but when we neared the place we found out it had been taken last night from the rebels and that our forces were still in advance and a great many right in the vicinity of the place. The cavelry & Artillery of this division went on in advance of this brigade and for [all] I know of the division.

Oh I tell you but the knapsacks pulled down heavy. And as soon as the boys got their tents pitched they sit down to rest and a great many went to sleep. And now all that can be heard is "Oh, how stiff I am" comes from all. But all is cheerful and good humor. Here comes the beef cattle of this division. They have been brought on when all is safe.

Well we came right through the main street of Fairfax on which is situated the Courthouse which shows the horrors of war. Most of the Citizens retreated with the rebel soldiers and their houses are used for barracks for the men and sheds for horses. Well I wish the provision wagons if there is any would come up so that we could have some Coffee.

The men of different regts keeps straggling in and by us. We are camped on the north side and near the road. Whup, the wind is raising. We are in quite a thick timber and in sight of Fairfax. Well the news comes that the rebels have evacuated Centerville and are evacuating Manassas but I shant credit the latter.

Well I must get up and stir around to keep of stiffness.

March 11, 1862

And a verry fine morning and we are here this morning. 8 o'clock. This morning revilee was beat at the dawn of day. Answered to roll, got breakfast. Struck tents and packed knappsack expecting every minute to forward march. But it has not come as yet but we were called into ranks and stacked arms, unslung knapsacks and broke ranks. Then in a few minutes we were called in again and received the [order] that we were not to go far from camp for the roll would be called often through the day and no time set when it should be done. Now I think this is useless for there is not a man I think that would desert.

Well I feel first rate this morning. There was about twenty five or thirty contrabands come to Kings headquarters last night. A great many of the officers got a male contraband [black servant][44] to carry their things and be waiters for them thereby giving the most or all of them work. And the others were sent on back to the rear to someplace I don't know where. And they brought the news of the rebels had left Centerville and were leaving Manassas and what they couldn't take with them they were burning. And they say they came from the other side of the latter place but I cannot believe everything they say.

Straggling soldiers keeps going by and all night the wagons were rattling along the roads and it is said that a great deal of artillery went by also. It is stated as a fact that our forces are in possession of Centerville. Oh but there is lots of soldiers and teams scattered all through the woods around here. The provision wagons came last night in time for our cooks to make us a cup of coffee apiece and it tasted good I tell you. I got a good nights rest after we had roll call last night.

March 12, 1862

And we still remain in the same place as yesterday and nothing of great consequence has transpired since I last wrote. Except that last evening the whole

Brigade went out about quarter of a mile west to a field and there had a Brigade dress parade. It was a fine sight with the second [Wisconsin] Regt band playing down the front and back and after the parade was dismissed our battalion drilled a few minutes mostly doublequick whilst the other battalion went to camp. This morning Capt [Callis] gave us a good lecture or advice rather to keep in camp for yesterday every other Co in the Regt was out getting & killing ducks, geese, chickens, hogs, cattle and taking beehives. But our Co only got two sheep and there was only two or three boys in the muss so last night the colonel gave the officers a good blessing for it and our Company got the least blame and the most praise for good behavior. And he also gave the order that nobody should go out of Camp under any pretense unless there was a noncommissioned or commissioned officer with them.

Troops still continue to pass. Yesterday there was two or three regts went back to the rear, they having been out scouring the country and came in for rest. But the worst feature about it is we had nothing but Coffee for breakfast, not a bite of bread. Oh yes, my tentmate gave me two or three pieces of crackers and some of the boys that was out yesterday had some meat and some that had money bought things of the sutler.

March 13, 1862

Well, we are still at the same place. One deserted secesh was brought into Camp last night and two prisinors just brought in this morning. One was a large stout man, the other a smallish man. They have on gray pants and one of them had a kind of brown Coat similar in shape to our common overcoats up north, the pants having a black stripe about an inch wide down the leg. Well, when some of the boys asked him how they averaged he replied pretty well with a smile on his face. There was a terrible crowd gathered each side and in the road evry man having something to say but nothing insulting.

Well last night we drew three days rations of crackers and with the meat and chickens brought in by the boys yesterday, we had plenty of meat. But I didnt get any of the chicken but plenty of the pig and veal. Our Colonels and field officers went to Manassas yesterday evening. The doctor went along also and found some medicines and our ordinance sargeant went out and brought in two secesh wagons pretty good ones and a good large chest made at Richmond and a rusty rifle but had a firstrate gun and a sword, a splendid one. But the scabbard being iron it had rusted badly. The belt was some rotton. But had been a splendid sword some day. There was four more contrabands came in last night. McDowel told them that they were free and to hire out if they could. Having all they could make they do so by all that comes into camp. The boys raised a flagstaff yesterday near General Kings quarters and he let them have the flag to put up and it is now flying. I expected last night to be marching before this time.

Well I wrote a letter to mother last evening. Also one for Wm Turnby to his father as he cannot write.

March 14, 1862

Still at the same place, plenty to eat. We had skirmish drill yesterday morning and in the evening Battalion drill. The best drill we have had. We are improving verry fast lately. The Colonel praised us up verry highly. Well I had the bad luck to have some crackers stolen from me while on drill yesterday. And I shall carry my haversack with me after this. Well the sixth [Wisconsin] dressed up one of their men and thought to make us believe he was a secesh and brought him out on the road with four men guarding him with their guns. And great crowd following and hollowing secesh prisinor but our boys got wind of it and there wasnt many went to see him as they usually do when a prisinor comes by. They thought that they would get up a great sell on us but it was no go. Last evening the second [Wisconsin] boys got a piece of a gunbarrel and a little cart and fixed it up as flying artillery and brought it out on the road and commenced canonading us with paper wads. They would shoot then run a little piece, shoot again and when they got opposite Gen King's headquarters they stopped and threw a few shell made of paper and then retreated.

The weather is misty this morning. We doubled tents with four others last night and pitched ours and had a half of a tent put up at each end. They are made with such precision that by turning one half tent cornerwise they button on nice and tight but either four or six or more must pitch togather to it. Well they are just mounting guard. The guard runs around the Brigade so that all the brigade is togather.

Well the forageing party is just starting out. There is so many goes from each Company evry day with a noncommissioned officer with them. Well the mail came in this morning but there was nothing for me.

March 17, 1862

And a fine morning and we are back to Arlington heights & I am well and rested well last night. Well there has a great deal transpired since I last wrote. Well on the 15th inst we got orders to march that day to Alexandria a distance of fourteen miles it is said. Well we got ready and waited until about noon before starting as there was so many to go ahead of us. It is said there is 70,000 to take shipping to go and reinforce [Union General Ambrose] Burnside but we don't know anything about it. But I do know that we took up our line of march about noon for Alexandria and marched and marched and it commenced raining soon after we started. And rained quite hard sometimes and then would hold up a little but never stoped all day and it raised the streams and evry little hollow had a good stream of water running and evry hole in the road was full. And we had to march right through as there was no choice in the ground. We had to wade right through it all and sometimes it was about knee deep.

The road was a good turnpike all the way sandy, gravelly and the water washing the sand into our shoes. It made verry hard walking.

Well we ploded along there being no end to the massive colums of all kinds of things. When we got to within three miles and a half of Alexandria and there we met with the 5th Wis Regt.[45] We went on about half a mile and encamped on a side hill in the woods by the side of the road. And it still raining all this time. And still raining and we were as wet as we could well be. We got some rails and made a fire. By this time it was dark. Oh but how they did crowd around our fire. There was about a dozen boys of us made a fire togather and it was a good one. Whew, the steam rose from our clothes enough to run an engine if it was condensed. And it was pretty sight to see so many fires and so many thousands standing by them as the fires would show their forms through the darkness.

We pitched our tents, myself and two others tented togather and layed togather. We were quite wet on going to bed which was about nine oclock. It kept raining until about twelve oclock when it stoped as the boys said that sat by the fire all night and didnt get to sleep a bit. And I woke up about the time it quit but went to sleep again and awoke at daybreak having made a pretty good nights rest. But how the steam rose when we got up. Well we dried our clothes, got the orders to strike tents and get ready to march at ten oclock having but what coffee we made in our cups, hard crackers, raw ham. And the Regts that was ahead of us comenced going by and about noon we started back. Some said we were going back to Fairfax, some said we were going to Arlington and the latter proved true. We come back the turnpike a couple of miles and turned of across a field and struck the Washington and Fairfax turnpike which we went out on on the 10th inst., about three miles west of Baileys Crossroads. And when we reach this place there was soldiers & wagons of all kinds of things without number. They were going to Alexandria and then we heard that this division had been ordered back to camp for a few days until the transports was ready and that we were to take shipping at Georgetown.

Well then we knew that we were coming back to Arlington which we didnt like much. There was a great deal of murmering throughout the division it is said, espicially by the privates. For having to come back to camp and when we got or our Regt got back, we found that our tents had been taken down, packed up and put in the stable. Also our extra blankets had been packed into boxes and put in the stable. Then we were ordered to come down in the woods about a quarter of a mile and camp which we done. And we got fires started. By this time it was dark and I and five others tented togather and three more boys struck their tents opposite ours and we built a fire between them in so as to do for both tents. I rested well that night and as it had been a fine day, our things had dried pretty well and I awoke this morning seeing the sun rise and today we have done nothing but have dress parade for which we went up on the old parade ground.

There was considerable orders read and some promotions read and a letter from Gen Mclelen [McClellan] to all troops under his command to the effect that we shouldnt lay idle any longer. And that we should probably have long and rapid marches and great fatigue and hardships to encounter. And a courageous foe to face. But he had great confidence in the men and thought they would do what they had sworn to do. Well it was an encouraging letter and we were to hold ourselves in readiness to march at ten minutes notice. Then the Colonel gave us some good advice and talked verry cheerful. Expressed himself as having a great Confidence in the men of his Regt and dismissed us. Capt took us into our old street and dismissed us and told us to look up our things and all public property was to be returned.

I found my blanket but not my boots and they was worth three dollars. But let them go it is no use to cry for spilt milk. And there is the stove, it will be a total loss for it will not pay to send home. I tell you but the old Camp looks shabby with the stuff that has accumulated and the pens that were built which the tents were sit on.

March 19, 1862

And we have just got our tents pitched amongst the stumps. Well to return yesterday morning. We went to work and packed up our extra blanket in good shape and they are to be stored someplace until called for by us and we drawed a loaf of soft bread and it tasted good after having lived on crackers for a week or more.

We got orders to march at four oclock and we packed up and started for someplace taking our regular load of blanket, overcoat &c and when we got to within about two miles of Alexandria we turned into a field and pitched tents and got lots of rails, posts &c and then we had to pack up again and march, it then being dark and we marched & marched until about 10 oclock and then we stoped, I supposed to rest. And as the woods all around had been cut down, a great many of the boys broke ranks and built fires and soon half of the Regt done so and some of them comenced to pitch tents and the officers never said a word against it but the colonel went back I suppose to get orders what to do. He soon returned telling evrybody to take care of themselves and there was the greatest confusion I ever saw. The whole brigade stoped, we being the lead Regt in this march.

Colonel Cutler [Lysander Cutler of the Sixth Wisconsin] commands this brigade now in the place of King and King takes the place of Mcdowel [Irvin McDowell] as Mcdowel takes a higher position. Oh how the boys cursed Cutler, but I guess he was not to blame for he done as he was ordered I guess. But he is disliked by the privates and a great many of the officers in the Brigade. We marched over some verry bad road and it being verry dark it was hard going. Well I had a pretty good nights rest and got up and waited until about eight oclock for the coffee and meat and we had to make our own coffee and a great many had no bread and I had but little and have none for dinner.

When we got breakfast we struck tents, packed up and marched to this place about a mile from the place we camped last night and we have pitched tents again.

March 21, 1862

5 oclock P.M. The sun is shining verry pretty. The first time for several days. Well, I didnt write any yesterday for I didnt get off guard until about three oclock and it being a verry rainy day I couldnt write. Well on the nineteenth inst about three oclock, I and Corporal Mcdowel [Edward F. McDowell][46] with five other men from other Companies in this regt went on Amunition guard. There being a train of eleven wagons loaded with amunition belonging to this brigade. There being six of us we only come on post evry five hours so that it was not hard work but it stormed all the while and as we came off post we went into the wagons and slept on top of the boxes of catridges as they are all rifle catridges. I thought to myself as I lay on them that they intended we should not lack for powders and pills while we were in dixie, for there were at least 30,000 rounds in the wagon I slept in and each soldier in this Regt has 5 rounds now in their boxes. Well it kept raining and rained most all of last night. And has been cloudy today until about an hour since when it cleared off. This is what is called the equinoxial storm and I think we will have fine weather now.

I received a letter and a paper last night. The letter being from Henry and the paper was the Grant Co Herald. The letter brought news of all well except bad colds and George was still alive and had had Doct Stedman from Iowa to see him. He thinks he can cure him and he differs from all other Docts that had been to see him. And the snow was the deepest he ever seen it, it being from four to eight feet deep and he thought that if I had been there to helped him break roads that I should have wished myself back to Camp in Dixie again. But I think he was mistaken about it. And Mother and Caroline said in answer to what I wrote about that they must have a pan of biscuit baked, plenty of potatoes and plenty of good butter. But be sure and not cook any beans. They said that I must whistle in time so that they could have a good dinner ready by the time I got there

Oh but my eyes are sore and pain me. The cause of it is the fires we sit by. Smoke so bad and there are so many of them all around us that it is verry bad although it has not been so bad today as the wind has not blown much today. We draw our coffee & sugar and make coffee in our tin cups, evry man by himself for this last two days and I like it better. For when we march and stop we don't have to wait until the teams come up and the cooks cook it. We drew three days rations of it and crackers yesterday.

Well it is getting dark. Oh, I never seen a prettier sight than those rugged hillsides present at present with the hundreds of fires and big fires too for there is a great plenty of wood, the stumps and grubs so thick we have to pick out places to pitch tents. I put some leaves in the tent for a bed and I will rest better tonight.

March 22, 1862

And a cloudy day after a rainy right up to this time. Two oclock and we are still at camp among the stumps as I know of no better name but some of the boys call it

Camp starveout on account of the scarcity of bread the first day we came here. Nothing unusual has transpired. Lieut [Samuel] Woodhouse has resigned and there is some excitement in our Co on account of that. The promotions that are likely to take place and it is said that Lieutanant [Henry F.] Young has been promoted to first Lieut and the orderly Sargeant [John W. McKenzie] is likely to take his place as second Lieut and so on through the sargeants and Corporals and there will have to be a new Corporal. This is the way it generally goes. It has had a great effect on some of the noncommissioned officers and some privates. They have been shaving and cleaning up all day. I suppose evry one thinks he is likely to be promoted. (The simpletons, Oh, what office or money will make a man do) There appears to be quite a hard feeling towards Young, but I stick to him and shall until he does worse than other officers which he could'nt do verry well. I think that it is no great loss to the company when we loose Woodhouse. I would as soon see him go as a private.

Well, there is such talk that we will leave here for Alexandria before twenty four hours for [General Fitz-John] Porters division is embarking now and was all day yesterday. Well, I suppose that we will soon draw three days more rations for all the boys are out of grub and we have had a loaf of bread and thirty crackers for the last three days rations and all ate up now and I traded with one of the boys some coffee for four crackers and all gone. The cause of us eating so much bread is that we do not have much other food. What we threw away at Camp would taste good.

Sometimes since we begun to march I think that things will go on better now if they do not. I for one will look into it and see if we draw our full rations. It will probably cause some hard feelings between myself and officers. But right is right and I want my rights and no more.

March 23, 1862

And it is a fine sunny morning and we have just been out on Sunday morning inspection. We are still camped at the same place. And still expect orders evry minute to march to Alexandria. We hear of troops embarking evry day which makes us impatient to be going. Our forces have Island No 10 in their possession which was a verry strong place but our guns are far superior to theirs, thereby shooting a greater distance. There was I believe only seaven of our men killed and the enemys loss is not known but it was verry great as our forces could throw shells into their forts and theirs wouldnt reach our boats. Commodore Fort commanded the expedition against them.

Well we drew 25 crackers [hardtack] and a loaf of bread and coffee and sugar for three days. We get more to eat that we used to. The loaf of soft bread is calculated for one day & the crackers for two days. We have done sometimes three days with only twenty five crackers. I tell you there is some exciting debates about the resignation of Woodhouse. And it is said that when his resignation was received that the officers said that a man that would resign just now when the country needed him most was better out of office than in for he had wronged his country by so doing and he wasnt to be trusted.

Oh, there is nothing going on but cardplaying and some quarreling about the games. When the boys purses got to low for one cent bets they went to betting and playing for buttons and got run out of them and went to playing for nails. And now they have drawn some sutlers tickets and they commence again to play for them.

Well it is evening and I have just been over to Fairfax Seminary which is about one mile & a quarter distant from here in a southeast direction. It is a verry pretty building, also verry large & has quite a high conspicuous spire. The whole building shows the best of workmanship. There are a number of small spires on it besides the large one. It is built in gothic style with splendid brick and laid in cement. In fact, I never seen a finer building. There are quite a number of buildings around it. Two verry large ones, I suppose for boarding houses. In fact all the houses I guess are occupied or have been by teachers, servants, pupils &c and the stables for horses belonging to the institution. It is or was enclosed by a fence enclosing probably five acres and various shrubs & trees growing therein upon it making a verry nice park.

There is a large church near or rather connected to the Seminary by a verandah. It is well finished inside, also furnished with an organ and all things required to make finished church. In the center hangs a large lamp with eight burners and shines like gold. I was in and took a look at it and found a man that has the care of it, the church, he being a polite sociable soldier. He giving us some interesting facts about the history of the Church. He said it was built in 1858 but I thought from its outward appearances that it had been built twenty years or more, but all the houses in this country even of the wealthier class of people look rough but inside they are better finished that the generality of house at the north.

Well, those buildings, especially the Seminary, is set just on the top of the hill that rises about one mile back from the Potomac [River], also back of Alexandria thereby being on such high ground it overlooks a great deal of country in the front. We had a view of the river for four or five miles and could see the steamers plying about in its placid [water]. Also some sailing crafts of all sizes. We could see part of Washington but not verry distinct, which was some seaven or eight miles up the river. We could [see] the up part of Alexandria with its streets teeming with soldiers, ambulances & baggage wagons &c and looking down the bottom or level plane which streatches back from the river were swarms of soldiers comprising Infantry, Cavelry, Artillery and ambulances, wagons loaded with provisions, forage &c. It was one of the finest sights imaginable to stand on the doorstep of the seminary fronting the river and look in any direction. I stood and gazed on the beautiful scene as long as I dare for I and four other boys left camp without a pass and we were likely to march at any minute so that hurried us a little. I turned my steps Campward thinking what a beautiful Country this was once.

Well we returned to Camp finding it about the same as when we left.

March 26, 1862

And 11 oclock & pretty day. And just come in from Company drill. We drilled two hours. It is a verry pretty day, sun shines quite warm. Well to return to yesterday. We had Company drill in the forenoon in the bayonet excercise and after dinner we got orders to get ready for review at two oclock in light marching orders. Got ready & formed line though verry imperfect on account of the stumps and brush piles. Started for the place we knew not where but terminated to or near Fairfax Seminary. The whole country seemed to be alive, so great were the number of men of all grades and in all positions of modern warfare. And the Drum Chorus, bands and the shrill notes of the Cavelry bugle, taking it all togather it was a fine sight as well as a fine sound. The review consisted of Mcdowels Corps or grand division numbering probably sixty thousand men or more. It took a great while to arrange the whole so as to pass in review without intermixing. A regt of men there looked verry small among such a great many. Before marching in review the officers rode by in front and rear of each line with the newspaper reporters following behind and Lord Russel [William Howard Russell] Reporter for the London Times[47] was with them. He was quite a ways behind being rather an awkward rider. It caused a great deal of sport. At any rate, in our ranks they just hooted at him. Well we passed in review and done it well and all did so for all are pretty well drilled now. We came straight home as soon as we passed in review. Well I must get my dinner.

Well got dinner and been out on battalion drill. We went out on the same ground that where the review was. But there being so many there drilling that our battalion had not much of a chance and after a few moves we came home.

Well there was rather a disgraceful thing happened to one or two of the privates in our Co. It is as follows. We had roll call when we fell in this afternoon and there was two absent without leave so the Capt put a sargent to watch when they come back and have them march up and down the road in heavy marching orders and one of the [men] done as the sargeant ordered and he was released when we came back. But the other not doing it, the Capt ordered him to do it and he would'nt so the Capt and a Corporal took him to the Colonels and prefered charges against him and then the Captain had to Detail a guard to guard him and if I was the guard I would not let him have any privileges whatever. For now that verry man will cause more or less guards to go from this Co evry day when there would have been no use of it. And he is a man that has shirked more times than one that I know of. There is some from evry Company in the Regt and they say that the Colonel has put some of them to carry wood for him, thereby they are of some use.

March 28, 1862

And a fine day. Company drill in the forenoon and in afternoon signed payroll. We had another review yesterday but only two divisions out of the three that was there on the 25th inst, the other division having embarked it is supposed. And we expect to verry soon.

Well, that man that Captain prefered charges against has had his trial and got his sentence which as follows. He must march in the rear of the Colonels tent for thirty days, four hours each day beginning at six A.M., march till 8, go on drill, then at twelve begin & march till two then go on drill. He has a guard over him while marching and has a 32 lbs ball in his knappsack besides his clothing. Well he marches in heavy marching orders which included evrything and the ball besides which makes a verry heavy load so this is a hard job. He had better obeyed orders and I think he must or will be sorry for not doing so and he commences his job this afternoon.

March 29, 1862

And it is snowing with the wind from the east. We have not drilled any today. The three other Regts in this brigade have been paid off and have just commenced on Co & of this regt so we will soon have some money. I think some of trying to learn to drum. Took one lesson today.

Well it is quite chilly today. The new recruits that have come in think that it is about as bad as Wisconsin for chilly winds and cool nights.

March 30, 1862

And raining at times and cold chilly wind blowing which makes it verry disagreeable. And it is hard to keep fire and it is hard to sit in our dog kennels as the boys call them. But they turn the water verry well and are better than none. We got our pay last evening and the boys are all astir for all the rain that comes and some of them are quite boozy from the effects of the paddys dyewater (whiskey) and how they get it I cant tell for the orders are against selling any to the soldiers. But they get it. And some of them has paid two dollars for a canteen full. And they hold about three pints. But let them go it. It costs me nothing.

Well I have paid my debts, all but twenty five cents and I have sent fifteen dollars home or rather put it into the orderlys hands and he attends to it. Oh, this is Sunday morning. There has been so much bustle that I had forgotten it. Our old Chaplain [Samuel Brown][48] has resigned and I guess gone home. If he hasnt he had better. I received another letter from Henry a day or two since bringing the news of Georges death, the which I was verry sorry to hear but it didnt come unexpected to me, knowing how he was situated. I ought to answer his letter but it is such a bad day for writing.

The papers this morning brings news of the capture of Island No 10. They have been trying to take it for about a week so the papers have been stating but I believe it is confirmed.[49] We do not get so much news as we used to when in our old Camp. But it is a good thing that [we] did move from there for the health of the Regt is better. There are but three men on the sick list in our Co and only one of them is in the hospital someplace, we don't know where he is. One of our Corporals. And there is one that has the Scurvy, it being caused by him being so lazy and dirty. Oh, he is awful nasty. He has been banished from the Company until he gets well. He is able to be about but he must not talk with anybody or go amongst the boys on any pretense whatever.

March 31, 1862

Co drill in the afternoon. The boys are quite jubilant from the effects of whiskey. They will get it anyhow for all it is forbidden fruit.

April 1, 1862

And a pretty day. We had Co drill in the forenoon and brigade drill in the afternoon. For the latter we went out to Baileys Crossroads. We had a good drill. Col Cutler can command a Brigade verry well. But he is not liked so well as King was. But King has the command of what was Mcdowels division.

Well we have some sport with an old man or he makes sport for us in the way of ballad singing. He has a bundle of them for sale and he sings them, therefore he finds ready sale for them. I bought a couple of ballads & a song book of him. The songs are patriotic ones. The title of one being "We're Marching Down to Dixie Land." The title of the other is "The Ship Moves Proudly On My Boys." He has been singing all day and still singing.

April 2, 1862

And a fine warm day. Co drill in the forenoon. Brigade drill in the afternoon. We went out to Baileys Crossroads as before. We had a verry good drill. Some doublequicking. There was great time in camp today by the boys rallying on the pedlars and taking evrything away from them and only letting them go with their wagons & baskets. It is said that they had a polite invitation from the General to leave Camp and if they didnt do it, they would be at the mercy of the boys and they did'nt leave so the boys rallied on evry one that was in Camp taking one and at a time until they cleaned them out. They didnt truble the women or little boys and girls or book pedlars. All they wanted was something to eat and some of the pedlars took the hint and went out of Camp a little ways. But when the boys had finished in Camp, they started after the others that were half a mile of and caught their horses and took evry thing they had that was eatable. It raised quite an excitement. But nobody was hurt unless it was by eating so much trash. I did not participate in any such doings but I suppose served some of them right. What started it first was some of them went to passing Counterfeit money on the boys and they rallied. Well the boys must have taken as much as 3 or 4 hundred dollars worth from them all. And so it ended.

Well we changed our Cooks again. We, the boys all stick out to not pay the old Cooks anything. So they resigned and would'nt work any longer at the buisness. And the Capt thought to scare us by threats and he could'nt make that win and then he tried cursing and that wouldnt win therefore he was beat. Then we voted and the boys voted evry way & anyway just to be against the Commissioned officers. And he could'nt make that win. Therefore he got quite exasperated and said—well now, I shall appoint to for Cook and they must do it and he would not show them much lenity. Then the boys laughed. The boys are hard against the officers and try to plague them. At last Cap said he wanted to know if we were willing to have the Cook paid out of the commuted ration fund and we didnt care anything about that for we never expected to get it. Well there it settled and all goes on right again. And we will not have to only by our own consent pay the Cook we now have. And it has been seen and I have seen it that there were a few men in this Co that got favored by the old Cooks and they hung on for the old ones but the boys beat them out. We are still at the old camp.

April 3, 1862

And fine morning and had Co drill. We expect to march tomorrow to Alexandria to take shipping. We had Co drill in the forenoon, Brigade drill in the afternoon. Our Major [George Bill] in command of our Regt until near time to quit when the Colonel [William Robinson] and Lieut Colonel [Charles A. Hamilton][50] came. The Colonel said a few words to Gen Cutler and then he gave the orders for each Company to take their regts home which they done. And so it ended.

April 4, 1862

And a fine morning. It puts me in mind of a Wisconsin morning in the month of May when I have taken my hoe in hand and went to the field to cover corn. Well we are packed up again ready to march, it being 2 oclock. This morning we were ordered to get ready for review and the forenoon drill would be ommitted so that we could get ready. But about ten oclock the order came that we were to march at three oclock. But we don't know where, but some say to Manassas, others say to Alexandria and some one place and some another. Oh, but I tell you, the Camp looks shaggy as there is always a great many things gathers one way and another. And a great many things are destroyed by the careless boys when we are about to leave a camp, such as boxes and barrels of the verry best kind. They might be useful to the few families that live in the neighborhood or might to some regts that may camp here in future but it [is] rather a rough place for a camp.

Well the Artillery has started to the front. I can see them going on the road. And I should judge that we are going towards Manassas from the look. I think that all the artillery belonging to Mcdowels Corps is going and then all the Infantry must be going too. Also the Cavelry must be going and still the Artillery goes by. Now the baggage wagons comes and there is a great string of them. There, there the drum begins to tapp which signifies that we will soon start.

Well, the recruits for the 5th [Wisconsin] Regt that got here the day that their Regt went onboard and our Capt attended to getting them something to eat until they might have a chance to join their Regt, which they have not done and now they have been put into the small Cos in this Regt and going in as soldiers. But they have done none of it as yet for our officers had nothing to do with them but keep them from starving and they found acquaintances in the Regt that let them sleep in their tent. One of them is Mr. Pointers brother in law and he tents with us for they cannot draw any tents or anything else in Regt.

Our ordnance Sgt says we are going six miles to the front but probably he don't know. Well I will quit for this time as I see the sixth [Wisconsin] regt is falling in and we travel by Brigade now on the march.

April 6, 1862

And a fine morning and we are about 2 miles to the front of Centerville and just ready to take up our line of march for Manassas they say. And they also say that we only go 9½ miles today and yesterday we marched 16 miles they say but I think we came 20. Well as I have time to write a little, I will return.

Well on the fourth we marched about 4 miles and camped. Hard times for wood and water and was dark by the time we got our tents pitched. Got small fires made so as to make a cup of coffee.

Well today we came about ten miles and crossed Bullsrun [Bull Run creek] early in the morning on a temporary bridge, the other being burnt by the rebels. This creek is quite good size. Well we came on seeing a great many dead horses all the way. Some of the boys say they counted 100 dead horses. We came to Manassas soon, found it had been burned with the exceptions of some two or three houses. It never had been a place of much note until the war broke out and now there are quite a number of small board buildings been put up by Government for storehouses. And there are a few sutler shops. This place has been quite a stronghold for the rebels but their forts are verry inferior to ours, never mounting more than half the cannon and verry poorly built. But there was quite a number of them. Also a good many rifle pits. I saw a pile of old wagon irons. It looked as if they had piled 20 or 30 wagons and then burned them. Nothing but destruction meets the eye. There the cars come. Government having finished the road to Bristoe.

Well we came on to Broad Run, a run about twice as large as Bullsrun and crossed on a temporary foot bridge, the artillery and Cavelry fording it, the footbridge being only narrow so that only one man at a time could cross, so that it took a good while for all to cross and we camped here, the creek affording plenty of water.

April 10, 1862

Well I having been deprived of writing for several days by the recent rains which have been intolerable for three days. Well we were ordered to pack up on the 7th inst to march two miles to a better Camp ground as we were encamped on a cornfield and it begun to rain and therefore it would have been verry muddy. Well we came and camped in the edge of the woods with plenty of railfence which was soon carried off. Well it rained the balance of that day & night, next day & night & all day yesterday. And last night it snowed in earnest. In fact, it snowed the greater part time but in Camp it seemed to melt which made it rain. I have passed three of the hardest days that ever I passed in the service. And what makes it more miserable is my eyes are nearly smoked out by standing by those miserable fires.

This morning when I opened my eyes I saw the sun was shining and it made my heart leap for joy. And now we have got our things out drying although they were not much wet as we were verry careful and those little dog kennels turn water verry well. The snow has disappeared and the wind is blowing nicely. And we are in better spirits. And on the 7th inst we had no bread until just night and some of the boys, as soon as we got here, they went out scouring the Country for some bread for we had plenty of fresh meat which the boys had got. We have to come down to nothing but bread, meat, coffee and only 11 crackers per day which is not enough for me. We have plenty of coffee & sugar, meat twice a day, beans once. This is the average. Yes we have had two messes of potatoes since we marched this time. Well some of the boys come in just dark with some meat that they had bought of the Negros as there is verry few whites around here. And evry day the boys are bringing in something. But as I don't chose to run the guard and help some of the boys get it, I don't get any. And they that get it, eat it. Our sutler was coming to us today but when he got to nearly here, the N.J. boys rallied on him and took evrything away from [him] so we have no sutler shop wherewith we could buy some luxuries.

We are camped within 2 miles of Bristoe Station and the cars run to Warrenton, 5 miles further towards the Rebels. Some of the boys say we are going back to Arlington but that is all a joke I guess, for the railroad can furnish plenty of grub and we are so near it that I can hear the cars as they pass. Well I must quit as my eyes hurt but my story does not link verry good for a few days past.

April 11, 1862

And a fine day with plenty to eat and feel well. And on Brigade commisary guard today but we do not have to stand guard only at night as we can watch the things in the daytime a sitting in our bough house by the fire. And I and Frank & John bought a cup of molasses and three lbs of crackers from the Brigade commisary and we had plenty of Coffee so we made out a good dinner for a soldier. We are near the railroad and there has [been] four trains past since 10 oclock this morning going on to Warrenton Station distant 10 miles from this place. Soldiers, both Cavelry and infantry have been going past all the forenoon, the infantry crossing on the Railroad bridge and the Cavelry fording the stream, it being the largest of any I have seen in Virginia. They come past on the road to the left of us and we are on the other road but I guess they went that way so as to cross on the bridge. Just now there had been a great drove of cattle (a great many hundred) went past. They were all beef cattle. It looks as we had ought to have plenty of beef but we do not get it. The Brigade teams are bringing lots of provisions.

April 14, 1862

And the day is overcast with clouds with the appearance of storm. Well we got orders yesterday morning to pack up ready to march at nine oclock to come six miles to the front. We came to the Railroad opposite the camp we left where the road crossed the stream. Crossed the bridge, come five miles to Catlets Station and camped in the woods within 40 rods of the station on the best ground that we have camped on since we left Wisconsin. It is a delightful place, we are in the corner of the woods and can look out on the green fields. In some of them fall wheat is growing nice. There is plenty of leaves to make beds of which is nice for us. And if we want, we can fall the wood on our fires so thick is the timber. To this station terminates the use of the road at present.

And there are a great many men working on a large bridge within a quarter of a mile of us. On the 12th inst, the 2nd [Wisconsin] & 19th [Indiana] were ordered out to guard the R.R. from the Camp to Catlet [Catlett] Station and we found them on the road in groups of 3 to 6 men. And when we got here we found the 19th camped and we camped by the side of them and the sixth camped on the right of us again. The country looks better as we advance. Around here I must say that it beats our native state. Hurrah, the sun is shining. Last night there was two company of our Regt ordered out to go, I don't know where but I suppose to guard something. I expect to guard things at the station. For they say that the boys destroyed fifty dollars worth of whiskey &c, and some of our boys was boozy last night and nobody knew where they got it, but now it is supposed they got it there.

The Camp has a lively appearance this morning and now if a man wants to go out of camp safely he must get permission of the commander of the Co. The Colonel has adapted the plan of having roll call any time in the day and all of those absent without leave are to be reported as such. There we have no guard around camp and I like that. There is quite a number of our boys sick again. I don't know the cause of it.

(To return) to the last time I wrote I spoke of so many troops going by. But that evening they commenced going back. It proved afterwards to be Franklins Division and they were ordered to Alexandria to take shipping to go to reinforce McClelen, he being down near York Town [Yorktown, Virginia] which the Rebels hold and is a verry strong place. I pitied them troops after marching out all forenoon and then going back to the rear again. Oh it is Discouraging but it looks as if we would go ahead this time.[51]

April 15, 1862

And we had the usual roll calls in the forenoon and at two oclock we went out to drill by division which was something new. The divisions comprising 2 Companies each and the Senior Commander of the division takes command. We drilled till 5 oclock and then the Regt formed and had dress parade. After the courtmartial of Lieutenant Bird of Co I of this Regt was read, we were dissmissed. come to quarters, got supper &c. The Lieut proved himself clear of all the charges that were refered against him by the Captain of the Co. [Captain George H. Walther] to the great joy of the Company which they made known by cheering when they got to their quarters as they don't like the Capt verry well. They made quite a noise. Oh joy to the world. The great battle at Pittsburg landing [Shiloh] terminating in the complete rout of the enemy and Johnson [Confederate General Albert Sidney Johnston] killed and [Confederate General P. G. T.] Beauregard wounded and since died therefrom. It was the bloodiest battle of the war as yet. I have forgotten but believe it was fought on or near the 6 & 7 inst. It was a glorious victory to our army. It raised the brooding spirits of many engaged in the war.[52]

Yesterday I took a walk round to the station and down to the new bridge.

April 16, 1862

And a verry nice day. Quite warm and still at the same place. And no drill today but got permission from the Col to wash. That is the whole Regt, all that wanted to wash their persons or clothes and get their hair cut to the length of inch and half long and all that shaved at all must shave. And well it was a general cleaning. And Cedar Creek affording plenty of water for those to swim that wanted to and being within quarter of a mile. Well we had a general good time of it.

Well I bought a morning paper this morning which stated that Beaureguard was not dead as yet but I shall leave those things for history to prove after the war is over and just write what we hear in our Camp so as to show what camp life is in time of war.

April 17, 1862

And a verry pretty day. Drill by division in the forenoon and battallion drill in the afternoon. Nothing of importance transpired. This brigade is building a bridge over cedar creek so we can cross. The Colonel made us a little speech in which he said that we were to go ahead, that we would be left all over the country to guard railroads &c and the rumor was that the enemy was within 12 miles of us, 30,000 strong says he. Mcdowel says that his old division shall have a chance to do something. If it is possible we shall have a chance to see Richmond. Well on the 16th it is said Pattersons [Union] Brigade went by on the right to one mile in front of us and camped. And I saw a large camp over in the woods when we were out on the hill a drilling. The report this evening is that we start in the morning.

April 18, 1862

And a fine day and not gone yet but hear heavy canonading off to the left of us and it is thought to be a battle going on. Boom boom they go, but it may be practice only. No drill today but had to form at 1 P.M. in our shirt sleeves without arms and evrybody was conjucturing but the general conclusion was that they was going to make us work on the bridge and it terminated so for we were marched round to a stone fence within a few rods of the bridge and set to carrying stone and filling up the butments that were built. I tell you when the whole of the 7th Regt got to work, the stones rolled in and the general enthusiasm prevailed, hollowing, yelling & cheering for the paddies and it was a picturesque sight. Well when we had carried a few stones each, the Colonel said rest. I didnt think the hole was full but it was and in 10 minutes more the bridge was half done. But when the second butment got about half full, it being quite large and the stone harder to get, a great many quit. But when the Colonel mentioned that they were to get whiskey when done, they all put in harder than ever and they all got started so that they filled it up in about 5 minutes and they got more stone than they wanted. The Bridge builders had evrything ready and we didnt work over two hours and we had a good strong bridge but verry rough. We came to Camp and all those that wanted got their drink of whiskey. It being quite warm, the boys went in a swimming and the creek or run (or Cedar Run as the Virginians call it) was perfectly alive.

April 19, 1862

And looks like rain verry much, did rain a little last night. Rumors that we are going ahead today. The railroad Bridge is finished and the track is repaired for some distance onward. Our old Orderly Sargeant [John McKenzie] has been promoted to Second Lieutenant and last night he came out and called roll for the last time for this Camp and the Second [Henry Young] promoted to first and he came out with one bar on his shoulder straps, the second having a plain strap on his shoulders. The Second Lieut made a short speech saying that he would stick to Co. F. let what might come but if any 14 men would sign their names to a paper requesting him to resign he would do it and he wouldnt wait for a majority. The boys gave three cheers. He was a little tight (a short name for drunkeness) and today both of the Lieuts is on a tight also some of the boys. I don't think much of the Lieuts or anybody that will get drunk. And in the evening the 2nd Lieut had to take charge of a lot of men to go up to General Kings headquarters to guard his things and he was in a pretty fix. He could walk and that was all. Oh it is ridiculous.

There is two Cos of this Regt out on picket someplace, don't know where. We had quite a shower in the evening, at night looks like clearing off. Simon Woodhouse, one of the Corporals of this Co come to us this evening from the hospital where he has been for some three weeks. Also James Clark came day before yesterday from Fairfax hospital where he had been since we marched through. He had the typhod fever.

April 20, 1862

And Sunday. Nothing done but lay around camp, rained some. A great many packing up their overcoats, sending them to Washington, some sending them home but I didnt get mine packed up.

April 21, 1862

And rainy. Revilee at 5 oclock in the morning and marched at eight. Still raining a little, went 2 miles and came to Cedar Run farther down than where we were camped and it was verry high. We made a temporary bridge and crossed. The teams forded it and it was all they wanted to do. It being noon, we stoped and got dinner, started, come on about 4 miles through fields and all ways to get through for it was the hardest traveling I have experienced. Then we came to another large creek which they couldnt bridge and we camped and still raining. We were all wet, put a good dry rail fire, soon made them warm. I had to go on guard after carrying big loads of rails, getting tent fixed &c.

Had to pack up and [go] to a house as guard where the headquarters of brigade was for the night. We had to stand in the rain and mud all night but made the mans yard fence suffer. He had been a rich man once but had nothing much left. He said that Union soldiers that went along before us had taken evrything they could make use of. He had quite a large house and it was full of officers. He said he was born on that place and had lived on it all his life and he was considerable gray headed.

April 22, 1862

Marched at 8 oclock and we guards had to go to our Companies and march in the Company. We thought that we would be put to guard the wagons and get our knappsacks hauled. But no such good luck. This morning the creek has run down so that they built a bridge which we crossed. The teams forded to our regt goes in rear of the teams as rear guard and we had to wait till 11 oclock for it was so bad crossing & three wagons tiped over but didnt break them except the covers a little. We marched about 1 mile, stoped for dinner and let the teams go ahead a little as the road was awful, the teams sticking fast evry few minutes. We marched till dark getting about ten miles for today and camped after dark in the woods. This was a hard day for me, and I came verry near giving out. Sgt [George W.] Cowan carried my gun some which rested me some. Me being on guard last night, not getting any sleep, not getting dry, it went hard with me.

April 23, 1862

And marched at eight oclock. The 6th regt goes in rear today. Better roads. Come good speed, resting as usual and I feel a great deal better. Nothing of interest transpired. The Negros at the farmhouses coming out and smiling and chatting. We stoped near a house last night & in the morning a number of them came out, tickeled half to death, saying now we put for Alexandria or Washington soon as you boys get by. When we leave a camp they come in to pick up things that is left by the boys, coats &c. And we marched on seeing nothing unusual until we came about ten miles where there was a cavelry picket and we seeing some dead horses and some new graves. They were the graves of our men, 8 of them that were killed in a skirmish on that ground on Friday last, early in the morning about 3 oclock. Here we have in sight of the Rappahannock [River] and coming on 3 ¼ of a mile we came to the town of Falmouth. Quite a village on the bank of the river. The bridge had been burned when the Rebels retreated on Friday. Our Artillery fired four shots into the town which made the secesh soldiers run. We came through the town, band playing national airs. We came 1 mile north from the town, camped until further orders.

April 24, 1862

And nearly night still in Camp and rainy day. Teams went out forageing, just come in loaded, plenty to eat but no sugar to sweeten coffee. The rumor is that the citizens of Fredricsburg have raised the stars and stripes. This town lays about three miles down the river from here. It is said the Rebels are five miles from the town.

April 25, 1862

And nothing done but the usual roll calls evry two hours. And some more Negros come in. They tell some funny stories about how they fooled their masters and run away. They all appear to be quite smart negros.

April 26, 1862

And a fine day. Nothing done but Brigade and Regt teams went out forageing, got plenty of forage. Rumors that we go out 5 miles from here to work on the R.Road. I got a pass, went to town, bought some flour of which there was plenty in the mill where we got ours. The town full of soldiers bought evrything that was for sale. We come back on a point where we could see Fredricksburg and the Country. The loveliest Country I ever seen without any exceptions whatever and it is calculated to be the richest part of Virginia. It is a beautiful sight for the meadows and wheat fields are green.

April 27, 1862

And a fine day, verry. And marched at 7 oclock. Come through the wood about half mile to the railroad and came back on it 4 miles to where the large bridge crosses Potomac Run. Crossed on some trees that had been fallen for the purpose and waited till the Col come up as the Major had had command thus far. Our Colonel was out yesterday to find a good place for a camp and he found a good [one]. Well we waited [for] him to come up near a strawpile and we all got as much straw [as] we wanted. When he come up, he taking command, marched us to this place which is by far the best place we have ever had. Good springs & and quite a large brook & plenty of wood. The Camp lays on a side hill just steep enough and easy to drain. The streets running up and down the hill with the brook at the foot of the hill and near to the open fields which are green. The R. Road is half a mile from us. The cars run up this far. Here the bridge being burned, they must stop. This bridge is near 300 ft or more long and 70 ft high and 3 spans in it. And it is the talk that we are going to work on it. And I think so as we have cleaned up our street, fixed things as we never did before since commenced to march. That looks as if we would stay sometime and we cannot go faster than the cars can bring provisions to us. When the other Regts come they found nothing but wet straw which made them verry wrathy, espically the sixth Regt. They just stamped & swore, cussed us and then cussed their Colonel and give our Col a good blessing, called him hoggish &c.

April 28, 1862

And fine day. Inspection of arms today and washing day for those that wanted to wash. The usual roll call, dress parade in the Evening. Great many orders read. Great many promotions. Our 2nd Lieut and some sargeants. One Corporal in Co B reduced to the Ranks for absenting himself from his Co 2 ½ days without leave. One man in that Company promoted to second Lieut and so on through the Company and some promotions in other Companys. The boys play football and other games for pastime. Co. D. has got to work on the R.R. today. Out of this Regt there is a Co out of each Regt in the Brigade evry day hereafter. Men have been detailed and built bridges, fixed roads out to the main road.

April 29, 1862

And looks like rain but mist a little. Co. D. gone to work on R.R. Our boys playing ball. Only one guard from a Co per day. No camp guard around our Regt. The boys are restricted from taking anything whatever from the inhabitants around in this vicinity of Camp under heavy penalty unless they pay them for it. I mailed a letter to Mother yesterday. Co D was out chopping logs for the bridge. We are mustered in tomorrow. No mail today nor for several days, bad getting mail. Fletcher Kidd the 8th Corporal of this Company has come. He has been on the sick list about two months. Has been verry sick part of the time. He has not marched a mile with us on the march, being in the hospital at Arlington and thereabouts.

April 30, 1862

And last day of April. Mustered in today and rainy like. As a Co was done, marched to camp. In the afternoon we went out to make a road up the steep [hill], the other side of Potomac Run to take two car trucks up on the track to bring logs from the woods to build the bridge. There was a Co from the Indiania Regt to take them off the track and let them down the hill & bring them across the creek. Then we had to take them up and put them on. They made a fuss about laying track which did no good but when our Co got hold of them we just pulled it up through mud, over rocks & with Lieut Young on it to tell us where to go, it was only sport, for the whole Co done their best to forward it which made it go easy for all of us. Got it done, come home. The Regt had gone out on dress parade. The orders was read concerning the bridge giving us or our Regt the center span to build and the 6th Regt one end, Indiania the other and the 2nd Regt have to build a bridge farther back on the road in another place.

Been kind of rainy all day. Two mails came in about an hour a part just at night the first having nothing for me, the next I got a letter from Henry Lander in Nevada Territory. He is well, doing well. And one letter from Sarah, all well but quite lonesome and mother living and going to live with her this summer. They are going to live [in a] house on the place as far as she knew. I wish I were back to help her some for she will have to turn out to do chores many a stormy day, verry likely.

Drawed our sugar & coffee and make our own coffee, the Cooks having nothing to do with it. Well it is dinner time (noon day). We are to hold ourselves in readiness to march at a minutes notice and 19 men left to guard and work on the bridge and if they take them out of the Co as their belong on the roll for guard duty, it will take me and I shall not like it at all. I would rather go with the Regt but I do and go as duty calls me. The rumor is that we are going to cross the river to Fredricksburg. This is a rumor only but I believe the other is an order so the boys says we are sure to march.

May 1, 1862

And nothing done. Men for Company called on for 19 men to volunteer to stay and work on the bridge by the officers of it. They got them with some little truble. Answered Sarahs letter. The Regt going back to last camp.

May 2, 1862

And I concluded to join the bridge builders. Changed with a man that wanted to go. Also a great many others changed. There is one hundred men to be left. 15 men gone out of the 100 to work on bridge. We have to go at noon. The regt got orders to pack up & march to the last Camp.

May 3, 1862

And a fine morning. Hard shower last evening after we returned from work. Got tents pitched before it rained. We 100 men are camped togather and a Lieutanant, Sargeant & three Corporals with us. Our work last evening was digging trenches. Got them done. We are to work half a day evry third day. There is 6 reliefs. I tent now with the two Black boys[53][Henry and James Black], not by nature but name. We got our tent fixed up good. Regt has gone but we heard our drums last night. We have Frank Boyanton in our Commisary and cooks [for] us boys, that is Company F. Boys.

May 4, 1862

And worked on bridge 5 hours. We are to get extra pay for evry hour we work. So we have got the better of the other boys. I got half bus. corn meal at the mill at Acquia Creek. We have Corn cakes, plenty of fish.

May 5, 1862

And rainy in the morning, clear at noon, fine day the rest. The boys comenced at 5 oclock this morning on the bridge. They relieved at noon and another squad goes on until plumb dark. The report is that the rebels are evacuating York Town and we must rush the bridge up as fast as possible. The cars came up last evening late with a load of lumber for the bridge. The first time they have been up. The bridge was just finished back at Aquaia Creek about three oclock and they came right across and they have been up again today.

May 14, 1862

And looks like rain this morning of which we have not had since I last wrote. We have had splendid weather ever since we begun work on the bridge. And I got into blacksmithing after I had worked about a day on the wood work and have been so busy ever since that I couldnt write verry well. The cars run up from the landing to this place from 2 to 5 times per day. Orley F and Frank Boyanton is at work on the water tank, the only watering [tank] on this part of the road at present. There are two others, men from Co. A helping them and my shop is right on the side of the tank. I have a blacksmith from the Indiania Regt to help me. There is a not a great deal of iron about the bridge it being trusselwork using the dowel pin instead of a tenant & mortice. Of the latter there is not one about the bridge.

The work will be so far advanced by noon that a footman can cross if he can walk 85 feet from the ground which is the height of it, instead of 75 as I have stated before, from the creek to the top of the cribs which are built of large fine logs. They are 30 ft long, 6 feet wide, is ten feet where the water is likely to raise, those are built, some of them not more than 3 feet high which are on the banks. The boss calculates to have the cars across by tomorrow night. We put in some verry long days work. We get extra pay, I don't know exactly yet, and ten hours is a days work. But some and I have put in 13 & 14 hours. I guess we will be paid by the hour and I don't know long I shall work, certainly as long as I can. Probably I shall get to work at the Rappahannock Bridge, it being over 600 ft long, just double the length of this one but not so high.

Well, my book is nearly full and sorry for it for I havent another. I must go to camp and get some paper. We, the Bridge builders, is camped about 130 rods from the bridge and I must stay near the shop while writing so that if anything comes that he cannot do alone, I can help him. Good by.

Volume 5

May 26, 1862 to July 2, 1862

In Pursuit of Devils

[*Inside front cover*]
Wm. R. Ray's Book
Private of Co. F, 7th, Regiment Wis. Volt.

A Resident of Cassville, Grant Co., Wisconsin

If this book I should happen to loose,
Please notify the owner if you choose,
And if the owner you cannot find
To the above named place send a line.
And when I do get this same book
You shall receive more than a pleasant look.
On a big tree root I am sitting
When all of this is written
Slowly in pursuit of the Devils
But the modest call them Rebels.
We have as yet had no affray
But we expected one today
The rebels is not far they say
Maybe only a little way
and here we lay in camp today
I wonder what the folks will say.
If this book I should happen to loose
Please notify the owner if you choose.

And if the owner you cannot find
To the aforenamed place drop a line.
And when I do get this same book
The finder shall receive more than a look.

We are slowly in pursuit of the Devils
But the more modest call them Rebels,
We have as yet had no affray
But we expect one today.
The rebels is not far they say
And maybe only a little way
And here we lay in camp today
I wonder what the people will say.
Maybe some say it is not quite right
If nae don't let the 7th have a fight
To bad do they want to see the sight

On a big tree root I am sitting
While all of this am writing

May 26, 1862, Camp in the Woods 6 miles in front of Fredericksburg

Well I must awake from my slumber as it were for it has been in the of not keeping up my scrapbook. Well all I can say is that we are in camp and it is a fine day and I must go back a week or so when I was to work on the bridge. Well we worked day after day until sent to our regt, which was on the 22nd [of May] and our Co being on detached duty in Fredericksburg guarding and chopping railroad ties in the woods, when they were not guarding the city. I put in 15 days work there. The 6th [Wisconsin] Regt boys was ordered back the day before us and we left the [Nineteenth] Indiana there to finish filling the cribs with stone I suppose. And it will be a hard job.

We come [to] the city getting there about 12 oclock at night and the conductor said we might sleep in the cars as they would stay all night and we did so and joined our Co in the morning. Which we found not far distant. Found them quartered in an old blacksmith shop. It being a two story building, it made good quarters when cleaned up. They had been there for 8 or 10 days and were well fixed.

And Mon the 23rd we got our regular $26.00 pay and we had fine times, plenty of milk and could buy the verry best kind of bread.[54] In fact, anything we wanted to eat, for the Yankees have come in with all kinds of merchandise. But before they come the town was almost destitute of luxuries, in fact, everything. A great many of our boys bought shoes at the stores for what the shoemakers said they could only and scarcely get the stock for. And I believe it was so knowing how other things was.

They said if they had had them shoes there last winter they could have sold them for seaven and eight dollars a pair. And I seen one deserter that had on a fine pair of boots. He said they cost him $18.00 dollars in Richmond. And we see lots of deserters that come in to us. There was a sergeant and two other privates with that fellow I spoke of having the boots.

I wouldn't stop writing and go out to the road to see Secesh soldiers so plenty are they getting. It is said that there was a troop of cavelry lay within a mile of us last night. There was firing out to the front this morning which caused a little excitement. But proved to be only those that stood on guard the day before. And they were shooting of their guns so as to clean them.

There was a bad and a most horrible accident happened in the city yesterday from the explosion of a magazine which killed a soldier that was guarding it. It caused great excitement throughout the city and there being meeting at the churches. They were almost broken up, they fearing that the city was being bombarded. But it soon cooled down in a minute. There was an overwhelming crowd gathered to the place of the disaster. It was as follows.

When the rebels left, they left some ammunition in a small brick building which they had used for a magazine and our army took possession of it and put ammunition therein and guarded it ever since we took the city. And this man being on guard was killed. He was blown on top of a building some 4 or 5 rods distant. One leg blown of close to his body & the other just below his knee. The hair was burned of his head. He had scratches all over his body and besmeared with blood, blood and dirt. There was not a thread of clothing left on him. I saw him & it was the most horrible sight I ever seen. It is beyond description. His brother was the first to get hold of him, he being on another post not far distant. I have not heard as there was any body else got even a scratch.

There were a great many soldiers at work a little ways off hewing logs. They didnt get even a scratch. There a great crowd gathered and great was the excitement and many were the oaths & curses heaped upon the citizens who probably were not to blame. It is thought and I think that the fire was communicated to it by a wire and some citizen did the firing. It has caused many warm debates between the citizens and soldiers and I wouldnt be surprised to hear of a fire in the city shortly. For his Regt was in the city & it set them perfectly mad in a manner. There were brick and pieces of wood lying scattered over the ground for a great distance. It broke a great many glass in the city in the vicinity of it. Well, he was carried off and the crowd was dispersed and a guard put around a good distance off so as to [keep] anybody, evrybody from going near. For it might billow again and keep so doing. For there is no telling what the rebels might have done and do again.

Well, I will leave you to imagine what transpired and the rest as I have given as good an account as I could and will turn my mind to the news of today.

Late in the evening when the scouting parties returned, they brought the news that they had been out twelve miles and didnt see a secesh soldier. That the R. Road track was all torn apart two miles from here and bridge was burned that was across some creek. I have not found out the name yet.

Well we are now encamped in the woods 6 miles from Fredricsburg.

Yesterday morning our Co got orders to join our regt and got ready but soon another order come that the Brigade was going to move across the river and we were to join them which we did, the colonel putting us on the right wing which is calculate to be an honorable post. Well, we marched 16 miles through the prettiest country I ever seen. Ditch fences with trees growing on the top. On each side of the road is this fence. The country is verry level and pretty. The weather was quite warm and the dust verry plenty. We passed pickets evry little way along the road.

May 27, 1862

And a fine morning but rained a little through the day with some sunshine. Stayed in camp all day & had rollcall evry two hours. Nothing of importance transpired in & around camp. There is a rumor that the rebels have driven [Union General Nathaniel] Banks to Catlets [Catlett's] Station and past to the Potomac River. And they had burned the bridge at Catlets and the village and 2 engines and 3 or 4 cars, and that Banks had to burn a bridge that he had made. But this I cannot believe but if it be true, I think that it was done on purpose to draw them on so as we could go on towards Richmond and thereby get them between Bank's and McDowel's divisions. Well let it be as it will, it caused some excitement. And as for McClelen's army I have not heard from it for several days. Therefore don't know how they are getting along.[55]

Our Co is quite small now. They draw rations for only about 70 men and the number of officers has diminished for we left a couple of privates and one sargent in the Foundry at the city. Some six or seven privates, one sargent & Lieutenant Young there also, who were to join the Bridge Corps which was being formed for McDowel's division and left four sick there also that were unable to travel. So upon the whole, Co. F. is quite small at present. Yesterday I mailed two letters, one to Sarah, the other to Richard Lander in answer to the ones I received which brought the news that they were all well in both families. And Sarah says she is going to keep the shop and tools for me if I want her to which I was glad to hear. And I told her in the letter I wanted it. I have sent $15.00 to Henry and kept the rest which makes $65.00 I have sent to him.

May 29, 1862

Got orders to pack up, ready to march which we did about 10 oclock and came back to Fredricksburg. Rested 1 hour in the street, bought all we wanted. I bought a warm peach pie for which I paid 25 cents. Then we crossed the river on the new wagon bridge which has been erected in the last week and we come on through Falmouth and back 7 miles on the verry same road that we went [out] on. And camped, it being about 9 oclock at night. The day being verry hot we rested often until sun down when we come verry fast. And me not being well, it was hard on me. The catarrh in my head troubles me verry much of late when I get my blood heated. I was completely given out and should have had to [have] stopped for the night if they had went much farther. & I spread down my bed and layed down feeling as though I should have to ride on the morrow. The Captain [John B. Callis] came around to see the sick fellows and called and talked with me quite a while, offered his help but as I needed nothing but rest, I thanked him verry much and went to sleep. It is said we are going to reinforce Banks, that is Kings division is going. It is said that Banks has retreated to the Potomac River and that [Confederate General Thomas "Stonewall"] Jackson was following him up. I have an idea that we are going to the rear of Jackson, thereby cutting off his retreat and have him between our two armies. It is said that Banks has been retreating ever since the 4th of the month and if this be so, he has done it on purpose to draw him on and get us in the rear so as to take Mr. Jackson and his all. The men that was left in the Foundry was called to the Co.

May 30, 1862

And a fine morning, continued so till near noon when the sky became quickly overcast with clouds and the thunder rolled & shortly we had a thunder shower which was a welcome guest for it cooled off the air, layed the dust which had been almost intolerable. & the heat being so great up to this time, there had been two men in the 2nd [Wisconsin] Regt sunstruck, one killed, the other being helpless. It continued showery all the afternoon. And we marched a good gait & stoped about 5 oclock and made a cup of coffee and started again. Marched till about 8 oclock and camped within half a mile of where we camped the first night when we went out. Coming about 20 miles today over the same road and the Colonel says we must be to Catlets station by 8 oclock in the morning.

I stood the march well today as I went to the Doctor and he excused me and I got my knappsack hauled. But the boys found an axe and as our Co had no axe, I concluded to carry it today & the cooks would put it in the box in the morning. I heard there was two men died on the road from the 6th [Wisconsin] Regt. Oh, it must have been awful behind the Brigade as there was so many that give out and got behind and I guess the ambulances was well filled today. There was 2 from our Co that rode.

We heard that McDowel was under arrest for treasonable acts but I cannot believe it but the people do not have any too much confidence in him as far as I know.[56] And there is such a rumor that Banks has been driven back across the Potomac with heavy loss and that Jackson is being reinforced and he has said and made it known that he would have possession of the Baltimore & Ohio RRoad if it cost him 60,000 men. And if reports be true that they are about out of provisions I don't wonder that they want to get into Maryland & Pennsylvania where they would have plenty of provision with forageing or just taking it from the well stored warehouses.

May 31, 1862

And cool and cloudy. We started at 6 oclock this morning. Come on to Catlets a good pace & camped near the R Road. The cars begin to come in and still keep coming until there is seaven trains and the soldiers is being put in as thick as they can stand and sitting on top as thick as they can sitt. It is evident that we are going on the cars and we are going to White Plain to help Banks. Evrything is a buzz and evrything goes on smooth. Oh, wouldnt it be nice if we could capture Jackson & all his arms & stores. There is several of our boys back yet and some came up this morning only. Had camped in old houses &c and the Doct has sent a team back for those they might find on the road. There will not be any behind that would walk for evrybody wants to go that can so as to see the sights and get a share of the glory if there is any won.

There one car goes loaded. There goes another load of 7 cars and it is as full and covered all over with soldiers as can be.

June 1, 1862

And cloudy & sultry warm. Now 2 oclock and still in Camp. No cars been up today, they finished taking about one half of the division last night. The last train left about dark. Today I don't feel verry well, a slight headache with some fever and I bought a box of Ayers pills so I have taken a dose of them. The Provost Guard took quite a number of boys out of this Regt to our Colonel for playing poker (a game of cards) and he had each one tell him how much he had both won & lost & he counted it up and made them divide so that evry man would get what he lost. He reprimanded them for breaking the law & praised them for telling the truth. For he said each man and his opponont told the story so near alike. There was 15 or 20 of them in the scrape. There was several playing poker in our Co. They jumped mighty quick, I tell you, when they heard of it. Oh, it is surprising. There is lots of boys wouldnt have their folks and sweethearts know for all they have earned in their service. Oh, it is shocking to see how wreckless the boys do get. I never had any idea of how wreckless the boys do get and even brutal in some cases. I don't wonder at the Commanders having so much guarding.

Well, no cars yet, there must have been something up.

June 2, 1862

And a warm morning. Looks some like rain. Got orders to march which we did about 10 AM for a place by the name of Haymarket, distant 13 miles from Catlets. Well, we traveled on resting evry little while. Continued warm & sultry till noon when we had showers and continued cloudy & sprinkling a little once & awhile which made it good traveling. I had to fall out in the forenoon but caught up and kept up in the afternoon. There was a great many out. Towards night & one of Gibbens [Brigade Commander John Gibbon] aides ordered the rear guard to fix bayonet and make the boys come in but no sooner had the guard fixed bayonet, then there [was] a shout went up from the Stragglers to fix bayonet and evry man done so. The Lieut or aid rode off in a hurry, perfectly dumbfounded at the boys acting so. I suppose he thought he could drive the poor tired out fellows but he had to leave there without saying any more. Those stragglers were over a hundred in number & from all Regts & Co in the Brigade. And some of the stoutest men amongst them that was outdone by the heat which was intolerable between showers.

I gave 25 cents to a man to carry my blanket. That lightened my knappsack so I kept up but it was hard work then. And now Cap Finnecums [Mark Finnicum of Company H] is under arrest for disobeying orders by giving the stragglers too much lenity, his Co being on rear guard and he couldnt be cruel to the boys. Now Gen Gibbens has arrested him for not obeying orders. But evry man from the Colonel down in the Regt will stick to him and help him out of it. The Col thinks a great deal of Finnecum and will see that he has his rights. Gen Gibbens has made his brags it is said, that he would bring down the boys to the verry letter but I guess he has or will find out mistaken.

Well we reached here at dark, camped within ½ mile of the town, made fire, got supper, went to bed. I commenced coughing then vomiting, kept on so steady till about midnight when I got easy & slept till morning. This has been another hard day for me but as soon as I get hearty I can stand it. I taking physic and traveling hard, it made it work pretty hard on me. Reported as soon as we got our tents pitched that we had to go back to Fredricsburg in the morning. This made the boys down hearted for we were in hopes that we should get out to help Banks catch Jackson. I kind thought it was so for the officers said so.

June 3, 1862

And Cloudy, warm & Sultry, no air stirring and we are still in camp. It is now three oclock. The railroad cars is running pretty brisk this place. Haymarket [Virginia] is a station. There being probably 20 houses & no more. There is one store, the only public house in the place. This Road is the Manassas Gap RRoad. This is the third RRoad we have been on and never got a ride since we come to Washington.

June 4, 1862

Lazed in camp all day (Oh pshaw a pencil is a bad thing to write with). Rained hard last night and run into our tent and did so with most of the boys. We were not wet much for I had taken the precaution to dig a small ditch around the tent but which proved insufficient for the heavy shower but luckily nothing but one end of one blanket got wet a little. Well, it continued to rain all day which made it awful bad for us. Well night came at last, had rollcall, went to bed. Today there was a great many boys went to houses to stay but they were brought in by the patrol guard towards night of which Gen Gibbens ordered out a verry large one. But they didnt catch any of Co F. boys although there was some out & several until after dark.

Got a paper today. [Union General George] McClellan had a fight within 5 miles of Richmond, drove the enemy back with great loss on both sides, they disputing evry foot of ground with their greatest efforts.[57] Well, I feel some better this evening. R Pierce [Richmond Pierce] is sick in his tent. I let him have some pills to take which helped him some he thought. Cap [Callis] went up to see him. Cap acts more manly that he used to. I think he has reformed a great deal for he attends to his buisness better than he used to. So I think, I cannot judge for others.

June 5, 1862

And cloudy with a little sunshine, sprinkles verry little once & awhile. We dried our blankets which were damp, cleaned our guns. That is all we have done today.

Oh, I forgot to tell you that this Brigade had to build a raft to get provisions across on, the creek being swollen by the rains to a river and the depot was on the other side. So this was the plan they had to adopt to get rations of which was scarce among the boys for the last week, our main and nearly all we had to eat was crackers & coffee. Well we had three small pieces of beef in the time about as much beef in the week as I have eat in one day at home. And today we had a mess of beans which I relished verry much as I am getting hearty again but still have bad cold and pain in my breast.

June 6, 1862

Got orders to march at 7 oclock this morning which we did and come back about 1 mile to the Warrenton Turnpike and started to Warrenton, a distance of 12 miles it is said from Haymarket. We reached the town a little after 4 oclock by the large clock on the Courthouse which we heard strike 4 when we were a mile of town. We camped right at the edge of town on a pretty little ridge, a verry pretty camp ground. As soon as the boys were dismissed from the ranks, great numbers started for town which caused a verry heavy guard to be called for around Camp which was six men from a Co. This took me on guard and we let no one in or out. So they caught some that were out. And when they got one, they put him on guard and relieved somebody of the Co. they belonged [to] and there were several relieved so.

Well the Country we came through today was unlike any we have traveled over before. Today it was hilly with small streams in the hollows & good springs coming out of the hillsides. Altogather the country shows we are getting nearer the mountains and the Country is verry pretty. We found considerable cattle in pastures today along the road. This would be a great Dairy country but it lacks the enterprising men. Evrything looks old and dull. What looks so pretty is the Country as it naturally lays with its groves. And as for the town, I have not been in it but from what I can see, I judge it is a pretty place. There is a great many shade trees in it. The old clock was great company through the night when on guard, striking the hour through the night and telling what time to go on and come of guard. I believe it could be heard strike 4 miles tonight so still & pretty was the night.

June 7, 1862

Got orders to march to a better Campground. Got packed up but the Colonel had been over while we were packing up to see the ground and it being worse than the one we were on he said we might pitch tents again and we would stay at the old camp. Well we must have a pass to go to town now or we are liable to be picked up by the patrol which is sneaking around all the time.

Well we had a hard shower just at night which flooded some of the tents driving the boys out. But I had ditched mine and kept it dry. Now as R. Pierce is sick I and Wm Smith is tenting togather. I am afraid that Dick will never get well so as to join the Regt again. I hated to see him leave us and go to the hospital which he done when we left Haymarket. Heavy guard today around camp. The Negros bring in cakes, pies, milk &c for sale but in small quantities. I got a pass, went into the town. It don't look verry well with its muddy streets and poor sidewalks. Only one street of any note. Town contains probably 400 inhabitants in time of peace but not near so many now & mostly women. This is a hot secession hole. There is 3 or 4 little shops but sold out most evrything they had.

June 8, 1862

And fine morning. Sunday and the boys that want to go are going to church at 11 A.M. & when they had been there a while they were ordered to their regts to get ready to march immediately. A commissioned officer had to go with each Co boys that went. About 20 of our boys went. When the citizens found the soldiers coming in they all left but three of them and the preacher. And we got ready and marched taking the road for Catlets [Catlett's] which is said to be 10 miles by railroad and 12 by the wagon road. We come on the latter, it being noon when we started. We came right through the main street of the town. The different bands of the Regt playing national tunes, the Inhabitants gazing on with wonder, some laughing, some crying, others cursing & frowning. The colored people seemed well pleased and a great many of the fair sex smiled on us espicially the young girls. Well, we came on & on resting evry three or four miles, the day being cool and the roads good. The officers calculated we came 11 miles when we camped on an old camp ground on Cedar Run. This, I think, was formerly a secesh camp. Well we were still 2 miles from Catlets. We reached this place and got camped & supper by dark. And after rollcall as I was just going to bed, the commisary come around wanting men to go with them to draw rations and I and 4 others went and with waiting and doing the buisness it took us till eleven oclock and having to get up at 4 in the morning it was tuff I thought. And the rumor is that we have to go to Fredricsburg tomorrow which will be about a thirty mile march but I guess we will not go that far.

June 9, 1862

Fine morning. Marched to where we camped on the 30 of last month as we went out to Catlets but didnt go around by Catlets as I stated yesterday but come across the Country. We layed in camp until 6 PM when we went on dress parade. Had a string of orders a yard long read to us. 3 men fainted away in the time. 2 of those were in our Co and at roll call Cap told us that revilee would be at four in the morning and we would have to start half past 5 oclock. Went to bed, had a good nights rest.

June 10, 1862

And started at half past 5 oclock and the instant we began our march it began to rain and continued a steady but slow rain till two oclock when we had reached the distance of 16 miles it was thought. We turned into the woods & camped and just as we got our tents pitched, it stoped raining and I washed my feet and pants, washed my shoes out and Bill made coffee and we ate dinner for we didnt stop for dinner today, only stoped some two or three times in all the march. I never stood a march better. There was not a man fell behind today from our Co. I would rather march in the rain than in the dust & hot weather.

June 11, 1862

And a fine morning and started at half past 5 oclock. They [say] it is eight miles to Falmouth. Well we marched on & on, resting as usual (except yesterday). We reached Falmouth about ten oclock, marched through & down the bottom about 1 mile, which brought us to opposite Fredricsburg and we camped on good ground but a limited supply of water.

Falmouth is a verry buisness place now. A great deal of buisness done there which [is] quite different to what we found it before. There being nothing to by [buy] then & now the streets is lined with shops of all kinds of shops. Plenty of apples for sale but pretty dear, only 5 cts a piece. The boys of the town met us half mile out with things [to] sell & followed us and in two hours time after we stoped we could buy anything we wanted. And the boys pitched in pretty steep for we have not had a chance to by anything to eat since we left here before.

Hello, there is a Fredricsburg papers for sale. I must go and buy one. Well, been & bought one for 5 cents. The Christian banner[58] is the name of it. It is printed on brown paper, looks verry odd. Well I have spent about $1.50 cts since we came yesterday. I bought a lb of fresh pork for which I paid 15 cents, had it for breakfast. Oh, it tasted nice.

Well we heard today that there was one Brigade left of at Warrenton, one left at Catlets so that left us alone and that Gen Gibbens had been appointed Military Govenor over Fredricsburg. And it appears so from what I can judge from the movements and I hope it is so for I am tired of running around all over the country and for nothing to as far as I can see. Oh, it is a miserable life the way we have lived for two weeks. We would of thought nothing of it if we had been after [Confederate General Thomas J. "Stonewall"] Jackson or any portion of the rebel army but so it is and we will have to put up with it.

Well the rumor that Mcdowel was arrested has proved false. But as far as my judgement goes I think he had ought to have been arrested. But he may be a true patriot for all his enemy's sayings and doings. Well up to late last night there was no other Brigade came in so I guess that Gibbens has been appointed Military Govenor of Fredricsburg and vicinity.

June 12, 1862

And fine day & quite warm. We have a brigade review today at 11 A.M. so we had fix up in good style and did better than ever we did yet on a review. It is a pretty sight with evrything shining. A multitude of pedlars and a great many of them have been taken up before the General for some cause, I don't know how or what. But I see they have all left dress parade at 6 P.M. All looks well. They come down stricter than ever. An order was read holding the Orderly sargeants of Co responsible for the cleanliness of men brought on guard by them. And the Col has now under arrest the Orderly of one Co for bringing unclean men on guard. And day after tomorrow there is to be a close inspection and any man found unclean, his Co shall be cut of from having any passes until they can come out clean. Now this is wrong to have the whole Co condemned on account of one man being dirty and it is not right to expect us to do as regulars when we are on the field and been marching and lying about in the mud like so many boys. Well we cannot better ourselves now. But it is hard when a man volunteers to do a thing to have the officers come down on them and have them arrested for any little thing. It was not so when King was our Brigadier General. But since Gibbons is over us, we find it different. Oh, damn this way putting regular officers over volunteers. It don't suit me at all.

Yesterday I got a letter from Henry and one from Newton. Our Regt has not had their mail for two weeks but now we shall get it oftener I hope.

June 13, 1862

And a fine day till 2 P.M. when it rained for about hour. And just as it begun to rain we got orders to get ready to march to the north & near Falmouth. Which we did & camped in a verry pretty grove of large timber and just rolling enough to drain which made it a beautiful Camp. It being dark by the time we got our tents pitched. In the morning about 3 oclock the order come to get ready to march in light marching order. The long roll was beat in the 6th and 2nd Regts. Then the news come that the rebels had driven our pickets in to the city and those two Regts went after and none of the others Regts went. And that was all we heard about it. I guess it was a false alarm. Those two Regts come back before night and seen nothing of any rebels.

June 14, 1862

And a fine morning and the inspection come of at 9 A.M. We were inspected verry close and they said we were in excellent order. And I know we did clean evrything the best it could be. The Regt officers inspected us. And the Col said last night he wouldnt have a guard around camp for he had confidence enough in us. And he would trust us to do our duty without being guarded as we had been when in the Brigade. For there he couldnt help having a guard if the Gen called for it so there is only a small commisary guard. After inspection we cleaned up the streets, each Co doing their own. And just as we got this done, the rumor comes that we move tomorrow as Gen Patrick [Union General Marsena Patrick] was coming to this place and as he camped there before, he was entitled now. Had 2 hours drill and dress parade. The Col issued an order that we were hereafter to drill one hour evry day, that hour being from half past five till half past six P.M., then dress parade. The ajjutant read a note from Gen Gibbons in which the Gen gave us (our Regt) great praise for their soldierly bearing and good actions and appearance and placed great confidence in us. But he disliked verry much the way the Indiania Regt acted by throwing away their clothing &c while on the march.

June 15, 1862

And fine day. Orders come immediately after revilee to get ready to go back to the Brigade at 8 oclock and camp on the same ground. This we done today. I had to go on guard as it is my turn but they didnt mount guard until after we moved which was about 10 oclock. It was commisary guard and 1 post in daytime, 2 at night. And there was thirteen of us so some of us come on only once & I was one of them. And I come off at midnight and come to my tent and slept till rollcall in the morning. When I went back today we had a mess of beans which was a rarity and we relished them well. I have ate 25 cts worth of oranges today, 8 in number. They are verry nice fruit.

Well they have called for guard from this regt & my tentmates had to go. They go in the Brigade guard. Oh, but the boys hated to leave that good camp.

June 17, 1862

Fine day, done the same as yesterday except that we had skirmish drill instead of Co drill as day before.

June 18, 1862

Fine day. Got orders to clean up for Brigade review by Gen King & Brigade drill. The Brigade got on the ground all ready for buisness about ½ mile from camp. When it clouded up and begun to rain and they dismissed the Regts. Colonels brought them, dismissed them and the water just poured down for a few minutes setting evrything afloat and runing some of the boys out of their tents that had not ditched around them. So that is all that was done today. Co C of our Regt is over in the city guarding. The officers is coming right down on us as if we were so many slaves now. I have had to go to the truble of getting a button brush which cost 30 cents and a box of Tripoli to rub the buttons & brasses with and now Co. B is varnishing their guns at their own expense and it makes them look so much better that the whole Regt will have to do it so I understand. And they are forcing leggins and blous [blouse or frock] coats on us and forcing us to wear them. It's a dime for this and a quarter for that and so it goes. And whatever the General says we must have, we must take it or be arrested. Our ajjutant [Frank Haskell] just as bad now as the Gen. The boys used to think considerable of him but they hate him just as bad now.

Well there was a verry disgraceful thing happened today. It is as follows. Three Corporals, G Henderson, F Kidd, & J Bradley and one private G Hickock [Griffin Heacock][59] was arrested for playing Poker or in other words Gambling. The Private was put under guard and the corporals arrested as a corporal cannot be put under guard but will be reduced to the ranks. Cap [Callis] has always allowed it to go on right in his face although it is against orders. And would have this time but the officer of the day watching around caught them at it unbeknown to either Cap or them and he addressed a line to Cap saying that if he didnt arrest them (the players) he would arrest him. So Cap, afraid of loosing his honor, put right out and done it to the great chagrin of the partys. This pleased me although I don't wish any of them any harm. But they have made great brags what they could & would do. They say if anybody writes back to anybody about this affair, they ought to be rode on a rail and one of the Corporals says he would shoot the man that would do such a trick. But just as likely as not, I might accidently write a few words about it when I write home. I am not afraid of any of them. Let them talk till they gray for I care not what they say.

It is said that the Col of the Indiania Regt [Solomon Meredith] has gone to Washington to see if he cannot get his Regt out of this Brigade and our Colonel has gone some place and been gone two or three days and the talk is that he has gone for the same purpose as the Ind. Col and if this be true, I hope he will succeed and we will be from under the old tyrant Gen Gibbons. It is him that causes the truble. He comes down on the regimental officers and they come down on the Co officers and as a matter or course, they must come down on us and that is the way it goes. I don't blame any of them for reminding us of keeping clean but I hate this putting on so much style. The boys call it putting on French airs.

Most of the Ind & 6th threw their extra clothing away and now they have to draw more. The Gen is bound to make us carry the extra clothing, thereby causing a great many to give out on the march and then they will have to haul them & their knappsacks too. And if they oblige me to carry so much, I will sitt down when tired and they have got to haul me.

June 19, 1862

And fine day, no drill but review at 6 P.M. by Gen King. It didnt rain so as to stop proceedings but sprinkled a little before going on review. The officers tried and did make most of the Co draw an extra pair of pants & extra pair shoes. But me with 5 or 6 others wouldnt draw them and we said we wouldnt until forced to and we expected to be marched to the guardhouse in the morning but were not. I have good shoes and good pants and I wont draw them unless forced to. And now they are trying to make us give ten cents apiece to get our guns varnished and there is a strong opposition against it.

June 20, 1862

And fine day. Done nothing but work on our guns & getting them varnished &c. They are stained a dark color first, then varnished them. It makes them look a hundred per cent better. Most of the Regt is getting their guns varnished. We did or all the Co did not get theirs done today. It costs 10 cts apiece. Warm day. The Private that was put under guard yesterday for gambling has been released and I guess the Corporals will not be reduced.

June 21, 1862

And fine day. Finished fixing guns and in the evening had undress parade. A great many orders was read and the three Corporals was reduced for gambling. When their folks hears it, it will make them feel verry bad for it is a great disgrace in a military point of view. And it is really in any place or position and it will stand in the army records as long as they live for they have betrayed the confidence of the officers. It is more disgrace than being Courtmartialed. It will most break the hearts of their parents who are verry pious folks and verry much respected in the circles in which they move. They are liked by evrybody that is acquainted with them and it being read before the whole Regt, it must have made them feel verry bad. And they are quite down hearted about it from appearances.

Well, I must turn from this disgraceful feature to one nearly as bad which occurred between Co B and our Co. It was this. One of our boys and a couple of B boys had some truble several days since and the B. Boys got drunk today and as one of our boys was going peacable through their street. And those drunkerds thought it was the same fellow that they had the truble with the other day. So they pitched on to him and comenced pelting him and drove him out of the street. This raised quite an excitement and most of the two Cos congregated around and one word brought on another until the two Cos came verry near having an irish row. I kept off a little way so that they should not get me in the fuss. Our Capt reported to the officer of the day what was transpiring and he sent guards to quell and take the imposters and when they went to take 3 or 4 of them, their Co pitched on to the guards and about whiped them out. Then the officer of the day come up and drew his sword and took command of the guard and bid the rascals walk off. Which they done through fear of being run through with the officers sword or the guards bayonet. It has caused considerable hard feelings between officers as well as privates. But if it had been the right fellow it wouldnt have been thought so hard of in our Co. But it was an innocent fellow they miss-used so if it had been the other fellow, a great many of the Co would have liked to seen him whiped.

I forgot to tell you the promotions. There was Wm A. Smith (my tentmate), Giles Parker [Calvin G. Parker][60] and F. H. Boynton were promoted to the places of the reduced Corporals. I have mailed 2 or 3 letters this week and wrote one today to Sarah & commenced another to Henry Lander.

June 22, 1862

And fine day and Sunday. The Cap got a pass from the Col to take the Co to Fredricsburg to Church or all that wanted to go. And most of them went but I didnt as I had a letter to finish and one to write to Isaac Lander which I did. & I don't like to be led to Church anyhow. And I finished the 3rd letter to send off in the morning.

Last night the boys serenaded the new Corporals using tin pans &c for instrumental music which they would beat on with the Choir singing. It caused considerable merriment in the Camp drawing a great [number] to see what Co F was doing. Co F is verry popular now throughout the Regt. Also noticed somewhat in other Regts by our Capt being verry popular amongst the white collars throughout the Brigade. But when Cap went to Gibbons to get him to sign the pass, he wouldnt do it saying it was out of order. And Cap determined to not be out done so he went to Gen King who signed it without a word of remonstrance and was pleased vis the Cap in taking such an interest in his Co welfare. And Cap does take great interest in our welfare of late I must say. But still he is the same of other folks, has his faults and one is he gives passes to a few two or three times to others once. But it would be a queer man that could satisfy evryone in the Co.

June 23, 1862

And fine day till about 7 P.M. when we had as hard a thunderstorm as we usually see and after raining hard for a half an hour, it ceased to a good steady rain which continued nearly all night.

We had no drill nor dress parade today. Our Capt got a pass to go to Washington. The talk is that the colonel sent him as a representative from the Regt to see about the state clothing to see if we shall have to pay for it or not. We hadnt ought to pay for it as they would not let us wear it out and it was an order from the United States secretary that no more troops should come in to the field with them before we got or the state pushed them on to us. If we have to pay for them the clothing bill for each man in this Regt will be not less than sixty or seaventy dollars and at the end of 10 months only at that.

We had orders to clean up the camp today as it would be inspected at two oclock. We all got trees and fixed about our tents each one fixing to suit himself. The street looks verry pretty now. I mailed my letter this morning. Lieut [Henry F.] Young was over to see us today. I was as glad to see him as a brother almost. He with a squad of the Engineer Corps is stationed in Fredericsburg. I wish he would come back to the Co. I should not wonder of hearing of Caps resigning then Young will come in as Captain which he had ought to have been at first.

June 24, 1862

And tolerable fine day. Rained a verry little through the day. Us fellows that worked on the Potomac Creek Bridge from our regt got paid today. I got $8.50 cts for my work being about 60 cents a day. This the extra pay over and above the $13.00 dollars per month and the other Regts will get theirs right along as fast as they can pay them off. This pay come in good play and pleased the boys verry much. And I can get in some of the money due me from the boys that sent clothes home with me. That is the expenses accrued by getting them home from the Bridgeport, the R Road station. But some of it I shall have to wait for till payday.

Had no dress parade, no drill today. Things went on all right today.

June 25, 1862

And pretty day. Co drill in the evening & from 4 till 5 oclock. Come in , got ready for dress parade but drilled battalion drill instead. Made some mistakes in the [drill] on account of the ajjutant who I think was some under the influence of liquor from the way he acted which caused some merriment in the ranks. We have to come out looking like a king in a manner. There is one dirty fellow in our Co. He has been sent back from guard mounting twice by the ajjutant and he has been put to carrying water for the Co until further order. He work evry day. Co C is over in the city guarding and has been for several days. I am going to send my dresscoat home if I can get it to town.

There was a committee of three officers around to examine the knappsacks and haversacks & canteens &c through the Regt. And they condemned our old knappsacks & haversacks and we are to get new ones and I hope they will be of a better kind than the old ones and will carry easier. I don't care if they get them so they will walk. One of the new Corporals treated the Co to a box of cigars. The boys keeps running to me to borrow money knowing that I got the most of any of them that worked on the Bridge. I could have loaned $1.00 cts if I had had it but I wont loan any but to my tentmate which I loaned one dollar. And my folks need it at home and to them it is promised all I can spare. I am going to keep plenty to do me.

June 26, 1862

And a fine but verry warm day. We had Co drill at the usual hour and battalion right after which lasted till dark. We rested several times. The colonel [William Robinson] talked and advised the soldiers as well as the officers what we had ought to do. We certainly couldnt have got a better Col. He is liked better evry day. He never gets wrathy and is always cool. He has a good command over himself as he has over his regt. And when any of the boys goes to him, he talks to them verry gentlemanly. He give one of our boys a pair of socks one day when we were on the march. He heard him complaining of sore feet and let him have them. And he helped the poor fellow who was badly crippled up on account of sore feet. This is something that I am not trubled with. The other Regts drills through the day so we have the best time of it.

Col told us also that the first blue suit we drew from was made a present to us but we should have to pay for the State clothes out of the money allowed us per year for clothing. I have drawed $36.00 & some cents in clothing from the United states.

We get splendid good bread. Verry nice. We get it as warm as we can eat it for the Bakery is only one mile. It is in Falmouth. My tentmate heard the Colonel say we were going to stay here till fall and there was some orders read last night concerning tools. I expect we will have something to do soon.

June 27, 1862

And fine & verry warm day. No drill today for our Co but some of the Cos drilled. The battalion was formed for dress parade but none of the Regt officers being present but the Colonel, we didnt have any. But he called the officers to him and appeared to be verry much vexed about something and talked in pretty strong terms to officers about their duties and that they had been rather slack of late. He admonished to be punctual and attend to their buisness, saying if the officers didnt take an interest, the privates would'nt in anything. We have to come out in the best of order on musterday which is next Monday the 30th inst when we will have two months more pay due.

The last rains raised the river so that it took away nearly all of the R R Bridge across the river here and they let the pontoon Bridge swing around to one shore to save it. We were down swimming this evening.

I forgot to tell you about how nice Bill [Smith] & I fixed up our tent. Well, we went into the woods and skined 4 large pine trees, getting the bark according to the size of the tent and staked up a piece on each side about a foot wide or more and sitt the tent on top of that and put a piece at the back end about two feet wide so that when the oilcloth was put up it closed up the back end entirely so that when it rained, it would not beat in. And we put a floor in of bark which will keep us dry when it rains and keep the dampness from us. We can sleep good on it. And in this Country, the nights are cool & no musketoes to truble. And we sleep under two blankets and about midnight we can get under the blankets & cover it up the same as I would last winter.

You may think me exaggerating but it is truth but there are some that have only one blanket between them and of course they cannot sleep under two. But I wont tent with a man that wont carry his blanket & if a man cannot carry it, there is a way provided for it to be taken along.

June 28, 1862

And fine day. No drilling, dress parade but we had to clean up tiptop for tomorrows Inspection which is Sunday. And the next day is muster. It is not much truble for me for I rub up my things evry morning and that way they keep in good order. But most of the boys after inspection lets their guns go till the next Sunday. Then they buy 5 cts worth of emery paper and scour up their guns. This paper leaves them rough and they rust again verry easy. But I use an oiled woolen rag, thereby leaves the iron smooth and oily. And it is not much truble to keep it clean.

Cap has got back from Washington, brings the confirmation of the first blue suit being made a present to this regt but we must pay for the State clothes.

June 29, 1862

And a fine day. Nothing done, no inspection as usual on Sunday, but we must get our accourtriments in good order for the muster on the morrow. We had a hard shower this evening & heavy thunder. The wind blew quite hard, only rained about 1 hour. Our tent didnt leak much for it is well pitched. I don't get many letter now a days but I must write one to Sarah soon but cannot send her any money I think, for the boys is without money and they come begging so hard that I cant turn them all off. For you know how it is. They will think it hard and I hadnt a chance to send it until after I got the last five dollar bill broke that I had. Then I couldnt send it but will send it when pay day comes.

Had dress parade as usual but not so many rollcalls through the day as we used to have. One of our boys has deserted it is thought for he has not been here since about 2 oclock on the 26th. The proper authorities is looking after him but I think he will get away. There is great talk about Cap resigning & going home and it wouldnt surprise me much for I have thought he would do so for a long time.

From what I can hear & see, I am in debt to Uncle Sam for clothing something over $7.00 cts which will have to be paid out of our next pay. But I am better off than half of the boys for the majority of them are over that and some are in debt more than the $26.00 cts and will have [not] a cent coming, but will have to pay some the next payday after.

I drew a pair of pants day before yesterday, also new knappsacks. Those we don't have to pay for. And I drew a new oilcloth and Bill did too. Our knappsacks a pretty good ones, better than the old ones but not the best kind.

June 30, 1862

Fine day, verry. Inspected and mustered in today. We were inspected verry close but prove ourselves to be soldiers and got the praise as such. No drill but dress parade at the usual hour 6 P.M. The Brigade quartermaster mustered us in this. This evening Cap told the boys that those that worked in Fredricsburg got their pay which was about $3.60 cts apiece but us fellows that worked on the bridge and was away from the Co didnt get any for [we] had got ours a week since.

Gen Gibbons was around looking at things and went to the Hospital to see the sick and inquired of the sick (three of which were from our Co.) how they got along and how they were waited on and why they hadnt cots to ly on instead of lying on the ground as they was. Well he quized them pretty close and told a pretty hard story but a true one and he seemed verry much dissatisfied. He then sent one of the waiters to have the Doctors come in and one of our boys that was just able to [move] about told us that the General gave him hell (in his way of speaking). Told them they ought to be ashamed to treat them so. He wanted to know why those that were bedfast were not sent to the hospital in Fredricsburg. And the boys complained a good deal about not having good eatables. He told the Docts they must do better and that they had money furnished by government to buy anything that was needed and he wanted them to use it for that purpose. And that there was a great deal contributed by societies and that they was entitled to a share. And could get it if he would. He going there in person and talking to the patients first, he got the true light on the subject. I rather guess he opened the Doct eyes and it is high time too. I suppose from what I have heard from other sources that he gave them to understand that that kind of work wouldnt do. I guess he is the only General or officer higher than our Col that ever was to the hospital.

July 1, 1862

And a fine morning. Cap got a pass for the whole Co to go to town to get their extra pay or pay for extra work. I had to take or did take Bills breakfast to him also to two of the other boys, all of which were on guard. Some of the boys when on guard goes without some of their meals on account of their tentmates not taking it to them. But now if I had a tentmate that would not bring my meals when there was no other way provided, I should not like it much and it wouldnt be right.

Well, we got started about 8 oclock, went across on the pontoon bridge and we could hardly stand up while on it for it bobed about so. The weight of our Co didnt seem to settle it a particle, but on the contrary was as light as a feather. There were men at work blowing up the boats with small hand bellows which they screwed on to a small pipe on the end of the boat or bladder or whatever they are called. There is three of those boats fastened togather and those three are about 16 or 20 feet apart and so on across. The framework begins on the boats lying timbers various ways. I hadnt a chance to examine it enough to give but this slight discription but those boats has to be watched and kept full of air. And they go over them evry morning as this morning.

We went to the R. R. Depot there. The boys signed the roll. Then we broke ranks, Cap setting a place for us all to meet when the whistle at the Foundry blowed which was at noon. We met at the place which was the Wisconsin Headquarters of the bridge Corps. Then it would be an hour yet before the money come and we were to meet when the whistle blowed which tells all parties tis time to go to work which is one oclock. In time Cap drew the money and it being in large bills so it had to be broke and Cap let the Orderly do the rest of it. But ere this, Cap give the boys till the whistle blew again which was 6 P.M. Then the working parties quit work. Well we got togather, come home.

Got here just as the Regt was forming for dress parade (as we thought) but proved to be drill. And we drilled till dark. Cap thought the Col would be mad but he did not appear so. The pass run out at 4 oclock but we didnt get back till half past 6 oclock. When the Cap went to see the Col after drill, Well says the colonel, I guess Co F will do for passes for awhile and rather smiled. Col drill the battalion alone and took it afoot. Had neither Lieut Col [Charles A. Hamilton] or Major [George Bill] or Ajjutant [Charles W. Cook][61] to help him. He done the work of all of them running from place to [place] doing all that was usually done by the other officers.

July 2, 1862

And a rainy day all day but steady, commenced early in the morning and rained till about midnight. Our tent kept us perfectly dry. That is it didnt leak any and at night we fixed up two oilclothes at front of tent which kept the rain off our blankets as the tent is so short that our feet comes outside when we lay straight. There was nothing done today. There is good news today in papers. I bought a Philadelphia Inquirer which stated that Mclelens right wing had fell and let the rebels have a great deal of ground which he had occupied for the last six weeks & while he was doing this he had his left wing pushed forward and planted quite a number of large siege guns in shelling distance of Richmond. He also advanced the center of his army. It is thought he done this to trap the rebels and everything he done towards that was successfull. The rebels thought they were gaining a great victory. Was just what Mclelen wanted them to think. It is supposed he has baged then ere this. He has his left wing on the James River now and he can land provision right in the camp of his troops. It is supposed he is going to take them more by strategy than by fighting. Jackson of the Shenandoah Valley has got his army to Richmond. The rebel prisinors assert and reassert that the streets of the city will run rivers of blood and be filled with dead before they surrender but McC it is has got the position now that he wanted and he can shell them when he gets a good ready. The soldiers wanted to stand, they not knowing what was up.[62]

Goodbye

What I have drawn

1 pair pants
1 hat
1 pair of shoes
1 blous coat
1 oilcloth
1 pair pants

Two pages from William Ray's Volume 6, detailing the August 28, 1862, encounter at Gainesville (Brawner's Farm). *Sherry Murphy*

Volume 6

July 3, 1862 to August 29, 1862

Spun Around
Like a Boy's Top

Wm. R. Ray
Private in Co F,
7th Regt. Wis. Volt.
From the Township of Cassville
 of Grant Co.
Of aforesaid State
July 3rd, 1862
Enlisted August 19th, 1861

July 3, 1862

And I now begin in my new book which is the 4th one since I enlisted. [Ed. Note: Ray lost count; this is his sixth book.] Well today is a pretty day. Nothing but dress parade today. The Colonel [William Robinson] having gone to Washington it is said, so the other officers got Cap [John Callis] to act as Colonel on dress parade which he did in good style. He telling officers to give the boys tomorrow to do as they liked best. And he proposed a sham dress parade to be got up by the boys and they must put the officers in the ranks and choose their officers from amongst the privates.

So shortly after dress parade, each Co elected their officers and they met in the center of the regt and elected the field officers from amongst the privates which were as follows. Maclin of Co. H [Victor McLin] as Colonel, Harris [Charles Harris] Co I as Lieut Colonel, [George I.] Henderson of Co. F as Major and [James O.] Mann of Co H as Adjutant. Our Co. Officers were as follows. John Dolphin as Captain, Wesley Craig as first Lieut, Griffin Hickock [Griffen Heacock] second Lieut, those are the Commissioned officers and the sargeants are Viz, C Bishop [Corydon B. Bishop], first orderly sargeant, J Schloesser [John J. Schlosser] 2nd, L Sixby [Levi Sixby] 3rd, L Stevens [Lewis W. Stevens] 4th, F.S. Kidd [Fletcher S. Kidd] 5th. The Corporals are viz, H Hentner [Henry Hudson] 1st, Wm R. Ray 2nd, J.D. Runnion [John Runion] 3rd, M Dexter [Milo Dexter] 4th, J Clark [James Clark] 5th, H Miles [William Horton Miles] 6th, J Leppla [John Leppa] 7th, G Eustus [George Eustice] 8th and last Corporal.[63] There was two Sergeons appointed from Co. G and that finished the officers. No, there is the Drum Major, he is to be appointed also which the Col will do. Well evrything is excitement tonight. I think we will make quite a demonstration on the morrow. All the officers is to give and did give up their Commands to the new elected ones. All the military that has to be done tomorrow is to mount the regular guard then the Regt does as it pleases. Oh, what a fine time we will have if things goes on right.

July 4, 1862

Fine morning. The sun rose pretty on the 86th birthday of this great and once happy Republic. Oh, awful to think of that a portion of it inhabitants have tried to & have Disgraced it to their utmost. Well about our proceedings of today. The first thing this morning was revilee and our orderly Sgt had us in line in proper time and called roll which he had fixed the evening previous. There was, as a matter of course, considerable laughter in the ranks but behaved well and obeyed orders which Our orderly said we must obey. And he couldnt refrain from laughing himself at the novelty of the thing. We broke ranks, got breakfast. The Drums beat the calls for us. I was much surprised to hear Corporal Rays name called not knowing that they had put me in. Hurrah, there comes orders, whats it for. For guard. 1 Corporal, 2 privates by order of Col Macklin [Victor McLin], J.C. Mann Ajutant answered the Orderly to the numerous inquiries. Guard to be mounted at 10 A.M. Corporal Miles was detailed with one of the regular Sargeants & regular Corporal, the two latter taking the privates, also all the officers in the Regt. And I tell you they had to work, it then being about 8 oclock and the Regular guard come off.

But as soon as we had got breakfast, the old cooks called on our Orderly to have somebody carry the breakfast to those that were on duty (as that is the way it is done). Orderly called at the top of his voice, J. B. Callis [Captain John Callis] and informed

William Ray's journal, recording events on July 4, 1862. *Sherry Murphy*

[him] that he had to carry the guards breakfast to him. This rather plagued him but go he must. Then there was water carriers & cooks to be detailed from the officers. For Cooks, the orderly detailed two Corporals and gave them their orders. They went to work willingly. Then the water carriers not being detailed, the cooks as usual began to hollow. When the orderly stopped their noise by detailing the orderly and first Corporal for to carry wood & water. They going to work as if they had been used to it. Then Callis comes back saying that the guards hadnt bread enough and he said he didnt want to go over there again (as the boys usually [say] when he sends them back to do anything). So our orderly told the old orderly he must go and he remonstrated against it. But our orderly said if he didnt go, he would report him to Cap Dolphin. So he concluded to go and started. Evrything going on right.

The sargents are getting the boys to cleaning up and they hunt up the old noncommissioned officers, get them in for policing and watched them the same as they always have done us. There. The Drums beat for our guard mounting. Our Orderly cries at the top of his voice, fall in guard. Which they done. He marched them up to the usual place of guard mounting where the guard was forming and the band playing without either time or tune. New Drum Major doing his best to time the music with staff causing considerable amusement and a great crowd gathers running from evry regt in the Brigade to see the fun. And the Drum Major trying his best to stop the music which he denounced in loud terms saying that there was no time to it. At last he gets them stopped and the crowds being so great, our Ajjutant had to station a guard around so that he could proceed to mount guard.

I forgot to tell you how the guards came out. Well they came out with their old dirty rubbish on the worst way and most comical. Our corporal had an old haversack for hat, got an old knappsack which had been thrown away, put it on with the canteen tied to the knappsack behind dangling about his legs and instead of a gun he had a verry large crooked stick, with paper stripes cut in a fantastic form on his arms. And it being against orders to go on guard without leggins, so they, some of them tied on an old knappsack on one leg and something else on the other and so it went. There being verry few guns or catridge boxes. Oh well, I cant give you a discription of the different uniforms or ununiforms rather for such it was. For it would take a large volume so great was the Diversity. Some with the crookedest sticks for gun that could be found, I think, as if they looked a week for them.

Well as I have stated the ajjutant got the guard placed around to keep the crowd back which was verry great by this time. The Drums begin to rattle with the usual signal of the Drum major. They beginning one at a time in a verry irregular manner. And evry man has his own tune and persists in playing it with the Drum major trying to keep time for all. At last he tires and signals for them to stop but no stop until he gives each one a severe punch in the ribs with his long crooked fantasticle, comical staff which makes them grunt and stoped their tune short off (great laughter all the while in the crowd). But guards and officers are sober, never crack a smile or as much as possible so as to make it go off better.

Well they went through the regular guard mounting form except that they added a great many new features. The Ajjutant finding fault with some of their guns (sticks) for not being clean (not having the bark of and splinters off, two or three of which he got in his hand). Well at last the ceremonies were all through. And the Drum Major could not keep all of his band still at the same time, not long at a time. And the continued & boisterous laughter altogather made it verry difficult for the ajjutant to make them hear his orders. Well at last they got ready to march the guard off. The officer of the guard takes command & commands guard doublequick march. The band beginning verry spirited and as usual evry one his own tune which made a terrible noise. The base drummer and drum major doing as usual try to keep time for the whole. Drum major making his staff fly with great rapidity. And the guard were chased (accidently) by a large Newfoundland dog (owned by Capt. Gordon) [Captain Alexander Gordon, Jr., of Beloit] which some of the boys had been holding behind a tent nearby and let him loose just as the guards come by. This scattered the boys all over and the officer of guard with sword drawn tries to defend the guard and gets run over by three or four of the guard which caused greater confusion still in the ranks of the guard. At last some of them with the officers got to the guardhouse, called roll, a great many missing. Officer of guard send sgts & Corporals of guard to hunt up the others, found some hid, others running yet. Some in the flight had thrown away their guns (sticks), got them all togather again.

Officer of the day comes up to give orders for the day to officer of guard which were as follows. Dismiss the guard and let them go to their quarters but be [ready] to fall in at a minutes notice if there should be any disturbance arise in camp. But before he dismissed them, he was to station guards in front of the field officers quarters which the regular officers had to give up to their successors in office. And our officers went into their quarters with all the honors that could be bestowed on them. The regular officers having to retire to other quarters and leave their arms and best suit of clothes for successors to put on. Which they did and commenced buisness in earnest issuing orders &c and shortly an order come for battalion drill at 3 P.M. and things went on all right.

Had roll call at noon. The officers fixing up and consulting about things &c and warning the [boys] to come out in tiptop order but to return two hours or right after guard mounting to police call. The Orderlys of each Co had orders to bring out the commissioned officers with shovels, axes, picks &c to police and all the field officers being away but the Lieut Col, he was brought out and a shovel given him. But after fussing about for about an hour and as fast as the ajjutant would get one in line another would run away and about half of the officers had got excused by the doctor and he couldnt make them work. And they bothered the ajjuttant so that he dissmissed by order of Colonel Maclin [Victor McLin] who reprimanded them some for their great reluctance. But if there was great need of any policing they would be called on. And here another trubel seized the officers, most of whom did want passes to go to the city. But now they couldnt get them for our officers would not make them out, thereby causing them some discomfiture where the Co officers did not get up to rollcall. Our colonel ordered that they should police the streets the same as they (the officers) had made us do it heretofore and several Cos got their streets swept and dirt carried off by the commissioned alone.

Well, time passed on and 3 P.M. came and with it the dress parade call, as the order for drill at this hour had been countermanded, and we were to have dress parade. The Orderly begins to hollow—fall in for dress parade. Most evry one falling in. Great excitement and noise. The Drum Major lead out his band and put them in right position. This time the music is better. There is both time and tune. The new drum major had on the old majors coat. The adj places the markers for the Color Co to form against. Which came out immediately, the other Co following & forming on in succession & in good style. The band playing national airs. Evry officer carrying out evrything in good order. Now the battalion is formed and awaiting the appearance of the Col. At last he makes his exit from his quarters and the crowd opens for him to take his place. And the crowd is so great and presses inward so hard that the ajjutant takes the guards out of Companies, the Captains taking the old officers. Several Cap were put on guard. They were placed in front of the battalion a good distance off to keep the immense crowd back so as to have room. I guess that verry near all the Brigade present. A great many officers and some mounted officers. The spectators kept quite still and the officers from other Regts helped to keep their boys still. That is to suppress laughter or cheering which would have amazed the proceedings if it had been allowed. They listened eagerly to catch evry word that came from our officers. All went right.

The band starts down playing a good tune. The Drum Major with his extraordinary comical hat sticking out in all shapes and of all colors most. I will leave you to imagine which you can better do than I discribe. And he puts on all the French airs he is capable of & uses his crooked staff in as neat a manner as possible. They played down on common time and back on quick time doing ample justice to both. Then begins goes the performances, has the battalion present arms to the Col. Col returns the Compliment with good grace & gracefully. He then put us through the manual of arms as is usually done on dress parade. Then ajjutant orders first sargeants to front and center which they do. Then he orders them to report which they did. Ordered them to their posts. Then he orders attention to order and proceeds to read the numerous orders which have been handed in, evry one hinting on something pertaining to military orders and moves heretofore made, and clothing and leggins and an order declaring all negros in the Union army white and shall be obeyed and respected accordingly. The orders were numerous and touching upon different things to numerous to mention. And the last was thanking the Commander (Col Robinson) [Colonel William Robinson] for the levity he has allowed us &c and expressing the greatest confidence in him as a man to lead us to the battle and complimenting him verry highly in evry way. Also the other Regimental officers.

Then the parade was dissmissed & officers assembled round the Col to receive instructions & orders. I don't know what they were but something pertaining to duties. He dissmissed and the orderlies of each Co bringing their respective Cos in as was usually done. Then the old Lieut Col informed the Capts of Companies that they were to take their Co down to the race ground which had been prepared for the Brigade and all kind of races to be run or anybody with anything. Free for all. We were marched down, it being half a mile and we formed on to the right of our regt around the track. Evry regt taking the place assigned them by the boss. The track was a round one. The mules without number was run, then the horses, then foot races were run. I guess evry officer in the division was there and the whole of Gibbons Brigade and a few privates from other Brigades but it was made for this Brigade only. But it being the only one in the division, so the officers collected. They made up a large purses for the fastest runners among men or horses or mules. A mule from our Regt got the first prize $10.00 cts and a man in the Sixth Regt that lived in the town of Cassville by the name of Ishmiel [John C. Ismael] got the first prize $10.00 cts for fastest runner but he was beat bad by Cap Richison [Captain Hollon Richardson][64] of Co A of 7th Regt. But he didnt run for the money, for officers were not allowed to run against the privates for money. But Cap just run for the fun of it and to see, he said, if he had lost speed any since coming to the army. He didnt want the money I think, but he would'nt have got it anyhow if he had. Well running continued till night. All kinds of races. As fast as one was off the track, another was on. Great excitement.[65]

About sundown we come home. Cap Dolphin dissmissed us. But it was sport I tell you, to see the great gang of mules start off at full speed. And the mules begin to kick off, tumbles riders and by the time they got around, there was quite a number riderless. Well our orderly & other officers officiated till roll call. Orderly called roll. Give up his office as well as the others. So ended the day. And I have left out a great many things that transpired. The [weather] was fine but rather warm. I enjoyed myself well but not so well as if the war had been ended and I were at home to go to some picnic. But however we made quite a demonstration. We done something that we could not do at home. But when we do get home, we will try to raise a Co for the next fourth after.

July 5, 1862

Fine day. Had battalion drill in the evening. Verry short one. None of the field officers be there. Our Cap had command, he being the Senior Co officer in the Regt and the next in seniority among the Captains. Took the next highest office. & soon we made a few awkward moves. Come in, had dress parade. The Col's going to let the Co officers drill the Regt so as they will learn to officiate in case of an emergency which might happen anytime.

July 6, 1862

And Sunday. Fine day. The Sunday morning inspection went through with no chance for our Co to go to church. There was a few of the boys went with other Cos that was going, they taking the letter F off their hats so that the guards wouldnt know but what they belonged to the Co they were then in. We had no dress parade. Most of the boys went to take a swim this evening. There was a funeral in our Regt this evening. He belonged to Co H. Complaint billious fever. It was carried on in military form with that doleful march being played by the band. It was a solumn procession.

July 7, 1862

And fine day, but quite warm. Battalion drill this evening in presence of Gen Gibbons. The 6th was out also. The rumor was that he wanted to observe the movements of both and the best drilled was to take the right of the Brigade but this is only a rumor as yet. But I think there was something contemplated about it or the Gen wouldnt of had it done so. Dress parade, several orders was read, one concerning cooking. It was as follows. That the cooks should rise an hour before revilee and have a cup of coffee ready as soon as roll call was over. And another order warning the officers about providing for their Companies and to see that they have plenty and that they will be held responsible for the execution of this order. This by order of Secretary of War. E. M. Staunton [Edwin M. Stanton]. This being done for the health of the troops. It is calculated to keep off fevers. There is to be no more squad cooking. There has to be two cooks detailed from their respective Cos and they are to do nothing else and are to be saving and attend to their buisness in good style. This causes a great deal of murmering in our Co. I don't know how it is in other Cos for a great many boys wants to make their own coffee and some wants to do one thing and some another and Cap cant please them all and that trubles him, I believe.

July 8, 1862

Fine day and no drill but dress parade. I went on Brigade guard in the evening at the usual time of guard mounting 5 P.M. Each Regt mounts their guards and sends them to Brigade guard mounting. They being closely inspected at the Regts and inspected at Brigade mounting also, going through a great many different and I think, foolish moves. At last we were through with it. Our Regts boys coming on the third relief. I do not know whether they had dress parade or not in our Regt.

July 9, 1862

Fine day. Verry warm. Last night was a hard night on me, it being verry warm and I not feeling verry well. Had taken some Physic (a dose of Ayres pills) the night before & they still worked on me. And have done so today which makes me feel quite weak but I worried it through till we was relieved by the new guard which was 6 P.M. I felt verry tired this evening. And was verry warm and close but most always for four or five hours in the middle of the day there is a nice breeze and so it was today. When I reached my quarters there was a letter from Henry waiting for me to read it which I done right after supper. Yesterday and today we only got half rations of bread. They say the Bakeries cannot bake it fast enough and besides we have poor living. I now would think what we got last winter would be good living if we could get [it].

July 10, 1862

Fine day. Nothing done today. Had dress parade. Orders read to be ready to march at one hours notice from now on and provided with 10 days rations. One in our haversacks, two days in each Regts teams and seaven in the Brigade teams. There is no news of any importance from Mclelen [McClellan's] army of late.

July 11, 1862

Rains a little this morning. Still in camp all day. Had drill in the evening at the usual hour. The Co officers acting as field officers. Gen Gibbons riding around looking on. We expect to move tomorrow morning.

July 12, 1862

Fine morning, not gone yet and I don't see as we are likely to go. I didnt rest well last night, the cause of it is I slept in a hammack and it was so soft and easy that I couldnt after sleeping on the ground so long. Making hammocks first started in Co C, 6th Regt [Prairie du Chien Volunteers] and they all got hammocks. The Brigade doctor seeing this issued an order for the whole Regt to have them as they would be much healthier. Then three or four of our boys made them and I laid down in one to try them and got up with the conclusion to make one. So I went at it yesterday morning to make it and did make it, taking my half of tent to make it. And find it much more comfortable living without a tent and with a hammock.[66]

July 13, 1862

And fine day. Nothing but dress parade. Went through the usual routine of daily duties.

July 14, 1862

Fine day, nothing but dress parade. The Govenors proclamation was read calling for 5 new Regts from the state of Wisconsin offering 2 dollars bounty to any man bringing in a volunteer to any one of those 5 new Regts & 3 dollars for those that joined the Regts that were in the field and one months pay in advance & also 25.00

General John Gibbon, Commander of the Western Brigade. *Generals in Blue*

cts of the 100.00 bounty. And one order was read to the effect that the several Regts in this Brigade was to have roll call at sunrise & form line on their respective parades by sunrise to be reviewed by the Gen & staff. Do so evry morning until further orders. This by order of Brig Gen Gibbons after which the Col made a little speech by way of encouragement but never said a word about marching. His speech was verry patriotic and calculated to inspire us with vigor and saying that there was a great chance for promotions from the army now in the field to take command in the new Regts. The Govenor promising this in his proclamation. I am sorry to hear that Recruiting goes on verry slow for the 20[th Wisconsin] Regt and hope that the people will arouse from their slumbers as it were and answer to the call of the President. The great truble is that the wounded & sick soldiers there in the hospital give the bad side to their friends thereby detering those that would come. I must say, though with great reluctance, that I fear they shall have to draft some but I hope not. I hope for the best and let time tell our fate.

I feel more like fighting than ever but as yet have not had a chance to show our boasted bravery but hope the [day] will soon come when we will have the orders to join Mclelen [McClellan]. To be sure we have hard fare but that is nothing compared to what we would have to do if conquered. My knappsack, I imagine, would'nt feel so heavy if we were marching to join Mclellen but probably it is for the best that we are lying here so long. I must write letters to all relatives and write verry patriotic, urging some of them to join if possible while they can be called Volunteers. Just think what a disgrace to be drafted to fight for all that is near & dear to us, life, liberty and the pursuit of happiness.

July 15, 1862

And fine day. Formed line according to the order of last evening. Gen [John Gibbon] came around on his prancing steed. Then we went to our quarters, got breakfast which was later than for several mornings in consequence of having that review. I think there is some clashing in the orders about coffee and the morning reviews because we cannot get coffee as soon as roll call is over on account of having to be reviewed so early. Had dress parade.

July 16, 1862

And fine day till about 5 P.M. when it clouded up and rained some which stoped our Brigade drill which we were to have at 6 P.M. it being put of till 7 in the morning. We had no dress parade. Had the morning review this morning. Breakfast come off as late as it used to. I comenced a letter to Henry this morning in answer to one I received last week.

Nothing occurred to break the monotony of our Camp life. We expect to march at any time. Our Regt got 4 new teams today which makes 13 in all in our regt. I don't know what they are going to do with so many unless they are to haul our knappsacks and I cant believe it for we have been deceived so often about our knappsacks being hauled.

July 17, 1862

And fine day. Nothing transpired. Had Brigade drill in the morning at 7 oclock. Had the morning review. Had dress parade in evening at usual time.

July 18, 1862

Fine day till evening when it rained as it done last night. Had no review this morning. Drill at 7 A.M. Dress parade in evening. Rained again this evening, just a nice shower. Today there was a team loaded up with knappsacks just for experiment to see how many could be got into one wagon. They got the knappsacks of three Cos in one wagon and went to Falmouth and locked the hind wheels of the wagon to come up some steep hills. The team proveing themselves able to draw that many with ease but when it comes to marching the knappsacks will be heavier. But one team can carry three Co's knappsacks anyhow. So we are to get our knappsacks hauled without a doubt.

July 20, 1862

Sunday, fine day. The Sunday morning inspection didnt come off. Cap got us off it some way. I got a letter today from Mother, she was not verry well. The feeling towards Cap [Callis] is bitter now, verry. He has sent one man, a good fellow, to Fredricsburg jail and he nor the Co not knowing what it was for. He stands verry low with the Co.

July 21, 1862

And fine day. Reville line as it is called in the morning. Brigade drill at 7 A.M. lasting till 10. Had battallion drill at 5 P.M. lasting one hour.

July 22, 1862

And fine morning, rained in the evening. The same maneuvers went through with as yesterday. The two Commissioners appointed by the Govenor to take allotments from the soldiers came today and the Major partially explained the nature of the law to the battalion saying it would be explained tomorrow. And I will wait till the morrow before writing it down.

July 23, 1862

And cloudy in morning but rained a little in the evening. Went the usual maneuvers today except having no battallion drill. In the evening, the battallion was formed into a hollow square and the nature of the allottment law explained by the Commissioner in person. He doing it verry plaine. It was simply this. That those that wanted to send money home, so much evry payday, could do it without expense and do it safely & expedistionaly. And there being rolls that you must sign your name, the amount per month or evry payday and the name & place of residence of the one you want to send it to and the paymaster will have one of those rolls and when a man steps up to get his pay, the paymaster looks at this roll, see how much the man has alloted to his wife, father or mother or whoever it may be and he deducts it and keeps it and sends it to the state treasurer. And he sends it to the person chosen in the town of the money owners or those to whom it is directed on the roll. And the man chosen to receive this money will distribute as directed.

I wrote a letter to Mother today in answer to one I received last week. I washed a pair of pants today for the first [time] in my life. I am getting so that I wash about as good as a woman. I have washed shirts &c often since I have been in the service. We have to come out in tiptop order now and I will willingly do it if they will carry my knappsack. I will keep a button & blacking brush, one of each and a box of tripoli & box of blacking. This tripoli is for cleaning our brasses, used with the button brush. And then there is emery paper & crocus cloth & oil &c for cleaning the guns. There is an extra pair of pants, one pair of leggins, extra coat and things to numerous to mention. But if they haul my knappsack, I will do my best.

Well, John Dolphin, my tentmate went blackberrying today and got a pail full of them. Oh, if we had plenty of sugar we could live good. Some of the boys gets apples and new potatoes.

July 24, 1862

Had the usual drills & revilee line formed in morning. There is to be a reconnoitering party sent out from this division. The second Wis Regt & Battery B [of the Fourth U.S. Artillery] & the 3 N York Regt out of Augurs Brigade [General Christopher C. Augur] started this evening, went across the River. Went, I understand, towards Gordonsville. The 6th [Wisconsin] Regt is to follow in the morning. Is what is called a reconnoisance in force.

Some of the Co in the Regt is allotting pretty largely, but our Co is doing verry little if any. They preferring to draw the money and I prefer to draw it myself. But if I had been going to allott any I should not have alloted any more than what I shall send when I draw it myself.

July 25, 1862

Fine morning. No reville line this morning. Battallion drill seaven oclock. The sixth Regt started at an early hour this morning. They went in light marching order as did the Regts of yesterday with two days rations in their haversacks as did the other Regts of yesterday. I went on guard to night. The two Regts here has to furnish the same numbers of guards as the whole [Brigade] used to until they return. It is now late & no news from the Regts. Last night about ten oclock we had a hard thunderstorm. I think I never seen a harder one. I attended a Society that is starting in the Brigade. The name is the Moral, Intellectual, Union Society. They are just organizing. I will see how it prospers. I think I shall join them. It is moral in evry way and if we stay in Camp much longer, it may be a good thing. None of the Commissioned officers attended except the Doctors of the 19th Inda [Indiana] last night.

July 26, 1862

Fine morning. I attended to my regular guard duty. When it came time to mount guard, it rained so hard they didnt do it but just sent the relief around and relieved us and we came home without going through the regular forms as usual in fine weather. It cleared off and was a pretty evening late in the evening. News came that the 2nd Regt had had a skirmish. But that the whole troop had not met with the enemy in any numbers. We are expecting to get our pay from one day to another.

July 27, 1862

And fine day. Formed revilee line this morning. This being Sunday we had no drill, had the Sunday morning Inspection. Come out in splendid order. Cap complimented us verry highly for our cleanliness, said we need never fear but that we would ever pass any inspection as long as we kept ourselves in as good order as this morning. Had dress parade at usual time 6 P.M.

John and I moved our hammocks to a better cooler place, there being a small ridge just wide enough for a tent or two hammocks. This ridge is formed by an old road running each side and they have washed out to the depth of 4 to 6 feet. Which causes a good drain thereby making it a dry place even when it rains. And it being a few rods from the Co. We have a good breez when there is any going. This ridge is nearly all occupied by those that have hammocks and the boys call it hammock Ridge. We are fixed up neat having our oilclothes stretched so as to form a tent over us down as far as our hammocks come. So we are better situated than if we were in tents for it cannot rain through and we are off the ground free from all vermin and the damp of the ground.

July 28, 1862

And fine day. No revilee line this morning. The Brigade has to change Camp. Well the quartermaster had some teams bring evrything that the boys wanted them to such as boards, tables and stools &c before we moved. Then the teams came back and got dinner, then hauled our knappsacks over here, which is about 1 ½ miles from the old Camp. We got here about three oclock, went to work, fixed up as well as we could. John and I fixed our hammocks up for the night. Then to fix up right on the morrow. It was clever in the Quartermaster to haul our boards &c over. John and I have two seats and a table which makes us verry comfortably situated for eating, writing &c.

July 29, 1862

And a fine day. Nothing done whatever in the way of Military duty except mounting a small Commisary guard. There is to be no Camp guard and we are to have roll call evry two hours. And those absent without leave are to be reported and dealt with accordingly. The whole Brigade put in the whole day making brush shades over their tents by sitting forks in the ground, putting poles on, then brush on that making a good shade over all the tents, the whole day. So large are the shades, John & I went to work & made a sort of cedar tent. At least the sides are made of cedar boughs which are verry plenty. The boughs are interwoven so that they look verry nice. The boys pronounces our quarters verry good & neat appearing & so I think. It has took a great deal of hard work to fix up especially for our Co for we had to carry all our materials whilst all the other Co had teams to haul theirs. Well we got fixed verry nice.

Each regt is camped separate from each other and the ground being laid out so that our and all tents are sett square. Evrything is done up in style all about the [camp]. The privates are next to the parade ground which is allways called the front, let it be which way it may, then the Co officers quarters about 5 rods back of the privates. Then the field officers about as much back of the Co officers & opposite the center of the Regt. The Camp is a large clover field and timber on three sides. The south side being open where the 2nd is camped and a little ways south of the 2nd is the 6th & on the north is the 19th Ind. They are all so covered up that you can scarcely see a tent. There is plenty of wood nearby and tolerable plenty of water.

July 30, 1862

Nothing much transpired. Formed the revilee line and had dress parade in the evening. The order was read that we would be inspected in the morning at 7 oclock. This being the monthly inspection. We done a little fixing up today.

July 31, 1862

Formed revilee line & then went in, got breakfast, cleaned up a little and the Regt formed on the parade and were inspected by the field officers except the Colonel who is sick and has been for some time. About half of our Co went out berrying after inspection. They brought in a lot of nice dead ripe dewberries. Improvements are still being made. I finished a long letter and mailed to Henry yesterday. I received a letter from R Lander & one from Sister Sarah, both of which I must answer soon.[67]

Hello, there is the glad tidings. Fall in to sign the payroll so as to get our pay tomorrow. We done it with a glad heart.

August 1, 1862

And a fine day. Formed revilee line & battalion drill at 7 oclock. Ordered to fix for review at 6 P.M. by Gen King which came off but in verry poor style for the weather being verry hot, the boys didnt care how they went. And in fact the officers couldnt make them do any better for they all worked togather and when they take a notion and hang togather, the officers never could handle us as they pleased. Kings Father was present at the review so it is said and there was a civillian with him I know, but don't know it was him only by hearsay.

Well we didnt get our pay today as we expected yesterday but the 6th & part of the 2nd was paid today. And they commence to pay our Regt tomorrow. John and I bought a peck or rather a haversack full of potatoes of one of our boys who had been out forageing on his own hook for which we paid 50 cts. They are new potatoes and are about the size of a henegg.

Our Regt is digging two wells. They have one nearly finished. This one is on the left wing and has plenty of water. The other one is to be on the right wing. I forgot to mention that we are clear on the left wing of the Regt which is second post of Honor. The cause of this being that our Capt is second in seniority. Capt [William D.] Walker of Co E is senior Capt of the Regt. When we got the Right wing, it didnt belong to us but we kept it for two months or more and now it seems hard to be clear on the left for we had rather be most any other place. It is the hardest place in Regt.

August 6, 1862

Well it is the 6th and fine day. And you will see that I have not written any of late. The cause of it being I was so unwell for several days back.

Well I must go back to the 2nd inst. Which was a pretty day, nothing done. The usual routine of buisness. And the 3rd inst it being the same. One of the wells is finished which has a good supply of water in it.

4th [of August] fine day, had Brigade drill in the morning. About noon the order came to get ready to march at 4 P.M. in light marching order except adding the oil blanket. And they were to take two days rations in their haversacks. The whole brigade went this time and I don't know how much more. 2 P.M. came and they came to postpone the start till 2 next morning when the whole Brigade was to move off towards Fredricsburg. It is not known to the line officers or privates where they are going but supposed to see the whereabouts of the enemy. It is calculated they will be gone 5 days and the cook of their respective Cos are to cook up rations & the teams follow them on Wednesday with the calculation to overtake the troop by Thursday morning when the rations will be due them. Evening and the boys are jubelant with the thought of going into new country. They are talking about the poultry & eggs that they will confiscate. They are taking salt peper &c in their haversacks to season them with. They will not be debarred from taking any little thing they want. And I guess they will put that order in force, that the troops are to live off the fat of the land.

5th of August. And fine morning. Had revilee at 1 oclock this morning, roll call &c. The orderly warning the boys to fill their canteens &c. Got breakfast, formed line at 2 oclock & started. There was considerable excitement. All those that were not hearty were left behind which included me & I couldnt have marched anyhow for which I am sorry for the boys will have a fine time. Our Col [Robinson] being sickly, the Command devolves of Lieut Col [Charles Hamilton] which the boys dislike on account of his inability to command them properly. But the Col is going in his carriage and if they should happen to get into an engagement with the enemy, he will get on his horse and take command if able to ride horseback which he says he means to try if it comes to fight. 10 A.M. A good many have come back to camp that have given out and still they come. For they march so fast that all that starts cannot keep up and when they cross the picket line, all those that are behind cannot get through so they must come back for they will not have the signal. And the pickets wont let them through.

All right with the boys the last we heard. Well the campguard has been reduced to 6 in number, there being well ones in Camp now to stand guard. But day before yesterday, the sick ones had to stand. There is a great deal of sickness in the Regt in that way. They will [be] sick for only 2 or 3 days & then able for duty. I missed the fever today as that is what I have had. Bedtime and all right.

6th [of August] And fine day. The teams started this morning at 4 oclock with the boys rations. Rather bad report in Camp. That is that Cap and 7 privates in the Regt was killed yesterday which gives the boys a chance to talk. But I don't & the boys dont credit the report much. The boys are sorry of Cap being killed if it is so but we wont allow ourselves to believe it. 6 P.M. sick call but the doctor is sick and the other two is gone with the Regt. Night and Lieut Lefflo [Christopher C. Lefler] of Co I who was not able to go with the Regt, has been up to Gen Kings to see him & hear how things was. He says all was right & they hadnt even had a skirmish unless lately which settled it in our minds that Cap was still alive. And this stoped the sorrowing but about noon today there was a report that they had a skirmish. We don't believe it. I wrote a letter to Sarah to day in answer to the two last me got.

August 7, 1862 [The Frederick's Hall Raid]

Fine day. All goes on right in Camp. The Doct that was left here is sick and a strange doct came and attended to the sick and went off again. I did not go up for I felt well except the sores on me and I went up in the evening to get some salve to cure them. A great many rumors at times through the day about the troops. And some of which proved true. Just at when one of our boys came in, he brings the news of a great many of the Brigade being taken prisinor. He came verry near it himself. As near as I can find out by this fellow whose name is Kuntze [Louis Kuntz],[68] he is well thought of in the Co and thought to be reliable. He says that on Tuesday there was a great many give out and came back to Camp which I know to be true. And they still kept doing so on Wednesday. But Tuesday evening he gave out and stoped at a house where there were many others stoped. He got his supper, paid for it. The woman of the house appeared to be a fine woman and treated him kindly. Here also, he fell in with a 19th boy and they stayed all night and got breakfast and they thought it a safe place and feeling as they couldnt walk so they would stay. So they stayed till about ten oclock, got something more to eat and just as they were eating they saw a cloud of dust rising down the road and didnt suspicion anything. But just as they were going to pay the woman, there rode up a squad of Cavelry and surrounded a wagon load of worn out boys from 2nd Regt that was just passing the house. They fired into the wagons and he seeing they were secesh, he run. When they hollowed halt, the 19th boy halted and obeyed their orders, laid down his arms and was taken prisinor. He, Kuntz, run for dear life. They fired at him. He heard the balls whistling & striking all around him but he kept on and escaped. But he says all those along the road was taken prisinor & that not being a few. They took all of our provision train but three wagons before coming up to this house. They just cleaned up evrything that was behind the main body of troops.

6 P.M. and the report is that our troops have taken our wagons back and 2 cannon. That our troops had drove the enemy back and &c. That our Capt was not killed and all good news, also that they are coming in this evening or early in the morning. Our doctor being sick so the [sick] or lame is not verry well attended to. I cannot get salve or liniment to put on my sores which is for the poison [ivy or oak].

Well about Kuntz. He ran and got into the woods and they came after him and just as he was going out of the edge of a woods, he seen some more after him so he gave them the slip again by crossing a hollow and getting into another grove. And then he saw no more of them. He stayed in the woods till sundown when he started for the picket lines and towards home. He reached the pickets after traveling about 3 ½ miles. They gave him the best they had. He stayed all night and in the morning he went back to the woods aforesaid after his catridge box, haversack and canteen which he threw away in his flight the evening before. He found them so he turned his steps homeward which he reached after dark with evrything he took away except his oilcloth which he threw away at first of his flight. He had a pass from the doctor which passed him through the picket line and the guards thereafter. If he had not had change along so he bought things to eat, he must have suffered for bread and that only for there was plenty of meat in the Country, also poultry & eggs &c but scarcity of bread.[69]

August 8, 1862

And fine day & no sick call this morning as the Regt didnt come back last night and havent come as yet this morning. Now 8 A.M. Sent mail out & got mail the same as when the Regt was here. 10 A.M. A couple of the boys have come in bringing the news of the Regt coming in soon. Here some two or three more boys come. There some more. Well, they coming in seperately, evry man for himself. Here Cap comes with two or three and they kept coming in for an hour. As soon as the regt got across the river, 2 ½ miles distant, the boys kept breaking ranks and coming ahead and stopping &c so there was no Regt at all to come into Camp.

I went and brought some cold water and kept at it until they all had plenty. They complain of being tired & sore all over, some lame and some one thing and some another complaint. They have had plenty to eat but hard marching and not much rest and verry little sleep. Most all of them laying immediately & sleeping from two to 6 hours. All stiff when they awoke. It being warm dry weather all the time and the dust intolerable and scarcity of water and the excitement at times & doublequicking some, and alltogather it was a wonder that some of our Co didnt die. But the orderly had roll call and all was accounted for.

I understand that the troops done all that was wanted. The Generals are satisfied for they say the object for which they were sent out for was accomplished and it was done without the 7th [Wisconsin] having a shot at the rebels except the few stragglers that were behind the troops, also behind the wagon train. The Secesh Cavelry to the number of about thirty attacked the wagon train but there being a Co of N.Y boys to guard them, besides a guard to each wagon which their respective regts sent. The N.Y. boys fought them while the whole train put on at the greatest speed for three miles when they came up with the troops so the rebels were defeated there. But they may have taken some of the stragglers prisinor. But this is not proven yet as I know of. But they did take two wagons from us that was loading corn at a crib. They took the teamsters also. This is all that our boys know of them taking from us in the way of property but they seem to think that there was as many as 60 or 70 of this Brigade taken prisinor.

As near as I can find out, the following troops were out Gibbons Brigade, Augurs Brigade, Hatches [Hatch's] Brigade & two Regts from Doubledays Brigade and two Batteries from the Division. This Hatches Brigade, I understand, came from Warrenton lately. They not belonging to this Divison. The Boys says they were going along and all at once they heard cannon in the rear. . . So they run back & the rebels retreated, then they come homeward reaching home next day which was Friday.

August 9, 1862

Had inspection today and at noon got orders to get ready to march at an hours notice. Then verry soon order came to march at 6 P.M. Then that was countermanded and we were to cook two days rations, have revilee at 2 oclock & march at 3 oclock. So we fixed up our knappsacks for they were hauled. Have to carry oilcloth.[70]

August 10, 1862

And started according to order. Some truble now to get all the knappsacks in one team for two Companies. We got along slow till about 6 oclock when we went good gait. Come back some 8 miles on the Catlets Road, then turned to the left, leaving a nice large brick church on our right. The weather verry warm and scarcity of water. As we traveled on a ridge, we stoped evry little way to rest. The ambulances are full of sick or given out men for all they sent quite a number around by railroad. We stoped twice, made coffee. Some say we go to Culpepper Courthouse, some say to Gordonsville. At last we got to the Rappahannock, the bridge being gone we had to ford it and it is now 8 P.M. Cold breeze. Had a shower. We were ordered to pull off pants, shoes and socks for the [water] was waist deep. Which we done, passed through a little town at the ford on the east side of the River. So we plunged in, went across but just on the top of the hill on east side there was a Regt stationed as guards to the several fords in vicinity. Also doing some picket duty. Well we put on our clothes, marched ¼ of a mile, camped on the ground with nothing but an oilcloth. The rest of the Division camped thereabouts. It now being 10 P.M. we stacked arms, spread oil cloths, went to bed. Have to get up at two in morning, start at 3.

Today the boys took evrything they wanted if they could find it such as horses, mules, chickens, ducks & geese & honey which there was a plenty. It is calculated we came 20 miles today. All stragglers from our Co come up.

August 11, 1862

And started according to order. Come along pretty brisk till the sun got up a ways. Then we had to rest evry little while. We didnt stop to make coffee until about noon, when we came up to a little place called Stevensville. There we lay till 5 P.M., made coffee twice. The boys took about a dozen beehives which were well filled. I didnt get any as I was off a little way under a shade tree for I was about ready to give up the ghost, I being unwell and the heat intolerable, it about capsized my equilibriams.

Well, I forgot to tell you that we heard yesterday that there had been a battle the 9th & 10th and that our folks was whipped and all kinds of rumors and kept hearing them but still doubted them till we came to this little town. And we have made a forced march and come to Culpeper too and seeing the battle ground off to the south west on verry high ground or on the side of the mountain for we have got to the hills and small mountains adjoining the Blue Ridge which we can see in the distance. The battle ground being 12 miles distant and some could see the flag of truce which they were burying the dead under. There is a great many rumors and all tend towards us being whiped.[71]

The boys got all they could get. Our Regt got most of the honey on account of us being near the house. The other Regts was quite a ways off. He was an old rich fellow they took the most from and all the Generals stoped there even to Gen King & they couldnt help but see the boys. But they don't care as long as the boys don't take what they cannot use or destroy. Well here it was proved to us that we had a battle and got the worst of it. And they were burying the dead. And there was to be no firing on either side till 6 A.M. on 12 inst when a few shots would be fired by us and to let them know whether we wanted to fight for the field or not as they held it yet.

Well now we knew what the forced march was for and didnt regret it any although they complaints were loud about soreness and sleepiness. The boys thought that they would like to see the fight go on in the morning. Well we started at 5 P.M. and marched westward resting evry little ways for the air was verry close. Well we marched on & on, good many giving out. And the wines and brandies furnished by Government to give the soldiers that give out on marches, the officers drink it up and now the doctors are so drunk they can hardly sit on their horses and they don't notice the poor fellows that are lying by the roadside panting and feel as though they don't care whether they live or die for such is their feelings. It acts odd on a man I must say for I once got behind a little one night but they Camped right off so I got along into camp and did and always have kept up. Our Second Lieut [John McKenzie] was tight, he could walk and that was all and was perfectly foolish which I hated to see.

Well we come on & on and a scarcity of water. At last long about 10 oclock we come to some camps which we had been told was only a mile ahead ever so many times by the officers and more expically by the Doct who told the stragglers so, so as to make them get along &c. Well at least we came to a dead halt for the road was blocked up and we stoped for near an hour. Oh great was the throngs. I never seen the like. Well we got started, come to the third Wis Regt who were camped by the roadside. They were verry glad to see us and we to see them. They said we were the only Wisconsin boys they had seen in the service. A great many found friends. They had been in the battle and had been out burying their dead that day. They had 180 killed and a great many wounded. They say as many wounded as killed. They have lost half of the Regt in one way and another the two days of the battle.[72]

Well at last we camped having come 10 miles, it being now about midnight. We camped as the night before. There is a great deal of talk about the battle &c and all expect to have to go to battle in the morning. We were soon asleep.

August 12, 1862

And fine morning. Evryody got up when he pleased. We had roll call after while and all of our Co was there all right. Got breakfast which consisted of coffee & crackers but we soon got some stinking ham which we ate with good relish. We had nothing but crackers & coffee on the march and what the boys foraged. I did not get any of that for I never felt like taking any extra steps. Well we soon got some fresh beef and we lazed around camp all day. And a good deal of complaint about sore feet &c. 6 A.M. come but the rebels have and are retreating. We had inspection of arms by the Captain just to see if they were all clear so as we should not get fooled in time of need. There is a scarcity of water. Ten came and no fighting. Our troops fired a few shot from a battery near the lines to see if the rebels wanted fight but we received no answer so we gave up the thoughts of getting to see the rebels. Not a drum was tapped today or any other music on account of the rebels might hear them thereby telling how many Regts there is here. No guard except wagon guard.

A great many visitors from the 3rd [Wisconsin] Regt to see their friends. They tell hard stories but true ones though. They have seen several fights but none so hard as the one of the 9th & 10th inst. They were in Banks command with all the fights in the Shenandoah Valley which will always live in history and to such I shall leave it to be recorded.

August 13, 1862

And fine day. Lazed in Camp till 3 P.M. when we had dress parade and moved our camp a few rods as also did the other Regt for we were camped verry close togather. Have plenty crackers, coffee & fresh beef. We have a nice camp now. Jackson still retreating so the rumor goes but we cannot tell. We or this division is to be reviewed by General Pope & staff and other Gens in this part of the army. Gen Pope wants to see the western troops so it is said.

August 14, 1862

And fine morning. Cleaned up. 9 A.M. came and with it came the order to fall in for to go on inspection.

August 15, 1862

And fine day. Got orders to be ready to march at 9 A.M. today but 9 came and the order was countermanded. We laid in camp [all] day. Had dress parade at 6 P.M. and the order was read to be ready to march at 9 A.M. on the morrow. Gen Gibbons being present, he spoke verry highly of the Regt. Also said that Gen Pope said that Our Brigade was the best in the service, the largest & best looking men.

August 16, 1862

And fine day. Got ready to march at 9 A.M. as ordered yesterday but we didnt start from our parade ground till about 11 A.M. as we had to wait for the rest of the Division to pass. When we started onward (as we call it) we came southward coming through the recent battlefield which stretched along each side of the road for 1 ½ miles. Oh how bad it smelled. The stench of dead horses of which there was many was intolerable. Seen a great many graves, mostly of our men. We came to within ½ mile of Slaughters Mountain and there camped in line of battle. That is this Brigade and the other Brigades also but in different shapes. Jackson has retreated to the other side of the Rappidan River. We have plenty of water but scarcity of wood if we should stay long for we use up the fences first.

Camped in a large clover field. Probably will move tomorrow. I ought to write a letter home. We have not had any mail since we left Falmouth. John and I have not put up our hammocks as we are not likely to stay long.

August 17, 1862

And fine day. This being Sunday, we had inspection, laid around camp all day. Done nothing but cook and eat such as new corn, apples and berries &c. No mail yet.

August 18, 1862

And fine day. Nothing done through the day but the general muster and Army of America is mustered today by order of Lincoln. We were mustered at 9 A.M., then in the evening we got orders to march. But the Regt didnt march till 9 A.M. next morning by a mistake in the Orderly.

I was detailed to go as the wagon guard. There about 40 from the Regt to guard our own train. Well guard formed, come to wagons on road. Found them all headed to the rear. Here I heard that we were going to retreat which I seen right off. It now being about 6 P.M. evrything is astir. The road full of wagons & now I kind thought that it would be a fight and if so I wouldnt get to see it. But cant help it. Must obey orders. Well we got started, came verry slow all night. The road was clogged full all the [way] and when there was a chance at the roadside, the trains would be six or seaven deep. Move a rod or two then stop and kept on so. We were just coming through Culpepper at daylight being only 7 miles from where we started, being 12 hours coming 7 miles. And in Culpepper, the town was crowded full of trains. Here we found out that the whole army was falling back. And it is said that Jackson is coming against us with 250,000 men that two to our one.

August 19, 1862

And still going on in the same way as last night. Oh how sleepy and tired. This going so slow is verry tiresome. About 7 A.M. we came to a small creek. There we found Gen McDowell superintending getting the teams through the mud which was verry deep on each side of the creek. He seemed to be in great haste which confirmed the belief in me that it was a retreat.

Well we came on and on all the day without even stopping to water or feed the horses. About 4 P.M. we came to the Rappahannock River. Here the railroad crosses the River. I come across on the Bridge. The trains forded it a little way below. We come on about 2 miles & stopped for the night was the order, expecting to have to go on in the morning. Here the news come that the Regt didnt start till 9 this morning and that they were all following. The whole army is on the backward move. Now we have come 17 miles in 24 hours without stopping to even water. Today our troops took an ajjutant Gen from secesh and brought him by the train. It is supposed there is 40 or 50 miles of train on the move today, if they were all in train shape, one wagon after the other and I don't doubt it.

My god, I hardly thought there were so many in the United States altogather. Lots of wagons broke down on the road. Some are burned, some are fixed up, just according to the men that boss the trains to give you some idea of the vast number of teams. Our Brigade has just about 100 teams and I suppose that is an average or thereabouts.

August 20, 1862

And fine morning, still where we camped. Got breakfast and shortly the Brigade made its appearance so the teams hitched up to accompany their respective Regt to camps. Here they come into the field. 10 A.M. & camped in line of battle, drawed & cooked our rations. 6 P.M. and got orders to march, packed up our knappsacks & loaded them into wagon. Wagon trains started as they did the night before when we retreated to this place. Night and we are not gone yet. The rebels have advanced on our troops and had a fight. Drove our Cavalry in, they making a charge two to our one. There has been some canonading today but with what effect it is not known to me except that some wounded on our side. The rebels seem determined and show out verry bold. I think there will be no general engagement brought on until we have reinforcements. We can hold our chosen position it is thought. The hills on either side of the [river] affording good situations for either party.

August 21, 1862

And fine morning, still in camp or not much of a camp as we have only a blanket apiece. We got breakfast, stayed around camp till near noon when we were ordered to start. & the rebels batteries & ours commenced to play of to the right. The shells of the rebels coming into a field opposite us to the west of us some 80 rods. So the Brigade got under way. We went right through the field with the shells flying over our heads and bursting when they hit the ground some 40 to 60 rods from us. We were under cover of the hilltop along here but presently we turned parallel with the flying shell, they passing to the left of & some right over our heads. But as it happened there was not a man in the Brigade hurt. But they were not shooting at us but at our battery which was planted on the hilltop near the river about a mile distant from us. Don't know how the rebel batteries were on the other side of River. We come some 80 rods parallel then filed to the right round the corner of a wood which we went along sufficient to admit the whole Brigade under cover of said wood. So we went in to woods, laid there till sundown. The artillery been at work all the time. But now ours has stopped.

We & the 19th [Indiana] went out. After filing around a point of timber we came in sight of our skirmishers which were firing as usual in skirmish & the rebel artillery still playing. We coming in full sight they commenced shelling us but all went whistling over heads. Verry soon we turned under cover of woods and they played at a battery that was coming across the field just then. But none of the shells hit them. Then just as we stopped, a shell came over the corner of the woods. Here it come, end over end, whistling & hissing and strikes the ground in about 20 feet of our Co & went on angling up the line, bouncing 3 times & landed in the ranks center of the Regt or where the ranks was for they scattered out of ranks, fearing it would burst. No one was hurt. This caused great merriment throughout the Brigade. But the shell didnt burst so we moved of up to the right farther out of shelling distance and there stacked arms, laid down at the foot of our guns which were stacked. The 6th & 2nd have been out skirmishing but have camped near us. So ended the day.

August 22, 1862

And a little showery and we are back to the same place as yesterday. This morning just afore daybreak we were ordered up and marched back here. So soon as it was light our batteries opened on them. They answered verry shortly. Here the shell came right towards us but mostly all fell short as they were not firing at us but at our battery on the hill right in front of us. Here we were allowed to build small fires to make coffee. There was some whistled over our heads. One came over & lit in the woods in the rear near a fire where the boys were at work. It hurt nobody. We stoped in the fields today. We changed position several times through the day. Just as the rebels did their batteries so as to keep from under their shells as much as possible. After two or three hours they gradually ceased firing & it then begun to be pretty lively times. Up to the right there they canonaded all the rest of the day and late in the evening there was a brisk musketry fire but with what success we know not. We hear nothing about whether we are successful or not. And there are verry few rumors. We know less than if we were not in the field as we have neither mail nor papers. We made coffee this evening but had to go back in the woods quite a way. We are verry scanty rations and are likely to be.

Well 5 P.M., rained a little. We camp here to night. Had three small crackers for todays rations. A little showery all night. As soon as dark the canonading ceased. There has been several persons hurt in the Brigade but not seriously. C Manning [Charles Manning], Co C, 2nd Regt,[73] an acquaintance of mine come from same town and the Major of the Indiana [regiment] lost his horse by a shell striking it, killing it instantly. So today passed.

August 23, 1862

And as soon as daylight our batterys, expicially the one in front of us commenced a vigerous fire. They firing a number of times before the enemy replied when they opened vigerously also. Their shells flying about us rather livelier than usual. We drew two days rations this morning. Some verry fat pork which pleased most of the boys as we had not had any salt meat for a week or so. And I made a frying pan of my plate by putting a split stick on for a handle and was frying my meat away back in the wood when the order was fall [back] for the rebels was shelling us rather closely. When I emerged from the woods, there was two wounded, Lieut Oakly [F.W. Oakley] of Co K & a private of same Co. The privates leg was badly jamed, the Lieut lost one arm, it is thought would kill him. So we move of a little to the right out of range and shortly moved back to the right again. 10 A.M. got orders to march, not known where, but terminated to Warrenton which we reached at dark. Here we heard and that the rebels had been in the town and through up to Catlets Station where our train was and had burned it and taken the guards prisinor. But this proved untrue. But there was 600 secesh cavelry attacked the train but the boys rallied and had quite a fight, drove them off. They burned 4 of Popes [Union General John Pope] headquarter teams and wounded some of the boys. One from our Co it is said. They wounded some secesh, took three prisinors. This all we know about it. There was some sick boys with the train. They rallied and hurled stone at secesh making them feel them. They fought with great desperation.

August 24, 1862

Marched down through the town & camped in field near good water. And orders as usual not to go out of camp on no pretence. Here we laid all day, canonading going on as usual, apperantly without ceasing. There was details were made by the Captain to get water & roasting ears so we had plenty of green corn &c. Nothing unusual transpired today.

August 25, 1862

And had good nights rest. John had the cholic verry bad last night so that broke me of my rest some. We laid in camp all day canonading going on as usual. We feel quite free today as we were permitted to pull off our accoutriments last night, we not having them off for so long it seems good. Ever since we first went under fire we have had to keep them on. Alphonso Kidd belonging to the Engineer Corps was up today. He brought the news of their corps destroying the RR bridge across the Rappahannock under fire of the Rebels. Our batteries was there, also some siege guns which made the rebels keep back a little until they destroyed the bridge. This was done to keep the Rebels from using it. Our forces is in possession of the place but evrything is burned at the station. This is called Rappahannock Station. The secesh displayed the greatest bravery. They shelled the boys pretty hard but not one was hurt. Our siege guns just riddled the ranks of rebels until they layed down in the tall grass. Then when a shell would light amongst them, a few of them would jump up and run for the woods. They kept the rebels busy carrying of dead & wounded.

August 26, 1862

And got to march this morning. We received the orders last night. Well we marched about sunrise coming to the front. We came about 3 ½ miles then canonading begun not but a little ways in front and heavy skirmishing also. We stoped and loaded our pieces. Battery B [Battery B, Fourth U.S. Artillery], our battery come by and the Sharpshooters belonging to our Brigade. They went by in haste as skirmishers and we turned into the woods and come into field. 19th [Indiana] & our Regt formed line battle and marched up almost a precipice and come into woods a little way, stoped.

Just as we did this our battery got position about 100 yards to our right around a point of timber on hilltop, commenced plying pretty quick time. The rebels answering vigerously. Verry soon a shell from them took one mans arm off, crippled another, went on over hill to where the horses was. Hit one in head, kill him, went into another and bursted, killing it and wounded two more. Pretty good for rebels but that was all the damage they done us in all day fighting to my knowledge. The sharpshooters keep up a vigerous fire picking off secesh till 4 P.M. when the Rebels started over to our lines with flag of truce.

Some of our sharpshooters that was distant from their commander kept up a fire on the enemy for a while. It is said that as soon as the flag come out the rebel skirmishers that lay in the grass not far distant from ours all rose up & beat a retreat. Our sharpshooters couldnt stand that. They let them have the contents of their guns. The rebels wanted a little while to pick up their dead & wounded but I guess all they wanted was to relieve their line of skirmishers from their perilous position as our sharpers would fell evry one that showed above the [grass] until the truce. They laying down and our boys got close as they wanted to.

Well hostilities have ceased for today except picket firing so it is said. Sundown we move up towards our canon and get out of the stench of a dead horse which we have had all day which is intolerable now. There boom goes the canon again over to our right about half mile. We can see it now as we have formed line in edge of the woods. Not allowed to make fire but just at dark one third of Co was detailed to go a mile into hollow to make coffee for the whole Co so we got plenty, went to bed.

The greatest silence prevails and must for there is only a line of skirmishers twixt us & rebels.

August 27, 1862

Laid same place till N. [noon] when we with the battery marched back toward Warranton. Supposed we were going back to rest but behold we came on through to within 4 miles of Haymarket. Stop, not allowed to take of accoutriments it now being about 2 oclock at night. We hear that the rebels are at Manassas.

Colonel William Robinson, the commander of the Seventh Wisconsin, was severely wounded at Brawner's Farm. *SHSW*

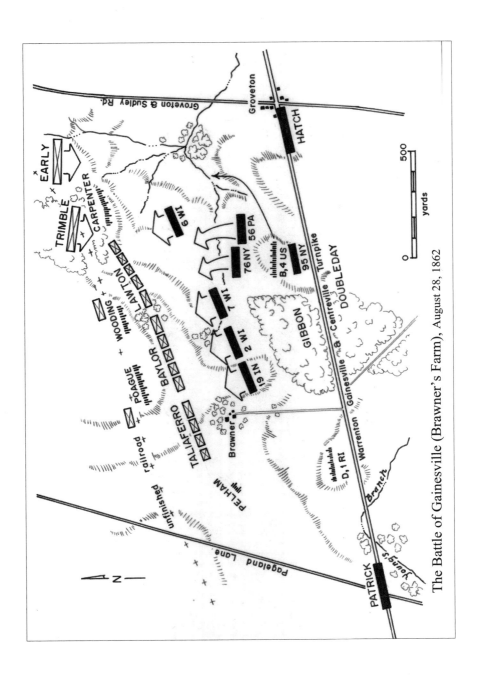

The Battle of Gainesville (Brawner's Farm), August 28, 1862

This view of the Gainesville (Brawner's Farm) battlefield looks north from the Warrenton Turnpike. The Seventh Wisconsin marched over these fields in its advance against Stonewall Jackson's Confederates. *Nolan, The Iron Brigade*

August 28, 1862 [The Battle of Gainesville or Brawner's Farm]

And at daylight we started, came 3 miles to rear of Haymarket, stoped got 4 crackers apiece & some beef. Didnt get to cook it. Marched some two miles or so, hear canonading to. Battery went ahead. We followed soon & the 2nd Regt had gone. We got in line of battle in the edge of the woods, marched up to the top of the hill, little confused. We halted to dress & and the flanks of the Regt being ahead so they had to about face, march back on line but before this there was three wounded in our Co. I saw two go down. Well just as I had faced about, there was a ball struck me in back of head & as it appeared to me, I spun around on my heels like a boys top and fell with my heels in the air and spun around again for a few seconds.

Come too, roll over on to my knees, crawled off to the rear a few rods, got up, walked till come to little gutter in small hollow, laid down to rest but the balls fell around like hail striking verry close so that wouldnt do.

Got up, walked of to woods, met with a fellow from our Co, helped me to the ambulance, found doctor, put me in ambulance. Pretty soon a shell came verry near and bursted disabling for use two of a N.Y. Regts ambulances. So we were driven off a mile farther and Doct commenced dressing wounds. Great many kept coming in, didnt get to mine.

I got tired of waiting, laid, went to sleep and about two oclock at night, Doct woke us up about 20 or more in number, saying that we should have to walk, all that could for or be taken prisinor, as all the ambulances but one had gone ahead filled with those that couldnt walk. So we started stringing along, those that were ablest going ahead, evry fellow for himself and the Doct loaded up and come. We had two or three to lead us. Me with two or three others soon got so far ahead as to loose the [rest]. We got in behind a Regt and went along.

One of our boys got into an ambulance belonging to this Regt. He was shot through the nose & face, ball came into his mouth, spit it out into his hand & didnt save it as I should have done, I think. So we marched on & on, gaining on the column for they would have to stop for I don't know what. But always so on march.

At last daylight come & still marching, come across some of our Co, kept with them till we caught up with an ambulance, 56th Penn and the Doct following it saw me, hollowed, had me come and get in as it was not heavy loaded.[74]

August 29, 1862

Now it is the 29 and we stoped & went on and stopped &c. Went off wrong direction some two miles. Sent after, went back, went by the Regt, got out but Lieut wouldnt let me stop and good he didnt as it proved. Got in, went on, stoped pretty soon at Manassas Junction. Here I had to get out as they had to go after some of their own boys. Well I got out, fixed a shade for a fellow from our Regt who was crazy with his wounds, having arm broke & jaw split, all was done with piece of shell.

I must get another book.

Major George Bill, one of the Seventh Wisconsin's field officers, was shot in the forehead at Brawner's Farm. *SHSW*

This book finished at U.S. Hospital Chester, Penn. Those four last pages written at this hospital. I have neglected noting down since I was wounded for my head has been so confused that I couldnt write.

I will send to the town half mile distant, get another book and sent this one.

Volume 7

August 29, 1862 to January 15, 1863

Wounded Thick
on the Grass

Wm. R. Ray
Co. F, 7th Regt, Wisconsin Vols

In U.S. Hospital, Chester, Del. Co.,
Pennsylvania Sunday September 14th, 1862

September 14, 1862

A fine Sunday morning. In the hospital at Chester, Penn and have neglected noting down what has transpired. Therefore I shall go back to the:

29th of August. Where I left off telling about the man that was crazy. Well when we got out of the ambulances, I fixed as good a shade for him as I could with my oilcloth, it & my canteen being all I had with me. The Doct having the rest I suppose.

Well this fellow being in so much pain that I concluded to go to the Regt and tell some of his Co boys. When I got there, behold our ambulance had come up & Doct also. I told them how this fellow was situated but the Doct didn't take much heed &

told me where to go which was a large tree about a mile farther on where he was getting them together for the ambulances to carry back about three miles to the main or only hospital. Well it was the hospital for Kings Division. It being a verry large spacious brick building and nice yard, also plenty of shade trees. This house was Beaureguard's [Confederate General Beauregard's] headquarters until their retreat from Manassas last spring.

Well there was men wounded in all places lying thick on the grass. The surgeons discharging their duty faithfully. My wound didn't pain me much so I got water &c and waited on all I could. There was 3 or 4 from our Co & a good many from the Regt that I waited upon in every way that I could. Also great many strangers. Well it got to be about 2 P.M. by this time and we lay around waiting on each other till about sundown when they furnished the greater part with a substantial supper, beef, bread & coffee. But those lying off from the house a ways as we was did not get anything to eat. I went to look after something for those that couldn't walk but was all gone so we had nothing but hard crackers & water still.

Well we, I say we, for there was two Boys from our Co that was given out came in. And they & myself fixed up beds for others as well as we could and got them pretty well situated for the night. Our wounds not dressed yet and 9 P.M., all right, most all asleep. The wagons and ambulances have been bringing in wounded all day and still continue to arrive.

I have forgot to mention about the battle that is going on all day verry fierce but with what success I cannot tell. There is as usual a great many rumors. There has been a great many troops went out this morning whilst I was lying under the tree heretofore mentioned. The battle [South Mountain, Maryland] was raging within six to 8 miles from here only. We could hear the canonading distinctly and a great deal of the time could hear the small arms. 10 A.M. and no advantage gained today.[75]

30th [August 1862] And this morning we got up at daylight, fixed around, got water & wet wounds &c as you may imagine. Missed my breakfast as well as some others but we all got coffee as much as we wanted. Quite a number had to eat hard bread. Orders comes that all that can must walk to the hospital back across the Bull Run which being about three miles to the rear. The cripples had been going for an hour.

Now I & G. Parker, J. Marlow, H. Miles [Calvin G. Parker, John Marlow, and William H. Miles][76] started leaving. F. Boyanton & E. Meartney (our orderly) still lying on the ground. They dressed our wounds in great haste yesterday but it was late in the day and couldn't be called dressed wounds but we were satisfied because there were a great many worse off than we except John Marlow who was hit in the face, his wound was well dressed. Well, we traveled on and on; the road was full of cripples. We stoped by a well, got drink, filled my canteen so as to keep my head and wet others wounds who did not have their canteen. But I determined to hold to mine as long as possible. Well at last we reached the hospital which was on top of a hill which was [hard] to climb but it paid well for there was a nice shade yard. The house not verry large. Here they had a quantity of negros cooking, so we soon got plenty of food, laid down in shade to rest. John Marlow, he in this march strayed of some other way. He being a fellow that don't seem to care how or where, he is contented all-ways.

Dinner soon came, a good one too, consisting of soft bread, soup and fresh boiled beef. All was good. I now had got my appetite pretty well sharpened, as I had not ate much for two days afore the battle. Here the wounded kept coming in all day by the hundreds and it might be thousands, for such numbers was there. They came from all parts of the army. This being the main [gathering place], a central point, it appeared as if every team in the army & I guess they was engaged in hauling the wounded, those that couldn't walk only. At last got supper and the officers gave us out some blankets, had to return them in the morning. So we laid with a verry [good] bed, three of us having a double blanket apiece. Everything was going on all right as we supposed.

We could hear the canon & some of the Boys that was out a little ways could [hear] musketry. The battle was terrific but not so bad as today [September 14, South Mountain]. It has been awful charging and recharging.[77]

31st [August 1862] And rained a little early this morning which woke us up that had no cover of boards over us. Well we got breakfast after a long while and we got orders for all that could walk had to do it. They taking our names, Co. & Regt. of evry man. They were called over and we formed into a squad with a noncommissioned officer in charge; they having the pass for their respective squads. So we get started at last, come along slowly but just as we were starting there came a train of ambulances, 150 in number & a great many of the nicest carriages in Washington to carry those that couldn't walk, of which there was plenty to fill them I think.

Well on we trudged. Verry soon those cowardly scamps that come from Washington got panic strick and turned their horses heads the other way started back saying at the top of their voice that the rebel cavelry was coming & there being a drove of along the road and the Boys that were driving them made a great deal of noise so upon the whole the ambulance drivers came verry near getting up a panic but it didn't move us old veterans, we just made fun of the city Boys of which there was 3 or 4 in every ambulance. But however they did not get far from this supposed enemy as the boss of the train came in great haste on horseback with his revolver drawn swearing he would shoot the first man that would not stop. Us cripples hooting them, calling them &c. Ah you city clerks & fops you would play smut. And great was the insinuations that was heaped upon the gentry at the idea of them starting back without their loads. For we were not scared a particle at the rumor of rebel cavalry coming. The boss turned them back and in a couple of hours they overtook us well loaded.

We traveled on & on, at last come to Centerville. There were lots of troops there which had fallen back the night past and early in the morning for the purpose of forming new line of battle, our troops being whipped on yesterday. Our Division (except our Brigade) was cut up badly and when ordered to retreat, it was a perfect panic, the troops running every way. Every man for himself and the Rebs take the hindmost. Here we got off the main road and went around like lost sheep till some officer who was kind enough to show somebody the road and we followed and got on the road all right again which soon brought us on to the turnpike leading [to] Fairfax courthouse. Hitherward all the teams were going here. I soon seen we had to go at least ten miles yet before getting on the cars. As I had been on this road twice before, I felt a little at home.

Well we traveled on and on ambulances passing back and forward going out empty and returning well filled, the trains lumbering along no end to them seemingly. At last we got [to] Fairfax then we had four miles yet to go. Here we turned square southward. As we were much in need of some water which was scarce on the road. Also something to eat, we not having anything since morning and some not anything then to eat. Well we traveled on & on thinking it the longest 4 miles that I ever saw. But the worst [was] there were so many lying by the roadside. Some only resting, some dead, some dying &c. This didn't seem to move me otherwise than to nerve myself to go on when I felt like lying down, caring not whether I lived or died, as my hopes for the Union was lost. Our army was well known to have been defeated which made us feel bad when we knew it was not for want of ambition in the troops. We knew it must be bad generalship.

Well at last we got to the station, there being only a few cars there and those were being fixed up for such as could not walk. The boss telling us that we should have to walk three miles further down to the next station. So after trying to get something to eat, in which we failed, we started down the track & got to the station about dark. Nothing here to eat and I was to tired to look after anything and it being dark so I and somebody made a bed and laid down went to [sleep]. When I awoke the boys had got on to the cars and left us fellows but the cars didn't start for a little while so I found a place on the outside, got on. It now was about 12 oclock and we started and went into Alexandria and we [were] ordered out of the cars and we marched along the street.

Some said we were to go on the boat, go to Washington and a lot of us got down there, seen no way to get aboard. Went to find a hospital somebody said we had to go to. Found it but no, we had to go on board the [boat] for Washington. So we went back to the landing and was showed the boat we had to get on. At last after standing ever so long we started and got on board. We had nothing to eat all this time and get no sign. Some hadn't a bite for three days. Well it is now daylight.

September 1, 1862

Well we laid around till about 12 N. The wounded have been coming aboard all the forenoon. There is another boat loading with wounded. They went to

Washington about 11 A.M. They have been bringing bread and butter & coffee aboard to feed the sick & wounded all day & they swear they will never get through they eat so much.

At last the wheels begin to turn and the boat floats out into the stream or the Majestic Potomac rather. She is headed up and away. We go passing many, many boats & of different kinds which almost covered the River. At last after about an hours ride we stoped at the pier. As we went up past the Navy yard there were hundreds of canon pointing towards us, also different directions, the most of them being field pieces mounted on those stupendous wheels such as is always used. There were many pieces, hundreds ready for the field. What signifies a few cannon being taken from us when we have such an armory as this to manufacture them.

Well at last we got off the boat and there was a guard placed to let no one go out but those wounded, with the idea of taking them in an ambulance. But they found that wouldn't do for there was too many so they let them go out enmasse, the Doct that come to receive us leading the way to the hospital. But here I got with Frank and he not being able to walk so I stayed with him and soon an ambulance came and took us to the Judiciary Hospital. There they took Frank and I into 7th ward. We were furnished new clothes and sent into the bathroom which I was verry glad to see as I was both dirty & lousy, couldn't help it. It was hard but honest.

So I got clean once more and had a good bed. Had my wound dressed which made my head feel well and when I went to bed I went right to sleep. The nurse woke me for dinner which was good and I ate hearty as they had brought me plenty. Slept most all the afternoon, had supper.

September 2, 1862

& a good nights rest, breakfast and looked round a little. Got outside of the hospital, bought some peaches of an old lady which tasted verry good as I hadn't any fruit for so long that was fit to eat. Then we were all called in to take the names of those that were able to go to Philadelphia which included Frank & I who wanted to go, so we were called out and formed line. There being about 100 from the hospital, so we were marched down to the Depot to take the train as we supposed right away but instead of that we did not get on till about noon. Then sit a couple of hours before started.

There were as much as two thousand soldiers there getting & I got my dinner in the soldiers retreat as did all others before getting on the cars. We went off and left several thousand waiting to go as soon as possible. Well we came to Baltimore. There we got out of the cars and walked through the city to the other station about a mile distant apart. This was a hard walk for many and useless walk because if we had stayed in the cars we should have been drawn through the same as the passengers were by horses, as engines are not allowed to go through the street.

Well when we got through to the station it was dark and we waited for about an hour then got on the cars. I bought all Frank & I wanted to eat, I being rather better of than many of the boys. I bought probably 50 cts worth of cakes and give to the boys in our car and that was all the supper they got. I didn't suffer only with cold and we were better off than the most of them for Frank had a rubber & two Wolen Blankets & so we made a bed down. Got in, had a good sleep before the cars started and still slept after they got started. We laid there most all night.

The cars started about midnight and run about half way here stopping verry frequently, and stopped as we supposed as usual. But we laid there till daylight.

September 3, 1862

And it was verry cold, everybody shivering and they had us in old freight cars so we couldn't get out verry handy but we laid there till the sun was two hours high. Nothing to eat, nearly freezing. It was hard. Some of the boys went to a house nearby and got some fish, bread &c. Some got out, made fires, made coffee in their cups as they used to when soldiering. As some of them had their haversacks, therefore, they had coffee, sugar and a few crackers. So some of them got along well enough but I could get buy nothing as there was nothing to buy and we had to do without.

At last we started. After while we got to Wilmington. There some boys were buying bread for the Soldiers so I sent 4 cents by a boy. He got me quite a loaf and as much butter as I needed. I was verry hungry but I couldn't eat it all. I never had anything taste so good as that did.

On we go, come to Chester 15 miles this side of Philadelphia. Here we were ordered to get out and did so, many of them getting back in when they found out that we were going to stop here. And if Frank hadn't been lame we should have got back in and went to Philadelphia which I am glad we didn't, so we came up here. They soon finished fixing a new ward up and we went in. We soon got our dinner which was good one, got into our ward. Numerous kindnesses shown us, furnished clean hospital clothes. Had to bathe again and got to rest again. Here for several days we were not attended verry good. That night, verry late, the Doct came around but I didn't get my head dressed so it went. But it didn't pain me much.

September 4, 1862

And had a good nights rest. About 9 A.M. the Doct came around, examined my head, ordered it dressed. Said it was not dangerous, said the bone was not cracked which pleased me. Everything went on right today. The nurses are verry kind. We had plenty to eat. Our wounds are to be dressed twice a day. The ward master is fixing up his books, making out a roll. The Regulations for the Governing this hospital have been brought in & hung up. There is rollcall at 6 in the morning & at 9 P.M. We are to have passes as soon as we get able to go.

September 5, 1862

A fine day. All goes on right. Go to our meals regular & have plenty good food too. Verry different from other hospitals. Today they assigned Doct Morton to take care of our ward, it being Ward E., No, 3. He was around this evening - appears to be a fine man, is verry cheerful and kind. He appears to have some feeling.

September 6, 1862

And fine day. All goes on right. The Doct comes around between 9 & 10 A.M. Then makes a call in the evening about 8 P.M. My wound is doing well.

September 7, 1862

Fine day. All goes on right. The same thing gone through as yesterday. And I don't expect any difference. They go through the routine of business over & over every day. Doct comes at the Regular time, there being a time for everything and it is done at that time & a place for everything and it is kept in its place. Oh, we are comfortably situated and can have anything we call for.

September 8, 1862

Fine day. All went on right. They are still fixing and finishing the ward. We have both warm & cold water brought in pipes to the bathrooms and wash rooms. Today we changed our place of dining from the main building to the general dining room and there we don't get only about half as many different kinds of food. Sometimes they tell me that there is only bread & coffee. Doctor goes his usual rounds twice a day and everything goes on right.

September 9, 1862

And about the same as yesterday. We don't get anything for supper but Coffee & bread. We don't have near so good living as we used to in the other dining room. Well the business is about the same every day. The Boys that are able get passes to be absent some 7 or 8 hours. It will be useless to note down everything over and over that passes day after day until about the 15th when I had an attack of the Fever. The Doct didn't tell me what kind but I think it was the billious fever. At any rate I had it four days. And the Doct stopped its ravages. While I was sick the Ladies [civilian nurses] paid great attention to my wants. They troubled me to much bringing me evrything they could think to eat. But no use, I wouldn't eat it until the third day when I begun to eat a little and kept improving right along. And soon went to the table to eat. I didn't wait [until] the Doct ordered me to as most of the boys do. There is plenty of them that will sit in the ward and have the nurses bring their meals to them just because the Doct don't order them out.

Whilst I was sick they attended on me as well as I could have been at home. And all are verry kind. Well I gained verry fast and soon was able to have a pass. I go to town most evry day. We have to change shirts twice a week, and change all round once a week. Change of bedclothes once a week. They are verry cleanly. All went on as usual until the 20th inst. when I got shaved. Had those straggling whiskers taken off. They had got verry long and I had no scissors to cut them off so I concluded I would get the Barber to take those off and let them come out evenly all over if they would. This barber comes round & those that have a mind to can get shaved, hair cut &c. And it is said that Government pays for it.

Nothing of interest has transpired of late. The new dining room has been finished and we go to eat there and get better food.

Everyday there is some going back to their Regts or somewhere. They say they don't send any more back to their Regts. At any rate they go to Philadelphia and I suppose the provost Marshall[78] does what he pleases with them. Put them to guarding someplace I guess, thereby relieving those new troops to go into the field and giving the old veterans that have been crippled or sick easier business & that business can be done by them as well as by the rugged soldiers who are just waiting for such to come, so they can go to see the Elephant. And I am sure if I can serve U.S. as well that way as any I don't care about going back to the Regt.

September 30, 1862

All right fine day. Reported myself for duty this morning and was put on duty after dinner to stand guard at the Ladies room, a verry nice place. The Ladies were verry clever, so I enjoyed myself verry well. Well all has went on right since I last wrote. I have written quite a number of letters and been rather negligent. Therefore have not written as much as I should had ought to have done.

A few evenings since, one of the patients of this ward came in drunk. He had been out on a pass to the town. And he made an attack on another patient, both Irishmen and had a little fight. The way they flounced around on the beds and chairs was wonderful. At last they got them parted and took the drunk fellow to the Guard house and next day he was sent to the Regt, so we got rid of him. He was a smart man and could converse on any subject. He was verry well read. Well he was a smart man but the Demon intemperance was hold of him and a day or two since the other fellow was sent off for drunkenness and there is several more Irish that gets tipsy that will soon have to get out for the wardmaster will not have such doings about him.

They still keep sending off those that are able & willing to go. And they keep enough so as to come on about evry third day. Standing guard is not hard work here. But I, being a little weak, it went as hard as when in the regt. I, as well as several others from our ward, will have to sleep in the ward for a while till they get beds for us in the guards room which is in the main building. There the guards have a hall, verry nice, large and light. It being a regular hall, it is a nice place. And is full.

They expect the surgeon General here to inspect the hospital affairs. He being a brother of the Chaplain of the Hospital. The Chaplain is not liked verry well but I have seen nothing wrong with him except he being the cause of breaking up the Ladies society which was a great benefit to the hospital. I don't like his profession. He wears the cross, he preaches & has meetings often through the wards & distributes books, tracts &c.

October 3, 1862

And rather cloudy, sprinkled a little. I am on guard today. Stood only four hours, went on at 11 A.M. come off at 1 P.M., went on at 5 P.M., come off at 9 P.M. and the Sargeant said he would set up & fix some and two others beds, they being from the same ward as me and I acquainted with them wanted and did get them in the same room. We picked us out a room but behold when night come they had put no covering on the bed so the Orderly sargeant said we should have to bring or borrow some blankets from our ward. But the wardmaster wouldn't let them come without an order. So as I was lying in my room one steward passed. I hailed him, wanted to know about it so he took me to the head steward and laid the Complaint for me and I told him how it was and what I done so he gives me an order for three blankets from the ward & an order for 6 sheets & 3 pillow cases to the washhouse. So one of the Boys went to the washroom and I went and got the blankets so we got fixed up.

There is another bed in the room, probably somebody accepts it. But if not we shall accept it and put the other bed out as it is too much crowded and 2 beds is all that is calculated to [be] in the room. The steward was surprised that we should have 3 beds in that room. Why says I, there is four. At which he laughed hartily. Well I was determined to not be out done so I attended to the thing myself and got well situated. All agreeable fellows.

We are living so fine and easy here, I'm afraid when we come to go to the Regt we will [be] so tender and not used to sleeping out that it will just likely as not make us sick as it does most of them that have once been to the hospital. Well no more for this time.

October 5, 1862

And fine day and it is Sunday. We drew our clean clothes from the orderly this morning. We got all just the same as at home except we were too late to get handkerchiefs & towels but we, if here, will be on hand the next time. Well we are getting along fine. Nobody occupies the fourth bed and we shall move it out on the morrow and then we shall be sure of having the room to ourselves as long as we stay here. There was a lot sent to Philadelphia yesterday, but they didn't pick on us fellows. In fact I am not able to stand up two hours when on pass & here I have to sit down some of the time.

October 8, 1862

And a fine morning. Quite warm. None of us roommates have been sent off yet. We have another roommate. He is the head cook in the Ladies room. He is apparently a verry fine man. We all get along verry agreeable together. But the cook does not stay here any in daytime, only sleeps here. I have been quite unwell since I last wrote. Had a bad Diaherea, but am getting better. I got a pass this morning but shall not go out till after dinner. Half a day will tire me out. Evrything goes on right. We come on guard evry third day. The man that cooks for us does it up right and we have plenty to eat. We are living too fine, for when we come to go away and sleep on the ground it will go verry hard and probably make us sick. But we must obey our superiors in office.

Well I don't know much to write about for I have speculated enough on the beauties of the place and its accommodations for a soldier &c.

I forgot to tell you we had some Rebels come to the hospital with about 150 of our men. They all were sick and wounded from the hospitals of Frederick city, Maryland. The wounded were those of South Mountain & Antietam and they were a bad lot I tell you. A great many had to be hauled in the ground and carried into the wards. A great many had hobbled about ever since the battle with only one stick and had broken legs. They were dirty, same as we when we first came. It has been about a week since they arrived here and they look quite different. There was about 30 secesh the most of whom are verry free to talk. Some have taken the oath of allegiance and others will, they say, when they get well enough to go out. Some of them say they always thought that they could whip us until they came north and they met so many new troops going all well dressed & well armed. That they must confess their weakness & inability to whip us but they say if they had had the strength in men and arms that we had they should have whipped us long since and I believe it myself.

October 13, 1862

And a cloudy day, sprinkles rain a little. Rained most all night last night. And was rainy yesterday and day before yesterday. And the day before that was quite rainy and that day I was on guard but didn't get wet as the guards was & will be furnished overcoats as long as they stay here. They are new coats but verry poor ones. But if they had been good ones, I should have drawn one to kept. But we have them as long as we stay here anyhow. The weather has been such that we were not uncomfortable with them on when out. And I am on guard today and have to wear them to keep warm.

We guards have been trying to raise a liberty pole[79] for the last week. The Sargeant Major commands the guards. And he bosses that also. And the fault all lays with him. Sometimes he is about half drunk and other days he is the other half. He is a sargeant from the regular army and acting Sgt. Major here only, and I think it will never be raised unless somebody else takes it in hand. I understand today that he was arrested for running the guard last night. He is a perfect tyrant over the boys and the boys will not stand it much longer I think. We are treated like gentlemen by all the other officers. Also by the Doctors.

I have not heard a word from the Regt as yet. And yesterday I wrote a letter to the Co. and directed it to the Co. also. I got a letter from Sarah [sister] yesterday bringing the news of her being married. She has married a German or in other words a Dutchman. Well I don't care if he is an honerable man. He wrote some in the letter it being German. I got one of my brother Germans to read it. He said it was good writing and good spelling. I wanted to know what his Education was. He said it was good, he thought, which I was glad to hear if it be true which I haven't a reason to doubt. She, as a matter of course, speaks verry highly of him. His name is Hottes. All I have to say is if he will prove to be a good husband it will be all right.

October 17, 1862

And day and right as usual. We had some rain last night. And it had been raining a little for several days. And cloudy all the time since I last wrote. I was on guard the 15th again but with my own consent. I expect to come on tomorrow but hadn't ought till next day. But they have sent of a good many and therefore we have less to do the duty.

We had to move out our beds day before yesterday to make room for some boys that they wanted to confine for running the guard. But they only kept them confined 24 hours and sent them to their regts. There was 3 Sergeants, 1 corporal and all. But we are back now and it seems good to be alone. We had to crowd to the guards room and there was so many & they kept up a great noise so that I couldn't read or anything. I tell [you] high living and not much work makes them feel well.

They keep sending off to the Regt. And I expect evry day when they will send me, and my roommates also expect the same but I don't want to go now till I get my pay as the Regt has been paid ere this. And if I should go I would not get my pay till the next two months is due. It is the talk that the paymaster is coming today or tomorrow and so it goes.

I got a letter from Henry on the 15th inst stating that they were all well & mother had written in it also. Her health being about the same it was when I left home which was tolerable.

We raised the Liberty pole on the 15th, also the flag and the chaplain made or rather read a speech as that is his mode of speaking. We had quite a lively time. Cheering, singing songs, drums beating, fifes squealing &c. There were three or four secesh that was able to get out and they were out to see it of their own accord. They sat looking quite dejected most the time. The several speeches were made. But there was nothing said by either the speakers or the vast crowd that would be insinuating.

But on the other hand the speakers said we had nothing against the southern soldiers personally.

The whole thing went off exceedingly well. It is the first Flag raising I have been to since I have been in the service. And that is rather queer, that we never all last winter had a flag up in the Regt.

October 27, 1862

And rainy day and has been a little so for several days but today it is raining hard. We have fine weather most the time since I last wrote. There has been nothing of importance transpired since I last wrote except that the house got fire yesterday. Got pretty well started but they soon found some fire men and soon had to good streams of water on it. It had got in between the plaster and floor & they had to tear off the plastering to get at it. It was caused by lying some brooms against the main pipe that runs from the heating furnace and the fire. This being in the quartermasters dept. It caused quite an excitement which soon subsided as were not long putting the fire out. It would have been an awful thing if this building had burned up and it would certainly have set the wards on fire. As the roof is gas tar it would catch from the least blaze. It would have been a loss to the Government of about $200,000.00 or thereabouts and would have been a great loss to the patients physically speaking but kind Providence smiled on us so we ought to thank him for that. For we still have good quarters.

Well, I am learning bookkeeping, therefore I am well occupied my many leisure hours. I am progressing verry well. If I stay here long I shall learn it thouroughly. There is lots of soldiers going off for duty someplace but they don't go to the army. As long as I can't go to the army, I will stay here as long as possible. I can't hear a word from the Regt therefore I don't care about going. Most of the secesh has been sent to Fort Delaware and there I suppose they will be paroled.

The paymaster has been here but those only that had been mustered got pay and therefore I got none but I hope my discriptive list will come by the 31st inst as that is muster day.[80] And those not having their discriptive lists will be mustered for the time they have been in the hospital only. Therefore if mine shouldn't come, I will get only 2 months pay, that time I have been in the hospital.

The weather is getting cool. They are putting stoves in the wards and they are badly needed.

November 19, 1862

Rather warmer than usual and cloudy, rained a little last night. Well it has been a long time since I wrote last. But I have been so busy with my bookkeeping since I last wrote that I did not take time [to] write about what was transpiring. But there has been nothing unusual transpired. We were mustered on the 30th of last month and I hadn't my discriptive list and I don't know as it has come yet. It hadn't a week or so since but it is too late now for to get 4 months pay because the payroll has gone to Washington to be signed.

Well on the 7th of this month we had a hard snowstorm of about 24 hours. Snow about 6 inches deep. In two or three days it was all gone. And we had mud for a week, then fine, fine weather and good getting about which made it more cheerful. They have sent off several squads but don't send me. But they always pick out the worst characters. Therefore I have had a good chance to study which I have improved and have got so that I can go right along with bookeeping in common buisness way besides learning to write a great deal better.

Well it seems as though it is too good the way I live but still it is harder on me than when at home. Be up evry third night, but when it is stormy weather we don't stand on the outposts. Guards only where there is shelter for them. I am on guard today and it is raining like Jahue. So the guards will be taken off, at least those that are outside.

All the soldiers that are here have drawn woolen clothing from U.S. clothing store and the guards have to pay for their washing hereafter. I have drawn 1 pair drawers, 1 shirt, a knit one it is verry warm. About ten days since they [sent] off 23 of the guard giving them plenty of clothing &c to keep them warm and the talk evry day is that some more is going but they havn't gone yet.

About two weeks since they got tired of so much noise in the main building that they moved us all out and quartered us in ward A3 and here we are now. They are good quarters. We have two common sinks for washing face and hands. And two bathing rooms with a large iron bathing tub in each room with soap & towels. But I have one of the latter of my own and use it myself. So we are well situated as I could wish with good beds, chairs and stands twixt our beds.

About a week since there was about 300 soldiers came from Philadelphia. All had been in hospitals there and not verry bad ones as they, the most of them, could walk or all of them. I was down with about a doz other guards to bring them from the depot and we waited and waited. Train after train came. At last at 7 P.M. they came and we marched them up. I, with two or three others, was rear guard and I stopped a carriage and had a verry lame man get in and just as he got in, the horse began to back and the man kept pulling him back. At last the carriage tipt over. Then I thought I had done it. But all were satisfied when he was getting in and none of them attached any blame to me, not even the cripple. And worse than all it was raining torrents and the road shoe top deep with mud. So we helped the man unhitch and he got on his horse and he was verry anxious to have the basket and in getting out the basket the mystery was solved. Lo & behold there was a jug in the basket. Then [I] knew enough. I took the cripple by the arm. And I had his knapsack on my back which I carried all the way and we plodded along, got here at last. And I make a point for the supper table.

December 2, 1862

And verry fine morning after a rainy day yesterday and quit a cold night but not so cold as I have usually experienced in Wisconsin on the first day of the first winter month. The ground didn't freeze to the depth of an inch after all the great ado made by the boys. And what made it appear cold to me was being on guard and having a slight [cold], therefore it affected me some. I stood in the main entrance hall of the main building. There couldn't a bit of wind strike me. But still there was that dead cold chill air that always haunts such places where the great heater of the world never has a chance to cast its congenial rays upon it. But however, I am relieved. Am comfortably situated by my stand. Pen in hand busying myself as usual when I have any spare time.

I am still at the hospital. And same as ever, don't know when I shall return to my Regiment. I am [on] duty as usual and that is about double what I would have to do at the Regt, I think. I have had no news whatever from the Regt for near a month. I wrote a letter to Lieut Young three or four days since to let him as well as the boys know how & where I was. Also giving him a polite invitation to look after my discriptive list and send it to me. Which had ought to have been done long since but has been neglected by somebody, I don't know who. I cannot now get but two months pay as I did not get it ere the Payroll was sent off to be signed.

On the 27th inst, or Thanksgiving Day, this Delaware Co. give us a splendid dinner of roasted turkeys, chickens, ham, ever so many different kind of pies & cakes & sauces. In fact it was what I call a Wisconsin Celebration No 1.

There the old cook blows his whistle, a little bit of a piece of iron with a mechanical hole in it, which when he presses his breath through with all the power at his command, makes a verry shrill sound which can be heard verry easily by those with good appetites. Then there is a rush for the dining room. The old chief cook of the whole mess of cooks is there & takes command & with him and his subordinates they get us strung along each side of the table. And no man to sit down until the said chief waves a little flag which he holds in his hand and stands on a stool higher than the Co. So we all got a standing position at a parade rest.

Then there was a man with a great big parchment in his hand got up on another stool. Also stating he had a series of resolutions to offer in behalf of the Ladies of the County. And he proceeded to read which he done verry poorly from some cause. But the resolutions were good. Exceedingly well suited to the occasion, rendering our heart felt thanks to the ever mindful fair sex. That through with, the chaplain went through with his services, according to the rules of his church, on such occasions, thanking the great Creator for permitting us to come togather to give thanks &c.

Then the chief waved the flag and we were all quickly seated and. And what we done I need not tell you, but leave you to imagine what we done. We ate a good meal. Then they brought us one thing after another until we had to leave our plates loaded, couldn't kept it for we ate as long as we could.

Well, Thanksgiving over with and we come back to the old thing again. Go on guard evry third day as usual. There was about one hundred soldiers sent away two or three days since. And some fifty today or night rather as they send them away on the twelve oclock train for some reason. I suppose so as to keep them from getting drunk on the road. As it is impossible to keep them from it when sent in daytime and they get evry guard out or as many as they have guns for to guard them down and until they get on the cars. Then the Provost guard takes them in hand until they get to Washington or Alexandria where the convalescent camp is.

I see by the statistics that there are sixteen thousand convalescent soldiers at Fairfax Seminary Camp or Convalescent Camp. And that they have been treated verry bad in the way of not furnishing them in wood, blankets &c wherewith to keep them warm. And Surgeon Gen. Hammond denies through the column of some of the papers of having anything to do with it. That it was not his business, but it was a gross neglect on the part of somebody but didn't say who that somebody was. Some of the boys writing back tell hard stories about the place, of them suffering with cold. And when I think of how well off I am it is quite a contrast. And I feel perfectly satisfied but I have yet to be dissatisfied of this place.

December 8, 1862

And fine day with about 6 inches of snow on the ground which fell on the fourth inst and has stayed so. So cold has the weather been that it has not thawed any except where the sun shines on the south side of the buildings. The thermometer has been down to 20 degrees below zero which is not verry common in this country. And the papers state of there being as much snow at Fredricsburg, where the army lays now as there is here and the thermometer as low. If so, some of the boys must have suffered for there is some that will not carry as much as will keep them warm. And are verry careless and think of nothing only as they want to use it. I never knew it so last winter. And it would be much worse now as the boys have nothing but their shelter tents. And maybe some of them none. I feel sorry for them, verry sorry.

We have changed our place of dining again. We have for 2 days but are going to eat up at the main building hereafter. They have stoped this cookhouse down here in the lower one. As the lower wards have been emptied there is no use of the kitchen going on just for the guards only. I am verry glad of the change for we have better victals and everything is cooked better and cleanlier looking. It is only such rations as we got at camp. But its all in the cooking. Poor rations well cooked eats well when a fellow is hungry. I am perfectly satisfied with my living.

The farmers are still husking corn here. I got a letter from Henry stating all well and that he was most done husking corn &c getting his falls work done earlier than usual. I also got a letter from Sister Mary [Mary Jane Ray] & all was well and that my Nephew Isaac Lander [son of Isaac C. Lander and Thurza Ann Ray] was dead. He died at the military hospital Keokuk, Iowa, he being in the southwest department. I was sorry to hear of it. His mother and one of his sisters went down to see him when they heard he was sick but he had been dead four days when they got there. I have got so many letters that I cannot think of them all. No, not half of them but hereafter I will try to keep pace with them, which I can probably do as I cannot write any more. For somebody stole the last and only paper I had and I have no money. Well, only one cent but I must keep that for seed.

December 12, 1862, [Battle of Fredericksburg] [81]

Fine morning but cold. About half of the snow has gone of and yesterday, in the middle of it was quite warm which melted it away verry fast. The weather is still cold where the army lays but has moderated so that they have made a move and shelled and burned the City of Fredericksburg and crossed and built bridges and crossing the whole army and it supposed that a great battle is raging today from accounts in the papers. Also stating the greatest and most heroic deed of the [war] being done by 100 men that volunteered to go across the river and take a squad of rebel sharpshooters that were stationed there to pick off our engineers and mechanics that were building one of the bridges which it was impossible for them to finish. There was more volunteered than could be used, they only wanted 100. So they started over in small boats and landed on the other side, fixed bayonets, charged on the rebels, drove them off, took 101 prisinors, come back.

The bridge was finished and the troops began to cross and there was enough troops thrown across to hold the place till this morning when all would cross to make battle if necessary. All of this was done under a shower of missiles thrown from our guns, 173 in number. They all opened at once and kept at it. All concentrated on the city. There was twixt 8 & 9000 shells & fired yesterday completely enveloping the city in smoke up to dark last night. Evrything was going on fine. The people are awaiting in anxious suspense for tomorrow mornings paper expecting to hear of a great victory.

December 14, 1862

And fine day. Quite warm. Last night was warm also and most of snow is gone off from the ground pretty much. There is exciting news this morning from the army. The Sunday morning Chronicle brings news of the army being hotly engaged and that our forces drove the enemy and held the ground they had gained, was still fighting desperately.

Now for some of the reports that was put in circulation this morning by some of the boys for a spell. And was a pretty good one. It was this. That the rebs had taken 15000 of the Penn. Reserve prisinor when in fact there is not that many of them or never was. But it caused some speculation in jokes which were cracked pretty freely of the reserve Boys of which there is a good many on guard here. It was thought for a good while that it was true. There was only a few lines in the paper about it. I suppose the news is suppressed. I was on guard yesterday. This being Sunday, I think I will to go to church tonight. Well I will have to wait patiently till tomorrow morning and see what the news will be. No more at present.

December 26, 1862

And evening. Well Christmas is past once more and New Years is close at hand. There has a great many things of interest transpired since I last wrote. The Battle than I spoke of when I last wrote is over, it being already placed on the pages of history by the historian as one of the Bloodiest of the war. 1,500 killed, 10,000 wounded and our army after 4 days battling, some times hotly engaged, at others not a gun fired by either side, were forced to fall back across the River on the same old line they occupied before crossing. Nothing gained, but knowing that the enemies works are impregnable. The army fell back and was all across the River ere the Rebs knew. Our forces took about 700 prisinors, and they lost about as many in same way. The wounded was all got off the field before we fell back and the dead was buried the two or three succeeding days under Flag of Truce as usual.[82]

The cry of the country against [Army of the Potomac commander Ambrose] Burnside is hard and there was a committee appointed to investigate it which didn't take long, for Burnside took all the blame on himself as his own defeat and says it can't be otherwise for the gallantry of the troops was unquestionable. They done all that could be desired by any Generals. I will leave it to the Historian to record the valor shown there and that hottly contested field. There has been nothing unusual transpired since the Battle.

December 29, 1862

And a verry fine day. It is warm and pleasant. But no snow as I have been used to see in a more northern latitude. There is nothing unusual from the Army. Don't know where [Union General Nathaniel] Banks is as yet but he will turn up some place with a crash.

Oh, I forgot to tell you about us moving into the new quarters that have been erected for us. We have the Regular bunks to sleep in now instead of a bedstead as heretofore. There is three in a Bunk. Myself and Sherart and a clever German by the name of Wehaug occupy one bunk. We moved in on the 24th inst just after dinner and that night Sister Tyler gave us a splendid supper. And the guards, through the orderly Sergeant, presented the Surgeon in charge John L. Lecoute with a gold ring as a token of Friendship. After which he made a few appropriate remarks. He was much surprised, and seemed greatly moved almost to tears. He said he felt verry much pleased knowing the sentiment of some of the people. He was much surprised to see such a good feeling toward him.

All the Doctors were present as well as the Ladies, the latter waiting upon the table. The affair passed off well and we had plenty of it. And after the supper was over we had a keg of Beer which some of the Boys imbibed pretty freely and we had a noisy time all night. Not much sleep for the weary. There was quite a number of light heads and evry night since we have had some drunken fellows. There is 84 men in the guards quarters which fills the bunks. There has been a Lieut detailed here for duty. The card shufflers are busy. Nothing else for today.

Oh yes, I got a letter from Brother Amos [Amos W. Ray]. Hadn't heard from him for 2 years. He is in the 16 Indiania Regt. laying near Memphis Tennessee, that being in the Department of the Southwest. Which I answered and answered a letter from Henry. Some days since, I received a letter from Sarah and all was well. I am on guard today. On the First Relief No. 6 post.

January 2, 1863

Well, New Year has come and past and nothing transpired to denote it except the wishing of each other a happy Year Years. We guards had nothing to eat but Uncle Sams grub consisting of fat pork, bread &c the same as we get on 'other days. Of late we don't get as good victals as we used to. We have lost our old and good cook, he wouldn't serve any longer. There has been from 2 to 6 and more of the guards drunk all the time since Christmas Eve. But this has played out for we took a vote on the Guard house affairs viz: That evry man that came home drunk was to be put in the Guard house and it was carried without opposition. And since that time we just shove them right in as soon as they raise the least disturbance. It causes some sport. But all submit to it. And it being a law of our own making, nobody can find much fault with it, if any. So things will go off better now and we will have to go on guard evry third day now only instead of evry other day as it has been since the day before Christmas.

There has been a good many parties and balls around here but all small ones, none of which I have attended. There was a watchnight meeting up to Upland, the small town about a mile from Chester. I being on guard could not go to it. Oh, I said we did not have anything unusual. But we did, for there was about a dozen Boys fired as many volleys as the old year was going out and the new one coming in.

January 6, 1863

And a foggy morning. We have verry fine weather since I last wrote. Nothing unusual has transpired. Three of the guards has volunteered to go to their Regts. Namely Wm R Ray and C Ladd & Burns. We expect to go today but may not till tomorrow. The Boys call us patriots and say they wouldn't go until obliged to. But I am sorry to say there is too much of that feeling throughout the Army. And I will go for I think it my duty as evrybody else that considers themselves able.

9 P.M. And waiting for the cars we are at the Provost Marshal office. We came down here starting from Chester about one oclock. Reached here 2 oclock and now expect to start for the depot any minute. There was 3 secesh prisinors came down

with us who are going to Fort Del tomorrow. There has quite a number gathered in from the different Hospitals in this City of Philadelphia. The old Corn Exchange Building is used for this buisness, they having built a new one. A splendid one too.

January 15, 1863

And fine day but windy. It having been so long since I have written that I must go back a few days. I am now at the Company and have been for 5 or 6 days. But have been so busy fixing up my quarters that I couldn't write.

Well to return to the Provost Marshals in Philadelphia. 10 P.M. we started for the Depot to take the 11 oclock train, but didn't get off till one oclock train. We had first class cars. The train starts, goes slow towards morning, overtake the train that preceded us & it had broken down. But still went slowly along and something got the matter of our horse so we went slowly.

7th [January 1863] And we arrived in Baltimore about 1 P.M., got good dinner at the refreshment saloon, started for Washington on 3 oclock train, went pretty brisk, reached Washington before dark, partook of a rough repast at the soldiers retreat and were sent in some poor quarters or verry cold quarters, put in a miserable night, couldn't sleep for cold.

8th [January 1863] Got breakfast at the same place as supper. We were then formed into a company, marched under guard to the boat that sh'd start to Aquia creek at 8 A.M. Got aboard and off we went. The guards coming aboard as the boat started. Reached there, 12N, were marched to a bord shanty where we were given dinner &c. Turned over to another guard & there we had to wait until we were sent after which was two days for Frank and I.

9th [January 1863] when the Provost Marshal [Military Police] of our, the first army corps, came after us & about a doz belonging to it. We went up to Falmouth Station on the cars. Then marched to the Provost Marshals office which was four miles. Raining Jehu like and had been all the afternoon. It was now dark and verry dark. The Provost Marshal said we must be sent to our Regts. And the Captain of the Provost said we couldn't go, that he would give us something to eat which he did. Ordered his cook to give us plenty of coffee and crackers which we ate with a good relish and he showed us a fodder pile which he himself had slept in the first night they came there so we made a bed in it and luckily it stopped raining, rested well.

10th [January 1863] And we were then singled out for our Regts and guard sent with us and the guard taking each right to his Co and getting a receipt from the Colonel of the Regt for the men.

So we started and came about 4 miles, found the Boys in good spirits & good health generally, rather better than usual and the company numbered 40 men which was much larger than I expected to find. There had most of the Boys got back from the Hospitals, found the boys in better quarters than last winter. And I got in with 3 other boys who had built their shanty for 4. And it wasn't quite finished so I turned in and helped them fix it up verry comfortable. But I am sorry to say that two of my tentmates are verry lousy and when we change camp or move I shall try to get in with somebody else or tent so as to leave them out for they are verry dirty Soldiers. And they might be clean, I think when we are in camp if they would try. They are two of them college educated folks too. Well after I got here I had to help them finish the cabin by banking it, build chimney, making a door, putting up shelves &c. Things too numerous to mention it. Anybody that has lived in the woods will know how it is done. Well about our Company officers. Lieut Young in command of the company and the only commissioned officer here now. As Captain Callis is in Wisconsin recruiting and hope he will never (unreadable) again.

[Ed. Note: back cover reads: "Turn to the front leaf." The following section is written on the first two pages of the diary.]

For the company was never in better condition than it is at present. and I am sure that we never had so good or so plenty food for we have a great plenty and we do just about as we please and run about almost where we please and are always here when there is anything to do and we have no trouble anyway whatever. And the company was never so obedient as it now is for everyone seems to like him and try to please him and he does the same.

Well about the camp. It is near Bell Planes [Belle Plaine] on the Potomac River and about 7 miles from where we lay last summer when we were in this part of the country. The camp is on a small ridge. The soil is rather sandy which keeps it dry and there is plenty of wood and water also. But we have to carry all of it up the hill and that goes hard. Well I have received no letters from home since I came to the camp. I wrote one to Mother & Henry yesterday. Well this Book is full and I will commence another so.

Good By.

1863

Private William Ray did not return to the Seventh Wisconsin Volunteers until the middle of January 1863. Because of his Brawner's Farm wound, he had missed the battles of Second Bull Run, South Mountain, Antietam, and Fredericksburg. When he finally returned to duty he found about 40 men in his Company F in their winter camp on a slight ridge not six or seven miles from where they had spent the previous winter. There were more than he expected, and the regiment had substantially changed during his absence.

Captain John B. Callis, who had organized the company, was back in Wisconsin on recruitment duty, and in command was Lieutenant Henry Young. Colonel William W. Robinson was back in command of the regiment after recovering from his Gainesville (Brawner's Farm) wound. Lieutenant Colonel Charles A. Hamilton was about to resign and return to Wisconsin to practice law. It was also understood that Callis was about to be promoted to major to replace George Bill, who had also been wounded at Gainesville and had just resigned. The Seventh and the other old regiments of the brigade had been much reduced by the hard fighting of the past few months, and a new unit—the Twenty-fourth Michigan—was added in October 1862. General John Gibbon was also gone, promoted to division command in another corps; in his place was Solomon Meredith of the Nineteenth Indiana.

Of more significance was another matter. No longer were the soldiers of the other regiments calling the Westerners "the Black Hats," but "The Iron Brigade of the West." The proud name supposedly dated back to South Mountain on September 14, 1862, when General George B. McClellan watched the brigade fight its way up the National Road. Upon inquiry, "Little Mac" was told the troops belonged to Gibbon's Western brigade. "They must be made of iron," McClellan said to another officer (or at least that is how he reported it later). The casual remark was overheard by a newspaper correspondent. "This brigade has done some of the hardest and best fighting in the service," the correspondent wrote a few days later. "It has been justly termed the Iron Brigade of the West."

But it was at Gettysburg, Pennsylvania, on July 1, 1863, that Meredith's First Brigade of the First Division of the First Corps won undying fame. There, the Westerners came on the run from the south that morning to be thrown into line northwest of the town. The Second Wisconsin, Nineteenth Indiana, Seventh Wisconsin, and Twenty-fourth Michigan plunged forward *en echelon* into a woods on a slight ridge to repulse James Archer's advancing Confederate brigade. "There are those damned black hatted fellows again," the Rebel infantrymen called to one another over the gunfire. To the north, the Sixth Wisconsin successfully captured hundreds of Confederates they had helped trap in an unfinished railroad cut.

The bloody morning success evolved into a desperate struggle early that afternoon. Three hours later the Confederates came at them again in thick lines of well-formed infantry. With loud yells and unstoppable tenacity, the Southerners smothered the Federal position atop Seminary Ridge. On the left, the Iron Brigade regiments stubbornly held on and soon found the enemy on three sides. "Come on, Johnny! Come on!" some of the Wisconsin boys shouted with an angry wave of a clenched fist. In the fierce and frantic shooting, in the smoke and swirl of bullets, the black-hatted soldiers fell back from one position to another. And soon the defensive line was gone.

In the press and confusion of the Union retreat, the shattered regiments of the Iron Brigade tried to keep together, moving through the streets of Gettysburg until, finally, they came to a Federal line being patched together near a cemetery on a low hill south of town. The Confederate pursuit sputtered to a halt in the deepening darkness as newly arriving Union regiments tramped in to take their place along the growing Federal line. The delaying fight of the Iron Brigade and other units, as well as the hesitation of the enemy generals to press their advantage, was decisive. The new Union position south of Gettysburg proved the key to victory. For the next two days the Confederate Army of Northern Virginia hammered Meade's Federal lines in a series of unsuccessful attempts to dislodge the Union soldiers before abandoning the field on July 4 and marching back to Virginia.

No brigade in the army had performed better service at Gettysburg than the Iron Brigade, but the cost had been frightful. Indeed, the "Iron Brigade of the West" had been shot to pieces. Within a few hours, some 1,200 of the 1,883 men taken into the battle had fallen. In the Seventh Wisconsin, of 343 engaged, 178 were among the killed, wounded, or missing.

One of them was William Ray.

Volume 8

January 26, 1863 to February 27, 1863

An Emancipation Act

[*Ed. Note: This book is in poor condition. Someone gave it to Ray for his use, but it already had notations and drawings written in it. Ray recorded his observations on the available space. This problem is compounded by the fact that some pages are missing. It begins as follows below, with some concluding observations on the Union defeat at Fredericksburg, Virginia, in December 1862, and Union General Ambrose Burnside.*][83]

* * *

... to trade off for Burnside but I don't wonder at the doing it for it was truth that we were stuck and they were ready for us where we were going to cross as it afterwards proved

January 26, 1863

And a . . . day & rained nearly all night. There was nothing unusual transpired. I got a letter from Henry today it being the first mail I have had since coming to the Regt. It stated he was well and he heartily endorsed the Emancipation Act which I am glad to hear. I made a washboard with a jackknife. You would smile to see the skills displayed on it. And I didnt get to use it today on account of the stormy weather and I expect to be on guard tomorrow.[84]

January 27, 1863

And stormy it being rain until toward night when it turned to snowing and snowed al night. I was on guard today, there being only one post and there being 10 guards. We only had to stand once a piece 2 hours & 20 minutes. I being the 8th one, I had to get up at 2 oclock at night. I was quite sick all the night up to an hour or so before when I got up and vomited and was better right away so that I felt a great deal better when I got on post which is some 40 rods distant from my shanty. In going there I had to go through snow nearly knee deep to my great surprise. There being some bales of hay there, I broke one open and got in thereby keeping my feet dry and protected from the cold. The time passed off well, by singing two or three Patriotic Songs such as the Ocean Wave, the Star Spangled Banner &c. The guard arrangement is verry good. The guards are allowed to go to their quarters and the Corporal or Sergeant which ever it may be comes & notifies them when their turn comes. That is even better than I should have asked had that Privilige been allowed me. When the time was up my relief came promptly and I returned to my quarters & went to Bed again, had a good nap.

January 28, 1863

And a fine day. Stoped snowing soon after daylight. When I awoke this morning the sun was high up. Probably one hour. The snow is going off verry fast under the rays of the warm sun. The report is that [Union General Joseph] Hooker has superceeded Burnsides which if true, we, I think, will soon have something to do in some way. Probably he may not do any better than Burnside but I hope so, if such a thing could be shone which I for one doubt verry much.

We are verry scarce of rations for several days but not bad off. We will have Plenty hereafter as they will have got it fixed again as it was before we march. I signed for a hat and a pair of pants and I have drawn me a new haversack so I will get fit out ere long. While out on that march I got a good knappsack that was being thrown away by a soldier and if I hadnt drawn a Blanket I could have got one the same way.

January 30, 1863

And nothing exciting. It is a fine day. We are likely to have soft Bread soon as the Brigade is building a Bakery. It is built with logs. It will soon be done I think as there are a great many at work on it. There is Bakers to from the Regt so that will save US the expense of hiring them. And when we march they can shoulder the musket again.

January 31, 1863

And fine day & I got at that long talked of job Washing. I joined fires with the Co Washman and he showed me a number of new tricks about washing. It was hard getting a fire started on account of the snow which has not all gone off yet. But pretty much so on the hillsides and we being in the hollow we had it to contend with which made it rather bad. But I soon got some water hot and went at it to try my new washboard which I was well pleased with. I soon rubbed out 6 or 7 pieces & got them on to boil. Then being quite hungry I came up to the shanty and got dinner which I had fixed and started to boil and left in care of one of the tentmates which he did well. Then returned and took the clothes out, rinsed them, they looked well. In fact I never knew how to wash before and I think when I get home I will not go verry dirty if I couldnt get them washed by some woman. But I live and learn and I have learned a great deal since I came into the Army.

February 1, 1863

And looks like storm. We got orders last night at roll call to start on Picket at 8 A.M. this morning. We had revilee early and got breakfast, got two days rations. That being the time we had to stay on duty. When going by headquarters we halted and new orders for forming and conducting a new picket line. Went on at great speed reaching the line at 10 A.M. the time set forth in the new orders. The distance to the lines is about three miles. In consequence of forming the new line it was late in the afternoon when our company got posted. We, our, the Left rear, we were quartered near a house and the officers made that their headquarters. There being a safeguard there, I was called upon to go and relieve him, by Lieut [Henry] Young, he being one of the officers that had command there. He saying that I should get some wood, as much as we should use as we would set the folks fire. This I gladly done for I didnt feel verry well having a bad cold at the time. And it was raining some and was likely to be a bad night. So I got plenty of wood, got my things moved in, soon was seated by a Blazing fire in the old fashioned Chimney and sat and chatted till about 9 P.M. when the Old lad had supper on the table and urged us to eat. That being my privilige as it always is a safeguards. So I and three or four officers sit down to the table. The supper consisted of Buiscuits & Pancakes (the latter made of cornmeal) ham and eggs, butter and the best kind of coffee. Supper over, we chat with the Family awhile. They consists of the two old folks and their two grown up Girls or young ladies, more properly speaking and they all were so ignorant that one person raised in the North would know more than them all. Oh but they were worse than any Negro that had been in the North 6 months. I never had an Idea before how Ignorant a person could be. But I see where the Blight of Slavery has been. There is Ignorance to the worst degree. The poor white is Below the negro if anything.

I wanting to go to bed (as a safeguard is allowed to sleep) the old woman showed me to a bedroom not forgetting to remind me if I heard the chickens squak or pigs squeal I must up and out to see what was the matter. And all I would have to do is get up look out the door as it was tolerable light, could see the pig sty and hen coop. I found my bed to be a feather bed. But not so good as a straw bed in Wisconsin for it was like evrything else about the Establishment. It looked as if it had been in use for a hundred years. The house had been a fine one in its day, it being large and three stories high. One of those being a kind of basement story. Evrything, furniture and all as I said before looked a old and the people now living here are verry poor. I thought I had seen the Vales of Poverty in my time but I never see such a one as that.

February 2, 1863

And fine looking morning. Rather cold last night. I got a warm breakfast similar to the supper last night. No other man but myself to sit down. I thought myself rather lucky to have two ladies and the Mother of them to breakfast with. It was such an unusual thing. But however I got along verry well for they were verry Ignorant. But were verry tidy and good cooks. Their victuals was cooked excellent such as it was which I have before named. Set around all day without any dinner. But had supper about dark, earlier than last night. The Officers are coming again tonight. This seems to be a resort for officers to get meals. Evening passed off about the same as last Evening. I had to get a good deal of wood as the old man is quite sick and they must keep a fire upstairs and they have fireplaces only and two going all the time so it takes a good deal of wood.

February 3, 1863

And fine but cold morning. Got breakfast as usual. But two or three officers of the Picket line breakfasted here. Expect the Relief soon. 10 A.M. and the Relief has come. I don't know what Regt, I believe 7th Indiania. A man was sent to relieve me. Before he got to the house the Old woman pitched out to him about getting some wood. Scared him half to death he said. He thought he was elected for 48 hours work. Pretty hard guard duty to have to get all the wood for the house when the guard at a house is not obliged to do anything and they are obliged to feed & give him bed.

Well I soon joined the company and was trudging for home, evry man for himself as they were relieved, they would start home. I reached home about 12 N. Built fire, got dinner.

February 5, 1863

And stormy, rather snowy. I am on fatigue duty today and had to work all day in the storm. Those who wished got two or three drinks of whiskey. I, as always, rather discouraged it if anything. We were putting [up] a shed for the horses and mules of our Regt. There being about 40 men at work at different things about it, we got it up. But that night, it being stormy, it blew down as I said it would when I saw how they were putting it up. For I am some acquainted with such work having done it at home some for cattle shed &c about the farm. I got pretty wet and didnt feel well to begin with & had not for several days. The shed was covered and sided up with pine instead of straw as at home.

February 6, 1863

And rainy this morning. About 1 P.M. cleared off. Was a fine evening. One of my tentmates came fatigue duty today and the fatigue party have to put up the shed again that we put up yesterday. This caused some merriment amongst the Boys. Twas a rather hard joke on us fellows of yesterday. They worked till noon & then was let off on account of the storm which soon stopped and was a fine evening. Today we was to had Inspection but it didnt come off on account of the storm. There having been an order issued to have Co Inspections evry Tuesday and Friday, and Regimental Inspection evry Sunday morning. So they calculate to get the Regt up in good condition by the next muster for Pay.

February 7, 1863

And fine day, verry. Nothing of importance today. But drawing rations &c. We drew Onions today, it being the first I ever got from U.S. But the Boys got them pretty regular for a while before I come back. We drew Potatoes also but those we have had evry few days. What I draw makes me two good meals & we draw them about once a week. I got a letter from my friend Shesart at the Chester Hospital and the certificate from the Hospital showing that I was mustered there came in the letter. He said things was going on as usual and that he was well. From him forgetting to put Washington, D.C. on it, it went to Cairo, Ill and then was returned to Washington which delayed it some. But, however, I got my certificate before the Paymaster come to see us.

February 8, 1863

And fine day. This being Sunday our Regt Inspection come of. The Major giving us praise for our cleanliness. Nothing else transpired in a military way. [William P.] Norman,[85] one of my tentmates and myself took a walk, went down the ridge striking the Potomac about 3 miles below here then came up the Beach, found quite a number of good apples that had been dropped or lost in the river from time to time and blown ashore. We came up the Beach to the lower landing in Potomac Creek then home, it being only ¾ of a mile from the Landry home.

February 11, 1863

And fine day. Norman and I got up a good pile of wood. Our tentmate C. F. Dean [Charles F. Dean][86] wont do anything. He don't bring even as much water as he drinks. Don't do anything whatever. Damed Lazy fellow. Perfect imposter, he wouldnt do his own cooking as long as I would do it. So I quit cooking with him. And day before yesterday D. Rector [Danforth Rector] come home from the Hospital, he having stayed here before he went there and before I came in, so he had a claim so that makes 4 of us now in this small place. And he is sickly so we have to do a good deal for him. But Dean is hearty and must do more or he and I will have a fuss and I have plenty to back me in it.

February 12, 1863

And little Rainy in the morning. But turned out to be a fine day. We drilled a little today in the manual of Arms.

February 13, 1863

And fine day. Had Inspection. We drew soft Bread yesterday again which makes twice that we have drawn. The first loaf I sold for 25 cents and the last one for 15 cents. I sold them because I was hard up for money and had plenty of hardtack. I got sutlers tickets, it being all the money we have nowadays. So I bought me a plate to eat off from and couple of papers of smoking tobacco. I got my Plate for 10 cents. But they always sold them for 15 cents. That was the fault of the new clerk which they have got. Lucky for me. We finished getting up our tree we had cut down.

February 17, 1863

And went on Picket this morning starting at 7 A.M. It having been snowing for an hour or so. The whole Brigade went this time. They have got a line so that it takes a Brigade instead of a Regt as heretofore. We walked pretty smart out there reaching the line about 9 A.M. and commenced Relieving. We went to the extreme Right which made about 2 miles more traveling than the other time out. Our Regt was right Grand Reserve. Only one Company on Picket and the first 2 hours our Company was on. Then Co B next and each man had only two hours out of the 48 and the other 8 Cos was on reserve all the time. We got all fixed about 11 A.M. and still snowing. It is now near six inches deep. We found verry poor arrangements which western enterprise soon bettered. The Boys said they couldnt expect anything better of down-Easters for they never seem to have the nac of getting along asaid western Boys. I was on the 3rd Relief which went on at 11 oclock at night and No 1 of that Relief. I stood from 11 to 1 oclock as we supposed. Having no timepiece, we guessed at it. We were Relieved from Post at 5 AM and went back to the first Reserve. That being our Boys that were not on post.

It quit storming about dark so I had a pretty good time but rather cold as I had to stand on a high sharp ridge and a keen cutting wind blowing which made the leaves and brush crack.

February 18, 1863

Come in at 5 AM, got breakfast which I ate with a good relish. Daylight comes & with it a mist of rain. Been a little rainy all day by spells but more comfortable than yesterday. Night come and sett in raining in earnest. We, Norman and I, got up a good pile of wood and I had taken my piece of surplus tent along so with one oilcloth & the tent, we fixed up a shelter so that we slept dry for all it rained torrents. Part of the time my Blanket was on top and got a little wet.

February 19, 1863

And cloudy but not stormy. Most of the snow is gone. Rained hard last night. Slept warm and dry. I soon dried out my wet Blanket for we had a good fire as we looked out and got plenty of dry wood last evening. Most of the boys put out & went to old houses around last night and stayed till the Regt come to relieve us. About 11 A.M. we started home, come across lots & through woods and saved walking near a mile and a half. We reached home about 1 P.M. I felt as if I had got home. We begin to think this is home at any rate we were verry glad to get back. The Boys say that it was the hardest Picket duty they ever done and I think I never see worse. One of our tentmates D. Rector came home the night before we did and he had a good fire. Somebody had taken 4 large sticks of wood from our wood pile. I don't know who it was but I hope that it will Burn on their fire. We can stand it and not break us.

February 20, 1863

Fine morning. Nothing done today but get ready for inspection at 4 P.M. and Dress parade just after. We had a Corporal promoted to Sargeant, 2 privates promoted to Corp, Frank Boynton [Francis A. Boynton] is the Sargeant, T.C. Alexander [Thomas C. Alexander] and J Black [John C. Bradley] Corp.[87] So much for Co. F. The two privates were as deserving as any two in the Co of the Promotion

February 21, 1863

And fine day. Had Dress parade. In accordance to an order read last night on Parade, there were 7 men Drummed out of the service of the U.S. in presence of this, their Brigade. They had been Court-martialed and that was the sentence. There was 5 of them had their heads shaved in presence of the Brigade and the ornaments and buttons torn off their clothing and then the Brigade was formed in two columns facing each other and about 40 feet distant apart and they were marched through with the Band playing the Rogues March. First there were six soldiers marched by the front with reversed arms then the victims formed in two lines and then 6 soldiers behind them marching at charge Bayonets. The whole of the Brigade drummers and fifers, they played the Rogues March clear through twixt the two lines. It caused some sport for us fellows & some of them didnt seem to care anything about it. One of them, the worst character, pulled out a quarter and offered to pay the Barber which he declined taking. When they came past me I took one glare at them and turned my head in spite of my wish to look. I couldnt stand it. Then we were dismissed. I came home well satisfied with the Proceeding. They were marched to the landing, I supposed to send to Washington and there let them go their way. As it happened, we had a fine day for the Proceeding which I hope I shall never witness again. I think, as also do most of the rank and file, that commissioned officers had ought to be served the same for the same offence. Which was (with the exceptions of one) for Limbering to the rear in time of Battle. And one for disobeying orders. I say Limbering as that is the name the Boys give it when a man wont go up to the slaughter-pen in time of Battle but show their heels. I read most evry day of some officers being dismissed from the service and evrything seems to be going on better of late. Gen Hooker comes out bold in evry order he gives.

February 22, 1863

And stormy day. This being Sunday there was nothing done. It snowed nearly all day. The snow got to the depth of 6 in. It will be rather a cold time for those fellows that had their head shaved. But they will soon get a wig when they get to Washington.

February 23, 1863

And fine warm day. Nothing done today in milatary matters. I and all my tentmates went, got one load of wood each. We have to bring it near half mile. But all of us can bring enough at once to do a day.

February 24, 1863

And fine day and I am on Brigade Guard. There is twelve Privates and only one Post in daytime and that is at the Guard house door to watch Prisnors, there being 9 of them. One of our Boys come in today, he being the first from our Regt this winter and it being the first Brigade Guard also from our Regt to my knowledge. It is a dreary job as only one can be gone at a time to meals &c and it is in a dreary place down over the hill from the camp. At night there is two posts, the other one being down at the Bakery a little further down the hill to keep the Boys from carrying off the dry wood. We now get soft Bread most evry day. They run the Bakery day & night. I got a loaf of good bread too when I stood there. One of the Boys from our Regt gave it me. I guess out of his own.

February 25, 1863

And fine morning. Expect to be relieved. But 9 oclock & 10 oclock came and no Relief. At last the Lieut went up and Behold they hadnt detailed any guard which they soon done from the 19th and it was about noon when they got there. The Boys thought they would have to go on Picket this morning but the order was countermanded so we fellows will have to go at last. But we wouldnt have to have gone this morning. But the third Brigade goes 4 days to the others two as theirs is the largest. So we will have to go on Friday morning I expect.

February 27, 1863

Went on Picket this morning. Fine weather but looked like rain. We reached the lines as usual in good time and our Co and Co B was assigned three Posts right where we struck the lines. The rest of the Brigade going on their Respective assigned them. We or our Reserve or at least our Co had a good place this time. We occupied an old cabin. The center of the floor having been torn out by others we had a good fire in it. It was a good I tell you for us fellows.

[Ed. Note: The last two pages have been partially torn out.]

. . . I must commence on my new book. I have just purchased one for 50 cts and I will bid this good bye until I return home if ever.

I missed one day as you will see but we were in camp.

This book was made a present to me. Quite a contrast in cost.

Volume 9

June 4, 1863 to August 7, 1863

Wounded at Gettysburg

[Ed. Note: Unfortunately, the volume covering March 1, 1863 through June 5, 1863, which included the Chancellorsville Campaign, is missing. According to Ray, he lost his diary while on picket duty.]

Wm R. Ray
Member of Co F, 7th Regt, Wis Volt
Resident of Cassville, Grant Co Wisconsin

1st Brigade, 1st Division, 1st Army Corps

Camp 4 miles Below Falmouth
Stafford County, Virginia

June 4, 1863

Just returned from Picket and I have had a bad misfortune. I lost my diary while on Picket and couldnt find it. I offered $5.00 reward to the man that would return it safely to me. Time will tell whether I find it or not. I must go back to the first of June.[88]

1st [June 1863] Fine day. We had Co drill in forenoon and in the afternoon we signed the clothing book for things that we got since signing last time. Nothing else of consequence.

2nd [June 1863] And go on Picket at 8 AM. We went on the left of our Divisions line and the 19th took the right where we went the last time. There not being enough Privates for the last Post so 7 or 8 of us noncommissioned officers stood 24 hours. It was near a large house, in fact in the large dooryard. It was a lovely Place and a large fine house, verry much so. I was on Post at a gate near the house and at night had to keep a close watch to see that there was no signals given. Evrything passed of well. The rebs come over bringing some papers and I traded one of mine with them. I got the Dispatch and some of our boys went over. One fellow out of Co K went over alone right among some 20 that were on the flank. He traded some things with them, I don't know what. They want coffee evrytime & for evrything. Two of Gen Wadsworths [James Wadsworth] aids [aides] came down just as he got over there and two of the Rebs come over landing right where the aids sit on the bank. They come out & shook hands with the Boys and we were as brothers as you might say. They to brought tobacco to trade for coffee. We chatted awhile, officers & all togather pell-mell. Then we were ordered back by our officers. Some of the Boys wanted to trade but hated to or feared to before the officers so they asked. The aids consented to it so they got some coffee. The aids was looking for Papers & found a couple at our Post. They found out there was three come over and they coaxed the Sergeants & then the Privates and all. But he couldnt find the third Paper which I had. And the Boys wouldnt tell. But when our man come back, they looked through their glasses at him which we found out afterwards was to know them when they saw them so as to arrest him when he got back. But we fixed it up so that we completely foiled them. They couldnt make him out or find him. They give it up saying that we Wisconsin Boys was too much for them, they would give it up. Our sergt told them if we had a paper we knew enough to keep it too ourselves. They went away not much wiser than when they come.

3rd [June 1863] And fine day. But rained a verry little last night. When daylight came they began talking again but they were verry still last night. We were relieved this morning, 10 A.M. The aids made us another visit this morning but they could make nothing. They give it saying it was no use. We were old soldiers that we worked together like a machine. So I got through again without them getting the much coveted Paper from me.

Twas this evening that I first noticed my book being gone. That is the worst thing that has happened [to] me. I dislike that the worst of anything. I breaks into my book so I may have the good luck to get it yet. I am going around to find it. I have stuck up a notice that I would give $5 reward to the man that brought it to me.

4th [June 1863] And fine day. We were relieved about 9 oclock this morning by the 31st New Jersey. They come in heavy marching order saying that the division was waiting for us to come in, that we were going some place. The march order come about 12 last night and that all the tents were struck preparatory to start when we reached there. We started home somewhat vexed to think that we had to march without having any rest. But I had a good nights rest as we were on the grand guard. When we got in sight we saw to our surprise that they were pitching tents again. And when we reached camp, the order was countermanded and glad were we. It is that only our [First Army] corps had such orders & that we were going into Maryland to relieve the 8th Corps and they were coming to take our place. They have been recruited up full and our corp was going there for that purpose, they being the smallest in the army. But no such good luck. That would be rather to much of a retired place for us. Oh no, we cant go. They cant do, it appears, without us. We had dress parade at usual time. I got the first number of the Madison Journal I signed for 8 or 10 days since.[89]

June 5, 1863

And fine day. We had Co drill in morning. We drill good. Lieut Sloat understands it well. We had Battalion drill in afternoon. Major Finnecum drilled us. He understands it well. The best drillmaster in the Regt. Went through a series of moves. Marched Battallion in line considerable. We have got so that we can march with a straight front. Straight as a beeline, especially when he has command. Drill over, had dress parade. Just at night we were ordered to be ready to march at 3 oclock in the morning. 3 days rations in haversack. Take evrything along. Many rumors. The general belief is to cross the river. It is said the 6th Corps is across the river. They crossed in the afternoon and took 500 prisinors with considerable loss to themselves. But how true it is time will tell. The camps that we could see has disappeared and it is generally believed the rebs have fell back towards Richmond.[90]

June 6, 1863

And fine day. Still hold ourselves in readiness to march. But night coming and with it the order to be ready to march in the morning at 3 oclock with 3 days rations. Our Regt only having such orders. Great speculation where we are going. Our forces are across the river opposite and above us. And it is said 2 divisions are across. But all we know is that we or some of our forces are across and we hear an occasional cannon fire. Old Hooker [General Joseph Hooker] is going to keep them on the qui-vive it appears.

June 7, 1863

And fine day. We lay around awaiting orders to march and got them. So at last at 2 P.M. we got the order. So we packed up, formed line. Gen Wadsworth comes along to see us then we see the 56th Penn come out ready to accompany us. Then we started, went up to Corps Headquarters. There stoped an hour. They load lots of mules with ammunition, hospital stores &c preparatory for the worst events. We start. One Co of the 2nd [Wisconsin] sent for as guard to the mules &c. We travelled on & on resting about evry 3 miles. We went a verry crooked road & evry imaginable way keeping in hollows and behind woods so the rebels might not discover us. We crossed the R Road about 4 miles from Falmouth, come on, struck the Catlets road. It coming on dark we stoped, made coffee. I forgot to tell you of 1 Battery of light artillery accompanying us.

We start again & march on taking the usual rests. But march verry brisk. At last we reached our destination for today. Hartwood Church, 7 miles from Falmouth and it is 11 oclock. We lay down for the rest of the night, We have marched about 15 miles to get 13. So ended today and a hard one too. Verry tired are we. We now see that we are going to the right of the army for some purpose. Some say one thing some say another. We were lucky having good water all the time and I had some lemons and I put some in my canteen having lemonade all the time. It went well here. We found out also that we are to be joined by more troops. We hear Hooker has some troops on the other side of the river yet. There is lots of troops all around here. So there is no general move.

June 8, 1863

And fine day. We got breakfast, started at 6 oclock, turned to the left leaving the Catlets road. We go up and towards the river resting evry 3 or 4 miles. Our Regt goes ahead today. When we started this morning another Regt joined us from the 6th Corps. We marched till about noon on this road then turned on another going toward the river. We went on some 3 miles, stoped within about 1 mile of the river. Here we stoped for dinner near a good spring. We had a scarcity of water today. Here it was said we were to cross. We lay about 2 hours. There is considerable troops here and we have passed troops all along today. Havnt got out of the army yet. There we are ordered to march around to the rear of some woods there to stay till further orders. So we stayed. When night come on, got coffee, put out fires for we were only about 1 mile from the river. We lay down. We marched hard today. We are to cross here it is said.

June 9, 1863 [Battle of Brandy Station, Virginia]

And fine day. We were awoke at break of day this morning to draw 3 days more rations & get ready to march at a minutes notice. Daylight comes & we build fires. Hark, there is Picket firing. There was a regt went by before we got up going to the river. There was not more than a dozen shots fired. We get Breakfast. News comes that our men is on the other side of the river. Our cavelry is going down & several batteries. 7 A.M. We start, go down to the River. The Infantry are crossing & there is several thousand cavelry formed waiting for us to get across and more coming. We have to wade the river, it being about 2 ½ feet deep in the deepest place. Some takes off shoes & socks, some roll up pants only. Most of them wade in just as they are, hollowing & yelling &c. We get across. Being the last regt today so we were the last infantry to cross.

Go ¼ mile, come to the little town consisting of a large mill not running and store. But nothing of value in it. Some two or three old ledgers showing that there had been considerable buisness done. One paper was found stating that he, Kelly, had entered suit in the circuit court against a man to the amount of $7,000.00 and evrything around showed that there had been great buisness done there before the war broke out. There was the mansion and a number of small buildings. The latter I suppose for the hirelings and negros. The mill was started, I suppose, for the purpose of spoiling the stones by letting them run togather. Well, we lay here till the cavelry went by, probably 3000 of them. They turned square into the country.

We started, went up the road running up the river. Went 1 mile, stoped for 2 hours. While we were stoped they run out scouts & skirmishers &c to feel for the rebs for we are going right toward where they were fighting all day today. And where we heard cannonading all day yesterday. But now we can hear occasional shots of small arms. We get up, start and march verry fast for probably 4 miles then stop. Can hear one shot, from our piece, we suppose. We can see our cavelry charge in among a few houses off a mile or so to the left of us.

We start again, go a mile or so and form line of battle. And we see away to the south our cavelry going along in same direction we [are]. Here the men that was detailed to go after water come up. We had carried their things along and then they come without water, we having no chance to get any since leaving the river. We can see our & the Rebel cavelry charging. Cavelry & artillery being all that is engaged. We right face, start again in towards the enemy. We cross the R.Road. I judged about 3 miles from Brandy station, this being the place we were to take, I understand. But our calvery couldnt hold it. They took it but the rebs charged on them with a superior force, strongly supported by Infantry which come on the cars just as our men got there. When our cavelry charged, the Rebs run the train back a ways. We went into an open field about 1 mile from the engagement, laid down here. Details was sent after water but returned with only a little muddy stuff.

After laying there a little while, we went back to where we stoped before. There we went behind the woods. And details for water again. We lay there about an hour, then ordered over to near the river about 2 miles off. We went out through the field again. But this time we could see no fighting, there being a lull. We have to carry the knappsacks of the men after water. We got over and formed behind a stone wall, the Battery in front on the hill. Here we see some sign of retreat. Cavelry goes out and others come in. We see several dead & wounded come in. We lay here about half an hour then ordered to cross the River and take a strong position. We started, got nearly to the river and ordered Back to support a Battery that was posted on the hill a little way from the river. We can hear an occasional shot of small fire arms. We lay here about half hour. The rebs fire several shots at us but do no damage. The rebs keep firing rapidly with one gun, that being about all they have used today in the way of artillery.

We are ordered across the river. We start, get down to the river the battery following us. We being hard up for water all day and as quick as the Boys steped into the river, they stoped to get a drink & fill their canteens. But an officer on the bank commenced yelling for us to go on but the boys didnt pay much attention to him. This ford is deeper than the one we crossed this morning. It being about 7 miles below here. We went up into the woods about ¾ of a mile, stoped. Evry one of our troops will soon be over. There is lots of cavelry. There is still skirmishing and occasional shot fired. We lay in the woods till night which wasnt long coming and we being wet up to the waist we were chilly. Then we started down the river. Good road. We travel down to Rappahannock Station some four miles I should judge. There camped, it being 10 P.M. This was a hard day. Crossed the river, traveled most of the day & without water or stoping to get anything to eat and expecting to get into a fight any minute. There is many things that I could write but time & space will not admit of it. It is said we accomplished the thing we went for.[91]

June 10, 1863

And fine morning. We got up at 6 oclock & started without breakfast to go only 1 mile. We went right up the [Orange and Alexandria] railroad and camped till further orders which didnt come today. We had good dry rails for fire & we cooked & eat & slept. It is a nice shady place not verry good water though but plenty. There was a great many, I guess most all the cavelry went by today. There was four rebel flags went by, four different regts carrying them. They being tied on their flag staffs below their flags showing those regts captured them. This shows that our forces done something. The rumor is that we took 400 Prisinors.

June 11, 1863

And fine day. Sprinkled rain a little just at dark. At half past 6 oclock we moved. Go up the railroad still till reaching Bersley Station [Bealeton Station] about 2 miles travel this morning. Here we rested some 2 hours. All or most of the infantry come up consisting of some 2000 men in all. The cars run to this station bringing supplies of forage & rations. They took the wounded on the cars here. We turn to the right on the main road to Falmouth. We rather thought we were going back to camp. But after going 1 mile we turned into the woods and camped. A good shady place. Water scarce and bad. We were told to fix up comfortable as we might stay here two or three days. So Tommy & I made a shelter of our oilcloths, got good lot of leaves for bed. We have a scarcity of meat having none today and being so much exposed we eat all we can get. But lucky for us, Tommy found some where some troops were camped.

We got orders about 5 P.M. to get ready to go on picket. Our Co & Co H & dozen men from Co B. We got ready to start & behold there was 4 men absent without leave. Sergt Boyanton & Corporal Schloesser were among them. But they come in soon after we formed. There was about a hundred men from each regt, our Major Finnecum having command. We came down the R.R. to where we left camp in the morning. There we waited till dark which soon come. Then we marched down to the river where the RR Bridge is. There we find a section of artillery. Here we find that we are here to keep the rebs from crossing if they should try it. Our Co was taken and sliped into the rifle pits. Also were others from other Regts. Then we lay down taking out our Blankets, evry man laying down in his tracks. Sentinels were put in front to give the alarm if anything transpired. But when we got back to the station as we come down, we drew 3 days rations consisting of crackers & pork, sugar & coffee. We got verry nice pork, verry.

June 12, 1863

And fine day. We lay around all day a few rods back of the Rifle pits. There being about 1,000 men in all. But last night there was only 2 or 3 Co in the pits. There was 2 men came over with a flag of truce on Pretence of seeing after two or three wounded officers. The guard at the bridge didnt take them under his care as he should have done but let them come on. I guess he, the sentinel, was a recruit. Fortunately an officer seen them and stoped them ere they got up the bank so as to see what force &c we had. He sent them back verry soon without the expected information.

Just at dark a part of the 3d corps come up and relieved us. There was a division. I suppose they calculate to stay awhile some say. Probably, some say, most of the army is coming up the river. We went back to camp reaching it about 10 oclock, found the Regt &c just when we left the evening before. The cars are coming in fast bringing supplies. We now see that this will be made a base of operations of a part or all of the army.

It looked like rain again this evening as it has for several evenings past but don't come.

June 13, 1863

And fine day but warm. We lay in camp till 2 P.M. when Gen Wadsworth come into camp & ordered us to march. Our corps is coming up by here. There has been a number of troops going by today. The report is that the whole army is coming this [way]. We went up by the station and on some 3 miles and camped it being about 6 P.M. Just before dark our Regt teams come up bringing our baggage that was left in the old camp. I got all my things but my tin pail, coffee pail. So did the Boys but some few little things. Captain [Henry Young] come up with the train as also did several of our Boys who were left in camp. We have plenty of good water here. I was glad, verry glad to see Cap come back. He brought good news from home. Mother is well. Cap says he never seen her look so well as she does. All the relatives were well & doing well as far as he knew. We got the mail this evening, the first for a week. I got a letter from Henry and all is well.

June 14, 1863

And fine day. We started this morning. Came to Warrenton Junction, traveled verry slow. We are front guard today of our corps. From here we come to Catlets Station. From here we come to Manassas Junction. We stoped at Kettle Run 7 miles back just at dark, just after dark to make coffee. We traveled verry slow making about 20 miles in 22 hours. We started at 6 A.M., traveled today & all night. It is said we have to report at Alexander tomorrow night. 3 corps do. This has been a hard day. But we knew the road well as we had traveled it last summer, some of it 3 times over.

June 15, 1863

And fine day. We wish for rain so as to lay the dust which is almost intolerable. We traveled all night, stopping at Manassas Junction this morning little after sunrise. Here we stack arms, make coffee. The Boys think that we will have another Battle on the old Bullrun [Bull Run] Battlefield as the rumor is that the rebs is trying on the same thing they did last year. But they havent got in our rear, that we know. I cant make out what is up unless the rebs is attacking us in superior force. And we have to fall back. We lay here till ten oclock when we started for Centerville which we reached just night. Distance 6 miles, slow traveling. We were rear guard today. Had a great deal of truble with the stragglers. We got to Bullrun Creek where we had coffee. Here we got some pretty good water. It is verry hot today. We stoped here about 2 hours. There were a lot of rebel earth works here that were made by them in 61 which interested the boys considerable. They were verry well made. The Boys huddled togather under the trees to cool off, they being verry warm. We start & cross the creek which is rather small and coming along verry slow. We have skirmishers out on each flank to pick up and start up the Boys that give out and crawl under some shade trees or another. And I imagine many fall behind to get taken prisinor so as to get out of soldiering for some 2 or 3 months &c. But we didnt leave many. Our officers got off their horses and let the worst ones ride.

The rumor is that [General John A.] Dix is coming on to Richmond by way of the Peninsula. And it is even asserted that he has Richmond. Time will tell what this move means. The Army is still in good spirits, seem to think that we may have a fight soon and I cant help but think it myself.

We come on slowly passing a number of graves which were made in the 2 Battles [of Bull Run]. We passed the house where I first had my wound dressed, 29th of last August. It then being used for division hospital. At last we reach Centerville, go inside the old rebel Brestworks and camp verry tired. Here we get good water.

We, our Regt, stands it well to what the others do for we got well broke in before they come to us. I went down to the creek, took good wash, put on a clean shirt which I bought from one of the Boys for 50 cents. It is a good shirt but he was about to throw it away and I hadnt changed since last Sunday week and both my shirts was dirty and hard worn. I think I shall take one to patch the other. I drew a new pair of shoes yesterday. My feet are nearly on the ground. But as long as it is dry weather I will not attempt to break the new ones while on the march as I wear the old ones in preference for the new ones would make my feet sore.

I was grossly insulted & abused this morning by Corporal Schloesser [John J. Schlosser]. He is a german & he done it without the slitest provication. But he is a large heavy man. I guess he thought he would scare me & he couldnt. He at last gave me a slight kick. I treated him well. Kept my anger down, knowing I would have him foul if I had a mind to arrest him and courtmartialed. He put up his tent on my gun and I wanted to use it for that purpose myself to make a shade and had no buisness about the ranks for he is color corporal. He was intruding on others besides me. We got started, one word brought on another. He talked verry harsh while I laughed and spoke kindly which enraged him so that he kicked me. I got what I wanted. This happened this morning and tonight I spoke to Cap about and got good satisfaction. He is going to attend to the gentleman right off. Cap said I done just right and for me to not let him run over me and if he ever abused me again to report to him and he would reduce him the ranks for it. Said I must not let him run over me. When I told all about it, he said I had ought to have knocked him down with a club, stone or anything.

June 16, 1863

And fine day. Don't it beat all how the dry weather holds on. I had a good nights rest. We get no orders to march as yet. About 10 A.M. we get orders to clean up for inspection tomorrow morning at 8 A.M. and evry man is to have on a clean shirt so the boys got their clothes washed up. But it couldnt be helped, our being dirty for we have had no time to wash up. We lay here all day. The sutlers to the different Regt come in today bringing a load of stuff which they quickly sold. Just at night they were ordered to Washington for we are to move in the morning early. There was some excitement in camp in consequence of the daily paper bringing reliable news of the rebs whiping our forces at Winchester under command of Milroy. The [rebs] surrounded him & he cut his way out with the loss of 2,000 killed, wounded & taken prisinor. Milroy's force was 18,000 strong. He fell back to Harpers Ferry and the rebs went into Maryland and on up to Pennsylvania plundering and destroying.[92]

The Govenors of the states bordering Penn and the govenor of Penn also call for men to repel the invaders. Great excitement throughout the north. The Regts of men that have went home volunteer to help repel the invaders. We now begin to see the intentions or partly so of our generals. They are going to keep a force between

Washington & rebs and harass them with a part of the rest. The report is that there is 30,000 rebs gone up there which I don't doubt. The rumor is Gen Dix of the Peninsula is coming up on transports with a part of his command. But this I doubt.

This place, Centerville, is occupied & fortified by our forces. This has been going on all summer. Since coming here, Cap has quartered with Tommy & I. His tent not coming up.

June 17, 1863

And fine day. But verry warm. Revilee was beat at 3 oclock this morning. Had roll call, got breakfast, packed up ready to start. Waited long time. At last at sunrise we start coming the much noted but small dirty looking village of Centerville. But when coming to the Alexandria turnpike, contrary to our expectations, we come right across it instead of turning on it. We took the Leesburg road, coming on at a good speed for some 4 miles when we rested, then come on 2 miles, rested again and so on. We come to a creek when we took a rest of about an hour. Those that chose made coffee. Tommy & I made tea as I have about ¼ pound for to have some on such occasions. When tired & weary, it tastes good. Then we started, come probably 2 miles when we were ordered to halt & countermarch which we done, causing some scolding & jokes. This thing & that was talked about to numerous to mention & numerous rumors about the enemy but we know nothing. Only that we come back keeping straight east. We come by the road. We went on as the road forked. This was unexpected. Then as a matter of course, the boys had some new speculations and Jake & I said I guessed the reason that we didnt go on was that the enemy was there.

We marched verry fast, verry and oh, how the sun poured down. Look either side the road, there you would see the boys laying, given out. Perhaps one faining a sunstruck man and others you would see pouring water on their heads & the Doctors constantly writing Passes or attending some sunstruck fellow. We march verry fast. The heat and dust is awful.

Present we pass Cap Richards (Gen Aid de camp) He tell us to not march so fast as it was no use & that we were going on three miles where we would find plenty of good water. And we should camp for the night. At this the Boys cheered up hollowing Bully for you &c. And we had a lively time, seemed to forget for the time that we were marching. We halt, rest some 20 minutes that being the time genrally. We go slower, resting often. At last after coming 2 miles on the road, we turn off to the left through fields, cross the Alexandria & Leesburg R.Road. But it is torn up, the trees burned, the rails carried off. We come about a mile through nice meadows and camp near good water in a large meadow. We come, it is said, twelve miles today. We had plenty of good water along the road today & came through pretty country and it is pretty here too. We reached here about 3 P.M. Some pitched tents temporary & some slept as usual in the open vis the weather being so fair. But I think we will soon have rain.

The paper of today bring bad news about the rebs in Maryland & Penn. Some of them were within 16 miles of Harrisburg. The people are responding to the govenors call as well as the Presidents.[93]

June 18, 1863

And fine, verry warm till about 3 P.M. an awful storm came up. Not much rain at but such a hurricane I never seen in Virginia. It blew tends down, scattered things Pell Mell for 15 or 20 minutes at the end of which there was a calm and rained quite a shower, then stoped long enough for me to get an early supper when another and showered till dark when it sett in as I thought for an all nights rain. But didnt rain much at last. We have no orders to move & stay here all day. Get a good rest. Ordered to clean up for Inspection at 8 A.M. tomorrow morning. We got ready.

The 6th [Wisconsin] Regt is out on Picket today. The rumor is that our forces had a fight at Snickers gap yesterday and whipped the rebs bad but this is only a rumor. We get no papers today. No mail since the night the Brigade joined us.

June 19, 1863

And a fine day. No rain but cloudy. We march at ten A.M. Come four miles, camped in a large field but not verry good water but plenty. We got orders to camp. It rained a little towards night. We get no papers today.

June 20, 1863

And fine day. Lay in camp all day. Quite contrary to expectation as we got up & fixed for marching by daylight but didnt go. We get orders to fix up for inspection tomorrow at 10 A.M. We get no paper. But many rumors what this corps done & that one done &c. But we know nothing.

General [Solomon] Meredith returned to the Brigade yesterday to the great Joy to all. We lay right by the side of the Alexandria & Leesburg R Road.

June 21, 1863

And fine day, cloudy. We had no inspection but got ready to march at an early hour. But no go. So about 10 A.M. our Regt was called on to furnish 100 men for Division guard & our Captain with them.

June 22, 1863

And fine day, cloudy. Our Boys were relieved from Division guard by the 6th [Wisconsin]. I was not on it but my tentmate. So I went in with Runnian [John Runion] for last night. We are ordered to clean up for Regt Inspection by tomorrow 3 P.M. We had dress parade & there we had an order read to us confirming the rumor that our cavelry had a fight yesterday at Ashbys Gap, whipping the Rebels, killing, wounding & taking Prisinor a number of the enemy. Took 3 Cassions, blew up one, took 2 guns, one a Blakesly gun. Our Cavelry behaved splendid making many charges and coming so close a number of times as to use the sabre freely. And at night had driven the enemy 5 miles from where they first attacked them. Our forces being the attacking party. Gen Pleasanton [Alfred A. Pleasonton] having command of the Cavelry forces, Gen [George] Stoneman having been relieved.[94]

June 23, 1863

And fine day. We clean up for inspection which came off at the time set. Inspected by Cap Ricardson [Hollon Richardson], Aid of Gen Meredith. He said our Co was rather better than any in the Regt. We had Dress parade at usual time. Several courtmartials were read. The charges in one of the cases was the expression of Disloyal sentiments. His sentence was hard but the general remitted all of it as he had always been a brave good soldier, never flinched from Duty and the Gen thought that he said it in a fit of excitement as his conduct had proved him to be anything but Disloyal. We are expecting to move evry hour in the day. I finished writing a letter to Mother & Henry. I have received since coming to this camp 2 papers & 2 letters, one each from Henry & Mother.

Co C and Co I of our Regt are out on some kind of duty. It is said they are guarding the Engineers who are building a Bridge across Goose Creek. We made out or our Cap did to get a paper today & the Rebs are rather fading back a little in Penn. And fortifying at Hagerstown, Maryland. And they seem to be less Bold and they appear to fear something in all quarters.

June 24, 1863

And fine day. We lay in camp all day. Tommy & I earned $1.70 cts today washing. We done washing for the officers. They wanted us to do it as we are the best of any of the Boys. We had Dress parade. We expect to march early in the morning.

June 25, 1863

And fine day till just night when it rained some. We were awok at just daybreak to get ready to march which we done. And about 6 A.M. the order was countermanded & we put up tents & about 10 A.M. ordered to get ready & march which we done. Come to Edwards Ferry. There the Pontoons were laid. We crossed. Here they are using the Canal bringing stuff for the army hereabouts which is not large. We come on some 4 miles, stoped, got dinner, traveled on resting as usual. Pretty warm. We come to Poolsville, a nice little town. We come through to another little town called Banesville and turned off the road a little & camped, it being just dark. It rains considerable now and for half hour past. We have to Pitch into the fence for wood, get supper with. U. Sam will have pay it. We have come, I should judge,

16 miles to. The rumor is that the rebs have crossed their whole army into Maryland & Penn., 80,000 strong.[95]

June 26, 1863

And rainy all day & rained most all night. We slept dry. We got up before day & got ready to march at daylight. But we didnt get started. 7 A.M. and kept raining. We come back through the town and took the Frederick City road and come on without stopping to rest till near noon when we stopped. Made coffee. Has rained steady most all the fornoon. We crossed the Manacca River just for making coffee here. There is a little village I suppose by the same name as the River. The Boys are short of rations. Have all that is allowed them but when marching we eat more especially this march as we don't get any vegatable food except the Bread. Our living consists of Bread, meat, sugar & coffee. When we stoped, Tommy went out to a house & got a couple loaves of Bread which we soon devoured. We get them for less than half what we could in Virginia. And it is so with most evrything.

We start, come on some 4 miles to within ¼ mile of Jeffersonville and camped in a clover field in rear of a fence & nice creek & good spring not far distant. The fence was soon torn down to make tent fixtures & fire, there being no wood near. We don't find so much timber in Maryland as in Virginia although this is a timbered country. But the farmers take most of the ground as it is thickly settled with enterprising farmers. Good houses, bad & good fences & good road to travel on in places, looks as if they had been working out pole taxes. We have to go into fields to camp now & I guess U.S. will have to pay the damages as they are a loyal people judging from the stars & stripes displayed in evry village, hamlet and many farm houses by the roadside. Evry place we are greeted with smiling faces from both sexes especially the fair sex which almost invariably have a flag in hand. We have seen many fair maids, verry many, some as good looking as ever the sun shone on. A striking contrast with Virginia for there passing through a village you would see a lot of negros half clad, looking out the doors and through the broken window panes. I look on those with sorrow & awe instead of admiration. There is many negros in Maryland but they are well clad & at work with their masters appearantly well satisfied with their Position. They don't come clambering over fences & following us as in many cases in Virginia.

June 27, 1863

And we march at 7 A.M., come through Jeffersonville & on to Middletown where we camped. It has rained a few showers today & is still showery. We are camped within 2 miles of the South Mountain Battlefield and opposite the gap our Brigade took and held for which Gen McLellen complimented us verry highly.[96]

June 28, 1863

And fine day till towards night when there was showers. This being Sunday and we lay in camp most of the day. So we had Inspection of arms. One of our Boys that was in this town in the hospital all last winter and was well acquainted got a pass and went in, brought out a lot of necessaries for the Boys such as tobacco. Well we begin to think we may stay here a few days when the order come to march immediately which we done. It being about 3 P.M. we start & come out on the Road back a ways when we turned through by roads & across fields &c. But always traveling so as to make no more damage than we could possibly help. We came to within 1 mile of Frederick City & camped just at dark in clover field as usual here. They brought some wood so that saved the fences.

Here the news is that we have to go to Gettysburg some 35 miles. And the rumor that Gen Hooker has been relieved from command & Gen Mead [General George Gordon Meade] is in command.[97]

June 29, 1863

And rained most of the day but verry steady. We started at 7 A.M., come verry fast, not resting much till we come 13 miles. Good when we stoped, made coffee, it being about noon. When we started, traveled Jehove like coming through Mechanicsville as all other town being verry Patriotic. Traveled on through rain & mud. But it is not bad traveling as we are on the turnpike as far as mud is concerned

for the mud is so thin that is not much truble to get through. At last we come to Emmettsburg a nice & patriotic Place. We go through the town & 1 mile & camp. That is the Brigade made camp but we go 1 mile farther on Picket and we stop for the night. And after throwing out a few outposts & we got supper, spread blanket, went to bed having come some 27 miles today so we think. &

Iron Brigade commander General Solomon Meredith oversaw a stout defensive engagement at Gettysburg on July 1, 1863, that may have saved the Army of the Potomac. *Alan Gaff Collection*

William R. Ray. Although Ray wrote on the back of this photo that he sat for it in the spring of 1863 (just before Gettysburg), the "W.V.V." on his hat, which means Wisconsin Veteran Volunteers, dates it after January 1864. *Sherry Murphy*

I guess that we think just about right to. The Colonel [Callis] spoke a few words of encouragement to us and said we might sleep but we must be ready at a seconds notice to meet the enemy if attacked. They say it is only 7 miles to the enemy.

June 30, 1863

And we marched at 8 oclock this morning. It is said we go 5 miles & camp & get rations. But we come only about 3 miles, turned into a piece of wood in a field. Here we lay the rest of the day. I was detailed with three men to go to a house as safeguard

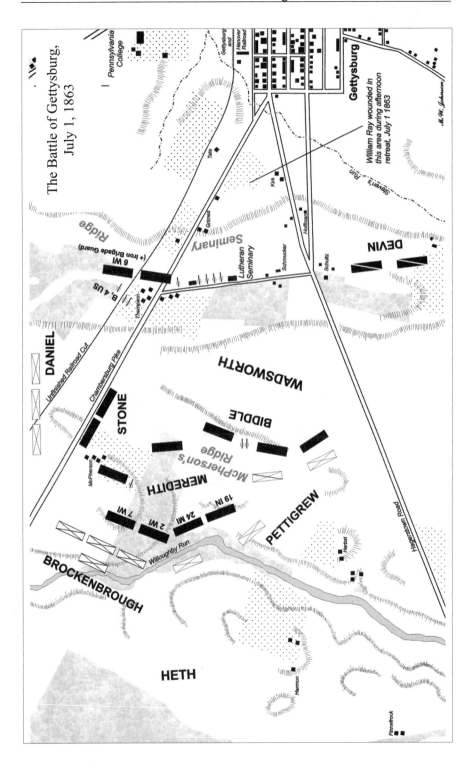

The Battle of Gettysburg,
July 1, 1863

Pennsylvania College

Gettysburg

William Ray wounded in
this area during afternoon
retreat, July 1 1863

M. W. Johnson

Steven's Run

Gettysburg and
Hanover Railroad

Tate

Kirk

Grimes

Hoffmann

Schmucker

Schultz

DEVIN

Ridge

Seminary

Lutheran
Seminary

Ridge (+ Iron Brigade Guard)
6 WI

B, 4 US

Thompson

DANIEL

Unfinished Railroad Cut

Chambersburg Pike

WADSWORTH

STONE

McPherson

BIDDLE

McPherson's
Ridge

MEREDITH

19 IN

24 MI

2 WI

7 WI

PETTIGREW

Herbst

Hagerstown Road

Willoughby Run

BROCKENBROUGH

HETH

Harmon

Forneck

where we got a good supper & some milk for which we paid 25 cts a piece. Just at dark orders came to march at 3 oclock in the morning.[98]

July 1, 1863 [First Day, Battle of Gettysburg]

And still rainy as it was all night. We didnt march till about 9 A.M. We went towards Gettysburg. After going some 4 miles we turned off into a field.[99] Cannonading begins. Soon our cannons reply. We get up near & see the cavelry supporting the Batteries. Went on a little farther. Halt, get dressed up in line of Battle. Go forward. Our skirmishers begin to fire. Soon we see the top of a rebel flag. We still advance. As soon as a man sees a reb he shoots. We fix Bayonet still going on. Pass right over their dead and wounded, they being in a hollow. We went on to the other hill topp. We took some prisinors.[100]

We then fell back from where we first started & the right of the Brigade swung around across a Big hollow and Bringing us & the 2nd Regt on top of the hill. All this time cannonading was kept up. We lay down. Lay there till about 3 P.M. when the Rebs advanced on our left, the left of the Brigade, also the left of the line of Battle. They flanked us. We had to fall back & they kept flanking us & we kept falling back till we got behind a Brestwork made of rails. It being only 2 ½ feet high so we got behind it and just mowed the rebs, all in front of our Regt was just mowed down. But their line being the longer they kept swinging around the end and getting a crossfire on us. We had to abandon that Place. Battery B [Fourth U.S. Artillery] was just in the rear of us when we lay behind the Rails and evry gun poured in the grape which swept the rebs. But there being no Battery on the left to help the Boys so they couldnt hold up under double their number. We retreated through the town or the Regt did.[101]

I was hit about ¼ mile out of town by a Ball on the top of the head, come near knocking me down. But I straightened up, went on, another Ball hits sole of my shoe cutting it nearly in two, it only making my foot sting a little.[102]

I come into town with the Regt & soon found a hospital. But it was the 2nd Division. I went in, stayed 2 hours. Soon after getting in it was surrendered to the Rebs, they having got possession of the town. I started out, soon found our division hospital down amongst the warehouses & Railroad depots & with many others, here I got some supper and attended to my wound as all was busy attending on worse than mine. There was a little shelling this evening. Night comes on and we lay on our straw, some dying, some having their limbs amputated, others waiting. I will leave the reader to imagine for it would take to long to give the particulars. I threw away my knappsack when hit and lost my haversack so I lost both Bedding & food. But I can get along for that.[103]

July 2, 1863 [Second Day, Battle of Gettysburg]

Sharp skirmishing all the time and occasionally a canon fired till 3 P.M. when musketry begins and the canonading which had been incessant for an hour now

This image looks west down the Chambersburg Pike from the western fringes of the town of Gettysburg. In the left distance is the Lutheran Seminary, near which the Iron Brigade made its last stand on the afternoon of July 1, 1863. William Ray fell wounded on the slope below the seminary. *National Archives*

ceased except when the Rebs would charge on our pieces and try to take them. The Battle raged til 10 oclock at night resulting in a complete victory to our arms for this day.[104]

Our men were so near the town ever since they took position that many bullets come to the Hospital which is on the opposite side of the town from them. There was many of their Soldiers laying around town till the fight begun when the officers come around. I suppose their provost guard and drove evryone out towards the Battlefield. Quite different to our officers who have always neglected that part till the last 2 Battles when they done the same thing. That thing of leaving the stragglers out of the fight has played out. The stragglers was what helped to defeat us at 2nd Bullrun Battle. For there the officers didnt look up those cowards and nearly half the army was stragglers. We couldnt tell whether we were defeated or not. But we knew from the sound that we were not driven much. Lots of wounded secesh going back. They don't say much, seem mum. That tells me that they were not victorious.

July 3, 1863 [Third Day, Battle of Gettysburg]

And sharp skirmishing all day till about 4 P.M. when musketry begins & cannonading ceases, it having been going on for an hour awfully. The musketry is awful for about an hour, terrible. Wounded secesh go to the rear in great numbers. Our line seems to be in the same place as last night. The secesh soldiers don't say much but think they will whip us. I told them that things will take a turn in a few days. They thought they would be in Harrisburg. But late tonight they let or their Gen [John B.] Gordon let our Doctors have his ambulances go bring some of our wounded of the first days Battlefield and they brought in a number of loads. Several of our Regt came in. But none of our Co. Poor fellows, I have often thought of them.[105]

They look bad, having nothing to eat or drink since wounded and some were wounded early on the first. Today we got as much as we wanted to eat for the first day since wounded. Many of the People left the town and took evrything with them. And others houses, the rebs entered taking evrything eatable & valuable and what few was left were either afraid or couldnt furnish anything. But there were a few that did bring [food]. They done well by us considering how they were surrounded.

The weather has been showers & sunshine & cloudy intermixed ever since the Battle begun till last night when we had hard rain. We all know that the rebs havnt broke our lines and the general impression [is] that they will retreat.

July 4, 1863 [Confederate Retreat from Gettysburg]

And rather stormy, rained hard last night. Well, I awoke this morning, found the streets deserted. All the Rebs gone someplace, ambulances, wagons & all. Then comes a Reb cavelry at great speed down the street saying at the top of his voice, keep in your heads, your skirmishers are coming and as he said it, crack went a gun.

The Ball went whizing down the street after him. Then comes our cavelry men dashing down the streets & in a minute or two the infantry. Some of the 11 corps. They run in evry Battle. But now they appear verry Brave. They searched evry Barn & house taking a great many Prisinors right in the town. I guess nearly as many as they took of our Boys when they could.

We are ordered to go out of the town to our own hospital in the country, back in the Rear. So all that were able started with a glad heart. Those that couldnt walk, ambulances took. I soon started & as I came along the streets soon teemed with wounded that could walk. Many of them badly wounded but they scratch & hobbled along. After going about 1 ½ miles I come to the Regt & Co. Found only 19 men left with Cap as a commander still. The rebs didnt hit him. They all seemed as glad to see me as if I were their Brother and I assure you I was just as glad to see them.

Cor Alexander [Corporal George Alexander] went over to the right wing of the Battlefield with me. There were quite a number still on the top of the ground & some had been Buried. All the wounded had been taken care of. They killed verry few of our men for they didnt fire much. But charged up the hill to try to break our lines. That why I suppose they are short of ammunition for there were verry few Ball in the lower side of the trees. But quite different on the upper side for there they were literally skinned and the more smaller ones just cuts off with the Balls. Some trees 3 inches diameter had so many musket balls in them that they fell to the ground all a mass of splinters. I was about a mile along the lines but being fatigued I couldnt go farther so we turned back without seeing the worst place right in front of our division. They didnt attempt to come up as it was verry steep there and I guess that is the reason it was given to it. They thought the rebs wouldnt attack, thereby give our division & the corps as much rest as possible. I believe our corps was not engaged at all, none of it.

Well when I returned I had a few parting words with the Boys and their good wishes & went to our Brigade Hospital where I found a good place for a field Hospital. It being about 200 yards in rear of the Brigade and large rocks on each side. A natural protection from the enemies Balls. Quite a secure place. I found Dr. Spaulding [Ebenezer F. Spaulding of Janesville] of our Regt, he being the only doctor in the Brigade since the Retreat. He dressed my wound with his usual carefulness & feeling; he is a verry feeling man. When that done, got a cup of coffee, small piece of Bread, they having not drawn any rations since I left them.

I started for the Hospital, they said 1 ½ miles but I traveled on near 3 miles fore getting to our Division Hospital, passing a great many on the Road. Found a good many of our Boys at the different ones and a good many going the same as myself. I found Tommy, my tentmate. He was hit in the first of the engagement. Went on to what was called our Division Hospital. But found that as all the others to contain troops from the army just as it happened. But there being a scarcity of food and no shelter, the barn & house being full and after getting wet to the skin I concluded to go on towards the town where the cars come to and stop the first place I got a chance. It being 7 miles to the town I thought I would go there tonight rather than stop outdoor. But after going 4 miles and inquiring at many houses along the Road, we found a wealthy farmer. He gave us privilege to stay in the Barn and we coaxed a loaf of Bread off him for which paid 30 cts. There was 9 or 10 Wisconsin Boys stayed in the Barn. We messed togather. It is now just dark.

We met many stragglers going up to the front, also the teams to the different commands going up with rations which the Boys need. All the teams have been parked at Westminster some 18 miles from the front till morning when they come up with the necessaries for the army. At evry house we stopped at, they were eat out and most evry house there was officers of the lesser grade too. I saw no Generals at private houses. But it was many of the Lieuts who think they are a little god. But you can find fools in the army as well as elsewhere. This has been rather a dull fourth to me as well as a hard one.

July 5, 1863

And we get Breakfast and start to town which is three miles. It rained nearly all night and if I hadnt started off I would [have had a] hard night. But as it was I done first rate. This morning I got my Breakfast at a private house. Also a loaf of Bread for the other Boys. We soon reached the town. There the citizens had a place to receive the wounded & keep them till the cars took them off. They took us in and give us some niceties in the way of Bread & Butter & apple Butter & other choice things. Then the cars were going out in half an hour so we got on. They were now pretty well loaded. We start, come to Baltimore which we reached at just night. All along the road at evry station, we were treated to something good with the People crowding around us & praising & pitying the soldier. But when we got to suburbs of Baltimore there was People by the thousands to look & talk to us. We were Besieged all the time by them. When the engine left us and the horses were hitched on, the crowds followed along and the streets in evry place was wedged full of People with one [thing or] another to give to the poor wounded soldiers who had been fighting for them &c. When we got in the city however & stoped, the Union Leagues guarded us to keep the pressing crowd back. The greatest enthusiasm prevails. We were given supper in the cars & evrything that the city could get up was poked at us. At first it was welcome. But they kept pressing us to take till we were tired. They, not content with our eating & drinking, they filled our haversacks & jackets. Some of the Boys got wine, but I was not so lucky. Just as well of as if I had got it. After we would take no more they lets us get out of the cars. The guard now had to Point the Bayonet at crowd before we could get through. But we soon got out by being loaded down with things. Cigars & tobacco were freely given away to chewers & smokers, in fact anything could be got by a soldier. Well we were marched to the Wests buildings Hospital where we got our wounds dressed and went to bed with the order to be ready to go off on the cars at 5 in the morning. I thought I might get to Chester Hospital again as we most assuredly would go that way.

July 6, 1863

And rainy this morning. We got to the cars after getting Breakfast but it was eight oclock fore we started. We come to Philadelphia stopping at evry station except Chester & there we made no halt whatever. We reached Philadelphia 2 P.M. and there we were besieged by an immense crowd again for two hours when we got into ambulance, went to the cars, come up to Germantown Hospital 8 miles from Philadelphia. Here we were ushered into the hospital, our names registered and sent into the different wards. I was put in ward E, have the first bed in the ward. We soon had supper after which we, our wounds were dressed and we retired. I felt right at home here. Things are similar to Chester Hospital. I like the looks full as well. And think I shall like it in time to come.

July 7, 1863

And rainy like. I awoke at the Beat of the Drum feeling verry much refreshed. Had a good nights rest, got a good Breakfast, got wound dressed, Poultice on it, sit down and write a letter to Mother. There is only one nurse to this ward as yet. But as soon as some of the Boys get able, they will be detailed as nurses. The Hospital was empty when we come. The nurses and all that was able to when the Govenor called on the Militia of the state went. The hospital guard was sent away and cripples put on guard. We ate and slept today, being somewhat fatigued by our long ride.

July 8, 1863

And rainy today. We have our wounds well taken care of. The Doctors being verry attentive & kind. We have good food, plenty of it. When there is not enough for you on the Plate, you call for more and it comes right off. The cooking is done excellent. Being done by females instead of males as at Chester. The coffee & tea is splendid, just as I used to get it at home. Females are employed at this Hospital for most work or all that comes in that a woman can do. Today passes quietly as it could. No other nurse. There is two Doctors for three wards and each one has half our ward. I wrote a letter to Captain today so as to let him know where I was so that if he chose, he might send my Discriptive list right along and through him, hear about the Regt & how many the Company will muster now. I am anxious to know.

July 9, 1863

And cloudy like till evening when we had a hard shower. I wrote a letter to Mary Jane today. The mail goes out twice a day. We draw paper evry day, 1 sheet, 1 envelope to a man from the contribution drawer which the chaplain has charge of.

We have to go to his office for it. The envelopes are franked by him so it costs us nothing to write home. We get some niceties evry day so far, they being contributed. We have a good kind wardmaster. He attends well to his duties.

July 10, 1863

And fine day till 6 P.M. when we had a hard shower. I wrote a letter to Richard Landar today in answer to one I received some 2 weeks since. My head is doing well. Has turned out to be a worse wound than was at first supposed. I washed my pants today preparatory to going out on a pass, there being a few issued today to those having pretty good clothing as we can get no new ones. I shall fix up my old ones. They are badly worn.

Nothing worthy of note transpired today. We have cheering news in the paper from the different armies in the field. The Army of Potomac is pressing Lee, & Rosencranz [Union General William Rosecrans] whipped [Confederate General Braxton] Bragg before Chattanooga, Tennessee & Vicsburg [Vicksburg, Mississippi] was surrendered to [Union General Ulysses S.] Grant on the 4th of July unconditionally with all things there with consisting of many guns & 21,000 Prisinors. History will chronicle it as the greatest event of the war. May success attend our Arms till we have none to oppose.[106]

July 11, 1863

And fine day, nothing transpired of note. I worked some today. Helped the nurses scrub the floor for exercise as I can get none otherwise. There is from 4 to 8 passes given each day but I concluded to wait a while before I applied [so] as to be sure to get one. My wound is doing well, it is properly dressed twice a day. Things goes on well. I was to church last night. The minister is Episcopalion, read his sermon which made it rather dull for me at least. It was a good discourse, well put togather but it doesnt sound right. He might Preach an age and it would have no other effect that to weary the audiance. We can get Paper evry day except Sunday. From 3 to 4 P.M. I wrote a letter to Sister Thurza-Ann today.

July 12, 1863

And fine day, this being the sabbath & the church bells are ringing in evry direction showing that the sabbath is much respected in this place. Many of the Boys that got passes come drunk & disorderly and I think I may say with truth that evry man in the ward got a drink or more by those that went out bringing it in, although it is strictly prohibited. There is some quite drunk. There is 2 Wis Boys in the Guardhouse now.

My God, when will sin cease. As long as our army is so wicked, we will never whip the rebs. God will not take the yoke from our necks although they be chafed. Me thinks sometimes that this war may last 10 years. Some say if we capture Lees army that will settle it. But I think not for the almighty is not Respected enough. Why, I have seen some as wicked acts as ever the Roman were guilty. Me thinks I can see the Downfall of the great Republic. Excuse for expressing such sentiments for I don't mean disloyalty but refer you to ancient History. For instance, Rome had just such insurrections as this we are engaged in and you there see things that has transpired similar to those transpiring in this Rebellion. & on account of their wickedness they were swept from the earth. And the wickedness I must confess is verry much the same. This is rather bold assertions while under Martial law but they are not made by a secessionist by any means. This war may end and we have peace, say 20 or even 40 years and then have another insurrection and completely overthrow the Republic. God forbid such to be the case. But me think it will happen on account of our arrogance & Pride. As a nation I mean & not individually. There has many of our Brave but wicked Boys fell in the last Battle and the almighty saw fit to Direct one of the Bullets so as to hit me again. By the way for a warning. The wise may talk & fools may laugh. But as for me, I Believe it has been sent on me as a punishment and shall continue to think so until convinced otherwise. But still I Remain in sin. It may cost me my life yet.

July 13, 1863

And fine day, rained a little last night. This is Sunday and we had inspection this morning. Our ward was pronounced in good condition. Our wardmaster don't understand evrything about the buisness. But he is a good kind nurse and all he wants is practice to become a good wardmaster. Evrything goes on as usual except we have one man in the Guardhouse. He has, with several others, has been drunk most ever since they come and if it is not stoped there will be some more of them in it.

July 14, 1863

And sprinkled a little early in the morning. But the rest of the day was cloudy only. After have my wounds dressed & getting my pass I, with an acquaintance which has been made since I was wounded, went out, it being nearly noon. We traveled around a while & got down to the Mclellen Hospital about 1 ½ miles from here towards Philadelphia. There we waited till the Horsecars come along when we got on. Paid 5 cents to ride to the city, about 5 miles. Cheap riding as well as verry nice. I prefer it to the steam cars. After strolling around till tired, went into a resterant and got a dish of oysters, my comrad taking clam soup. I being tired and head pained me so I concluded to rest. And comrad wanting to go down the street, so we agreed to meet at the depot at 4 P.M. which we done just in time to take the cars. We get to Germantown. Conrads finger pains him so, he go into the hospital and I start to do my Buisness. Got portfolio & some paper & envelopes & bottle of ink & shoe brush & blacking, all of which I was in need of. Then I come in, getting into the ward just in time to turn round, to go the table. I like this place full as well at Chester Hospital. I meeting with so many Boys from the Brigade & they must all treat & as I wouldnt drink strong drink, I request lemonade or beer &c. Such as is harmless or smoke with them. So through the day I got so much as to not want much supper. I shall I think, go alone the next time. Which will probably be a week as there is about 60 of us & only 10 a day can get passes. It is verry nice. All you have to do is get outside the yard and you can ride on the horse cars anyplace, most for about 1 cent per mile.

July 15, 1863

And fine day but rained most of last night. I wrote a letter to Henry today. All goes on right. I happened to be out at the gate today and a fellow come along, sell Blackberries. I bought 2 qts for 20 cents, come into ward & treated the Boys as long as they lasted which wasnt long I assure you. I have commenced today to study grammar. I bought one yesterday, give 37 cents for. I have got the first page by heart for to commence. But it remains to be seen what I can do without a teacher.

My comrade had his finger amputated this evening. He was under the influence of chloraform about 2 hours, time enough to take off all four of his limbs. At Gettysburg I seen a surgeon take off a number of limbs and about 10 minutes was all he wanted to take of a leg. Last evening they took one of the Boys fingers entirely out & the nurses say he didnt wake up till this morning, being under the Influence some 7 or 8 hours. The Doctors want to practice, I guess.

July 16, 1863

And fine day. We had church this evening. The sermon was delivered by an old man of that town. I don't know his name. The Doctors took off another finger this evening for a fellow.[107]

July 17, 1863

Fine day with nothing to report but the rumored fall of Charleston SC. But our forces are at work at it undoubtedly.[108]

July 18, 1863

And fine day. Nothing new today. 10 of the Boys a day get Passes. There is some Boys in the guardhouse from our ward. The guardhouse is full most of the time, generally for drunkeness.

July 19, 1863

And fine day. This being Sunday, we had Inspection. Evrything was in good order. After Inspection, the Boys get their passes. We had church at 1 P.M., By the Chaplain Smith of the Hospital.

July 20, 1863

And fine day. I got a Pass today and 2 more Boys that are verry friendly. But I know or at least can imagine what makes them such warm friends. I have money and they have none and I could'nt get rid of them. They hung to me like a leach and would suck just as hard. The next time I go, I shall try to go alone. I wanted to go to the State ageants. But they wanted to go someplace else and so it kept going all day. I wanted go visit the Mint and Independence Hall and various places of Interest, all of which I might of done if it were not for the leaches I had with me. We stayed in the city till about 4 PM when we come back, got in the Hospital just time for supper. And after supper went out again. Stayed till near 8 oclock then came in that being the time my Pass run out. Not verry well satisfied with the days travel. But I got a good lesson which I shall try and use.

July 21, 1863

And fine day but little cloudy. Nothing occurred worthy of note. One of the Boys of this ward came in drunk, got in the guardhouse. The wounds as a general thing are doing well. Mine's getting along exceeding well. It will be healed up in 10 days or so. There is quite a number of the Boys detailed out of this ward for guard & Police. The Police are go clean up the yards & all grounds about the Hospital, scrub the entrance halls &c.

July 22, 1863

And fine day. Nothing occurring. Our wounds dressed twice a day. Good care.

July 23, 1863

And I had a Pass today. Run round through the town some & got a dish of clam soup which is a rich dish. And some fruit &c of which the markets is pretty well stocked. I was up on corner Clinta street to a Bayonet factory. There saw the rough iron taken and put through the different processes going through probably 15 hands. Comes out bright as any silver dollar and smooth as glass. I was around to the german town waterworks, saw the large pumps at work forcing the water 230 feet up from whence it run away 2 miles & half to the Reservoir.

July 25, 1863

And fine day. Nothing unusual today. But scrubbing the ward floor. That's done once a week or every Saturday so as to be nice and clean for Sunday morning Inspection. I rec'd a letter from Amos yesterday and answered it and today I received one from Lucretia which I must soon answer.

July 26, 1863

And answered the letter I received yesterday. We had a nice little shower this evening, then cleared off again. We had the Sunday morning Inspection & passed as good. Had church at 1 P.M. after which the Passes were given out to return at 6 P.M.

July 28, 1863

And rained a little in the evening, a nice shower. Evrything passes of right. I got a letter from Mother & Henry which I answered. Mother was a little unwell but Henrys folks was well as usual.

July 29, 1863

And rained a little shower in the morning but turned out to be a fine day. I had a pass today and run around considerable. Was down in the country a little. Run about good deal, seen the country which is verry pretty.

July 30, 1863

And fine day. Quite warm. Good many gets in the guardhouse for one demeanor & another. They say there is about 40 arrested now, mostly for drunkeness. It pains me to see so much of it, this is a worse place than the field for sin & wickedness. There are many on the Blacklist. They cant get passes and there has been different arrangements made in the pass system. There is ten passes issued evry day. They begin and take all as they go right along skipping those that's got their name on Black list. In that way I will get more passes than heretofore. For I will get to go out tomorrow again as my bed is first.

July 31, 1863

And rained a little in the morning, but cleared off about 9 oclock. I got a pass today, got it earlier than usual, half past ten. So I and one of the 19th Ind started, went down to the city on the steam cars. From the depot we went to the Navy yard, going most of the way on the horse cars or street cars as some call them. Go any place in the city for 5 cts. There we saw 2 or three large crafts in course of erecting and one a Monitor with 2 turrets. A verry large one. She is pretty well along. Most of the wood work is done here. I saw many cannon of all sizes & kinds, also ammunition for same. But we could'nt stay long, got only a slight look at the things. From there we went to Chestnut St and on up to Independence Hall. We entered, found many curiosities. We went up in the steeple where we could look all over the city. Fine View. But just as we reached the Hall the Bell rung the alarm for fire and when we got on top of the steeple we had a fine view. The firemen running with their engines, hose &c for extinguishing the fire. But they soon came back as the fire didnt get much of a start.

August 2, 1863

A fine day. Verry warm as it has been for several days. I got a letter from Henry to that had been to the Regt. It was written on the 6th July. So that had no news of consequence as I have got letters of a later date.

August 3, 1863

And fine day with a nice shower in the evening, rained quite hard. There is quite a number of the guards sent of today also some from the wards that were convalescent and some taken from the wards and put on guard. There was 3 of each from our ward. We have pleasant times here. But there is one thing about it that I don't like. There has been a pack of cards brought in and wardmaster threatened to burn them once when he caught them playing. The players contended that it was no worse than checkers. And I don't know but it is just as bad to play any other game as cards. They don't gamble any place for pastime only. We have several checker boards in the ward, some have half a dozen and I think it is more sin to play a game at cards for pastime than to play checkers. But when the Doctors come in some of them asked him about it. He told them they might [play] cards or checkers either if they wouldnt gamble. But they must be kind to each other and not get up any bad feeling twixt each other or he would discard both.

For my part, I wish Dan (the Ward master) had of prevailed for I don't like cards any way. They have ruined so many men & are ruining thousands evry day. There is a good deal of grumbling about passes. But they have to take their regular turn now. Dan having got a Pass Book, we eat, drink and sleep and most of us are happy. Maybe all. But I don't think. There was a number released from Prison today. Some had been there for days and others only as many hours according to the offence they had committed.

I forgot to speak about Being to church yesterday. As usual the chaplain after sermon, read the Presidents Proclamation, proclaiming to the 6th of August as fast day or thanksgiving and enjoined it upon the people of showing a respect for it & to meet at their several places of worship, there to offer Prayers to the Almighty for his mercies &c as all such Proclamations requires of the people. After which the Chaplain invited all to be present that were able to attend &c. The chaplain is a nice & for what I know, a good man. He appears so, But his preaching is some like a schoolboys Proclamation for it appears not but what somebody has written & he reads it off or Proclaims it as I used to my poetry &c, what little it was when at school.

Well about my grammar. I don't get along verry fast for I find this is to much bed lam and then my mind runs on military things and I believe I could study anything of the military kind. I think I will get a copy of Tactics & see if I can study them which I think I can for I come in contact with nothing else much for my mind to run on. I wouldnt be much surprised. I joined the service again soon after my time is out. I shall try studying the tactics and I expect to go out tomorrow and get me one.

August 4, 1863

And I got a pass today. The weather is verry warm. I got my Pass about 11 AM, went right, took the 11 ½ tram steam cars for Philadelphia. Soon arrived there. After rambling for a while I come to corner Vine & Green Streets. There I waited a few minutes for street cars which soon came. When I got aboard, went down to the Fairmount water works 2 miles distant. Upon getting there & entering at the large iron gate. Many nice walks & seats. Nice grass plots twixt the walks. The grounds is shaded with all kinds of trees. The sun having verry little chance to strike the ground. In about the center of this flat is the fountains with a number of brass spouts where the water issued going to the hight of ten to fourteen according to the size of the tube the water issues from. The largest tubes throws the water highest.

After sitting a while to rest and watch the water &c, gaze on the different trees and shrubs. It appeared as though I could never get done looking. The scene beggars description. It is a lovely spot. The Mount is to the right as you enter the gate on top of which is the Reservoirs. They cover a number of acres. After gazing till tired, I went to the works which pumps the water to the top of the Mount. The works are a series of large water wheels of great power. The water giving the necessary power. The Pumps and machinery & cars all run by the wheels. There is a number of Pumps of great capacity. Near here, right in the side of Mount stands a bust of a man holding a large serpent in right hand. Out of its mouth issues a large stream which rises as much as 20 feet or more and out of the toes of the bust water issues with as much force. This is thrown out hard and falling about 40 feet from the feet of the bust. There is an enormous power used to work the whole thing. I am not capable of describing it accurately.

From here I went upon the mount where I could see most all over the city. Good view up the river. See all the water works plain. Here I see that the grounds cover about 15 acres I should judge. Here I find the Reservoirs smooth & placid waters. They are fenced in by a strong wooden paling fence and outside of this is a road wide enough for 4 persons to walk abrest. It is graveled and each side of the road is the Kentucky Bluegrass growing rank. This is all around it. Then down about 20 feet below is another such a road running two thirds of the way around the other third. The ground rises abrupt to level with the other road above. Around the outer edge of this walk is a row of nice large shade trees, mostly soft maple. But some of all kinds. This is also a verry nice walk. More comfortable than the upper one for it has no trees near it & is kept clear of tall grass & weeds. There is nothing to fall or blow in the water nor no chance for the birds to light. From this 2nd walk, the ground slopes of nicely & covered with the same kind of grass to the foot of the mount, probably 80 feet. There is, I see, another fountain about opposite on the other side of the Mount from the one I have mentioned before. But this is only spout but a large one. There is not many trees on this of any considerable size. It appears to have been lately improved. Many of the trees are small. Well I cant now give a better discription of the grounds. To sum it all up, they lovely beyond discription. At least so of by me. I thought myself well paid for my day travels.

I got down to the Race street depot. There I took the cars, come up to the 9th street, went to depot. Returned home which I reached half past 7 P.M. half an hour before my Pass run out. I am tired but amply paid for it. I went alone today & enjoyed myself the best I ever have. So ended the 4th of August & my Birth day. But I didnt think of it all day.

August 5, 1863

And fine day. Nothing of consequence occurred. My wound is doing verry well. I have no bandage on my head now. It is most well. They have got a cannon here for firing tomorrow to celerabrate Thanksgiving day. It is an iron piece that was captured from the British when the Battle of this Place was fought or as you may, the Battle of Germantown.[109] It has a verry old look. Is about a 6 pounder. It is kept on purpose for such occasions. Evrybody that can get out is taking a look at it. Evrybody takes a lively interest in looking at it. We expect to have great times tomorrow.

August 6, 1863

And fine day. But as usual of late, verry warm. We got our usual breakfast. Nothing of interest transpired till 12 N. The cannon fired & kept firing evry 2 ½ minutes til 30 rounds was fired. After which we had dinner rather later. We had in addition to our usual dinner, ¼ of a common pie to a man and about a spoonful of tomatoes & cucumbers apiece. Those were cut up & vinegar on them and that is all we had after all the talk about our great dinner we was to have. And the Pie caused some truble for a few got 2 pieces. By chance I was one of the lucky ones this time and then all wanted and there was not [enough] for [all]. Come verry near having a fight about the thing. It terminated disgraceful in my estimation. I wish that there wasn't a pie brought on the table.

Nothing transpired till sundown when a few more rounds was fired. It was posted outside the hospital enclosure on a vacant town lot. When it was fired it jarred the whole hospital. It cracked twice as loud as a twelve pounder would in the field. They pounded grass, green grass into it on top of the load. That made it crack loud. It was a pretty still evening and rather cooler than usual. The town boys have a little gun of some kind that they are firing with. It is a 1 or 2 pounder I should judge. We had an appropriate sermon from the chaplain at 8 P.M. It was well suited to the occasion. He enjoined us to be thankful & offer up thanks to the almighty for our existence as a nation and for the great victories he has vouchsafed to us &c. He went on to considerable length. We finished up the excercise by singing the Star Spangled which all joined in as most of the soldiers can sing it.

August 7, 1863

And fine day. Verry warm. But not so much so as several days since. I got a pass today. Got it about 10 A.M. rather earlier than usual. And I start for to find the old Germantown Battle field. Get out on the street after going through 2 guards and showing my pass to each. Went up the street some three fourths of a mile. Came to an old stone wall looking verry old in which was a gateway. Had been a gate there sometime. Here we turned in, went up to the house that the massacre was in. It stands back from the street some 100 yards, a lawn intervening. But not much care taken of it. There is also a great many trees of different kinds & sizes interspersed of it making alltogather rather a pretty place. There has been no Improvement whatever since the Battle. The Grand daughter is living in and owns it. The old man in his will enjoined it upon any and evrybody that lived in the house to not disturb anything whatever. The house is a good & large one. Stories high. Built of stone & plastered. The old negro that was working there, he took some pains to show us the bullet marks on the house. Also several cannon ball marks. As near as I can get it, the English come & surprised our troops & just massacred them & got possession of the house. And our fought them from the outside. History will tell you about it. But I got to see the much noted place. There [are] a number of busts of persons. They are Italian marble & carved in Italy. Bullet mark on them.

Two pages from William Ray's Volume 10, detailing his experiences in the hospital following his wounding at Gettysburg. *Sherry Murphy*

Volume 10

August 12, 1863 to January 14, 1864

The Veteran Question

Wm R Ray, Member Co F
7th Regt. Wis. Volt.
A Resident of Cassville, Grant Co of aforesaid state
At present a patient in USA Hospital, Germantown Pennsylvania

August [12] 18, 1863

Well I must return to the 12 inst. That being the day I got my other diary full and not getting a pass for several day, did not get a book and forgot when I was out. But had a pass today so got it.

August 13, 1863

Many of the boys getting 15 day furloughs. All a fellow has to do if he wants a furlough is to ask for somebody is going evry day sometimes 10 or 15 a day.

August 15, 1863

And fine day. I got a pass today. Went down to the State Agent and from there to the mint. Stayed there couple hours, found the managers and officers verry courteous. Showed me around the building. Seen them making copper cents. They were not coining in the other departments. But got to see the machinery and the coins of different nations and all nations. Some verry old pieces. Also many specimens of all kind of mineral, one piece of lead ore from Galena, Ill. And copper and iron from Lake Superior mines. I was pleased to find my state so well represented in the cases in the way of minerals. Evrything is neatly arranged in glass cases so they can be seen but not touched. I had to register my name on going in. Admittance from 9 A.M. til 12N only. This stares you in the face as you enter, it being posted on the right hand door. I got there half past 11 A.M. I considered myself well paid for my trip.

From here traveled homeward taking rather a circuitous route the better to see things to be seen. And came into the hospital at last without getting a diary. Done most of the traveling in the street cars. Traveled some 15 miles today I should think. I got a letter from Henry and mother. Well and doing well. Henry had got nearly done harvesting & had good crops.

August 17, 1863

And fine day, rather cooler today. We had hard rain last night and a change in the atmosphere. I think we will have some cooler weather now for a while. Some more furloughs came today. I think sometimes of trying to get one but then I think the cost is to much for a weeks pleasure. Twill cost me at least $40.00 on my trip there & back and then to think how much iron that would buy if I work at my trade when I get back or how many acres of land I would buy if I chose to farm it for a livelihood. Or how long it would school me if I chose to go to school. Any of those, if I chose follow them as a business would require all the capital I could raise so I think I had better save it. $40.00 is not picked up just whenever a fellow wants it.

August 18, 1863

And fine day. Had a pass today. Got about 10 A.M. went out a little while, come in to dinner, stayed in till after supper when I went out and got this book and returned.

August 19, 1863

And fine day. Had a hard thundershower last night. The air is nice and cool this morning. I have a good time now. My wound almost healed up and nothing to do but study tactics of which I purchased a volumn, containing the maneuvers through School of the Soldier & Company Drill and Battallion Drill. I calculated to study it as my [mind] seems to run on something of the military. I tried studying grammar but no go for not but war matters could I think of, so I will study such. I got a letter from Sarah yesterday and today I got one from Henry & one from Amos. He is still at Vicsburg still. He spoke of seeing Richard Lander, Isaac Ray & they were well.

Henry, I am sorry to hear is rather unwell at present & Sarah has been quite sick, but was better. The folk was done harvesting generally and I was glad to hear that the crops was a good average yield.

I also got a letter from the Co. From F. A. Boyantan. The Regt was at Rappahnnock Station. Done nothing except a little picket duty. There was 20 of the boys only, no ranks, but they were in good spirits. I am glad to see Frank and also the boys so patriotic. Frank is verry much so to my surprise.

August 20, 1863

And fine day. Things goes on as usual. I had a pass but didn't go out. I did not put in for one either. The weather is some cooler for the last 2 or 3 days. The showers we had done that. It is quite pleasant sitting in the wards now. I bought me a new hat for 75 cents. It is only a cheap one. Bought it so as to send my old one home and I thought that it would last me till I got to the Regt. Then it not being in uniform I should have to draw a new one. So I didn't want a verry expensive one to throw away. Some of the boys that went away on furloughs are coming back, their time being up.

August 21, 1863

And fine day. I had a pass today. But didn't use. I have seen most of the places of interest round here & in the City and I can't see what the boys find so enticing out. But Oh, it's the liquor that entices them and many at a fearful rate too. Evry day there is some going into the guard house for drunkness. A day or two since the fellow that I associated with some got into the guard house for drunkeness. He was, I thought, about the best fellow I could associate. But I will have to give up going with anybody. When I go out, go alone then I will not be disgraced with being in their company. Oh what will this world come to.

August 22, 1863

And fine day. But rather warmer today. Some more of the boys that had furloughs come back today. I wrote a letter to Henry today in answer to one that I received from him and mother. I also [answered] Mary Janes letter & wrote to William in the same sheet. Evrything is quiet. Goes on right. I sett up about evry third night. There is four volunteers evry night. There is two that has to [be] waited on, one has his arm off & he has the fever. Also he is verry bad off. He will die, I think. The other one is shot through hand. He is doing well. Have to pour a pint of water on the wound evry quarter hour & that is all, so he don't take much care. I have set up a number of times. Do many little things around the ward for the boys that can't help themselves. There is only three in our ward that has to be waited on.

August 23, 1863

And fine day, pretty warm. This being Sunday, we had the usual inspection. Also the usual sermon. But I didn't attend for church was called before we got through dinner, so late was dinner. Then I wouldn't go. It was about 1 oclock when we had dinner. I finished reading my testament through today. Mother will be glad when she hears it. But at the same time, I might have read it through several times since I have been in the service. I still keep studying tactics. I am getting along well with them. I can do much better at it than at grammar, for I am more conversant with it of late & my mind is turned in that direction more.

August 24, 1863

And fine day, quite pleasant today. The fellow that had his arm taken off and has been sick [with] the fever for three week died about noon today. He died verry easy without a struggle. But Oh, what a condition he was in. Nothing but skin & bone. It is a hard sight. I didn't notice a man much dying on the battlefield but this looked hard. He being a German & Roman Catholic he had the Priest in to see him some four or five times and just before [he] died he came again and administered the last tribute. He went through different motions &c to numerous to mention. But it seemed to have the desired effect. It was verry soluemn and impressive. There were quite a number of his friends in to see him. If he had been under the care of Doctor Crall (our doctor), I think he would not have died for he has had several bad cases and they got through all right and didn't [get] the fever. He uses water on the wounds. But the other fellow Downs don't believe in. He poltices instead of water. And I believe that is what caused his fever, then death.

There is a sutler shop opened this morning in the yard, he having built a shop. It comes verry handy for the boys, if he will sell as cheap as out in the town.

August 25, 1863

And fine day. Nothing of consequence transpired. I had a pass today. Went out an hour or so after supper. We had a number of showers today, a verry hard one while I was out. Come verry near being wet to the skin, got a little so as it was. We have had so much fine weather of late that I almost forgot to mention it.

August 26, 1863

Fine day. Quite cool. I slept with two thicknesses of blanket over me and about half the day could wear my coat without being uncomfortable at all.

August 27, 1863

And fine day. Our ward & Ward F can't get passes today nor no more till we find out and bring notice to the Head Doctor who it was come in through our ward. There is one man pretends to know. He will divulge the secret I guess, although he & some of the boys are a little ornery. And he, to Plague them a little by keeping them in, won't tell till he gets ready. The boys really abused him and commenced on him before they had a right & that had its influence so he wouldnt tell till he got ready. And I don't blame him much.

August 28, 1863

And fine day. Had several little showers today. We get no passes today. The boys are getting somewhat excited about it in both wards. The Doctor says unless we get the rouges we can't have a pass for 60 days. That they must stop running the guard and coming into the back windows & the 2 rogues belong to neither ward that are being punished. But they come into our ward window on purpose to throw it on us. The Guard couldn't tell which of the two wards they come into so Ward F comes in for a share. I have told the Boys repeatedly that they hadn't ought to go out there nor allow others to & we got blame for it many times when the boys come from other wards & went out on purpose to keep the guards from coming into their ward to look them up. Thereby they would miss punishment and blame. But our boys damed anybody that would inform on any soldier going out the window. They were so short sighted that they couldn't see what it would come to. But I thought that they couldn't always break the rules and not be catched. I tell them they brought it on themselves & laugh at them while they curse all and evrything. Oh I will be glad when I get out of the service just on that account.

The news in the morning paper is cheering. I buy a paper every morning. Gilmore [Union General Quincy Adams Gillmore] has taken Forts Wagner & Sumpter [Sumter, at Charleston, South Carolina]. The work has begun in earnest. Sumpter is crumbling to the ground. I wrote a letter yesterday to Sarah & John & the day before a letter to Amos and the day before one to Mary.[110]

August 29, 1863

And fine day. Rained a little towards night. A shower only. The boys got passes today. The fellow that knew one of them fellows that came into the ward through the window went and reported him so they put him in the Guard house and they put another fellow in. But some say he is not the right one. But let them fix that as they may. We get passes again. And some of the boys that made so much fuss about it didn't want to go out then. But that is human nature. Some more come back that have had furloughs. But none of the boys are getting furloughs. They are waiting till after we get pay which we expect about the 10th of next month. I hope so at least for I want to stay till I get it, before going to my Regt.

The Doctor gave me a chance to go on guard if I chose, instead of going to the Regt. But I choose to go to my Regt after being paid. I may have done wrong to myself in refusing for it is a good place here. But I think of the boys in the field and the hard fare & hard times they have. And that I ought to be there to share it with them and in some ways make it easier on them. And being a noncommissioned officer, if it is of the Lower Grade, it will have it influence. And by such staying away others will be kept that would not. I don't mean to convey the idea that I have any influence. But I think it is the other way with me. At least if I should have any influence, I would be as much surprised as when I got the menial office that I now hold. The office is only a secondary consideration in my estimation.

In a letter I have from my Co. I find there are many of them taken prisinor that were not wounded. There were two that died from their wounds & 8 wounded, also Lieut A.A. Kidd. 6 were missing or taken prisinor rather. 2 of them were slightly wounded. The others had nothing the matter but fatigue and that was so with all of them that got away. I guess there is not much sympathy for those that were taken prisinor that were not wounded.

August 30, 1863

And fine day. Quite cool, cold enough for frost last night I thought. But I don't know as there was any. The boys get passes and all goes on right. I expected a letter today but didn't come. I havn't had one for near a week. Think is time. We are to be mustered tomorrow. Most of us for 4 months pay. I for one have $52.00 due from my Uncle.

August 31, 1863

And fine day. We were mustered today. All went off right. And we soon expect to get our pay. There is a number of the boys off one way and another. Some has overstayed their time on furlough. This is the last day of the summer months & I expect in one year to be in the State of Wisconsin on my way home from the Capitol, that is if I am permitted to live so long.

September 1, 1863

And fine day. Still continues cool. They are fixing to send of a lot of fellows. There is as many as 30 in the guardhouse. All of those will be sent and a number from the wards, probably me. For I refused to go on guard, choosing to go to my Regt when I got my pay. They are drawing clothing, fixing to go. The fellow from my Co that has been in the guardhouse for near a month, he is going for he has to go for his misdemeanor or he wouldn't have went. I think he never would volunteer to go. I would have went if we had been paid, although my head is not quite well. So I concluded to stay.

September 2, 1863

And fine day. The boys started at 10 A.M. today for their Regts. 76 in number, they made considerable noise & threats. Many apparently much chagrined at the having to go. At last they started. After dinner we commenced signing the payrolls. I have signed it. We expect to have our pay by the 10th next.

I started a letter to Mother today and a daily paper to Henry. The paper had a long argument in it on the Slavery question which I thought he would like to read. Our sutlers shop comes verry handy. I frequently indulge in a few cents worth of what I now call luxuries (viz Tomatos & onions &c) which we get verry reasonable, for which I pay cash, a thing that verry few of the boys have now. I still buy a paper evry morning. The only one that buys papers in our ward now. I expect evry morning to hear of the city of Charleston being in flames, but it don't come yet.

September 3, 1863

And fine day. I had a pass today. Was out a couple of hours and while out I got my hair cut & a shave and hair cleaned. All of which I paid thirty cents for. I took my old hat out and expressed it home, it having the ball holes in it that gave me my wound. I received two letters today. One from Mother and Sarah and one from Minnie Spander in answer to one I wrote her some time ago. I feel in a verry good humor this evening having got two letters.

September 4, 1863

And fine day. Nothing worthy of note transpired. All I want now is to have my pay & then be sent to the Regt. I want to see the Boys, it will seem like going home almost. I am anxious to go when I get paid. We expect it soon about next Tuesday they say. Our Surgeon in charge has been assigned to duty elsewhere & Dr Betton been appointed in his stead which seems to please most of the folks working here. They didn't like old Curtis as they called him. They thought he was to tyrannical. But I thought he done first rate. I guess the truble was he made evry one do his duty. And some didn't like to be made to, and they raised a howl. And most people is apt to believe an evil report about a man sooner than a good one. I don't or can't find any fault now the way things is carried on. But at first I felt inclined to find fault more than otherwise. But I begin now to see I was wrong.

September 5, 1863

And fine day. Cool and pleasant with nothing transpiring unusual except scrubbing. This being Saturday, they get ready for Sunday morning Inspection which is as sure to come as day itself. I have taken some cold, by getting my hair cut. Some says it is by getting whiskers out (by the way of a joke) but really my face is just about as free from whiskers as when I left home.

September 6, 1863

And fine day. Verry. We had the usual Sunday Inspections. And church service. Our new Surgeon in charge give church passes to all that want to attend church out in the town. But some of the boys come drunk on such passes. They get them, they tell the Surgeon, to go to church. But alas, if they do, they visit some grog shop afterwards. I repeatedly have to receive jeers and scornful looks from many in my opposition to them. But I have give up saying anything, for it don't do any good as I can see. The majority & a verry large one too of this ward has been under the influence of whiskey many times and there is one Orderly Sergeant that is drunk two thirds of the time and I am ashamed to confess that he belongs to the Badger state.

September 7, 1863

And fine day. But no pay yet. Now they say we get it Wednesday. Well twill surely come soon. I have mailed a letter to Henry today. Also one to Lucretia, she having got home and wrote me to that effect. So I answered it right of. I also got one from Caroline. I received two & mailed two. I was much surprised as well gratified to hear from her when writing from home.

I had a pass today but didn't use it. That drunken Sergt that I spoke of yesterday tried to have me go out with him. But no. I could read him. He knew I had money and when he got me into some saloon or shop he would either want me to treat him or he would treat and then leave me to pay it. I have been fooled more than once that way by fellows having no money. And if a fellow goes out and buy a few apples or peaches there will be, perhaps, be a dozen soldiers standing and all looking askance at you. And most certain some will say: Say Billy (or who ever it may be) aint you going to treat. Then if I shouldn't treat, they would commence some redicalous and make game of a fellow on the streets. This is one reason why I don't go out knowing what bad repute the soldiers have got into this town. There has several scandalous affairs transpired in this town by the soldiers. And I can't blame them for they certainly have cause to complain.

September 9, 1863

And fine day. The cool weather continues. There has been a change in the Surgeons. The Surgeon that was in charge of the hospital (Curtis) & the surgeon of our ward has gone to Charleston or rather Morris Island and Downs, the surgeon of the other side of the ward has taken charge of this side. The boys don't like the change but most of them has got well or nearly so, they don't want much attendance so don't make much difference.

September 10, 1863

And fine day. A surgeon from Headquarters is here examining all the Patients. Those that are hearty and well evry way are put down for the Regt. But those that are invalids are put in the Invalid Corps.[111] Some for the first & some for the Second Battalion & those that are not well of course remain till well. I being one of the latter on account of the heat hurting my head. He put me down for to stay here till cool weather. But I thought if I took a notion which I am somewhat likely to, that I might go before that time. I wrote a letter to Sergt F.A. Boyanton in answer to one I got some time since. One of the Ind. Boy got a letter yesterday. It stated that we were going to have a Brigade flag presented to the Brigade on 17th of the month & a picnic if the Johnys didn't truble them.[112] They expected President Lincoln would be there. But I hardly think it. I expect they will have a great time. I would like to be there. I hope they will enjoy themselves well.

September 11, 1863

And fine day. We got our pay today. I got mine in full $52.00. But after getting it I couldn't get out to express it home. They let nobody out whatever. I judge from that that they are going to send some off, probably tomorrow. Many of the boys vow they will break guard. But that is rather dangerous buisness.

September 13, 1863

And fine day. We had no Inspection today. Church service as usual. But by some fellow from the country from the way he spoke, I thought he was a Methodist. Gave a verry good discourse. Quite different from the Chaplains reading Sermons. He spoke offhand and may [many] said they wished he was the Chaplain. They liked him well.

September 14, 1863

And fine day. Had a little shower about noon which made the air cool. This morning they are around notifying the boys that are going to their Regts. Dr Patterson, knowing that I wanted to, told the Surgeon in charge and he sent for me to come up. He wanted to see me. I went, found Patterson at the door to introduce as one volunteering to go. He received me verry kindly and complimented me for so doing. He put my name down. I gave him $50.00 to express home to Henry & told him I wanted to draw some clothing so he had the clerks fix it so I could get some. Many others wanted clothing, but they could not get it, I being the only one out of some 70 that they would let have [any] and they accommodated me in evry way they could, I being the only one volunteered. I drew to 2 pairs of drawers & 2 shirts & pair of socks.

At last about 10 A.M. they got us together and all ready in the front yard. And with giving us one thing and another kept us there till near noon when they gave us a lunch of bread & butter & hot coffee. After fooling around an hour or so waiting for the train we marched out to the depot. The cars soon come & we got aboard. Great time shaking hands and cheering & many acted verry unkind towards the doctors, blackguarding them & the hospital and evrything about it. But I felt quite different. I considered I had been taken care of and well treated in evry respect as much so as could be expected.

At last the cars start & such yelling that old depot never heard before or the town either, for they was at it ever since they come out of the door of the hospital & kept at it till we got to the Provost Marshall in the city which is a large 5 story brick building. They put us up in the fifth story and there they kept yelling and the Bottle was passed pretty freely as it had been since out of the hospital yard. Here we had to stay till five oclock. Before this time arrived, another crowd numbering about the same came in from some hospital in the City & and some of them as well as many of our boys got pretty tight by this time & got to scuffling & playing and hollowing. We were so thick in the room that you could stir us with a stick. Their fun soon turned into a fight & the guard at the door yell for the sargeant of the guard. He come up but the Boys took him off the drunk man so he went and got a number of guards, the officer of the guard coming along. They come up & the Sergeant took hold of him again and some of the rough started again. But the officer, nothing daunted, drew his sword and told them to stand back or he would cut them down and ordered his men to load, which they done. But while the officer and guards were engaging their attention, the Sergeant got the drunkard down the stairs. When the officer drew his sword, whiskey Bravery soon wilted & would have submitted to most anything. So they soon got kind a civil.

Five oclock came & we marched down to the Depot, a distance of 3 miles. The Bottle was still passing around & many verry Boozy and evrybody on the sidewalks was knocked off by the boys pushing each other against them. And evrything no matter what was kicked off the sidewalks. They were cleaned off on that 3 miles. We got on the cars at half past 6 oclock & started & the Boys as noisy as ever. We come on slowly stopping at the different stations & switches at some of which we had to wait till other trains came up. We reached Baltimore 4 oclock and laid till daylight.

September 15, 1863

And fine morning. This morning about 7 oclock we were marched over to the Union Relief association, got Breakfast with the calculation of starting at 8 oclock. But trains kept leaving till 10 oclock when we were permitted to go. After reaching the Depot last night the Boys lay pretty still, most all asleep. We come to

Washington. Reaching there about 3 P.M., got our dinner at the Memoriable Soldiers Retreat then were put into the Barracks adjoining or Barracks No 1. There the Boys rested some, were not so noisy. About 6 P.M. we had supper and they tell us that we have to go out to convalescent camp in the morning which we were glad to hear. About 9 oclock they brought in about 50 conscripts & Substitutes and this started the noise again and it was kept up till near midnight when I got to sleep.

September 16, 1863

And fine day. I rested pretty well the latter part of the night. Last night 2 Regts come in, the 3rd & 5th Michigan. They went into other Barracks, they had breakfast before we. We got it about 8 oclock and about 9 we marched out to take the cars. After marching half mile & laying by the side of the Road an hour or so, the cars come along & we got on & come here. We reached here about noon. We were formed in two ranks and all Paroled Prisinors that hadn't been exchanged step to the front. Not a man here by that name. Then all those that wanted to go to their Regts step to the front and there was about half of them steped out. We were marched of & our names taken. And we were sent to Camp Distribution. Then the Doctor examined those left & pretty soon most of them come over. But of the whole that got to stay in the convalescent camp, there they have good Barracks. But here we have the Sibly [Sibley] tent.[113] They are verry good shelter.

Here we go, evry corps to themselves. So of course we go in the first row of tents. The first corps tents is full so we have to go into 2nd. We expect to go away in a day or two. Here we get dinner consisting of Bread & Coffee, Meat & Potatoes. There is a couple of cooks. They draw, cook & deal out the rations and there is a fellow acts as orderly Sergt. He calls the roll when we fall in for meals and a fellow missing roll call, he misses a meal for evry one. So that keep the Boys verry verry punctual. This Department consists of three camps, namely Convalescent camp where those that are not able to go to the field stop. Distribution camp where those that are able to go to field are sent and there wait till the corps commander sends for them. Camp Parole where those that are Paroled go to till they are exchanged. There is a guard around the whole thing which is done by the 3 & 4 Penn Reservers [3rd and 4th Pennsylvania Reserves]. Then the inside guards are invalids. There is a guard twixt our camp & Parole to keep us from mixing.

The camp is neat & orderly and evrything works like a charm. It is a nice camp and kept nice. Quite contrary to what I had been lead to believe by rumors, but I understand that it is better than it used to be. There is evrything carried on here. Most evry Profession except a lawyer. There is dentists, Barbers, Sutlers, Milk pedlars &c all useful. There is no few Pedlars or anything that is a nuisance to Soldiers. I am glad to hear & see things carried on so well. Evrything is neat & clean & the food is well cooked. That used to be the worst place a Soldier passed through. But now it is carried on scientifically & will I think gain a good reputation in time to come. This is all done by the negros, that is the working part is.

I forgot to mention that there is a camp for Deserters & I am sorry to see it full. They are sending thousands of them to the army. The Draft is what catches those thats been deserting since the war commenced. They are most all being caught. When they get here they have to labor evry day working on the Railroad, cleaning the camp & all kinds of work and when the authorities thinks Proper, they are sent to the army. Then when they get there, they are courtmartialed and have to abide by the sentence, let that be what it may.

September 17, 1863

Nice shower in the afternoon. Another lot of fellows come in today, and some went away. All belonging to the Sixth Corp. Fifth corps Boys went to their Regts. Myself & one from the 19th Ind & 3 from the 2nd [Wisconsin] occupy one tent.

September 18, 1863

Some convalescents come in today. One fellow that belonged to the 19th [Indiana] that we left drunk in Washington came with them. He was sent into the Barracks to stay till examined. We get our meals regular and get plenty such as it is. It is rather rough living. There is plenty of evrything to buy. But money is rather scarce. It wont pay to buy when evrything costs so much. I took a walk today, clear around the whole camp being about a mile around. I found evrything that a camp needed. They bake the bread right here in camp. The cars come right into the Camps.

September 19, 1863

Another squad come in today. Some more additions to the first, the first corps men [First Army Corps] number 175 men in this camp. The news from the Army is to the effect that they are not fighting and I should think that they would send for us.

September 20, 1863

And fine day. But verry cool. This is Sunday but we have no Inspection. I went to night meeting. There is meeting here 3 times evry fine day through the week. I wrote a letter to Mother today. There has been a great Revival here and it is still going on. The news tonight from the front is that they are fighting.

September 21, 1863

And fine day. Evrything as usual. Lot more fellows come in today. The report that our men were fighting proved to be untrue. Nothing more than skirmishing. I wrote a letter to Mother & Henry today.

September 22, 1863

Fine day. Twas verry cold last night. The street Sergeant put 6 more men in with us. So our tent is pretty full, 11 of us. The news from the Southwest is not the best today. According to the papers, the Rebs has given Rosencranz [Union General William Rosecrans] the hardest Battle he ever had with them. But he held his ground by hard fighting. I hope it is true. I should dislike to hear of him being whipped now. Oh, the Western Boys will fight hard, I tell you. They are men.[114]

September 23, 1863

And fine day. Nothing of interest today till about 2 P.M. when orders come to draw what clothing we wanted. And the cook to cook one days rations. So we, the 1st Corps, drew clothing. I drew a haversack only. I wanted a half tent & oil blanket. But could [not] get them.

September 24, 1863

And fine day. I arose this morning with joy in my heart and got ready to start at 8 A.M. I drew my hardtack once more again, the first for near 3 months. There is about 200 of us. We start with a few guards, go to Alexandria. At 11 oclock we get on the cars. They are loaded but we crawl on and into them, there being about 200 armed men on each train to keep off guerillas if they should attack us. There is four trains and they keep pretty close together for mutual protection. We start, run out stopping at stations along the road, reaching Culpepper about dark. Here we get off and a Lieut takes charge of us. Calls the roll & forms us in line & we march off about 1 mile to Gen Meads [Meade's] Headquarters where we find out we will have 9 miles to march to reach the corps. So the Lieut said we could camp. But if any of us choose to go on he would get a cavelry escort & let us go. But we chose to camp. So we come a few rods, camp, built fires, made coffee & went to bed. I seen many places along the road where I have often been & where we have camped &c, for instance, Bristow & Catlets & Bealton & Rappahannock Station & many other places where I have traveled by. When we neared the Rappahannock River we see the characteristics of the camp viz Soldiers graves and dead horses. Most of the latter emitting a verry offensive smell. I find the country pretty much the same as when I went through here last August a year ago. I was then on wagon guard. There is 2 fellows of my Co. with me, [Benjamin] Hayden and [Henry] Hudson.[115] We camped together last night. There is not many troops around here. Our lines I understand are about 12 miles from here.

September 25, 1863

A fine day. We arose early, got breakfast, drew rations and started for Corps Headquarters 7 miles, they say. We marched along pretty good jog, resting once & a while. Reached the headquarters about noon and after calling the roll & making out a list for those belonging to the first Division, we started for Division Headquarters. Where roll is called again and a guard sent with us to our respective brigades. And from there a guard was sent with us to our Regt. I found only three in camp and the three officers. The others being on Picket. Those fellows that were taken Prisinor haven't got back yet. The Boys are well, 2 that was slightly wounded had got back. Cap [Captain Henry F. Young] is rather unwell and looks bad as he has for a number of weeks. Alphonse Kidd [Alphonzo A. Kidd], Second Lieut is a little lame yet from his wound. The Picket line is only 1 mile and Sergt Boyanton [Francis A. Boynton] being up here on Business I went down with him when he went.

I found the Boys in good situation and living well. They had fresh mutton & Pork, there being plenty of it around here amongst the farmers. The Country round here don't show the affects of war so much as in most Places in Virginia. I had a good supper of green corn and fresh meat.

September 26, 1863

And fine day. Got breakfast. I went on Post for 1 of the Boys. I thought I would try it again. I find the Boys living like Brothers. They seem to be verry much attached to each other. They may be said to be the escence of the 107 men we left the State with. They are or seem to be well satisfied with their lot. They seem to be more devoted with their work than I ever saw them. I see a number of Rebs on the other side of the River.

This River is small, fordable in many places. The Picket lines are each side of it. But quite aways from it along where we were Posted. The Rebs were a mile or more from us. There was one come over to the next Post and they took him back to the Rear. He either give himself up or they took him. I thought he came over to exchange papers only. We were relieved about 5 P.M. by some N.Y. Regt and come to camp. There is a rumor that our Corps is all that is here & the Army is moving in some direction.

September 27, 1863

And fine day. This being Sunday morning we had Regt. Inspection. I have no gun yet. But I went on Inspection. We were Inspected by Major Finnecum [Mark Finnicum], he being in command of the Regt. The Col [William Robinson] is commanding the Brigade & the Lieut Col (Callis) [John B. Callis] was seriously wounded at Gettysburg & has not returned, he being at home now. I never saw such a Brotherly [feeling] amongst men before. Officers and all. It does my verry soul good to see it. I can never forget how Brave the officers was at Gettysburg expecially Lieut [William E.] Sloat. He gave the cowards and stragglers no Peace at all, kept driving them to their Regts. And them that their Regts was too far away he put them in our Regt.

September 28, 1863

And fine day with nothing unusual transpiring. Nearly evrybody expects we will retreat soon to the other side of the Rappahannock. But it don't come yet. I find things more pleasant than I expected. I am sorry to see Cap so sick. He is just able to get about.

September 29, 1863

And fine day. We have nothing else but fine weather now. There is plenty worse in store for us and it is sure to come. About 10 A.M. we broke camp and came to the rear about a mile to a better camp where we camped & there being lots of old camps hereabouts, we found plenty of boards & boxes. Jake & I started out and left John to fix up a shed over the tent, we having pitched the tent before & got fork & poles for the shed. Jake got some boxes & I got some. Also a good frame for a table which we fix up and now have the best table in the Regt. We got some Virginia feathers (cedar boughs) which makes the bed a great deal better. We are comfortable fixed verry much so.

The rumor is that three Corps has gone to reinforce Rosencranse [General William Rosecrans]. Let that be as it may. There is not much show of advancing. Rosencranse was beaten without a doubt & that seems to put quite a different face on things. But it will come out all right.[116]

There is one thing I am pleased to see. There is not so much wickedness in the Army as there used to be. There is not half the swearing and the tracts and Religious Papers is read a great deal. Altogether I can percieve a great change in the Soldiers morally speaking. I am glad to see it and before this war is over, I think there will still be a greater change. I can now verry frequently see soldiers reading the Testament which used to be a rare thing.

September 30, 1863

A fine day. 7 Privates & 1 Sergeant from our company for Picket today. They started out at 1 P.M. At 3 P.M. we had drill. There being so many out on Picket that we were formed into 4 companies. We had a good drill of about 2 hours and dress parade.

October 2, 1863

And stormy day, verry. Rained all day verry bad. The Boys come in off Picket some before dark and some long after dark. The latter were so unfortunate as to get lost. But they got in all right. They had an awful time. They were wet as rats. Jake was out. I kept supper warm for him. But found it difficult for the rain put the fire almost out. John & I had the tent in good order having done evrything to make it comfortable that we could.

October 3, 1863

And fine day, contrary to my expectation when I went to bed last night. I awoke this morning to see the sun shining. About 9 AM we had Co Inspection after which John and I made ready to wash some clothes. About the time we got ready the order [came] for all to wash that wanted as Saturday from this [time] on would be set apart for such duties and there would be no drill or duty. So John and I got all we could and went at it & washed till about 2 P.M. when the order come to get ready to go on Picket, to be on Reserve. We relieved the 2nd Regt so we first went to camp, got ready and set off. Come out about 3 miles finding the 2nd in a pretty camp which we took as soon as they went out. And fixed up nice for there is any quantity of boards & boxes here. We are here as a support for the Picket line. One third of the Regt is under arms all the time so it is not verry heavy duty. I believe I could content myself here the rest of my time in the service so pretty is the camp. We certainly are well situated.

I believe I havent noticed about the Regt getting new guns. We now [have] the new Springfield Rifle, a splendidly finished piece. They look to nice to use in the field. The finish on them would entitle them to a rack in a gentlemans Parlor. The Boys are verry proud of them and take the best of a care of them.[117]

The Army carries 8 days rations now. I drew enough today to make up mine. I had to put crackers in my knappsack. That with the wet clothes made me a verry heavy load.

October 4, 1863

And fine. Jake, Jack & I fixed up our tent today. We had plenty of boards and fixed it nice. The mail comes today but nothing but a paper for me. There is a guard around camp. I am on guard at 4 P.M. and until tomorrow 4 P.M. This is my second time as corporal of the guard. There is considerable excitement amongst the Boys about going into the veteran Corps: if the majority of the Regt will reinlist for 3 years and get $402.00 Bounty and be allowed to go to the State to Reorganize & Recruit. There seems to be a good many that will go.

October 5, 1863

And fine day. And we had great times today about this veteran corps. The Regt fell in & went out to meet the Brigade to decide about [the veteran corps]. I being on duty, I could not go. They were out a couple hours, had letters & speeches read from different General and there was a number of speeches from the officers upholding the scheme. And when the Regt come back the Major made them a long speech supporting the scheme. He recommending the officers to draw up a paper stating the thing fairly and let those sign it that wished to enlist. And if they got a majority they were sure to go to the State. They got up considerable excitement and I believe it will work. But as for me, I don't know what to do with it. For Mother requests that I shouldn't enlist again. And I shall hate to see the Boys all go and me go into some other Regt. I consider a Mothers wish should be complied with. But I think she would rather see me coming home with the Co than go amongst strangers. At least I would rather to go home & I believe I shall if the majority goes, taking the Pay into consideration. It is Big, upon the whole it amounts to $25 a month.

October 6, 1863

And fine day. Great excitement about reenlisting. The papers were drawn up and most of the Co signed. But I wouldn't at first until I had a little talk with Cap. The Boys, some of them, made considerable sport of me because I didn't [want] to go. But I talked with Cap and he advised me to go. He said that when they got back to the State and got furlough to go home and when he come to see Mother she would want to know why William didn't come. And he would hate to tell her that I wouldn't come and she would think right off that something was the matter twixt him and me. He seemed to think that she would rather I would come home with the Co. And I finally thought so to. And I guess Cap was about Right. I hope so for I want to go with the Boys. I certainly should dislike to go into another Regt. To be sure I could worry through 11 months most any way but I would rather go with the Boys. If Mother is satisfied then I can go it.

Most of the Regt has signed & the major made us a speech, a verry Patriotic one. I think when we come to start there will be many more go along. They cant stand the Pressure. I can't anyway. This going home & getting a furlough and getting the Big Bounty and more than all this, we will belong to the Veteran Corps and have the Badge of Honor to wear. And the honor of belonging to the Veteran Corps is something. Taking it all togather I must go and the more effect it will have on the war will be as good as a hard Battle and perhaps many Battles. Just think the old troops going in again after having such hard times, it shows our hearts are in the work. The thought will make the Rebels tremble.

October 7, 1863

And rather stormy. Just at night set in & rained verry hard. The excitement continues unabated about the reenlisting. There are a few that try to put a damper on the thing. But I guess they will fail. The Boys generally want to go. Some of the Boys have been back to Camp. They say the 6th [Wisconsin] and 2nd [Wisconsin] don't go into it so strong as we do. They are between a Hawk and a Buzzard about it. I want to go the more I think about it. Going in under the same officers is what just suits me. Our Co officers are good and well liked in the Co. There are some to be sure that don't like them. But evrybody has their enemies. This carrying 8 days rations has played out. Our ration wagon come out today. We were glad to see it for we wanted some Pork verry bad.

October 9, 1863

And fine day. We were relieved today by 19th Ind [Indiana] and come back to camp. We carried a lot of boards back and fixed up our tent good, raised it about 18 inches which makes it verry nice.

October 10, 1863

And fine day. We had to get up last night to draw rations, 5 days which makes 8 days so we have to act commisary now. We got orders and marched at 8 A.M. Went out to where we were on duty supporting the Pickets. There we layed down. Now we think we are going across the River shortly. But it didnt come. We lay around till 2 P.M. when we went into camp, got dinner, drew Beef, got supper, expecting to march every minute. But the impression now is that we are going to retreat. John & I boils our beef, Jake being detailed to go on Picket when we went into camp.

8 P.M. we are ordered to pack up & the few teams that are here are going to the rear. We now think it's a retreat. We lay around till 9 P.M. when we are ordered up, start to the rear. We hear our Brigade is to go in the rear which proved to be so. We traveled along slowly to near Stephensburg when we camped. It being after midnight we lay down till 3 when we were ordered up and started on our march. Ordered back after a few taking a few steps. So we sit around & get breakfast.

Come daylight & still don't start. We get early dinner, 12N & start. March along good jog when we see away off to the right about a mile our cavelry forming to fight the Rebel cavelry. Boom goes the cannon of both. Then we see a great smoke & a few shots. Now they are fighting hard. We can't see them they being just over the hill. But the quantity of smoke tells us old veterans that they are fighting hard. As we rise on higher ground going through the town we see our cavelry coming back and forming. This is all done while we was going ½ mile. We come through the town, find another Battery posted to the right on the hill. We travel on Briskly. The constant cannonading doing a great deal to keep many from straggling.

We leave the main road to the right, taking the road to Kellys Ford. We come briskly till the head of the column reached Mountain Run where we stacked arms and waited for about a division to cross, they having a sort of a Bridge made & run across 1, 2 & 3 at a time. But when our Brigade come to it, we plunged right in and in 15 minutes the whole Brigrade was across where it took long for a Regt of those Yankees to cross. We come briskly to Rappahannock, cross on Pontoon Bridge just below the fort. We being the last of the corps, it is said that only our corps is on this road.[118]

It appears to me that the whole army is falling back to the Defences of the Rappahannock. We find cannon in the forts to defend the Bridge. We come out about half mile & camped. Tis dark, we get supper, go to bed without pitching tents. Last night the same, laying on our tents. There has been constant firing of cannon all the time and just as we cross, it appears to be just up the River near Railroad Bridge. Tis said here that our forces burned the Bridge. The Boys are verry tired, some having rued that they joined the Veteran Corps. But I don't for I looked for this & even worse if it could be worse. It isnt the distance we marched, but the laying around for 2 days and 1 night. Tis more tiresome that marching 20 miles each day and having good nights sleep. I look for worse times than this. Glad twas no worse.

The Boys was glad when they got across the River for we were in a bad fix if attacked while on the other side & I must admit that I lay down to sleep feeling more safe and as though I might sleep all night. Many of the Boys expressed themselves in this way. I am glad I have got into America again and begun to whistle &c.

October 12, 1863

And fine day. We lay around all day nothing of importance transpired. About 2 P.M. most of us pitched tents to get a shade & if all well to stay to sleep in them which we did till about 12 oclock that night.

October 13, 1863

And fine day. We marched at 1 oclock this morning. We marched till we reached Warrenton Junction. We got here about 10 A.M. & got breakfast and layed till about 2 P.M. when we marched and came to Bristol. Reached here about 10 P.M., we camped. There is lots of troops on the road and the roads and fields are full of wagons, cattle and Batteries, all on the retreat. But is all goes on orderly. No confusion. There is some truble in crossing the creek. We got over them dry. But the wagons and Batteries got across slowly. But I guess all right. I think the Rebs won't get much although they follow close. But our cavelry keeps them at bay. We hear all day at intervals some canonading. Evrybody appears to think we will be enough for them when we get as far as we want to go. We will turn around and fight them. From appearances we will fall back as far as Centerville.

October 14, 1863 [Battle of Bristoe Station]

And fine day. We were awoke at 4 AM this morning. Drew rations, ordered to march. But the Adjutant General thought we might have time to get our breakfast. He thought. But there was no order to that effect. But do as we choose about [it]. They all & I with them put in and got it. Had plenty of time. We drew 4 days rations which makes us 8 days still on hand. About 5 we marched. And marched along pretty lively to Centerville. Coming by Manassas Junction and crossing Bull Run Creek at Blackburns Ford, the same place as last summer. We waded right through, never stoping to pull off shoes. But this morning soon after starting, we crossed Broad Run. This is quite a stream. Here the officers told us to pitch in and get across the best way we could and would form on the other side, which we done verry quickly in half the time we could [have] done any other way. We reached Centerville about 1 P.M. & took position on the left of the Corps which had formed line of Battle on the heights here. We seem to be forming to act on the defensive until all our trains get by. They have been going rapidly. The constant cannonading to be heard some 8 or 10 miles off. But not heavy say overall a shot evry 5 minutes hurries things. Great many reports about things. Both our losses & gains, none of them to be credited. We got dinner about 2 P.M. Heavy canonading begins and going upon the little hill in front, looking away across the valley some 10 miles to a ridge, we see the smoke & hear the noise of a number of guns and from the appearance of the smoke, we conclude there is some infantry engaged. But probably nothing but cavelry.

3 P.M. The fight now is going on which appears to be more than an ordinary skirmish and is interesting the officers some. It is watched with intense interest. They are seen to shift position but we can't tell which side it is.

4 P.M. And still they fight. Evrybody is beginning to think we may be called on.

5 P.M. & fight is over & said to be in our favor. The excitement, what little there was, has cooled down.

6 P.M. And a few shots is heard in the direction of the Battlefield. We commence to get supper. The teams still go back and some are being parked just over the hill. The Boys begin to pitch tents thinking we will stay here all night. I go after some tent poles, John & Jake getting supper. We draw fresh beef. When I get back I found all ready to move. But twas only ¼ mile to the right & rear to get into some Rebel Brestworks. Those that were cooking supper stayed to finish it. John was amongst them and after we got here, Jake went back to help John bring the supper which soon came and we ate with a good relish.

Pitched tent, went to bed, it now being about 9 P.M. There has been a few shots since dark. I was verry unfortunate today. I lost all the meat we all had. We had it in a bag and carried it in turns & I forgot to pick it up when starting after resting.[119]

October 15, 1863

Rather stormy but not bad. Light showers. Appearances of a great storm soon. Nothing unusual transpired last night. We lay behind the brestworks till about 4 P.M. when we ordered to get ready and march. Just before we marched, there was some firing twixt the Rebs and our men at long range. We marched about 1 mile to the right and took position behind good Brestworks. Looks like we will have a stormy night. Got supper and pitched tent, went to bed with orders to keep our cartridge boxes where we could get hold of them at a minutes warning in case we should be attacked. We can see 1 line if not 2 lines of battle about 1 mile in front. The fight yesterday turned out to be all in our favor. Took 5 pieces of artillery, 450 prisinors.[120]

October 16, 1863

And stormy day, heavy showers all day at intervals of an hour or so. Just after dark verry hard shower with heavy wind. This evening we drew Beef and John & I bought some so we have plenty of meat, which we need verry bad especially in bad weather. In cold stormy weather we can eat a third more meat. We fixed up our Brestworks some and made some new on our right. We, I guess, are ready for the Rebs. But I think they will never attack us here, for this is an open field for a mile in front our Brigade. We feel quite safe here.

Gen. [Solomon] Meredith come back today. He was wounded at Gettysburg. Has not been with us since. He made the Boys a speech. They had gathered around his headquarters to see him.

October 17, 1863

And fine day. The sun shone out bright. Fine time for those that got their blankets wet to dry them. But we kept ours dry. We drew 5 days rations more today and considerable extra to make up for our losses and waste, which we have from carrying them so many days. No fighting today. From the papers we hear all is right. We lost comparitively nothing in our retreat & worsted the enemy evry time they engaged our forces. General Mead is too much for Lee this time. Lee was 3 or 4 hours too late to get into the rear of Mead. As they say, he was just in time to be to late. Evrybody has great confidence in Mead.

October 18, 1863

And fine day. We got orders this morning to be up & ready to march at 5 A.M. We got ready and waited most all day for the order to march. But didn't come. But about 3 P.M. we got orders to pitch tents which we done. And nothing transpired the rest of the day.

October 19, 1863

And stormy till about 10 A.M. when it cleared off. The sun come out warm and twas a pleasant afternoon. We got the same orders this morning as yesterday morning. But we fulfilled them this time. A little after daylight we marched taking the Warrenton Pike, come to Haymarket, we come by Gainesville and the old Battlefield. We got here. By the roadside see many graves, one with the head out. We camped near Haymarket. Most of our Regt went out on picket, out on the Warranton Pike. Here we can hear fighting twixt our & the Rebel cavelry. 25 of us were posted as a reserve, I with them. The Picket line was soon formed. Fighting continued all the time, sometimes verry fierce, some artillery firing and lots of small arms.[121]

A man comes down the road post haste. Our sentinel that was posted on the road stops him. He wants to know where our corps headquarters are. Sentinel tell him. He orders his orderly to go tell Gen. [John] Newton that our cavelry is hard pushed & one Brigade cut off. So he goes off. We still hear hard fighting, it being only 1 ½ [mile] away. Our cavelry falling back, takes position near us on a hill. Some wounded goes by. Good many riderless horses, their riders, many of them being dismounted as skirmishing. Our cavelry falls back, leaving us outside. The firing nears us. Zip the shell goes over our heads, bang two or three burst right amongst us. Several fall without bursting. Wounded one man.

We ordered out, leave in a great hurry, evry man for himself. We get into the road going to camp. The major of the Picket line tries to form us as skirmishers but he couldn't do much. The Boys was too much excited. At last the rebel come to here. Ball whiz all around us. The Major orders double quick and starts himself. He being mounted, of course he outrun us. We soon see the regt which we made to join, which were forming line of Battle. The whole is aroused. We heard the reb charge on our cavelry or our cavelry charge on them. I couldn't tell which. But I know they [had] us fellows nearly surrounded once. But when they saw our Infantry forming they give back. So I guess most of them got in. All of our Co did. But many the balls that whized by my ears & heels. Our cavelry fell clear back and the Rebs didnt choose to tackle us when formed in line of Battle. After we got rightly formed we lay down till about 2 P.M. when we fell back to the other side of the town and bivuacked, taking a strong position, I suppose as rear guard. I thought we would fall back to Centerville.

I guess the rebs rather worsted us today. They having Infantry to support cavelry is what done it. And our cavelry has been fighting them all day without any infantry to support them and they were pretty well exausted. Well, we bivuacked one third of the Regt under arms all the time and the others to sleep with their cartridge boxes on and guns by their side.

October 20, 1863

And fine day. We were all ordered up at 4 oclock this morning and got breakfast to march at 5. But we didn't march. Then we got dinner there. Our Co. went out to relieve Cos. A. D. who were on Picket all night. We went out about a mile, found them in a nice place with only one Post. We relieved them, they went back to camp, we stayed there till about 3 ½ P.M. when we were ordered to form with the other pickets up on the line which we did and went up to the town. The corps was marching by going towards Thoroughfare gap. Here we waited till our regts come along when we fell in & come along. We marched verry slow, coming verry slow. At last we get to the gap and through it going verry slow, taking a byroad, the teams going on the main road. Tis about 1/3 mile through the gap. After getting through the gap we turned of to the left, went up onto raise in the ground and bivoucked in the open air, it now being about 12 oclock or midnight. We have come about 7 miles and has been a hard march

October 21, 1863

And fine day. We lay here in camp till after dinner when we moved about 1 mile southward & went into camp. We here have a fine situation on high ground, a creek at the foot of the hill and plenty of spring water. We made some improvements in our tent. I cut my piece in two & sewed a piece to the end of each others making them 2 feet longer. And I had picked up a piece on the road and cut it just the size to fasten up one end so we now have plenty of room and can sleep without our feet being outdoors. We haven't heard any fighting today. I think the campaign is about over and there seems to be a good deal of that feeling. We drew 3 days rations this evening. We now have 7 days rations on hand.

October 22, 1863

And fine day. We lay in camp. Some of the Boys are foraging on their own hook which causes the Headquarter guards good deal of truble. They having to watch and arrest such as they see them stealing from the farmers. This country here in the mountains has not been disturbed much as yet. But now the henroosts & pigstys are soon cleaned out. There is a hill near by. And there is a strong guard kept there to keep the Boys from stealing. What they have they sell, such as they have to the Boys at a reasonable price. The Boys are fixing up their tents. The indications are that we may stay here awhile. The cars came into the gap today. The Boys have got to running about so that we have roll call evry 2 hours to keep the Boys in camp.

Some shoes come today & I drew a pair of No. 8 but they are one size too large. I shall try to trade them for a smaller pair. I got a letter from Mother day before yesterday & one from Henry today. They are well. I am verry hard up now. I have no money, no stamps, no envelopes. Truly hard up. But I don't suffer any so I don't get far wrong. Good health and plenty to eat.

October 23, 1863

And fine day. Till just night when there was quite a shower and continued showery till bedtime.

We lay around & done nothing today. Some of the Boys done their washing. I have to wait till tomorrow for the kettle so as to boil the clothes or I should have washed today. I understand that our line of Battle is on the Rappahannock River again. The Rebs having fallen back and are sending their troops or a good share of them off to the Southwest to oppose [General Ambrose] Burnside's who are doing great damage to them by the way of tearing up 4 miles of their main R. Road and still at it.

October 24, 1863

And stormy all day. Had reville at 5 A.M. and orders to march at 7 A.M. which we did after getting breakfast. The rumor is that we go to Bristol [Bristoe] Station. We start, come back through the Gap and up to Haymarket on the RR track. Here we rested, having rested once before. Then we start, come by Gainesville and to within 2 miles of Bristol Station when we rested, having come all of 6 miles without resting. And we come nearly doublequick. The Boys say they never marched so before & I guess we wouldn't have rested then. But we had just waded Broad Run which was so swollen by the rain that it was up to our hips and raining all the time so we stoped to let the stragglers catch up. Then started, come through the Battlefield of the 14th Inst which I have spoken of before. Here we see many graves and dead horses and a goodly quantity of Iron &c which is characteristic of such fields showing that it was a small Battle, rather too much for a skirmish.

We come by Bristoe Station or the place rather, everything being destroyed. All there is there now has just been fixed by our men, they now having a large force at work on the road, the Rebels having destroyed the road completely. We went on out to Brentville 4 miles from Bristoe. Reached there about 4 P.M. When we were getting our supper, we [were] ordered to go back to Bristoe when we get our supper. Just after dark we started and went to within 1 mile of Bristoe having to wade Kettle Run or now it is a river, so swollen is it by the rain which has been incessent all day. This make three times we have waded up to our hips. We turned off the road in the low pine woods and bivaucked. It is now 9 P.M. We have made 20 miles today. And having so many wet things to carry (tents &c) that we are completely tired out. Greater part of the Boys say they will not go into the Veteran Corps now. That they will serve out the 10 months and go home for good. But as for me, I am just as much a veteran as ever I was, real stanch veteran.

October 25, 1863

And fine day. The sun shone out bright and warm which was a fine thing for us fellows. We lay in around till noon when most of us put [up] our tents. We drew rations today to do the month out (viz 3 days) having several days on hand. This being Sunday, we have church services. All the Chaplains in the Brigade have joined & we now have Brigade services all at the same place. This being my week for drawing rations for the Co, I couldn't well attend church. Now all the noncommissioned officers have to draw a week apiece. The boys are getting lots of Percimmons. They are verry plenty this year. The mail come in today. I got a letter from Henry. Alls well as usual. He has got the $50.00 I sent him and 50 cents more. The Doctor at the Hospital must have made a mistake. I left him 30 cents to pay expressage. But he sent all that and 20 cents more. I allways knew he was a gentleman or I wouldnt have trusted him to sent it. I got a Post Stamp in same letter.

October 26, 1863

And fine day. We lay in camp all day. I, with some of the Boys went down to Broad Run. Got some grapes & washed hands & face. Some of them not washed since they left the Gap. Late in the evening for an hour or so there was heavy canonading off to our left. Probably a skirmish. The officers are making out the payrolls for the months of Sept & Oct. I must write a letter now as I have got some stamps and traded one stamp for 3 envelopes.

October 27, 1863

And fine day. I drew 3 days more rations today. Today there is considerable canonading off on our left. Probably a skirmish only as it lasted only an hour or so. The rebels, it is said, are all on the other side of the Rappahannock except a few roving bands of Gurrillias.

October 28, 1863

I and John washed all day. Done our own & Jakes & for the officers and several of Boys. We had nothing but a small kettle which made it slow work. I washed one without washboard & that made my hands sore. Then while John was washing some, I took my hatchet, walked up to a cedar tree and in less than half an hour I had a washboard that answered the purpose as well as a zinc one. So we got along first rate. Jake got dinner for us. Also supper.

October 29, 1863

And fine day. We have a detail of 2 to 3 men out of a Co. for picket now. There was rations of whiskey issued today by the commissary & some of the Boys didnt drink any and others drank their rations so the consequence was that some 2 or 3 got tight and made a great deal of noise and towards night the Brigade got verry noisy and just at night there was a Brigade guard put on. I guess old Col Robinson (he is commanding the Brigade now) thought that if they couldn't behave themselves we would give them something to do. This is what I think, only I may be wrong.

We drew soft bread today which pleased me as well as the Boys verry much. We have straightened & cleaned up camp & the indications are that we will stay here a while. I wrote a letter to Mother today and sent it along with Henrys which I mailed today. We now have our mail regularly evry day.

October 30, 1863

And fine day. We still draw soft bread. I drew all kinds of rations today that is allowed, even to dried apples & pepper &c the first since we left the Rappidan [Rapidan]. John went down to the Butchers and bought us a verry nice piece of beef for which he paid 10 cents and with what we draw will keep us in beef for quite a while. We drew some verry nice bacon today. They are giving us lots of good rations now.

Our going home has played out. We cant go, so the War Department say. So the Veteran Buisness is played out and we stay 10 months more and go home for good. The President has called for 300,000 more men to be raised by Volunteering by the

4th of Jan next. And if not raised by that time there will be a draft to fill it up. All those are designed to fill up old Regt. Go ahead old Abe, I will support you in that.

October 31, 1863

And stormy in the morning till about 10 A.M. when it cleared off and was fine the rest of the day. We were mustered at 10 A.M. today for 2 months more pay, $26.00, by Maj Finnecum [Mark Finnicum of Fennimore]. We had no Inspection as we used to. He only called our names. The Regt is small, the largest Co is only 26 men for duty & we are next. We have 23 for duty. I get the [Wisconsin] State Journal regularly but not much other mail.

From todays paper we hear the Rebels have been whipped again this time by Joe Hooker. He is in command of 2 or 3 corps on the Virginia & Tennessee RR. They attack him at midnight. He drove them 5 miles &c.[122]

As for the Armies in Virginia, the Rebs are on the other side of the Rappahannock and ours just on this side. We (the 1st Corps) are on the Reserve like as near as I can hear. We have pretty heavy picketing. I guess to inside Picket for the RRoad mainly to keep the Gurrillas off.

November 2, 1863

And fine day. Today there was a detail sent out of each of the Regts that were in the fight at Gainesville to rebury the dead. They found them almost naked, many of them quite naked. There was 2 went out of our Co.

November 3, 1863

And fine day. We had election today for State officers. There was nothing unusual transpired. We still have heavy Picket detail evry 2 day and Brigade guard evry day. There is amusement for the Boys now. There having been a great deal of Foraging done by the Boys since we came here and now there has been an order issued that the officers of this Brigade will have to go without their pay until they find the men that killed the cattle &c or they themselves must pay the damages which is $50.00. This the officers swear they will not pay & they say they can't find out who did kill them & I don't know what they will do. But somebody will have to pay it I guess. For they say they are known to be Union People without that had their stock killed. I don't wish anybody harm but I would like to see something done to stop this pillaging in the army. I have always detested it and do now.

November 4, 1863

And fine day. I get some logs to fix up tent. I wash shirt, drawers & my pants. My tentmates are on Picket. They went yesterday morning. There is nothing going on except most of the Boys are gambling playing what they call Cap Poker. They have no money but value the caps [musket percussion caps] at 10 cents each and play for them and redeem them payday.

November 5, 1863

And fine day but windy today. There is a Sergt, Corpl, Private out of our camp for Picket. I was the Corpl to go. We went out at 9 AM. All the Boys from our Regt Cos are on Reserve this time out. We stay till about 3 PM when we were drew in to camp to march. But we found they had gone so we went on & overtook them on the road to Catlets Station [Catlett Station] road. We, our Brigade bringing up the rear & on wagon guard, we were divided up half a Regt in a place. We got along slow getting to within 1 mile of Catlets at midnight. Here we camped for the night. Came 6 miles.

November 7, 1863

Coming along the Rail Road to several miles south of Warrenton Junction when we left it. We are leading the Corps today (our Regt is). We come along pretty brisk, resting once & awhile for to let the wagons get along. We are to go to Morrisville they say, which we did or near it. And turned into the field, made coffee after which the order come to camp for the night. The weather being fine, not many of us pitched tents. Just made down beds in open air.

They say we come about 12 miles today came most of it in the forenoon at which time we hear cannonading up the Rappahannock (river wards) which is kept up steady all the afternoon and towards night it grows more fierce. And by going out from camp a little, we can hear musketry or small arms, perhaps cavelry. From appearances I guess we will go to the Rappahannack River & take up line.[123]

November 8, 1863

And march at daylight, come to Kelleys Ford & cross the river on a Pontoon Bridge. Went about half mile, got dinner. Here we hear that our forces took 3 cannon & 1500 prisinors yesterday when that fighting was going on & that we whipped the Rebs badly. We start again and march along, pretty good jog, till we reached Brandy Station. Here we turned to the left and went about 1 mile, formed line of Battle and Bivaucked in rear of our arms, it now being just dark. The whole army has crossed the River last night & today & I hear ready to give battle if need be. There has been considerable firing today away upon the right at times. Pretty heavy especially as night comes. But ceasing soon after. The rumor is that we are victorious.

November 9, 1863

And fine day. But rather windy. There was a few flakes of snow today which started most of the Boys to pitching tent and after getting most of them pitched, the order come to march immediately. Which we did taking the road to Rappahannock Station 6 miles distant. None of the army but our corps appears to be going. The officers tell us if we get to the Bridge first, we cross first and get camp sooner. So we put out nearly doublequick & did reach the Bridge first & just before dark we crossed without stopping. Came up the river some 3 miles & bivouacked in the woods opposite Beverly Ford. We reached here about 7 P.M. We started at half past 4 P.M. having come at least 8 ½ miles in 2 ½ hours. There has been no firing today.

November 10, 1863

And cold, windy and cloudy. Snowed a little here last night. But looking over the other side of the River to the Blue Ridge, there we can see the snow plainly. The mountains are perfectly white. But none to be seen on this side. Twas verry cold last [night]. We lay around till about noon when we draw 3 days rations and get dinner & move camp. Going about ½ mile in some nice thick timber and camped in good order, if need be to stay all winter. Have orders to cut no timber till further order. It appears that our corps is on the reserve certain. Tis said only our corps on this side & there was only 1st & 2nd divisions of it. We left the 3rd division at Bristoe when we come away. Just at dark tonight, the sergt major come around for a detail of 7 men from our Co to go and work on the Rail Road. To start at half past 6 in the morning, take six days rations with them. They were supposed to have 8 days rations but none had it and taking the Regt through twill not average more than 4 days. But the order is to take plenty. Let that be what it may so all those that were going to work drew 3 or 4 days more rations. There is some 50 or 60 to go out of our Regt tomorrow.

November 11, 1863

The Boys started this morning according to order of last evening. They all appear glad of the chance to change buisness and they think we will not have to move soon. And that also pleases them for we havn't much rest since I came to the Co and now we will be apt to get it. To be sure we will have to work about half the time and Picket one quarter of the time for each and evry man. But we will be content with that and glad to have it to do nothing worse.

This morning about 8 oclock the Paymaster come and we signed the payroll and then they were sent to the men on Picket & those that went to work for them to sign them & in the evening about 4 oclock we got our pay. Our Regt was paid first this time. The Captains drew the money for those on duty as usual. I got all that was due me on clothing account, $13.80, making in all $39.80 & I collected what was owing me otherwise till now I have $57.00 and some yet due me. I shall be able to send home $50.00 and give some to the war widow Mrs. Simpkins. Her husband, James [W.] Simpkins was a member of our Co and was killed at Antietam.[124] He was a good soldier & was much respected in the Co and the Co concluded to get up a contribution in the Co.

November 12, 1863

And fine day. The boys are settling up & paying each other which they always do and signed their contribution for the war widow. Some giving 25 cts & on up to $2.00. I gave $2.00. I was the only one that gave that amount when I signed. I did think of giving $5.00 but Cap thought $1.00 was enough as we could get up another sometime hence. That what she would get this time would do for sometime as they, the officers, would give $5.00 apiece which would be $15.00. I made me a washboard & fixed up a tub. Put handles, preparatory for washing tomorrow.

November 13, 1863

I & Jake washed today. We washed John clothes for getting & bringing our dinners to us. We wash for others to the amount of $1.10 which being divided leaves each with 55 cents for his days work or rather about 5 hours and our own washing which in all is as good as 75 cents for the day. We get 10 cents apiece for washing.

We, in our tent, had a big quarrel yesterday. Jake & John doing the most for I left there. Twas on account of John neglecting his duties as tentmates. He has not done much of late. I suppose like most of us he has his lazy fits as well as working ones.

November 14, 1863

And fine day. There was a detail for Picket this morning and I, not being detailed to go, and not wanting to go on work to the Railroad so I change with one of the Boys & come on Picket. The R Road squad will go out the morning we come off Picket, but 3 hours earlier. We started at 10 A.M., came to the lines. Here we was counted off, 15 out of our Regt squad to go outside of the lines to the lookout post some half mile in advance. Here we have a nice place, one Post in daytime, 2 at night so that will not be hard work. We have good water and plenty of good wood. All went right till just dark when it commenced to rain and thunder & lightening & we had one of the hardest storms I have seen in Virginia and it tapered down to a steady rain & rained about half the night. I was on Post through the first & worst of it. We only stand an hour at a time. I sheltered under a big tree. But get wet almost to the skin and when relieved found the fire at quarters almost out, the Boys having crawled into their shanties and let it go out. But I went to work and amidst the rain, I soon had a good fire. And sat around kind comfortable till 12 oclock when I went groping my way to my post, it being so dark that I could not see the man so I had to whistle. He answered me & in that way found the post to stand another hour but didn't rain much this time.

November 15, 1863

And rained some in the morning but cleared of about 10 A.M. and was kind a pleasant. Nothing of note transpires about in this vicinity. But we hear some firing away down the River. A skirmish I suppose. Some of the Boys went into camp today, got the mail. But none for me. But the [Wisconsin] State Journal which will come good to read.

November 16, 1863

And fine day. Nothing of interest transpired till about noon when the officer of the day came and had the picket line advanced outside of us thereby doing away with the lookout post. & we went on the Picket Reserve. But still had one Post to stand amongst 7 of us and we stood 2 hours so we came on only once in the night. Twas pretty cold tonight. I went on at 6 & stood till 8 oclock so I had all night to sleep.

November 17, 1863

And fine day. About 10 A.M. the Relief came and after being relieved we came to camp. Found the rest of the Co had gone on fatigue duty which proved to be working on a fort at Rappahannock Station. The Boys that went to work on the R Road come back when only out 5 days. They having got the Road finished to the River. And on the other side the road is not torn up for we drove the Rebs away so quick that they had not a chance. John went on Picket so there is one out of our tent most of the time.

November 18, 1863

Jake and I done a big washing today. We made $1.60 apiece besides our own washing. About 10 AM they made another detail to work on fortifications and sent for Jake but when he got to camp, they had sent another man so he came back and helped me finish which took us till nearly night. Worked verry hard.

I expressed my money this evening. The Chaplain starts with it in the morning for Washington. There has been men sent home to Recruit from the Regt from our State. Cap [Hollon] Richardson is the commissioned officer from our Regt, then there is a Sergt & Private from each Co. George Eustice (Sergt) and Private C. B. Bishop [Corydon B. Bishop] from our company went to recruit. They started yesterday morning at 8 oclock so now we are certain that the Veterans scheme has played out.

Gambling is going on at a great rate. Most evrybody but me is at it. Boys in our Co set up all night, at least some do, to Gamble. Tis really shocking to see to what extent it is carried on.

November 19, 1863

And fine day. There was a detail made late last night to go on fatigue. But this morning the order was countermanded with the explanation of marching. But we laid in camp all day and done nothing. We drew 2 days rations of soft bread today. We have lots of rations now and that is good.

Today the ceremonies and dedications of the National Cemetary for the fallen brave of the Battle of Gettysburg. The President is to be there and the Govenors of each and all the states that had soldiers there (except Rebels states) and in fact each & all or evrybody that chose to go or could go.[125]

November 20, 1863

And fine day. We that were to work yesterday, went today. Our work was filling up all the old Rebel works around Rappahannock Station both on this & the other side of the River. We get done 8 P.M. and the Sergt of the Engineer Corps wanted us to help the 2nd Brigade finish their job. But we wouldn't which caused some words & we came home. We done a big days work & the Sergt said so, but he feared that if we didn't stay, the others would leave. But we came home. We expressed our money today, the chaplain taking it to Brandy Station. I sent $50.00 to Henry.

November 21, 1863

And rainy day, all day. Rained some last night also. Tis a verry disagreeable day. We keep good fires in front of our tents which makes it more comfortable. We got no dailies today or yesterday. The reason I don't know unless they expected to move. & the Main Army may have moved but our Corps didnt. Cap Bird of Co I [Joseph N.P. Bird of Wautoma] come to the Co this morning, he hasn't been with it since the Battle of Gainesville. He was badly wounded there & he is now lame.

November 23, 1863

And fine day. Nothing of note transpired till just night when the orders come to be ready to march at daylight on the morrow morning. So we drew our rations from the Co commissary, he having kept the rations in the boxes till we wanted them to use as they will keep better there than in the haversack.

November 24, 1863

And stormy. We didnt march as was ordered last night. The storm preventing I suppose. The Pickets were drawn in this morning but went out again at 10 A.M.

November 25, 1863

And fine day. We lay in camp today. I got a letter from Mother and Lucretia. They were both well as usual. Mother had rented the same rooms of Sarah she had 3 years since, & her & Lucretia are going to live together which I am pleased to hear. I think they will live verry comfortable.

November 26, 1863 [Mine Run Campaign]

And we marched at daybreak, crossed the Rappahannock at the R Road Bridge & traveled on nicely till within ½ mile of Elys Ford on the Rappidan River. I should judge we come 15 miles today. We came through the timber most of the way making altogether a rather a pleasant march. We reached the ford about 10 P.M., bivauck by the roadside. Tis said by the Commisarys that the 5th and 2nd Corps crossed today without opposition.[126]

November 27, 1863

And fine day. We got up at 2 A.M., started to march at 3 A.M., crossed the Rappidan River and traveled most all day on different roads coming, I cant tell where. We lay by the roadside for about 2 hours and got dinner. All this time there is skirmishing of to our left & front. Some ways off though.[127] Then we started and marched another direction, come on to the Orange Co Pike. Shortly after camped. It now being about 10 P.M. and we are right by Meads Headquarters.

We had a little brush with the Gurilles. Our Brigade led the corps today and the Gurrillas attacked the 5th Corps wagon train. They being just ahead of us so we got in line & marched through the woods. Our skirmish line drove them back so we didn't get a shot at them. We pushed them so hard they couldnt get off with all the wagons so they took the mules, set the wagons on fire. And while we were there, 4 or 5 ammunition wagons blew up. Twas a pretty sight if twas our own. The pieces flew & the shells burst in evry direction.

November 28, 1863

And rains some today. We got up at 2 A.M., marched at 3 AM, come to Robinsons [Robertson's] Tavern. Here we turned of the road and stoped, it being daylight now. We lay here till about 9 AM when we started through the woods. Skirmishers ahead. Came about 1 ½ miles when we were halted, formed line, our skir [skirmishers] firing pretty brisk with the Rebs. We lay here all day. Our Batteries threw a few shells & the Rebs replied with a few shots. When it ceased & all was quiet except skirmishers firing constantly. We lay in a hollow & by going on the top of the hills, we can see away across a big field. There the Rebs are plenty. Our men have planted lots of canons on the top of the hill. Night comes and all quiet. Our Brigade skirmishers captured 3 Reb cavalry men when we advanced this morning. They are fine looking men.

November 29, 1863

And fine but cold day, sharp wind blowing. We have big fires and keep comfortable. This morning at daylight we moved out of the hollow up on the hillside in a good position, so as the hill will shelter us from the enemies shells if they should open on us or reply to our guns if they open. Which they did at 8 A.M., threw a few shots and the Rebs made a feeble reply. And soon all ceased and nothing but skirmish firing. There is a few comes in wounded & one or two killed today. The day passed off without any heavy fighting. But the usual amount of rumors. But there is one consolation. That is that we know [Union General Ulysses S.] Grant is doing just about as he pleases with Rebs, he having whipped them bad.[128]

November 30, 1863

And fine, but cold north wind blowing. We as usual expected the thing would open this morning but only our guns threw a few shots and got no reply. But a Brass Battery kept up a desultory fire with one piece at the enemies Pickets or skirmishers and so the day passed off. We drew Beef this evening and a little later we drew 5 days rations of sugar, coffee, meat and hardtack & salt. Some or most of the Boys was out of rations. Some had no bread for 4 of 5 meals back. I, having more than I would eat, gave some 25 crackers to them. I have a good large haversack and took care of & drew all I get. While some of those hungry chaps was playing Poker instead of drawing their full rations.

December 1, 1863

And fine day. Still a raw wind blowing, but tis from the south today. Things passed off pretty much the same today as yesterday until about 2 P.M. when we drew beef again. And got orders to be ready to move. So we went to work & got a good [meal], John having got 25 cents worth of beef liver from the butcher.

4 P.M. And we relieved the Penn Reserves. They form the 3rd Div of 3rd Corps. And we marched out, taking the road and come to Germania Ford on the Rappidan which we reached about 10 P.M. When we got there, the 2nd & 7th [Wisconsin] had to go on Picket up the road on the other side about 1 ½ miles so we crossed the River, come up. The 2nd going on reserve, we went out to the front and turned off the road into the woods & camped. One man from a Co had to go on Picket, there being only two Posts. The others bivoucked and twas not long ere we was in bed. We come over some verry rough road. Come about 9 miles. The Boys think tis a retreat. But I hardly think the Army will retreat tonight. But it may for the rumor is that Longstreet has come back from the Southwest with his Corps de army. And if so, I think we have not forces enough to cope with Lee. If we cant, why we draw so many forces away from Grants front, which will give him a still better chance.[129]

December 2, 1863

And fine day. We found when we got up, we found the whole army has come across this side of the river, a good share coming along this road through the night. We lay here till about 10 A.M. When the rest of the Brigade coming up, we fell [in] and went along. Taking a kind of a byroad, went to Mortons Ford. Got near the ford, turned into the woods. Made coffee, expecting to go to Rappahannock Station tonight. And that we had been sent here to guard this ford to keep the Rebs from crossing till our trains &c should get back. But night and we bivouked. We heard 2 or 3 canon when we first came here. & that is all for today.

December 3, 1863

And fine day. We lay here till 12N when we marched to Mountain Run. Crossed it and camped. We are now within 2 ½ miles Kelly Ford. We once thought before we stoped, we would put the Rappahannock between us and the Rebs. We found many troops along the roadside putting up winter quarters. We begin now to think that the campaigning is over for this fall. We hope so at least.

December 4, 1863

And fine day we lay in camp till 12N when we marched about 1 ½ miles on the road to Kellys Ford and turned into the woods & camped. Good water, plenty of wood. Evrything indicates that we will go into winter quarters. But there is no order for it. But the Boys went to work and by night some had up enough timber to build their shanties. Jake & I got up a few logs. John has left us or we left him to tent by ourselves.

December 5, 1863

The Boys are busy building their quarters, & some are waiting till further orders. I and Jake for the latter and till some of the Boys get done so that we can get the axes. But lo & behold about 3 P.M. orders come to pack up and be ready to march at a minutes notice. So all work ceased. We wait & night comes & bedtime. But no orders so we lay down. Some were cursing, some laughing. The former for having to leave their half finished shanties & the latter pleased because they hadnt done any more & also that the others were so foolish as to go to work without orders.

December 6, 1863

Verry cold night last night. Today passed off and we stay at camp but the order of last evening still unchanged. But the Boys couldnt rest. They put in a good day on their shanties. Some have theirs raised. Generally four are going together & building so that 2 tents will cover them. Therefore they are 7 by 10 feet inside, generally.

December 7, 1863

7th And fine day. & the order of the 5 inst still unchanged & the Boys still at work on their shanties. Jake & I got up our logs today, thought we wouldnt wait any longer. We had an ax to use all day so we got all our logs. We split them so they will build up & make much nicer house than round poles. We worked verry hard.

December 8, 1863

And fine day. The same as yesterday. Today we get up our shanty as far as to where the gable ends will begin. That order is still unchanged but the teams are unloaded and the officers are building quarters. Today there was a small Picket detail made one man from a Co. Tis inside Picket line.

December 9, 1863

And fine day. And we still continue work on the shanties. And we now think we will stay here all winter. Some of the Boys have got their shanties finished. And our next neighbors asked us into theirs to sleep till we should get ours finished which we expected. And found it much more comfortable than sleeping in the tent.

December 10, 1863

And fine day & things same as yesterday. I got my chimney commenced today & got the cover on.

December 11, 1863

And fine day & things as yesterday except I had to go and draw rations, this being my week for the buisness. This Brigade more expecially this Regt is agitating the Veteran Corps question again and many are going into it.

December 12, 1863

And windy, cloudy and looks like twas preparing for a big storm. Jake & I are about ready for it. We slept in our house last night. We will soon have it done. We are taking considerable pains with it & the Boys generally pronounce it pretty nice. There is Big news from the Southwest. Our troops have captured great many prisinors.

December 13, 1863

And rainy day. Rained hard last night. Jake went on picket today & now I have to work alone today. Our chimney smoked some and I fixed it some today and it goes better. I must hurry with my work & write some to the folks. I have not wrote for so long that they may think hard of it. But I cant well help it for I am so busy that I cant do it.

December 14, 1863

And fine day. But verry muddy under foot. I put a bunk in today & still keep doing a little. I have joined the Veterans if the Regt does. But not if the Regt don't go to the State within 100 days to reorganise and Recruit. But on no other terms.

December 15, 1863

And fine day. Jake come in off Picket and brought some nails & lumber that he picked up around some old houses that had been torn down by the Soldiers. Such has been the fate of many of the empty houses around here. We made a door & put up some shelves today and done little things now that a man wouldnt think of if he were not building. We have a Pane of glass. We will have to make a frame for it so we will have a window, a luxury that none of the other Boys have.

December 16, 1863

And fine day. The regt turned out today and policed the streets and grounds and I had to go also. Cap sent Jake to borrow a spade and shovel to ditch our street with. So after I was done policing, I went to work and daubed the shanty. Jake doing my part of the ditching street so as I might get it done, which I did by night. Now we have it daubed both inside and out and find it verry comfortable. Finished the days work by hanging the door.

The street needed ditching verry bad. Although the ground is considerable inclined (to the east), the water does not run off. The cause I suppose is the soap clay which lies about 3 inches under a gravel soil. This clay will hold water equal to a bucket. The Boys at first thought it would be great stuff for daubing their shanties. But it proved an utter failure for it cracked so bad as to leave almost as much open as before. But lucky for me it was proven before I wanted to use any. The top soil almost as good as lime & sand. It becomes verry firm when dry.

December 17, 1863

Stormy day & latter part of last night. Jake had to go on Picket again this morning. The duty is verry heavy now & for a week past. There is a detail evry day to build Corderroy [corduroy] road[130] on all the principle roads to be used from the RailRoad Station to all headquarters. I got wood &c & read a little in the newspapers. The talk now about the Veteran is that we cant to go home as an organization. That we cant be spared out of the field. So I for one don't go. But there are several going from the Co.

December 18, 1863

And fine day. I got my shoe mended today which had a hole in the side. Our drum major is the cobler for the Regt or at least for those that choose him. I bought 3 candles today. They will do till we draw again. I put a latch on the door & ditched some around the shanty & built a porch over the door today. Got wood &c.

The Sutlers are coming up now. There is two up now & selling in 6th & 19th. I tried to get a coffee pot but they were all sold. We need one verry bad. I witnessed the shooting of a Soldier this afternoon of the 2nd Brigade. I neither know what his name is or what Regt. The 2nd Brigade was brought out under arms in military style. But our Boys went out just as they pleased. There being no order for us to go, we could use our pleasure. Most of the Brigade went out. Twas about ¼ mile from camp. All was ready & evrybody straining their eyes to catch a glimpse of the doomed man. At last we hear the band, playing the death march. At last they appear coming up the hill in front. There he is, the Boys say, between the Platoons and the Chaplain from our Regt walking by the side of him.

Now they reach the top of the hill and stop within a few paces of the coffin which sits with the foot of it at the head of the grave. He walks out, seats himself on the head of his coffin (and I suppose is blindfolded, the crowd being so great that I couldnt see that part of it.) Now all is ready & the band ceases to play. The Provost Marshal raises his hat from his head, up comes up the guns of the first Platoon. Then he passes it to the left which is for Aim, then drops it which is the signal to fire which they done at the same instant. And the man drops back on his coffin. The Doctor runs up to see if he is dead. Takes hold of his arm, feels of his pulse. And all is right. The guards are sent off & a crowd gathers round the lifeless corpse of a deserter. Rumor is that he deserted twice & some say three times and went as a substitute two or three times. The crowd disperses and 2nd Brigade goes to their quarters & tis all over with.

So the day passed.

December 19, 1863

And fine day. Jake come in of Picket. He has to go on Picket half the time now, the duty for the Co is so great. He sleeps two nights in the shanty and 2 nights on Picket. We are still trying to get into the Veteran Crops, still keep the thing warm. Maybe we will get it through yet so that we will get home. After Jake come, we got dinner & he & I went to the creek taking about $2.00 worth of washing with us which we done by dark. We worked verry hard to get it done. Tomorrow is Sunday and I will try to rest some.

December 20, 1863

And fine day but cold, the ground or rather mud froze hard enough last night to bear up a team today for the first time this winter. The Brigade was called out this evening & Col B Robinson (he is commanding the Brigade) made them a speech explaining the Veteran Corps arrangement. Also the commandants of the Regts said a little and a Private in the 6th Regt come out and made a good humorous as well as comical speech, caused considerable laughter. And also gives us some good sound advice and he appealed to our Patriotism. Said twas our duty to sustain the Government & that he was going to reenlist &c. And upon the whole I believe he made as many Veterans as all the rest. Major Finnecum (he commands our Regt now) told them that we had enough to take us home (viz, ¾ of the Regt) and that we meant to go &c. The major as also the Co officers are doing all they can.

December 21, 1863

And fine day, but cold. Didnt thaw much today. Jake went on Picket again. I would [have] had to went if they had called on me for a Corporal. But they didnt. I will certainly have to go verry soon. For I havent been yet. Most all of our Co has put their names down to join the Veterans corps. I wrote a letter to Mother today. I done a little more to my shanty today. Just putting on the finish. You will wonder what kind of a finish when I tell you that a hatchet & jackknife was all I had to do it with. But nevertheless you would be surprised to see how comfortable we have it. Shelves & pegs to lay & hang evrything on that we have. And they are quite numerous, more so than I thought they was before I got them all out of the knapsack & haversack & my pockets. Tis amazing what a soldier does carry.

December 22, 1863

And fine day. But still as cold as ever. This morning I went out to the Picket line to take Jake some provisions, Beef & loaf of soft bread. He had rather a scant days rations to take with him. I took some rations for John Bradly [John C. Bradley] also. He being the other man from our Co. I found them away down to the mouth of Mountain Run, about 2 miles from camp. They were verry glad to see me come with the rations. I found them in a pretty good place right on the Bank of the River with plenty of wood. When I returned to camp, I built the chimney 20 inches higher which makes it draw better. It don't smoke now. I [have] Joseph Stonehouse, a man from the next tent to sleep with me.[131] His bedmate has gone home on furlough of 15 days. There is a number from the Regt gone home. The Papers today bring the report of the Rebel General [James] Longstreet being dead. Tis a report only, as yet.[132]

The Regt was called out this afternoon and the Major read the Articles of War read to us. He also told us that all was progressing well for us going home as Veterans. This evening I feel rather sickly. But I guess tis such as I often have. I will be over it in a day or two.

December 23, 1863

And fine day. When I got up and looked out the window I see that has just snowed enough to make the ground white. Joe slept with me last night also. Jake got in from Picket about noon. We intended to wash some after getting dinner. But lo, when we were eating, the Sergt come in, telling us to be ready to march at a minutes notice. But not to take off our tents till further order. We finished dinner and talking over the probabilities of the case, then packed up. Found my knapsack pretty heavy. We having several days since drew a new tent apiece & I got a new pair of pants. I got a pair of shoes, but they being too small, I sold them and my tentmate drew a pair of boots and they were too small for him & just fitted me so I bought them of him. Give him $3.25, that being the price of them & he took my shoes, they being better than his, paying him the money. Nips me rather short but he has plenty, so I will not suffer.

Well we waited for the order till supper time, got supper and dark come and no march. Now we know we will stay here tonight & the rumor is that we are going to change camp, only we go the other side of Brandy Station, go into quarters of some other corps. But that we don't march till morning. But if we don't go, I will wash tomorrow. Tis rather bad that we have to leave our good shanty. I don't expect to find as good a one if we should go into other quarters. But the Boys don't grumble much as they expect to go home in a week or ten days. The rumor is that the mustering & paying officer is at Div Headquarters ready to muster & pay us off & that Gen. Mead says he will send us home right away and I don't care so much about having my shantie if all this transpires. Tis said that none of the other Regts is going into it.

December 24, 1863

And fine day but cold. We marched at 6 A.M., come to Culpepper. We marched fast & rested only once. We reached here about 1 P.M. and our Regt was selected to stop in the town to guard it and be quartered in empty houses. So we turned out, come into the town & waited for orders & until the cavelry leaves that are guarding the town. We waited till near night but received no orders. So we wanted our dinners & the Major took us a little ways out of town & we got it & stayed there all night.

December 25, 1863

And fine day but cold and the cavelry didnt leave the town today. But we got quarters in an old mill which we cleaned up, making it more comfortable. But there being no fireplace or stoves, we have to have our fires out doors. The teams hauled wood for us. We will have to stay here till the cavelry goes out, then we take their quarters. The officers are working at the Veterans Papers. Today passes off without any of the excitement usual on Christmas Day except the many drunken cavelry men. They are having a great spree. They say they got privilige to stay in the town over Christmas, when they expect to leave. The cars are coming in pretty brisk, heavy laden with army supplies. Our corps is camped near the town & the Brigade just in the edge of it.

December 26, 1863

A rainy day, but the team furnishes plenty of wood so we keep large fires. Several Cos has got houses and gone to themselves. The officers are still at work at the Veteran Papers. We have high hopes of going home soon, probably 3 or 4 days.

December 27, 1863

And stormy day, mud ankle deep all over town. The officers took fright at an order that Mead sent or misconstrued the meaning and stoped making out the Veteran Papers. Some of them was so vexed that they burned the papers and it caused considerable merriment amongst the Boys. Some were sorry, some were glad & the officers mad & the Boys crack jokes still harder. The cavery don't leave the town today. Some more of the Cos find quarters to & our Boys find one but when they went to clean it out they found it occupied with some furniture and a woman living in another house claimed it and sent for the Provost Guard. And we thought we had better let it go & give it up for today & sleep in the old mill another night.

December 28, 1863

Better weather but cloudy. We were not relieved as we chose to stay here on guard. The Commisary officer offered to get us permanently detailed if we were a mind to stay and get some more men and they promised to make us comfortable. So we consented & there were six more men sent down & they went on & relieved the others. So they will come on evry other day. There had ought to been 2 more non commissioned officers as it is pretty hard duty for us, but we can stand it. The officers has got to understand that order of yesterday & it has no referance to us. So they went to work at the Papers again.

December 29, 1863

And fine day. Our guard duty is the same and going all right. The captain of the Commisary is going to get us a nice little house that stands near the Depot to live in. When we get in there we will have a comfortable place. It is occupied by 3 cavelry men. But the captain is going to try to get them out. I signed some of the Papers for enlisting in the Veteran Corps today & [so] did most of the Regt.

Our Co has got a little warm house. They had to build a chimney in it. It is a verry comfortable place. The cavelry has left the town & the 14th N.Y. have come in to do duty that we was to do if we were not going home.

December 30, 1863

And fine day. 200 of the 8th Illinois cavelry who have reenlisted into the Veteran Corps went home this morning. They left the Depot in high spirits & our

Regt expects to go soon. We expect to be mustered tomorrow. Mustered out of the service & in again & mustered for pay.

December 31, 1863

And stormy day, showers. We were mustered today & are veterans now & expect to get our pay tomorrow. I went up to the quarters to be mustered. I with 23 others in our Co are fast for 3 years or during the war. The Boys seem happy to think of getting home once more. The order is for us to go as soon as the buisness can be done & the officers are working at it day and almost night. They are in as much of a hurry as the Boys for being off. I am still on guard at the Depot. The Sergt runs the guard in the afternoon & fore part of the night, then I run it the other 12 hours of the 24.

January 1, 1864, New Year's Day

And a verry cold day. Last night the ground frooze verry hard. Twas the coldest night I ever experienced in Virginia and the citizens say that it is a rare occurrence.

The Boys had great times last night. At least those that could get enough of the creature (Whiskey). Many were the orders that were filled for Whiskey at this depot and many more that were refused. Nothing but an order from the Commisary Captain will get anything here. Today passed off without anything particular.

January 2, 1864

And fine day but a cold raw wind blowing. 6 companies of the Regt has been paid off in full, Bounty &c. And our Co will be paid tomorrow & the talk is that we start home on the 4th inst. That all the government property will be turned over on the morrow & suchlike. But time will tell the story and it alone will. Today the 6th N.Y. Cavelry took the cars for home, they having reenlisted. Well I must stop to get some dinner & supper. I only get two meals a day now. Thats as much as I have an appetite for.

January 3, 1864

We got our pay today & expect to go to Washington tomorrow on our road home. We thought we would be relieved today but were not.

January 4, 1864

And stormy day. We guards were relieved this morning. Went to our Companies & got ready to start home. But we missed the first train so we had to go on the platform cars [on] the next train which came along about 11 A.M. & we came verry slowly to Alexandria which we reached about 7 P.M. & were taken to the

Soldiers Retreat, got supper. This Retreat is a verry nice one. Evrything is neat & clean. At 10 P.M. we took the train for Washington, arriving there in due time and were quartered in No. 4 Barracks. There being good fires in the stoves, it was somewhat comfortable. Here we are to stay till we draw clothing &c.

January 5, 1864

And fine day. We stay in Barracks all day. Most of the Boys getting Passes & going out & buying clothing such as they want. Most of them are buying fine hats. The Boys are having a good time generally.

January 6, 1864

And fine day. We drew clothing today. I drew an overcoat and dress coat in the line of clothing & a knapsack & haversack & I bought a hat & vest & the pants I had before. So now have a new suit. But have got to get the pants altered when I get to Madison. We expect to go tomorrow. The Boys run around the city and were not molested by the Provost Guard. All they needed for a pass was to have the figure 7 on their hats.

January 7, 1864

And fine day. And we don't get off till dark when we start and load into old cars. But there was a stove in each one so they were comfortable. & after sitting till about 11 oclock when they hitched on & took us through to Baltimore which we reached about 4 A.M. Sit in cars till daylight when we were marched. . . .

January 8, 1864

. . . to the Retreat, got breakfast. Then were quartered in a large warm room till near noon when we were marched to the North side of the city and took the cars for Pittsburg [Pittsburgh]. It being nearly night when we start, so we come by Harrisburg but didnt stop. But we come to Little York before this & Doctor Palmer [Henry Palmer of Janesville][133] treated us to supper. He is in charge of a large hospital here. Here I met with one of our Boys that was wounded at Gettysburg.

January 9, 1864

And fine day. And today we reached Pittsburg just dark and were taken in the Retreat & got good supper. Then we were quartered in an empty building to stay all night most probably. Many of the Boys went to the Theatre, but I made down my bed and went to bed till about 11 oclock when the Boys just returned from the theatre and awoke us to get up and go on the cars for Chicago. Which we done, got started out about 1 A.M.

January 10, 1864

And fine day, but tis cold. We are getting so far north that there is a great difference twixt here and Virginia. Many of the boys while they were at the theatre had their knapsacks stole from them. Several had new suits in them, some as much as $50.00 worth of clothes. We come on as far as Lyons where we got breakfast but had to pay for it. And we come on till near noon when the cars run off the track & smashed some of them pretty bad but hurt nobody. The two hind cars were thrown square across the track. The Boys joked the officers pretty hard (they occupied the last car) said that they got the car drunk, as we knew they were having a jolly time over the Black Bottle. About 6 P.M. we get started now for Chicago. Ride all night stopping at the many stations &c.

January 11, 1864

And we reach Chicago at just dark after riding all day. We here found out that we could come on right off as soon as we could get our supper, which we were allowed to get as we pleased. The Major gave us leave so we would just get back to Co on the train was all he cared for. We all got around and into the cars about 9 P.M. & the cars started. Now we see snow plenty. Also cold enough. But we kept good fires. Now we will soon see the state line. The Boys are tired. They lop down & go to sleep verry soon after getting on.

January 12, 1864

And fine day and [too faded to read] [Arrived in Madison] There we found a fine, good dinner awaited us in the large dining hall near the depot. We partook of & I assure you we done justice to it. We were then formed and marched up to & around the Capital square. The Drum Corps playing Patriotic tunes all the while. And from there to the Capital Hall which were opened for us. Tis a verry nice hall and roomy enough for the whole Regt. But to return, I forgot to tell you about the Govenor [James T. Lewis] giving us the reception speech welcoming us home. His speech was short but to the point.[134]

The officers went to work making out our furloughs & the Boys went & come as they pleased all over the city. The figure 7 would pass them through the guards. We boarded at the taverns or got our meals there costing from 30 to 50 cents per meal. I got a tailor to fix my pants. I also bought a comfortable pair of gloves, collars & necktie &c. Evrybody seems to be glad to see us. Although they are not acquainted with many of us.

January 13, 1864

And we get our furloughs. Some start home on the freight & accommodation train. But I, with many others, concluded to wait till 4 P.M. & take the Express Train which we did & reached Bridgeport at 8 P.M. There we met with a farmer by the name of Wood [Reuben R. Wood of La Crosse]. He was formerly Captain of Co C, 2nd Cavelry and we rode with him to Patch Grove. Paid him 25 cts apiece. We reached here 11 P.M., went to the [small hole in page] Horse Tavern. Waked them up, got in & got to bed.

January 14, 1864

And rather stormy. We got up late, got breakfast & hired the man of the Tavern to bring us to our homes. Cook come to Lafton. There we met with Sam Woodhouse, our old Leiut, he is keeping a grocery. Then Frank Simons [Franklin Simmons, Company K][135] And I came on. The teamster brought me within half a mile of Mothers when I paid him $1.60 and come on, reached here 3 P.M. Found Mother and Lucretia at home and also Sarah & her Man & Mary and they are all well. I will leave it to the reader to imagine how happy we were. I have given a verry brief account of my homeward tour. I reach home safe and sound. I am verry thankful for it. I found things quite different in Sarahs family, she having a German for husband. Mother is well situated. Cornelia (Amos child) is with her, she is only a small girl & Lucretia is with her also. She is a great help to Mother. So upon the whole I am well satisfied with things. Mother lives in the room George built for her before I went away.

Well I must stop till I get another book.

1864

The winter of 1863-1864 marked the third year in a grim civil war of unexpected magnitude. To the men of the Seventh Wisconsin and the rest of the Iron Brigade regiments, it seemed there was much yet to be resolved. Ulysses S. Grant, the Union's most successful general, was promoted to command all the Federal armies. Grant decided to leave the Western Theater for Virginia, attaching himself to the Army of the Potomac to face General Robert E. Lee. The Army of Northern Virginia was just a handful of miles away beyond the Rapidan River, still very able and ready to turn back any Union offensive effort. In the Wisconsin camps there was quiet discussion of a possible Confederate invasion of Kentucky or Ohio—or even another offensive against the Army of the Potomac by Lee's army.

The Iron Brigade itself was thinned by its heavy losses at Gettysburg in July 1863, but many of the wounded men were returning to the ranks and fresh recruits were arriving to flesh out the unit. More troubling to the old hands was the assignment of a series of Eastern regiments to the organization, ending the tradition of an all-Western brigade. Only some 700 remained of the 5,000 volunteers who had left Wisconsin, Indiana, and Michigan during the early weeks of the war. The old brigade was no longer the same unit that had performed such magnificent service at Gainesville, Antietam, and Gettysburg. Although Ray and his comrades could not have known it, the Iron Brigade would never again be the decisive force in battle it had once been.

But it was the "veteran question" that dominated the soldiers' talk. War department clerks in early 1863 began raising alarms that many of the volunteer regiments—including the early regiments of the Iron Brigade—were reaching the end of their three-year enrollments. In the Army of the Potomac alone, the enlistment of 77 regiments were set to expire before the end of August 1864. Worried army officials decided to offer veteran reenlistments to the men in ranks. If three-fourths of the men on the roster of a volunteer unit would reenlist, the order said, each soldier would receive a $402 bounty paid in installments (this at a time when privates collected $13 a month), and the "veteran volunteers" would be sent home as a regiment to enjoy a 30-day furlough.

After weeks of discussion, the soldiers of the Sixth and Seventh Wisconsin regiments voted to "veteranize." The early volunteers of the Second Wisconsin, however, decided to go home, and the Nineteenth Indiana fell victim to a clerk's error and was, despite vigorous protest by its members, merged into the Twentieth Indiana, ending the Hoosier connection with the Iron Brigade. The total reenlistment rate for the Seventh Wisconsin was 211 of 249, and 227 of 290 in the Sixth Wisconsin. One of the new "veteran volunteers" was William Ray.

Some of the heaviest fighting of the war was just ahead for Ray and his comrades, and the bloodshed would continue almost without respite until Appomattox. In some respects Ray was a lucky man: he suffered his third combat wound early in the fighting at the Wilderness—and missed some of the heaviest fighting of the war that followed.

January 17, 1864 to May 30, 1864

Back to the Front

Wm. R. Ray Diary
Glen Haven, Grant Co. Wis.
January 21st/64

A Member of Co. F. 7th Regt Wis. Veteran Vol
Reenlisted Jan 1st 1864

January 17, 1864

And fine day & at home. & tis the Sabbath day. Has been long time since I had a Sabbath at home.

January 18, 1864

And fine day. Went down to Henrys today, found them well and getting along fine. The 3 oldest was gone to school (viz) George, Viola & Florence. This district has a got their new schoolhouse finished & keeping school in it.

January 19, 1864

I & Henry went to town. Found many of my friends, some I knew & some I did not know. But most all appeared to know me. We stayed in town late waiting for the mail to come. I purchased flannel for two shirts which Mother is going to make.

January 22, 1864

And fine day. I go down to Glen Haven to see the place & see about buying a house & lot. Found 4 or 5 for sale. But didnt like some & one of them I liked verry well. But twas more than I cared about paying out. & I don't think much of the town as a place to live in. The Society is not the best kind. Returned by noon, got dinner. Wm Henry took us up to Isaacs. We reached here about 3 P.M. Found all well, with an increase of one verry recently. It is about a week old. I found the family small to what it used to be some years. Since I went to the army, one died in the hospital, the other is still living & well. The family is well.

January 23, 1864

We stay at Isaacs all day & visited &c. I went to singing school last night to the old schoolhouse that I got all my schooling in. The old place looks kind a natural. But I found verry few of the people that I knew. Those that were children with me have grown up and gone hither & thither. Some to war and others have grown up entirely out of my knowledge. So much so that I was made acquainted with several of my old friends and couldnt recognise them. There are a verry few men. Mostly ladies. This is the only place that I have noticed the deficiency. Tis really great. We had a good sing of it & came back. I enjoyed myself verry well.

January 24, 1864

I with Clark & the girls went over to Mark Scotts last evening. Made a short call. I found their family small to what it used to be. Only one of the children at home. One is married & all the rest are dead.

January 25, 1864

And still fine warm weather. I stayed at home. Henry came up on the afternoon & I concluded to go down to Cassville with him tomorrow to see about the Bounty the town is to give the soldiers, viz $100.00.

January 28, 1864

And fine day. I am at home. I looked over my book &c today. Found them in good order. Found many things to please me. I am glad to see that they have been so well taken care of.

January 30, 1864

And fine day. I went to town today, got over to the Price farm. There I met Henry at the Blacksmith & he was going to town so I rode in. They had the meeting of the citizens but when I came away they had not raised much more money. They had about $1100.00 raised to buy 15 recruits with. I did not get my money. But I shall try hard to get it. I fully calculated to get it. & I went home with Henry calculating to settle with him.

February 3, 1864

A fine day, thaws a little. And at home. Come to the conclusion that if folks wants to see me, they may come & see me. A neighbor calls occasionally.

February 4, 1864

John (Sarahs husband) and I went down to Cassville today. We called at his sisters (Mrs Gingre) and got dinner. Then we looked around to find a house for sale. Found a number & comparitively cheap. One I concluded to buy if I and the owner can bargain. He asked $350.00. But I offered him $250. After bantering some time he fell to $300.00 so I left him & come home to confer with Mother about it.

February 5, 1864

I went down to see Capt [Henry] Young . He was not at home, having gone up to Mr. Ramseys to see a number of Recruits for our company off. He returned however & I had a little chat with him and with Firman & his wife, being acquainted with all. Henry coming along on his way home from Beetown where he went this morning. Called at the mill for his grist, so I jumped in & rode home with him. After partaking of dinner he came up to Mothers, I thereby having a ride home. After staying a couple of hours he returned home. In the meantime he & Mother settled, he & I settled, he coming out some indebted to me. He gave me his notes.

February 7, 1864

And fine day. This is the Sabbath day. There was church at the schoolhouse today. But I didnt attend. Time is flying swiftly. My time to return to camp will soon be here. I must start on the morning of the 10th inst.

February 9, 1864

I & John went to town. I didnt buy the house &c but fixed things so that Henry can buy. I didnt get my town Bounty as I expected as I have to get a duplicate from the Ajt State Gen [State Adjutant General] to show that I am credited to the town.

February 10, 1864

I started for Prairie du chien. John took me down to Henrys with the team. Then we started about half past 11 oclock. Came on good speed, reached Praire du chien about 5 P.M. Put up at the Masion house. Here I found Frank Boyanton [Francis A. Boynton] & several others. One of their neighbors brought them down.

Twas harder for me to leave home this time than before. Something unexpected but duty to my country compels me so to do.

February 11, 1864

The train started at 9 A.M. I took passage for Madison. When we got to Bridgeport, lot more of the Boys come aboard. There is most of the old soldiers aboard now and our officers & a number of acquaintances. We came on to Boscobel, took on a lot more and kept picking them up & when we reached Madison, Frank Boyanton took our names, said he would go up to the Ajt. Gen. [Adjutant General's] Office and see & get our papers if he could. I got another ticket for Milwaukee & went on with the Boys. We reached here about dark. Put up at the Menomince house. The Boys scattered in different houses. We start at 8 A.M. in the morning for Racine.

February 12, 1864

We take the 8 A.M. train for Racine which we reach at 10 A.M. Come to camp, verry few here. The Quartermaster assigned the Cos their quarters. Co F., or at least quite a number of [us], took peaceable possession of one Barrack. The Boys scattered into the city as they have to board themselves until tomorrow when we get rations. I went up town late this evening. But came back & I with about a dozen others slept in the Barracks. We had a verry good bed as there is plenty of straw.

February 13, 1864

A fine day but windy. Captain came today, also the 1st Sergeant. Cap brought the duplicates & I set down & wrote a letter to Henry & sent him the duplicate to draw my local bounty, as also told him to buy a house & lot in Cassville. Tis a corner lot on Bluff Street (forgot the name of the other street) where most of the travel comes around that corner. It is a pretty place & water near. The house is one storie high with two good rooms and about as pretty a place as there is in the town. Henry will now have $200.00 in cash in his hands of mine to pay down. Today we drew rations. There is no guard around camp & the Boys go & come as they please.

February 14, 1864

This is, as evrybody knows, Valentine Day. There is a goodly number Boys got in & there is a guard placed around camp with orders to let nobody go out without a pass signed by the Lieut Col [Mark Finnicum]. But there was many got out for all that; & some committed depredations on the citizens such as tearing paling of the fence & breaking gates down & breaking windows &c. & at night there was a patrol went through the principle streets & got a number of drunken rowdies and they too had molested citizens. & it is for this that the guards has been put on. The citizens I find verry courteous & sociable people. They talk & chat with all that behave themselves. But we will soon be brought in bad repute on account of the few Devils.

The appearance of the country is quite different to what it is in the western part of the state. Here there is no snow and don't appear so cold. But there has been a wind blowing ever since we come here. The soil is verry sandy & quite dry in many places. Our camp is near the lake shore just south of the town. Tis a pretty place for a camp & the several groves in & about camp makes it look much better.

Our water is good but rather softer than what we have out west. And is furnished by a well in camp. The officers made us another visit today & we had the first Rollcall which will be kept up. There is 43 present & more to come.

February 16, 1864

And verry cold day, hard wind blowing. It as much as we can do to keep warm. There is a rumor that we start for dixie tomorrow.

February 17, 1864

Clear but cold wind blowing. We got ready and started. Took the cars & off fore Chicago at about 9 A.M. which place we reached about noon, got dinner at the Refreshment Saloon. Was waited on in a verry genteel manner by the fair sex. After getting dinner, marched to the depot of the Pittsburg, Ft. Wayne & Chicago R.R. Got on good comfortable cars. At 3 ½ P.M. start on another ride of 480 miles. We paced along as usual. The Boys seem happy. Not a single case of sickness in the Regt.

February 18, 1864

And fine day, rather frosty. It seems as though we are doomed to some misfortune evrytime we travel. And it come on us at about 9 A.M. this morning. About 20 miles this side of Ft Wayne the cars run off the track caused by a rail breaking. The Engine went over safe. The first cars, which contained the baggage, run of the track and the tender & car behind not running off, held it from going down the embankment. & it running on the frozen ground & across the ties smashed the running gear all to pieces from this. Back some 4 or 5 cars was on the track all right, ours or the one that most of our Co. was in being the hind one of that number. And then there was three 3 off, the first one behind ours run off, pitched down the embankment which is about 8 feet high, falling on its side & rather disturbing the equilibrium of some & others, it gave them a pretty good idea of astronomy when they fell out of their seats & their heads striking in various ways against obstacles. But luckily no one was verry seriously hurt, but the affair drew Blood on several.

They soon clambered out the door but it tried the climbing propensities of some. The next 2 cars stoped right side up on the embankment. Here we had to stay until 1 ½ P.M. In the meantime they had got a number of men & 2 pairs of new truck. The trucks were put under the baggage car, the broken one having been first removed. At this time 1 ½ P.M. we started, this affair having delayed things so that we were delayed at many places waiting for trains to pass. We drew bread & cheese today.

February 19, 1864

Weather is milder. We ride all day today, delays frequent. Nothing particular occurs, except the thieving of several little things as glasses &c, out of groceries. They being drunken reckless fellows and unhappily for our Co. there is several such fellows at it. We drew bread today. We did expected to reach Pittsburg tonight. But we will not I guess. But we have good cars & are comfortable. We come home as far as Chicago on what they call Pick cars. They being freight cars with four windows in a car & 3 bench seats running lengthwise & we thought when at Chicago that we would have the same till we got in those. Those we have now are second class.

February 20, 1864

And still fine, weather mild. We reached Pittsburg just dark. We were well received by the citizens. We marched to the Refreshment Saloon and got a good supper after which we gave 3 cheers for the hospitality received at the hands of the patriotic citizens of Pittsburg and 3 more for the Patriotic State of Pennsylvania. We then went back to the Depot for the purpose of getting on the cars. But there being different arrangements so that we had to march a short ways down the street where we got on second class cars. This was quite unexpected to us for we thought sure that we would have to take Pick cars here. 9 P.M. the time for starting & we did start. Come on all night rather slow though having to wait for trains at different stations.

February 21, 1864

And fine day. We still are going till nearly midnight when we reach Baltimore. We march to the Refreshment Saloon. There we were quartered in the building for that purpose. We were delayed at one place today, 3 hours waiting on the workmen to finish a new bridge they were putting in. I was somewhat surprised to see men at work on a job that they commenced this day on account of its being Sunday. But as it took them only one day to build it, I should have thought they might have put it off one day. But probably twas a necessity that compelled them to do it. I was verry glad to have a chance to lie down a few hours as I am almost sick with a bad cold and I have been so for 4 days. I have not enjoyed my ride well at all, havent ate but 2 meals in that time.

February 22, 1864

When we were awoke for breakfast I see we were among & with the 57th P.N. [Pennsylvania] Fine fellows were they too. We went to breakfast. Twas verry good but I couldnt eat it. Drank a cup of coffee, got up & went into the city, found an oyster saloon, got a good dish of Oysters which tasted verry well to me. Cost 25 cts. Then returned to quarters. We stay here till 4 P.M. when we started out. Got on the cars & after an hour or so we start for Washington. Come slow, stopping at the different stations, reached Washington 9 P.M. Got supper at the Retreat, marched to No. 4 Barracks where we spread blankets. The 9th N.Y. Cavelry came with us also.

February 23, 1864

We stayed in the Barracks all day getting our regular meals at the Retreat. We drew garrison & camp equippage today and those wanting clothing drew it also. Just at night the order come for us to start to the front tomorrow morning at 9 A.M.

February 24, 1864

We get breakfast, march to the cars, get on and soon we are off for the front, coming by way of Alexandria, stopping a little while here, then buzzing onward, stopping at the different stations. Come to within 1 & ½ miles of Culpepper. There we got off. It is now about 3 P.M. Here we stopped a couple hours. Then marched up through Culpepper and 2 miles west to near the old Brigade or what is left of it. Here we camped, it being now about 7 P.M. Now we have to pitch tents as well. I & B Hayden [Benjamin Hayden][136] my tentmate, we made bed and spread tents over us.

February 25, 1864

And fine day. We draw rations & straighten up, forming streets preparatory to building cabins. Gen [Lysander] Cutler was over to see us and ordered all the teams axes &c we wanted to build with. There was a number of teams come & our Co got one. I was detailed to go with the choppers & we put in a good days work. But as usual I had the misfortune to get my left hand bruised pretty bad.

February 26, 1864

I was sent out with the detail again today at the Captains Request on account of me being out yesterday & knowing the woods. So I went & we put in another good [day]. My tentmates got a set of good logs so we can put ours up tomorrow. My hand is quite sore. But I didnt have anything to do but boss the work. The recruits went out to drill one hour. There is about 100 in the Regt & 22 of these belong to our company. And the officers say there is 20 more coming to our Co and 200 to the Regt.

February 27, 1864

Our Co. has houselogs enough so we don't have to go out chopping. We got our shanty up and the tents stretched over it. So we sleep in it tonight. The recruits go out to drill a little again this morning. The Boys are verry busy at their shanties.

February 28, 1864

We got up our chimney & finished the cabin with the exception of the door which we cannot make for want of boards which are impossible to get. So we have to hang up one of our Rubbers [rubber blankets]. We have the best cabin in the Co. We are well situated. My tentmates are B. F. Hayden, H Brinckman [Henry Brinkman] & R. Lesler [Richard Lesler]. The two latter are recruits & good fellows.[137]

March 1, 1864

Stormy day. Ended with a little snowstorm & frooze some. I forgot to tell you the 6th [Wisconsin] Regt came yesterday and are camped near us. They are building quarters. We come in the right time to get evrything ready ere the storms come.

March 3, 1864

Drill the same as yesterday. Our sutler come up today with a good stock of goods and those needing articles can get them. I wrote a letter to Flora Lander today.

March 4, 1864

And fine day. We had company drill in the forenoon & Battalion drill in the afternoon, it being the first of the latter we have had. I got a letter from Mother and Lu today with $4.00 in it. Both being welcome guests. They are well. But verry lonesome since I left. They miss me more than ever before.

March 5, 1864

We have squad drill in the forenoon, I having a squad. We drilled in the manual of arms and Battallion drill. It is surprising how fast the Recruits learn.

March 6, 1864

I go on picket today. Start 8 AM, reach the picket lines about 10 AM. We have to go about four miles. Tis rather a poor place, timber being scarcc.

March 7, 1864

And fine day. I was on duty most of last night as Corporal of the guard. This guard is put on in the night only so that if there is firing on the picket line, this guard can alarm the reserve. At 10 AM we of the Reserve got relieved, those that have been on the picket line. I and another corporal having to run one Post. I posted the men till midnight then he posted them the rest of the night. There was two posts & 8 men making 4 reliefs.

March 8, 1864

And stormy in the morning, fair in the afternoon. The new Pickets come about 10 A.M. & relieved us & we came home. I found dinner most ready. I am both wet & hungry. There is drill this afternoon but I don't have to go.

March 9, 1864

And fine day. We had the usual drill. There has a lot more recruits come today, 6 for our Co & they are boys from my neighborhood. They have to go in with others till they get a shanty built. Two of them is going to stay with us.

March 10, 1864

Stormy till near noon when the rain set in steady the rest of the day. I am picked on to go with those last recruits into the timber and boss the job of getting the logs for their shanty. We went out & chopped them and the team come & we loaded them & come home wet as rats. Found my dinner waiting for me. It being so wet done no more today. There was two went on picket from our shanty, Lesler & Hayden and then we took in two more making 4 of the recruits. The reason was they couldnt find a dry place but ours that they can get into. So I took them in. They were wet & hungry. Our boys generally have poor shanties. But we keep nice & dry in ours.

March 11, 1864

We had drill in the morning only. The Boys pitched in & helped the new recruits put up their shanties. I worked for them in the afternoon. I built the lower part of the chimney. Then rain coming on, we had to quit work & get wood & water & I got supper. I will finish their chimney tomorrow. They will be able to move into it tomorrow. Oh, I am almost out of Patience waiting for letters.

March 12, 1864

We had squad drill in the forenoon & in the afternoon, Battallion drill. The Col formed us in Brigades & we had Brigade drill. To do this we were formed into one rank, making two Co out of one. I was left guide of one company

March 13, 1864

And fine day. This being Sunday we had Regt Inspection by Lieut Col Finnecum. Things in good order. Cap called on me to drill those last 6 recruit in the

Inspection of Arms so that they wouldnt be entirely ignorant of the motions. I got a letter from Henry. They were well. In it he states about buying the house & lot in Cassville for which he gave $300.00, $215.00 down & gave his note for the other $85.00. He paid $115.00 for me. So I credited him that or he has taken up one of the notes I hold against him. And the other I will either pay him or let him take up another of the notes I hold against him. He has got a warrantee deed in my name and is going to get it recorded.

March 14, 1864

Squad drill in forenoon. I had a squad today under my instructions. We had no drill in the afternoon. We cleaned up camp. I was detailed on general Police as corporal of it. We cleaned up about all the officers quarters. The team hauled off the trash. It took us pretty much all the evening. I wrote a letter to Mother and Lu today.

March 15, 1864

And cold & cloudy & windy. Disagreeable weather. We had squad drill in the forenoon. We were drilled in one squad. Corp Runion [John Runion] had command of us. None but the recruits were out. I acted as right guide on the drill. In the afternoon we had Brigade drill of 2 hours. Col. Robinson drilled us.

March 16, 1864

We had company drill both in forenoon & afternoon. Lieut Sloat drilled us in the evening. I wrote off a good patriotic song. The title of it is Brave Boys Are They. I wrote a letter to Henry today informing that I was satisfied with his purchase of the house & lot for me.

March 18, 1864

cold & verry windy. We had squad drill in forenoon & in afternoon had Co Drill & drilled Skirmish drill a little, Lieut Sloat commanding. Lieut Kidd was out with us also. He generally goes out with us. About 3 P.M. we had orders to pack up and be ready to march at a minutes notice with 3 days cooked rations. We got ready but at same time all seemed to think we would not march & we didnt. About 7 P.M. the order is countermanded which we hailed with joy.

The Co. has been divided off into 4 squads, & a noncommissioned officer put over each squad. I have the squad on the left or fourth squad. Sergt [Jesse] Roberts has the first. Corpl [Thomas] Alexander the second, Corpl Runnion [John Runion] the third & I the last & fourth. There is two new corporals in our Company, viz I. Raymer [Isaac Raemer] & N. Bradbury [Nathan Bradbury]. Corpl Alexander is acting Sergt now. Capt got a letter from our first sergt L. G. Parson [Lorin G.

Parsons].[138] He is at Annapolis M.D. as are other Boys belonging to our Co except Corpl Schloesser [John J. Schlosser]. He was sent to Georgia before the exchange.

March 20, 1864

And fine day. I go on picket today. We went through the routine &c and reached the picket line 11 A.M. I, as well as all our Boys, were on Reserve. This being Sunday, they have the Sunday Morning Inspection. And tis just 2 weeks since I was on before. At light I get the Boys at our fire to go out & get a lot of wood for the night. & we have good fires. One third of us have to stay up all night. My squad stays up till 12 P.M. when I wake up the Corpl of the other third & we got to sleep.

March 21, 1864

And cold, chilly, wind blowing from the Northeast. Twas cold night. At 10 AM we go on Picket line & I with 10 men are on one post. 2 Beats making 5 Reliefs we attend. The officer appointed an assistant for me, so he posted the Boys half the time. I done it the forepart of the night and he the latter part. I started with the Boys out to get wood. Made them all go so we had a good fire which we needed for it was cold.

March 22, 1864

Cold with wind blowing. We look with longing eyes for the Relief which came about 10 A.M. Found out 2 of my tentmates gone on picket. I forgot tell you about one old Soldier & 8 recruits more coming to our Co in the evening of the 19th ult. I didnt know any of them but one of them knew me. His name is Hutchison [Albert M. Hutchinson].[139] I had seen him once or twice before I come to war. They are at work building their shanties. Just night & begins to snow hard and keeps it up till bedtime.

March 23, 1864

The snow fell last night about 10 inches deep. It is going off pretty fast today. No drill today. I got a letter today from Mother & Sarah. They were well & Mother expected to move to the new home in town soon. Thurza-ann & Isaacs lost their youngest child by death.

March 24, 1864

We get our pay today. Regular $63.00. The snow is going off fast. We expect Gen Grant around today to review us. We have to keep in readiness all the while.

March 25, 1864

And rainy today. I wrote a letter to Mother today. We drill squad drill today. I drilled one squad in the afternoon Co drill. I got excused this afternoon from drill for the purpose of getting my boots half soled. But couldnt, the shoemakers have so much to do. We have none in our Regt so we have to wait the option of others. I got a letter from Flora Lander this evening & they have mourning in the family. The youngest having died since I left.

March 26, 1864

And fine day. We had squad drill in forenoon & in afternoon had Co. Drill. Gen. [Ulysses] Grant hasnt come yet & perhaps wont.[140] I received another letter this evening. This is from Sister Lu. She is well and writes a good long letter. I like to get her letters are so cheerful. She is ready to start to learn her trade & wants some money which I promised her & today I started the money to Henry viz $60.00 & told him in the letter I wrote him today to let Lu have $20.00 & help her find a good place to learn the trade she chooses. But she don't speak of her and Mother moving into town as yet.

March 29, 1864

We had the long expected Review today. There being only one corps of Infantry and the Cavelry belonging to it as also the artillery. We got out there, tis about 3 miles from camp, and got fixed & Grant came around & reviewed us. Just then the rain began to fall & we started home without going through the usual Preliminaries, Marching in review &c. We done nothing in the afternoon. Oh, I forgot to tell you about us fixing up our Shanty. Daubed it over and put on eave troughs.

March 30, 1864

And fine day after a hard nights rain. We had Co. Drill in the afternoon. But twas rather windy. I sent for a Gold Pen of Mortons Make No. 5 first quality. Cost $3.00. I sold my old one for first cost to one of my tentmates.

March 31, 1864

A fine day but cloudy. Squad drill in the forenoon. I drilled one squad in the afternoon Battalion drill. Capt comdg us. Col. Finnecum drilled. Col Robinson has returned to the Regt and Brigd Gen Cutler has returned to command the Brigade as also Gen [James] Wadsworth commanding the Division, the latter the Boys are pleased to hear of coming back. He is well liked by the greater part. The commands stands pretty much the same as at the Battle of Gettysburg.

April 1, 1864

And fine in forenoon but rained in afternoon. We had Co drill in forenoon. None in afternoon. This as evrybody knows is April fool day. And a numbers have realized it in truth causing no little fun. But I didnt get fooled I believe. But having an empty

Pill Box, I wrote those words on a small piece of paper (this is April fool day) and put it in the bottom of the box and lid on, wrapped it up verry nice and threw it into the street. And somebody picked it up. But I don't know who as I couldnt keep watch all the time. But he would be fooled.

April 2, 1864

Stormy. Both rain and snow but cleared off at just night. I and [Henry] Brinkman had to get wood today. We have no drill today, it being so stormy. Mail comes but no letters for me. But two papers from Mother. They are the Northwestern Christian Advocate, a religious paper. I was detailed on guard but twas too stormy I guess for they didnt mount guard and I am not sorry for my boots leaks in both mud & water. I hope the shoes will soon come that have been signed for.

April 3, 1864

And fine day. Today being Sunday, we had the usual inspection. I am on guard today. But will not come on much duty as I am supernumerary. There was 3 recruits and one old soldier come today. The old soldier was the one that went home recruiting. He got only one recruit and has been gone 4 months. He is rather lazy fellow. He came to stay with us to stay till he gets a better place. Brinkman went on Picket today.

April 5, 1864

And cloudy & cold. We had drill same as yesterday. I drilled a squad today. I wrote a letter to Mother today. Brinkman returned from Picket. I had a good dinner ready for him of Beans & Pork. Ben went on Picket today so that fellow that we took in can stay 2 days longer with us & I will have somebody to sleep with me for Ben is my Bunkmate and when he is gone it is rather cold sleeping.

April 6, 1864

And stormy, a little so. We have Co drill in forenoon. Lieut Sloat comd'g and squad drill in afternoon. We are warned to get evrything in good order for a riged [rigged] inspection by an officer from Division Headquarters. He is to inspect the whole division & report the 3 best Regts & 3 worst ones and as a matter of course we don't want to be the worst ones.[141]

April 7, 1864

And fine day. We had squad drill in forenoon & in the afternoon, each & evry Co. went out to shoot at a mark. Each Co by its self and having their own marks. We had an orange box & I should judge shot 200 yards. We hit it many times, shot it till it would hardly stand up. There was many good shots. I hit the Box once & came close to it several times. & after spending an hour or so at it, we had Battallion drill of 2 hours making in all a hard drill. Brinkman & I washed today, made $3.10. He got excused from squad drill and I didnt so he done about two thirds of it and all I would take was a dollar although he wanted to give me half. He is a first rate fellow, a man evry inch of it. Ben came in off Picket today. O, I forgot to tell you that I bought a watch last night for $8.00. It was an old quartur watch & today I traded it off for a cilender escapement [watch] & gave a dollar to boot. I intend to keep trading till I get hold of one that just suits me. I want to get a Patent Lever [watch] if I can.

April 8, 1864

And fine day. We had the much talked of Inspection today. There was two officers. One examined & inspected us, that is our accoutriments & clothing. The other one had a paper & pencil in his hand and those that were best were marked No 1 and some No 2 and one in our Co No 3. I was amongst the first.

April 9, 1864

And rainy all day as well as last [night]. We are having a great deal of rain lately. I wrote a letter to Henry today in answer to one I got the 5th inst. I put in my time reading or writing whilst most of the Boys are lolling around or playing cards & fooling away their time.

April 10, 1864

And fine in the morning & raining most of last night. This being Sunday we have Regt Inspection. About 5 P.M. begun to rain. We had church in the evening 3 P.M. the Chaplain gave us a verry good discourse.

April 11, 1864

And cloudy & chilly, wind blowing from the north. I am on guard today. But was sent to my quarters. The officer took off 6 men & Sergt & Corporal & sent the rest to their quarters. There is only one post. Co. Drill in forenoon by Lieut Kidd. In afternoon Battalion Drill. I wrote a letter to Sister Thurza-Ann today. Brinkman went on Picket today. We have elected Ben as cook for the shanty & the rest of us are to get wood & water.

April 14, 1864

And fine day. At 10 AM we go out on Picket line, relieve those that have been on the last 24 hours. They were all 2nd [Wisconsin] Boys on the Post but me. We got along fine. I run the Post the forepart of the night & the other corporal the latter part.

April 15, 1864

And fine day. We get relieved at the usual hour by the new Pickets & come home. I found a good mess of turnips & beef awaiting me which I done justice in due time. This time while on Picket all the coms & noncom officers of our Regt were with the second. Our Boys went on the left. So I got home about half hour before the others. There is a rumor afloat that we are to all be courtmartialed. But I guess tis all a rumor. I don't know what it is for and another thing I don't care for I know that I have done my duty. Therefore my conscience is clear. I found when I got home that I had 3 or 4 papers & a box of pills awaiting my return which I, of course, was happy to see. But I would have been more so if they had been letters. But I must be content as well as thankfull that I have as many as I have. My correspondents are more numerous now than I can do justice. For I seem to have lost the zeal I once had about letter writing.

April 16, 1864

And fine day. We have no duty today. After this we are to have Saturdays of each week for washing and cleaning up for the Sunday morning inspection. I put in my time today reading & scribbling. I got shaved today.

April 17, 1864

And fine day. This being Sunday we have the usual Inspection & also the usual church services which were given by the Chaplain of the 7th Ind Vols. He is a gifted speaker. Much more so than our Chaplain. He gave us an excellent discourse & after singing dismissed [us]. Then we had a sort of singing school for practice. We have pretty good now. No letter for me today. I expected some.

April 18, 1864

And fine day. We had Brigade Inspection today & was pronounced in the best of order. Had dress parade at the usual hour. The Col. Drilled us some in the Manual of Arms. This being something new I thought I would mention it.

April 19, 1864

And fine day. In forenoon we had Co. Drill. In the afternoon shot 5 rounds apiece at [a] Mark & was to have Battalion drill. But the Col. give off to let us clean our guns. I mailed a letter to Mother today & at night when the mail come in I got a letter from her. She is well as usual & in the same envelope one from Lu. She was well & expected to start to learn the Millinery trade the next week. My money got home all right and Mother got the ten dollars I owed her & Lu got the $20.00 I was to let her have.

April 20, 1864

And fine day. We had Co. Drill in forenoon. But I drilled a recruit in the Manual of Arms so I didnt go on with the Co. In the afternoon Battallion drill. We drill in the Skirmish drill the whole Battalion at the same time. All the sick was sent off this morning. This indicates that we will move soon. I wrote a letter to Brother Amos today in answer to one I received last October. I wrote one to Mother also today.

April 21, 1864

And fine day. Had Co. drill in forenoon, Battalion drill in the afternoon. The drill same as yesterday. Dress Parade in the evening and we come out in style I tell you. There was an important order read. It is as follows. Any Private or non commissioned officer that can get a good recommend from his Co. & Regt. Officers can go before a Board of Officers to be examined if they are or will be qualified to hold a commission in a negro Regt., by going to the Free Military School at Philadelphia for 30 days. If they pass they will get a commission.

April 22, 1864

And fine day. Had Co. Drill in forenoon all doublequick. I had 20 recruits by myself drilling them in the Manual of Arms. In the afternoon had Battalion drill. I rec'd a letter from Henry this evening. They are all well as usual. The money I sent got through safe. I let Lu have $20.00 of it.

April 23, 1864

And fine day. This being Saturday we have no drill. But had to turn out on review for the Govenor [James T. Lewis]. The review lasted about one hour and half. The Govenor look the same as he used to. I answered Henrys letter today and mailed it. We have such fine weather now & have had that we expect to move any hour.

April 24, 1864

And fine day. But just after dark commenced to rain & pretty hard wind. This being Sunday we have the usual Inspection (Regt'l). We had church today. The chaplain distributed a lot of small books & Papers. The Col. when looking at my gun on Inspection say that [it is] a good & clean one. It being the only one in the front rank he remarked about cleanness. Rumors are beginning to fly about when & where we will move. The officers turned in all surplus kettles, axes &c today. Oh, I forgot to tell you about me comencing to study the tactics in earnest. I have recited 3 lessons. Wm Booth hears me recite & explains to me &c.[142]

April 25, 1864

And fine day after a nights rain. Had Co drill in forenoon. We have to drill in heavy marching order so as to accustom the recruits to it.

April 26, 1864

And fine day. Had Co. Drill in forenoon. Capt drilled us. Battallion drill in afternoon. I acted as left guide to the Co. I made several mistakes by not being used to the buisness on that part of it. A lot more recruits come today. 2 more for our Co. There is one private from our Co. got a recommend, viz. Wm. Booth, to go before the Board to be examined to go to the Military school. Also the Sergt-Major and Corpl Homes of Co. A [Lewis P. Holmes of Columbus].[143] Those three from the Regt. I still continue studying tactics and am making great speed.

April 27, 1864

And fine day. We have Co. drill in forenoon. In afternoon Battallion drill. We had target firing this afternoon also. I got one mark of merit. Among some 20 men, not half the Co hit the Board. We shot 200 yds and the wind was sideways and blew pretty hard. This was disadvantageous to us.

April 28, 1864

And fine day. Drill the same as yesterday except no firing. I wrote a letter to Mother today in answer to one I got several days since. In [it] she wanted to know about the walling of the cellar under the house. And getting the house painted. Ordered the cellar walled but not the house painted for it would cost $30.00 & I don't feel able to pay that just now.

April 30, 1864

And fine day. We go on the line about 10 A.M. and take the third post of the right reserve. That being the one we were on. We have all sorts of rumors concerning both our forces & the Rebels. This being the last day of the month they are having muster in camp for 2 months more pay.

May 1, 1864

And fine day. We were relieved at the time. Come home. I found a mess of beans waiting for me which I done justice. I also found a letter from Mother and a pair of socks awaiting my return. The socks I was not in need of just now but they will not come amiss soon. Rumors about marching still afloat. This being Sunday we have church at the usual time. The sermon was a good one given by a Chaplain from the 2nd Brigade. I attended. I wrote a letter to my niece L Lander today.

May 2, 1864

And fine day. We had Co drill in forenoon, Battalion drill in afternoon. Rumors about marching.

May 3, 1864

And fine day. But in the evening had a perfect hurricane. We get orders at dark to pack up all but blankets. That we expected to march about midnight. Sure enough after tapps we drew rations & got ready & marched at midnight.

May 4, 1864 *[Opening of the Overland Campaign]*

And fine day. We marched on briskly till 8 A.M. when we stoped & got coffee. Marched on crossing the Rappidan [Rapidan] & Germania. Rested 2 hours & slept. I went & washed my feet & face. Then we marched to Gordonsville & camped. It is now four P.M. We get supper (Ben & I) and go & take a good wash. The rumor is that the Rebs is retreating (hope so). Rumored that [Union General Benjamin] Butler is coming up from Ft. Monroe on Richmond. The Boys stayed the march well & have heavier knapsacks than usual. We came 24 miles today. All think Grant is doing it right. It is a beautiful evening.[144]

May 5, 1864 *[Battle of the Wilderness]*

We march at pretty early hour. We march & figure around & get into line of Battle about noon (being about 3 miles from Quartzville). We advanced on the foe through a dense forest. After going about 1 mile or so we came on to them.[145]

They fired at us pretty brisk. We done the same for a while & then charged on them, drove them & kept driving them for a mile or so when they got support & routed us completely.[146] We took many Prisinors while driving them and they took some when they drove us. But the most they took from us was wounded. While we got verry few of their wounded. They fired into us pretty brisk for a while. But we outrun them & got back to some brestworks & here the officers, what there was there, and a few of the Bravest Privates got a few to rally. And they of course gave confidence to others so it was not long till we had a line of battle 1 mile long & the old colonel come up. He took us back to the rear where the rest of the corps (the 5th) was forming a ncw line.

Here the whole Brigade formed & also the division. But just as we commenced retreating, the rebs gave me a shot.[147] One buckshot taking effect in the calf of my right leg, laming me some. But they couldn't catch me. I seen them all settled. They all prevailed on me to go back for I could scarcely walk. I came to the rear, found a hospital established by a good spring. Here I got a cloth, put around my leg & the Doctor, being a regular, he didnt pay much attention & said I could carry a gun again, didnt need to go to the hospital. But I couldnt see it & as soon as one of our Div.

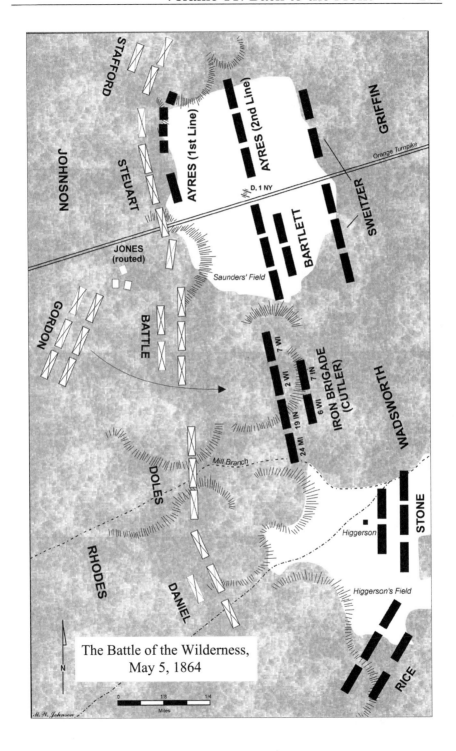

The Battle of the Wilderness,
May 5, 1864

N

0   1/8   1/4
Miles

M. W. Johnson

This image of Saunder's Field was taken after the end of the war. It looks from the Union position across the Orange Turnpike (visible in the foreground) and the field up the slope to the woods beyond, which marked the position of General Richard Ewell's Corps. The Iron Brigade went into action in woods that extended out of view on the left side of the photo. *USAMHI*

Ambulances come, I got in and come to hospital which is about 3 miles from the main line of battle. Here I found things fixed to receive us. There being tents & flags being pitched for to go under. But about this time the firing is awful to hear. They keep fighting without intermission. The wounded comes in verry fast till dark when I go to sleep but wake up several times hear firing. Pickets firing.[148]

May 6, 1864

Hard fighting all day.[149] Most of it at & near Parkers Store about 2 miles [away.] The contention is for the Plank Road running to Gordonsville. Our division has been in it today again and been cut up worse than ever. We havent gained or lost ground yet, we hold them and they us. The rumor is that Burnsides [Union General Ambrose Burnside] come this evening with 40,000 men.[150]

May 7, 1864

Hard fighting all day. We start for Fredericsburg [Fredericksburg] at night & those that can walk do & others ride in ambulances & wagons. We march most all night & stop & rest.[151]

May 8, 1864 [Spotsylvania Court House Campaign]

And fine day. Fighting again today. We come to within 2 miles of Fredericsburg, stop & rest. It now being 2 A.M. of the 9th [8th] the rumors is that the rebs have fell back. We hear cheering all along the lines. But it is verry distant.

May 10, 1864

And fine day. We stop in the city most of the day. Towards evening they get the bridge laid and all the wounded pile into the wagons & we start for Bell Plane [Belle Plain]. There is communication men now & the teams are to go back to the front loaded. We traveled half the night & camped within 8 miles of the landing.

May 11, 1864

And fine day. We rise early, go to Bell Plane [Belle Plain]. Here find the Sanitary Commission making coffee for the wounded. I soon got some & some bread. Had breakfast, lay around all day waiting for my turn to come. But there being always worse wounded so I didnt get of. So I & another fellow from our Co. fixed up a shelter, went to bed. Still raining a little & the wounded still coming on. Many from yesterdays battle which was hard. Evrything is favorable in front. The Rebs have fell back. There is busy times here now getting forage & provisions loaded on the teams for to go to the front.

May 12, 1864

And rainy all day. I & my tentmate get breakfast & try several times to get on the boat but always full or something the matter. But at last after noon we got on. Got started up the river. We get dinner on board. Come on up good gait, get opposite Alexandria & boat comes out & hail us to know if we are wounded. Yes. Land here then. So we landed & got off the boat. Ambulance brought us to Union House hospital.

[*Ed. Note*: book ends—continues on paper]

May 13, 1864

And fine day. My diary being full I have to take a sheet of paper to post up with till I get some money from home which I have sent for today in a letter I wrote to

Mother. I also wrote a letter to F.A. Boyanton [Boynton] today & the Co. Also. We have good attendance & my wound is slight. Soon be well. But I don't like the situation of the Hospital at all. It is right in the City surrounded by the dirty dingy looking buildings. Not even a spear of grass to be seen unless we look across to Potomac into another state. There, there is a good scenery, fine landscape. If the hospital was over there, it would be nice writing in the hospital good enough. But all we can see stirring is a verry few citizens & some negro brats. Few invalid soldiers &c. The streets are not crowded as usual with soldiers.

Old Grant has them all at the front & evry day there is thousands going to the front. The soldiers that have heretofore been in the Forts around here doing nothing are going to the front now. They will reinforce the army considerable. I have seen to my knowledge as many as 10,000 go down the river. The news from the front is verry cheering. Our forces are still driving the enemy & he had asked for a flag of truce for 48 hours to bury his dead. Grant told him he hadnt time to bury his own dead & that he would advance on him and did advance on them, & drove them.[152]

May 14, 1864

And rather rainy. Little showery enough to cool the air. & the wounded still come, a number of boatloads have passed up the river today. Some have stoped here at this place but most of them go to Washington. The boats go down loaded with troops, provisions & forage & come back loaded with wounded. This has been an awful battle or will be when finished. The Surgeon of our Ward was around wanting to know if we wanted a furlough. If we did, say so & we would be likely to get one. The transportations will be furnished to those wanting it by the Quartermaster.

May 15, 1864

And showery, sunshine & showers at intervals, not what you might call a bad day. Things goes on all right. But our diet is light, exceedingly so. My wound is doing well. There is great many troops going to the front. I should think there has been some 5,000 troops gone down to Bell Plane today & so they go evry day.

The news from the front is cheering. The report is that Secesh Army is completely routed. How true this is I cant say. Time will tell. One thing certain we are whipping them bad. 7,000 prisnors at Bell Plane & most of their dead & wounded. This we know but to say anymore is only guessing. Butler is driving them.[153] [General Phil] Sheridan has got into their rear & destroyed the R. Road. & 1,000,000 rations &c. Property to the amount of 10,000,000 dollars & this we know. There is not so many wounded coming up today as usual. There is a number our Generals killed & wounded. Gen [John] Sedgwick killed, Commandant of the 6th Corps. Gen. Warren wounded, Commandant of 5th Corps. Division Commander viz. [Union General James] Wadsworth (our Division Commandant) Rice killed & [William W.] Robinson wounded. On the Rebel side according to their paper,

[James] Longstreet & [Confederate cavalry commander J. E. B.] Stuart killed. [General Robert E.] Lee & [General] A. P. Hill wounded. & a number of their Genrals captured. & also a few of ours. The rebels Bradley [Tyler] Johnson of Frederick, Maryland and Stewart [Confederate General George Hume Steuart] captured.[154]

May 16, 1864

And fine day with little showers occasionally. The troops continue go down but come up. I guess most of the wounded have come up. The news from the front is to the effect that there was no fighting on Friday & Saturday. But evrything was in our favor. The roads were verry muddy caused by the recent rains. They had great deal of it while here there has been little. The roads are in rather bad condition. But the army is well supplied.

Things went the same as yesterday around the hospital. But today papers don't say the army is routed but are in force & in strong fortified position & ready to fight. But it is confirmed that they are short of rations and ammunition. Verry bad off for the former. Longstreet is badly wounded. This is confirmed. As also that we have 8,000 Prisnors.

May 17, 1864

And rather rainy. Things pretty much the same as yesterday. A few wounded still continue to arrive & pass up to Washington. I see from the papers that there are quite a number of our Regt in the Hospital at this place & Washington.

May 18, 1864

And fine day. Things around here the same as yesterday. There are a great many troops going to the front. The news from there is still cheering. Lee is still in force opposing Grant. But Grant is wide awake & I think will give Lee all he wants. Both are fortified. But Grant intends to advance as soon as the roads will permit.[155]

My wound is almost healed & I will be able soon to go to the front. And I wont be sorry. I will be glad to get away from here for things don't suit me. This having dinner at 1 P.M. and supper at 5 P.M. I don't like. But I can stand it as long as I stay. I want to hear from home first.

May 19, 1864 [End of Spotsylvania Campaign]

And fine day. The news from the front is to the effect that Grant attacked Lee pretty vigorously. But with what success is not known. This is the news in the evening papers. We will see in the morning if the morning papers have any official reports. That being the only news that can be depended upon.

May 20, 1864

And fine day. The news from the front is favorable. There was some fighting on the 18th & we captured two lines of the enemys brestworks on the right & some 200 Prisnors. But twas not known whether we gained anything particular by it. But we held our own. The boats are running up to Fredericsburg & the Railroad from Acquia Creek [station] to Fredericsburg is running. There was a number of the slightly wounded & those that were well were sent away today. Tis said under Arrest for leaving the field without sufficient cause. But I know that the fellow that was here with me from our Co. B., Bryan, had sufficient cause, but they took him. I was as able to go as he but they didnt see fit to take me.

May 21, 1864

And fine day. The news from the front is favorable. They are doing nothing now but a little skirmishing. The Army is well rationed. & all the wounded have been got off the field.[156]

Butler has fallen back from besieging Fort Darling & his command captured Brigadier General [William Stephen] Walker (rebel) of Texas.[157] So far the loss of Generals has been about equal on both sides. Gen. [William] Sherman has whiped Johnson [Joseph E. Johnston] again at Rome [in Georgia] & captured a few Prisnors & Johnson has fallen back again & Sherman still follows him up like the hunter on the tigers track.[158]

Our cavelry has cut evry R.Road around Richmond & intend to keep them so. Also the telegraphs. We have a wounded Rebel in our room. He don't like to hear of them being whipped. But when I told him that Butler had to fall back, there was a great change in his countenance. He is a true Rebel but at the same time pretty smart. He thought to fool me some by appearing ignorant about things. I saw his game & done the same. Then afterward I would tell him all about the place, so that rather beat him. He appeared to know nothing about Vicsburg [Vicksburg, Mississippi, which surrendered to Grant on July 4, 1863] but I got him the same way as before. It rather took him down, so I guess he wont feign ignorance anymore. He can talk pretty well. But he has to give in most of the time. We get along fine. Through all our talk we don't get angry with each other. Live well together well.

May 22, 1864

And fine day. Things are about the same as yesterday. There has been no fighting the last day or two. There is not so many troops going to the Army now and a few wounded coming up. They are the worst cases that come now. Those that wouldnt bear moving sooner. We have recaptured most of our wounded from the rebs. That is, those that were badly wounded & left in the field Hospitals.

May 23, 1864

And fine day. There is nothing unusual transpired today. There has been no fighting but slight skirmishing. There was several boatloads of wounded come up today. But none for this place. The news appears to be suppressed if there is any.[159]

May 24, 1864

And fine day till just evening when we had an awful storm of both wind & water, the former being verry hard. The news from the front is that Lee is falling back. That our forces have got as far as 7 miles the other side of Bowling Green, nearly half way from Fredricsburg to Richmond. I am beginning to look for a letter from home, waiting patiently.

May 25, 1864

And fine day. The news from the front is good. Lee has fallen back to a position between the north & south Ann [Anna] rivers. Our Army capturing about a thousand Prisinors more. There has been a little fighting with their rear guard which is verry strong. There was a large number brought to this hospital tonight of badly wounded. Some verry bad cases. They have been laying at Fredericsburg a number of days and half starved. Some have the fever. They are a heart rending sight. They are as poor as a snake.

May 26, 1864

And fine day. The news from the front is cheering indeed. We have drove the Rebs again. What I spoke of yesterday is confirmed today. The Rebs cant tell what it means. This flanking movement of Grants which he will persist in doing rather beats them. Prisnors that we have taken say that evrything has been removed from Richmond to Columbus, South Carolina. That it is nothing more or less than a mere fortress now. Even Jeff [Confederate President Jefferson Davis] himself has gone to a more genial clime as also his cabinet. They are beginning to be afraid we will capture Richmond.[160]

The Johny we have in here with us cant see it though. He says we will have harder fighting to do than what we have done yet. Grant is changing his base from Fredericsburg to Port Royal, which is, I believe, 15 or 20 miles below the former place. And he is going to evacuate as soon as the wounded are removed & going to take up the road &c. This I think a wise plan for he will have shorter communications to guard & when he gets down far enough he can change the base to Po [Pamunkey] River or somewhere in that neighborhood.

There was a large number of wounded come into the hospital last night. It is full now. They are awful to behold. The verry worst cases, some with maggots in their wounds. I have turned in to help them or the nurses. We got one new one in our room. That being the only vacant bed. We had a number of ladies in to see us today

May 27, 1864

And fine day. The news from the front is cheering. Our fellows is gaining still & our supplies are going it is said to Port Royal. And evrything is progressing rapidly. I have turned nurse today & will be till I hear from home when I shall leave here for my Regt. But I must if possible hear from home before going. I expect a letter tomorrow. I am waiting with all patience. The fellow that I have to attend to is shot through the ankle. It is a verry bad wound & worse than all he is a perfect baby of a fellow. There is lots of troops going to the front today. There has boat loads gone down. At least 3000.

May 28, 1864

And fine day. Nothing unusual transpired. My patient is verry trublesome. But I put up with it knowing he wouldnt say so if he was well. Our Johny Reb is still with us. His friends still come in to see him, always bringing him something evry time. But he is verry clever. Always divides with us fellows. The news from the front is highly cheering. We still hold our own & a little more. Port Royal is our base for supplies now.

May 29, 1864

And fine day. Evrything is going about the same. I expect to go tomorrow to my Regt or make a start. This being Sunday we have the usual inspection. All is right &c. There is more troops going to the front & some wounded coming up. Our forces have entirely evacuated Fredericsburg and Acquia Creek and Port Royal is the base now.

May 30, 1864

And fine day. Things as usual. I got a memor [memoir] and one book from Henry which I sent for sometime since. It comes in good time for have been writing Diary on note paper.

The report is that our Army has recrossed the North Ann [Anna] River and march down & captured Hanover town on the Paxumakey [Pamunkey] River. This is supposed to flank Lees Army.[161]

May 31, 1864 to August 28, 1864

The Petersburg Mine

Corpl. Wm R. Ray
Co. F, 7th Rgt., Wis. Vols.

Residence
Cassville, Grant Co., Wisconsin
1st Brigade, 4th division, 5th Corps, Army of Potomac

Enlisted Aug. 29th 1861, Reenlisted Jan 1st 1864
Wounded at Gainesville, Gettysburg & Wilderness

May 31, 1864

I got a pass and went out in the town a couple of hours which I enjoyed much. I got my hair cut & face shaved. But the heat hurts my head verry bad.

June 1, 1864

I don't get off for my Regt yet but will hail that day with joy. I have a repugnance to nursing. The news from the front is that our corps was within 7 miles of Richmond, had a fight & repulsed the Rebs. Our transports have reached West Point & White House so the supplies will be got to the army without truble. Home of the army is on the same ground as when under [Union General George B.] McClellan. Evrybody seems to think Grant is capable to cope with Lee.

June 2, 1864

And fine day. I have another room to take care of now with 4 patients in it. & I am a regular nurse now, have to come to it. The news from the front is good. Skirmishing evry day.

June 3, 1864

And fine day. I get along well with my new duties. Long for the time to come when I shall go from here. There has been some hard fighting. Our corps being engaged. Our corps lays near Mechanicsville on the left of the army. I see the names of T. C. Alexander [Thomas C. Alexander] & I. C. Raymer [Isaac C. Raemer] among the wounded in the Washington hospital.

June 4, 1864

And fine day. The news from the army is good. I got a letter from Lu today. Minnie Lander wrote a little in it also, by the way reminding me that I hadnt answered her last letter. So I set down & answered it. This being Saturday I will have to scrub up the floor &c preparatory for tomorrows inspection. The Johny Reb that was with us went to the Prisnors hospital at Washington today. We were verry intimate friends. He being a good clever fellow. His visitors came and to see him but he being gone so they gave us the cakes, berries &c that they brought.

June 5, 1864

And fine day. Nothing unusual transpires. We have the usual inspection. I have another room with 4 patients to take care of.

June 6, 1864

And fine day. Some more wounded come in but none to my rooms. The news is rather cheering. But not so much so as heretofore for we don't gain so much. Those that come in today came for the White House landing being wounded on the 3rd inst there being a hard battle that day [Cold Harbor]. But not much since beyond skirmish.[162]

June 7, 1864

And fine day. The news from the front is that we are within 40 yards in some places of their brestworks & slight skirmishing going on all the while. There was a large number come into this hospital late this evening from the Battlefield of the 3rd [at Cold Harbor]. I got 2 verry bad cases in my room. There is one that will die I think. His thigh is badly fractured near his body. The other is flesh wound. They are both helpless. Oh, but I have hard work now. I have 6 helpless men & 2 that can help themselves some & they being in two different rooms makes it worse. I long to go to my Regt for I don't like the buisness but the Doctor cant spare me at present, he says.

June 8, 1864

And fine day Hard work verry & bad work. The man that has his thigh broke, I had to clean. His wound was teeming with maggots & they were half over his body having eaten holes right into his flesh. The stench was awful. But I rolled up my sleeves & went at it. Used turpentine pretty free. I soon had him clean. Twas an awful stinking job. I soon got the poor fellow comfortable as he could be made. The Doctors don't do anything for him but give him stimulants. I guess they think his case is hopeless. He wants me to write to his wife which I shall do as soon as possible.

June 9, 1864

And fine day till towards night when there was a light shower. Things went on all right today. I had a pretty hard days work to day. I wrote a letter today for the fellow I spoke of yesterday. His name is Farrell of the 28th Massachusetts.[163] He is verry low. The Doctors I think have left him to die for amputation would be sure death. I wrote her just how he was. Thought it wouldnt be right to do otherwise. There was more wounded come today. But none to this hospital.

June 10, 1864

And fine day & hard work. The old man is still alive. But failing fast. The wounded continue to come in. There was a few come in to this hospital. But I got none. The news from the front is devoid of interest. Slight skirmishing continues and still fortifying.

June 11, 1864

And fine day. This morning at 4 oclock I was awok by the night watch to get up & take out the old gentleman to the dead house & prepare him for the undertakers. I with 3 other nurses soon did it. So goes another soul, a sacrifice to the cause we so much cherish.

June 13, 1864

I get a pass today to go to Washington for my pay & did so. But when I arrived and enquired for it they wanted to see my certificate from the surgeon in charge of the hospital I was in. But this I forgot to get. Therefore, I could show nothing as evidence that I hadnt been paid at hospital so my errand was fruitless in that way. A Co. K fellow of our Regt went over with me & he was in same fix. So after running around the streets a while we steered for the Smithsonian Institute, which we reached in due time. After taking a rest under one of the many large & pretty shade trees that beautify large lawn around the spacious building, we enter. On the right hand side of the door there is a large book on a stand in which the placard above it invites us to register our names &c which we done & went on gazing around for couple of hours & still didnt get done looking. But the shades of evening were coming on so we leave the place feeling well satisfied with our trip & wind our way toward the Ferryboat dock which we reach in time to be just a little to late. Then we had to wait 2 hours till when it returned. When we got aboard & soon started for Alexandria which we reached in course of ¾ hours & come to hospital, it now being nearly dark. I will make another try for pay in a few days.

The 2nd Wis came in to Washington today. Their time is out. There is about 100 privates & a few officers. I saw several of my friends. They were gay and happy fellows & I don't begrudge them their happiness. God speed them is my prayer.

June 15, 1864

And fine day. I got another pass for Washington. I went over and got my pay. There was some 40 cents stoppage against me for little things I lost. I went to the Treasury to draw my money & went around through the building looking at the different Departments. Found it far superior to anything I ever saw and a great deal larger & from there I went to the Patent office, looked at the different things till I got tired & returned on the 6 P.M. boat. Found things all right.

June 17, 1864

The news from the front is cheering. Grant has crossed the James River south of Richmond & thumping away at Petersburg. Rumored that they took it.[164]

June 18, 1864

And fine day. All is right. The news is that Smiths Corps took Petersburg yesterday morning. But the Official Dispatches don't confirm it. It rather puzzles the Rebs to make out what Grant is doing, he having flanked him again. This move across the river shows a masterly man has got hold of the Boys & they think so too. How I would like to be with them now.[165]

June 19, 1864

Things as usual. The news front is that we have the outer works of Petersburg only 1 mile from the city. The city could be burned anytime now. Grant rather surprised Lee this time. But not quite enough to get the strong works. Petersburg is only second in importance to Richmond to the Rebs in VA.

June 20, 1864

And fine day. I got a pass today & went to Battery Rodgers at the lower one of the City and visited Richard Calvert. He is a member of the first Battalion Wis. Heavy Artillery [Company A, First Wisconsin Heavy Artillery]. They have a nice camp and well situated in every respect. He is coming up to see me soon if I stay here. I had a good companion out with me today. We had a good [time] & at night went out to the Theatre. Had a pretty one. 25 cents admission fee. I also saw Sergt Enlaw of Co C. [Oscar W. Enloe], my Regt. He is just returning to the Army from home on recruiting service. He having been home since last November. Twas 11 P.M. when I got to bed. I got my photo taken today. [It is likely that this photograph is the one appearing as the frontis in this book.] Got 1 doz which cost $3.00.

The news from the front is that there has been another hard Battle. Our forces are still confronting the Rebs & confident of Final success. They are represented as being in the Best of Spirits which I don't doubt in the least.

June 21, 1864

And fine day. I am at work still. I spoke to the Doct again this morning about sending me to my Co. & he promised to send me tomorrow morning. But I hope not too early for Richard Calvert will be up this forenoon & I want to see him ere I go.

June 22, 1864

And fine day. I do up the morning work & quit work, prepare to go out on pass, but the Doct being so busy amputating a leg &c that he couldnt sign it so I went out without it. Went on an old one. But didnt have occasion to use it. Richard came up about 10 A.M. and we went up to see Charly Chipman [Charles F. Chipman][166] one of my Co. Found him doing well. He will be apt to loose the use of his arm. & after talking over things &c we returned to hospital & got dinner, taking my friend down to dinner with me. After dinner I was called on to go so I got on knapsack &c and started. Dick went with me to the Provost Marshalls & after shaking hands &c we parted though much to our dislike. I think a great deal of Dick. He is a fine fellow. He sent his love to his brother & best respects to the Co &c. Well they put me in with a lot of fellows that had been Courtmartialed & bounty jumpers &c. Bad company. But at 3 P.M. the ambulances come & we go to Camp Distribution. Reach here about 4 P.M. and after going through the routine characteristic to entering the camp we were assigned our Barracks, each corps by itself. I was put in No. 36 Barracks. Here I met with Webster [Mathias Weber], cook of our Co.[167] Verry glad was I to see some of the Co go to the Regt with me. He has been to the Germantown Hospital. He says it is a bully place. I know it was when I was there.

June 23, 1864

And fine day. We ly around the Barracks all day &c. There is a squad detached to work evry day. But I didnt come on. This is a verry warm day. I went down & got my hair cut again. Was too warm with so much on my head & then went & got the Shoemaker to halfsole my shoes & I calculated to go to the field well fixed.

June 24, 1864

And fine day but verry warm, exceedingly so. We lay around the same as yesterday & as we may expect to do until sent away. I took my pants to the Tailorers to get the stripes put on to be done in the evening. But when I went after them she had just returned from Washington. She having been over to see her brother, he being wounded and in the Hospital. So she had done nothing to them. But am to go tomorrow morning. I wrote a letter to Henry today, sent him my photograph. We have rather poor rations here. They are cooked and we go to the dining room & eat. I buy milk morning & evening.

The news from the front is without interest. Nothing but skirmishing at times. We hold our own and gain a new position on some part of the line most evry day.[168]

June 25, 1864

And fine day & things about the same as yesterday. The news about the same except that Sherman has captured Lookout Mountain [in Tennessee] & 1000 Prisnors & 12 cannon from which place he could count the houses in Marielle. But afterwards abandoned it.[169]

June 26, 1864

And fine day. About 4 P.M. we have a fine shower which cools the air some, which had been exceedingly oppressive all day. The order come late this evening for us to go to the army tomorrow with 5 days rations.

June 27, 1864

The weather exactly the same as yesterday. We got our arms & accoutriments & rations &c and 9 P.M. start for Alex. [Alexandria]. Go about a mile & meet orders to go back to camp and await further orders. This we didnt like much, at least those that wanted to go. But twould one day more perhaps for some to play off on the Doctors and perhaps get rid of going &c. 6 P.M. and still here yet. But go tomorrow.

June 28, 1864

And fine warm day. & we start at 8 A.M. for Alex. The band belonging to the camp accompanied us for ½ mile and discoursed some fine music which the Boys steped to in admirable order. We reached Alex. 11 A.M. We come slow. Here we get catridges & tents &c and now are fully equipped. We lay here till 4 P.M. when we go aboard the Gen Hooker. About 300 & the other 6 or 700 aboard the S.R. Spaulding, an ocean steamer. 5 P.M. we tie loose & start. A soldier on the Spaulding jumped overboard. They stop to pick him up & we run ahead. Presently the Spaulding come up & passes us. The Boys on her bow & hooting up. But our engineers got up steam & run past them. Then we hooted them & in a little while they passed us again & hooted us & so on evry few minutes. Kept up racing till dark when the Spaulding went ahead for good as the wind was blowing pretty hard & our boat being a river boat set so high & light that the wind affected her speed. Dark & we are past Bell Plane.

June 29, 1864

And fine day. We run all night. I slept verry little last night. This morning about 9 Oclock we past fortress monroe [Fort Monroe][170] and the Ripraps [Rip Raps]. The channel runs between them. Here there is a great many ships of all kinds and sizes and both English & French man of war vessels lying there. We come on up the river, noticed the noted places such as Harrisons Landing &c with great interest. At last we reach City Point & go on up to Bermuda Hundred & there we anchored. This being the place we were ordered to. But were ordered back to the City Point and went up to the wharf, tied up and stayed on the boat all night. I seen many things of interest today. But cannot now dwell on the different subjects.

June 30, 1864

And fine day. We get off the boat about 10 A.M. & draw some more catridges & start coming on verry slow stoping about evry mile. The heat was great & the dust greater. I never saw dust so deep. It is from two to four inches deep and there being a strong wind blowing. So the dust flew so as to perfectly blind us some times for rods. It was an awful march. We stoped to make coffee about 4 P.M. & when done we start on & soon come in hearing of skirmishing. Here we halted, closed up & went on rather thinking that we might get into a fight ere we got to the Regt. Soon we come to the Brestwork fartherest in the rear. Now the fight became general along for a mile or so. Here we stoped awhile & went on again a mile or so & so on for several times.

At last got to fifth corps headquarters where the names of those belonging the corps were called & marched in to the yard that incloses the fine mansion here that belonged to the different divisions & from here we went to Division Headquarters. It being dark now & from here we were taken to Brigade headquarters & then the Regt & Co., our Brigade being in the Brestworks.[171] So we had to go right up to where the bullets fly. But it being dark they couldnt see us. Sergt Roberts went over with us. There was two besides me for our Co. I found only 20 of the boys in the Co and 4 or 5 of them had returned from the Hospital 4 days before I did.

Whiz, whiz, the bullets go over our heads. But we don't fire. Our brestworks are high enough that they cant hit us if we keep in them. Occasionally a shot from the Artillery. We have some morter on the right & they throw shell occasionally which fairly makes the earth quake. Some light right in the Reb works, play havoc with them indeed. About evry one does so we can beat them at that.

July 1, 1864

We lay in the ditches all day. Cook & eat. We can have a good liberty by way of stirring around if we are of mind to risk our lives which the Boys do a great deal. A ball whizing past never stops anything unless it hits the man. Never stops conversation at all. I was amazed to see how indifferent the Boys are to things passing. The Boys got verry friendly for a spell today. They all stoped shooting and got up looking at each other.

There is one place about ¼ mile to the right of us where the line makes a bulge forming a horseshoe and brings our works and the Rebs within 150 yards of each other here.[172] A man from each side sallied forth with a paper and someone in our Brigade to the right of us fired. At that they run back to the works and the Boys in the Brigade hollered kill that fellow that shot &c. Most evrybody seems to think he deserved death for shooting on such an occasion. But in two or three minutes they sallied out again & this time they met, shook hands & exchanged papers & returned and then the usual shooting commenced. There is less shooting evry day & the Boys are more and more venturesome on each side. They will get friendly soon so that the pickets will not have to lay in the ditches all day. That will be a great relief to the poor fellows & myself to when I come on which will be soon verry likely.

We have only one officer left, 2 surgeons, 1 corporal, myself being the one. Cap [Henry Young] is with the Co but him & Lorin Parsons are away making up the rolls papers for the Co. This being muster time. Lieut Kidd is Division Ordnance officer & Lieut [William] Sloat is wounded. Three of the Boys that were Prisnors have returned while I was away. They were Sergts [Lorin G.] Parsons & [Calvin G.] Parker & private James Farmer[?]. Sergt Parker was killed in the great charge made on the 18 of June & his body now lies bleaching between the two lines. He just took the flag two or 3 days before to carry.

July 2, 1864

Today we lay back in the woods. The 2nd Brigade come in last night last & relieved us we having been in three day. That being the way they are going to manage it. We have to relieve in the night time. We came back here about ½ mile in the rear of the Brestworks. Had a good nights rest last night.

July 3, 1864

And fine day. We lay in the shade, cook & eat &c. Towards evening I & [Henry] Brinkman took a walk up around towards Division headquarters. & to the Sutlers. I got a bottle of mustard & 25 cts worth of lemons, that being only three & came around by several batteries that throws a shell occasionally & then home. Make some lemonade. We have plenty of ice here, there being a verry large Reb Icehouse near here so we can get as much as we want. Have ice all around in trenches & all the hospitals have plenty. So much for Reb hospitality. There is rumors of great things tomorrow. First what the Rebs will do, 2nd what we will &c. But it is only rumors. There may be some demonstrating as it is 4th July.

July 4, 1864

And fine day with nothing unusual transpiring except some of the officers getting drunk. I am sorry to see some of the officers is so bad repute. Especially Cap [Henry] Young. He is not liked at all by the Boys. They all seem to be of the same opinion. They all have a great deal to say about his drinking &c. We got some pickled cucumbers & onions this evening. They are verry nice. So much for the Sanitary Commission & we got 4 cans of preserved turkey, beef & tomatoes & once before get Sourkraut &c. We live well now. Verry. I wrote a letter to Mother today. Mail goes out evry day & comes in. We have a nice place here. But the bullets makes us a visit occasinally. But no one hurt. They come spatting around on the trees.

July 5, 1864

And fine day. & in the brest works again, this time in the rear line. We came in last night about ten oclock, relieved the 2nd Brigade, they having been in three days. Those trenches are not so commodious as the front ones. They being narrow we cant stretch out when we lay down. I expected a letter from home today but did not come.

July 6, 1864

And fine day. We lay in the works all day. There is verry little firing. Today none in our front. But there is a Reb sharpshooter away to the right that is verry annoying. He wounded two men in one Regt with one Ball. At least we suppose twas him for the common guns will not do execution so far. The programe being changed again so that we were relieved this evening at dusk only staying two days at a time in the works now. An inspection ordered tomorrow at 2 P.M., the rumor in camp is that our Division is going to Harpers Ferry & that the Rebel General Ewel [Richard S. Ewell] is near there with his corps. One more of the Boys come to the Co today & he said he met one Division of the 6th Corps going to City Point and they said they were going to Harpers Ferry. No mail for me today again.

July 7, 1864

And fine day. We lay around & attend to the duties of camp &c. I wrote a letter today to Mother but didnt mail it waiting to get a letter from her this evening. We make camp today, cleaned up &c so that it looks nice & we are comfortable now. We are down in the wood a little farther now so that we don't hear the Balls now & can rest more easy. We drew rations this morning. Got onions & krout &c. We got good rations now. Brinkman went over & got some butter & tobacco. I have got to smoking as bad as ever & Brinkman smokes some too. But I have to borrow a pipe when I smoke. I thought I would quit when I got to the Co. But cant do it. The fellow that I took the vow with got to chewing before me smoking & he owns to it & says he will pay me the $5.00, the being the amount of forfeited by the one that done it first.

July 8, 1864

And fine day. I am on fatigue detail. We started out at 4 A.M. there being 40 out of the Regt & a corresponding number out of each Regt in the Brigade. We go to Corps Headquarters & there get an ax for two men & come up the left of our line to near the 2nd Corps about 2 ½ miles to the left of our Brigade. Here we were set to work chopping down timber in front of two large forts which are being built. This is done to give the gunners a fair range if the enemy should break over our brestworks that are in advance of us. Still we work in the rear of our lines. The boys work well. We have cut many acres today. We have each Regt Detail divided up into three reliefs & I have charge of one relief & each relief works two hours at a time.

I forgot to mail my letter that I wrote yesterday & I have none come yet. This evening about 5 oclock there was a fierce little Battle on the right of Burnsides Corps & the cananading extending down the lines opposite us. But musketry. There was several wounded though, I saw them going in. The report is that the Rebs charged on our work but couldnt take them.

I got a paper of the 7th today & it has the official account of the Destruction of the Pirate *Alabama* (commanded by Capt [Raphael] Semmes by Kearsage [*Kearsarge*] commanded by Capt Wilson [John A. Winslow], US Navy. The Alabama has been spreading death and destruction among the American commerce on the seas for 2 years. But she now lies at the bottom of the sea as also many of her crew. But Semmes & some of the crew got away. But it is thought we will get them. The British ship *Greyhound* was watching the fight & when the *Alabama* sunk, the *Greyhound* picked Semmes & some of his crew up & landed them instead of turning them over to the Americans. It is thought that was the plan arranged between Semmes & the Capt of the *Greyhound*. Time will tell what they will make of it.[173]

July 9, 1864

And fine day. We are chopping again today & when night comes on we come home. Find the Boys packed up ready to go into the trenches. But we are going to stay & we have been out working our number of days & so tis nothing but right to let us lay in camp.

The 2nd Brigade has been in the works three days. I cant tell how they are running the thing. They have changed it so often. I was up the road today to see the large fort they are building to sweep the ground that we have been clearing. The fort is 500 feet square & there is a large number of men at work on it. They work like Beavers & evrything seem to go on with a will worthy the cause.

July 10, 1864

And fine day & warm. We are longing to have rain. The ground is so dry & the water is getting so scarce. We lay in camp all day. The Boys in the Brestworks come down once & a while. This being ration day, I & the Boys here drew the rations & took ours out & sent theirs up to them. We drew two heads of cabbage & about 2 quarts of curry & about half bushel of onions turnips & beets togather. We are getting pretty well fed now. I got a letter from Flora Lander today & mailed the one I wrote to Mother several days since. I forgot to mail it till then.

July 11, 1864

And fine day. Nothing of interest transpires today till night when the Brigade comes into camp being relieved by the 2nd Brigade. The news today is not cheering. The Rebs are at Harpers Ferry & in Maryland. There is great excitement amongst the people. The Rebs are destroying a great deal of property & driving off all that can walk such as horse & cattle.

Tis said the 6th corps has gone up to Baltimore & the rumors is that the Rebs are forty thousand strong & consist of the best troops in Lees army.[174]

July 12, 1864

And fine day. We changed camp today & fix a good camp. We are more comfortable. I and two other fellows from their tents made a good shade over our tents which makes it comfortable. The news from Maryland is anything but cheering. The Rebs are there in force without doubt & mean mischief. They are at Frederick City, MD & Hagerstown, Pennsylvania doing great damage.

July 13, 1864

And fine day with a verry slight shower in the evening. Just enough to say that water fell & a great deal of thunder & lightening. We lay in camp as usual. Cook & eat. We have some vegetables to cook, Turnips, cabbage, beets, onions. Just about a mouthful of each. But we are thankful for small favors. Take all together it will make a good meal. But such messes might keep us rid of the scurvy & other Diseases incident to living without vegetables.

The news from Maryland is by no means cheerful. But it is some consolation to know that it is not as bad as it might be. The Rebs has been checked a little. Gen. Wallace [Union General Lewis Wallace], he being in command in that Department.[175] But they were too many for his force & he was forced to fall back on the Defenses of Baltimore. Great excitement prevails throughout both City & country. The Govenors of Penn. & MD have called for troops to drive the invaders from the states & the people are responding in Maryland with a will, especially Baltimore. She has turned out 10,000 citizens armed & to work on the Defences of the city. The rumor is also that they do not intend taking the City but make a feint on it & slip by to Washington & take it first. The rumor is that the 19th corps has gone up there also. The papers is full of rumors & rumors only. The papers are two days old when we get them. We have the paper of the 11th. I expect by this time the tide is turned. When the old Veterans of the 6th Corps get at them they will get out of that.

I expected to hear from home this evening but didnt. I am waiting patiently for some letters to answer. I have such a good chance here. I took a cracker box and made me a table & bench so I am ready for writing in earnest.

July 14, 1864

We lay around camp & attend to duties. At night go into the Brestworks. We get a lot of reading matter today from the Christian Commission. Captain brought it to us. This a great wonder but I think he does not make quite as much fun of Religious Matters as he used to. He don't seem to sneer at such things now. He shows some respect now. I wrote a letter to Henry today. Got no news from home yet. And now the rebs have cut all the Railroads coming to Baltimore from all sides except the one coming from Washington and we will not get much mail till the communications is open again. The news is not verry cheering. But both Baltimore & Washington are still safe. The Rebs have been so near the latters Defenses that our forts opened on them making them halt & the 6th Corps got up & deployed & drove the Rebs 1 ½ miles. All is safe now about the latter place.[176]

There has been a great deal of work done on the work since we were on before & tonight they are working. There is 2 forts built in the line of trenches & six mortars just behind us so that taking all togather we cannot do much more digging. There is 3 lines of Brestwork, 2 in rear of us. We being in the front line this time out. The ground is litteraly like a sive sitting on a board so thick are the works and holes.

July 15, 1864

And fine day and cool & we are comfortable. Along towards night some of our pieces opened & by & by the Johnys threw a mortar shell & it burst near one of our mortars & we soon answered it with four at once & they answered again & so kept on for a few minutes. Our Mortars threw about 30 shells in the course of an hour or so. The Rebs threw about half as many. When one of ours would burst amongst them we would yell & when theirs would burst amongst us they would yell. Some of theirs burst right in our trenches. But wonderful to note there was not a man hurt by them. But we had the last shot & we rather beat them for we blew up their magazine. I tell you it sent a shower of sticks, dirt &c all around. We afterwards see the Johnys gather around the hole. I expect some of their friends was buried in the ruins. When it blew up we yelled at & jeered them & they opened a number of pieces but our boys dried them up soon. Ours almost invariably giving the last shot. The mortar shells look pretty as they raise from our mortars. We can trace them clear over till they burst. They go verry slow to that a canon shot does. For we cant see the latter.

Engineers of the army was inspecting the works today. They were quite a while around here. This appears to be a prominent place as there is lots of forts just about here. They continue to work & build something most evry night. The news from Maryland is by the way of an official dispatch & that was that the Rebs was crossing back into Virginia & our troops was pressing them. We couldnt get any papers today & no mail. One of our Co went out & exchanged papers with the Rebs. Their papers has nothing about the moves except what is copied from our papers. They know nothing of the Operations of their Army in Maryland except through our papers.

July 16, 1864

And fine day with signs of rain. We have things about the same as yesterday except that the Rebel shells did not drop right amongst us. But went over and came verry near our mortars. Our boys had the two last shots today & Johny wouldnt reply. Our shell was seen to burst right in or near their mortars. I guess we were rather too much for them. One of their shell struck in the Brestwork in rear of us & after going in several feet flew out & up into the air almost out of sight & off to right angles to the way it came over & went about 40 rods before it lighting. The Battery man went over & got it & put it in & threw it back to the Johnys. When night came & with it the 2nd Brigade we come to our camp & Bivouck for the night The news from Maryland is better. The Rebs are retreating & both cities are safe.

July 17, 1864

And fine day and we enjoy the comforts of camp as well as we can. But what we fixed up the last time the 2nd Brigade carried off. So our camp is bare. There ought to have been a guard left here to watched the camp. When we got breakfast this morning we built brest work in front of our camp so if the Rebs begin to shell, we will have somewhat to lay behind for they can shell these woods all to pieces if they (the Rebs) had a mind to.

July 18, 1864

And fine day. We fix & clean up camp a little &c. Last night about 10 P.M. we were ordered to pack up & be ready to move at a minutes notice for a Johny Deserter came in & told our generals that the Rebs were massing their forces some place on our line to charge & break through. & in about an hour we moved out & our Brigade formed in 2 lines in rear of all the work & at the bottom of the hill & send a detail to the Pioneers Crops. Got shovels & picks &c and built brestworks & good one also in about an hour & then laid down to rest without unpacking so as to be ready for them. But we lay there all night & no alarm so that makes 5 lines of Brestwork on this hill. We came to camp at daylight & that is all about it. I had my doubts about the truth of the thing for he was a Private only & they are not apt to know much about the moves of the army. I know we don't. But some times such is true & it is best to be ready. It was some of a disappointment to the Boys. But a happy one I guess.

We live well now. We drew potatoes & cabbage &c, things in the Vegatable line. So that we have two or three meals out of a drawing if we boil them. But most of the Boys fry evrything. Fry. Fry. But I & my tentmate (a Dutchman) boil a good deal. Our icehouse has ceased to supply us, it [the ice] being all gone. We get our mail but none comes for me.

July 19, 1864

And fine till toward noon when the rain began to fall & continued for several hours & twas a verry nice gentle rain. I was in hopes that twould rain several days for we need it bad. But we may have some more yet before it clears off. Just at dark a detail was made from our Regt for fatigue. & they went & worked on a new fort they are building on the front line and on the right of our Division. The fort is for mortars, some say 200 pounders & some say 100 pounders &c. I got a paper evry evening a most or rather I furnish the money & some of the Boys go after them as the paper boy don't get around to us ere his papers give out, so they have to go to Corps Headquarters after them. The news is not exciting. & nothing unusual except the confirmation of Sherman being in front of the fortifications of Atlanta GA & had take 3 or 4 thousand prisnors & the report is he has taken 6000 since. But the last I doubt.[177]

I got 2 letters last night. One from Henry & one from Mother & Lu. They are all well & doing well as could be expected. The crops are almost a failure. The wheat entirely so. My [heart] leaped for joy when I heard my name called in calling over the mail & then again the 2 time, but when I come to read them I find that they are the answers to the ones I wrote at Camp Distribution. The others of which there is quite a number was sent to the Hospital & they have not been forwarded to me as they should have been.

July 20, 1864

And fine day. We go into the Brestworks at 10 A.M. & relieved the 2nd Brigade. There is roads cut now so that we can come up & the Johnys not see us. There has been a great deal of works made here since I was here before for the mortars &c.

There is the usual firing on our right & bombarding &c all around us. The work is beginning to look complete. Some verry nice ones & strong too. There is a great many gabions and fascines used in the construction of these works.[178]

Just at night there was a detail for Picket made out of our Regt. I being the noncom out of our Co. We went out to the line by the flank & took our positions in the different pits as we came to them, there being a Sergt & two men on the first post & I being the first Corp, I acted as Sergt (as there was no Sergt on the detail). I had command of about half dozen pitts on the right of the line. We found one pit in a bad condition, mud ankle deep & they had piled in a lot of green corn to dry it up & that made it worse by the way [of] a stench. So I took one of our two for to go & get a spade or shovel from the Brestworks & I posted out the videttes [guards or pickets] about 50 yard in front of the pits, one from each pit. They had to stay on till midnight & then I would relieve them with the others & when this done, the man got back with the spade & we cleaned out our pit & fixed it up quite comfortable. & I took the spade along the line to let the others fix theirs. But theirs was in good order, they having the tents over them in yesterdays rain.

I got another letter from Mother & Lu tonight. They are well as usual and evrything is going on about as usual. Evrything in the way of living is raising to a high pitch. I got a paper this evening & I see the President has called for 500,000 more troops to volunteer & gives them fifty days to do it in & then the sweeping draft. I don't like that. I want the draft for people will not volenteer verry fast. For evrybody most is waiting for the draft and my belief is that they will continue to avoid. The news is nothing of importance.

July 21, 1864

And fine day. We lay, sit, stand or walk around just as we please. The Johny don't fire at us at all in our front & we don't. We tried several times to trade papers but the officers or the men wont let us. There is orders against it. I had a paper & wrote a lot of stuff on the margins. It was of the scissorine [?] style. We can cook here on the line or go back to the Brestworks & do it. There was considerable shelling today & our canonier done well. I had the consolation of seeing 5 of the Johnys go off wounded & the Boys says they saw more. Lots of our shell light right in their work & also did some of theirs. I saw one of our men away on the left carried off in a blanket. I guess he was killed. Some Johnys come in & they say if we stay here a month longer our canoniers will be able to hit a copper cent a mile so direct do they shoot. We hollowed back to them when they hollowed to us & had a great deal of sport. Towards night they threw three shells over & none of them burst and our Boys wanted to know of them if they didnt want us to bring them a coal of fire to light their fuses with.

July 22, 1864

And fine day. We have nothing unusual transpired. The news is good. We have captured or rather our Calvelry under [Union General George] Crook has captured 300 wagons from the Maryland raiders & killed & took prisnors, a great many of them & done them a great deal of damage &c and still pursuing them. Making altogather a glorious affair for the Federals. The Rebs are making the best of their way to Richmond.

The news from Shermans Department is glorious. He having got within 7 miles of Atlanta. And the news from Tennessee is glorious. [Union General William Sooy] Smith has whipped [Confederate General Nathan Bedford] Forrest three times & 2500 men & lots of guns &c from him. This last was mostly a cavelry expedition.[179]

There is another verry important piece of buisness been transacted. It is the going of Col Jaquess [?] & another man to Richmond & back. They being sent by the President. But it is stated not for the purpose of making peace propisitions but it still leaves the public in the dark as to the object of the errand. But the full particulars are to be made public some time in the future. They were entertained in the highest style at the Spottwood house, that being the leading hotel in Richmond. They had gold fork & spoons on the table & plenty of wine & they stayed 3 days & tis said cost the Rebel government $500 in their money. They visited the Prisnors & report them as doing as well as could be expected. Both on the Island & in the Prisons

July 23, 1864

And fine day. We are relieved this evening & go to camp, find the camp in order there having been a detail sent in to police the camp &c. The news is cheering & reports of Atlanta being captured by Sherman.[180] I comenced to write a letter to Lu & Mother today. The usual canonading continues & the spades are still used with good effect. There is being lots of roads cut from the different camps to the works &c.

July 24, 1864

I, with all the Co, am on detail today. We are tearing up the RRoad (that is the Norfolk Road) through the long deep cut near our camp & making a wagon road in it. We all got hold & turned it upside down at the same time laying it by the side of the grade. We done this in the forenoon & in the afternoon we were digging the road. Dig four feet into the ground & throw the dirt up on the side next the enemy thereby making a bank about 8 feet high which is sufficient to screen the teams as they go up to the front. This like many others runs to the main line & this main road runs the length of the Army. By having those roads we can move troops &c without the Rebs knowing it. This is a good plan but takes a great deal of work. The Boys work good saying they would rather die than fight. The news today about the same as yesterday.

July 25, 1864

And rained some last night. Most all night. We were awoke again early this morning to get ready for fatigue. I did not have to go this morning. Sergt [George] Eustice goes today and noncom for each Co each day. They are digging road today again. We don't get much rest now. Well we would rather do that than fight. I finished my letter to Mother & Lu today & mailed it. Today is kind a cool & pleasant. The news is about the same as yesterday. All reports about Atlanta the same, captured &c.

July 26, 1864

And fine day. We are on fatigue today again. The whole Brigade. But I am on as noncom for our Co. We are digging again today & the Road is most finished. We worked hard all day not stopping for dinner. I formed the Co into 2 reliefs & relieved evry hour so the hour that they was off they got dinner. When six oclock arrived we quit & go & get supper & just dark we are ordered to pack up & go to the Intrenchments. Which we done with some grumbling. We being out of the [works] only three days & working all that time goes pretty hard. But we can stand it.

The news is good. We have good authority of Atlanta being taken with a hard battle. 2000 loss on our side & 6000 on the Rebel side. The latter we hold entire. The Rebel Gen [John Bell] Hood having superceded Gen Johnson [Joseph E. Johnston]. He ordered out the army to give battle which they did in earnest & got badly whipped. Sherman carries evrything along with him. Success to him. Things around here are about the same. Dig, dig & keep digging.

July 27, 1864

And fine day. We go through the usual routine of duty as usual when here. The Boys call it being relieved now when we come into the works. They think being relieved to use the spade is not what it is cracked up to be. So they have just changed it. About last night, one third of the men in each and evry Co have to be up. We are divided in to three reliefs. & a noncom to each relief. I was on the third relief and have to wake all up at 3 oclock & be under arms till daylight.

There is about the usual amount of shelling with the usual precision on our part. The rebs don't throw much over us today. The Batteries in the rear of us not throwing any, so Johneys don't when they cant elicit a reply.

July 29, 1864

And fine day. Things the same as yesterday except they are unusually buisy today with the spade & seem to urge the men with the spades pretty hard. There is something unusual to transpire soon to break the monotony as we are pleased to term

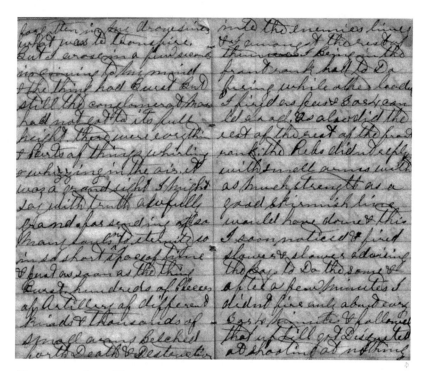

Two pages from William Ray's Volume 12, detailing the July 30, 1864, explosion of the Petersburg Mine. *Sherry Murphy*

it now when there is not more than 2 or 300 killed & wounded. The rumor at just night is that all the works are to be filled which have been vacant & sure enough about 10 oclock they commenced the buisness. I was on guard, the first relief last night. But tonight I am to unwell to be on duty & got the captain to excuse me. & I had been sick all day, something like the belious fever & Im afraid I will be sick. The Boys got tools a fixed up, their work good tonight. The report about midnight that we are to give Battle in the morning. & tomorrow morning dawn is the time or rather half past 3 A.M.

July 30, 1864 [The Battle of the Crater]

And fine warm day & verry warm in the way we verry much dislike as you will see presently. 3 A.M. all awoke ordered to pack up & get into our works preparatory to open at half past 3 oclock. The signal to open would be the blowing up of the fort in the Rebel line which our forces had just finished undermining &c. to blow it up. They having been to work at it about a month. It is situated on an angle of their works so that they can enfilade a good distance of our line with several guns.[181]

Half past 3 come & it didnt go up & four come & didnt go. We wait rather impatiently & some gazing at it all the while.[182] I set down at last & we began to think the thing was put off for today. But half past 4 arrived & with it the shaking of the ground where I sit & kind awakened me. I rocked to & fro, looked at the ground to see the crack that might engulph me the next minute. I couldnt think for a while what it was. Had quite forgotten in my drowsiness what was to transpire. But I arose in a few seconds in coming to my mind & the thing had burst. But still the conglomerat mass had not got to its full height. There were evrything & parts of things whirling & whizzing in the air. It was a grand sight. I might say with truth awfully grand for sending so many souls into eternity so in so short space of time. & just as soon as the thing burst hundreds of pieces of Artillery of different kinds & thousands of small arms belched forth Death & Destruction into the enemies lines & I amongst the rest of them, I being in the front rank had to do firing while others loading. I fired as fast as 3 or 4 could load. As also did the rest of the rest of the front rank. The Rebs didnt reply with small arms with as much strength as a good skirmish line would have done. & this I soon noticed & fired slower & slower advising the Boys to do the same & after a few minutes I didnt fire only about evry 3 or 4 minutes & followed that up till got disgusted at shooting at nothing & sit down. But the greater part of the Boys thought it was fun to fight the rebs behind our own brestworks. At least when they didnt fire any. I say Bravo for them but I tried to get them to fire slow. But no & verry shortly the officers taking notice of the situation ordered us to not fire only as we could see one of them. & so we done it & when we would ease a little they would begin to show themselves again & then they got perhaps a hundred shots & they almost invariably fell. There was some good shots made.[183]

There was another noticeable feature which I soon noticed. That was that the Rebs replied verry weakly to our Artillery. They would fire one shot to our side (I dare say) 100. & after several hours our artillery slackened a little & kept on till they fired only an occasional shot & we began to do about as we had done before the Battle.

But to return to 5 minutes after the fort blew up & the Boys yells, see our Boys have the fort. No, yes, yes, yes, those are the Blue coats. I looked & they were massed just on front of the ruins of the fort & lots of Greybacks coming Prisnors. Soon they forward. They go over the ruins. Some few Rebs run & many come into our lines. See, see, see our men go over the ruins. All the union flags on the farther side of the fort. Our Boys cheer. We hold it. Fire fast. Don't let the Rebs raise over their Brestwork. But the Rebs are having a hot fire into the flank of our men from down their line. But tis so far off we cant reach them. Our men pile over & into the fort & we see Rebs come in. Our men begin to fortify themselves. We see the Rebs in great agitation runing towards the fort. But keeping their heads well down. For they got a hundred shot whenever they showed their [heads] and when they passed the embrasures in their forts.[184]

I tell you about 7 A.M. our side was Bright. But the Rebs I knew were reenforcing from the left. They would come down to the hollow about opposite & turn & go up it & get back over the hill and go up one by [one] to the right & formed in the woods. This I could see & told our officers so. But I surmise that they didnt heed it any considering the source it come from. Twas not high enough in Authority. But about 8 A.M. it showed itsself for they come out in two, two or three lines of Battle & charged down the open plane. Oh, how they did fall from the galling fire our Brave fellows poured into them. They break. Confusion and many turn back and many others come on up close to the fort. But only to be defeated. Killed. Wounded & many take prisnor. A few went back. Our boys cheer. We still hold the fort. In about an hour another 2 or 3 lines charge down & met the same fate of the former. This time as well as the other, great many of our men run. But there was enough stayed to hold it for a while and many that had at first run now reformed & charged up driving & capturing most of the Rebs. By this time things began to look dubious for there were so many that run & many killed & wounded by the galling flank fire the Rebs had on them. Our fellows after the first charge of the Rebs seemed to be confused & appeared as though they had no officers to command them. By the Bravery of a few out of each & evry Co., perhaps they held it. There was, I guess, about 8000 of our men on & about the fort at one time. But now 9 ½ oclock & there don't appear more than a thousand.[185]

10 A.M. And the Rebs come out & charge on both sides of the fort & our men run so that they couldnt hold it & perhaps 400 of the Bravest of the Brave had to surrender. Which they did. Then our fellows poured the shot & shell into them when they see the Rebs had it back again. Oh, how our Boys cursed & damned them & damned the officers for not reinforcing our Brave fellows when the Rebs would charge on them. There is something wrong says the Boys. The Boys yell to much commisary allowed, meaning of this that the officers were to Drunk on commisary Whiskey. For last night when our Brigade Ammunition team came up with ammunition they brought a Barrel of whiskey. I suppose thinking that would be needful to insure success. But the Rank & file didnt get a smell.

By this time we had nearly quit firing as the Rebs wouldnt show themselves above the Brestworks at all. Only now & then a man & our fellows would send a number of ball after him & not unfrequently bring them down. Well we are ordered to assume the defensive & give up the offensive for the Present. Evrything is lost that was gained early in the morning.

The Boys begin to cook coffee & prepare & eat breakfast and 11 oclock dinner togather. Things look rather dubious. The rumor is that we have captured a line of their works on the left but I don't place much confidence in it. The firing has ceased except the usual desultory fire as before the Battle.[186]

The news from the north is anything but good. The Rebs have whipped our forces & drove them back to Harpers Ferry & still confronting them. & it is anticipated that they (the Rebs) are going to make another Invasion of Maryland. But our fellows are preparing to give them a warm reception. But the news from Sherman is good. That is that he has closed in around Atlanta & cut off all but one road of escape & that the cavelry has started for that & are almost sure to cut it. He defeats the Rebs in evry attempt to suprise him &c. The Army is in high spirits. They ought to be surely.[187]

(Evening) And the things are as usual. Except the conflicting rumor about the Disaster and who the blame rests upon &c. There was one Divison of Negro troops in the Battle for the fort. The rumors about how Brave or how cowardly they are &c. But the best founded rumor is that that Regt of negros did run. Their officers run first & this seem to be the truth for it is not denied and evrybody believes it. For many of the negros stayed & fought without any officers to command them. Tis said by the 37th & 38th Wisconsin that was in with & fought with the negros. That the negros done as well and many instances better than some whites because they fought without officers which our Boys is not apt to do. & when the Rebs captured them they put them in a squad by themselves &c. Well I saw two squads going away & there is rumors that they didnt take a negro prisnor & when they did they abused them & even cut out their tongues &c other barbarities. I as well as most of us think the negro will fight if he is commanded by good officers. I say try again. The negros seem to hate the defeat as bad or worse than we do.[188]

July 31, 1864

And fine day somewhat cooler than yesterday, sprinkled rain a little once today. We were relieved last night about 9 P.M. & came to camp & had a good nights rest. We lay in camp today till about 2 P.M. when were ordered to pack up to be ready to move at a minutes notice which we soon done & come about 2 miles to the left. & after laying around and resting an hour or so we were put into camp for the night in front of a large fort on the hill. We got supper & laid down without taking the blankets for now. Twas verry warm & sultry. Tis said we are to do Picket duty & garrison this fort. That is our Brigade and the troops that are here are to move out and we go into their camp. They are nice camps. Shades built over the tents & many things fixed up which they will have to leave. They will come good for us. But at the same time I am sorry to see them have to leave things for I know how it is by experience.

Today there is not much said about the fight. The rumor is & I think it is true that our Genrls sent in a flag of truce to care for the wounded & bury the dead. But the Rebs only received it & returned it & when it was nearing the work they fired on it. They are verry cross. They wouldnt let our fellows do anything to relieve the wounded (so the rumor is) but give them water. The reason, I suppose, is that they have none but what is inside their works, as they near come over them so they can take care of theirs anyway in spite of us & our poor fellows must lay there & suffer. Tis horrible they say to look on the dead & wounded. They lay piled up. I could see in the evening after the Battle that the ground on their side of the fort looked quite blue and know it must be as the fighting was done on such a small space. & we cant see what was done on the other side of the fort as right there, the line turns.

August 1, 1864

And fine day and we are still here in front of the fort. Get breakfast & then get ready & move into a camp used by a Battalion of sharpshooters in rear of the fort. They are just moving out & leave many things that will be useful to us. We come in & Brinkman gets a nice place with a good bunk already made. Tentpoles &c. We just pitch our tent over them & go to work to fix up a table & made a stool &c and fixed up generally. Then policed all around, got cleaned up. So by evening the camp has a homelike appearance. All the tents have a shade over them. Take it altogather, the camp would be hard to beat. All the Regts have been assigned to the camps that have been evacuated by other regiments. All nice camps. There is plenty of wells that have been dug by the occupants of the camps & altogather the Brigade has a nice place & we have to garrison the fort. But none is camped in it. But there is a guard kept on it. There is one line of Rifle Pitts along here, they being small ones & they are only guarded lightly. So we can man the work & lay in camp for our camp is within a few rods of the works & the Picket line is 2 or 3 miles out. Therefore if we are attacked, the Picket firing will warn us in time to run to the works. We are almost on the extreme left of the line now & we are almost out of hearing of the fire of Musketry on the right where we used to lay. We were on the right of the Corps & now I guess we are on the left of the Corps.

The news today is to the effect that the Rebs are going into Maryland. The news from Sherman is about the same as yesterday, still grasping around Atlanta. The mail comes & with it a letter for me, or rather a small bundle. A pair of socks with a box of pills & a verry nice little needlebook in them & in the needlebook a nice little letter from Sister Lu. In the letter she says all is well and that Mother was not at home. She being on a visit to Thurza Anns & Marys & all the relatives in that neighborhood. I was delighted to hear from home again & know all was well & Lu seen from the letter what I wanted & she sent me the things.

Sergt Eustice went over to the Pioneer Corps & got a kettle to wash & when he was done, I got it & Brinkman & I went down and washed evry bit of our clothing (but coats) & boiled them & now we will be rid of lice perhaps for a few days at least. & we washed our persons. We feel much better. Most all of us have got what we call the ground itch which is caused by being so dirty. Our clothes is packed full of dust & our skins is caked with dirt. All of which we could not help till now. & perhaps we will have a chance to get clean if the Johneys will let us. At least I think we will act on the Defensive for a while now until the army is recuperated as also to get in some of the men that have been called for.

August 2, 1864

We lay in camp all day. Do a good deal of policing. Our camp is in fine order. There was a detail for Picket made taking about half our Co & we have to guard the fort too. One out of each Co for the Fort. I got 2 letters from home, one from Mother & one from Lu. They are well. They sent me a sheet of paper & envelope in each letter. I wrote a letter to Mother but wouldnt mail it for I thought I would get one from home. Brinkman has gone on Picket.

August 3, 1864

And fine day & nothing unusual transpired today. There was a fatigue party went out & cleaned out the trenches that we are to occupy if the enemy come to attack us. I finish writing the letter to Lu today & mailed it. The paper brings the sorrowful news of the Rebels being in Maryland & Pennsylvania again & they have burned Chambersburg, a nice thriving city in Pennsylvania & committing various depredations to numerous to mention & the news from Sherman is meagre, he being in about the same position as yesterday.[189]

The news from this Army is various. But the supposition was when the last dispatch was sent by the correspondents of the Press that we would be in Petersburg in a day or two. That dispatch being sent when we had evry prospect of winning. But tomorrows paper will have the failure. The rumor that the Rebels wouldnt receive the Flag of Truce has proved untrue for they did & allowed us to bury the dead & care for the wounded. Tis said 150 of the former & 40 of the latter were found in & about the fort or at least between the lines. There is a rumor the Paymaster is coming.

August 4, 1864

And fine day & this is my Birthday making my 26th. And also Thanksgiving day. But I think there wasnt much given in the Army if there was at home. The news is nothing exciting except from Maryland. The Rebs are there in some force. But how much they don't know. I got a letter from Richard Lander. He is well & at Memphis. He has been out on the great expedition which whiped Forrest so bad & tore up the Mobile & Ohio R.R. & done a big thing. I am on guard today as Corporal of the Guard. Only three men on guard at the well.

August 5, 1864

I didnt get a paper today. But tis said the news is the same as yesterday. The papers is filled with the particulars of our failure here & the Rebs in Maryland &c.

August 6, 1864

A fine day & verry warm towards evening. I go on Picket this evening. We start from camp at 3 P.M., go to Brigade Headquarters where all the Regimental details meet & from there we go to Picket line. Reach it half past four, it being about 1 ¼ miles & we are posted, I with 4 Privates on one post. There is a cavelry camp in our immediate front & most of them is out on Picket 4 or 5 miles in front of us so we are in secure place for Picket. One man on post at a time so we have pretty heavy duty.

August 7, 1864

And fine day with a slight sprinkle in the evening. But not enough to do us any good. Evrything goes on right & we are getting along fine. We are still in hearing of the firing of the 9th Corps & we are still 1 ½ mile south of our camp. I was quite unwell last night with headache & pain in bowels. But feel great deal better today. I feel quite at a loss for news. Get no paper & even no reports or rumors. I feel hungry for some news. I wrote a letter to Mother today & I hear from some of the Boys that come out to get apples &c from the orchards outside of the Picket line from a mile to mile & half, that I have a letter in camp. But they forgot it. The Boys will go out anyhow & they get some pretty good apples but generally they are verry poor. They, like evrything else in Virginia, are verry poor.

August 8, 1864

And fine day & warm. The Brigade of Cavelry that was here was relieved today by another Brigade & they went back to the rear to go into camp & recuperate themselves & horses. 1 of the Boys went into camp today & brought out the mail. I got 2 letters, one from Mother and one from Henry. The folk are well as usual. I see from them that Isaac Lander has sold his farm again, this time for $3,000. He has made $600 by taking it back from the man he sold it to last spring. He has the crops off the place &c. That was a lucky hit for him that Thomas wouldnt have it. But he don't say who he sold it to this time. He and Henry are talking of going out west to look up a new home. I wish I were there to go with him. But there is no show for it now until the war is over or I am discharged.

August 9, 1864

And fine day. Rather cooler today. Good signs of rain but it passed around us. There was a great deal of thunder & lightning. We were relieved last evening about dark & came to camp. I find my tentmate has gone on Picket. I guess they have changed the program so that we, our Brigade, does Picketing all the time on a certain part of the line & the 2nd Brigade on another certain part. For the last two or three nights there has been a detail out to build a fort in the front on the Picket line away down to the right where the works are close together. The Rebel works within a quarter of a mile. I wrote a letter to Sarah & John today.

August 10, 1864

And fine day with nothing unusual but the report of that Mobile is taken by [Admiral David] Farragut.[190] I wrote a letter to Mother today.

[*Ed. Note*: End of Diary. Ray's next page contains the following list:]

First Relief:

Atkinson, Alexander, B. Bryan, Cook, Brinkman, Delp, Mchugh, Hutchinson

Second Relief

P Bryan, Booth, Rice, Lesler, Endicott, McDonald, Garner, Bronsetter [Branstetter]

Note: 200 cartridges wanted in Co. F to make 40 rounds each

Picket Guard:

1. O. Clark, 2. H.M. Pulver, 3. D. Borst, 4. D. Birdsill
2. Relief
B.C. Tolison, Co E
G. Donaldson, A

[*Ed. Note*: The sheets of paper in the back of Volume 12 contain the balance of Ray's diary for this period.]

August 15, 1864

And fine day, somewhat cooler today. We had an awful hard shower about 10 to 11 oclock last night. Run me out of bed, the water come about 2 inches deep in & under my bed. So I got up and crawled on to some poles & got some sleep, some of the Boys was up all night playing poker & other kinds of gambling. We lay in this camp all day today. I now hear we were to go to City Point last night & get on transport to go some place. Some say to Fortress Monroe. But we don't know where & others say we come here to act in the same capacity as the 2nd Corps so as to be in supporting distance of either flank of the Army. We are expressing our money home. The Chaplain is here to take it to City Point & there he will put it in the Agents hands and get the receipts for it &c. I sent $100.00 to Henry & with what I had coming to me in the Co. I will have $25.00 left me to dispose of for such articles as necessary. [See Appendix 2]

Just night and we have had an awful hard shower, harder than the one we had last night. The water run in a flood all over the ground. This will effectually lay the Dust which had become intolerable. Brinkman & I fixed up our tent & I went to an old camp near by & got some boards & put a floor in it. So we will have a nights rest if it does rain.

August 16, 1864

And fine day. Pretty warm. We don't go away today. But about 10 AM we move a little ways & make a new camp & are likely to stay here a few days at least. We will have to make shades over our tents if we stay long here so as to keep the sun off. We have plenty of good water here. The troops that was in those camps, I must give them great credit for their enterprise they showed by providing themselves with good water. Our Boys have never dug a single well in any of our camps. Our officers don't take hold of such things as they ought to. They lay around, seemingly without energy enough to eat & drink. I have often spoke of digging wells. But nobody takes any notice of such things. Our Col is good enough but the line Officers are lazy, verry.

August 17, 1864

And fine day with a shower in the evening. We lay in camp as usual and evrything is quiet. The Boys are patronizing the Sutler pretty well. I commence to write a letter today to Sister Lu, but didn't get it finished.

August 18, 1864 [Start of the Battle of Weldon Railroad or Globe Tavern]

And fine but verry warm day. We marched at just daylight. Come to near the front and then turned down marching Southward towards the left flank of the Army. I find our whole corps is going. The Divisions that were in the works being relieved by so many of the 9th Corps. After getting pretty well towards the left we went outside of the works and on outside of the Picket line. We have to rest often, the heat being so overpowering. See several sunstruck.

The rumors are many & of a great variety. The general opinion is that we are going to the Weldon RailRoad to bear it up and perhaps hold it. Soon the word comes that the first division hold the Railroad & have tore up 1 ½ miles of it. We soon come in sight of it & see that it is done. We stop for dinner. They fly around and get dinner, all pretty near given out. Just before stopping, one of our Co. (Webster Cook)[191] was sunstruck. We soon got a stretcher & carried him off & under a shade & put him in care of the doctor. There was only just men enough left in the Co to carry him off, all the rest being stragglers. I come verry near being one of the latter, but kept up.

We can hear skirmishing up the road a mile or so towards PetersBurg which I think we can not be more than ten miles from. After getting dinner we start and go up towards the firing. We soon get where the bullets whiz past over us and they are fighting hard. We hear our Boys cheer & the Rebs cheer. The wounded begin to come to the rear but not verry fast. But more stragglers. The Provost Guard stops most of them, letting none through but the wounded & our Boys stop many. We are in support of those fighting.[192]

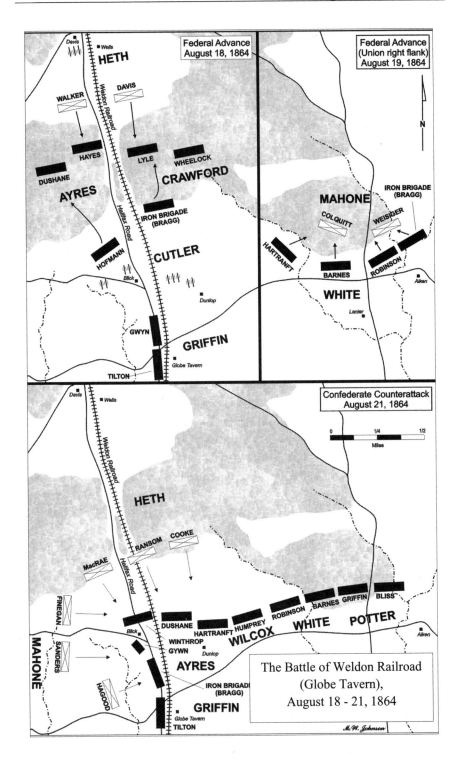

Federal Advance
August 18, 1864

Federal Advance
(Union right flank)
August 19, 1864

N

Davis
Wells
HETH
WALKER
DAVIS
HAYES
LYLE
WHEELOCK
DUSHANE
CRAWFORD
AYRES
IRON BRIGADE
(BRAGG)
HOFMANN
CUTLER
Blick
Dunlop
GWYN
GRIFFIN
Globe Tavern
TILTON
Weldon Railroad
Halifax Road

MAHONE
COLQUITT
WEISIGER
IRON BRIGADE
(BRAGG)
HARTRANFT
BARNES
ROBINSON
WHITE
Lanier
Aiken

Confederate Conterattack
August 21, 1864

0   1/4   1/2
Miles

Davis
Wells
Weldon Railroad
HETH
RANSOM   COOKE
MacRAE
Halifax Road
FINEGAN
MAHONE
SANDERS
Blick
DUSHANE
WINTHROP
GYWN   Dunlop
HARTRANFT   HUMPREY
ROBINSON   BARNES   GRIFFIN   BLISS
WILCOX   WHITE   POTTER
Aiken
HAGOOD
AYRES
IRON BRIGADE
(BRAGG)
GRIFFIN
Globe Tavern
TILTON

The Battle of Weldon Railroad
(Globe Tavern),
August 18 - 21, 1864

M.W. Johnson

The Boys drive & are driven &c for a couple of hours when our line, all but a strong skirmish line, fall back & same in front of us. March off to the left flank where the rebs are driving them back a little & we march up in as pretty a line as ever I seen to the edge of the woods & halted & built work. The fighting is over except skirmishing & our Batteries throw a shell once & a little while. We must lay on our Arms all night ready for any emergency. So they order us. Night comes on & all is quiet except the skirmishing. The Rebs we captured says their generals tell them that they must have the road back at all hazards & they will try it tomorrow.

August 19, 1864

And stormy mid morning but fine in latter part of day. Rained considerable last night. We lay in the works till daylight when we, our Brigade, moved off to the right about 1 mile & formed line of Battle in thick woods. Considerable skirmishing in our front. We get breakfast & about 9 A.M. we march of to the right again & begin to establish Picket line & keep at it till the whole Brigade is on. But we missed our way a little & had to swing around till we joined on the left of the 2nd Corps Pickets, they being on the left of the old line of works, our Regt joining them. This line run mostly through thick woods & being some 2 ½ miles long I think. We build fires & get dinner & all is fine till about 3 P.M. when the Rebs come in on the line about the 19th Ind. & 24th Mich. Break through & capture a lot of them & our Regt fell back into a good position ready to receive them if they come but they didnt come. They soon met with some troops that stopped them & sent them back in a hurry capturing a good many & recapturing many of our men.[193]

We soon reestablished our line, but could find no body to connect with on the left of us. Our Lieut Col & Major & some of the Boys went out & by night captured 23 men & three officers. & night coming on & we our Regt alone, twas thought best to fall back to the 2nd corps Pickets which we did & got inside the line. We bivouac for the night having to furnish some Pickets. We get supper through the rain & go to bed, making the best of things as we can. Get no tidings from the Brigade or the rest of the Corps. This has been a hard old day for us. Forming a new picket line is hard buisness & then having it broke &c. I don't wish to see many such I tell you. I believe our Regt didnt loose a man.

August 20, 1864

And we are awoke early & get breakfast. Examine our guns to be sure of them going. We march out & form Picket line again & after considerable truble get our left to join with some of the 9th Corps which came in here last night. Our Regt is half mile farther ahead now than it was yesterday. We having to do so, so as to join on the left. We stay here till about noon when a regt from the 9th Corps relieves us & we have to report to corps headquarters. We marched off rather pleased to get out of this unwelcome place. We come back along the line & quite surprised were we to find lots of troops & Brestworks where the day before there was nothing. We now see too that there has been much more of a fight than we thought for and they drove our fellows too. But they didnt hold the ground long. For our Boys soon sent them back howling. As we passed over the ground could see dead Rebs & guns &c. Such things on all Battlefields.

We reach corps Headquarters & are sent to the Brigade which we found about half mile from here across the R.R. & glad were we to see each other. Each one thought the other was captured. But when we come to get togather we find that only about 150 of the Brigade has been captured. We took our place on the left of the Brigade which soon moved up into the works they were building. We occupy a part of them which we have to [get] finished & did finish & then went to work, get supper & camp in rear of the works. One third of the Co. having to be up all night. I was detailed to go after rations & we had to go about 2 miles to the rear. We started about 5 oclock & didnt get back till 9 oclock, there having been so much rain & travel on the roads that twas almost impossible to get along. We had a hard time of it. I was detailed to stay up with the first relief. But Corp Alexander kindly volunteered to take my place considering I had been out after rations and had such a hard time of it.

I am completely disgusted with the way things is going this evening. The Boys could or did buy whiskey & many of them got drunk & 3 or 4 of the Boys that went with me for rations got drunk & didnt get in till long after I did. I hope there will not much of it get into the ranks for if we have to fight tomorrow we want all sober &c.

August 21, 1864

And fine day till towards night when we had thunder showers. We had a fight today. The Rebs charged in front of our Brigade. But they didnt get verry near for our murderous fire just mowed them down and there being a ditch in front of us about from 2 to 300 yards, they got into what was not wounded or killed & they commenced to come in & we ceased firing & a lot of the Boys rallied out & took the rest prisinors. Our Regt got about 100 of them and a number of officers , a lieut, Col & Major with them. And as soon as this was over another Brigade charged on the 2nd Brigade & they met with the same fate or worse for they captured a flag and more prisinors than we. & in a few minutes another Brigade charged rather on the left of the 2nd Brigade & around the flank which they partially succeeding in getting around when they met a hot fire from another line in this front that they were not expecting. & a couple of Regts of 2nd Brigade doublequicked to the left & come partially in the rear of the Rebs. When they threw down their arms & Capt Daily [Dennis B. Dailey] of Gen Cutlers [Lysander Cutler] Staff went up to the rebel General [Johnson] Hagood & demanded him to surrender. Hagood turned & shot Daily giving him a mortal wound it is thought. Our Boys shot Hagood & the Rebs picked him up & they were shot down. & another set done so & met with the same fate & so to the fourth set of men when they go off the field with him. & after the

Rebs threw down their arms, lots of them took to the woods & got away. But many of them bit the dust before they got out of reach. So we captured about half this Brigade & this ended the fight.[194]

We, our division, smashed up the Rebel division pretty well. We have half of them inside our lines & they attacked us away to the right but got repulsed. So we gain all around today. They evidently don't like for us to hold this road. Some say they don't care much about it. But I think they wouldn't fight so hard for it if they didnt care much about it. I guess most of the Army is here for I saw one division of the 2nd corps & the 9th corps is here and they say they are all in position. Looks like work. Any hour may bring on a Big Battle. Evrything seems to be in good order and all quiet except some skirmishing. There is a good many complaining kind a sick & with the Diaherea &c. In the fight, our Regt just had one man wounded. And his time was out to within 7 or 8 days. He is rather unlucky. But not so much so as if killed.

August 22, 1864

Fine morning after a big rain last night. At sunrise we were called under arms. To be ready for what might come as they were going to advance our skirmish line. But the skirmishers met with no resistance. So after they had gone as far as they wanted we were dismissed & got breakfast. We lay in the works all day with nothing unusual transpiring. They warn us to take good care of our rations for we may not get them so regular & just at the right time, for the roads are bad & likely for no better. & the Rebs might truble us some & the rumors are so numerous that it is not worth while to give any of them. We got mail today. I got one from Flora Sander. Brings news of all being in usual health. I also got 2 papers from Mother

August 23, 1864

And fine day after a hard rain last night. We move back a few rods this morning so as to get a better position for the left of our Brigade & get a place to build a Fort. After moving there was a detail made to dig down the old works & make the fort which we worked at till about night. Then our Regt was dismissed so as to go on Picket or a heavy detail from it rather, I with 6 privates from our Co, this taking about all there was left in camp for there has been a lot of men at work building abbatise [abatis] in front of the works. Most evry body seems to be at work strengthening the works. This looks like staying here. We will soon have them as strong as those in front of Petersburg. Well we go on Picket. Our Regt picketing for the Brigade. I with 3 privates on a Post & we have to keep awake all night which is pretty hard duty & one man on Post.

August 24, 1864

And fine warm day after a pretty fair night, but did make out to rain a little though. There was quite a little fight away down on the left some 2 miles or more about 10 oclock of last night which served to keep us awake pretty well. Today passed off with nothing unusual but eating roast corn which we get outside the Picket line. The day wore away till at last sundown came & with it the Relief which we were pleased to see. In due course of time, we relieved & got together & come to camp. But when we got back to where we started from the evening before, the Boys were not there. The Brigade had moved out & camped in rear of the 2nd Brigade, other troops taking their place. But we soon found the camp and bivoucked which I was in need of. The Boys have been working most all the time since we left. They were out chopping down timber last night. Some of them were out near us & the sound of their axes & their merry laugh done much to drive of the dreadfull monotony. The thick woods & the fear of the enemy coming in & the darkness with a sprinkling of rain made picketing anything but agreeable.

August 25, 1864 [Battle of Reams Station]

And fine day after the usual nightly rain. Till we were awoke at 3 A.M. to get ready to move camp & join the 3rd Division which we are attached to now. Our Division is broken up. The 2nd Brigade is in the 2nd Division. Our Division has always been small & now that Gen [Lysander] Cutler is wounded is a good time to break up the Division. Gen Cutler was wounded on the 21st by a piece of shell on the upper lip slightly, so I don't [know what] Brigade we will be now. [Samuel W.] Crawford commands the Division. The old Pennsylvania Reserves & Buctails [Bucktails] are in it. They are good troops. I feel somewhat gratified to know that we are with them.

Well we lay around till noon & didnt march. But soon the order come and we went to the rear about 1 ¼ [miles] & camped in a nice wood near a creek. Nice place. I went to work & fixed some & then concluded to wait till near night when it gets cool. But Behold, about 4 P.M. ordered to pack up which we did & marched out to the work someways to the left of where we lay before, but near the Railroad. Here we stoped a while. Pretty soon we hear skirmishing away down to the left. Soon big guns crack & firing more rapid. We ordered up & march off to the left. The firing increasing till now it has assumed the shape of hard battle.[195]

We march on directly towards it for 1 ½ miles when we halt & a Battery goes by. We expect some thing to do soon. We lay waiting & can hear the Battle raging furiously. Both Artillery & Musketry. But it begins to cease. Now begins again. They say & I should think the Rebs charging on our men. Pretty soon a General comes back and shortly we are ordered to go back, that all is right. We have drove the rebs off but they seem to be fighting yet. But it stopped ere we got to camp. We come back to the same place & camped & verry tired was we too. We found our tentpoles allright &c. The Rebs are getting in a bad fix I think. For they never would charge on our works so before. Things must be getting desperate with them. Tis said they made 3 separate determined charges on our Boys works.

I got a letter from Lu this evening & a good one too was it. I was much delighted. I read & reread it. Seem so good to hear from & sympathizing heart once & a while.

August 26, 1864

And fine warm day after the usual nights rain. We packed up & marched all this morning, knew not where we were going. But supposed not. We marched out on the field near corps Headquarters & fussed around a while, forming line here & there. The whole division got here after a little & General [Gouverneur K.] Warren come out & I soon seen we were to be put in position which we soon were & details made to for picks & spades to build works. They are facing to the rear exactly. To what we had the day of the fight. There is a large field here of about 4 miles circumference & the road running through the center & we have it fortified nearly all around now. Our division doing the last. Well we worked hard all day & have now some of the best Brestworks we ever had. Those in front of Petersburg are poor by the side of them. The rumor today is that the 2nd Corps got whipped yesterday evening after we started back to camp.[196]

[Ed. Note: The following entries were written on several sheets designated as pages 9-14, and inserted at the end of this volume. Discovering where they fit into Ray's narrative was a mini-mystery. As it turned out, Ray completed these entries on August 28, 1864, expanding on his experiences of the earlier fighting of August 18-21. One of the clues was provided by Ray's mention of being lost in the woods, and eventually reaching the brigade, "much to their surprise." A member of the Sixth Wisconsin wrote about the same experience, describing how the Seventh Wisconsin was "gobbled" up by the Rebels, but that "the 7th regiment got back, having given the Johnnies the slip and taken some prisoners." Another clue is Ray's reference in Volume 13 for August 28: "well, I have caught up with my diary. I was once a week behind . . . ."]

. . . have orders to put out Videttes Posts and make ourselves as comfortable as we can. Now away off to our left the rebs are charging, an awful deadly fire & a terriffic yell & all is still for 2 minutes or so & then two or three pieces of artillerry belch as the death and destruction & slight skirmish fire. We think the enemy have been repulsed. We are in a verry bad position now to for both our flanks are exposed to attack & we have the enemy in front & not an officer knows anything about the position & are without orders. We are in a critical position & we all know it but we do the best we can. It has rained most of the afternoon & we are wet to the skin & now it rains a torrent. List, there the enemy charges again in the same place. Away I should think ¾ of a mile to our left. Heavy firing for 2 or 3 minutes & all is hushed except the yelling of the fiends & the same thing appears to have been enacted as the first charge but the artillery seems to be firing this way.

And we begin to be more anxious, would to heaven that some orders, so we will know our fate. But no, nothing but anxious suspense. & we here in the dense forests & evrything wet & to make it doubly dismal, we cannot see our hand before us. We cant find each other only by calling or whistling & in walking about fetch up against this bunch of briars or that prickly pear & perhaps a big tree, face scratched, hands scratched & clothes torn. All this time the skirmishing goes on both away to our right & left & all still in our front. There, List, there another charge. I think tis our men this time. There! Tis the same thing over again only the noise seems to get farther away & now all is hushed. They have fired their last fire and have met, or one side or the other has given. We listen, our hearts throb. There! Tis over, they have began skirmishing again & we are pretty certain our boys have drove them this time. It is now near 10 oclock P.M. & all appears to be settled except the skirmishing, which of course will continue night.

Well, I take of my knapsack after finding a big leaning tree & take off my oilcloth & put around my shoulders & seat myself on knapsack. Now conclude I will have some sugar & hardtack & some water that I had carried in my canteen all day. I ate with a good appetite as I had not had anything since leaving camp except nibbling on a cracker once & all the boys were in same fix. As you will perceive, I have made no mention of such a thing being allowed but we cant complain for we know that it has not been advisable to do so & now we dare not build a fire.

Well, after eating I lay down on the leaves, sticks &c and put my oilcloth over me & try to catch a little sleep. But to no use. The rain pours down. I feel the water soaking through my clothes from underneath but to tired to move. Well, time wears on & midnight nears. I have a watch but cant see the hands. All the good it does me is that I can lay & hear it tick, tick, & keep me company. List, what is that. I hear footsteps. Somebody says to somebody on the next Post to the right of us that we are ordered to get out of this, that the enemy is in our rear. So some start off for themselves but I knew that wouldnt do so I called out for us all to get togather & then we could resist the better the enemy. & desired company F to find the first sergt, he was in command of the Co. & let him take care of us. He was not far off & most of the Co. got togather and many others besides. None knew where to find their company so they fell in. & the sergt said for us to stay there till he went down to the left aways & see the Major. He was commanding the Regt.

So the sergt soon returned & with orders for us to stay till the left wing come to us which wasnt long. & by this time pretty [near] all the Regt had got togather & we found out from some of the Boys that had just captured some Rebs that they were stragglers in the woods only so we breathed easier. & now arose a controversy about which the camp was, but twas soon settled by some one taking the lead & we wandered & wandered & still wandered & found no Brigade. So we concluded to

Bivouck till morning, which we done after putting out a strong guard & putting a guard over some prisnors we had taken just before stopping. We were all lost so I with 2 others spread our bed & crawled in. It now must be 2 A.M.

5 A.M. [August 18, 1864]. And we are awoke by the officers to get up and get ready to march. Which we done quickly feeling much refreshed. It is just light now & I take out my watch to wind it up and it is stoped at about 5. I wind it up & set it by guess. We form in marching order. Putting the Prisnors behind the Regt with a strong guard & the Major made us a little speech saying that we were to fight and not be taken Prisnor but if we must surrender we would all go togather & this was just my sentiments & also most of the boys. We wandered around for some time and most evry rod we would capture one or more Rebels. At last we run on to a squad of about 50. They threw up their hands imploring, saying don't shoot, we surrender & we took them in. A number of them was wounded , some on horses with legs broken. We put them under guard & wandered on & came upon some of our men that had Rebel prisnors & then on Rebels that had some of our men Prisnor & so on till we had as many rebs as what we numbered ourselves. & now we are getting so many we can hardly guard them. Fortunately they are verry docile for they are lost & we disarm them as soon as captured. They don't seem to care about anything but something to eat. We divide with them. They eat hard tack with avidity. We come across a lot of our Soldiers that have a few rebs & they turn them in to us & some of them fall in with us & some start of for themselves in which they are verry foolish for in union there is strength. At last Major & 2 or 3 start out to find some sign of troops& soon met with 2 officers that had been sent out to look for us & past them there came some cavelry charging through the woods. But they proved to be ours that were in search of such as were lost for the army was falling back. We were piloted straight to the brigade which had fell back ½ mile & fortified. We found them, much to their surprise. They thought Rebs had us. We got breakfast & then the brigade fell back with the army & we came back to our old camp. Reached it at 5 P.M. evening of 28th.

Glad to see it.

Volume 13

August 27, 1864 to December 31, 1864

They Cry "We Surrender!"

Corp Wm. R. Ray"
Co. F. 7th Regt, Wis. Vet Vols.

Camp near Yellow Tavern on Weldon R.R.
A resident of Cassville, Grant Co, Wisconsin

August 27, 1864

And fine day. After the rain of last night we lay in our works or tents rather which are pitched in camp style in rear of our verry strong works. We have a day of comparitive rest today. It being the first since the 18th ult. May lay here sometime. The Boys that didnt reenlist are counting the hours till their time will be out. Pay to go with them. They will be discharged on the 2nd of September.

There is many rumors what the Rebs have done, doing & going to do & the same of us. But I guess the 2nd corp got drove a little on their left.

August 28, 1864

And fine day & we missed the rain last night & today. All day without a sprinkle. We lay in camp same as yesterday. Gen Warren was around today looking through the camp & works &c. There is a well being dug near the camp so we will have plenty of pretty good water & I will send my last Diary home by the same mail. I have not heard from the last one I sent. But I suppose it will be all right at home. But the folks have forgotten to mention it in their letters.

Well I have at last caught up with my Diary. I was once a week behind when we were so busy & had so much rain & having to write on a sheet of paper so it were unhandy. But now have my new diary I can keep up.[197]

August 29, 1864

And fine day & rain last night again. We lay in camp today. Had general inspection today. It being the first since I came to the Regt, I think. I wrote a letter to Flora Lander in answer to hers I received sometime since, as also answer to one I got from her today. Answered them both in one. And answered Henry letter that I recd yesterday. They all brought news of the folks enjoying the usual health. & Henry has been out on the Milwaukee & Prairie-DuChine [Milwaukee and Prairie du Chien] R.R. & find him a new home which he done. Bought a nice farm of 80 acres near the town of Boscobel & within a quarter of a mile of the R.R. From the description he gives I think it a pretty place. He says he can get land cheaper on that road than on the Road in Iowa, where he was sometime since. My tentmate [Henry] Brinkman went to the Hospital yesterday. He has been unwell for several weeks past and is now quite low. Diheria being the disease.

Half of our Brigade is out today on fatigue duty working on a large fort near where we had the fight on the 21st. We are strongly fortifying this place. There appears to be a feeling that we must hold this place against old hazard himself.

August 30, 1864

And fine day. We have had no rain last night or today. Been a verry pretty day & we were out on fatigue duty today. Working on the fort. We worked 6 hours, there being 2 reliefs. This fort is a verry large one & completely commands the Railroad for several miles. Twill be a formidable work when done. I had command of a squad of 10 men of Co G. They were mostly Indians. They were the best working squad I have been over. We were let off at 6 P.M., came home & got supper &c.

The orderly & Captain have gone to make out the Muster Rolls & also the papers for those boys that their time will be out on the 2nd of Sept. We have had 2 promotions in our Co. Lately. Albert C. Morse,[198] Wm Atkinson to be Corporals.

August 31, 1864

And fine day. We lay in camp today. Had muster for pay at 2 P.M. & 5 P.M. We move down into the woods some ½ mile & camped in good order. Ben Bragg [Benjamin F. Branham][199] saying we will stay here sometime if the Rebs didnt drive us out & that we had better fix up camp pretty good. So I & my tentmate made a bunk &c, upon the whole making things quite homelike with plenty of good boughs on the bunk &c. The Boys that are going home are joyous. The news in the papers is good. There has been no battles but some skirmishing &c at different points. There is a rumor in camp that Fort Morgan at Mobile [Alabama] has surrendered and all the Prisnors, munitions of war &c to the Union forces. This is an important capture. Union is victorious all around.[200]

We expected some to hear from the Democratic Convention today. It sit on the 29th to nominate a man for President. We will probably hear tomorrow. But through the Press, [Union General George B.] McClellen seems to be the favorite. The Peace men are trying hard for their man. But they will be hard up to beat old Abe [Lincoln] when the election comes off. There is a rumor that the Draft which was to come up on the 5th of next month is put off so it is doubtful if old Abe gets my vote. But we must be patient and try to think all is for the best. At least so I do. I feel in as good spirits as ever.

September 1, 1864

And fine day. The Boys that didnt reenlist started home this evening & a happy set of fellows were they as whiskey could make them. I should have been ashamed to left the Company in the plight they did. Well they are gone & peace & prosperity to go with them. I have no desire to go home to what I thought I should & considering the company I should have had to gone in made me think less of it. They were all good soldiers & all stout men but some of the worst gamblers in the Co. were among them. The Col. went with them. I rec'd a letter from Lu today which I partly answered.

The Democratic Convention have not decided on a candidate for President yet. But the supposition is that McLellin [McClellan] will be nominated. There has been some change in the affairs in the Co. Sergt [Loren] Parsons & [George] Eustice has gone home. Sergt [Thomas] Alexander is acting orderly now. Boynton being wounded & [Jesse] Roberts[201] is on the Pioneer squad. So there is only one Sergt in the Co. & he was lately promoted. I am first Corporal now.

September 2, 1864

And fine day. We were awoke at 1 A.M. this morning to pack up & be ready to march at 2. But didnt till three when we set out. Went out to Corps Headquarters & turned to the left. Went down to the left flank of the army & massed outside the works & stoped, it being daybreak now. We lay here till near sunrise when we marched back to Corps Headquarters & turned off to the left & went out to & outside of the works where we had the fight on the 21st, & massed here again. This time there is a division of cavelry ahead of us & some of them gone on a reconnaissance & the remainder near us as a support to those gone out. & we, if need be, a support for the whole. Ours (the 3rd) division being here. After laying here some 1 ½ [hours] the cavelry comes in with a few Prisnors. They having been out some three miles & found the enemy & strongly fortified. So we retraced our steps for camp which we reach about 10 A.M. & verry tired too, to find our turnips, beets & soap &c which we drew yesterday, gone. Some of the Engineers are in camp near us & they must have come & took them while we were gone. They were too heavy to carry on a march. We drew last of rations, sanitary articles &c. There was a detail for fatigue this afternoon for to work on the fort. [We] will be finished tonight, I understand. I finished my letter to Lu today & mailed it. We have lots of whiskey & Quinine furnished us just as much as the Boys will drink. I never tasted it but the Boys say that quinine they think is the main ingredient so bitter is it. Some of the Boys will drink it anyhow even to get drunk. This the Doctors says is to keep off fever &c. Perhaps it is good but I cant see the point. I think the remedy is worse than the disease. I will risk the latter at any rate.

September 3, 1864

And fine day. & we are in camp. Nothing unusual transpires. The usual detail of about half of the Co. to work on Fortifications. Good news to chronicle. Fort Morgan surrendered to our forces on the 23rd with all the things pertaining &c. And there is a rumor that Sherman is in Atlanta, that the 20th Army Corps occupies the city & that there has been a hard battle & Shermans Army cut Hoods in twain & that our forces have been victorious in evry instance &c. Big thing if true. We have regular mails that arrives & departs daily and evry thing goes on well.

September 4, 1864

And fine day with things the same as yesterday. Perfect quiet in camp. The order is for all to make bunks to sleep upon &c. But as I have mine I am not included in that order. This being Sunday we have inspection &c. I have catched up with my writing, have answered a letter of Amoses today which I got six week since. The news in the papers is good. Still rumors of the capture of Atlanta and Early is retreating down the valley towards Richmond & Sheridan pressing him closely. It is thought if Early gets down here they will try to drive us from our position. But this we think they cant do.[202]

The Democrats nominated McLellen [General George B. McClellan] for President & [Congressman George] Pendleton of Ohio for Vice President. I don't like the nomination much. But if Abe puts the Draft, I will vote for him. Then he will show that he is a friend to the soldiers & is going to make the grumblers at home help us. But if he don't do it, he must make peace soon for our armies are going down sadly. But trust that all is for the best.

We are fixing up camp nice & digging a well so we will have nice cool water &c. We have a creek nearby which we wash in. I got a kettle from the Pioneer yesterday & washed & boiled all my clothing except coat & will now be rid of lice &c which we all have a plenty of. We drew clothing today. I got a pair of drawers, that being all I have need of at present. I picked up one of the many good shirts that the Boys throw away because they are dirty, and washed & boiled it & thereby saved $1.50. Nothing like economizing in these times.

September 5, 1864

And fine day & warmer than usual of late. & I am on detail for fatigue duty. We have been chopping timber down so the guns from a large fort can command a field which it hid. The hot sun rather gets me down. I give out coming home & had to rest. My head trubles me a great deal now in hot weather. I fear I shall have to give up soldiering, some of those hot days at least go on the list of invalids. The papers today being the official report of Ian Slocum [Union General Henry Slocum] stating that he with his Corps occupies the city of Atlanta & that there had been a big battle & our troops had been victorious. But stated no particulars of the affair. The spirits of the army is good & we get plenty of rations. & those of the Boys that will drink quinine & whiskey get all they want & evrything goes well. I guess the officers expect an attack as the order is this evening for us all to have 50 rounds of ammunition for the teams was going to the rear. & evry man must stay in camp & be ready to slip on his accoutriments in a moment.

The 7th Ind [Indiana] Regt of our Brigade starts home tomorrow & they are making speeches &c, having a pretty joyous & noisy time. I say let them be joyous. Our Brigade is verry small now. But I hope it will soon be recruited up. There has been no recruits from our state got on the last call for this army. The most of those going into the army to go to the army in the Southwest. But the Regts from other [states] especially the eastern states are being filled. The N.York papers says there is a 1000 men going through that city evry day for Grants army & it is estimated that there 1000 landed at City Point daily. But none for our Regt as yet except convalescents.

September 6, 1864

And fine day & cool, cloudy & rather pleasant. Nothing unusual transpires except that there is no detail for fatigue today. We are having a pretty good time now. Something like we used to have when we thought soldiering a hard buisness. The Boys are in good spirits over the good news from the southwest & the papers as yet gives no account of the Draft being put off, which we fear will be done yet for I think it would be a deadness to the Army. I wrote a letter to Lu today.

We have plenty of Sutlers about us now. Our sutler has come up, but the Boys don't trade with him much for he don't trust & the Boys don't have money & those that have money go to other places to trade. We want to get rid of him because he wont come up as other Sutlers do, but comes when payday comes near.

September 7, 1864

And fine day & cool. We lay in camp & no detail today but Guard. There is one out of each Co for guard to see to the cleanliness &c of the camp. I got shaved today. My tentmate is the Barber. He shaves for the Regt or all that he can. He charges 10 cents each. Makes considerable money. I sent for a new pen to N.Y. City. Twill cost me $1.40 & the certificate calls for a pen worth $6.00.

September 8, 1864

And fine day with nothing unusual transpiring. Except that the Rebs took 50 of our pickets at daybreak this morning. This happened not far from here.

September 9, 1864

And fine day. I am on guard today. I with 3 men is all. I have to attend posting them, there being only one post. It is just a nice job for at tattoo, I take the guard off & put it on again at reville in the morning.

September 10, 1864

And fine day. The cars come up to within half mile of camp today. They will be up to Corps Headquarters in a day or two & the corderoy roads will soon be done. And the telegraph wire is up so we will be in town soon. This morning about daylight our men away down on the right charged and took about 100 of the Reb Pickets in. This is to pay them for what they got from us a day or two since.

September 11, 1864

And fine day. This being Sunday we have Co. Inspection at 10 A.M. And half an hour later we have church. The Chaplain gave us a good sermon. The day passes off quietly in camp. But the details that are working on the corderoy road near our camp make considerable noise. This evening the cars got up to Corps Headquarter & on reaching there they whistled loud & shrill a number of times. As much, I suppose, to chagrin the Johnys as anything else I suppose. The whistle fairly said, we defy you Johny to come & take us. I guess it rather surprised the rebs. Things are going nice.

We can still hear the Picket firing in front of Petersburg. The rumor is that Mobile is taken & so say the Rebel Pickets. & now I think they must own our superiority, now that we have both Mobile & Atlanta in our possession & Sheridan still keeps the Rebs south of the Potomac. The Rebel Press tries hard to stave off the loss as an insignificant thing but still other papers own it & I guess they will have hard work to ram it down their soldiers that it isnt much &c. I wrote a letter to Mother today.

September 12, 1864

And a fine day & the Regt is out working on the corderoy road. We do up considerable. The cars are running up constantly now with supplies &c. The rumor is that Deserters coming in says that Lee has changed his headquarters to Reams Station & a good part of his army has gone with him & that they expect to strike us a hard blow one of these days. And the papers of today say that the rebs have ordered all the Gurrilla Bands in Virginia to report to Lee to help him in his next Battle & it is surmised that part of [John Bell] Hoods Army is coming up here & if all this be true & they should draw [Jubal] Early out of the Valley pretty sudden & bring his force with all the others combined, Lee might truble us some before Grant could get the 6th & 19th Corps back here. But we must trust in the good Lord and to Providence some and be patient for we certainly have good reason to be thankful for past victories.

The draft is ordered forthwith in those Districts where they have not showed a willingness to volunteer. But in many parts of the country they have filled their quota already.

I got a letter from R Lander. He with his Regt is now at St. Charles on White River, Arkansas. He is well & hearty &c. But the letter brings sad sadness from cousin (Amos Eubanks). He is about to loose his eyesight. At least he is nearly blind at times. He is 1st Lieut of the Co now.

One of our officers, our 2nd Lieutant Alphonse A. Kidd is leaving, mustered out of the services today and is going back home. He has in my opinion rather deceived the boys and the Company some by not staying as he promised when we reenlisted. But I say, let him go home if he wants to. We can do as well with his room as his company. I never thought much of him anyway. He is governed entirely by the Almighty Dollar.

September 13, 1864

And fine with nothing unusual. The rumor that Mobile in Alabama is taken needs confirmation yet before I will believe it. I wrote a letter to Miss Ryan of Oldham Co. Kentucky soliciting a correspondence with her & also one to Henry & one to Lu. We give the camp a general police today. The whole Regt turning out for the purpose. We have a verry nice camp now.

There is still heavy details working on the roads. They are making a double wagon road here opposite our camp where there is some low ground. Cap Young is talking of going home and if he does I say the same as I said by the 2nd Lieut. But at the same time I dislike to see Cap to go. He is a warm friend of mine. I would rather see him stay.

September 14, 1864

And fine day. We lay in camp today with nothing unusual except that we move camp about ¼ of a mile & got a better camp. There was a guard left at the old camp till we could to go back & get what things we wanted. For other troops was coming in there. Ben & I brought our bunk & table over & set them up here & by night we had all things fixed up as before except that Ben hasnt his Barber chair set up. This is a much nicer camp than the other. We will soon clean it up & there is a well nearby which will furnish us plenty of good water but not so good as the other. The rumor is that all that belonged to the Old first corps is drawed away from the front. Some say they are reorganised & going off to some other Department. & others contradict it & say that we are formed into two Div's & still belong to the fifth Corps. & I think the last is most likely of any of them.

September 15, 1864

And fine day. & we clean up camp & fix things ok & about 3 P.M. we are ordered to fall in & stack arms which we done. & we were not allowed to leave camp & the rumor with it that the rebs was moving around to our left and might attack us &c and we must be ready. But dark came & nothing but some skirmishing in front. The cavelry & some infantry have been out all day & just now they are returning to camp. What they done I don't know, but they didnt do much fighting. So soon after dark we took in our guns & the excitement was over. But there was a shot once & a while through the night.

I still keep up my practicing writing & am now studying arithmetic. Caroline sent me one. It is Rays intellectual. It is mental arithmetic and the hardest one. But I am progressing well in it & then I still read my Testament & the daily papers &c. I got my pen that I sent for to N.Y. & didnt suit me so I sold it for $1.60 & have now sent for some certificates. I sent $1.00 which will get 5.

September 16, 1864

And fine day. There is still some slight skirmishing in front of us. But nothing serious. There is a rumor in camp that the Reb cavelry come around our left so far that they took 2600 of our beef cattle & had got off with them. If this be true it is a good haul for them. It will do them three times the good that it will do us harm. & that is one reason why we should keep supplies from them. But there is great hope of them being captured back again.[203] We live under a suspense all the while. We expect the rebs will attack us. We, I think, are ready for them. So let them come. The news is unimportant. All the main armies seem to be laying still & I think they need it. We get plenty of rations, plenty of beef & good beef too.

September 17, 1864

We had Regt Inspection and were in rather better order than yesterday. There was church today. A strange chaplain preached.

September 18, 1864

We made a general police of the camp and it look nice. Hereafter we have Co inspection evry day till we get in the best order and Co drill in forenoon & afternoon Regt drill except when we have Brigade drill. & that is ordered 2 times a week. I got a return from New York getting five certificates for my $1.00 & none of them calls for an article of less value than $4.00.

September 20, 1864

And fine day with the same drill as yesterday. We find that we have lost a good deal of our proficiency in drill. I had a little truble with one of the noncoms yesterday & in the scuffle got my foot scalded a little. He came to and did appropriate my fire or rather one I built to boil my pants which were in the kettle at the time, ready to set on the fire & I concluded that I would have it & I did have it too & he didnt get his dinner there. I gained my object. He is a fellow that makes a practice of running from fire to fire & never bring a stick of wood & now he will not truble me much more I hope. He abused me with his tongue shamefully & he is a fellow that I have accommodated with frying pan, hatchet &c like fixings till I was tired. Besides loaning him a pair of socks he has never returned & now he has money borrowed of me & more. That all he is a fellow that talks scandalous about me to my back. But some people are so stupidly ignorant that a person must take compassion on them.

We have good news from [Union General Phil] Sheridans Army. He has had a Big Battle with [Confederate General Jubal] Early & whipped him bad, taking some 2 thousand prisnors on the field & killing and wounding as many more & capturing 3000 sick in Winchester & killing a number of generals &c. Great Victory.[204]

September 21, 1864

And fine day. Brigade drill in forenoon & Co drill in afternoon. I got excused from drill in afternoon by the doctor. My ankle is too sore. I must halt.

We have review tomorrow. Our brigade will be reviewed by Gen Warren. I hardly think I shall be able to go, hope I shall though. We will have to put on style now as long as we lay in camp. The rumor about the Rebs capturing about 2500 of our cattle has proved to be true. They did get them & took them off with about 30 of the herders prisnors. I spoke to Cap today to let his cook (Perry Gilbert)[205] to go to the commissarys & get me some flour & he said anything I wanted & Perry could get for me, he might. I thanked him for his kindness &c. Perry got the flour for me today, got about 3 pounds for 20 cents. It will make several messes of pancakes & gravy a number of times. I got it for the latter for mostly. It is verry kind in Cap to accommodate me so much. Privates are not allowed to buy. But in this way they don't know but it is to be used by the officer. If privates were allowed to by promiscuity they would buy it all from the officers & the Quartermaster could'nt furnish so much. It would take too much transportation.

September 22, 1864

And fine day. But tried hard to rain early in the morning but cleared of so that we had a good time for the review which came of at 3 P.M. I am was excused by the Doctor, not able to walk much. & what little I do it is with pain to me. I could'nt even to go to see the review it being out on the plane towards Corps headquarters. They returned about 5 ½ P.M., saying they had a good drill. Gen Warren drilling them himself. There was only our Brigade. There was several Brigades on the field ahead of ours & gone home as only one could maneuver at a time so little was the space.

September 23, 1864

And fine day. Things as usual. The Drill &c, Co in forenoon & Battallion in afternoon. Good news from Sheridan. He has whipped the Rebs in 2 different Battles. The first day, the 19th inst, whipped them, took pieces of artillery & 2500 Prisnors & 3000 Sesh & wounded in Winchester [Virginia] & still pursuing them. & Was a splendid & decisive Victory. The Boys call it a ratification of the nomination of Abe &c. And I forgot to mention the 8 generals (Rebels) that was killed & wounded. 4 of them killed. Our loss not known as yet except Gen [David A.] Russell killed & two others wounded & of rank & file supposed 2000 killed & wounded.[206]

I wrote a letter to Henry today in answer to one I Rec'd yesterday. He giving me a full & interesting account of his trip to Madison and his buying a new home or farm rather near Mezamonia [Mazomonie] which is 22 miles west from Madison on the R.R. Isaac Lander went with him & bought a farm on the opposite side of the town or east rather, Henrys being on the west side. Each is half mile from the town. The town contains about 800 inhabitants & is improving verry fast. There is a sett of enterprising Capitalists in it. Good schools &c. The latter is a great item to both familys. There is lots of children in them. I think it will be a good place for Lu to sett up a shop in the way of millenery business &c. Henry has not got my money yet. But I think I must have forgotten to address it so as it would to Cassville & they have sent it in the Package that went to Lancaster.

September 24, 1864

And fine day. & the usual drill &c as yesterday. There is good news this morning by special order from the War Department announcing still another greater Victory in the Shenandoah Valley by Sheridan & the brave troops under his command. Whip the Rebs, took many prisnors, hadnt time to count them as yet & 16 pieces of artillery, Battle flags &c. This makes 21 pieces of Artillery & supposed about 10,000 Rebels placed hors de combat & this is a splendid Victory. Another grand satisfication meeting. The papers today gives a verry full and interesting account of the Battle of the 19th inst &c.[207]

September 25, 1864

A fine day & the paymaster has come & is paying the 6th [Wisconsin] Regt. He will hardly get to ours today. We have signed the payrolls. We get orders to pack up about 3 P.M. & to go over and relieve some of the 9th Corps about 1 ½ miles of to the Northward. So we come, found them packed up & in line. We went into their camps & they went off someplace. Rumor says that they as well as all the troops that have been in reserve are going up to the right to help Butler. He having whiped the Rebs & took the R.R. between Petersburg and Richmond &c. And another rumor is that they have whipped Butler & took part of the canal he was digging &c. If they have done the latter, it is bad for us. The Boys we relieved say the rumor here was that the Rebs was evacuating Petersburg so we cant tell much about how things stands. But we have heard some firing up there.[208] There is something going on.

September 26, 1864

We got paid today. I didnt like to walk over to the Paymasters, it being half mile. So I told Cap to draw it for me & the Paymaster put it in an envelope with the other Boys money that went on Picket last night & Cap don't care about opening it till they come in so I have not got mine yet. We know nothing more about what is transpiring than we did last night. I got a letter from Mother today bring the news of her being well &c and 25 cts worth of postage stamps.

September 27, 1864

Fine day. & we are about the same as yesterday to news &c. We cant get any papers. Why it is so I don't know. We must arrange it some way so as to get one or more from the news store. There was some firing on Picket today & 1 negro surrendered.

September 28, 1864

And about the same as yesterday, some little picket firing. One negro killed & 3 wounded by the rebs. They don't fire on our boys at all and they are right joining the negroes.

September 29, 1864

Pretty much the same as yesterday with the exceptions of a little fighting on the right. But I guess it didnt amount to anything. Perhaps wounding a few. We are expecting to move evry minute. We were packed up most all day. There is many rumors afloat. Just at dark there was an order read to some troops that are massed in rear of us that part of our Army on the right had crossed the river & took a lot of strong works on Chapins [Chaffin's] farm & 15 pieces of Artillery & 300 Prisnors. This is a spendid victry. & the rumor is that they took the last line of works around Richmond &c. But I don't put any confidence in the last. I could hear artillery going by to the left all night fast & the cars came in fast. There is something up more than usual.[209]

September 30, 1864

And fine day & we got up at 4 A.M., got breakfast & pack up & stay so till about 3 P.M. when we move up to where we were camped before & other troops took our place & all those troops that were here abouts last night & yesterday have gone to the left. We heard heavy firing last night away off to the left just about west of us [Peebles' Farm] & then we supposed that some of our troops were out there & now, 5 P.M. the news is that the movement to the left is a perfect success & evrything is going all right. We are ordered to pitch tents thinking how lucky we are to not have to be in the fight although it was not verry severe. There was some wounded come in this afternoon. There was another little fight on the right last night.

October 1, 1864

And stormy, cold & disagreeable verry. Fall weather in earnest. We were awoke last night at 11 P.M., got up, packed up & after waiting a while for the order to march we got orders to rest till 3 A.M. I went to bed or rather laid down & put my oilcloth over me & had another nap. Was awoke about 4 A.M. to march. We are ordered out to the Von [Vaughn] road & build works & hold the road. We marched out, I being still lame. I trudged along taking my time. But the distance being short (only two miles) I didnt get far behind. The Boys reached the road about daylight & found some work that had been thrown up about enough to hold half the Brigade. This included all but 2 companies of our Rgt & all to the left had to build works. This was lucky for the 7th & those on the right of us. We built works &c sufficient to protect us. There is skirmishing all day in our front but nothing more. But away to the left there has been several hard little fights & rumor says that our forces are successfull evry time. & now tis night & we, the old man rumor says, have captured 3 lines of their works & all still glorious &c. We feel that we have been verry fortunate in this advance. We have had the best time of any of the corps that is our Brigade.

October 2, 1864

And rather cloudy, but at times the sun comes out verry warm & towards night cleared off. There has been about as much skirmishing as yesterday but not quite so much artillery firing. We do nothing today except there being a detail to work on some brestworks on the left of the Brigade. There being a space of ¼ of a mile or more that there is no troops & that is why we are fortifying so that can stretch our line if need be if there is no troops comes to fill it up. I got a letter from Henry today & all is well &c. He said I might direct my next letter to his new home, Mezamonia. He is going to have a sale the 10th of October & would leave immediately for Mezamonia.

October 3, 1864

And fine day. We are quiet or tolerably so all along the lines. A shot occasionally from artillery & also from the skirmishers. There is a heavy detail from the Brigade today working on a large fort right in front of us. It will be a strong one when finished & it is to be finished as fast as possible. The Boys work with a will. Gen Warren told them that they might want to use it in the course of 24 hours.

My foot is still lame but improving fast. The papers bring good news from all quarters. Sheridan is still driving Early &c and our troops under Butler on Chapins farm still hold their position. But the Rebs have charged on them with 3 heavy lines of Battle & our Boys hurled them back in confusion & great loss to them &c. All good & glorious &c.

October 4, 1864

And fine day. Quite warm. We have nothing of importance today. There is a heavy detail to work on the fort. About 3 P.M. we get orders to pack up & move out of the works. There was some others from the first division come in. We waited here till dark for orders where to go. In the time had 3 or 4 horseraces. Gen [Edward] Bragg himself being the first. [Bragg had taken over brigade command on June 7, 1864.]

Well just at dark we started & came to our old camp near the railroad. Reaching here about 9 P.M., found our camp torn all to pieces, not a bunk left. I being still some lame, I did not [arrive] here for sometime afterwards & verry tired too was I. There is great speculation about where & what we are going to do. Evrything seems to be going on the same as usual, if any difference it is livelier.

October 5, 1864

And fine day. We lay in camp till 3 P.M. when we came over to the works & where we were prior to the advance & relieved the negros. We get the verry same camp as before and I the same bunk which I remodeled a little. I and Ben soon had up a table & are comfortably fixed &c. There is a heavy detail from our Regt for picket. We feel quite at home here & long to stay awhile. The campaign is over again I guess & we now hold a line 44 miles long & two thirds of the way around Richmond.[210]

October 6, 1864

Things going all right. Some firing on Picket line. But we are so used to that, it don't make much excitement in camp. There is nothing unusual to chronicle unless it is that the Boys are going in on Sutler goods & living fat. I indulged a little today by the way of buying half package of flour. This flour is put up in 6 lbs packages & cost $1.00 & all we have to do is to mix it up with water & bake it. Ben & I made a nice mess of cakes. It is a great invention. The boys call it patent flour. I got a letter from Lu today. She & the relatives are well. I mailed one to Mother today also.

October 7, 1864

We lay in camp as yesterday except those on Picket. We have nothing to do. We drew clothing today. I got a pair of shoes & haversack & all the Boys that hadnt blankets drew them & also knapsacks & such things necessary for winter.

I got two pens today from New York that I sent after & sold them right away, making $2.80 clear on them. I shall send for some more & I have done so well. I get them on the certificates that I got some time since. They cost 20 cents apiece & I have to send $1.15 on each certificate & get the article called for, so I get them cheap.

October 8, 1864

And fine day & things about the same as yesterday. I sent for 3 more pens today. I wrote a letter to Lu today in answer to one I got sometime since. The picket line in our front was pushed out some half mile farther today & thereby gaining a much better position. Now the line is in the edge of a wood with an open field in front & on the top of the hill. & the Rebs fell back with little or no resistance to our advance. We in camp were under arms all day so as to be ready for what might possibly come. But the Rebs didnt try to regain the ground they lost.

October 9, 1864

And fine day after a verry cold night. I got a letter from Lu & Mother, also one from Florance. All is well, Lu expected to be in Mezamonia the next letter she writes. It has been my luck for the past few weeks to get a letter from her a day or two after writing but I can remedy this by answering sooner the previous letters. There is a rumor that Hood has got in rear of Sherman. But the rumor is not credited here. The news is not of much importance otherwise. But all is well. The rebs has not yet tried to drive our picket line back.[211]

October 10, 1864

And fine day but cold nights of late making two blankets necessary for to sleep warm. We go on Picket today & find the line in a good place & things nice except that we have to go back to camp for water.

The Regt being so small, the noncoms, at any rate of our company, condescend to stand post & I with the balance. But this I generally do so it did not matter much for me. Things all quiet on our part of the line. But away up the right, considerable picket firing. Two posts have one Vidette out in daytime & at night one from each. I & Sergt Alexander & 3 Privates are on this post. I got my first State Journal [newspaper] today that I subscribed for some few days since. It is the weekly.

October 11, 1864

And fine day & all quiet in our front & going on well &c. We commence to fortify our posts today & the Pioneers to chop a little timber down in our front.

We draw rations today it being my turn to do so. We had to go clear back to camp. The Rebs & our Boys got into conversation this evening, our boys cheering for Abe [Abraham Lincoln] and they for Jeff. [Jefferson Davis] & our Boys for Little Mac [Democratic Presidential Candidate George B. McClellan] & they the same. They seemed to be pleased when we cheered him. Then our Boys cheered for Butler & they said to hell with him &c&c. And so on, things to numerous to mention. Dark coming on they stoped & only then it was verry pleasing to hear them. Up about 1 mile to our right constant picket firing all last night until at last the Rebs charged down on our men who sent them back in a hurry. The firing was quite brisk intermixed with Artillery.

October 12, 1864

And fine day. The relief come about 10 A.M. & we came to camp & settled down for a little rest. I answered Lu's letter today & mailed it. I had my warrant as Sergeant presented to me today & as a matter of course I was much gratified. And feel grateful to Cap for the honor he has confered on me & also the confidence he puts in me & I shall try to do my whole duty. My tentmate being sick when we went on Picket & went to the hospital, so I had to get another tentmate & I got J. A. Drew [Jacob A. Drew].[212] He used to tent with me last fall & I liked him & do still. He is a man of passable morality.

October 13, 1864

And fine day but rather misty and cloudy towards night & twas cold. I wrote to Mother today & also sent my warrant as Corporal home with the letter. The news from all the armies is good. Especially from Sheridan. His cavelry whipped the Rebel Cavelry & took 11 pieces of artillery & 300 prisnors & drove them all through the mountains.[213]

Hood is in rear of Sherman. But the supposition is that Hood is past where Sherman wants him for he has six weeks rations & a good large army. There is no uneasiness for his safety.

October 14, 1864

And fine day & we expected to have Inspection today but it didnt come of. It is the monthly inspection. I got a letter from Mother today.

I got the stuff from home I sent for to line my blanket. Twas verry cold last night & I and my tentmate concluded to put up a chimney which we done & have a good one too. I build it & some of the Boys thought I was a stonemason & so neat was it built. & it draws good. I will now sleep more comfortable. We carried the Brick about 40 rods from an old mill that is burned down. We now have the nicest chimney & tent in the Regt.

October 16, 1864

And fine day. We go on Picket today. The whole Regt. getting on the line about 9 A.M. & we have to stand about 3 hours apiece in 24, noncoms & all stand & I with them. I command the Co today being the Senior Sergt on duty with Co.

October 17, 1864

And fine day & all quiet on the line. We have fine weather now. There was a little cannonading last night away up to the right. Sergt [Jesse] Roberts has returned to the Company. He has been with the Pioneer Corps all summer & the Boys, & I with them, would rather see him there than with the company. But however, I can stand it. The Sanitary Commission issued onions today. We got about 1 pound apiece. Good treat. The rumor is that [War Department] Secretary [William] Stanton is going to visit the lines today. Some say he has been on the Picket line but this I doubt some.

October 18, 1864

And fine day. We are relieved this morning & by the same men that we relieved. The 2nd & 6th Regt. This makes only 2 days off. This is pretty heavy duty. We came into camp & all right. & I write a letter to Mother. Drew rations, I having to do that this time. The report that Stanton was coming around was false. At any rate he didnt come from some cause. But he is in the army some place.

October 19, 1864

And fine day & we are enjoying ourselves the best we know how. The Boys are fixing for cold weather. Most evry tent in our Co. has a chimney & are building them & fixing up tents &c. Ours is verry comfortable. I wrote a letter to Mother today & sent a Harpers Weekly also. It had the Chicago Platform Illustrated. It is a good get off on Democracy of the Present day. I took a walk out today to get a kettle to Boil some rations in. I went to a number of Sutlers & didnt find any. But found some Blacking Brushes & bought one as we need some more in the Co so that when we have to fix for Inspection we will not have to wait so long on others for brush &c. I have got the lining sewed on my blanket & I find that it adds fully the warmth of another blanket & adds only one pound to the weight of it. I sleep as cozy & warm now as when at home in a feather Bed.

October 21, 1864

And fine day but cool & likely to storm soon. All is quiet on the lines except an occasionally a shot at the Boys. They fire now where our Boys is. But our Boys don't fire back so they will soon stop it. We fell in & stacked arms along the works ready to receive Gen Grant & Mead [Meade] but they didnt come & we were somewhat disappointed. Sheridan has been whipped & then turned again and whipped the Rebs recapturing 20 pieces of Artillery &c and capturing 23 more & lots of wagons &c and 1600 Prisnors & they are still coming in. The Rebs where we were on Picket said that [Confederate General James] Longstreet had gone up to whip Sheridan & he did. But twas a dear one to him. Sheridan will soon be as high up in the Pictures as Grant if he keeps on.[214]

October 22, 1864

And fine day & all quiet &c. The Boys come in off Picket today & nothing especial to chronicle. I got the certificates for Jewelry that I sent for & they called for articles worth from 5 to 7 dollars. But I sent for the Pens of highest price for they sell the best of anything I could get. I had to borrow $81.00 to send for them or rather make out enough.

October 23, 1864

And fine day & all is quiet. This being Sunday we had Co Inspection. And at 1 P.M. we had church. The chaplain having returned from his furlough home, we will have church regular now. He gave us a good discourse. I got 2 letters today, one from Richard Lander & the other from Cornelia, my little niece, some 12 years old. She is living with Mother (her GrandMother). All was well & doing well. Richard has got back to Memphis Tenn. He had been sick & was sent there to the Hospital.

October 24, 1864

And fine day. And on fatigue duty today. I & 2 Corpls & 14 men. We are rebuilding Parapets or Brestworks, putting them up better & in a better location. The Boys don't work verry hard & some of them don't do anything. F. A. Boynton, our first Sergt got back last night, also H Brinkman. They have both been to the hospital. The latter was sick. But the former was wounded & is now minus 2 fingers on the left hand. He looks well. There is lots of the boys coming back. Our Co numbers 30 now.

October 25, 1864

And fine day & there's a heavy detail to work on Fortifications. I don't have to go today. The next Sergt went. Evrybody seems to think that there will be a move soon & others think not till after Election. I wrote a letter to Cornelia today in answer to hers.

Dark & I am detailed for Picket tomorrow with 3 Corpls & 14 men. Rumors that the army is now moving. Tis only a rumor. F.A. Boynton acted as Lieut for the first time today. He is going to make a good officer I think. I shall be glad to see him in Command of the Co. Capt [Henry Young] has gone to command the Division Pioneers or rather Div Pioneer officer.

October 26, 1864

And fine day & we go out to the picket line. But it had been relieved by some of the 3rd Brigade and after waiting sometime for the officer in command of us to go to camp to see what he was to do & returned, we came back to camp. We put in for things that we needed badly in the way of Ordnance & Camp equipage &c. I put in for a knapsack as mine was somewhat worn. We now know that there is a move on hand. In fact troops have been moving today. Night and we have orders to be ready to move at 4 in the morning. Revilee at 3 oclock. Cap has been returned to the Co again.

October 27, 1864

And fine day till towards night when rain sets in & continues most of the night. Last night about 12M we were awoke to get our things we had signed for & get our mail. I got 2 letters, one from Mother & one from Lu bringing news of all well &c. Henry & family & Lu have got to their new home.

Well for what we done today, Revilee at 3 A.M. March at 4 taking the road to the left, to by where we had the fight on the 21 of August & on to the Vaughn road, going on it a ways, turn to the left, come inside of the fortifications which are verry strong & travel on inside them for several miles, come to where they turn square to the right & run round to the front line. This being the rear line we traveled by. Here on this corner where we go out is a large fort named Fort Cummings. We have been traveling rather slow until now & we now travel pretty brisk. Soon hear skirmishing which seems about 1 ½ miles off, going on hear it plainer & more of it. Come to the 2nd Division Hospital. Few wounded here. With skirmishing in front & ahead we now think we will soon have something to do but we keep on. The Major [Hollon Richardson] says we have or rather that [Union General Winfield Scott] Hancock has taken the road.[215]

We come to an old sawmill & cross the creek on a dam newly built. Just on the rebel side is a weak line of brestworks which our men hold. We cross, go a little ways, form line of Battle across these works, rest a while & send skirmishers ahead.

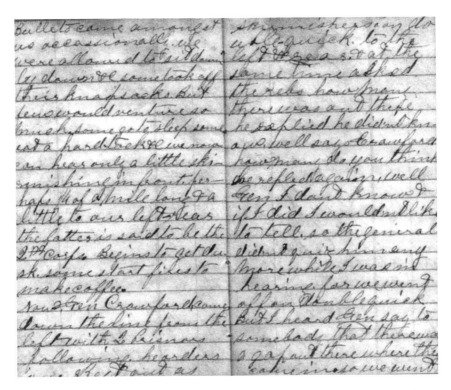

Two pages from William Ray's Volume 13, detailing the Hatcher's Run engagement, one of the major encounters of the Petersburg Campaign.
Sherry Murphy

We follow up to a creek which we cross & then have to recross & from now on till about 4 P.M. I cant tell where we went.[216]

We marched all the time, first by the flank, then in line &c. So many different moves I cant recollect, with skirmishing first to our right, then front, then to the left & sometimes in our rear &c. And twas all the time in the woods with thick underbrush & a shower of rain about 1 P.M. Just enough to wet the brush & that wet us. At last we formed line & pretty heavy skirmishing in front. We now thought we had got to the desired place for the reb bullets came amongst us occassionally. We were allowed to sit down, ly down &c. Some took off their knapsacks but few would venture so much. Some go to sleep, some eat a hard tack &c. We now can hear only a little skirmishing in front perhaps ¼ of a mile long & a little to our left-rear. The latter is said to be the 2nd Corps. Begins to get dusk. Some start fires to make coffee.

Now Gen [Samuel] Crawford came down the line from the left with 2 Prisnors. He orders our Regt out as skirmishers on double quick to the left & rear & at the same time, asked the Rebs how many there was out there. He replied he didnt know. Well, says Crawford, how many do you think? He replied again, well Gen I don't know & if I did I wouldnt like to tell. So the general didnt quiz him any more while I was in hearing. For we went off on doublequick. But I heard Gen say to somebody that there was a gap out there where they came in. So we went out, formed line to protect the flank of our Brigade & pushed ahead. We are ordered in doublequick. Come to a few rebs. They cry don't shoot, we surrender. They were taken in &c and from now on a little ways kept taking in a few stragglers. Sergt Roberts captured one & here we stoped & formed a good line & Roberts went to the rear with his Prisnors. The Major sending word to the general that he was awaiting orders. Roberts soon come back & went to the Major with some order I suppose.

But at any rate, we were not relieved or ordered back as we had anticipated. But ordered to put out Videttes & make ourselves as comfortable as possible without fires. I soon made me a bed by just taking my rubber of my knapsack & lying down, spread it over me with my knapsack for a pillow. But I could not sleep for we was wet to the skin. As I said before, twas raining all the time now. It being now about 10 P.M. I should judge, I thought—what a contrast now with this time last night. Then I was lying in my tent with a blazing fire in the fireplace. But I should have mentioned that since about 8 P.M. there has been hard fighting up on the left some 1 ½ miles from [here], tis said with Hancocks men. There was several charges made but we cannot tell how they made it. But the firing is in about the same place as before the Battle so we have not lost much ground I guess.[217]

11 P.M. And they up on the right & Lieut Deerbon commanding, got scared & run along the line nearly to our Co, telling them to get to the rear for the rebs was in their rear & he put off with a squad of them that would follow him. & the scare come on down the line to our Co & I told the Boys not to run but let the Major know about it. So Roberts, he knowing where the Major was, went down & told him. So he ordered us togather & we go, a great number of us for some run of at first mention of it. But now we are togather & start for the Brigade as we suppose. But after wandering around for an hour or so and being completely lost, we halted and the Major ordered a guard to take care of the Prisnors we had & guard the camp. We lay down as best we could, the water pouring down at times. But I was soon asleep it by this time being Midnight.

October 28, 1864

And we were awoke at daybreak, get up, get ready to march. Have a guard detailed to take care of 7 prisners we had taken. And before starting the Major said to us, he wanted no straggling & if we were attacked to fight & no giving back. That if we were taken we would all go togather. So we start, evry little ways we take a Rebel Prisnor or find one of our men & he being a Prisnor or perhaps two or three. Soon in our wandering, we come upon a goodly squad of about 66 Rebs & about a dozen men of a Maryland Regt guarding them. They, too, was lost so they made signs to surrender & we took them & kept on and soon seen some more which we tried to get but they run like deer. But some of the Boys got sight of them & they were Blue coats & they, I suppose, thought we were rebs so they run. This being something I did not see a reb do for they would stop as quiet as lambs. Here we halted and a few went out to recconnoiter, they soon found out where we were & came back with several officers of the Brigade that were sent out to look for us.

We soon started, came to the creek we crossed in the morning & here we stop to make a Bridge which was soon done for our forces had built it & crossed & torn it up so this looked like retreating. So by this time most of the boys had come to us one way & another & we had about 100 Prisnors.[218] While here there was heavy skirmishing not far off. So having the Prisnors securely guarded, we start & going about ¼ mile we come to the old Brigade & I tell you twas a welcome sight. They were building works &c, preparing for what might come. The guard turned the Prisnors over to the Provost-Martials & the 24 Mich was ordered out to relieve the 6th Wis on skirmish line & we took the place of the 24th & were ordered to take of all but cartridge box & rest & get something to eat & dry ourselves. For we were verry wet & we hadnt been by fire since we left camp, so it felt good. We got breakfast & ate hearty. This being the first meal we had had, we just nibbled a cracker for the last 24 hours. Here we get an inkling that it is a retreat.

About 10 oclock we are ordered up & we start for the rear & now the Major tells us that we are ordered back to our old camps. This made us feel good & I felt much better for I was quite sick last night & until I got breakfast. But now feel all right & we march a great pace & come back to camp resting only twice on the way. We reach our old camp at 4 P.M. & happy we were to get here. We found our chimney standing. But all boards & boxes were gone. They are a Soldiers furniture. But the Boys & I with them were thankful that the chimneys were left & didnt mourn over the loss of so many boards &c. Well, we get supper &c and enjoy it well. So ended our short & hard but verry eventful campaign. But lo, some of the Boys & a Lieut of Co. D that we thought was taken comes in. They all together brought in & turned over about 80 or 90 more Rebs & the scattering ones in all, we can safely count on 200 Prisoners. But we or Co E lost one man taken prisnor, that being the total loss of the Regt.

October 29, 1864

And fine day & we rest today. In the evening the officers laid out a new camp a little back & on the top of the hill & with it we had orders to build good comfortable quarters. So we Policed off the ground a little & Picket out our lots. We camp by wing having two rows of shanties & a street of 60 feet between them & evry shanty is to be built about 6 by 10 feet & about 5 feet high. We can vary a few inches if we wish and we have 12 feet in width on ground to build on & all our chimneys on the same side & evrything in uniformity. I got my Pens today that I sent to New York for. They came in good order & I sold them all in an hours time. But my money is gone & I cant get any more or I could do a good Buisness just now. But will try it on Payday which will soon come for we will be mustered tomorrow for 2 months more pay. I also got a letter from Henry. They are well.

October 30, 1864

And fine day. Capt Young went over to the intrenching tool wagon & got an ax for evry tent so we could go at it & put the Shanties up in a hurry. We got ours raised today. We took considerable pains & we have the nicest in the Co so far. We worked hard today, made good use of the Axes which were returned at 5 P.M. The whole Brigade & I don't know how many more, are at work building. The Place begins to look like a city.

October 31, 1864

And fine day. And we are to work on our Shanties. We borrow an ax now & then & when we havent tools to work with we do something else. But are getting along fine. The news in the Papers is that we extended our line 3 miles on the left & our last move was a perfect success & captured 900 Prisnors.

We were mustered today instead of yesterday as I before stated we would be. But we didnt stop work & we are getting along fine. We will be able to move in tomorrow.

November 1, 1864

And fine day & we are still at work like Beavers. But we work to a great disadvantage by not having tools, have to borrow & lend &c. We are not so fortunate as to have an ax. One of my tentmates had an ax but give it to Cap to carry & that was the last of it. But in such a time as that we would throw away all such things. We got the tents on today & the chimney built & moved in & will sleep in it tonight.

But I havent told you my tentmates yet. They are George Booth & Thomas W Blunt.[219] They will sleep togather & I will have to sleep alone for the man I was tenting with, J. A. Drew has been detailed to the hospital. I am sorry to have him go away for he is a good fellow & so are Tom & George. I think myself verry fortunate in get men of good morals & steady fellows. They always will do their share & which will make us live happy &c.

November 2, 1864

And fine day & we are at work on Shanty again. We slept in it last night & I took cold. I had to sleep on the floor. Jake stays with me yet till he gets his finished. He is building with the Hospital Steward, [Leonard] Davis.[220] The news through the Papers is good. Gen Grant in his Official dispatch says the last move is a complete success, evrything is going right all around.[221]

November 3, 1864

And verry rainy day, especially in the latter part. I washed my shirt & drawers today & rubed the skin of one knuckle & made a blister on another. We done a little finishing on the shanty today. It is most finished now. But evryday we can see something needing to be done to add to the comfort. For instance, made couple of stools & hung the table to the wall so as to be let down at pleasure. And for a door made a frame & tacked some pieces of old rubber on said frame. One of the Colporteurs[222] came around today with religious papers & writing paper & envelopes &c. He seemed to be an agreeable man. I like to have such come around occassionally. I got a State Journal today so I have the news from the state.

November 4, 1864

And fine day after 10 oclock but rained a little in the morning. We worked a little more on shanty today, fix, fix &c. We have a full sett of cooking utensils as follows. 1 frying pan, 1 6 quart pail with lid, 1 2 quart coffee kettle. That makes the sett, we can fry or stew. The latter articles I just bought, Bucket $1.50cts, Coffee Pot $1.00cts & George had the pan. I take cold evry night since I came into shanty. Hope it will not continue long. I wrote a letter to Mother today. Rec'd one from Lu too, she was well. But had met with a slight disappointment in getting a room to start buisness. But this I hope she will soon overcome & get started at her trade.

Well most all have finished building. Officers & all. Evrything goes to show that we are to stay here. Evrything is quiet on the lines, there is a detail evryday to work on fortifications.

November 5, 1864

And fine day & we clean up the street today. By chopping off the stumps close to the ground & sweep the ground clean, get the trash &c into piles prepartory to hauling of with a team. I wrote a letter to Henry today. [See Appendix 1] The news in the Papers is nothing exciting.

November 6, 1864

And fine day. And we finish policing the street and we have a nice camp. All goes on well. This being Sunday, we have Co. Inspection. Today appears most like Sunday of any for a long time. We sit in our shanties and read, write & converse and we enjoy ourselves well. But our health is not the best. We have bad colds & Tom is most sick abed but we will soon get over this I hope.

November 7, 1864

And rainy bad day but we are dry & warm. The detail to work on fortifications work. George is on today. Last night we had to get up for the Rebs raised a fuss away up on the right. Tis said they charged our works twice & were repulsed. & last night half of the different Regts in the brigade had to be up all the time. We, the right wing, was up till 1 oclock and then we went to bed & the left wing watched, but the Rebs didnt truble us the night. Tis said our men took 600 prisners. The Rebs want to do something to effect the Election but we will watch them. I received a letter from Mother today & answered it. Mother is well but Cornelia is sick with the chills & fever, which I am sorry to hear. We are having good living now since we got our mess kettle. We have soup half the time. We have flour. I bought a ball & we drew potatoes, so with Beef, Pork, Potatoes & flour we have some good messes.

November 8, 1864

And rather rainy today. The Election goes off quiet but with considerable sport with some McLellen men. Our Co went 22 for Lincoln & 3 for Mac and the Regt went about the same proportionately, Lincoln getting 4 fifths majority. I was one of the Clerks & Corp [Albert] Morse the other of the Election. There was not much Electioneering & considerable fun. I expect they at home are having exciting times. My hope is that Lincoln will be Elected and I believe I shall realize it. There is many Deserters from the Rebs coming in. Most evryday some come into our Brigade. The Boys with the Big hats wont fire on them they say & in fact our boys & them are verry friendly on the Picket line. They say they cant trust the others.

We draw rations. We get good rations now, some vegetables.

November 9, 1864

And rather showery. Nothing especial transpired. I got a letter from Cornelia. All well. I wrote one to Lu in answer to one I recd sometime since. There is lots of Deserters from the Rebels coming in evry day.

November 10, 1864

And fine day. Nothing unusual except going on Picket. I & both of my tentmates with most of the Co, we get on a guard post. We have to stand an hour a piece at night & set up by the fire one hour.

Fatigue Detail [from Company G]
  1. H. Christman [Henry Christman of Milwaukee]
  2. — Parry
  3. B Peck [Benson Peck of Durand]
  4. Eley Cadatt [Joseph or Alexander Cadott of Sterling]
  5. H. Sioux [Henry Sous of Osceola]
  6. A. M. Attwood [Abner M. Atwood of Grand Rapids]
  7. J. King [Joseph King of Polk]
  8. J A Samuels [George Samuels of Barre]

9. H. Felix [Henry Felix of Centralia]

10. J. Buck [John Buck of Barre]

November 11, 1864

And fine day, we & the Johny are verry friendly, trade papers &c frequently. We built us a Bough house & fire right in front which makes it comfortable. The firing is kept up all night away up on the right.

November 13, 1864

And fine day. Last night orders come that we must have no communications with the Rebs as there was contraband news in the papers through some source. It is that Sherman has Burnt Atlanta & left 2 Corps to look after Hood & started someplace with the other 5 Corps supposed to be going to Charleston or Mobile.[223] I got a letter from Lu today. She is as well as usual & is going to start a shop soon.

4 P.M. And we are relieved by another Regt & come home & are soon comfortable.

November 15, 1864

And fine day. We have Brigade Review today. Come out in pretty good style considering our bad clothing. We will soon have our new clothing now. There is Rebs coming in evry night.

November 16, 1864

And fine day. We have Co. Drill in forenoon & in afternoon. Inspection by Division officers & right after Battallion drill & then Dress parade & then supper & oh, what a good supper, consisted of a delicious soup & so ended the day.

November 17, 1864

And fine day & the same drill as yesterday. But George & I got excused from Co. Drill to fix up the end of our cabin so I could take the oilcloth of to use & we made a good job of it. There is slight rumors about moving & I expect that we will have another move before winter sets in unless it comes soon. We can buy anything we want at the Commissary so we can live better, for we can get vegetable. George went & bought 25 cts worth of onions & we have some fine soups &c.

November 19, 1864

And rainy day & no drill. We have drawn our clothing so there is considerable washing going on. I washed my old pants last night & will wear them on fatigue so as to save my new ones. I drew a coat also & will wear the old one on fatigue also. I wrote a letter to Miss ——— [left blank]. Most all think there is a move on foot &c.

November 20, 1864

And rainy day. This is the holy sabbath day. But no inspection. Nothing known of the move. Rumors various & Rebel deserters.

November 22, 1864

There is rumors that we will have 100 recruits inside of a week. We will be glad to see them & as many more as the state will send us.

November 23, 1864

And rainy day & uncomfortable weather. We do nothing today. I put my time in studying my arithmetic & writing a letter to Henry. We have got things fixed up so now that I can put in a good deal of my time improving my mind.

November 24, 1864

Rainy today & rained great deal last night. There is rumors of a move but I guess this will stop it. There is some troops moving but I guess they are only changing a little.

November 25, 1864

And cloudy but no rain but rained hard last night. The recruits came today that we have been expecting. We got 100 & the 6th [Wisconsin] Regt got 180. We got mostly substitutes & the 6th, drafted men. As a general thing they are stout men & mostly Norwegians & clearly evry one are foreigners. They came so late that they couldnt be assigned to their companies. we took them into our Shanties & let them sleep on the floor. Evry shanty took 2 of them.

November 26, 1864

And fine day. & the recruits were assigned to the different companies, the weakest taking them so as to equalize all the Co of the Regt. Our Company is the largest & we didnt get any. & I am glad of it for we will not have squad drill now. If we had got any I should of had a good deal of the drilling to do.

We have roll call 3 times a day now & things will be carried on according to regulations hereafter. We have a new sutler. The Major got a new one & told Mr. Shirrell the old one that he didnt want anything more to do with him. We can get anything we want now on credit & it will be a great accommodation to the Boys.

I and my tentmates buy a few needy articles but don't go in verry extravagant.

The recruits are verry busy putting up their Shanties & the boys help them some. They drew tents today & will camp out till they get their shanties up. We will have no drill till then.

November 28, 1864

And fine day & the same as yesterday. The recruits draw clothing so they will be in uniform with us. They were in Military uniform but they lacked the big black hat. They draw caps when mustered in but our Brigade wears hats so they must wear hats too.

The Rebs still continue to come in. Three come in & went through our streets today to be turned over to the Provost Martials & then to be sent to City Point where they will have a chance to take the Oath of Allegiance & either go north or to work in the quartermasters Department, they having their choice.

The Rebel Papers says that Dutch Gap Canal is finished & they expect to see Grant Pitching into them. & that is the rumor in our army too. The weather is the finest I ever saw it. Tis verry pleasant. There is troops moving now. The 9th Corps is going by to the right of us. I don't know [how] far to the right though.

November 29, 1864

And fine day & things about the same as yesterday. The recruits still at work at their Shanties. There is some more troops going to the right & some to the left. Tis said only the 2nd & 9th Corps changing Places.

The rumor is that that fleet of Men of Wars men went through the canal this morning. How true it is we cant tell. But we can hear the heavy roll of canon up in that direction. They are no common pieces either. All is anxiety about the move.

There is great rumors of Peace propositions being offered to the Rebs. Some say he should not offer them. That they are the ones to sue for peace. & I think we had better show mercy & then if they wont why then, Pitch in & give them hail Columbia.

The rumors from [Union General William] Sherman is through Rebel sources & that is to the effect that he is, to use the Johnys words, just tearing the guts out of the confederacy. This is cheering to us & hope he will continue to tear.[224]

November 30, 1864

And fine day as ever there shone on the earth. Nothing of importance today. The recruits are still at work building their shanties. This is the last day they will have. They will have to drill some hours evry day after today. But our Co will not have squad drill for we have no recruits. The rumor is to the effect that there is 200 more coming to our Regt. Let them come, we will welcome them.

December 1, 1864

And fine day & the recruits have their regular 4 hours drills daily from now on. Our Co. don't drill & perhaps we will not till the recruits in the other companies gets drilled enough to have Co. Drill. Then we will have to come out. There is another heavy detail for Picket out of our Regt today. The boys don't know what to make of it. Our whole Co except the sergts.

December 2, 1864

And fine & I am alone today same as yesterday & have a good time writing, studying arithmetic & I wrote a letter to Lu today. There is lots of Johneys coming in. There has about 20 come in today & yesterday & some of the South Carolinians which are supposed to be the best troops they have.

December 3, 1864

And fine day, a verry light shower last night. The boys come in today from Picket & they count up to the number of 27 Rebs that have come in on our Division Picket line in the 48 hours they have been out. But there is orders strictly Prohibiting any communication with them anymore at the Present. Captains Young, Johnson [James Johnson of Columbus] & Lieuts Weaks [Charles E. Weeks of York] & Camel of our Regt were mustered out of the U.S.M. Service today and they start home tomorrow. Success to them but some of them promised to stay with their Cos till they went home. But I cant blame Capt Young any for his buisness at home was in such a bad condition that he must go & him going gives me a chance to rise some in the scale of Military Promotion. For the Orderly sergt will be first Lieut & the first Lieut will be Captain so there will be a new lot of promotions in the Co. There is but one line officer left in the Regt that come out when it did, all the others have gone this way & that. & now we are commanded by officers that have risen from the ranks. We have almost a new sett of such officers & this pleases me & most all of us. I like to see men that have carried the knappsack so long have a chance to make something now

December 5, 1864

And fine day. This being Sunday, we have inspection. Inspected by Sergt Roberts, Boyanton [Boynton] not being able. He is still verry unwell & I fear he will never be able to take command. The rumor is that we are going to move out of these quarters & the 6th Corps which has just come from the Valley are going to take our place & we are to go out & build new quarters & as night draws near a brigade comes up & camps for the night on our Parade ground. & to wait till morning when we will go out. Tis said about 1 ½ miles & will have a much better place than here. We are ordered to be ready to march at 5 A.M.

December 6, 1864

And fine day & we move out according to order. March to the rear & come outside of the rear line of works, march out about 2 miles southeast of the camp & go into camp by pitching our tents on the ground. This seems hard but tis honest. We now are pretty certain that we are going on some kind of a raid, some say to the South Side Road & some say to the Weldon road & others say to the right of the army, the other side of the James River, but time will soon tell. We draw rations late this evening & have orders to be ready to march at half past 5 in the morning. I got a letter from Lu this evening.

December 7, 1864

And fine day, little cloudy & like rain but didnt. We marched at the appointed hour, go out to the Jerusalem Plank road & follow on it marching pretty fast till about 2 P.M. when we stoped having come about 15 miles. Here we get dinner & lay here till about 5 P.M. when we start going pretty fast. After going 1 ½ miles we come to the Notaway river which is considerable of a stream. Here we crossed on Pontoon Bridge & go to within ½ mile of Sussex Courthouse. Here we camp for the night. We calculate we have come 22 miles today & we are verry tired. Great discussions arises as to where we are going. But most all seem to think we are to strike the Weldon RR and follow it on down to Weldon where we are to meet with Porters fleet. But we have met with no opposition as yet.[225]

December 8, 1864 [Reconnaissance to Hatcher's Run]

Cloudy, sprinkles a little once & awhile. But not enough to do any harm to marching. We arose early & march at 5 A.M. following the same road past the courthouse for several miles when we turn square to the right & take the shortest road for to strike the RR which the women & negros at a house on the corner say is 7 miles. We march past & the boys keep well closed up. After going some 5 miles we hear firing. There says our cavelry has struck the rebel Pickets. Which proved to be so for going a little way, we halted in sight of our Cavelry drawn up & a battery come rattling by & took position in the cornfield to the left of us. But we soon marched on & the battery limbered up without firing a shot & followed us there being the other 2 brigades ahead of us. The 2nd Brigade was throwed into necessary shape & sent the rebs a flying. There being only a few cavelry, said 300 only, we hurried on & soon emerged into a large open field and the cry runs along the ranks that the cavelry have burned the RR Bridge across the Notaway [Nottoway] River & looking away to the right about 1 mile we see the Bridge burning. This cheers up the Boys & going a little up on the rising ground, we stop & get coffee & eat Persimmons which are plenty & watch the bridge burn & speculate on whats to be done for about 3 ½ hours which brings 6 P.M.

We have supper & start out to go 2 miles which brings us right to the RR where the track is turned upside down & looking away to the right & toward the River we see different parties burning the ties & bending the rail by heating them with the ties. We stack arms & the right flank of the Regt goes to destroying the road & the left is on guard. & now as far as we can see, we see the work of Destruction goes on. & it is now verry dark & tis verry cold. As soon as we get away from the fires which are verry warm, we shiver with cold. The wind blows a hurricane. At last orders comes for us to make ourselves as comfortable as we can. All is quiet with the pickets & so we make bed & lay down but cant sleep for cold. The wind pierces right through our clothing. Lucky for me that I brought my old coat along to wear over the other. It makes considerable difference in the warmth. We now see with our own eyes what is our buisness here & wonder what will be done tomorrow.[226]

December 9, 1864

And fine day. We march at daylight. Here the Boys killed a fine cow they captured & some got & some didnt. We march on down the road for 5 or 6 miles & find it destroyed or troops at work destroying it. Some have been at work all night. At last we get a share assigned our Regt & we soon turn it upside down, which we do as fast as a man can walk & get it about half burning. We stop and get dinner & then finish it & then set around the fires & smoke & chat & speculate on what next to be done & things to numerous to mention. There being a big pile of corn near by, the boys are appropriating it & parching & roasting it & the officers are feeding their horses out of it & soon the Butchers bring along the beef cattle & they are herded on the pile. We lay here till 4 P.M. & for some 2 hours, troops have been passing & now again we hear some skirmishing, the first today. We start out & our Brigade streatches out on the road again & tear up about a mile more. This being left next to us. This we soon do & then come back to where we lay in the afternoon & went into camp for the night. & as soon as camped a detail is made to go out & forage & [after] about 3 hours, the four that went out from our Co came in with a lot of as nice beef as I ever tasted. We had all we all wanted. I having carried my big stew kettle so I said if some one would get the water I would set up and cook it full. The water was soon brought & I got about 10 pounds to cooking. & about this time the rain begins to fall pretty fast. And rained all the time I was cooking which was till about 11 P.M. & while cooking, I roasted and ate near 1 pound so hungry for beef was I.

The camp is pretty noisy, most of the boys that went out got liquors of one kind & another, viz. Peach Brandy & apple brandy & applejack &c. All the best of liquors & some have used them rather too freely. Well I got into the tent & go to bed.

December 10, 1864

And we are up early & get ready to march at daylight. But don't march till after 10 A.M. All the time since 5 A.M. this morning, troops, wagons &c have been passing back so we are pretty sure that our raid is at an end and a number of the boys are so drunk they can scarcely walk & some dead drunk & the Doctor gives them a Potion that would sober them. At last we fall in & start, get on to the road & our Regt is taken as flankers. So we strung out & marched outside of the road, keeping in sight of the column. We marched on till dark without stopping much, when we camped in a large field with plenty of water & rail fences near by. Soon have large fires which we need for the rain of last night & it all freezing, making a heavy sheet which kept dropping from the trees all day keeping us wet & many of them had wet blankets. We got supper & enjoyed ourselves well as we could for we are verry sore & sleepy.

Just as we were camping, the enemy came upon our rear guard which they had Pressed hard all day. But didnt gain anything & now our Boys thought they would pay them for their termerity so the rear infantry laid down to each side of the road in the fence corners & the cavelry was ordered to fall back in disorder & let the rebs come on. & when they got well in between our fellows, our Boys fired, killed 4, wounded 5 & captured several. So this made them mad & saucy & watchful so our Gen thought we had better take a better position. So our Regt was thrown around to protect the right flank & a Picket of 20 men & proper number of non commissioned officers were put out. I was the Sergt of the Picket & this took considerable time. So now twas after 10 P.M. We made 3 Posts of the 20 men. I run one Post till 2 A.M. then woke the corporal & I went to sleep. It has rained most all the time and now is raining. I take rails & lay them in the fire, dry & warm them & lay them down, put my rubber over me & have short naps till daylight.[227]

December 11, 1864

When I got breakfast & we have orders to be ready to march at 7 A.M. All quiet. We are about 4 miles from the courthouse. We join the Regt & start after evrything else is gone by. We have to be rear guard today. So we march on slow on account of the teams being stuck in the mud but we get along. At last strike the Plank road which makes us feel better for we know that we go back. The Pioneers & cavelry obstructed the road behind us with falling trees. At last coming to a large field, we formed line of battle & drew rations & get dinner. From now on we would march a ways & then form line of Battle & so on till we struck the river about sundown.

We now had formed line of battle 10 times & never fired a shot. The Rebs were scarce & afraid to show themselves. We crossed the river & after going about ½ mile through the worst kind of mud, we halted & once for today could say we felt a little safe. & now a division of the 2nd Corps takes the rear. Well we start & march 3 miles or so, having to go clear past all the other troops to get a camp. We halted and camped for the night & verry glad were we too. We got supper & pitch tent & go to bed. I being on Picket last night, I feel like sleeping tonight. We feel quite at home here. We had a hard time of being rear guard & now all the army is in rear, we feel good. We calculate to go home tomorrow or back to where we started from.

December 12, 1864

And fine day & we were awoke at daylight to get ready to march. Which we done without hurry & waited till about 9 A.M. & the 3 Division came along. We start in & march slow. The road is hard frooze. Twas verry cold last night. We march on till noon when we turn into the timber & make coffee & after staying here near 2 hours, we start. Now we see that there is no troops in rear of us today. Again we march on steady & reach the camp outside of the works (the one we left when we started out) about 4 P.M. and happy as could be to be where we can get rest. We have to camp out as the 6th Corps occupies our quarters yet. We pitch tents & get supper & mail comes. I get 2 letters from Mother & one from Lu & the State Journal & 2 papers Mother sent.

December 13, 1864

Cold & windy. We lay in camp & most evry tent has a fire in front which makes it verry smoky & causes us to have sore eyes. There is many rumors as to what we are going to do & will do and where our new camp will be. & some say we are going to make another raid. But time will tell what we will do. The weather is verry cold.

December 14, 1864

And showery, cold & cloudy, verry disagreeable. We lay in camp today with the usual rumors. The news is good from all the armies, Sherman is all right.

December 15, 1864

The usual rumor about what we are to do. Officers say that Gen Bragg has been out & picked out a good camp for the Brigade & that we are going to it tomorrow.

December 16, 1864

Warm day. We pack up & in due time we start & come to our new camp about 2 miles east of where we lay & it is a fine camp, right in the woods & fine chance for building. After considerable truble, we get in the right shape & camped till we get our Shanties built to spread them on. The Major got 5 axes to the Co. & we had to put handles in them. But we having an ax of our own, I & George & Richard went to cutting logs & let Thomas do the cooking &c. Richard Turnbull[228] is the man I took in to bunk with & make the four in number. & he is a fine man, good morals & quiet.

December 17, 1864

And fine day. We work hard today & get up the body of our shanty & we are getting along fine. The Boys are getting along fine. We let Thomas do the work of cooking &c & we work on shanty.

December 18, 1864

And a verry little showery. We get our shanty most ready to put our tent on. But we have [to] sleep on the cold damp ground one night more. Some of the Boys that had an auger got into their shanties tonight. We have an auger in our Co. but the others have been using it some & we will get it tomorrow.

December 19, 1864

And a little stormy but not so much so as to stop us from work. We got moved into ours today. I built the chimney. We had to build it of mud. By building a framework & packing in mud around them and build a fire in & burn the wood out & that will bake it similar to a brick. Making a good chimney & it draws well. I believe I have just hit it.

December 20, 1864

And fine day. & we keep finishing our shanty which is near completion. We rested well last night on our new bunks. All are at work & getting moved into their shanties &c. The news from all quarters is good. Sherman has reached the defences of Savannah & has invested the city. & Thomas has whipped Hood & captured many thousand Prisnors & guns &c. And still capturing.[229]

Evrything goes well now. The rumor is that Jeff Davis is seriously ill & evrything in hubbub about Richmond.

December 21, 1864

And the same as yesterday. We are short on for rations caused by us eating so hearty while working hard on our shanties & we have to buy some. There has been an order issued to the effect that no more whiskey shall be issued except on an order from Corps Headquarters. This I am happy to see & the time will come I hope & believe when there will none be allowed at all. Then we will soon have peace.

December 22, 1864

And fine day. About the same routine of duty. There was a Picket detail from our Regt today & Thomas & George was on it leaving me & Richard alone for the next 48 hours. I got a letter from Mother today. Also a pair of socks & the Journal. All is well, they are having verry cold weather up there now. The thermometer has been down to 30 Deg below zero.

December 23, 1864

And rather cold & cloudy. Things the same as yesterday. I worked some for the Chaplain today fixing up his big tent comfortable. There was 20 recruits came for the

Regt & we had to take them in amongst us, so Richard & I took two. They sleep in Georges & Thomas Bunk & they will be assigned to companies in the morning.

December 24, 1864

And fine day & all is well. We did not get any recruits in our company. George & Thomas come in, the Pickets being relieved. The Boys are talking, wondering & wishing about tomorrow & what they will do. There is going to be nothing done here that I can hear of to make it noticeable as Christmas Day. But we, for all that, will enjoy it the best we know how.

December 25, 1864, Christmas Day

And a fine Christmas day. & nothing unusual transpires. We have the army rations for dinner &c. I put in most of the day writing letters, one to Henry & one to Mother in answer to some I received not long since. I wrote Henry to send me a box of stuff such as Butter & honey &c and what they thought best. Some of the boys had boxes come in good order too, so this encouraged me to send for one. We had church services today at the usual hour & prayer meeting at night.

The news is good, it is from Rebel sources that Sherman has captured Savannah with 17,000 prisnors & all its stores &c pertaining to it. And Thomas has captured 13,000 of Hoods men & 61 pieces of artillery & still following him. All is well all around & the goose hangs high. The last Herald N.Y. has a full & graphic account of the operations of both armies which verry interesting. I & my tentmates have read it. It is many columns long.

December 26, 1864

And fine day. & the whole Regt. is on Police duty cleaning up the parade ground & all grounds bordering on the camp. All have their shanties & some are putting up shelves &c for convenience sake. The camp presents a fine appearance. The ground is excellent & the camp is so admirably laid out & the buildings so well planned & as well done, that with the few scattering trees of evergreen makes upon the whole a verry pretty & pleasant camp. I hope we will be permitted to enjoy it till we go home which some of the Boys think will not be long. But I must say I can not think so, I think the people are not punished enough. I got a letter from Cornelia today. Also a pair of gloves from Mother. All of which I glad to get. She & Mother was well.

December 27, 1864

And fine day. I am on guard today as Sergt of the Guard & also commandant, there being a corporal also to help me. The Privates are recruits, evry one, & are as green as can be concerning guard duty. So I have to teach them. There was another detail for picket from our regt. The picket duty is light & we have only a little way to go, something like half mile.

December 29, 1864

And fine day but chilly. I help in making out 2 more of the rolls today. We got along fine. I wrote most of the day & find it considerable of a job to write out one roll. There has to be four made out, so there will be one to make out tomorrow.

December 30, 1864

And fine day, but cold. I help the Lieut finish the rolls which proved to be an all day [job], almost. They will be ready & in good order by tomorrow when we will be mustered for 2 months more pay.

I promised the Chaplain some time since that I would fix up his Bunk when he was ready & so he called on me today, but I couldnt go for I had to help finish the rolls & when we got the rolls done, I had to take the company out on general Police to sweep up & carry off rubbish that lay about the camp & with this finished, my work was finished so I cleaned up my gun & accoutriments ready for the Inspection & muster tomorrow. Lieut F.A. Boynton came up yesterday so as to muster out & muster in again as Captain & also to muster for pay. He look better than when he went away but he says he is no better. The sore under his arm is worse, it has turned to a regular abcess and a bad one too. He expects to go back to the Hospital soon, he says he has good treatment there.

December 31, 1864

And stormy & cold, verry unpleasant. We were mustered. We fell in in the street without arms & marched up to the Colonels door & there he call the roll off the muster roll & those present answered & then returned to our quarters. Soon there was a detail for Picket taking 2 of my tentmates, viz Tom & George leaving Dick & my self all alone. So we will have a fine time writing &c. I finished writing a letter to Lu which I commenced several days since.

There has been great many promotions of late & among the rest our old Sergt major has risen to Adjutant & William Booth, a Private of our Co has been promoted to fill his place. Well this as evrybody knows is the last day of the year & the last day of the week & last day of the Month &c as also being New years eve. There is nothing transpiring to note but I expect if I were home there would be. How are they that are in civil life tonight. Well I cant say as I am unhappy. I enjoy myself verry well, sitting & chatting with my good tentmates.

1865

The Seventh Wisconsin spent the winter of 1864-1865 near Yellow House on the Weldon Railroad near Petersburg, where the Army of the Potomac and the Confederate Army of Northern Virginia remained locked in a deadly embrace. Lieutenant Colonel Hollon Richardson became the fourth man to command the Seventh (the others were Joseph Vandor, William Robinson, and Mark Finnicum), but he was not mustered as colonel.

With the coming of warmer weather, the armies began to move. The Seventh Wisconsin saw more fighting on February 6-7, 1865, again at Hatcher's Run. A few days later the Sixth and Seventh Wisconsin were ordered to garrison duty at Baltimore, but the order was countermanded at the last minute and the two regiments were assigned instead to the First Provisional Brigade along with the Ninety-first New York Infantry.

On the first of April 1865, Lieutenant Colonel Richardson's Seventh Wisconsin participated in the fighting at Five Forks, Virginia, on the extreme right of Lee's stretched line. The attack, launched against an entrenched enemy, drove them through an open woods and an open field beyond before occupying the captured Confederate trenches. The next morning, Grant's hammer stroke south of Petersburg along the Sixth Corps' front collapsed Lee's lines and triggered the evacuation of Petersburg and Richmond. It was the beginning of the end. On April 9, after a long forced march, the Iron Brigade enjoyed what one historian described as "the proud satisfaction of assisting in the capture of the famous army of General Lee, at Appomattox Court House." The long war was finally over.

William Ray and comrades returned to Washington and participated in the Grand Review before being ordered to Louisville, Kentucky, where they arrived on June 22, 1865. There, the men of the Sixth and Seventh Wisconsin regiments mustered out, their proud service at an end. The men of the Seventh left for Wisconsin on July 2, 1865, and were given a hearty welcome home by its citizens in Madison three days later.

In the final tally, the Seventh Wisconsin had a total enrollment of 1,630 in ranks over the four years. Of these, 281 were killed or mortally wounded in combat, a grim 17.2 percent. In total, the regiment lost 1,016 killed or wounded during the war, including 34 who died in Confederate prisons. The Seventh Wisconsin's three heaviest battle losses were suffered at Gainesville or Brawner's Farm (42 casualties), Gettysburg (37 casualties), and the Wilderness (55 casualties).

Of the soldiers who mustered out at Louisville in 1865, only a handful remained of the volunteers of 1861. One of them was William Ray.

Volume 14

January 1, 1865 to June 14, 1865

We Are the
Iron Brigade Yet

William R Ray
Co. F. 7th Regt, Wis Vet Vols

A Resident of Grant County of Aforesaid State
Enlisted August 29th 1861
Reenlisted Jan 1st, 1864

January 1, 1865

And happy New Year to all is my best wish & God grant it. Last night as the old year was going out & the new one ushering in, the Brigade Band played a number of good & sweet airs around the camp, the night being clear & still. The sweet strains of music as it floated along on the light breezes made me think of home & how it would be to be there but I didnt allow myself to think too long on such Pleasures for fear that I might get homesick & that is a disease I have been so fortunate as not to have much while I have been in the service.

There was another picket detail today to relieve those that went out yesterday. I suppose for the purpose of letting them have some of New years to them selves.

There has been a rumor around to the effect that deserters from the rebels brought the news that Old Jeff was going to surprise the world today but we have seen nor heard nothing uncommon. There was some firing today but nothing of importance. There still continues to be many rumors about peace & and some important ones, if true.

This being Sunday we have Inspection. Captain Boyanton has returned to the Hospital, he not being able for duty. I am sorry to see him so but it cant be helped.

January 3, 1865

And fine day, rather cloudy. Nothing new but that the recruits begins to drill today. The first since coming to this camp. We got our overcoats that we sent off last spring to be stored. They are welcome articles we needed long since.

January 4, 1865

And fine day. We have Co drill in the afternoon. George went on Picket. There was about an inch of snow fell last night. This is the first we have had this winter. The weather is much like Nov weather in Wisconsin.

I had a new Soldier, a substitute, an entire stranger offer to loan me some money so I took 2 dollars of him. He didnt know my name but said my appearance told him there was honesty in its owner. This I, of course, considered flattery. I told him my name & thanked him for his kindness &c. So we were out of bread & we got the Lieut to buy us a quarters worth (viz 4 loafs). The order allowing us to buy at the Brigade Commissaries has been rescinded so we have to get the officers to buy.

January 5, 1865

Rainy day, showery. Recruits are drilling All the Boys are out of money, so we don't get many dailies now, so we don't know what the news is. But nothing special I guess for all want rest & so we may not look for much for awhile but all is well.

January 6, 1865

And verry stormy, hard rains. We would have had a big time today if it had been fine. There was going to be some medals presented to members of the 6th & 7th Wis Regts for meritorious conduct. But tis put off till tomorrow. There is a good many returning to their companies now from the hospitals &c. 1 came to ours today. Our Co reports 17 Privates, 8 corporals & 3 Sergts for duty now. Sergt Jesse M Roberts was mustered today as 1st lieut so we have two officers now.

January 7, 1865

And fine day, rather cool. The presentations of Medals did not come off today & is put off till Monday next to allow some distinguished gentlemen time to get here that were coming. I wrote a letter to Vina M Lander today in answer to one I recd sometime since. I recd a letter from Lu today.

January 10, 1865

And Inspection of camp today & all is right. Some of the Cos are making sidewalks of timber which makes them verry neat. I got a can of butter from somewhere, I suppose from Sister Lu. It come through the mail & weighs 2 pounds, it is verry nice & sweet, taste good.

January 11, 1865

And rainy but not bad. I got a letter from Lu & one from Sarah & Mother & one nice box of fruits which Lu sent me & the letter tells me that she sent me the butter & with all I will have good eating for a while.

January 12, 1865

And fine day. And one of our tentmates T.W. Blunt, his furlough came last night. He started home this morning. We commenced to make sidewalk in our street today. I wrote a letter to one of my Nephews H. W. Lander, he is in California & I forgot to put the postage sufficient on it. I put on only 3 cents but should put on 10 cents & it may not go. This is one of my mistakes. Dick is at work on the Brigade commisaries house & has been for several days & he got us a quarters worth of bread, soft bread.

Capt F. A. Boynton came up from the point today. He is going to stay with us now as long as his health will permit. He is pretty well & looks as well. I am happy to see him looking so well. I hope he will be able to stay with us as long as he is in the service. Wrote a letter to Sister Lu today.

January 13, 1865

And fine day & we finish the sidewalk & ditch the street &c. Have dress parade in the afternoon at the usual time, viz 4 ½ oclock. Capt Boynton is Officer of the day. This being the first time he has officiated in that capacity. He done well, exceedingly so. He makes the gayest officer we ever had in the Co. Evrything goes on well. The papers bring us no exciting news but good. The Rebellion is still on the wane & Treason's going down. I wrote a letter to Cornelia today in answer to one I received sometime since. I have got so behind with my letter writing that a letter lays sometime before I get to answer it. But calculate to catch up soon.

January 14, 1865

And fine day & nothing especial today. We had dress parade today at the usual hour. The Report on the condition of the several camps of the Brigade was read & the

Gen gave us his praise for our tidy camp. & there is a little piece concerning it in the Daily N.Y. Herald and it gives us great praise also & we have the nicest camp I have ever seen.

It is rumored on pretty good authority that Grant has relieved Butler & sent him home to report to his wife & children & from there to the Adjutant Gen by letter. This for the failure of taking Wilmington, N.C. and that Grant has gone in person with the noble fleet to take it. But this is only rumor but for all generally believed.[230]

January 15, 1865

And fine day nothing unusual. Dress parade in evening. This being Sunday, we have inspection by Cap & all in the best of order. I had the best gun I have had since being in the service.

January 16, 1865

And fine day. We had orders early this morning to get ready for the Presentation of those medals but about noon the order was countermanded & we ordered to be ready for Brigade drill at 2 P.M. which came off. We had a good drill of 2 hours & returned home in high glee. We have to go outside the picket line for to get a field large enough & then it is too small but has to do.

Colonel Morrow [Henry Morrow of the 24th Michigan Infantry] commanded us, Gen [Edward S.] Bragg not having returned from furlough home. Our Capt commanded the Co. for the first time on drill & I acted a new part today in the way of acting left general guide of the Regt. This buisness was entirely new to me but however I got along verry well.

January 18, 1865

And fine day, same drill &c as yesterday. Sergt T. C. Alexander got his commission as 1st Lieut in Co H. Good news. Fort Fisher has been captured by the Union forces.[231] I got a letter from Mother & a package of dried beef which is excellent.

January 19, 1865

And fine day. Sergt Alexander turned his book over to me and to assume the duty of Orderly or first Sergt. But nothing but the duty for the present & the first thing was to take the guard detail out to mount guard. Had Brigade Inspection at 10 A.M. all in good order. All my duties for today have been new ones to me but I got along well. I got a can of cake dough from home today which is verry nice when cooked. My Sister is verry kind in so doing. I have many little things of comfort which I should'nt have were she not to send them.

January 21, 1865

And rainy day & we do nothing. Look like we would have a big storm. We have no guard mounting when the weather is bad. I get along well with my new duty. But I find some opposition. There is some of the noncoms headed by a sergt that rather likes to cross me & cause me some truble. They have some bad motive, I don't know what it is but I think it is jealousy. I may be wrong. They got up a petition & most of the Co. signed it to have the next sergt I C Reamer [Isaac C. Raemer] promoted to Orderly & was going to present it to the Captain but they didnt & it is well for them that they didnt. For if they had he would reduced the noncoms to the ranks. Why they should have such hostility I cant tell for I never laid a straw in their way & done them no harm in any way whatever. But let them work, do their worst. I can live that opposition down & will try hard to use all well, both friend & foe. I have got to obey my orders & they have got to theirs.

January 23, 1865

And fine day, but cloudy, ground verry soft & muddy. The same as yesterday duty. I had the boys sign up the clothing book. I find my work double what it was & much more perplexing than what it was before taking the Orderlyship. But I have not lost my patience as yet.

There is great rumors of peace afloat now. & great number of Deserters coming in with the usual story of starvation, hardships.

January 24, 1865

And fine day with the usual duty. There has been considerable firing down on the James River this last two nights. Tis said the Rebs had a pontoon bridge across the river & was crossing & their troop to this side & Gen [John] Gibbons found it out & began shelling them & tore their Bridge to pieces & their gunboats ran down to protect it & he sunk one & run one ashore & the other & ably got away so he made a big thing.[232]

January 26, 1865

And fine day & the same as yesterday. Capt has put in for a furlough. There is a great many going home now on 20 day furloughs. There is 5 percent allowed to go all the time till further orders.

January 27, 1865

And fine day. Things going OK. There is rations of Whiskey issued now evry day. It has a good potion of quinine in it. It is given for the health of the men. Capt Boynton has gone home on a leave of absence for 20 days. I get along verry well with my new duty. There is two or three of the noncoms that are rather trublesome. But they have to obey their orders, the same as myself.

The Lieut is sick today & tonight he is quite bad. He had some writing to do & called on me to help him so I went up & helped him all I could.

January 30, 1865

And warm & sunshine, fine day. Peace Commissioners are in our lines from the so called confederate states. There is 3 of them so rumors says. Evrybody seems to think they will make her win.[233]

January 31, 1865

And fine day. All the men not on duty are at work on the shanties that are being built for the recruits which we expect tonight. Let them come, they are welcome.

My 3 or 4 enemies have been at work again & got up a request[234] for me to hand the Co. Books over to the Lieut now commanding Co. But this I paid no attention to at all. But the Lieut seen I didnt do it (for I believe he was connected with the plan to overthrow me) he took it upon himself to take me to task about it. So he called me up to his quarters & I could, I think, see deceit beaming in his countenance & he said he want confidential & so mite it be & ever will be. But the main point was to get me to give over the books & which he requested & I complied with, though I must confess much to my chagrin. I felt wrong & I was wronged but I knew no redress at present time. I, perhaps, may have some chance when Capt comes back for redress & I may not. I must in accordance to my oath to the U.S. put up with it & grin & bear it. So I return to the rank of file closers & let Isaac C Reamer [Isaac C. Raemer], the next sergt have the Co to run. I can read the verry hearts of the men that acted so by me. They cant look me in the face.

February 1, 1865

And fine day. I have nothing to do. I feel easier, not fatigue or guard or any other details to care for. Orderlyship is not so verry desirable but I am a poor man & the other four dollars a month on the wages is an incentive to strive for it. But the labor is Terible.

February 2, 1865

And rainy, cold, bad day & nothing of importance transpires. We drill Co. Drill now in forenoon & in afternoon & in afternoon, battallion drill when the weather is good. We expected Thomas Blunt back last night but he has not come yet. He will be reported as a deserter tomorrow if he don't come before that time. But the ice in the Bay trubles the boats so that it may be he is ice bound as they have been several times this winter. There is men going home on furlough & men returning most evry day.

February 4, 1865

And fine day & I am on guard today. We had the regular guard mounting & twas done up in good state. Lieut Alexander is officer of the guard. Things goes on well, was not trubled much today. I had to fall in the guard only once to salute the officer of the day.

About 3 P.M. orders came to get ready to march at a minutes notice. Shoes were issued to those wanting & 3 days rations issued & by dark all was ready. But no order came & Tattoo was beat early & all went to bed. I, being on guard, had to sit up half the night to post the guards. And about 12 oclock there was a detail made for picket to go & relieve the Picket that was out. So they could come in & get ready. I went to bed after giving the watch & guard over to the Corporal & the order come to be ready to march at 5 in the morning with Rubber & woollen blankets only. Leave the rest & a guard would be left & the adjutant told me I was to stay as Sergt of the guard & there would be 1 more from each Co to help us & that the Corporal was to wake up the drummers at 5 in the morning.

February 5, 1865

And was awoke by the drums at 4 A.M. The Drum Major made a mistake & got up an hour too early. But I went to sleep again & was awoke about 5 A.M. to eat my breakfast, which done & the boys got ready. George is the only one that goes from our shanty. Tom & Dick being excused for lameness & they have to go on guard. I have to make a guard out of what is left. Soon the order comes to fall in at half past 6. That time arrived & they fell in & the Col gave them a few words of advice & they started of going to the west-ward.

There is 3 corps (viz the 6th, 2nd & 5th corps of Infantry & a corps of Cavelry) going. So say rumor. Big, think can do something if they try hard. Night & we can hear away off towards Reams Station hard fighting. Both musketry & artillery hear it for near an hour & then all is still. Many camp rumors but they are not worthy of notice, don't believe any of them.[235]

I get along well with the guards. I am commandant of them. Lieut Alexander went with the Regt.

February 6, 1865

And fine day We have pretty fair time here in camp. But verry anxious to hear from the Boys definitely. We have rumors evry hour but we cant rely on them. They had a hard fight last evening we know. & tis said was beaten back some. There has one man come in. He has been hit with a spent ball. He is a German & don't know & can tell less about what has transpired.

February 7, 1865

And rainy bad day. Sleeted most all day. Bad time for the army, especially for the wounded. There was some hard fighting yesterday & pretty reliable news from the front. Rumor say Lieut Alexander was wounded & taken prisnor & a number more killed & wounded. All the casualties in our Co was Corpl George Atkinson slightly wounded in hand and all. They met with strong resistance & I guess rather got the worst of it. The rumor is that 2 corps from the Southwest has come here. The guard buisness is running harder for the boys are mostly sick & they tire of such constant duty. There has some boys come in that have slight wounds.

February 8, 1865

And fine day & most all the sleet has melted which makes the ground verry soft and where there is any travel, tis muddy. One of the boys of our Co was into camp today [& he corroborates the report of] Lieut Alexander being wounded & Prisnor & Corporal [George] Atkinson slightly wounded, the former of Co. H & the latter of our Co. F. As near as I can find out only 3 have been killed out of the Regt and some 10 or 12 wounded. But tis said that our Regt has lost the least of any in the Brigade by them being on skirmish line most of the time. Our Co has come out bully so far. They say our troops are fortifying & are likely to stay & that we will have to go out there if they do.[236]

There was 64 recruits come this evening for our Regt & a sett of good looking men too. The Quartermaster assigned them to Co for the present & I drew & dealt out rations to them, for our commisary Sergt has gone out with the ration teams to the regt. But I got along amazingly well. I have been verry busy today. I have evrything to attend to or most evrything. I consult the Quartermaster some on things I know nothing about.

February 9, 1865

And fine day. And some of the Boys come into camp today & they represent the thing in pretty fair light. Our troops have fortified & are going to hold the line. There is talk of our boys coming into camp to get their things & then return & build quarters on the new line.

February 10, 1865

And fine day & the rumor still prevalent that our Div is coming in to camp & at night they did come. We heard of them coming & went to work to build fires in each shanty. The recruits that we sent out yesterday came back with the boys & they have to be taken into the tents till theirs is covered. Tis rumored that we all have to go tomorrow to the new line.

General Edward S. Bragg
Generals in Blue

February 11, 1865

And we did'nt go from camp till about 10 A.M. & we were ordered to Meads station to take the cars for City Point & the boat for Baltimore for special duty by order of Gen Hallack [Union General Henry Halleck]. An honor confered on us for our daring bravery at Hatchers Run & other times before. But I could not see that we would go to Baltimore & when I got on the cars I thought we would go to City Point. But when we got down there, only 1200 could go so the recruits were taken out & when we got on the Boat, the recruits was sent too, on another boat. But we bunked on the Boat & lay there all night. But were ordered off in the morning & could not go to Baltimore but no orders to go anyplace.

February 12, 1865

And cold and windy. We got on the cars about 1 P.M. & come back to Crawford station within ¾ of a mile of our camp we left the day previous. Here we went into the woods & got dinner & started for to hunt a new camp away down on the left someplace. We are likely to be put into other brigades & we know not where. Loud are the curses against old drunken Bragg. We think he is to blame for us not going to Baltimore. The boys are quite downhearted. Well, we marched about 5 miles & went into camp near the old division for the night & until further orders. Tis verry cold. We, the Co., fixed up a wind brake & built huge fires & were soon comfortable. But nothing compared, says the boys, to what we would have been in Baltimore. But we must abide by our fate. But old Bragg. Oh dear, what Blessing is showered on his head by most of the Boys. He has played truant to the men that won him his star.

February 13, 1865

And weather same as yesterday. We lay in camp today & in the evening a picket detail goes out of our Regt on picket. We do nothing today but speculate on our future destiny, we mightily fear the old brigade is broken up & we have to go into some others. Bless Old Bragg.

February 14, 1865

And the weather fine & warm. We lay in camp all day. The officers goes out with the Colonel to look up & lay out a camp returning at night with the glad tidings that we will move early in the morning about 1 mile & go to building quarters again & that we, the 2 Regts, the 6th & 7th Wis are formed into a Provisional Brigade & be commanded by the Colonel of the 6th Regt, Col Kellog [Colonel John Kellogg]. So we are the Iron Brigade yet. Those troops that have gone was not with the brigade when it won the name of Iron Brigade, so we don't calculate to let them have it yet. & we are afraid that Old Bragg will go & get our Brigade flag & parade it around with what the please to term the Iron Brigade. But if he has got the great part of it with him, it is not the Iron part.[237]

February 15, 1865

And weather rainy, but we come to our new camp & find it laid out verry nicely, but in a muddy cornfield with considerable corn yet remaining on stalks, plenty of wood & water near. We go into camp in the woods till we get our cabins up. We pitch tent & go to work to get out timber. We took two of the nearest & best trees we evr could find. We split them into slabs as thin as we could, cut them 8 by 12 feet long. We didnt find much truble in splitting them. We quit pretty early & got up a good lot of wood & built a huge fire in front of our tent & got supper. Eat it, chat awhile about cabin &c & go to bed. There is only three of us now. Dick, he had a sore knee & went to hospital when at City Point. We all sleep togather now & will sleep warm though tis raining & cold.

February 16, 1865

And rainy day, verry disagreeable. But George & I work most of the day & Tom cooks &c, takes care of things. Our 2 Regts are organized completely now & we go by the name of Provisional Brigade.[238]

February 17, 1865

And fine day & we worked moderately hard. We work just as if we could leave all we have done any minute & we calculate to go. We are in no great hurry. The boys say we are getting the best cabin in the Regt & we are getting along fine.

February 18, 1865

And fine day. We still work away. I took in a German one of the last recruits that come in with me. He appears to be a fine man. Cant talk much English but has been in America some years. Has got quite Americanized, handy with tools & with all, I think I have made a good choice.

February 19, 1865

Still at work leisurely. Got cabin up, chimney partly built. Getting nice cabin, best in Co & as good as any in Regt. Great news from the South. [Union General Robert] Foster has got Charleston & Sherman got Branchville & Columbia both in South Carolina, the latter the capital of state. Sherman & Foster is going just as they please. Lee was sending off a large body of troops to operate against Sherman which caused this Army to make the last move so as to draw them back. And it did do it.[239]

February 20, 1865

And fine day and same as yesterday. The rumored good news of yesterday was read officially today. There was great cheering in the other Regt when it was read. But our Regt as usual said nothing. Some as they turned to go to their work made out to say Bully in a common tone.

There was one of the old Vet come to Co. today from hospital. He has been missed in Co. much for he was our Phunny feller. His name is [Webster] Cook. He was sunstroke when we took the Weldon R.Road.

February 21, 1865

And fine day & we put the cover on our cabin & moved in but have considerable finishing to do yet. Many little things to numerous to mention. We have a better chance to build this time than ever before. The sutler brought up some nails & our Co has an auger of its own & plenty of axes & they are in pretty good order too. We have two in our mess. Our chimney draws good & evrything seems to go well.

February 22, 1865

Fine day & we put in a floor, put up shelves & Pins. Hang up different articles, finish our bunks which makes them neat & comfortable. This is Washingtons Birth Day & some of the officers are having a spree. But not ours for many of them don't taste liquors at all & the others are moderately temperate. Just at dark we have orders to pack up & be ready to march at a minutes notice but don't go yet.

February 23, 1865

And fine day. The new is good. The armies from all quarters is doing well. I answered Mothers letter today & have got our cabin so near done that we can live comfortable in nothing more to do except put up the door & that we will do sometime when we get other matters arranged that are more necessary. We have a rubber blanket up for a door which answers verry well.

February 24, 1865

And cloudy & sprinkles of rain once & a while. We are ready for a good roof, warm & cooky. The official telegram of the capture of Wilmington N.C. was read today to us but as usual our Regt didnt cheer but all around us they was howling. I wrote a letter to Lu today in answer to one I received near two weeks since.

All of our Co. have got into their quarters & we have cleaned up our street & we begin to feel quite at home.

February 25, 1865

Stormy day. We are ordered out in line at 9 A.M. Break rank after stacking arms and go to our quarters there to await the tap of the [drum] for to fall in to go out on Review Corps Review. But the storm continued & the order was countermanded & we stay in cabins most of the day. I write & study my arithmetic &c. I got a letter from Florence and answered one that I got day before from Lu. I got two papers from Mother today. The North Western Christian Advocate.

February 26, 1865

And misting rain in morning but afternoon fine. We have nothing of importance but good news of Shermans moving on & on all the time & Rebs falling back & so it goes. I wrote a letter to Henry today in answer to his which I read a little while since.

There is great rumors about the paymaster coming but he don't come as yet. I have not faith in the rumors, for he has often been reported to be coming but don't get here. I hope it is so to be sure & hope is all, but let Government keep the money if they will end the war.

We had dress parade this evening & orders was read for to be four hours drill evry day hereafter from 9 to 11 A.M. and from 2 to 4 P.M. & all the usual camp duties such as policing & the regular guard mounting &c.

I was going to wash some today but forgot it was Sunday. Then when I thought of it, as a matter of course, I didnt wash but spent the day reading testament, studying arithmetic, writing &c.

February 28, 1865

And rainy day all day. I was on fatigue today as Sergt of the detail. We were out in the woods getting out timber for Corderoy Road. Found bad timber & had a bad time generally. Got wet to skin & come home about 3 P.M. This is the last day of the month & the muster for pay come off today. Just dark & the paymaster has come, is at the Col's now.

March 1, 1865

And rather rainy and I got my pay today & collected some that was owing to me. They have paid up pretty well. I sent $10.00 to Mother in a letter & paid off my debts & been settling up generally.

I was called on by the Lieut to help him make out the Muster Rolls. Twas my turn to go on guard but the other sergt was sent. I guess he was not able to do him much help. I sent for a pair of Stripes & Chevrons to a firm in Harrisburg, Penn.

March 3, 1865

And stormy like day & do nothing today in the way of work. I write to N.Y. today for some certificates. I am going into the Pen Buisness again to try to make something. I sent $2.00, that will get 11 certificates. I have also sent to T. B. Peterson, Philadelphia for the U.S. Army Regulations.

The news in the papers is good. But there is a rumor in camp that Sherman & 10,000 of his has been captured but I don't believe it. There is a great many Deserters coming into the lines now. They average 125 daily in the Army of Potomac. Lieut got his furlough late last night & was off at just daylight this morning for home.

March 4, 1865

Rainy day. This is Inauguration Day. Lincoln & Johnson will be in office for 4 years. There is report that Sheridan has captured rebel general Early & his army.[240]

March 5, 1865

And a murk misty, cloudy day & nothing of importance. Our Rolls was a little wrong and the 1st Sergt called on me to help him right them which, as a matter of course, I did. I bought me a Patent pipe for which I gave $2.50 for it is a neat & good smoking one. I thought as I had not bought one for several years, I could afford it now.

I wrote for a copy of the Army Regulations today for which I sent $2.50. Don't know the price but am confident of its being enough. I am studying Arithmetic & tactics, reading the papers &c, keep doing something all the time.

I forgot to tell you about the late Promotions in the Co. Webster Cook & Thomas Blunt have been promoted to corporals & Corporal Morse promoted to Sergeant. The report of Shermans being captured is false.

March 6, 1865

And fine day & I am on guard. We have no guard mounting. We have 2 Post on the color line & one in front of the colonels quarters & they are all recruits so. So I and the Corporals have to teach them the duties of a guard which we find laborious for many of them cannot speak a word of English. The news is good & all is well. The Recruiting in the State of Wis is Brisk.

March 7, 1865

And fine day & I was relieved from guard at the usual hour. We have review today. Was reviewed by Generals Mead, Warren & Crawford. Our Division only was on this ground. The other divisions of the Corps had grounds other places to the left. It passed of verry well, was verry fatiguing for we had to wait a long time for the Gens. Tis currently reported our Regt is going on Provost duty at Corps Headquarters. Some say to Army Headquarters.

March 8, 1865

And stormy day, rain most of the day making the streets & roads a perfect slough of mud & water and altogather was a verry unpleasant day & do nothing of importance.

The news from Sheridan through the Papers is good. Say he has captured 1800 men & Early with them & drove the other pell mell. I got a letter from Philip Brother. He wanted to know of me where his brother Frank was. But I couldnt tell him. I have answered his letter. I am pleased to hear from the old boys & would be much so to hear from L. C. Parsons, Ex Sergt [Loren Parsons] for he is owing me some & promised to send it to me when he got his money changed. It has now been 6 months since then & I guess that he has not it now to send.

March 11, 1865

We have inspection this morning & not in verry good order & are to have Co inspections evry morning till we can come out better. This pleases me, I like to see disipline. I sent for a copy of the Army Regulations yesterday & sent $2.50.

March 12, 1865

And fine day. We have the inspection this morning & come out in better order. There is some of the men that would have to do better if I had command. I do dislike a dirty soldier when it can be helped & there is some that will get a blessing when I come to review their conduct. God forbid that I should get so debased as to use my time up gambling when I should be doing duty.

March 13, 1865

And fine day. We have inspection again today & in good order today. The Sergt comd'g Co does verry well. But he don't punish the delinquents & he should. He & I gets along well togather with the buisness of the company but I cant stand the other two. Bradburry [Nathan Bradbury] & [Albert] Morse & especially Bradburry for he is an Idiot and what is worse is a verry selfish man of the worst stamp.

We had 5 recruits come to our Co this evening & they are all Germans. We had to take 2 into our cabin as we had a floor. So it goes. Those that fix up comfortable have to be put on. There is one cabin with 3 noncoms in & they have the poorest one in the lot. They are Sergts Reamer [Raemer] & [Nathan] Bradbury & Corp [Cyrus] Alexander.[241] The 2 latter are my worst & I guess only enemies. God forbid that anything should happen them but they are sure of their reward.

March 14, 1865

And a fine day. I am sent out with the old men to chop logs for the recruits cabins for they must go on drill. Bradburry took command of them & heretofore they did not like him for they say he don't know anything about the drill. But he puts on more airs that a frenchman at dinner.

We get the order to be ready at 1 P.M. for review which we did & march over to Humphry Station on the R.R. About ½ distant where we find the 1st & 2nd Divisions preparing for review. & we got into shape too & after waiting 2 hours or so, Gen Warren & Lady with a number of his staff reviewed us. After which we marched in review & all passed off well & we returned home verry tired. Found rations ready to be given out & orders to hold ourselves in readiness to march. & get supper, draw rations &c. Verry tired. The review well paid me for going, twas a gay time. William Booth has just returned from furlough & the cabin is full of boys asking questions &c. And twas late ere we got to bed. He brought my watch back well repaired. It cost me $3.50 & I now have a good timepiece.

I & Jake got our pens we sent to New York for. The dozen cost us $20.00. I paid him $10.00 & I got the certificates I sent for & send the money for pens & watch chain. They certificates cost $2.00 & I now have sent $15.00. I have met with good success selling those I had so far.

March 15, 1865

And fine in after part of the Day but rainy in forepart. We done nothing in forenoon & Battallion drill in afternoon. I sent $50.00 by Express to Henry to give to Lu. I was intending to send more but have nothing to spare now. I spend nothing but for necessary expenses.

March 16, 1865

And fine day. Squad drill in forenoon. Sergt Morse drilled the recruits. I wrote a letter to Cornelia & one to Lu and in afternoon had Corps review at the same place as the last & it went off a good deal better. Tis said that Secretary Staunton & Gens Grant & Mead was there but we not being allowed to look sideways when passing the reviewing Officers so I couldnt see them.

We are still under marching orders. Drew two day rations in evening. Many of the Boys sent their overcoats home & some their blankets. But there was no order for them to. So I thought I would keep mine yet till the order comes for I like to be comfortable & not expose myself to the inclement weather which might cause me to be sick. I got 2 letters today , one from Lu & one from Jennie, the young lady Spright & the State Journal & we in our tent get a daily, mostly the New York Herald. The news is good. Sheridan played hob with the rebs & so is Sherman. Some part of the army under him has whipped the Rebs. I think it was Gen Cox's command.

March 17, 1865

And fine day. We have drill in forenoon. I drill the squad without arms & there was battallion Drill in afternoon. But as the last recruits drew their guns, I had to give them a lesson in the Manuel of arms. We expect to march evry day but we still occupy our shanties.

March 18, 1865

And fine day. I am on guard today. Have the regular guard mount done up in style & I had 2 corpls to help me & we had to run the guard according to Regulations & as I had a copy of them, I let the Corpls read them & instructed them all accordingly. & I had occasion to near the Col once in posting a guard & he took me to task & began to question me about the duties as mine & the Sentinels also & I answered all but one. He, I guess, soon satisfied himself for he didnt ask many for I happen to know. I answered Lus letter, also Cornelias. I felt quite sick tonight. The guard having to lay out there all night, which is a new feature in affairs. This being the first time & it goes tough to the Boys. I and the officer of the guard is the only ones that ever had such things to do. All the others are recruits.

March 20, 1865

And fine day. I am on fatigue or rather Police. The men that came off guard yesterday morning have to sweep the camp & carry off the dirt and Police the camp generally.

I got a letter from Mother today which I answered & sent her $5.00 more. I also got a letter from the Hon. Senator Young. He being an old acquaintance of mine & I am please to hear from him. He is well & in the Senate chamber helping to make laws to Govern us.

March 21, 1865

And fine day. Have Co drill both afternoon & forenoon & they were poor ones. The Sergt don't seem to have verry good command or he don't exercise his authority as he should.

There is great peace rumors going today & tis said on good authority that Old Jeff & Lee wants to meet Lincoln & Grant at City Point & that Grant sent for Lincoln immediately & they was to be there last night.

March 22, 1865

And fine day. We have Co drill in forenoon & Battallion drill in afternoon. News is good from Sherman & Sheridan, the latter having reached Whitehouse Landing on York River & will rest his command for a time till U.S. Grant finds him something else to do. Which I think will not be long. From appearances, I think we will not move verry soon for our Sutler has come back as also some others.

March 23, 1865

And fine day but verry windy. The hardest wind I seen in the last year. Tore the tents of a number of cabins but mine stood the storm well. The dust was awfull, almost putting the eyes out if one steped out. Taking it altogather, twas a verry stormy day.

The 2nd Corps was reviewed today & tis said Lincoln was there. If so, he may have come down to confer with Jeff & Lee. When he gets a good ready, there is great talk of peace by evrybody & I hope it will come. The Rebels are coming in as usual. There has 3 come in to our Brigade today, two brought their horses & the other had to leave his to keep from being captured by the chasers that were trying to catch them.

We had Inspection as usual this morning & Co. drill right after but no drill in afternoon. Twas too windy. I wrote a letter to Lu today & one to Hon. M. K. Young in answer to his verry kind & encouraging letter. I am happy to know I still have a friend in him. He used to befriend me when I was a mere Boy & evinces a readiness to still do so. He said if I had applied to him for the favor 3 week since, I could have got a commission.

March 25, 1865

And fine day. We got orders & did march at about 7 A.M. We had to go without breakfast. We went out to Army Headquarters, about 6 miles, for the Rebs broke through our lines at daylight & got nearly to the R.R. They took 2 of our forts & the works between & was just playing hob & our fellows come in their rear & gobbled up a lot of them. Some say 4,800 & we marched around on to a plain nearby & formed for review, was reviewed by President Lincoln & Gen's Grant & son & Mead & Warren &c and all the big ones. & after that we marched up to the right & towards Army Headquarters again & got some coffee & then they began to fight away to the left about 3 miles from here & we fell in & marched down to support them. When we got there & stacked arms, the order came for us to go to camp & twas just dark & we took a straight road for it which we reach about 9 P.M. all tired out.

Just as we started back, some 200 Reb Prisnors came by & now evrything seem to have settled down to the usual quiet.[242]

March 26, 1865

And we had orders at 5 A.M. to get up & be ready to march at a moments notice which we done. & soon after daylight we formed on the Parade ground & stacked arms & come to our quarters & keep in readiness to march at the tap of the Drum. We lay so all day & at night ordered to make ourselves comfortable & to go to bed which we done. There has not been much firing today but tis rumored that the Rebs massed in front of the 2nd Corps today & consequently stoped our fellows from charging as was intended today.

March 28, 1865

And fine day. Have inspection by the Brigade Commander. Just at night we have orders to be ready to march at 4 in the morning. So we drew rations & went to bed.

March 29, 1865

And fine day. Was awoke at 4 A.M. & got ready to march at 5 ½ oclock & we did start going towards the left, marching on pretty brisk. Had the order of march read to us while resting at time. Marched on till near night when the head of the column run against the Rebs & brought us to a halt but the 1st Div soon cleaned them out. & we went out to the Boydton Plank Road & our Regt was sent out to help the 147th N.Y. guard the road. But were relieved after building work & getting supper went back a ways & camp for the night, it being 11 P.M. & raining some.[243]

March 30, 1865

And rain all day & just at night our Regt sent out on picket. Still raining, evry ravine is flooded. Get picket line formed dark comes. Hear fighting away off to the left, our cavelry, I guess.

March 31, 1865

And still raining. About 9 A.M. we are drawn in & join the Brigade as they come along going towards the left. After going a mile or so we stop & rest. About hour, skirmishing begins in our front & our Regt is ordered out double quick & advance. We come on to the enemy and fighting begins & great confusion too. The Recruits are wild with a few exceptions. Soon all are running & the reb hurling in the lead & we retreat across the creek in great confusion, some going the way we came & others wading & swimming. But I watched & found a shallow place, got over with wading.[244]

[Ed. Note: Unfortunately, Ray's entries for April are missing because he was acting as an orderly and with the army on the move, he had little or no time to write. See Appendix B, which contains Colonel Kellogg's official report of the activities of the brigade during this period, as well as Colonel Tarbell's report for the actions of the 91st New York Infantry, which was brigaded with the Seventh Wisconsin. Its experiences were very similar to those of the Seventh.

After the sharp fight at the White Oak Road, Ray's brigade participated in the action at Five Forks, which broke through the far right anchoring position of Lee's lines. That event triggered the Confederate retreat from Petersburg and Richmond, ending the long and bloody siege. The Army of the Potomac followed Lee west and trapped his men at Appomattox Court House, where Lee surrendered the Army of Northern Virginia on April 9, 1865. President Lincoln was assassinated three days later on April 12, 1865 in Washington, D.C., while watching a play at Ford's Theater.]

May 1, 1865

And fine day. & we were awoke early to get up & get Breakfast & be ready to March at 1 A.M. And at that hour the rest of the Brigade came up the road & we fell in & marched about 2 miles & stoped about 3 hours & got coffee. When we started again & marched about 6 miles to Wilson Station & camped, the sun about an hour high.

Well I have lost one month. I have been unable to keep the book posted up as I have been acting orderly since the first of April. The Sergt (Reamer) [Raemer] was killed on the 31st of March, that was acting orderly. But there is several of the Boys that have kept their Dairy up & I shall have to get them to copy it for me.

May 2, 1865

And up early & fine day. We march at 6 A.M. & marched pretty fast. Rested about evry hour for about 10 to 15 minutes & we stoped and got coffee abut noon & marched till sundown & camped within 6 miles of Petersburg for the night. Today we marched parellel with the RR.

May 3, 1865

And fine day. And we marched at 7 A.M. to within 1 mile of the city where we rested a while. Started again marching by company in line & so we marched through Petersburg along the principle streets & marched to within 6 miles of Richmond. We have had good roads all the time. But the Pike between these two cities is splendid. We camped for the night.

May 4, 1865

And fine day. Up and march at ½ after 6 A.M. & march to the city of Manchester right opposite Richmond & camped & draw rations. They say we stay till tomorrow.

May 5, 1865

And fine day & we got ready to march & some started. But the order was countermanded & we went into camp & stayed all day & some few got passes to go to Richmond. They were all officers. Shermans Army is coming up this way to Washington & we are bound for the same place & I guess will be mustered out.[245]

May 6, 1865

And fine day. We march at 8 A.M. after drawing clothing. We marched through Richmond the same way as Petersburg. Went by Libby Prison & Castle Thunder & many places of note.[246]

May 8, 1865

And fine day & the same as yesterday. Today we reach Bowling Green, a small town on the Railroad. We are now within 20 miles of Fredericksburg. I got a pass today & fell out, not being able to keep up, but came up in the evening.

May 9, 1865

And fine day & marched at usual hour. I got a pass today & took my time. I got my knapsack hauled in the ambulance but couldnt get a ride myself for they were so full. We reach Rappahannock River just below Fredericsburg & cross it & the ambulances go into park just at dark near the river. I was not able to go up to the Regt tonight so remained with the Ambulances & slept under one. We made a long march today & done it well. But it wore me out as I am sickly now. Cant eat much & feel weak. The nurses came around about 9 P.M. with tea & farina which I relished highly.

May 10, 1865

And fine day. & march as usual. But I couldnt get a new pass today as I was not up to the Doctors at the Regt & I couldnt ride today. But still get my things hauled. I feel some better today. We make a good march today & the ambulances park near the Regt tonight & I get to the Regt to stay all night.

May 11, 1865

And fine day. & march as usual. I get a pass today & get my things carried again. But have to march. We get along fine today till about 5 P.M. when we have the hardest thundershower I ever saw. The lightening struck a man & 3 horses not far from me & killed the man & one horse & hurt the others verry bad. The rain continued & the trains was delayed crossing the Ocauocon [Occoquan] Creek & I got so far ahead & got dark & I lost the road as I thought & the teams getting stuck all along & the ambulances don't come up & I am wet through to the skin. All my things being in the ambulance, in this condition I make for a fire & when I get there, find a house near & get Permission from the man to go in. Found the house pretty full but found room & got to the stove & got some coffee from a stranger. Made a cup of coffee & set by the stove all night. We are now about 6 miles from Fairfax courthouse. 22 miles from Alexandria.

May 12, 1865

And fine day after the hard storm of last night. I got breakfast at the house this morning & a good one too, for which I paid fifty cents & then started. Got as far as the Barn. Found 3 or 4 of our Regt there & among them the Sergt Major. & we started, overtook the Brigade at Fairfax Station but didnt join it & kept wagging on as best we could. Got to the courthouse & there I got a can of oysters for $1.00. & as the Brigade was resting, we made dinner of the oysters & a good dinner, too, was it. & started on coming slowly & resting evry little while & about sundown came up with the Regt in camp near Balls Cross Road about 2 miles from Acquaduct Bridge.

We are now about 5 miles from Washington in a nice camp. I feel a great deal better today but have got something like the piles coming on me.

May 13, 1865

And fine day. We lay in camp all day & the sutler comes up. Many rumors & among them one that we are to have no review but go home as soon as we can get transportation. Plenty of pedlars, can buy most anything.

May 14, 1865

And fine day & tis Sunday & we have Preaching & we were ordered to clean up, for it was expected that the Govenor would be over to see us. Rumors again that we are to march to Baltimore & there get transportation.

May 15, 1865

And fine day. Are ordered up at 4 A.M., be ready to march at 6 A.M. But we only moved camp about ¼ of a mile & got a verry pleasant camp & tis said we are to stay here till we go home. The Govenor has not come yet. But is coming. I wrote a letter to Lu today in answer to 2 I got sometime since.

May 16, 1865

And fine day. The Govenor came today & made us a Speech. He has a fine appearance & spoke well & encouraging. Said we would be home soon he thought. But we couldnt go just yet. He didnt stay long.

May 17, 1865

And fine day & we have a close inspection. Tis monthly Inspection. We have fine time here. Nothing to do & plenty to eat & can buy most anything. But money is scarce now, verry. We thought we would move today. But I guess we will stay here now.

May 20, 1865

And Sunshine & rain today alternately. Co drill in forenoon only. I was on fatigue detail today with a squad of 20 men. In the evening, Secretary [Lucius] Fairchild called on the Col & the Regt was turned to receive him & he in turn made a little appropriate speech, though much to the point.

May 21, 1865

And fine day and Battallion drill in afternoon & I was absent from it unintentionally. I went down to the creek to wash & when I came back they were at it. We were called out in evening to fix for review. By making 5 companies out of the Regt so as to just fill the streets on the Review on day after tomorrow. But there being so many men absent that we couldnt do it. This being Sunday the Chaplain gave us a short discourse.

May 22, 1865

And a little rainy out but not much. So we were formed again this morning & fixed the Regt into 5 companies & drill Co. drill so to prepare us to march in review tomorrow & in the afternoon we drill Battallion drill preparatory for the review.

We have had no soft Bread for a day or two & the Boys are grumbling some. We have had soft Bread for a few days & so it goes hard to eat hard bread now.

Evening & we are formed again & inspected to see if we come out in good order which we did & were dismissed with orders that reville would be at 3 A.M. & we be ready to march at 4 A.M.

May 23, 1865 [Grand Review in Washington, D. C.]

Did so but didnt march till after 5 A.M. when we marched to the city by way of long Bridge up through the city. Formed ready for review, stacked arms & rested till further orders which was about 3 hours coming. & then we fell in & marched in review. We marched by the front some two miles when we came near the Acqueduct Bridge at George town. There came on to the Pontoon bridge by the flank & crossed & after crossing rested a while & then up & on. Come to camp about 3 miles from the Bridge, reached camp about 4 P.M. The streets & evry available place to see was crowded with Spectators & prominent among them was the President & cabinet & the heads of all the different departments & Bureaus & all the Foreign Ministers & Consuls &c. There were boxes fixed so as all the Officials could have seats where they could [see] all with ease.

The whole thing went off quietly & without a blunder. The Cavelry went through first, then our Corps & then the 2nd Corps & lastly the 9th Corps. The Pioneers & Pontoonices with all their kit were along & laid the Bridge early in the morning, making a complete review of all things pertaining to the Army &c. Shermans army is to go through the same Routine tomorrow, the 24th. Today was a grand affair. I wish I had time & space to comment on it.

May 24, 1865 [Grand Review of Sherman's Army]

And fine day. At roll call the Major called us into line & said the General was much pleased with the actions of this Regt yesterday & he would pass all over the Bridge to the city that wanted to go & that we were to get ready about 7 A.M. & be in good order. & we were ready at the time & went & the General with us & he took us up on to the Avenue & told us to break rank & go where we please & report at the Bridge at 6 P.M. so as we could get over before 7 P.M. I started with several of the Boys to see the Passing colums of the 15 Corps which just began to pass. But soon lost them in the densely packed crowd & didnt see but 2 or 3 of the Co. all day. After loitering around till tired & hungry, I sought an oyster saloon which I soon found on a corner. Went in & ordered a Peck of steamed oysters which were delicious. After which I took a stroll up street towards the Capital & in due time with hard labor I made my way to it. & entered the magnificent building & traveled in it for a couple of hours. & being weary besides feeling unwell, I came out & down on to the street. Got on street cars, start for Georgetown opposite the Bridge some 1 ½ [miles] distant which cost 6 cents.

Shermans Army marched & went through the evolutions just as well as we did. The Corps was much larger than ours, mostly four Divisions, yellow flag represents the 4th Division. The flag of the 15th Corps is verry remarkable one. The badge on it is the catdridge box & the two words written in a circle over it, forty rounds. It called forth many remarks from the dense crowd. All day long they could be clapping of hands, cheering heard. About 4 P.M. the column ceased to pass for all had gone passed & the crowd began to disperse.

I now turn my face towards the Capitol to go & view it awhile. I wend my way up through the crowd. At last I reach the foot of the hill the Capital is situated upon. I pause to rest for I am verry much fatigued from standing all day. After a pause of a few minutes I climb the steep ascent & enter the capitol from the north & wandered in it an hour or two & seeing too many different thing of Beauty to Describe or even name them here. Twas a grand sight & among the grandest were the Pictures. The Building is Magnificent but not entirely finished. But workmen are at work all the time on it. I want about a week to explore it to my satisfaction. It is all built of large blocks of Marble. Tis splendid. Tired, I sit down on the steps at north entrance to rest a few minutes then to go down on to the street & take the street cars for the Bridge which is reached in due course of time, but with having to wait often for the streets to get clear. At last reach the Bridge, tired & almost sick. Come on across without hinderance & feeling sick, I am a long time getting to Camp having to rest often. Reach camp & sick enough too. Rather like the Billious fever.

May 28, 1865

And fine day. Had inspection in forenoon. Had preaching at 6 P.M. by the chaplain from Massachusetts, he being on a visit to the Army & gave our chaplain a call. Preached a good Sermon, great rumors about going home but nobody knows when.

May 29, 1865

And fine day. I am on guard today as Sergt of the Guard. Have the regular guard mounting, putting on style now & we do it too. Evrything about the camps goes on nicely except there is a good deal of whiskey drank & our Captain, I am sorry to say, does his full share of it.

May 30, 1865

And fine day & I am relieved at the usual hour 9 A.M. and feel quite sick too & get worse through the day. I have a hard fever from 10 A.M. till 5 P.M. when the fever leaves me & I feel better. I sent for the Doctor once but he was not there & but come about 5 P.M.

May 31, 1865

And fine day. And feel some fever today but not so much. I am getting better of it. I am excused from duty. They had dress parade. The men in the regt whose term of service expires prior to the 1st of October (there is 4 drafted men in our Co among them) have went up to be mustered out of the service.

Great rumors concerning going home & all's on tip-toe & excitement all the time. Many betting that we will go by the 9th of June.

The Presidents Proclamation is published today concerning the Rebels. In fact is an amnesty Proclamation to include such & such & so & so &c &c &c. I got a letter from Mother & Sarah today.

June 1, 1865

And fine day. I feel pretty well today. But have to take medicine yet. I am excused from duty. I wrote a letter to Lu today. Sergt [Bruce] Bryan[247] has got a furlough of ten days to go to Philadelphia & started this morning. Many rumors about going home but no orders to go yet. The troop feel gay. They have torchlight processions & many such things that can be made with candles or powder. They are verry noisy till midnight evry night. All expects to go home first.

June 2, 1865

I feel a good deal better today. Dress parade & guard mounting is all the moves that are made, no drill. Troops going home all the time. Those that were mustered out of our Co & Regt are awaiting transportation to go home. I wrote a letter to Mother today, also one to Sarah. Mother is verry anxious to have me come home. Gen. [Henry] Morrow took the Brigade out today & made them a speech. Told them what to do & told them to behave themselves as well when citizens as when Soldiers &c.

June 4, 1865

Nothing unusual today. Many rumors about going this & that place &c. Nothing definite. Troops going home evry day by thousands. I commenced a good job today. It is taking the Military history of evry man in the Company or that ever was in the Company & what became of him &c. Sergt Bryan has returned from his furlough. He has been no farther than Washington. And all he got the furlough for was to get his pay. He had to try twice for the furlough & had to or did lie the biggest kind. Lied as I wouldnt have done for forty. Such men always get their reward in due season.

June 5, 1865

And fine day & the Order has come at last to send us to Louisville, Ky to report to Gen Logan [Union General John A. Logan] & we expect to go in a week or so. And what we will then do is hard to tell. Some say we are to be mustered out there & others say we & a lot more Wis Regts are to be consolidated & many such rumors.

June 6, 1865

A fine day & I am quite sick again. Had a verry bad diarhear last night & it holds on today. I am excused today by the Doctor. Feel verry poorly.

June 7, 1865

And fine day & the same as yesterday except that those men that were mustered out have gone home. The extra duty men are being returned to the Regt & everything is be made ready for the move for we are to go to Louisville beyond Preadventure.

June 8, 1865

And rainy some today. I feel a great deal better today. I finish my history of the Co today. That is what the Discriptive Book says about each man. It was considerable of a job.

June 9, 1865

And fine day & nothing done not even dress parade. I wrote a letter to Mother today. We are going to loose some more of the Regt for there has an order come to discharge all men that have been in confederate Prisons & that will take some 60 or 70 men in our Regt. I feel better today again & think I will get along now.

June 10, 1865

And rainy day. Showry, nothing new transpires today except the Order putting off the time of our starting till the latter part of next week. Oh yes, we drew a lot of Sanitary clothing today. I got none of it for there was too many that had more brass in their face for begging than I & some got a complete new suit, that is drawers, shirts, socks & Suspenders. & in the evening drew a fine large mess of cucumber pickles & some potatoes all from the Sanitary Co.

I forgot to tell you there is only 2 of us tenting togather that is myself & B. Haydin [Benjamin Hayden]. The other two put them up a tent & I was verry glad too for one of them, Sergt Bryan is such a profane & immoral man. I dislike to tent with him. He is acting Orderly still & I guess will be promoted to it soon as the Orderly is discharged. & he may have it too for I wouldnt have the truble for the extra $4.00 a months & I am not fit for an Orderly in this company for I am just the contrary in disposition to most of them, for they are profane Gamblers, that is the officers & most of the noncommission'd too & I am the reverse.

June 11, 1865

And fine day. We have the Sunday morning inspection at the usual hour, 11 A.M. and we are ordered out on parade ground without arms to hear preaching from the Massachusetts chaplain. The same one that preached 2 week since. The boys or most of them were vexed at having to go out so, & they wouldnt sing so he had to do it all. Which made it rather dry. But he gave us a good sermon & many that were vexed were not sorry for attending. I tell you, it is no use to try to conceal the fact hat this Regt is verry wicked, yea debased. I am sorry to have to chronicle it so but truth must come. There would have been a verry small congregation if they hadnt been ordered out. I must give the colonel credit for so doing & hope he will continue so to do. I wrote a letter to Mother today & told her to be patient about me coming home. For I now thought I would not be home before the 4th of July and perhaps not then. I hav'nt so high hopes of coming home at so early a day & at one time. I got a State Journal today. It is a welcome visitor now when I have time to peruse it.

June 12, 1865

And fine day & nothing of importance transpires. Have the regular guard mounting & dress parade style but no work. The 6th Corps has been behaving themselves bad this last day or two. They have been rallying on evrything that is eatable in the sutler shops &c and now we have to have a patrol day & night to protect our Division Sutlers & commissaries &c. I have not heard of our corps taking part in any such buisness. We, the corps, is verry orderly. There is rumors now that Logans men or some of his veterans have mutinied & burnt part of Louisville & that he telegraphed to the War Dept that he didnt want them to send anymore Veterans there. But this I think is all Bash. I hope we will go.

June 13, 1865

And Showery most of the day but cleared off late in the evening. Nothing done today, all's quiet. Many vague rumors afloat. 700 of the 91st N.Y. H. Art. started home this morning. They came under the last order for mustering out troops, they belonged to Brigade but do not now they having been consolidated with the 147th N.Y., that is the Veterans of both Regts. Have wrote a letter to Minnie Lander in answer to one I received some 2 months since. I received a letter from Lu today bringing the good news of her doing well &c. And I received a neat Pocket Diary from Lu also, this I sent for to have it here by the time this one was full. I have guessed it exceedingly well.

June 14, 1865

And Showery today & nothing transpired today. Those men that were to be discharged have not been. The Order has been countermanded much to their Chagrin. I would of been happy indeed to see them go for I think it is due them considering how they have suffered while in Prison. There is another rumor that we are going to start on Friday next, but no one knows where to, some say to the state & some say to Louisville. Let that be as it may, I would be glad to start to some place. I want to get home so as to start in some kind of buisness & be at home where I can live better & enjoy myself better. There is no place like home, let it be ever so humble. I know my Dear Mother would be as happy as myself to have me at home.

[*Ed. Note*: The following Florence Percy poem, "EMPTY-HANDED," was clipped from a newspaper and placed in the pocket at back of diary.]

> Sitting here with forehead bowed,
> Feeling but my heart's dull aching,

I can hear the fierce and loud
Tumult of the jostling crowd
Following—never overtaking—
Hear the thousand hurrying feet,
With their restless beat and beat—
Life's strong surges, rolling, breaking
Over many a storm-wrecked fleet,
Many a hope that knows no waking.
All my voyaging is o'er,
All my fair ships wrecked or stranded,
And I wait upon the shore,
Empty-handed.

Far a way a river laves
 Mossy rocks with tender sighing,
And a patient pine-tree waves
O'er two unforgotten graves;
 Toward the spot where thou art lying,
Oh, my love, my life's lost saint,
With a wordless, wild complaint
It is my soul forever crying!
Oh, my child! my heart grows faint
Calling thee, with grief undying!
Love, and faith, and hope are flown—
All my spirits need demanded,
And I sit here all alone,
Empty-handed

Volume 15

June 15, 1865 to July 16, 1865

[*Discharged July 13, 1865*]

Home and
a Mother's Kiss

Sergt William R Ray
Co. F, 7th Regt, WisVet Vol. Inft
A Resident of Cassville, Grant Co Wisconsin
Enlisted August 19th / 61
Reenlisted Dec 28th /63

Was wounded at Gainesville, Va, Aug 28 /62
and at Gettysburg, Penn July 1st /63 and at Wilderness, Va, May 5th /64

In Camp on Arlington Heights Va

June 15, 1865

And fine Day & we lay in camp today & late in the evening we draw enough rations to make up 8 day & be ready to march at 4 A.M. in the morning. We were called and after Tattoo & formed line to let Lieut Steward [James Stewart], commandant of Battery B, 4th US Regular Artillery propose Enlisting into the Battery to us. But I think he didnt get 1 recruit for the Battery & here the Col told us we start for the west in the morning. March to Washington & there take the cars. I & another man from another tent get the big kettle & boil all our meat togather.

June 16, 1865

And fine day. & we march at 5 A.M. & go to Washington where we find the cars ready & some of the Brigade loading on. There is 10 Regts in the Brigade and five Different states Viz. Wisconsin, Indiana, Michigan, Ohio & Minnesota & a good deal of speculation as to where we go. Some say we will go right on through & not turn off at the relay house on to the Baltimore & Ohio R.R. which will take us west. At 11 A.M. we get aboard the cars & start, being the last train out except the Baggage train which we left behind. When we get to Relay house we turn on the Baltimore & Ohio R.R. & come on through a hilly & mountainous country. The road running up a good mill stream which is well used for Manufacturing Purposes. Dark comes on & I & Ben fix for sleep. We are on top of a box car, a verry good place & lay down.

June 17, 1865

A fine morning. Just daybreak & still among hills & by the side of the Potomac River. About sunrise we come to Harpers Ferry. Here we see the Shanandok [Shenandoah] which makes a confluence with the Potomac and right between the two, on the point is the Village of perhaps a 100 inhabitants & many burned buildings & debris of all sorts. Most all the Government property is a pile of ruins.

We follow up the Potomac a ways then turn of into the country leaving the river to the right. But strike it again in an hour or 2 & follow on all day. Road verry crooked & through many deep cuts & most of the way the hills & bluffs have been cut down to make road. On the opposite side of the river is the Chespeak & Ohio canal which is in use. There is a great contrast between the speed of the canal boats & the train. All the way we find no towns of importance except Martinsburg, Va & Cumberland, M.D. Here we were furnished good coffee by the sanitary Com. When we go on, stopping & different watering stations & passing most of the other small stations with out stopping. They are numerous but no buisness at most of them. Poor farming country. But splendid water powers all along the rivers & creeks. We go slow all the time waiting on switches for as high as 10 trains to pass us sometimes.

The road is a good one. Near night we have to wait a long time for there has a train run off the track ahead of us. We being near the river, many of the boys go in swimming. At last we start, run slow and Ben & I got to bed again same as last night.

June 18, 1865

Awake to see a fine morning & along the river still & Big Mountains. River getting small, getting pretty well up to the head of river. . . . Worn out with fatigue I lie down & cover up for tis cold enough for 2 blankets.

June 19, 1865

Awake this morning to find us going down the mountain. Pretty well down, quite large streams & more improvements along the road & the towns look neater & Brisker. Through some 23 Tunnels today. Many Bridges and get along fine.

June 20, 1865

We lay around camp till noon when we get dinner & right away the order comes to fall in which we do & march through the town to the Boats & get aboard without delay & start of down the Majestic Ohio. Boat not crowded, things O.K. Parkersburg is a dirty place but apparently a Buisness place. Not more than 2000 Inhabitants I should think. I watch & gaze on the hills, fields, meadows &c with delight.

June 22, 1865

And fine day. All is well & we see more towns, stopping at none till we come to the city of Cincinnati. Here we stop & the Col vouched for our good conduct to the Gen & allowed us to go into the city free. The Boat would stay 15 minutes & perhaps ½ hour & it stayed the latter. & we started on down the river, not land again till we get to Louisville. All the Boys but one or two come on Board, none left of our Co. Some companies left. But 3 noncommissioned of our camp, the Orderly Sergt & another sergt & Corpl., but they got on the next boat & come on.

June 23, 1865

Awoke this morning to find us still going & within 10 miles of Louisville. Soon reach it & land & go ashore & are marched into a street in the shade to await the other troops coming ashore & some that have not arrived. Here we lay till noon & then ordered to the other side of the river to go into camp & some go out to the boats they came off but we go up to the ferry Boat & go aboard and cross to the town opposite to the city (Jeffersonville I believe). Here we go ashore & march up the river from the town 2 miles & go into camp on the Bank of the river, a verry nice Place for a camp. & as soon as the arms is stacked, the boys break for the river & are soon Bathing. But I didnt indulge for I was too warm & the march from town almost played me out. Twas so warm & my head is so easily hurt by the heat & it is getting worse. I am getting almost afraid of the sun as I was of Rebel Bullets and it was one of them that causes me the pain when my Blood gets warmed up a little. By Breaking my skull.

June 24, 1865

And fine day. We lay in camp & do nothing. But there is a pretty heavy detail from the Regt for guards. We have a camp guard & a Patrol to patrol the road to & in the town for the, or some of the, Boys don't behave well, but on the contrary, verry bad & molest the folks so they call for protection. The Col said he would not have a guard if they behaved themselves well. But as they wouldnt, why he wasnt to blame for having a guard around camp. I went up to the Doctors call this morning & got excused for time to come or rather till further orders. I am not able to do much this warm weather, the sun hurts my head so.

June 25, 1865

And fine day, once & awhile there a shower passes around us but no rain for us, weather warm. There is camp guard still but it is lighter than usual. There has been considerable excitement up today in the Regt about going to Arkansas. There is 4 Regts to go out of [Henry] Morrows Command & our, or most of our, officers want to go. But the rank & file don't & there was some loud & harsh talk about it. Two thirds of our co says they wont go if they pay them first & if they don't pay them till they [are] down there, then they will leave & most of the noncoms in our Co as well as the other Co say they wont stay. Some of the officers was around talking but the Boys just told them right to their face that they wouldnt go. I never said I would not go. But I don't want to go & don't know as I will. I put in for a furlough today to go home & am going if I can get my pay. I want to be there by the 4th of July.

June 27, 1865

And fine morning. The Col called us out last evening & told us that he had exhausted the last effort to get us out of the service & now he was going to resign & go home but would have rather gone with us, if we could have gone. He talked to us verry feelingly.

June 28, 1865

And fine Day. My furlough came last night approved for 25 days & I started with 3 others of the Co for the city of Louisville to get our Pay if we could & if we couldnt we were not going. But one of them did go. He borrowed some money. But we couldnt get our pay as our Payrolls had not come to this department yet & were not likely to so as we could get pay. For we are not to be paid off till we are mustered out so the paymaster Gen said. So that is some assurance that they calculate to send us soon to our homes. God grant it may be so. So when I found that out, I turned my steps homeward which I reached about 1 P.M. verry much fatigued from the effect of the heat on my head. We hold furloughs & cant use them which is a rough joke on us. I studied on it whether to go out in the country a few miles & hire out for a few days or not but concluded not as I cant stand the heat. The farmers are paying from 1 ½ to 3.00 a day for hands, the latter for Binders & the first price for hoeing. Good wages but cant go the work. So to draw rations, I must report for duty, which I did with reluctance for I calculated on seeing home & friends on the 4th of July.

June 29, 1865

And fine day with a shower in the evening. The order that there has been so much talk about for the last few days came at last about 1 P.M. The order came to muster the 7th Wis out of service & report to the state & there be paid off & receive our Discharges. & the Col, after reading the order, made a few timely remarks. & amongst the rest said he wanted none of this drunkenness, he wanted to go home better than they came down here from their Veteran furlough. He would tie up the man that got disorderly, let him be private or officer to which the Boys say bully. He advised them to brush up & get shaved & hair cut &c &c. Go home like men. At the end of his speech we gave three cheers & the Boys kept yelling & playing for an hour or two. I gave three rousing cheers. The Boys all feel well. The Col said he would make an effort to get to the state by the 4th of July. We are waiting on the muster out rolls now & I suppose we will work night & day.

June 30, 1865

And fine day. & we are hard at work making out the Musterer out Rolls & I worked most of last night on them. The Col says we can be in Milwaukee by the 4th of July if we get in the Rolls by tomorrow night & we are doing our best at them. But some of the Officers don't care much about going so soon & our Captain is one of them. I do believe he would keep us in the service as long as he wanted to stay if it were in his power to do so, even to the end of the term of enlistment. & he is about half drunk now & he well knows that he cant earn his living as easy at home & don't seem to care much about us anymore. Such men get their reward in due season.

Myself, Corp Alexander & Private Morse, Best Pensmen in the Co, are putting the thing through about as fast as can be done. But Cap seems to try to delay us with his mistakes & other trifling matters.

July 1, 1865

And arose early & ready to work on Rolls but Cap is still sluggish. Wait on him. Get to work at last & do a hard days work but with some mistakes being made. We have to do some over and I am quite unwell today so upon the whole don't feel in the best of humor. & just at dark when getting my supper, just about to give up working at it for this day, Cap comes and wishes me to make out the discharges for the Co. & he has set a lot of men fixing up a place in a roomy tent for me to write on & is going to furnish candles & I am to have Corpl Hayden to help me by reading of the Discription of the men from the Discriptive Book. Well, we go at it & have 49 of those papers to make out tonight. Fix for a nights work & all are ready to help me & all I asked them to do was to bring a canteen of cold water & then for all to leave the tent. That was all the help I wanted of them which they done. But some were verry anxious about having theirs made out first.

July 2, 1865

And fine morning But didnt awake till sun an hour high. Worked at Discharges till Break of Day & got them finished & then went to bed tired most to death. Didnt have a good nights rest as you may imagine. All is to be ready by 9 A.M. to muster out & was ready. Mustered out & all the things belonging to U.S. turned in by Noon. We are to start at 2 P.M. for home. That hour there is a great shaking of hands with acquaintences in the 6 Regt [Sixth Wisconsin] who have come over to see us. We fall in, form line & the Col makes us a speech & telling to be good soldiers &c and reiterating what he said the other day about Drunkenness. Says he will enforce it. We start with light hearts saying we are citizens which we are in reality, although we don't get our Discharge till we get to the state and are paid of. Get on to the main road leading to town. There we find the Division drawn up on each side of the road to give us our last farewell honors & which they done in good style cheering us lustily as we passed. We reach town & depot & take the cars, box cars but have seats in. This being Sunday, there is no trains running except Soldiers so we don't stop much. Reach Indianapolis about midnight. Run pretty fast & over a rough road. I have been quite unwell today. Have the Dierhea quite bad & nothing but hard tack & pork to eat & water for drink & poor quality. Cars not stopping, we couldnt get fresh water.

July 3, 1865

A fine day. We reach Chicago about 11 P.M. & after marching around some on one street & another we find the Soldiers rest. But can get no coffee & we lay down outside for the night - bivauck along the walk between the two buildings. The walk would hold our Regt. We are to go out on the 9 A.M. train for Milwaukee.

July 4, 1865

And we are up early but have to wait till 8 A.M. before we get Breakfast when we march down & get on the train & we go to Milwaukee at a good speed. But it was 11 A.M. ere we got off. We reach Milwaukee about 3 P.M. when we are marched down to near the Fair Building & stacked arms in the street & rested for an hour or so. When we were marched into the dining hall of the Fair Building & partook of a excellent dinner, having the ladies to wait upon us & they were verry nice, young ladies too, exceedingly sociable. & after dinner a number of welcoming speeches from different prominent men of the place, also one from Gen Catter[Cutler] & another from [Charles] Hamilton (formerly our Lieut Colonel but resigned some time since). After which our Major thanked the People of Milwaukee for their generosity in giving us so good a dinner. After which we were invited to step into the fair where we could go free into every department. & here I wandered & looked & wondered &c till I got tired & went out on to the street to walk around town some. & when I returned, the most of the Regt had taken Arms & gone down to the depot where we were to stop for the night. We had freedom same as a citizen, to go & come as we pleased. The citizens show us evry respect in their power. I feeling quite unwell today, I stoped in the depot & went to bed early. I was abused this evening by the Orderly (Bruce Bryan). He detailed me to go on guard & I told him I were not able to do duty & says he, God damn you, what ails you, to which I never made an answer & he went & detailed some one else, one of the Corpls to act as sergt on that occasion. This is the first time was ever abused by any orderly, sergt or anyone else for not doing duty & he had no provocation to do so. The Soldiers Fair is certainly a grand affair & it is for a grand purpose. Tis for raising money to build & endow a home for the lame soldiers of the State. I hope it may prove a complete success.

Oh, but I must tell you about what transpired after we come down to the depot. Col Hamilton treated the Regt to 2 kegs of Beer & now at this time (dark) there is quite a number drunk. What a pity to see some of those otherwise fine young men make a Beast of themselves. Not a drop would I taste.

July 5, 1865

And fine day. We reached Madison about 4 P.M. & here I found 3 of my Nieces & one Nephew on the train that was ready to start to the west. They had been up here on an excursion & are just ready to return. & I find them well & hear from them that the folks at home are well. They live only 25 miles west from here at a town called Mazomania.

We get supper about 6 P.M. after which we march up to the Capital Park, going around 3 sides of it ere we enter & all the while we are marching, there is a Brass piece being fired as rapidly as possible. Over the Gate [by] which we enter the Park is stretched a wide piece of cloth & the inscription (Boys, we welcome you home) painted on it in large letters. We formed in column in close order & the Govenor & Executive Department made its appearance on the stand, which after Col [Hollon] Richardson introduced, we welcomed with clapping of hands &c. & the Govenor proceed to speak & welcomes to our State &c, and all the Executive Dept followed with the exception of (Gen) (now) Secretary [Lucius] Fairchilds, he not being present. & the Mayor of the city not being able to attend on account of Illness, sent a Representative & a verry good one too. Made us a good speech & last of all, Col Richardson rises & makes a good & humorous speech. I think the best speaker on the stand. He thanked them for giving us such a welcome & and upon the whole made a right good speech. Says he, all welcome us Boys, the Loyal & the Copperhead welcome us. But why do the latter welcome us. Because we have quit fighting their friends (Loud Laughter & hurrahs) & they frequently cheer him.

I felt real Bad when we left the Depot but by the time the reception was over, I was well pleased. For evry dept of the state was represented & each one in his speech gave some interesting statistics & especially the Treasurers was, for it is him that knows about our Pay. Truly I feel as though I had done a great work in going to war.

Surely we, the Army, has saved the nation & the citizens say so & they seem to feel so. They act nobly by us, Soldiers are first-class.

Well, all over & we march out of the Park & take the shortest route for Camp Randall, which I find considerably improved & a great deal larger, good Barrack up. Before assigning us to our quarters he (the Col) told us we must behave ourselves & he would put no restricktions upon us & that we had liberty to go where we pleased. But not to home & on the morrow he would give those passes that lived near here if the Paymaster didnt pay us for a few days. We will know tomorrow when we do just get pay. Hope soon for we want to go to our homes. Well Co K & our Co take a Barrack & we find them roomy & well finished but too warm. I soon go to bed quite fatigued for tis dark. Many set up discussing about going home tomorrow &c what has transpired since they was last here &c.

July 6, 1865

And fine day & we draw rations of evrything allowed by Regulations. About noon our Co Rolls come in to be rectified. Cap leaves us again, he being about half drunk now. Says he will be back by 3 P.M. & wants evry man here to sign the Pay rolls. He came at the time & we had the rolls ready & signed them. At same time, said we could not get Pay till next Thursday & the Col said we could all go home that choose too. So after signing the Rolls, there was a bustle to get ready for the 4 P.M. train. That is the Boys of our Co. But I having no money was not in a hurry. But was studying some way to get some money to pay my fare.

So I start up to town & the thought struck me that I might leave my watch to get repaired at Jewelers & let him have it as security for a few dollars. & I found all of it. I come across, I believe, a Gentleman watchmaker this time for he was verry respectful. I got 3 dollars of him & now I start for camp & give up going till the morning freight train & feeling faint & wanting something tasty for supper, I bought 10 cents worth of herring & found they just suited my taste & perhaps will cure my diherea. Reach camp, find half of the Co gone home. I made some coffee & ate a hearty supper and feel first rate, better than for several days.

July 7, 1865

And fine day. And I arose early this morning, got Breakfast & got ready to go to depot. & start, find nothing but freight trains going out this morning at 8 A.M. Wait till near 8 and go and get aboard of the conductors caboose. Train is off & the train reaches Mazomanie about 10 A.M. I had to pay 50 cents for riding. Well after putting my knapsack in the warehouse till I find some of the folks, I start out. Come to a Barbershop, go in, get shaved & inquire of him [where] Miss Ray the Milliner lives. He didnt know, unless lives the next block. & put for it & walked right in, supposing it was Lus shop. But Behold I see no face I know & the ladies are as much surprised till I inquire of them & they said Oh, you are Miss Rays brother. To which I answered in the affirmative. They extended hands to shake which I had no alternative but accept & so they proffered to go with me to Lus. But a gentleman came along & he took it up, directed me to the place which I soon found. Only Minney there, Lu having gone out. But soon returned & glad to see me. As I was here, I got dinner here & then went up to Thurza's & found all well but her & she was rather unwell. I get supper here & then come back to Lus & Lu comes up to Henry with me. & I find Henrys folks well & happy to see me as I am them. But I forgot to say that Clark hitched the horse & buggy & brought me up. I brought my knapsack up here too for I allow to make this my home till I return to Madison. I am happy to see the folks, indeed I am, but Mother is not here & I cant go & see her verry will till I get discharged. I have made several new acquaintences today. The young ladies are verry numerous in this town & good looking ones too.

July 8, 1865

Made many new acquaintances. I have a splendid chance here, I believe to get a partner for life or in other words, Enlist for life. Great many young people in this town.

July 12, 1865

And fine day. On the train. We soon glided to Madison. I went down to camp & I got some dinner or rather finished it. & I find out that I can draw the money that is due Mother from the State Volunteers Aid. & so I and another man of our Co go up to the State Treasurers Office & draw what is coming to us. I drew $19 for Mother. That paid all up to the 13th inst., the day we are to be discharged. I came back to Barracks to stay all night. Not a thing to make a bed & go in with one of the Co. that had a rubber only & tis verry cold night. Indeed, we are to get our pay tomorrow.

July 13, 1865

And fine day, but verry verry cold. Indeed, last night I suffered with the cold. We get breakfast & the Boys begin to collect in & by 9 A.M. they all got in & the Officers come & we formed line for the last time. The Col made us a Speech, his farewell Speech & twas a good one. He said all that was good to say, gave us good advice &c and to always remember we belonged to the old 7th. He made a verry feeling speech & he felt it too as also did the Boys. I could not refrain from sheding a tear (& I was not alone). He cautioned them against intemperance, Idleness & Bad women. Those either seperately or altogather would spoil any Man. Make him unfit for any society. Well he talked like a father to a wayward child. I wish I could Pen evry word of it down in this Book for a guide to myself. After the Col, the Major Hagt [Hoyt?] & after him, Doctor Ayers & after him our good Chaplain spoke a few well timed remark as also verry feeling ones.

When he was through, we marched up to North of the Capital & halted & are to be paid of soon. But an order soon comes that they will not commence to pay till 1 P.M. and we can go where we please till then, which we did. I took one of my particular friends (A.H. Conner) [Andrew H. Connor][248] and went to a eating saloon & stood the treat to a good dinner as twould [be] the last one we could eat togather. Well, they begin to pay off & so on. It comes F Co turn. We march up into the building & one by one as his name is called, goes up to the counter and gets his pay & discharge & becomes a citizen once more. I felt a thrill of joy run through my heart & veins when I grasped the Discharge & some $334 & some cents. I steped out of the room & went to settling up which was soon done. & I did not owe much & I had good success in getting what was owing to me so I am straight with the world except I want $3 of a man in our Co. & he is good as old wheat.

Now 5 P.M. & too late to go out on the train so I will wait till morning & go down on the freight train as far as Mazamanie. I go to the Boarding house where a number of our Boys stop & put up for the night & I set up till 12M to see the Boys of Co. that were going off on that train. What a time they had playing cards & drinking & carousing. I got sick of it but 12M come & they off & I go to Bed, verry tired.[249]

July 14, 1865

Up early for breakfast & go down to the Depot & wait till the 8 A.M. freight-train goes out. I will go on it. I get into the conductors Caboose & we of. Arrive at Mazamanie. I find Lu well & Caroline up making her a visit.

July 15, 1865

And fine morning, but cool enough for an overcoat. Carried my Knapsack. The Express soon came & I was off in a jiffy. Reached Pr Du chine [Prairie du Chien] about 7 A.M. & found the Boat ready to start down the river. I got aboard, take Deck Passage, cost $2.00—just double what it was 4 years since. Soon reach McGregors, Iowa and soon arrive at Clayton, Iowa & touch there & off, are soon at Gullenberg, Iowa, & soon we reach Cassville, my native town & home. Soon as the Plank touches shore, I leap on & am ashore which I find overgrown with grass & weeds and only one dim path up the Beach to the street. I meet with only one man I know, Mr. Rankil (Merchant). He seemed verry glad to see me. I start for home. & on reaching the gate see Mother standing in the door. I tell you I felt a thrill of joy run through my whole frame when I opened the gate & approached the house. I thought evrybody is not Blessed with such a home, a kind Mother to greet them with a Kiss.

July 16, 1865

And fine day. This is Sunday & no Inspection today. Oh what a Blessed thing to be a citizen once more. Don't have to turn out at the will of our Officers (although it was right & proper to do so) for officers I have none to Obey.

William R. Ray, with no more officers to obey, in later life. Exactly when he sat for this image is unclear. On the reverse is the inscription, "From your loving Father." *Sherry Murphy*

William R. Ray's gravestone (left) at Horseshoe Bend, Idaho. His wife's gravestone is on the right. *Photo taken by Erni Stivison*

Epilogue

After the war, William Ray lived with his mother in the house he had his brother purchase for him in 1864 with money he had sent home during the conflict. He continued to write in his journal. His first few months at home were spent repairing his house and improving the land. He also apprenticed as a blacksmith, with the idea that he would one day have his own shop. Because he had wisely sent home much of his pay during the war, he had the ability to support himself and his mother, but he continued to be frugal and accounted in his journals for everything he spent.

The years after the Civil War were similar to the years that follow any war. It was difficult to get good work. Like most young men, Ray wanted to establish himself in a home with a wife and family. Many of his journal entries are about young women, but he is always discreet and rather evasive about his relationships with them. Several entries concern a "Miss Winsor," who is one of the ladies he courted. The entry on October 29, 1865, reads as follows:

> In the evening I called on Miss Winsor, had a little chat. Hello. When Whap. Soon another young Gentleman came in. Found upon being made acquainted with, his name was March. He made himself quite agreeable & at home &c. But I outwinded him if nothing more to my great pleasure. I didn't give a darn about him coming there but the Joke of it was I was not going to be outwinded. Neither was I By jove, which is a source of some pleasure to me.

Although Ray occasionally wrote of his wartime service in his postwar journals, he did not do so in any detail. He referred once to "writing military history of evry man in the Co for our old Chaplain Eaton. I promised him I would do so & sent it by mail," although this history has never come to light. He noted that town meetings were held to discuss whether or not "Jeff Davis" should be hanged, and contact with soldiers with whom he served warranted occasional mention. His most frequent references to his wartime service had to do with his health—especially his head wounds, which were aggravated by hot weather.

After three months in Cassville, Ray decided to move from Wisconsin at the end of October to find land in Iowa for homesteading. He found work in a blacksmith shop for a time until beckoned home by his mother's failing health in April 1866. She passed away in May of that year. After her death Ray convinced his brother-in-law, William Weaks, nephew William Henry Ray, and Giles Weaks and their families to move to Iowa with him, where they all settled in Spirit Lake. The entries during this time describe many hardships, some of which he compared to his experiences during the war.

William Ray married Emma Charlott Fenton (whom he referred to as "the Intended" or "my Dulce") in a civil ceremony on September 7, 1868. He wrote little about the courtship, but did describe some of the arrangements prior to the wedding. Oddly, Ray's journal entries thereafter rarely mention his wife or family, focusing instead on his efforts as a homesteader and the cost of daily living. The entries stop abruptly on October 11, 1868. A few pages were completed at the end of November 1871 when he left on a stage and train trip for Ogden, Utah, but once again end abruptly on November 30, 1871. If he kept journals thereafter, they have yet to be found.

Ray eventually settled in Idaho at a place called Horseshoe Bend, where he took up farming. He and Emma had ten children during their marriage. His diaries were left with his daughter, Emma Charlott Ray Ellis, and found after the death of her son, Clyde Ellis, in 1985.

Ray was admitted to the Soldiers Home in Boise, Idaho, on December 10, 1896. His application claimed that he was not able to "earn a support by manual labor because of Gun Shot Wound in Head and Right Leg with complications of catarrah and present condition of anemic." His application also showed that he was "receiving a pension of $8 per month" (certificate 175009 at the San Francisco Agency). A surgeon's certificate for re-admission to the facility dated February 1, 1899, stated that Ray was unable to support himself by manual labor by reason of "age, debility from gun shot wounds, and catarrah." He lived for another ten years and died on April 2, 1909. The cause of death was listed as "senility." He is buried at Horseshoe Bend.

His wife, Emma Charlott Fenton Ray, died February 27, 1918, in Horseshoe Bend of senile dementia.

Seventh Wisconsin Regiment

This regiment was called into camp during the month of August 1861, and placed under the command of Colonel Joseph Vandor of Milwaukee.

The following is a list of the Field, Staff and Company officers:

FIELD AND STAFF

Colonel Joseph Vandor, Milwaukee

Lieut. Colonel William W. Robinson, Sparta

Major Chas. A. Hamilton, Milwaukee

Chas. W. Cook, Adjutant, Madison

Henry P. Clinton, Quartermaster, Brodhead

Henry Palmer, Surgeon, Janesville

D. Cooper Ayers, First Assistant Surgeon, Green Bay

Ernest Kramer, Second Assistant Surgeon, Madison

Rev. S. L. Brown, Chaplain, Beaver Dam

COMPANIES

Company A—Lodi Guards

George Bill, Captain, Lodi

Hollon Richardson, 1st Lieut., Chippewa Falls

M. B. Misner, 2d Lieut., Columbus

Company B—Columbia County Cadets

J. H. Huntington, Captain, Fall River

S. L. Bachelder, 1st Lieut., Fall River

H. P. Clinton, 2d Lieut., Brodhead

Company C—Platteville Guards

Samuel Nasmith, Captain, Platteville

A. R. Bushnell, 1st Lieut., Platteville

E. A. Andrews, 2d Lieut., Platteville

Company D—Stoughton Guard

E. F. Giles, Captain, Stoughton

C. W. Cook, 1st Lieut., Madison

A. T. Reed, 2d Lieut., Stoughton

Company E—Marquette County Sharp Shooters

W. D. Walker, Captain, Montello

W. F. Bailey, 1st Lieut., Portage

W. B. Manning, 2d Lieut., Marquette Co.

Company F—Lancaster Union Guards

John B. Callis, Captain, Lancaster

Samuel Woodhouse, 1st Lieut., Lancaster

Henry F. Young, 2d Lieut., Lancaster

Company G—Grand Rapids Union Guards

S. Stevens, Captain, Grand Rapids

Homer Drake, 1st Lieut., Grand Rapids

Lemuel Kromer, 2d Lieut., Grand Rapids

Company H—Badger State Guards

Mark Finnicum, Captain, Fennimore

C. M. H. Meyer, 1st Lieut., Grant Co.

Robert C. Palmer, 2d Lieut., Grant Co.

Company I—Northwestern Tigers

George H. Walther, Captain, Dodge County

A. S. Rogers, 1st Lieut., Spring Lake

J. N. P. Bird, 2d Lieut., Green Lake Co.

Company K—Badger Rifles

Alex. Gordon, Jr., Captain, Beloit

F. W.Oakley, 1st Lieut., Beloit

David Shirrell, 2d Lieut., Beloit

The numerical strength of the Seventh Regiment when it left the state:

Field and staff: 9
Company officers: 28
Non-commissioned officers, musicians and privates: 979
Total: 1,016

This regiment, unlike those that had gone before it, was mustered into the United States service by companies, by mustering officers Brevet Maj. Books and Capt. McIntyre. The Seventh was fully equipped by the state with the exception of arms; received orders September 4th [1861], to move forward to Washington City, on the morning of the 21st broke camp and started; arrived in Washington Oct. 1 and was assigned to Gen. King's Brigade, McDowell's Division. This Regiment comprised a splendid body of men, and was well officered.

Report of the Adjutant General, 1861

Appomattox Campaign Reports

Reports of Col. John A. Kellogg, Sixth Wisconsin Infantry,
commanding First Brigade.

HDQRS. FIRST BRIGADE, THIRD DIVISION,
April 27, 1865.

CAPT.: In compliance with orders, I have to make the following report of the operations of my command from the 29th of March to April 25, both inclusive:

On the morning of the 29th of March, 1865, the brigade broke camp, situated near the military railroad about two miles from Humphreys' Station, and moved in a northwesterly direction, to a point about half a mile from the Boydton Plank road. At this point the brigade was halted and massed in column of regiments, right in front. Some firing being heard in my front the men were ordered to load, soon after which the command was moved into position in line of battle as follows: The Sixth and Seventh Wisconsin Veteran Volunteers forming the front line, in rear of the Second Brigade (commanded by Gen. Baxter); the Ninety-first New York Volunteers, divided into three battalions, moved on the left flank of the brigade, ready to be deployed either on the left flank of the line of battle or in rear of the first line, as circumstances should require. The enemy being driven from their position on the Boydton plank road by the troops in my front, my command was moved to a position near that road and crossing the same, the Seventh Wisconsin Veteran Volunteers, under command of Lieut.-Col. Richardson, being advanced to the road, the balance of the brigade being in line of battle about eighty rods to the rear, connecting on the right with the Second Brigade, under command of Gen. Baxter, where we remained during the night.

On the morning of the 30th of March the brigade was moved to the Boydton plank road and threw up breast-works, remaining there during the night.

On the morning of the 31st of March, &c. On the morning of the 2d of April the brigade moved to the South Side Railroad, only to find the position evacuated by the enemy. The command without halting here moved on the railroad track three or four miles, the mile-board marking thirteen miles from Petersburg, when, by command of Gen. Crawford, commanding division, the command moved at a rapid rate in a westerly direction about five miles, when the enemy were found in strong force in an entrenched position on the Burkeville road. By order of Gen. Crawford, commanding division, I deployed in two lines on the right of the road, my right resting on a wood, my left connecting with the Second Brigade, commanded by Gen. Baxter. The Seventh Wisconsin Veteran Volunteers, commanded by Lieut.-Col. Richardson, were deployed as skirmishers, with orders to cover the extreme front of the line of battle. By this time it was quite dark, and the enemy not being able to distinguish our uniforms, were at a loss to know whether we were Yankees or not, and before they had obtained the desired information the troops were in position to attack or resist the same, as circumstances would require. Upon ascertaining who we were the enemy opened fire upon my portion of the line; my men replied and immediately advanced toward the enemy, and halted within a few rods of their breast-works. The enemy ceasing to fire, I reformed my lines, and the men lay upon their arms until daylight.

On the morning of the 3d of April we again took up the line of march in pursuit of the flying enemy, who had beat a hasty retreat during the night, but failed to overtake them, and late in the evening bivouacked for the night.

On the morning of the 4th broke camp at an early hour, and took up the line of march in pursuit of the flying foe, reaching the Danville railroad at Jetersville Station in the afternoon of that day, finding it occupied by the cavalry under Gen. Sheridan, and the enemy in strong force just beyond. Here the brigade was formed in line of battle, and the troops, weary and footsore, having traveled all day without food, labored nearly all night, throwing up breast-works, remaining in this position, resting and waiting for an attack, until the morning of the 6th, when we moved out to attack the enemy, who was found to have made another hasty retreat, but without overtaking him.

April 7, still following the enemy, the tired but gallant column pushed on, following the west side of the Appomattox to the high railroad bridge just after the enemy had crossed, the structure itself having been fired and three spans destroyed by the enemy.

On the 8th made a long forced march, the most tiresome I believe ever made by troops, being impeded by the wagon train of the Twenty-fourth Corps, the infantry being obliged either to march through the thicket or mix in promiscuously with the wagon train. Camped that night in line of battle. On the morning of the 9th again started in pursuit of the enemy, who were brought to bay near Appomattox Court-House. But before we were engaged, the enemy, tired, dispirited, harassed, and surrounded, surrendered at discretion.

A tabular and nominal list for each of the engagements, of casualties, I have already had the honor to forward. In conclusion, I beg leave to submit the following list of names of officers and men of my command who have distinguished themselves, and to ask for them a suitable recognition of their services (see regimental lists and previous reports). For further particulars, I beg leave to refer to my reports for thee 31st of March and 1st of April, already forwarded.

I have the honor to be, & C.,

J. A. KELLOGG, Col., Cmdg. Brigade

Capt. HARRISON LAMBDIN,
Assistant Adjutant-Gen., Third Division.

*   *   *

HDQRS. FIRST BRIGADE, THIRD DIVISION,
April 25, 1865.

CAPT.: In compliance with field order of April 13, 1865, headquarters Third Division, I have the honor to submit the following report of the part taken by my command in the action near the Boydton plank road ont he 31st day of March, 1865:

On the morning of that day my command, consisting of the Sixth and Seventh Wisconsin Veteran Volunteer Infantry and the Ninety-first New York Veteran Volunteers, pursuant to orders from the division commander, moved from their breast-works on the Boydton plank road in a northwesterly direction, across Gravelly Run about a mile, where the brigade was massed in column of regiments, right in front, in a thick wood near an open field, and remained in this position about half an hour. The command was then ordered to deploy in line of battle on the left of the Second Brigade, commanded by Brig.-Gen. Baxter. In compliance with said order I directed the brigade to deploy on the first battalion, but before the movement was completed two regiments only, to wit, the Sixth and Seventh Wisconsin Veteran Volunteers being in line, the Ninety-first New York being treated as three battalions, not yet having time to deploy, I was ordered to deploy the two Wisconsin regiments and arrest the troops belonging to the front line, consisting of a portion of the Second Division, who were flying in confusion from the field. This order I found myself unable to execute, the men breaking through my line and throwing my own command into confusion. I then ordered the Sixth and Seventh Wisconsin to close their intervals, and formed them into line of battle, and directed them to open fire, and sent orders to the Ninety-first to deploy on second battalion (the Sixth Wisconsin Veteran Volunteers). Both of these orders were promptly executed. The brigade remained thus in line of battle, firing rapidly upon the advancing enemy until both flanks were turned and the enemy firing upon both flanks and rear of the command. I then directed Lieut.-Col. Richardson, Seventh Wisconsin Veteran Volunteers, to change front, so as to meet the fire on his flank, which was executed, but the enemy appearing in so large force in my rear, I directed the brigade to retire across Gravelly Run in as good order as possible. In retiring to this position my command was somewhat broken up, owing to the fact that the enemy was in their rear, compelling them to fight their way back. I claim that my command were the last organized troops to leave the field.

The Sixth and Seventh Wisconsin Veteran Volunteers were formed as they arrived on the front line next to the creek, near the bridge crossed by the troops in the morning. The Ninety-first New York Volunteers fell back across the creek farther to the right. One battalion, commanded by Lieut.-Col. Denslow, formed in an interval between the troops of the Second Division, where they remained the balance of the engagement, doing good service. When the firing had ceased I reformed the brigade in the rear of their first position and ordered them to lie down. We remained in this position about one hour, were then again moved to the front across the battle-field of the morning, and went into camp about half a mile in advance of the same.

The following-named officers are entitled to special mention for gallantry, viz: Col. Tarbell and Lieut.-Col. Denslow, Ninety-first New York Veteran Volunteers; Lieut.-Col. Kerr, commanding Sixth Wisconsin Veteran Volunteers, who was badly wounded while cheering on his men; Lieut.-Col. Richardson, commanding Seventh Wisconsin Veteran Volunteers; also First Lieut. J. A. Watrous, acting assistant adjutant-general, Second Lieut. C. W. Atherton, acting aide-de-camp, and Capt. H. T. Garfield, brigade inspector, members of my staff. The conduct of these officers came under my immediate notice. Lieut. Watrous was wounded and taken prisoner while discharging his duty. Lieut. Athereton and Lieut. Watrous each lost a horse, shot under them, which, with the horse of the orderly, make three horses lost from my headquarters on that day by the fire of the enemy.

My two orderlies, William Holloway, Company K, and Henry A. Hackett, Company H, both of the Sixth Wisconsin Veteran Volunteers, behaved in the most gallant manner, Holloway having his horse shot under him.

There are others, both officers and men, deserving special mention. The names of such officers will be found submitted in my report of the 23d instant for brevets, as recommended by their regimental commanders. My loss in killed, wounded, and missing was large for the time engaged, amounting to 8 officers and 290 men. I transmit herewith a tabular and nominal list of casualties occurring on that day.

I have the honor to be, very respectfully, your obedient servant,

J. A. KELLOGG,
Col., Cmdg. Brigade.

Capt. HARRISON LAMBDIN,
Assistant Adjutant-Gen., Third Division.

*   *   *

HDQRS. FIRST BRIGADE, THIRD DIVISION,
April 10, 1865.

CAPT.: In compliance with orders, I have the honor to submit the following report of the operations of my command on the 1st instant.

On the evening of the 31st of March the command encamped near the battle-field of that day, about one mile and a half northwest from the Boydton plank road, in column of regiments, right in front, facing the north. About daylight in the morning of the 1st instant, in accordance with orders, I changed the front of the brigade, by change of direction by the right flank, facing the east, and moved in colum, faced by the rear rank, in a westerly direction about three quarters of a mile, through an open field, my right connecting with the Second Brigade, commanded by Brig.-Gen. Baxter. At this point, by direction of the general commanding the division, the command was changed from the order in column and moved left in front, in a southwesterly direction, following the Second Division, Fifth Army Corps, to a position on Gravelly Run, near the Moody house and Gravelly Run Church, where, by order of the general commanding division, the brigade was formed in two lines of battle, the Sixth and Seventh Wisconsin Veteran Volunteers holding the front line. The right of my line connected with Gen. Baxter's command, the left with the Second Division, Fifth Army Corps. Receiving orders to that effect, I advanced my command to a road about half a mile in my immediate front, at which point it executed a left wheel. Here we became engaged with the enemy, the command moving forward and firing as it advanced, driving the enemy before us. In moving through a dense thicket and wood, the connection became broken between my left and the Second Division, causing a large interval, which was taken advantage of by the enemy, who threw a force on my left flank and opened fire, evidently with the desire of arresting the forward movement of the line of battle. I ordered my front line to continue the advance, and ordered one battalion of the Ninety-first New York Veteran Volunteers, forming a portion of my second line, under command of Col. Tarbell, to deploy on the left flank of the brigade, covering that flank, with orders to move forward and engage the enemy at short range. This order was promptly executed, holding the enemy at bay, until the Third Brigade, commanded by Gen. Coulter, came up and filled the interval. My brigade now occupied the center of the line, between the brigades of Gen.'s Baxter and Coulter, and continued in that position until we found the enemy entrenched. We then drove them from their works across an open field, pursuing them closely about three-quarters of a mile, taking many prisoners and killing and wounding many of the enemy, when, in compliance with orders, the brigade was moved into camp for the night.

I cannot speak too highly of the officers and men of my command; all did their duty. I desire especially to mention Col. Tarbell and Lieut.-Col. Denslow, Ninety-first New York Veteran Volunteers; Acting Maj. Whaley; Second Lieut. William H. Church, acting adjutant; First Lieut. Thomas Kelly, commanding Company H, and Lieut. Davis, commanding Company F, of the Sixth Wisconsin Veteran Volunteers—who were conspicuous for gallantry and daring on that day. Also the members of my staff, who were all that I could desire. Every order was correctly transmitted, and no one faltered in his duty. Lieut. Sherley, Ninety-first New York Veteran Volunteers, temporarily serving on my staff, had his horse shot under him while gallantly discharging his duty.

I have the honor to be, very respectfully, your obedient servant,

J. A. KELLOGG,
Col., Cmdg. Brigade.

Capt. HARRISON LAMBDIN,
Assistant Adjutant-Gen., Third Division.

* * *

Report of Col. Jonathan Tarbell, Ninety-first New York Infantry.

HDQRS. NINETY-FIRST NEW YORK VETERAN VOLS.,
In the Field, near Appomattox Court-House, Va., April 12, 1865.

CAPT.: I have the honor to submit my report of the movements of the Ninty-first New York Veteran Volunteers from the 29th ultimo to the present time, premising that the regiment has not at any time been detached, so that its movements are embraced in the history of the First Brigade, Third [Division], Fifth Army Corps, to which it belongs.

Being in camp about two miles from Humphreys' Station, on the U. S. Military Railroad from City Point, early in the day of the 29th ultimo the regiment, with its brigade and division, entered upon the grand campaign which has just closed so gloriously. Marching in a southwesterly direction, the advance met and drove the enemy near the Boydton plank road late in the afternoon of that day, the Ninety-first, with its brigade, being formed in line of battle, but the retreat of the rebels rendered its engagement unnecessary. The 30th was a very rainy day, and was spent in camp, at night throwing up entrenchments at the crossing of the Boydton plank road over ———— creek to intercept a probable movement of the rebels in that direction.

On the 31st the march was again taken up, leaving the earth-works in our rear. About 9 o'clock in the morning the advance met and engaged the enemy near the Quaker road, the Ninety-first being in column by battalions, with its brigade, in a dense wood a short distance in rear of the troops engaged in action. In the temporary absence of the brigade commander giving the Sixth and Seventh Wisconsin Regiments new positions, a brigade from the front, denoting a rapid retreat, broke through my battalions to the rear. The movement being imminent I took the responsibility of deploying my regiment into line of battle, which I did to the right of the third battalion, advancing my line about ten yards to the brow of a small declivity having a little ravine at its base, when I at once opened fire briskly, checking the enemy on this part of the line and turning him off to our left, remaining in this position until all other troops had left the field and the enemy in large numbers had passed my left considerably to our rear, when I directed my regiment to retire. I have since learned that orders had been sent to me to retire some twenty or thirty minutes before I moved to the rear, but the gallant acting assistant adjutant-general who started with the message for me fell wounded before reaching me, observed by some of my officers, but at the time unknown to me. At a log house in a clearing in the line of retreat an attempt to check the enemy was made, in which a portion of my regiment participated, my colors, myself, my lieutenant-colonel, Capt. Felthousen, and others among the number, in vain. On the brow of a high declivity farther in the rear a successful stand was made, and here a large portion of my regiment took an active part. Lieut.-Col. Denslow with a number of men and officers assisted in supporting a battery on its right, while others, under my own direction, officers and men, were in the line on the left of the battery.

The enemy was here checked, the troops reformed, and another forward movement at once entered upon, passing over the battle-ground beyond the Quaker road and encamping for the night without further engagement on our part.

April 1, at daylight, the march was resumed, resulting in turning the rebel right, compelling the enemy to evacuate strong and extensive earth-works, and to a hasty and evidently unexpected retreat. On this morning the regiment broke camp at an early hour in obedience to the orders of the proper commander, marching with the brigade and division by a circuitous route several miles to the rebel right and rear, halting near what was said to be called the Gravelly Run Church, where the troops were formed in line of battle about 2 p.m., the Ninety-first New York forming the second line of this brigade, in rear of the Sixth and Seventh Wisconsin Regiments, connecting on the right with Gen. Baxter's (Second) brigade, Third Division, advancing thence directly on the enemy about 3 p.m. After marching thus in line of battle a short distance, the enemy's fire was drawn, and soon after the left wing of the Ninety-first was moved up to the first line of battle, on the left of the front of the brigade to which it belongs; shortly after the right wing was also moved up to the first line, both in obedience to orders of brigade commanders. The firing of the enemy was sharp, close, and continued, but the Ninety-first, with the other troops, advanced steadily, sometimes on the run, driving the enemy, who was not allowed to make a stand. Arriving at right of the enemy's entrenchments, a portion of the Ninety-first took an active part in the capture of four pieces of the enemy's artillery. Under the lead of its officers, headed by its colors, the regiment promptly charged thence across a large, open field, where the fire of the enemy was particularly severe and where the most of the casualties of the day occurred. Following in this charge, over the rebel works and across the field, Maj.-Gen. Warren close to, and next to him, over the rebel works and across the field. On the further side of the field the rebels disappeared from sight by a hasty flight into the woods, and so far as the Ninety-first was concerned, nothing further was seen of the enemy that day. The advance was continued till within two or three miles of the South Side Railroad, when a halt was ordered, and where the Ninety-first was the first regiment reformed. It was not long after dark, and the troops were halted to be reformed. This done, the Ninety-first went into camp for the night, with its brigade and division, marching back some four or five miles for that purpose.

During the advance and though fighting all the way, the entire line of battle successfully made a left wheel, by refusing the left and advancing the right, the Ninety-first performing its appropriate part in this splendid movement.

I respectfully submit that my officers, without exception, behaved throughout in the most gallant and resolute manner, while the men rushed on with loud cheers at almost every step. My color-bearer, Sergt. Patrick W. Mullen, Company I, is entitled to especial notice for his coolness and steadiness; he went at my side over the enemy's breast-works into the open field spoken of; but, as far as I can ascertain, Corpl. Egbert H. Caswell, Company I, was the first man of the regiment to spring over, calling on his comrades to follow. Sergt. Henry S. Lodewick, Company K, and others took part in the capture of the enemy's artillery beyond the right of the regiment.

April 2, our men marched with the other troops to the east two or three miles, where we halted, receiving the news of the evacuation of Petersburg. During the forenoon we were put on a rapid march to the west, reaching the South Side Railroad only to find it evacuated by the enemy. The troops without halting were started on the track of that road, the mile-boards marking thirteen miles from Petersburg, following this track on a swift walk three or four miles, when information was received of a column of the enemy to the west, after which the already tired, foot-sore, and hungry troops were hastened without a moment's delay and at a pace which even flying fugitives could not outdo, overtaking the rebels late in the evening of that day. The Ninety-first went into camp with the other troops in line of battle, its right on a wood and swamp, and forming the second line of its brigade. Late in the evening the Ninety-first with other regiments of the brigade became engaged with a party of the enemy in the woods on our right, in which my regiment lost 1 killed and 15 wounded. The engagement lasted only a few moments, when the rebels retired.

April 3, we started with the other troops in pursuit of the enemy, who had retreated during the night, following by forced marches, and though the way was strewn with the evidence of a hasty flight, we failed to overtake the enemy that day, and at a late hour after dark bivouacked for the night.

April 4, again pursued the enemy, reaching the Danville railroad at Jetersville, Station, finding it in possession of the Union troops, and the enemy in strong force just beyond. Here the First Brigade, including the Ninety-first, threw up strong breast-works, awaiting and wishing an attack.

April 6, at 6 a.m. marched out to attack the enemy, who was found to have made another hasty retreat, but we followed on his track, making a long and forced march of about thirty-two miles.

April 7, still pressing the enemy, following the west side of the Appomattox, approaching the High Bridge, so called, over that stream soon after the passage of the enemy.

April 8, farther pursuit of the enemy and guarding the trains.

April 9, started with the train, but were detached at an early hour and sent to the assistance of our troops engaged with the enemy on the Lynchburg road, but success crowning the efforts of our brothers before we reached the scene of action, we were not engaged. On the afternoon of the 9th the enemy surrendered near Appomattox Court-House, where the Ninety-first is in camp with its brigade and division.

From the best calculation that I am able to make, the distance actually traveled since the 29th ultimo exceeds 150 miles. . . .

The following are the casualties Ninety-first New York Veteran Volunteers March 31 and April 1 and 2: March 31, killed, 25 men; wounded, 106 men, 3 officers; missing, 16 men. April 1, killed, 6 men; wounded, 38 men, 2 officers; missing, 6 men. April 2, killed, 1 man; wounded, 15 men. Total, killed, 32 men; wounded, 159 men, 5 officers; missing, 22 men.

Respectfully submitted.

J. TARBELL,
Col., Cmdg.

Endnotes

Volume 1

1. The Regiment was called into Camp Randall at Madison in August 1861 and placed under the command of Colonel Joseph Vandor of Milwaukee.

2. Baltimore secessionists attacked the Sixth Massachusetts Infantry on April 10, 1861, as it marched through the city to board a train for Washington. Four of the soldiers were killed and 39 wounded. Twelve civilians were killed and dozens wounded.

3. The main staging facility for Wisconsin regiments. It was located at the old state fair grounds at Madison and named for Alexander Randall, the state's first war governor.

4. One of the main bridges over the Potomac River leading to Washington, D.C.

5. The color company is assigned a position in the center of a regiment in line of battle, and the duty of the soldiers is to protect the unit's flags and color guards.

6. **Foot**, Waterloo, enlisted August 19, 1861, discharged disabled August 9, 1862; **Parsons**, Tafton, enlisted August 19, 1861, mustered out September 1, 1864, wounded Gettysburg, mustered out September 1, 1864, term expired. *Roster of Wisconsin Volunteers, War of the Rebellion, 1861-1865*, Vol. I. (Madison, Wisconsin, 1886), 559, 560.

7. The family home and estate of Robert E. Lee seized upon his resignation from the Union Army. It is now the site of the Arlington National Cemetery.

8. **Brother**, Patch Grove, enlisted August 19, 1861, mustered out September 1, 1864, term expired. **Thorpe**, Potosi, enlisted August 19, 1861, detached to Battery B, 4th U.S. Arillery from November 28, 1861, discharged March 17, 1862, for disability. *Wisconsin Roster*, 558, 561.

9. **Shipton**, Waterloo, enlisted August 19, 1861, discharged February 22, 1862, disabled. *Wisconsin Roster,* 561

10. The regiments of the Western Brigade, except for the Seventh Wisconsin, which is listed in Appendix A, are as follows:

THE SECOND WISCONSIN VOLUNTEERS

Company		County
A	The Citizens' Guard	Dodge
B	The La Crosse Light Guards	La Crosse
C	The Grant County Grays	Grant

D	The Janesville Volunteers	Rock
E	The Oshkosh Volunteers	Winnebago
F	The Belle City Rifles	Racine
G	The Portage City Guards	Columbia
H	The Randall Guards	Dane
I	The Miner's Guards	Iowa
K	The Wisconsin Rifles	Milwaukee
K*		Dane - Milwaukee

(*Replaced original Company K in January 1862 after it was detached and converted to heavy artillery).

THE SIXTH WISCONSIN VOLUNTEERS

Company		County
A	The Sauk County Riflemen	Sauk
B	The Prescott Guards	Pierce
C	The Prairie du Chien Volunteers	Crawford
D	The Montgomery Guards	Milwaukee
E	Bragg's Rifles	Fond du Lac
F	The Citizens' Corps Milwaukee	Milwaukee
G	The Beloit Star Rifles	Rock
H	The Buffalo County Rifles	Buffalo
I	The Anderson Guards	Juneau and Dane
K	The Lemonweir Minute Men	Juneau

THE NINETEENTH INDIANA VOLUNTEERS

Company		County
A	The Union Guards	Madison
B	The Richmond City Greys	Wayne
C	The Winchester Greys	Randolph
D	The Invincibles	Marion
E	The Delaware Greys	Delaware
F	The Meredith Guards	Marion
G	The Elkhart County Guards	Elkhart
H	The Edinburgh Guards	Johnson
I	The Spencer Greys	Owen
K	The Selma Legion	Delaware

THE TWENTY-FOURTH MICHIGAN VOLUNTEERS joined the regiment in late 1862 and was raised mostly in Wayne County, Michigan.

11. **John R. Callis**, a native of North Carolina, was a businessman in Lancaster, Wisconsin, at the start of the war. He came to Wisconsin with his family when he was 10. He organized and was elected captain of the Lancaster Union Guards, soon to be Company F of the Seventh Wisconsin. Promoted to lieutenant colonel, he was severely wounded at Gettysburg. Callis was discharged December 28, 1863, and pensioned for a total disability. He returned to Wisconsin and purchased a flour mill at Annaton. He became a major in the Veteran Reserve Corps in 1864, serving in an administrative capacity. Following the war, he entered the Regular Army and was stationed in Alabama. He resigned in 1868 and was elected to Congress from Alabama's Fifth District. He later returned to Lancaster where he operated a real estate and insurance business. He was elected subsequently to the Wisconsin Legislature. He died on September 24, 1898, at Lancaster.

12. **Whitney**, Mt. Hope, enlisted August 19, 1861, promoted corporal, died April 7, 1863, at Frederick, Maryland, of disease. **Boynton**, Waterloo, August 19, 1861, promoted corporal, sergeant and first lieutenant, wounded Gainesville and Petersburg, Virginia, mustered out July 3, 1865. *Wisconsin Roster,* 558, 561.

13. **McCartney**, Cassville, enlisted August 19, 1861, wounded Gainesville, discharged March 8, 1863, wounds; **McKenzie**, Mt. Hope, enlisted June 27, 1861, second lieutenant April 1, 1862, wounded South Mountain, resigned December 27, 1862. *Wisconsin Roster,* 558; **Cowan**, Ellenboro, enlisted June 27, 1861, discharged December 26, 1862, disabled; **Sloat**, Lancaster, enlisted June 27, 1861, promoted second lieutenant December 27, 1862, wounded Bethesda Church, resigned September 13, 1864, wounds; **Henderson**, Glen Haven, enlisted August 19, 1861, wounded South Mountain, discharged October 25, 1862, disabled; **Runion**, Potosi, enlisted August 19, 1861, wounded Gettysburg and killed June 1864, at Petersburg, Virginia; **[Alphonzo] Kidd**, Millville, enlisted August 19, 1861, wounded at Gettysburg and the Wilderness, promoted to second lieutenant January 5, 1863, resigned September 10, 1864; **[Fletcher] Kidd**, Melville, enlisted August 19, 1861, wounded South Mountain, discharged December 7, 1862, disabled; **[Samuel] Woodhouse**, Beetown, enlisted August 19, 1861, resigned April 1, 1862. *Wisconsin Roster,* 558; **[Simon] Woodhouse**, Beetown, enlisted August 19, 1861, discharged November 3, 1862, disabled; **Bradley**, Ellenboro, enlisted August 19, 1861, mustered out July 3, 1865; **Halbert**, Lancaster, enlisted August 1861, wounded at South Mountain and died September 20, 1862. *Wisconsin Roster,* 558-561.

14. **Clark**, Cassville, enlisted August 19, 1861, killed September 14, 1862, South Mountain. *Wisconsin Roster,* 539.

15. The battle at Balls Bluff, Virginia, October 21, 1861. **Colonel Edward D. Baker**, an ex-Congressman and friend of President Lincoln, was killed while making a demonstration against Confederate forces opposite the Potomac River fords near Poolesville. The death of Baker caused a political storm and resulted in the arrest of Union General Charles P. Stone for his handling of the action. Mark M. Boatner III, *The Civil War Dictionary* (New York 1988), 41, 800-801.

16. Federal losses were 921 with Baker and 48 others killed, 158 wounded and 714 captured or missing. Boatner, *Civil War Dictionary*, 41.

17. **Garner**, Waterloo, enlisted August 19, 1861, mustered out June 30, 1865; **Pierce**, Waterloo, enlisted August 19, 1861, wounded South Mountain and discharged June 10, 1862, disabled. *Wisconsin Roster,* 559-560.

18. Civilian camp vendors officially appointed to supply soldiers with a long list of items such as food, newspapers, books, and tin plates.

19. The four regiments reached Washington in uniforms of militia grey. As the state uniforms deteriorated, the various items were replaced by Federal clothing. The uniform issued those first months became one of the distinctive features of the Western unit. It consisted of the Model 1858 black dress hat of the regulars, nine-button dark blue frock coat, sky-blue trousers, white leggings or gaiters and white gloves. The change occurred over a period of time and it was Colonel Lysander Cutler of the Sixth Wisconsin, while acting brigade commander, who first began the issue of the famous black hats. The brigade's second commander, General John Gibbon, ordered the distinctive uniform for all of the companies of the brigade and added the white gloves and gaiters.

The brigade also drew attention in the Washington camps because it was the only all-Western unit in the Army of the Potomac. Always at odds within the brigade were the volunteers of the Second Wisconsin, which had seen service at First Bull Run, and the soldiers of the Sixth Wisconsin. Both organizations wanted to be recognized as the top regiment of the brigade. The Sixth Wisconsin became known as "King's Pet Babies" (because of suspected favoritism from brigade commander Rufus King) or "Calico Sixth," because of the colorful homemade shirts worn by some of the backwoods boys. The Second was the "Ragged Assed Second," due to the worn condition of the trousers worn by the men. The Nineteenth Indiana became "old Posey County" or "Swamp Hogs No. 19," while the Seventh Wisconsin men were called "Huckleberries," because they were always talking about pies and good things to eat. Lance J. Herdegen, *The Men Stood Like Iron: How The Iron Brigade Won Its Name* (Bloomington, IN., 1997), 33-37, 70-72; Lance J. Herdegen and William J. K. Beaudot, *In The Bloody Railroad Cut at Gettysburg* (Dayton, OH., 1990), Appendix Three by Howard Michael Madaus, 301-367; Alan T. Nolan, *The Iron Brigade* (New York, 1961), 292-295.

20. **Rector**, Patch Grove, enlisted August 19, 1861, wounded Gainesville and Gettysburg, mustered out September 1, 1864, term expired. *Wisconsin Roster,* 560. **Day**, Ellenboro, enlisted August 19, mustered out September 1, 1864, term expired. *Wisconsin Roster,* 559.

21. **Miles**, Harrison, enlisted August 19, 1861, wounded Gainesville and Cold Harbor, mustered out May 26, 1865. *Wisconsin Roster,* 560.

22. The report was only a camp rumor.

23. **Hudson**, Beetown, enlisted August 19, 1861, wounded Fredericksburg, Virginia, mustered out September 1, 1864, at expiration of term. *Wisconsin Roster,* 559.

24. Graefenberg Pills were a patented medicine created and sold by the Graefenberg Institute in New York. The following is taken from an ad in *Scientific American*, November 16, 1861: "What is claimed, and what is borne out by facts, is that the medicines are the result of the highest medical skill adapted to the compounding of simple and entirely vegetable medicinal preparations. The treatment is the most judicious application of these simple vegetable productions in aid of the great and equally simple laws of nature governing the human system in health and disease. In ninety-nine cases out of a hundred the Graefenberg treatment will certainly cure."

"CERTIFICATE FROM THE GOVERNOR OF VIRGINIA. I, William Smith, Governor of Virginia, certify and make known that Joseph Prentice, who signs a certificate relating to the Graefenberg Vegetable Pills, is the Clerk of the Court of this State. The said certificate embraces the names of the most reliable and responsible people in this community, and certifies to the invariable curative action of the Graefenberg Vegetable Pills, in the following diseases Bilious Complaints, Asthma, Constipation, Dyspepsia, Erysipelas; Low, Nervous and Simple Fevers; Gastuic Fevers, Gripes, Heartburn, Headache, Indigestion, Hysterics, Liver Complaint, Nervous Disorders. Neuralgia, Rheumatism, and all diseases arising from want of action in the digestive organs. And I further testify that full credit and faith are due and ought to be given to said certificates. In testimony whereof, I have subscribed my name, and caused the Groat Seal of the State to be affixed hereunto. Done at the city of Richmond, the twenty-second day of November, in the year of our Lord one thousand eight hundred and forty- eight, and of the Commonwealth the seventy-third. WILLIAM SMITH, Governor."

Volume 2

25. "You know that it was the largest review of troops ever had in America, that sixty thousand infantry, nine thousand cavalry and one hundred and thirty pieces of artillery passed in review before McClellan, that the organizations marched by 'battalions en masse,' and that it took from 11 o'clock A.M. Until 4 P.M. to pass the reviewing officer, and that the President, the members of the Cabinet, and all the celebrities, foreign and domestic, were present." Rufus R. Dawes, *Service With The Sixth Wisconsin Volunteers* (Marietta, OH., 1890), 30.

26. The Fifth Wisconsin was originally attached to King's brigade and there was discussion of having a "Wisconsin Brigade" made up of the Second, Fifth, Sixth, and Seventh Wisconsin Volunteer Infantry regiments. However, the Fifth Wisconsin was subsequently transferred to the brigade of General Winfield Scott Hancock. *Adjutant General Reports*, 46.

27. **Atwood**, Lancaster, enlisted August 19, 1861, died November 24, 1861, of disease. *Wisconsin Roster,* 558.

28. **Harville**, Tafton, enlisted August 19, 1861, transferred Veteran Reserve Corps January 25, 1864, and mustered out August 29, 1864, term expired. *Wisconsin Roster,* 559.

29. **Overton**, Tafton, enlisted August 19, 1861, discharged September, 1862, disabled. *Wisconsin Roster,* 560.

30. **Raemer**, Harrison, enlisted August 19, 1861, promoted corporal and sergeant, wounded Gettysburg and North Anna, killed March 31, 1865, Gravelly Run, Virginia. *Wisconsin Roster,* 560.

31. **Atkinson [George]**, Ellenboro, enlisted August 19, 1861, wounded South Mountain, Wilderness and Second Hatcher's Run, mustered out July 3, 1865. *Wisconsin Roster,* 558.

32. **Smith**, Tafton, enlisted August 19, 1861, wounded Gainesville and South Mountain, discharged December 11, 1862, disability. *Wisconsin Roster,* 561.

33. President Lincoln's annual State of the Union message to Congress.

34. **Largent**, Patch Grove, enlisted August 19, 1861, discharged December 31, 1861, disability. *Wisconsin Roster,* 560.

Volume 3

35. **Gleason**, Waterloo, enlisted April 22, 1861, detached to Battery B, Fourth U.S. Artillery, June 1862 until mustered out June 28, 1864, term expired. *Wisconsin Roster,* 354.

36. Generally, speaking, "Seeing the elephant" was a description used by soldiers to denote seeing combat for the first time.

37. **Nickerman**, Prairie du Chien, enlisted August 19, 1861, wounded Gainesville, discharged November 29, 1862, disabled. *Wisconsin Roster,* 560.

38. The new muskets were Austrian "Lorenz" Model 1854 rifle-muskets, reamed to .58 caliber from the original .54. Companies A, D and F claimed to have 93 in their original .54 caliber. Quarterly Summary Statements of Ordnance and Ordnance Stores-infantry, Record Group No. 156, National Archives; Vol. 5 (quarter ending June 30, 1863), 43 and 98. The Sixth Wisconsin and Nineteenth Indiana were issued .58 Model 1861 "Springfield" rifle-muskets and the Second Wisconsin .54 Austrian Lorenz rifle-muskets.

39. **Johnson**, Lancaster, enlisted August 19, 1861, detached to Battery B, Fourth U.S. Artillery from September 9, 1863, until September 1864, mustered out September 1, 1864, term expired. *Wisconsin Roster,* 560.

40. Ray's reference to Roanoke was in relation to General Ambrose Burnside's amphibious landing on the North Carolina island on February 8, 1862. Bowling Green, Kentucky, was abandoned by the Confederates on February 14, 1862 and promptly occupied by Federal forces. Another Federal force led by General U.S. Grant attacked and captured Fort Donelson, Tennessee, on February 13-16, 1862. The subsequent unconditional surrender by the Confederates opened the Cumberland River to Federal control of Kentucky and western Tennessee. Patricia Faust, *Historical Times Illustrated Encyclopedia of the Civil War* (New York, 1986), 272.

41. Ray is mistaken. General John B. Floyd did indeed ingloriously flee Fort Donelson and leave others behind to surrender the place, but he was not captured by Grant at Savannah or anywhere else. He was relieved of duty in March 1862, however. General Albert S. Johnston, the commander of the Southern forces in that theater of operations, was not with the army at Fort Donelson.

42. **Atkinson [William]**, Ellenboro, enlisted August 19, 1861, mustered out July 3, 1865. *Wisconsin Roster,* 558.

Volume 4

43. **Turnby**, Melville, enlisted August 19, 1861, detached Battery B, Fourth U.S. Artillery from November 28, 1861, to discharge March 17, 1862, disabled. *Wisconsin Roster,* 561.

44. Contraband was the name given to fugitive slaves who sought protection with the Union soldiers. Union General Benjamin Butler first applied the term "Contrabands of war" when he refused to return them to their masters upon learning they had been used to build fortifications. Faust, *Encyclopedia of the Civil War*, 161.

45. The Fifth Wisconsin was called into Camp Randall from June 21 to June 25, 1861, and was sent to Washington July 22, 1861, the day after the Federal defeat at Bull Run. It was first

assigned to Rufus King's brigade, but later became part of Winfield Hancock's brigade, William F. Smith's division. *Adjutant General Reports*, 45-46.

46. **McDowell, Edward F.**, Millville, enlisted August 19, 1861, killed August 28, 1862, Gainesville, Virginia. *Wisconsin Roster*, 560.

47. William Howard Russell was one of the most prominent British reporters of his day. He arrived in New York City in March 1861 to cover the American Civil War for the *London Times*. His writings eventually angered both North and South, and Russell left America in the spring of 1862. Faust, *Encyclopedia of the Civil War*, 649.

48. **Brown**, Beaver Dam, enlisted August 1, 1861, promoted chaplain September 15, 1861, resigned March 24, 1862. *Wisconsin Roster,* 539, 545.

49. The Battle of Island No. 10, Missouri, was fought April 7, 1862, about 60 miles below Columbus, Kentucky. Confederates fortified bluffs overlooking the Mississippi River and constructed batteries on the eastern side of an island there (Island No. 10). The Confederates surrendered the next day to a Federal force including General John Pope's Army of the Mississippi and Flag Officer Andrew H. Foote's flotilla of six gunboats and 11 mortar boats. The capture opened the Mississippi River as far south as Fort Pillow, Tennessee, and resulted in the capture of about 3,500 men with all their equipment. Faust, *Encyclopedia of the Civil War*, 386.

50. **Hamilton**, the grandson of Alexander Hamilton, resigned March 1863, still carrying a bullet in his leg the doctors were never able to remove. He returned to Milwaukee to practice law, then went to New York because of his father's ill health. He returned in 1875 and was elected to the Wisconsin Legislature and a judge. Nolan, *Iron Brigade*, 197, 350, note 33.

51. At this time, General George McClellan's Army of the Potomac was in front of the Confederate earthworks at Yorktown, Virginia, on the tip of the peninsula formed by the York and James rivers. He had hoped to use the water route to surprise the Southerners and move quickly up the peninsula and seize Richmond.

52. The Battle of Pittsburgh Landing or Shiloh was fought April 6 and 7, 1862, when Confederates under Johnston and Beauregard attacked a force commanded by U.S. Grant. The surprise attack was almost successful. Johnston's Confederates made sizeable advances on the first day, but were unable to overwhelm Grant's determined soldiers. Johnston was mortally wounded and Beauregard took over command of the army. Reinforced that evening, Grant attacked the following morning and drove the Confederates from the field. Beauregard was not wounded in the battle. Shiloh was the first large-scale battle of the war, and its horrendous casualties shocked both warring sides. Faust, *Encyclopedia of the Civil War*, 684-685.

53. **Black [Henry]**, Liberty, enlisted August 10, 1861, wounded South Mountain, discharged April 7, 1863, disabled. **Black [James]**, Liberty, enlisted August 19, 1861, detached Battery B, Fourth U.S. Artillery from February 9, 1863, deserted May 3, 1863. *Wisconsin Roster,* 558.

Volume 5

54. The monthly pay was $13 for a private.

55. The rumors refer to several skirmishes during Thomas "Stonewall" Jackson's pursuit of Nathaniel Banks to the Harpers Ferry area following the Confederate victory at Winchester, Virginia, on May 25, 1862, during what is now commonly referred to as the Shenandoah Valley Campaign. For an excellent account of this campaign, see Robert Tanner, *Stonewall in the Valley* (Mechanicsburg, PA, revised edition, 1999).

56. According to Captain Edwin Brown of the Sixth Wisconsin, McDowell was "headstrong" and "too anxious to retrieve this defeat at Bull Run." Another officer said the general's "reputation was peculiar. I have seen him attempt to handle a division . . . only to get his brigades and regiments so divided and twisted that he completely lost control of his command; his horse was always blundering over a fence into a ditch until at least there was a general impression with the men that couldn't be shaken, that this man who never tasted wines or liquors or even tea and coffee was a drunkard. They also believed him to be in some way in criminal communication with the confederates and it was current gossip in ranks . . . He wore a peculiar light colored and conspicuous hat that the enemy might distinguish and not hurt him. The charge of drunkenness and disloyalty was equally absurd, but McDowell's great success, was as a society man in command of a department after the war." John Marsh, "Early Days of the War," *Milwaukee Sunday Telegraph*, December 12, 1886.

57. The battle Ray is referring to was Seven Pines or Fair Oaks, fought just outside Richmond. With his back to Richmond, General Joe Johnston was heavily pressured to strike out against McClellan. Heavy rains had flooded the Chickahominy River, which left a portion of McClellan's army isolated below it. Fortunately for the Federals, Johnston's attack was bungled from the start and inartfully delivered. Casualties were heavy and included Johnston himself, who fell severely wounded at the end of the day on May 31. His successor for one day was General Gustavus Smith. That night, President Jefferson Davis appointed General Robert E. Lee to command the army.

58. A newspaper put out by the printers serving in the four regiments of John Gibbon's brigade.

59. **Heacock**, Beetown, enlisted August 19, 1861, corporal, mustered out September 12, 1864, term expired. *Wisconsin Roster,* 559.

60. **Parker**, Patch Grove, enlisted August 19, 1861, wounded Gainesville and Gettysburg, killed June 18, 1864, Petersburg, Virginia, *Wisconsin Roster,* 560-561.

61. **Cook [Charles]**, Madison, enlisted August 19, 1861 and resigned December 28, 1862. *Wisconsin Roster,* 538.

62. Ray is referring to a series of large engagements outside Richmond known as the Seven Days' Battles. The campaign was the brainchild of Robert E. Lee, who discovered that McClellan's right flank was exposed north of the Chickahominy River. Thomas "Stonewall" Jackson's Valley soldiers were brought from the Shenandoah Valley to fall upon the Federals with the idea of trapping and destroying part of McClellan's army, or at least punishing and driving it away from Richmond. The plan went awry, but did succeed in driving the large Army of the Potomac away from the Southern capital and down to the James River. Surprisingly few studies of this campaign exist. The best general account is Stephen Sears, *To the Gates of Richmond* (New York, 1994). An excellent multi-volume series of essays can be found in William Miller, ed., *The Peninsula Campaign of 1862: Yorktown to the Seven Days*, 3 vols. (Savas, 1994-1998).

Volume 6

63. **McLin**, Fennimore, enlisted September 13, 1861, leg amputated at Gettysburg, mustered out September 1, 1864, term expired; **Harris**, Plainfield, enlisted August 2, 1861, detached Battery B, from September 13, 1862, to August 1864, mustered out September 1, 1864, term expired; **Mann**, Clifton, enlisted August 25, 1861, discharged January 17, 1864; **Dolphin**, Glen Haven, enlisted August 19, 1861, detached Battery B from September 13, 1862 to September 1864, mustered out September 1, 1864, term expired; **Craig**, Potosi, enlisted August 19, 1861, killed September 17, 1862, Antietam; **Bishop**, Millville, enlisted August 19, 1861, wounded Gainesville and Wilderness, mustered out September 1, 1864, term expired; **Schlosser**, Glen Haven, enlisted August 19, 1861, prisoner Gettysburg, died March 19, 1864, Andersonville, Georgia, of wounds; **Sixby**, Glen Haven, enlisted August 19, 1861, sergeant, killed Gainesville, Va., August 28, 1862; **Dexter**, Ellenboro, enlisted August 19, 1861, wounded South Mountain, discharged November 28, 1862, disabled; **Leppa**, Potosi, enlisted August 19, 1861, wounded Second Bull Run, died of wounds; **Eustice**, Potosi, enlisted August 19, 1861, wounded Gainesville, mustered out September 1, 1864, term expired. *Wisconsin Roster*, 558-561, 566, 567, 569.

64. **Hollon Richardson** was born in Poland, Ohio, December 25, 1838, and moved to Chippewa Falls in Wisconsin in 1859. He entered the army as first lieutenant of Company A, Seventh Wisconsin Volunteer Infantry. During the course of the war he served in several capacities and was promoted to colonel of his regiment. Richardson was wounded eight times and was the only Wisconsin man breveted three times for distinguished service in the field. He was one of only two men, of all the officers of his regiment, who remained a member of the Seventh Wisconsin the entire war. Following his muster out, Richardson settled in Baltimore and practiced law. In 1870, he returned to Chippewa Falls. In 1900, he moved to Seattle, Washington. During the Spanish-American War he was a civilian employee of the Quartermaster Department and traveled several times to the Philippine Islands. He died in Seattle in 1916.

65. Rufus Dawes of the Sixth Wisconsin reported: "July 4th was celebrated with festivities and merry-making. Gibbon's brigade gathered upon a large plain, where there was horse racing, foot racing, and other amusements and athletic exercises. There was a great mule race, a sack race, and a greased pig." Dawes, *Service*, 51.

66. The hammocks are probably due to the fact the Prairie du Chien company contained a large number of Mississippi River raftsmen.

67. The consolidated morning report for July 31, 1862, showed the number of men present for duty in John Gibbon's brigade was 40 companies, 2,664 men, plus about 150 commissioned officers. Dawes, *Service*, 53.

68. **Kuntz**, Tafton, enlisted August 19, 1861, killed September 17, 1862, at Antietam. *Wisconsin Roster,* 560.

69. General Rufus King on July 24, 1862, ordered General John Gibbon to make a reconnaissance to Orange Court House and to ascertain the force of the enemy at that point. With three regiments of infantry, sixty sharpshooters, one battery of artillery and a squadron of cavalry, Gibbon proceeded to within five and one half miles of the court house and camped.

As he withdrew after ascertaining the whereabouts of the enemy, he was pursued and attacked by enemy cavalry.

The second reconnaissance, or "Fredericks Hall Raid," was also under the command of Gibbon and began August 6, 1862. The aim was to destroy a portion of the Virginia Central Railroad. The Sixth Wisconsin, with a small force of cavalry and artillery and under the command of Lysander Cutler of the Sixth Wisconsin, proceeded to Frederick Hall on the Virginia Central and destroyed two miles of track. The men penetrated to within 30 miles of the enemy's lines. Gibbon's force was about 3,000 and included six companies of the Harris Cavalry and two guns of Garish's New Hampshire Battery. Quiner, *Wisconsin*, 258-259, Dawes, *Service*, 53.

70. The order directed Rufus King's division to join General John Pope at Cedar Mountain, 45 miles distant, where Union General Nathaniel Banks was engaging the corps of Confederate General Thomas "Stonewall" Jackson.

71. Although Jackson outnumbered Banks at Cedar Mountain, he only managed to squeek out a limited victory. Banks lost nearly 2,400 men while Jackson suffered nearly 1,350 casualties. For an excellent account of this fascinating battle see Robert K. Krick, *Jackson at Cedar Mountain* (Chapel Hill, 1990).

72. The Third Wisconsin went into battle with 423 men, of whom 107 were killed, wounded, or missing. See *Adjutant General Reports*, 111, E. B. Quiner, *The Military History of Wisconsin* (Chicago, 1866), 486-487.

73. **Manning**, Waterloo, enlisted May 20, 1861, wounded Gainesville and Rappahannock River, transferred Veteran Reserve Corps July 1, 1863. *Wisconsin Roster,* 355.

74. Called Gainesville by the Federals and Groveton by the Confederates, the engagement at dusk August 28, 1862, is more commonly known today as Brawner's Farm. The fighting erupted when Confederate General Stonewall Jackson opened fire on Rufus King's brigade as it marched along the Warrenton Turnpike near the old battlefield of Bull Run. Heavily outnumbered, the four Western regiments stood their ground for 90 minutes with the two lines at times only 50 yards apart. The Second Wisconsin was the first engaged. The Nineteenth Indiana went in on the left of the Second, the Seventh Wisconsin on the right. The Sixth Wisconsin was slightly to the right of the three regiments. The Seventh Wisconsin lost 164 of 580 engaged, including Private William Ray. Reports later showed 725—more than one-third of the brigade—were killed, wounded, or missing. Eight of the brigade's 12 field officers were wounded, including all three field officers of the Seventh Wisconsin. *OR* 12, pt. 2, 378. Colonel William Robinson was shot through the body; Lieutenant Colonel Charles Hamilton through the thighs, but maintained his seat in the saddle as his boots filled with blood. Major George Bill suffered a slight head wound.

The Second and Seventh Wisconsin were consolidated under Lucius Fairchild of the Second Wisconsin, the senior field officer still on his feet. The brigade was lightly engaged the next two days and covered the retreat of the defeated Union army. "The best blood of Wisconsin and Indiana was poured out like water, and it was spilled for naught," Rufus Dawes of the Sixth Wisconsin said later. Herdegen, *Stood Like Iron*, 95-113.

Volume 7

75. The fight at Gainesville (Brawner's Farm) where Ray was wounded revealed Jackson's location to Pope, who spent much of August 29 assailing his strong position along an unfinished railroad cut. The battle became known as Second Bull Run (or Second Manassas). It was a bloody fight often waged at close quarters, but Jackson successfully beat back Pope's attacks. Ray's Western Brigade took part in the attack and suffered additional losses. The Seventh Wisconsin, for example, lost 164 men killed, wounded, and captured during the campaign. Unbeknownst to Pope, however, General Lee and the balance of the Army of Northern Virginia arrived on the field around noon that afternoon and had taken up a position on Jackson's right flank.

On the day Ray was writing this entry, the battle of South Mountain occurred (September 14, 1862). Federal soldiers discovered a misplaced copy of Lee's campaign plans wrapped around several cigars, which prompted McClellan to advance in the hope of destroying his enemy while widely separated. The slow-moving McClellan forced Turner's and Fox's Gaps in the South Mountain range after a sharp and prolonged engagement. It was while the Western Brigade was advancing up the National Road that the Second, Sixth, and Seventh Wisconsin, and Nineteenth Indiana, were given the name "Iron Brigade" by General George McClellan. For a more detailed account of this, see Lance J. Herdegen, *The Men Stood Like Iron: How the Iron Brigade Won Its Name* (Bloomington, Indiana, 1997), 145-146.

76. **Marlow**, Hurricane, enlisted August 19, 1861, wounded Gainesville, discharged June 16, 1863, disabled. *Wisconsin Roster*, 560.

77. The battle Ray heard raging most of the day was in fact much more intense and bloody than the September 14, 1862, fight at South Mountain. Pope attacked again on the morning of August 30, but was beaten back with heavy losses. With Jackson holding firm, Lee launched Longstreet's First Corps against Pope's left front and crushed the Federal army. Pope lost some 16,000 men to all causes, while Lee suffered about 9,200 casualties. The defeat cost Pope his command. For an excellent account of this campaign, see John Hennessy, *Return to Bull Run: The Campaign and Battle of Second Manassas* (New York, NY., 1993).

78. Ray is referring to military police.

79. Liberty Poles became common during the Revolutionary War when Americans, known as "Liberty Boys," erected poles sporting liberty caps to mark the repeal of the Stamp Act.

80. The Descriptive List was a regimental document which allowed a soldier to be mustered for pay.

81. Following John Pope's disastrous outing at Second Bull Run, McClellan had command of the troops during the Maryland Campaign, but lost the confidence of President Lincoln following his lethargic pursuit of Lee's army after the fighting at Antietam on September 17, 1862. General Ambrose Burnside was appointed to lead the Army of the Potomac on November 7, 1862. Although he doubted his abilities to lead an army, Burnside assumed the post and decided to attack Lee around Fredericksburg, Virginia, midway between Washington and Richmond and moved his army accordingly opposite the city.

82. The rumors Ray heard and read were again incorrect. With Lee's army deployed on the heights behind Fredericksburg, Burnside crossed his army over the Rappahannock River and attacked. Wave after wave of Federals were mowed down in the attempt to breach the

Confederate front. The only success came on the Federal left flank, where Jackson's Southern line was temporarily pierced. Casualties were about 12,600 for the Federals and 5,200 for the Confederates. Fortunately for the Iron Brigade, it did not directly participate in the attacks of December 14. Total casualties for the brigade were 65 killed and wounded, most from the long-range effects of artillery. *OR* 21, 138, 475-477.

Volume 8

83. It is disappointing that Ray's journal is missing pages for much of the period dealing with the army's tenure under Union General Ambrose Burnside and Ray's return to his company. Following the Federal defeat at Fredericksburg, the Army of the Potomac settled into winter camp at Belle Plain along the Potomac River. The men constructed wooden shebangs and settled into a routine of drills and picket duty as the army waited out the winter. Ray also missed the futile march through inclement weather that became known as Burnside's "mud march." By the time the army returned to its camps on January 23, 1863, many of the Wisconsin men were exhausted and sick from exposure. The march also coincided with a general crisis of confidence in Federal leadership and enthusiasm for the war. Burnside was subsequently removed and a new commander, Major General Joseph "Fighting Joe" Hooker, elevated in his stead. Hooker was the commander of the First Corps at Antietam. A new regiment, the Twenty-fourth Michigan, reinforced the diminished Iron Brigade after Antietam. One of the changes instituted by Hooker made the Western regiments the First Brigade of the First Division of the First Army Corps, Army of the Potomac. It was a move greeted with quiet pride and some boasting. See Nolan, *Iron Brigade*.

84. The Emancipation Proclamation was issued by President Lincoln following the Union "victory" at Antietam. It declared that as of January 1, 1863, all slaves in rebellious sections would be free and that the government would not repress those attempting to gain their own freedom. Faust, *Civil War Encyclopedia*, 242.

85. **Norman**, Madison, enlisted September 19, 1862, absent sick at muster out of regiment. *Wisconsin Roster,* 560.

86. **Dean**, Harrison, enlisted August 19, 1861, wounded Gettysburg, transferred to Veteran Reserve Corps January 15, 1864, and mustered out September 1, 1864, term expired. *Wisconsin Roster,* 559.

87. **Alexander [Thomas C]**, Millville, enlisted August 19, 1861, wounded North Anna, promoted first lieutenant Company H, January 6, 1865. *Wisconsin Roster,* 558.

Volume 9

88. The missing pages include the fighting of the Iron Brigade during the Chancellorsville Campaign. The regiments left their camps in late April and marched to Fredericksburg, where they were selected for a mission to cross the Rappahannock River in pontoon boats, and seize and hold the Confederate entrenchments on the opposite shore until engineers could construct a bridge. Several attempts failed and finally First Corps leader John Reynolds ordered the

brigade to storm the Confederate positions at FitzHugh's Crossing. "It now seemed that the Rappahannock must be reddened with our blood if the crossing was to be forced," said one Black Hat. Led by the Sixth Wisconsin and Twenty-fourth Michigan, the First Division, commanded by General James Wadsworth of New York, quickly crossed the wide river, capturing several dozen Confederates and taking the high ground. "It was the grandest fifteen minutes of our lives," said one Badger. "Worth a man's life to enjoy." The brigade missed the heavier fighting in the Union defeat at Chancellorsville. Total losses for the Iron Brigade were 10 killed and 39 wounded. The Seventh Wisconsin had two officers and one enlisted man killed and one officer and three enlisted men wounded. William J. K. Beaudot and Lance J. Herdegen, *An Irishman in the Iron Brigade: The Civil War Writings of Sergt. James P. Sullivan, Co. K, 6th Wisconsin* (New York, NY., 1994), 74-89; Marc Storch and Beth Storch, "Like So Many Devils": *Giants in Their Tall Black Hats: Essays on the Iron Brigade* (Bloomington, IN., 1998), 86-100.

89. The rumor circulating during the closing days of May and early June was that Confederate General Robert E. Lee was planning to once again invade the North. The rumor was true. On June 4, Lee shifted two of his three corps west out of Fredericksburg toward Culpeper Court House, leaving only A. P. Hill's Third Corps behind to watch Hooker's army. Also important those days was the arrival of hats for the new Twenty-fourth Michigan, making the Wolverines true "Black Hats."

90. Hooker had indeed pushed men across the river at Franklin's Crossing, above Fredericksburg, where he found Hill's Confederates in position. Skirmishing there would continue for several days.

91. Desperate for information, Hooker dispatched Brigadier General Alfred Pleasonton and his cavalry, supported by infantry and artillery, some 11,000 men, to find out what Lee was up to. Pleasonton's troopers crossed the Rappahannock at a pair of fords and attacked Jeb Stuart's Southern cavalry early on the morning of June 9, 1863, just seven miles northeast of Culpeper, Virginia, along the Orange and Alexandria Railroad at Brandy Station. Pleasonton's action triggered the largest cavalry action of the entire war. Charges, counter-charges, and hand-to-hand fighting marked much of the contest. The fighting ended late that afternoon with about 500 Confederates and twice as many Federals killed, wounded, or captured. Stuart and his men held the field by a razor-thin margin.

92. The information reaching Ray was generally correct. Called the battle of Second Winchester, Union forces commanded by Major General R. H. Milroy were attacked at the city in the northern Shenandoah Valley by Ewell's Confederate corps when Milroy delayed his retreat to Harpers Ferry. E. B. Long, *The Civil War Day by Day: An Almanac 1861-1865* (New York, 1971), 367.

93. The vanguard of Lee's army began crossing the Potomac River on June 16, 1863. Hooker wanted to shift the Army of the Potomac north of the capital and bring Lee to battle, while Washington officials wanted Hooker to relieve Harpers Ferry and follow Lee. This disagreement eventually proved to be the beginning of the end of Hooker's tenure in command of the army.

94. General Stoneman was relieved of command for his inept handling of the cavalry of the Army of the Potomac during the Chancellorsville campaign. Alfred A. Pleasonton was promoted to major general on June 22, 1863.

95. Lee's army was strung out from Pennsylvania down to the Potomac River, and the bulk of his cavalry under Jeb Stuart was beginning a controversial ride that would carry he and his men away from the main army and out of much of the campaign. Longstreet's and Hill's corps began crossing the river the day before (June 24), while Ewell's Corps was skirmishing near McConnellsburg, Pennsylvania.

96. Ray is referring to the time in September 1862 when General George B. McClellan referred to the Westerners as a brigade of "iron." Herdegen, *How the Iron Brigade Won Its Name*, 145-146.

97. Ray's news was correct. Lincoln and General Halleck, his chief of staff, had their doubts as to whether Hooker was up to the task of stopping Lee's invasion. When Hooker offered to resign over a dispute on how to handle the army, Lincoln accepted on June 27, 1863. George Gordon Meade, commander of the army's Fifth Corps, was selected to command the Army of the Potomac. Changing leaders in the middle of a campaign was a dangerous gamble.

98. The Iron Brigade crossed into Pennsylvania on June 30, halting at Marsh Creek, south of Gettysburg.

99. The men were up at dawn the next day and shortly after 8:00 a.m. Wadsworth's Division began marching up the Emmitsburg Road toward Gettysburg. The Second Wisconsin was in the lead followed by the Seventh Wisconsin, Nineteenth Indiana, Twenty-fourth Michigan, and Sixth Wisconsin. Riding with the division was General John Reynolds of the First Corps, commanding the advance wing of the Army of the Potomac. Nearing the town, the Black Hats heard distant artillery fire and hastened the pace. Reynolds rode ahead.

100. Shortly after 10:00 a.m., just as two Confederate brigades closed on Gettysburg from the northwest, the brigade column reached the Codori House one mile south of the town. The column soon crossed a ridge to the south of the Lutheran Seminary Building. The Sixth Wisconsin was halted in reserve. The four other regiments, moving in a line of battle, en echelon, at the double-quick moved up the slope of McPherson's Ridge as Federal cavalry pulled back. At the crest, the Second Wisconsin slammed into James Archer's Confederate brigade, which was marching east below (or south of) the Chambersburg Pike. General Reynolds was killed early in the fighting while urging the Badgers forward. Archer's Confederates were surprised by the sudden appearance of Federal infantry (they were expecting cavalry and militia) and were knocked backward. Several hundred were captured in the rout that followed, including Archer himself. North of the Chambersburg Pike, the division's Second Brigade was driven rearward by Joe Davis's Confederate brigade, but the timely arrival of the Sixth Wisconsin and a quick charge on an unfinished railroad cut ended the threat and slaughtered hundreds of Davis's men. Captured in the cut were more than 225 Confederates and the battleflag of the Second Mississippi Infantry.

The Iron Brigade formed a line just east of Willoughby Run in McPherson's Woods. For good accounts of the opening action, see Herdegen and Beaudot, *In The Bloody Railroad Cut at Gettysburg*, and David Martin, *Gettysburg, July 1* (Conshohocken, PA., 1996, revised edition).

101. With Ewell's Confederate corps sweeping in from north and northwest of town, General Lee realized that he had a wonderful opportunity to destroy part of Meade's army. In

the middle of the afternoon he ordered a sizeable attack against the line held by the Iron Brigade and other troops on Seminary Ridge. The assault drove the defenders back step by step to a last-ditch position along some rails piled in front of the Seminary Building. The collapse of the Union line north and west of the town (held primarily by General Oliver Howard's Eleventh Corps) came about 4:00 p.m.

102. William Ray was wounded just as his regiment began the retreat into the town. Colonel William Robinson of the Seventh Wisconsin assumed command of the brigade with the wounding of Solomon Meredith of the Nineteenth Indiana. The brigade's regiments (and the rest of the First and Eleventh Federal corps) retreated to the Union rally point at Cemetery Hill and later Culp's Hill.

103. The brigade missed most of the heavy fighting of the next two days, but the stand on July 1, 1863, allowed the Union army to secure the high ground south of Gettysburg. It was that position that proved decisive in the next two days of fighting. The Iron Brigade carried 1,883 men into the battle and suffered 1,212 killed, wounded, and missing. These heavy losses were the highest of any brigade at Gettysburg. The First Minnesota had the highest percentage losses at Gettysburg (fighting on July 2), but the Twenty-fourth Michigan had the highest total loss with 399 out of 496. The Seventh Wisconsin took 343 into the battle and lost 26 killed, 109 wounded and 43 missing for a total of 178, or 52 percent. William W. Dudley, *The Iron Brigade at Gettysburg, Official Report of the Part Borne by the 1st Brigade, 1st Division, 1st Army Corps* (Cincinnati, privately printed, 1878); Nolan, *Iron Brigade*; Herdegen and Beaudot, *In the Bloody Railroad Cut at Gettysburg*.

104. After the successful first day of fighting, Lee determined to attack again the following day. The attack was launched en echelon, beginning with Longstreet's Corps against the Federal left flank and moving up the line on Cemetery Ridge, brigade by brigade, as each thrust sought out an opportunity to break apart and rout Meade's army. The fighting was exceptionally heavy and prolonged, and ended only after dark with a Confederate dusk attack on East Cemetery Hill. Although the nighttime attack was successful, it was not supported and the Southerners were forced back off the eminence. There are many good accounts of the fighting on July 2. For an excellent and very original and thought-provoking examination, see Scott Bowden and Bill Ward, *Last Chance for Victory: Robert E. Lee and the Gettysburg Campaign* (Conshohocken, PA., 2001).

105. Ray is describing (in very general terms since he did not witness the fighting), what is known to history as Pickett's Charge. Lee made one of the most controversial decisions of his career to assault the center of Meade's line on July 3. A massive artillery barrage was launched about 1:00 p.m.—not 4:00 p.m., as Ray writes—and about one hour later Lee's Southern infantry stepped off from Seminary Ridge for their attack against Cemetery Ridge. The attack was a spectacular failure and cost Lee many thousands of killed, wounded, and captured.

106. Meade pursued his beaten enemy toward the Potomac River, which was so swollen the Rebels could not cross it to safety for many days. Lee dug in his army and waited for Meade to attack him, which he declined to do. On July 13, Lee was finally able to withdraw below the river, officially ending the campaign. Lincoln was not pleased that Meade allowed the badly wounded Confederate army to escape, but the Army of the Potomac had been almost as crippled during the three days at Gettysburg.

There was not a major action fought between Generals Rosecrans and Bragg in Tennessee, as Ray believed, but Vicksburg, Mississippi, had indeed surrendered to Grant on July 4, 1863, and the stronghold of Port Hudson, about 100 miles to the south along the Mississippi River, surrendered four days later.

107. Although Ray was not with his regiment, the day marked the end of the all-Western character of the Iron Brigade. The 167th Pennsylvania was added. The new men were Easterners, nine-month men, and were about to be released from service. The action marked the addition of a series of non-Western regiments to the brigade.

108. There was substantial fighting going on that July in and around Charleston as Federal forces inched closer to bring the city under siege. Federal forces attacked Battery Wagner (the primary subject of the movie "Glory") on July 11 and 18, 1863. Although modest gains were made, the city remained defiant—and in Rebel hands.

109. The fight at Germantown took place on October 2, 1777, when General George Washington tried to attack General Howe's British army. The plan went awry, however, and after a sharp engagement Washington retreated. Americans losses were some 152 killed, 521 wounded, and over 400 captured. The British casualties numbered 537 and 14 captured.

Volume 10

110. Although General Quincy Gillmore was making progress, he had not captured Battery Wagner or Fort Sumter, although the latter masonry fort was indeed crumbling under the barrage of Federal heavy guns. Ironically, the crumbled brickwork actually strengthened the defensive position, for once the walls had become piles of rubble, there was nothing left that could be done to the bastion with artillery.

111. Created in April 1863, the Invalid Corps consisted of worthy disabled officers and men who were or had been in the army. Faust, *Civil War Encyclopedia*, 383.

112. The special flag was made by Tiffany and Co., New York, from money raised by Wisconsin, Indiana and Michigan residents living in Washington at the time. The anniversary of Antietam, September 17, 1863, was originally set for the ceremony, but was delayed when the brigade moved to Culpepper. The Iron Brigade flag has been restored and is now in the Wisconsin Veterans Museum in Madison, Wisconsin.

113. A cone-shaped canvas tent invented by Major Henry Hopkins Sibley of the 1st U.S. Dragoons. It was able to accommodate 20 soldiers. Faust, *Civil War Encyclopedia*, 687.

114. Ray is referring to the battle of Chickamauga, which took place on September 19 and 20, 1863. Although the armies fought to draw the first day, Bragg's Confederate Army of Tennessee was reinforced with two divisions from James Longstreet's Corps of Lee's Army of Northern Virginia that night. The Federal line was breached the following day (largely as a result of a Federal command mistake that left a large gap in the line) and except for a gallant stand on Snodgrass Hill by a segment of his army, Rosecrans's men were routed from the field and bottled up in Chattanooga, Tennessee. It was a stunning Federal loss that threatened much of the year's gains in the Western Theater.

115. **Hayden**, Lancaster, enlisted August 19, 1861, wounded Gettysburg, mustered out July 3, 1865; **Hudson**, Beetown, enlisted August 19, 1861, wounded Fredericksburg, mustered out September 1, 1864, term expired. *Wisconsin Roster,* 559.

116. Following Rosecrans's defeat at Chickamauga, President Lincoln decided to send the Eleventh and Twelfth Corps from the Army of the Potomac, under the command of General Joseph Hooker, to help rectify the situation around Chattanooga.

117. The model 1861 rifle-musket.

118. On October 10, 1863, Meade decided to probe beyond the Rapidan to discover where Lee was moving his army. Unbeknownst to Meade, Lee was on the move and headed west and north, triggering what would be known as the Bristoe Station Campaign. Skirmishing was heavy much of the day.

119. Ray's entry is about the engagement at Bristoe Station, Virginia, where elements of Hill's Third Corps of the Army of Northern Virginia attacked retreating rear units of the Army of the Potomac. Hill's assault was rashly delivered and his men suffered heavy losses to no effect.

120. Casualties for the Bristoe fight were about 1,300 Confederates and 550 Federals.

121. Ray was listening to the sounds of the cavalry fight at Buckland Mills, where Jeb Stuart's Southern cavalry routed General Judson Kilpatrick's troopers. The engagement was the last serious encounter of the Bristoe Station Campaign.

122. Ray is referring to Hooker's nighttime battle at Wauhatchie, Tennessee. The Federals trapped in Chattanooga were attempting to open a line into the besieged city when James Longstreet's Confederates (detached from Lee's army for service in the west) attacked Hooker in Lookout Valley on the night of October 28-29, 1863. The Federals beat back the confused attack, which was one of the most important nighttime engagements of the war. Losses from all causes were about equal: 420 Federals and 408 Confederates.

123. The fighting Ray could hear was Meade's effort to thrust across the Rappahannock River at Rappahannock Station and Kelly's Ford. The result netted hundreds of Southern prisoners, and essentially reestablished the lines as they were at the beginning of the Bristoe Station Campaign.

124. **Simpkins**, Millville, enlisted August 19, 1861, and was wounded at South Mountain. He died October 8, 1862. *Wisconsin Roster,* 561.

125. The National Cemetery at Gettysburg, Pennsylvania, was formally dedicated November 19, 1863. President Abraham Lincoln's brief address is one of the most recognized and admired speeches in history.

126. Meade crossed the Army of the Potomac over the Rapidan River in an attempt to turn Lee's right flank and catch him at a disadvantage. The movement and handful of engagements that followed are known as the Mine Run Campaign, after a meandering creek in the region.

127. The skirmishing Ray heard was (as it eventually turned out) the only serious fighting of the campaign at Payne's Farm, where a division of Confederates under Edward Johnson held off almost two corps of Federals (Third and Sixth) in a confusing and sharp four-hour fight.

128. Ulysses S. Grant, victor of Shiloh and Vicksburg, replaced General Rosecrans in Chattanooga and went over to the offensive on November 23, 1863, against Bragg's Army of Tennessee, which was dug in on a broad semicircle overlooking the embattled city. Within

two days Bragg's army was routed off Missionary Ridge and knocked back into northern Georgia. Bragg resigned on the last day of the month. The campaign firmly established Grant as the preeminent Northern general and led to his promotion to lieutenant general and commander of all the Union armies the following March, 1864.

129. After Payne's Farm, Lee had withdrawn his army into a line of powerful entrenchments behind a creek called Mine Run. Although Meade determined to attack him there, one of his corps leaders balked when he saw the Southern lines and pleaded with Meade to cancel the attack. Meade wisely heeded the advice and decided to withdraw, effectively ending the war in the Eastern Theater until the spring of 1864. James Longstreet's Confederate corps was still in Tennessee and would not rejoin Lee until early in 1864.

130. Corduroying a road was a system of laying logs and branches to allow soldiers and wagons to pass over muddy spots.

131. **Stonehouse**, Beetown, enlisted August 19, 1861, wounded Petersburg, discharged September 27, 1864, disability. *Wisconsin Roster,* 561.

132. The report was false; Confederate General James Longstreet was alive and well.

133. **Palmer**, Janesville, enlisted September 7, 1861, mustered out October 7, 1865. *Wisconsin Roster,* 538.

134. A native of Clarendon, New York, Lewis came to Wisconsin in 1840 where his father had large land holdings. He settled in Columbus in 1845 and after a political career was elected governor on the Republican ticket in 1863. *Dictionary of Wisconsin Bibliography* (Madison, WI., 1960), 229-230.

135. **Simmons**, Cassville, enlisted September 9, 1861, wounded Gainesville, mustered out July 3, 1865. *Wisconsin Roster,* 574.

Volume 11

136. **Hayden**, Lancaster, enlisted August 19, 1861, wounded Gettysburg, mustered out July 3, 1865. *Wisconsin Roster,* 559.

137. **Brinkman**, Potosi, enlisted January 4, 1864, mustered out July 3, 1865; **Lesler**, Potosi, enlisted January 2, 1864, mustered out July 3, 1865. *Wisconsin Roster,* 558, 560.

138. **Bradbury**, Harrison, enlisted August 19, 1861, wounded Wilderness and Gravelly Run, mustered out June 2, 1865; **Roberts**, Beetown, enlisted August 19, 1861, promoted to 1st lieutenant December 13, 1864, wounded Five Forks, discharged June 1, 1865. *Wisconsin Roster,* 558-560.

139. **Hutchinson**, Tafton, enlisted January 20, 1864, wounded Wilderness, transferred to Veteran Reserve Corps April 24, 1865. *Wisconsin Roster,* 559.

140. President Lincoln on March 10, 1864, appointed Ulysses S. Grant to command all armies of the United States and promoted him to the rank of lieutenant general.

141. General James Wadsworth announced he would publish in general orders the regiment in his division that stood first in soldierly qualities, discipline, cleanliness, and condition of arms, but the time for the inspection was not given. The Sixth Wisconsin was later cited as "first in excellence in the division" on a ruse. When the order came to brigade headquarters, it was discovered by Colonel Edward Bragg of the Sixth Wisconsin, who gave

his regiment advance warning. Bragg said later the inspector "stopped at my tent and waked me up, and I pretended that it was the first I had heard of an inspection, and grumbled about their playing such tricks on us. . . . [The inspector at an 1885 reunion] admitted that he expected to take us unawares, and wanted to know how we got ready. I told him they always kept themselves that way in camp, to which he answered, 'Bosh!'" Dawes, *Service*, 245-246.

142. **Booth**, Potosi, enlisted January 2, 1864, promoted to sergeant major December 14, 1864. *Wisconsin Roster,* 558.

143. **Holmes**, Columbus, enlisted July 15, 1861, killed June 2, 1864, Bethesda Church, Virginia. *Wisconsin Roster,* 542.

144. The brigade, now assigned to Warren's Fifth Corps with the breakup of the First Corps, broke camp early May 4, 1864, and joined the column crossing the pontoon bridges on the Rapidan River the next morning. By that afternoon, the men were camped near the crossroads of Germanna Road and the Orange Court House Turnpike on the eastern edge of the heavily-wooded region known as the "Wilderness," which consisted of second growth timber, tangled brush, swampy creeks, and few roads and farms.

The general rumor about General Benjamin Butler was correct. Grant's overall plan was a multi-pronged effort to bring victory: William Sherman's armies would move against Joe Johnston in North Georgia while Meade and the Army of the Potomac struck General Lee in Virginia and another column moved south up the Shenandoah Valley. Ben Butler's 40,000-man Army of the James, meanwhile, took transports up the James River and debarked at Bermuda Hundred, just fifteen miles below Richmond.

145. On the morning of May 5, 1864, the Iron Brigade moved along the Parker's Store Road. By midmorning, the Federals encountered a strong element of Lee's Army of Northern Virginia, and for the next 48 hours the two armies fought one of the bloodiest engagements of the war. General Lee had reacted immediately to the Federal crossing of the Rapidan by shuttling his army eastward along two major and largely parallel roadways, the Orange Turnpike on the north, and the Orange Plank Road about one mile to the south. Lee's intent was to strike Grant's army as it snaked southward through the Wilderness. Richard Ewell's Second Corps of Confederates on the Orange Turnpike ran into General Gouverneur Warren's Fifth Corps near Saunder's Field, triggering the fight. William Ray is describing the opening of this engagement. See Nolan, *Iron Brigade*; Sharon Eggleston Vipond, "A New Kind of Murder," *Giants in their Tall Black Hats: Essays on the Iron Brigade* (Bloomington and Indianapolis, IN., 1998). For an excellent account of the battle, see Gordon C. Rhea, *The Battle of the Wilderness, May 5-6, 1864* (Baton Rouge, LA., 1994).

146. Wadsworth's division went into action about noon or shortly thereafter just below the Orange Turnpike and south of Saunder's Field. Cutler's Iron Brigade held the north or right flank of the division just above a small creek called Mill Branch. The Seventh Wisconsin held the far right of Cutler's brigade (and thus the far right of the entire division) and attacked that portion of the enemy line held by Cullen Battle's Alabama brigade and George Doles's Georgia brigade. With the assistance of other troops on their right from another division, the Seventh Wisconsin played a material role in driving back John M. Jones's Confederate brigade (which is what Ray is describing briefly in his account: "charged on them, drove them & kept driving them for a mile or so . . ."). Jones was killed in the attack. The Federal advance soon became confused in the heavy terrain and drifted steadily leftward (or to the south). This

left the Iron Brigade exposed to a heavy flanking fire that tore apart several regiments, including the Wisconsin men, who fell back to a line well to the rear. Cutler noted in his report that his brigade lost "very heavily in killed and wounded." See *OR* 36, pt. 1, 610-611. He was not exaggerating. The Seventh Wisconsin suffered its worse loss of the war in a single battle at the Wilderness with 27 killed, 155 wounded, and 35 missing. Losses at Gettysburg, which are considered heavy, totaled 21 killed and 105 wounded. William F. Fox, *Regimental Losses in the American Civil War* (Albany, NY., 1889), 397.

147. It is likely that Ray was wounded by a Georgian in John B. Gordon's Brigade, which launched an assault at this time against the largely isolated Iron Brigade.

148. The fighting seesawed back and forth the rest of the afternoon without either side gaining a lasting advantage. While Ewell's Southerners were battling Warren's Fifth Corps and thereafter John Sedgwick's Sixth Corps, much of the balance of the Army of the Potomac was fighting a mile or so to the south against A. P. Hill's Third Corps, deployed astride the Orange Plank Road.

149. The battle opened again on both fronts on the morning of May 6, 1864. The most critical fighting that day took place to the south along the Orange Plank Road, where a large Federal attack broke the Confederate lines and routed the right wing of Lee's army. Only the timely arrival of Longstreet's Corps saved Lee's army from what would have been a catastrophic defeat. Division Commander James Wadsworth was mortally wounded later in the day leading an ill-fated charge on the Rebel works. Brigadier General Lysander Cutler, the first colonel of the Sixth Wisconsin, assumed command of the division.

150. Ambrose Burnside's Ninth Corps was already with the army and joined the fighting on May 6, 1864.

151. By the night of May 7, 1864, the Iron Brigade and its attached artillery, Battery B, Fourth U.S. Artillery, were on the move south down the Brock Road toward Todd's Tavern and Spotsylvania Court House. Unlike every other commander of the Army of the Potomac, Grant decided to fight it out that summer. Instead of Richmond, Lee's army was the objective. As he would several times that May and June, Grant moved by his left flank around Lee's right in an effort to seek favorable terms of engagement.

152. Ray was correct: Grant was indeed "still driving the enemy." On May 12, 1864, Grant launched one of the largest surprise attacks of the war against a large salient in Lee's line at Spotsylvania. The attack captured thousands of Confederates, including several generals. The assault almost split Lee's army in two. The Iron Brigade was involved in the fighting near the Bloody Angle, which fortunately for William Ray, he missed entirely because of his "slight" wound suffered on May 6. The Seventh Wisconsin during the Spotsylvania campaign lost another 19 killed, 58 wounded, and three missing. Fox, *Regimental Losses*, 397.

153. Unfortunately, Butler was not driving anyone. After muffing an opportunity to cut an important rail link and capture Petersburg or perhaps even Richmond, Butler was fought to a standstill at the battle of Drewry's Bluff on May 16, after which he withdrew. The Confederates, led by General P. G. T. Beauregard, threw up heavy entrenchments on Bermuda Hundred and "bottled" up Butler and his Army of the James, largely removing the threat to Richmond and interior Virginia. For an excellent account of the Bermuda Hundred Campaign, see William Glenn Robertson, *Back Door to Richmond: The Bermuda Hundred Campaign, April-June 1864* (Newark, DE., 1987).

154. General John Sedgwick, commander of the Sixth Corps, was killed by a sharpshooter while visiting the front lines on May 9, 1864. Jeb Stuart was mortally wounded on May 11, 1864, but not captured, and James Longstreet was severely wounded during the fighting on May 6. Neither Robert E. Lee nor A. P. Hill were wounded.

155. The Spotsylvania Campaign was winding down by May 18, 1864. After several Federal attacks were beaten back, General Meade stopped attacking and General Grant decided to begin sliding around Lee's right flank a second time. His position at Spotsylvania was just too strong to crack.

156. Grant was marching east and south, and Lee was moving to confront him, planning to stop and dig in opposite Grant along the North Anna River.

157. General William S. Walker was actually a native of Pittsburgh, Pennsylvania, but was raised by his uncle, Mississippi Senator Robert J. Walker. He was a veteran of the Mexican War. Faust, *Civil War Encyclopedia*, 799.

158. General Sherman's three armies were enjoying significant success against Joe Johnston's Army of Tennessee in North Georgia. Johnston, who routinely preferred to withdraw instead of fight, continually fell back or was turned out of his prepared positions.

159. On May 23, 1864, Lee and Grant fought a battle on the North Anna River near Hanover. The engagement was not decisive in any sense, but it did reveal to Grant that his own position there was not a good one, and he determined to sidle east and south once again.

160. Grant was steadily wearing down Lee's army and getting a bit closer to Richmond with each major move, as Lee attempted to keep the Army of the Potomac on the outside of the arc of maneuver. Richmond was still firmly in Confederate hands, however.

161. Grant's main force at this time was along the Topopotomoy River and confronted Lee's line along the Chickahominy River. By this time Grant was only a handful of miles from Richmond—just as close as McClellan had been in the late spring of 1862.

Volume 12

162. The battle of Cold Harbor to which Ray refers took place on June 3, 1864, just a few miles outside Richmond near the field of the Seven Days' Battles. Tiring of flanking operations and believing that Lee's army was weaker than it really was, Grant ordered a massive full frontal assault against the enemy lines. In about one hour's time he lost at least 6,000 men to all causes, while Lee's losses are estimated at about 1,500. Unlike so many of the battles since the beginning of May 1864, the Iron Brigade did not materially participate at Cold Harbor. Since the opening of the 1864 campaigning, the brigade had lost 902 killed, wounded, and missing. Nolan, *Iron Brigade*, 274.

163. The soldier Ray mentions was a member of the 28th Massachusetts, which was one of the regiments of another legendary outfit—the Irish Brigade. The brigade's soldiers "fell in heaps" at Cold Harbor and its commander, Colonel Richard Byrnes, was killed there. *OR* 36, pt. 1, 390-391.

164. Using a ruse, Grant stole a march on Lee by crossing the James River and moving against the vital railroad center of Petersburg, without which the Confederate capital could not be held. He constructed a long pontoon bridge over the wide river and began shifting his men

out of their lines toward the James on June 12, 1864, with the actual crossing beginning two days later. It was one of history's greatest military movements.

165. William "Baldy" Smith's men had not taken Petersburg, although they had an excellent opportunity to do so. After successfully fooling Lee, the vanguard of Grant's army under Winfield Hancock marched for Petersburg. Smith, whose corps belonged to Butler's army on Bermuda Hundred, had orders from Grant to assault the city, and Hancock's corps could have assisted. Unfortunately, confused orders and other events, including excessive timidity, prevented the capture of the lightly defended Petersburg on June 15. Heavier fighting took place on June 16, but no full scale determined assaults to capture the place were made. Additional attacks and fighting took place on June 17, although by this date Lee was convinced Grant was below the river and had begun reinforcing Petersburg. The best opportunity to end the war in the East that summer slipped away. The Seventh Wisconsin lost 17 men at Petersburg on June 18, 1864, and 10 more in the fighting on the Petersburg line over the next few days. Fox, *Regimental Losses*, 397.

166. **Chipman**, Cassville, enlisted February 6, 1864, wounded Wilderness, transferred to Veteran Reserve Corps, April 24, 1865. *Wisconsin Roster,* 559.

167. **Weber**, Potosi, enlisted March 3, 1864, died of disease July 28, 1864. *Wisconsin Roster,* 561.

168. After the initial effort to capture Petersburg fizzled, both sides rushed up additional reinforcements and dug in. Grant's efforts were intended to extend his lines south and west of the city, stretching Lee's thin army and severing the several rail lines that fed the capital and enemy army.

169. Ray has confused the names of the engagements and areas of Sherman's battles in Georgia. At this time the Federal armies in Georgia were pressing against Joe Johnston's Kennesaw Mountain defenses, which were just a handful of miles from Marietta, Georgia. Sherman assaulted Johnston's men on Kennesaw on June 27, 1864, and was repulsed with heavy loss. Lookout Mountain, in Tennessee, fell to Joe Hooker's men the previous November during the fighting around Chattanooga.

170. Fort Monroe was erected during the 1820s and 1830s for the coastal defense of the United States. Its guns swept the waters of Hampton Roads, where the James River reaches the Chesapeake Bay. Faust, *Civil War Encyclopedia*, 277.

171. By the time Ray returned to the lines, the Fifth Corps under General Warren was holding a stretch of entrenchments southeast of Petersburg, with its right near the Jerusalem Plank Road, and its left near the Norfolk and Petersburg Railroad.

172. This area of the line was part of Burnside's Ninth Corps sector. Unbeknownst to Ray, Federal engineers were at this time extending a lengthy tunnel under the works there with the intention of packing its end gallery with tons of gunpowder and blasting open a breach in the enemy works.

173. The Confederate raider CSS *Alabama* was sunk by USS *Kearsarge* off Cherbourg, France, on June 19, 1864. Faust, *Civil War Encyclopedia*, 3.

174. Ray is referring to a large detachment of Confederates under Jubal Early sent by Lee to the Shenandoah Valley to thwart Federal efforts there and hopefully drain off Federals from around Petersburg. This column, about 14,000 men, moved north of the Potomac River and

was operating in Maryland and threatening Washington, D.C. Horatio Wright's Sixth Corps was dispatched by Grant to counter the threat and protect Washington.

175. The battle to which Ray is referring was Monocacy, fought on July 9, 1864, southeast of Frederick, Maryland. There, Early's Confederates, about 10,000 strong, were confronted by General Lew Wallace's scratch force of about 6,000. The Federals were routed after a spirited fight, but the engagement delayed Early's advance toward Washington. Wallace lost about 2,000 men, most of them captured or missing, while Early lost about 700 men to all causes.

176. On July 11, Early's exhausted Confederates approached the outskirts of Washington, D. C. Skirmishing broke out there, primarily around Fort Stevens. Since it was late in the day, Early ordered an assault for the following morning. Troops from the Nineteenth Corps had recently arrived from New Orleans, and elements of Wright's Sixth Corps (from Petersburg) were pouring into Washington just in time to confront Early. Once he realized he was outnumbered by Army of the Potomac and other veterans better than two-to-one, Early decided to withdraw, ending the threat to Washington.

177. By July 17, 1864, General Sherman was below the Chattahoochee River just a handful of miles from Atlanta. On that day President Davis, unable to get a firm answer from Joe Johnston as to how he planned to arrest Sherman's relentless march into Georgia, sacked him and elevated General John B. Hood in his place. The news from Georgia was decidedly in favor of the Federals.

178. Gabions were cylindrical baskets about three feet high and two feet in diameter. Facines were bundles of saplings used mostly for the sides of trenches.

179. By July 22, 1864, Sherman had waged two major battles against Hood's Confederates, the first at Peach Tree Creek on July 20, and the second two days later called the battle of Atlanta. Casualties on both sides were high, but Hood could not afford the losses he suffered. Ray's news about William Sooy Smith was incorrect. Smith led a cavalry expedition from Tennessee into Mississippi and was beaten by General Nathan B. Forrest at both West Point and Okolona, Mississippi. The disaster embarrassed and enraged Sherman.

180. Sherman had not yet captured Atlanta.

181. The mine was originally the brainchild of Lt. Col. Henry Pleasants, a Pennsylvania officer and former coal miner. Pleasants convinced his superiors that the plan to dig a 500-foot shaft and fill it with explosives undetected was possible, and the plan eventually secured the blessings of General Grant. The men began digging the shaft on June 25, 1864, which was completed on July 23, 1864. Several more days were needed to place the powder charges. The Confederates knew the Federals were digging a mine and unsuccessfully sunk a number of countermines in an attempt to locate it. For an excellent account of this engagement, see Michael Cavanaugh and William Marvel, *The Horrid Pit: The Battle of the Crater* (Lynchburg, VA., 1989).

182. The fuse failed at a splice and two brave members of the 48th Pennsylvania Infantry volunteered to enter the shaft and light it.

183. The explosion took place about 4:45 a.m. when four tons of gunpowder blew a hole in the Confederate lines about 170 feet long and 60 to 80 feet wide. The blast carried men, horses, dirt, rocks, and artillery pieces high into the sky in a giant mushroom cloud of debris. The unfortunate Southerners surprised in this manner comprised some nine companies of

South Carolinians from the 19th and 22nd regiments. About 300 of them were killed or wounded instantly.

184. General Burnside had been training a division of black troops under the command of General Edward Ferrero to rush and enlarge the expected breach in the line, but Generals Meade and Grant believed that if the attempt failed they would be accused of recklessly using black troops in a desperate affair. As a result, just before the attack was to begin, Burnside was ordered to use a different (white) division of troops. Burnside's most inept subordinate, James Ledlie, a notorious drunkard, drew the short straw. Although his men bravely charged into action, Ledlie remained behind in a bombproof shelter, imbibing alcohol. The white soldiers were not trained for the task, and instead of bypassing the large hole in the ground and driving forward, they poured into it, where they soon found themselves trapped.

185. Once the Confederates recovered from the initial shock of the massive explosion, they promptly coordinated to strike the flanks of the attackers and contain the breach. Southern artillery was fired into the attackers from several directions and infantry began smothering the area with musket fire. Burnside, meanwhile, continued feeding troops into the small space (including Ferrero's black division), which simply packed them into and around the smoking crater so tightly that they could barely move. The Southern counterattack was led by General William Mahone, whose division sealed off the tear in the line and held the attackers in place. Many atrocities took place in and around the Crater, especially when the Southern troops discovered that many of the trapped attackers were black. Much of this was clearly visible to William Ray.

186. By 1:00 p.m. the attack was over and those Federals who could ran the gauntlet of fire back to their lines. Casualties were extremely heavy. Federal losses totaled almost 4,000 from all causes, while Confederate losses probably came in around 1,500. Another excellent opportunity to divide Lee's thin army in two was wasted.

187. On July 28, Sherman fought the third of the three large scale battles for Atlanta in eight days at Ezra Church, a hard-fought defensive victory. Atlanta was now all but doomed.

188. Ferrero's black soldiers fought exceptionally well that day, and indeed "barbarities" took place; many of the blacks were shot after they surrendered, or were not allowed to do so.

189. Confederate cavalry under the command of John McCausland burned part of Chambersburg, Pennsylvania, on July 30, 1864.

190. On August 4, 1864, Admiral David Farragut guided a fleet of wooden warships and iron monitors past Confederate forts and defeated a smaller Confederate fleet. The battle for Mobile Bay shut an important Southern port and led to the capture of the ironclad CSS *Tennessee*.

191. **Cook** [Webster], Beetown, enlisted August 19, 1861, wounded Wilderness, mustered out July 3, 1865. *Wisconsin Roster*, 559.

192. Federal operations to cut the Weldon Railroad, which ran south from Petersburg into the deep South, began on June 22, 1864. After the first attempt to cut the line failed, Grant suspended operations until mid-August, when Warren's Fifth Corps (including the Iron Brigade) left its entrenchments on August 14-15 and headed south and west. Early on the morning of August 18, Warren's four divisions advanced against weak opposition and seized Globe Tavern, about six miles south of Petersburg, and the heavy fighting began. The Iron Brigade was led at this time by Colonel Edward S. Bragg, who had replaced Colonel

Robinson in June 1864. The brigade moved north against Henry Heth's Confederates with its left flank near the railroad.

193. The Confederates shifted heavy reinforcements south to meet the thrust against the Weldon line under the command of A. P. Hill. The Iron Brigade went into action on August 19 on the far right near the Aiken house against Confederates led by Alfred Colquitt and David Weisiger. The fighting was heavy and fought over very confusing wooded terrain. The sharp Southern attacks drove back the Federals, although Warren was able to counterattack and reestablish his positions. Remarkably, losses in the Seventh Wisconsin were very light.

194. The Iron Brigade had been pulled back and was now facing west parallel and on the west side of the railroad after element's from Burnside's Ninth Corps replaced Warren's troops near the previous day's fight. The brigade's position was strong and behind good field works. The attack repulsed by Ray and his comrades was led by Johnson Hagood's South Carolinians. Dennis Dailey was in command of the two companies of the Second Wisconsin that remained with the brigade after the Second was mustered out. At the battle of Weldon Railroad on August 21, 1864, Dailey rode into the Confederate line demanding Johnson surrender. He was shot from his horse by General Hagood (Hagood was not wounded in the encounter). Dailey recovered from his wound and was among the Second Wisconsin men merged into the Sixth Wisconsin in November 1864. William J. K. Beaudot, "The Bravest Act of the War," *Virginia Country's Civil War Quarterly*, Vol. VI, 1986. Federal losses in the attack were minimal compared to Southern casualties.

Several members of the Iron Brigade were detached during the Weldon Railroad fighting to serve nearby artillery pieces.

195. Reams' Station was a stop on the Weldon Railroad about two miles below Globe Tavern. Fresh (but tired) Federal troops from Hancock's Second Corps were dispatched to break up the rail line south of Warren's Fifth Corps. Ray was hearing a battle involving Hancock's troops and the attacking Confederates under A. P. Hill. After several attacks, one of which broke through the Federal lines, the Confederates were beaten back.

196. Hancock's Second Corps managed to repulse Hill's troops but at a heavy cost. Federal losses were about 2,400 men, half of whom were missing or captured; Hill's losses are unknown, but were not as heavy.

Volume 13

197. This is the reference mentioned in the previous chapter that helped identify the subject matter of the loose pages in the back of Volume 12.

198. **Morse**, Tafton, enlisted August 19, 1861, wounded Laurel Hill and Petersburg, mustered out July 3, 1865. *Wisconsin Roster, 560.*

199. **Branham**, Potosi, enlisted August 19, 1861, detached Battery B, 4th U.S. Artillery until January 1864, mustered out July 3, 1865. *Wisconsin Roster, 558.*

200. The garrisons of the forts defending the entrance to Mobile Bay—Gaines, Morgan, and Powell—were placed under a quasi-siege and ultimately surrendered. Fort Morgan was the last to fall on August 23, 1864.

201. **Roberts**, Beetown, enlisted August 19, 1861, promoted to 1st lieutenant December 13, 1864, wounded Five Forks, discharged June 1, 1865. *Wisconsin Roster,* 558.

202. The rumors were finally true. The final major battle for Atlanta was fought at Jonesborough on August 31, 1864, and Confederates evacuated the city that night. General Philip Sheridan, Grant's cavalry commander, was sent to the Shenandoah Valley to deal with Jubal Early's Confederates.

203. Ray is describing (with remarkable accuracy) what is commonly known as Hampton's Beefsteak Raid. The cavalry operation, September 11-16, 1864, took place south of the James River at Coggin's Point and netted about 2,500 head of cattle and 300 prisoners at the cost of only 61 casualties. Ray was correct; the food was desperately needed by Lee's army, and the raid was a morale booster for the embattled Southerners.

204. The news was correct. Although outnumbered, Early managed to mount a stout defensive effort against Sheridan's fumbling offensive on September 19, 1864. Eventually Federal numbers began to tell and the Southerners were driven from the field with heavy losses. Federal casualties were about 3,600; Confederate losses were about 4,000. Several high ranking generals fell on both sides, including Confederate General Robert Rodes and Federal General David A. Russell, both of whom were killed.

205. **Gilbert**, Tafton, enlisted August 9, 1861, wounded Gainesville and mustered out July 3, 1865. *Wisconsin Roster,* 559.

206. After Third Winchester, Sheridan followed Early's routed army south to Fisher's Hill, where another major action was fought on September 22, 1864.

207. The second battle Ray is referring to was Fisher's Hill, where Sheridan attacked Early's Confederates on September 22, 1864. Sheridan routed the Confederates and, from all outward appearances, seemed to have ended the Southern threat in the Valley. Sheridan's losses were only about 500, while Early lost almost three times that number.

208. General Benjamin Butler was penned up on Bermuda Hundred, and did not sever the railroad between Petersburg and Richmond, nor was the former city being evacuated. The canal to which Ray refers is the Dutch Gap Canal, which Butler's men were digging across a 175-yard neck of land in an effort to bypass Confederate batteries at Drewry's Bluff.

209. The fighting involved two major actions in a two-pronged Federal offensive north and south of the James River. The battle of Fort Harrison was the result of Grant's attempt to pierce the outer defenses of Richmond and convince Lee not to reinforce Early in the Shenandoah Valley. The Federals captured Fort Harrison, which was considered so important that both Generals Lee and Grant were at one point directing tactical operations. Other attempts were beaten back. South of the river and closer to Ray's position was the fighting at Peebles' Farm, which was an attempt to stretch the lines further west in the hope of cutting the Southside Railroad. Several days of effort eventually stretched the lines another three miles to the west and south, but the railroad remained in Southern hands. Casualties were heavy on both sides. A fine and detailed study of these actions can be found in Richard Sommers, *Richmond Redeemed: The Siege at Petersburg* (New York, NY., 1981).

210. Ray is not far off. By October 5, 1864, the Federal lines stretched from a point well west of the Weldon Railroad below Petersburg up to the Appomattox River, and from up around the northeast side of Richmond, a distance of more than thirty miles.

211. The rumor was in fact true. After the evacuation of Atlanta, General Hood moved his army north astride the Chattanooga-Atlanta Railroad, behind William T. Sherman, where he broke up the track in the hope of cutting Sherman's supply line and forcing his withdrawal. He was unsuccessful.

212. **Drew**, Orion, enlisted August 19, 1861, wounded South Mountain and mustered out July 3, 1865. *Wisconsin Roster*, 559.

213. Ray is probably referring to the fighting at Tom's Brook in the Shenandoah Valley, where Federal cavalry under George Custer and Wesley Merritt attacked their Southern counterpart. Several hundred prisoners were taken and the enemy was driven many miles.

214. Although Sheridan and many others believed General Early's Confederate army was no longer a major threat after Fisher's Hill, they were wrong. On October 19, 1864, Early launched one of the great surprise attacks of the war at Cedar Creek. Sheridan was absent from the army at a conference. The Confederates drove the Federals for several hours before Sheridan returned, rallied his divisions, and routed Early. Federal losses were about 5,500 to all causes, while the Confederates lost at least 3,000 (this number is probably low). General Longstreet did not play a role in the fighting, although he did return to the Army of Northern Virginia on October 19, 1864, following the crippling wound he had suffered in the Wilderness on May 6, 1864. Cedar Creek was the last major battle of the Civil War in the Shenandoah Valley. For a good account of this action, see Theodore Mahr, *The Battle of Cedar Creek: Showdown in the Shenandoah* (Lynchburg, VA., 1992).

215. Ray was part of a major movement of three corps at the end of October 1864 when Grant acted again to cut the Southside Railroad, which fed Lee's army. Ray's brigade (part of Warren's Fifth Corps) was engaged near Hatcher's Run, with Parke's Ninth Corps (formerly under Burnside) operating on the right, and Hancock's Second Corps operating on the left along the Boydton Plank Road.

216. The heavy fighting was indeed Hancock's Corps, which was heavily engaged on the Boydton Plank Road at Burgess' Mill (also called Hatcher's Run). While Parke's Ninth Corps was holding the Confederates in place, Warren's and Hancock's corps were ordered to encircle the southern and western end of the enemy line and roll it up. There was a lack of cooperation and coordination between Warren and Hancock, however, and the attack was beaten back. The critical Southside Railroad and Boydton Plank Road remained in Southern hands. Federal losses were about 1,800 to all causes; Confederate losses are unknown, but were probably lighter. Ray's Iron Brigade saw only light action and lost one killed, 10 wounded, and eight prisoners. *OR* 42. Pt. 1, 507.

217. The men marched down the Vaughn Road to the Armstrong house, and there crossed over to the south side of Hatcher's Run, where they formed the line of battle described by Ray. The subsequent advance by the Iron Brigade met little resistance.

218. The brigade crossed Hatcher's Run again on a bridge built during the night. Ray is wrong about prisoners. In reality, the brigade had captured 224 prisoners, "belong principally to [General William] Mahone's division." *OR* 42. Pt. 1, 507.

219. **Blunt**, Patch Grove, enlisted February 25, 1864, wounded Wilderness and Petersburg, killed March 31, 1865, Gravelly Run; **Booth [George]**, Potosi, enlisted January 2, 1864, mustered out July 3, 1865. *Wisconsin Roster*, 558.

220. **Davis**, Stoughton, enlisted July 1, 1864, from Company D, absent sick at muster out of the regiment. *Wisconsin Roster,* 539.

221. Grant may have claimed success, but the movement's objectives (to cut the Southside Railroad and capture the Boydton Plank Road) had not been met. Still, Lee's battle lines were stretched much longer, and the threat to his supply lines was greater than ever before.

222. The American Tract Society, a nondenominational Christian publishing house, was founded in 1825 by the merger of several small printing establishments. Believing that a very effective and inexpensive way to reach most of the world's peoples with the story of Jesus Christ was through the printed page, the Society produced Christian books, booklets, magazines, and leaflets. Each year the Society made available to prisons, hospitals, and missionary organizations free materials for their distribution. Military servicemen in seven major wars were provided Christian literature by the Society as well as the cadets at West Point, who received Bibles each year. In the 1840s, the Society began distribution of its materials through messengers, known as Colporteurs. These men, preferably single, were usually ministers or seminary students sent out and supported by various societies. Occasionally called on to preach, their primary tasks were distribution of materials and fundraising. Financial support for the Society's ministry depended (as they do now) upon the charitable contributions of their Christian friends.

223. Sherman left some troops behind to watch Hood's Confederate army, which was moving through Alabama and into Tennessee, while he struck out across a largely undefended Georgia on his famous March to the Sea.

224. The rumors were true. Sherman's men were burning and tearing up railroad track, bridges, and private property in the drive through Georgia. On November 22, General Slocum's wing captured the capital of Georgia at Milledgeville.

225. Ray and his comrades were taking part in a major move by Warren's corps to destroy as much of the Weldon Railroad to the south as possible, to deny its use to Lee.

226. The destruction of the line continued throughout December 9, 1864, and included the burning of a bridge across Three-Mile Creek. During the entire operation the brigade lost nine men to all causes. The brigade returned to its old camp by the evening of December 12, 1864.

227. According to the brigade's commander, General Edward Bragg, the attack on the rear guard took place on December 12, and the Rebels consisted of cavalry. *OR* 42, pt. 1, p. 508.

228. **Turnbull**, St. Croix Falls, enlisted January 13, 1865, discharged June 2, 1865, disability. *Wisconsin Roster,* 561.

229. Sherman was investing Savannah, Georgia, which was evacuated by the Confederates on December 20, 1864. In Tennessee, Hood's Army of Tennessee attacked General John Schofield's Federals at Franklin and suffered one of the bloodiest repulses of the war. Schofield withdrew to Nashville and Hood's men followed. There, General George Thomas and the Army of the Cumberland attacked Hood's weakened and demoralized army on December 15-16, routing it completely. Thomas's victory was one of the most decisive of the war. For all practical purposes, the Confederate Army of Tennessee, the primary Southern field army other than Lee's Army of Northern Virginia, had ceased to exist as an effective fighting force.

Volume 14

230. General Butler was indeed finally relieved of duty. He had been placed in command of an attempt to capture Fort Fisher, a large bastion protecting the last Confederate port of Wilmington, North Carolina. The Christmas Day 1864 attempt was a fiasco from start to finish. That very visible failure, coupled with Lincoln's successful reelection, finally allowed the Federal high command the luxury of sacking the political general on January 7, 1865.

231. A new mammoth effort against Fort Fisher began on January 13, 1865, with a massive bombardment from a large naval flotilla. It continued the next day. Thousands of troops landed on the sandy beaches and stormed the bastion on January 15, 1865. After several hours of hard and often hand-to-hand fighting, the fort fell. The best account of the entire Wilmington Campaign, including the fighting that followed the fall of Fort Fisher, is Chris E. Fonvielle, Jr., *Last Rays of Departing Hope: The Wilmington Campaign* (Campbell, CA., 1997).

232. What Ray actually heard was the battle of Trent's Reach, a fascinating affair that involved an attempt by the three ironclads of the Confederate James River Squadron (and assorted smaller wooden vessels) to break through the obstructions on the James River and attack Grant's supply base at City Point. It was a move born of desperation and failed utterly.

233. The Confederates Ray refers to were delegates selected to discuss possible terms for settling the war. They were Vice President Alexander Stephens, John A. Campbell, and Robert M. T. Hunter. The trio met with President Lincoln and Secretary of State William Seward aboard the *River Queen* at Hampton Roads. The conference was not successful in reaching a resolution to the conflict.

234. Paper in back of journal in pieces reads as follows:

Camp 7th Regt. Wis. Vet. Vol.
Wm R. Ray

Sir, we the undersigned members of Co. F. do not consider you a competent man for the place in which you are now acting and we politely request you two return the company Books over two the commanding Officer of the co with a request that you be Relieved By So doing you will greatly oblige all concerned.

R. A. Turnbull	
Thomas W. Bailey	William Branstetter
Cyrus Alexander	Charles Livens
William Atkinson	Andrew Bishop
Isaac G Reamer	Richard Lesler
Nathan Bradberry	Bruce Bryan
Albert H Morse	James H Endicott
Joseph Wilkinson	Peter Bryan
George W McClare	Perry Gilbert
Michael Inlough	Clarance H Fitzgerald
George Booth	Andrew H Connor

235. Ray was listening to another major effort by Grant to reach the Boydton Plank Road and hold it. This time the area around Hatcher's Run was reached without difficulty on February 5, 1865, by elements of the Second and Fifth Corps. Lee attempted to block the move, but was unsuccessful doing so. The fighting was moderately heavy. This action is known as Hatcher's Run or Dabney's Mill. The fighting intensified on February 6, 1865. Warren's Corps was eventually pushed back by Confederate reinforcements, but the Federal lines had once again been lengthened appreciably.

236. Federal losses for Ray's brigade at Hatcher's Run (which Ray missed) were heavy, totalling 213 from all causes. *OR* 46, pt. 1, 66.

237. Edward Bragg, Ray's brigade commander, came into the army as a captain in the Sixth Wisconsin and quickly climbed the chain of command. He became a prominent Congressman after the war and had a long political career. Colonel Henry Morrow of the Twenty-fourth Michigan, and many of the soldiers, blamed Bragg's drunkenness for causing the delay which led to the Sixth and Seventh Wisconsin not being sent with the Michigan regiment. In fact, the decision might have been the result of an earlier request by division commander Samuel Crawford that the Western regiments be retained. The War Department had asked General U. S. Grant for a brigade of reliable troops for special duty. General George Meade selected the brigade with the Western regiments, but Crawford asked the orders be changed. *OR* 46, pt. 2, 513, 519-20, 532-33.

238. The brigade included the 91st New York Infantry (the "Albany Regiment"), and was the First Brigade (Kellogg), Third Division (Crawford), Fifth Corps (Warren).

239. Sherman had indeed captured Columbia, South Carolina, on February 17, 1865; Charleston, South Carolina, was evacuated by the Confederates on the same day. Lee had dispatched his cavalry commander, Wade Hampton, to help raise troops in that area and try to arrest Sherman's progress.

240. Phil Sheridan's cavalry met Jubal Early's remnant army one last time at Wayneboro, Virginia, on March 2, 1865. The troopers easily defeated and dispersed the Southerners, effectively ending Early's Civil War career. He was not, however, captured by Sheridan.

241. **Alexander [Cyrus]**, Patch Grove, enlisted December 31, 1863, wounded Laurel Hill, mustered out July 3, 1865. *Wisconsin Roster,* 558.

242. The Confederate attack was a desperate gambit against Fort Stedman, east of Petersburg. Lee ordered the assault in the hope of breaking through Grant's lines and ending the siege of the city. Although the initial thrust was successful, it quickly bogged down in confusion and strong Federal opposition put an end to the affair within a few hours. Federal losses were about 1,500 from all causes, while Lee lost about 4,000 soldiers, the majority of them prisoners.

243. Unbeknownst to Ray and his comrades, the final campaign of the Civil War in the Eastern Theater was underway. The move was part of Grant's effort to keep Lee's lines stretched to the breaking point while he tried to turn the Confederate far right.

244. On March 29, 1865, Crawford's division, including Ray's brigade, advanced north and west from the Boydton Plank Road into a morass of woods and streams fed by Gravelly Run, which lended its name to the fighting that day (also called battle of White Oak Road.) The division approached White Oak Road before it met heavy attacks by several small

Confederate brigades and was driven back in confusion. According to Colonel Kellogg, Ray's brigade commander, his men were "the last organized troops to leave the field."

245. General Sherman was attacked in North Carolina at Bentonville on March 19, 1865, by a patchwork collection of Confederate outfits under the command of General Joe Johnston, who was reinstated to command at the request of General Lee. The three-day encounter ended with Johnston's retreat, which also ended the major fighting in that theater of operations. Johnston surrendered to Sherman at Durham Station in North Carolina on April 26, 1865. For an excellent book on Bentonville, see Mark L. Bradley, *Last Stand in the Carolinas: The Battle of Bentonville* (Campbell, CA., 1996).

246. Libby Prison and Castle Thunder were tobacco warehouses used as prisons in Richmond, Virginia.

247. **Bryan**, Beetown, enlisted January 23, 1864, wounded Wilderness, mustered out July 3, 1865. *Wisconsin Roster, 558.*

Volume 15

248. **Connor**, St. Croix Falls, enlisted January 18, 1864, wounded Laurel Hill and mustered out July 3, 1865. *Wisconsin Roster, 559.*

249. The Seventh Wisconsin had 1,029 in ranks when it left the state and reached a total overall figure of 1,932 during its four years of service. It lost 385 by death, 12 missing, 44 by desertion, 106 by transfer and 473 by discharge, mustering out a total of 912. William Ray's own Company F had a total enrollment of 174 over its four years with 31 killed in battle and 13 additional deaths from disease or accident. Fox, *Regimental Losses*, 117; E.B. Quiner, *The Military History of Wisconsin in the War for the Union*, (Chicago 1866) (reprinted 2000 by the St. Croix Valley Civil War Round Table), 482.

Bibliography

MANUSCRIPTS AND RECORDS

Descriptive Book, Seventh Wisconsin Infantry. U.S. National Archives & Records Service.

Morning Reports, Seventh Wisconsin Infantry. U.S. National Archives and Records Service.

Charles King Papers, Carroll College Library, Waukesha, Wis.

Rufus King Papers, Carroll College Library, Waukesha, Wis.

National Guard, Adjutant General's Office, Regimental Descriptive Rolls, Ludolph Longhenry Papers, Private collection.

Order Book, First Brigade, First Division, First Army Corps. U.S. National Archives and Records Service.

Order Book, Seventh Wisconsin Infantry, U.S. National Archives and Records Service.

Jerome A. Watrous Papers, State Historical Society of Wisconsin.

CENSUS AND NUMERICAL RECORDS

Alphabetical List of Soldiers and Sailors of the Late War Residing in the State of Wisconsin, June 20, 1885. Madison, Wis., Secretary of State, 1886.

Dyer, F.H., *A Compendium of the War of the Rebellion*. Des Moines, Iowa, 1908; New York, Thomas Yoseloff, 1953.

Fox, William F., *Regimental Losses in the American Civil War*. Albany, N.Y., Albany Publishing Co., 1889.

Roster of Wisconsin Volunteers, War of the Rebellion, 1861-1865. (2 Vols.) Madison, Wis., 1886.

Wisconsin Census Enumeration, 1895; Names of Ex-Soldiers and Sailors Residing in Wisconsin, June 20, 1895. Madison, Wis., Democrat Printing Co., 1896.

Wisconsin Census Enumeration, 1905; Names of Ex-Soldiers and Sailors Residing in Wisconsin, June 1, 1905. Madison, Wis., Democrat Printing Co., 1896.

BOOKS

Annual Report of the Adjutant General of the State of Wisconsin, Madison, Wis., William J. Park & Co., 1866.

Aubery, Doc [Cullen B.], *Recollections of a Newsboy in the Army of the Potomac.* Milwaukee, 1900. [Contains the monograph, *Echoes of the Marches of the Famous Iron Brigade, 1861-1865*].

Beaudot, William J.K., and Herdegen, Lance J., *An Irishman in the Iron Brigade.* New York, Fordham University Press, 1993.

Beecham, Robert K., "Adventures of an Iron Brigade Man." [Paste-up of a series of articles appearing in *The National Tribune*], 1902.

Beyer, W.F., and O.F. Keydel, eds, *Deeds of Valor,* (2 Vols)., Detroit, Mich. The Perrien-Keydel Company, 1906.

Boatner, Mark M., *Civil War Dictionary. New York, 1959.*

Buell, Augustus, *The Cannoneer; Recollections of Service in the Army of the Potomac.* Washington, D.C. The National Tribune, 1897.

Byer, F. H., *A Compendium of the War of the Rebellion.* Des Moines, Iowa. 1908.

Cheek, Philip, and Mair Pointon, *History of the Sauk County Riflemen, Known as Company "A" Sixth Wisconsin Veteran Volunteer Infantry, 1861-1865.* [N.P.], 1909.

Coddington, Edwin B., *The Gettysburg Campaign.* New York, Charles Scribner's Sons, 1968.

Current, Richard N., *The History of Wisconsin : The Civil War Era, 1848-1873.* Madison, State Historical Society of Wisconsin, 1976.

Curtis, O[rson] B., *History of the Twenty-Fourth Michigan of the Iron Brigade.* Detroit, Winn & Hammond, 1891.

Dawes, Rufus R., *Service with the Sixth Wisconsin Volunteers.* Marietta, Ohio, E.R. Alderman & Sons, 1890.

Dawes, Rufus R., "Sketches of War History." Military Order of the Loyal Legion of the United States, Commandery of the State of Ohio, *War Papers,* Vol. III. [Reprinted in: *Service with the Sixth Wisconsin Volunteers.* Dayton, Ohio, Morningside Books, 1984.]

Dictionary of Wisconsin Biography, Madison, State Historical Society of Wisconsin, 1961.

Dudley, William W., *The Iron Brigade at Gettysburg, 1878, Official Report of the Part Borne by the 1st Brigade, 1st Division, 1st Army Corps.* Cincinnati, privately printed, 1879.

Faust, Patricia, ed, *Historical Times Illustrated Encyclopedia of the Civil War. New York, Harper Perennial, 1876.*

Fitch, Michael H., *Echoes of the Civil War as I Hear Them.* New York, 1905.

[Flower, Frank A.], *History of Milwaukee Wisconsin. Chicago,* Western Historical Co., 1881.

Freeman, Douglas S., *Lee's Lieutenants.* (3 vols.) New York, Charles Scribner's Sons, 1942-1944.

Gaff, Alan D., *Brave Men's Tears: The Iron Brigade at Brawner Farm.* Dayton, Ohio, Morningside House, 1985.

Gaff, Alan D., *If This is War: A History of the Campaign of Bull's Run by the Wisconsin Regiment Thereafter Known as the Ragged Ass Second*. Dayton, Ohio, Morningside Press, 1991.

Gaff, Alan D., *On Many of Bloody Field: Four Years in the Iron Brigade*. Bloomington, Indiana, Indiana University Press, 1997.

Gaff, Alan D., and Maureen Gaff, *Our Boys: A Civil War Photograph Album*. Evansville, Indiana, Windmill, 1996.

Gibbon, John, *Personal Recollections of the Civil War*. New York, G.P. Putnam's Sons, 1928.

Gramm, Kent, *Gettysburg: A Meditation on War and Values*. Bloomington, Indiana, Indiana University Press, 1994.

Hennessy, John J., *Return to Bull Run: The Campaign and Battle of Second Manassas*. New York, Simon & Schuster, 1993.

Herdegen, Lance J., *The Men Stood Like Iron: How the Iron Brigade Won Its Name*. Bloomington, Indiana, Indiana University Press, 1997.

Herdegen, Lance J. and William J.K. Beaudot, *In the Bloody Railroad Cut at Gettysburg*. Dayton, Ohio, Morningside House, 1990.

Hurn, Ethel Alice, *Wisconsin Women in the War Between the States*. Madison, Wis., Wisconsin History Commission, 1911.

Johnson, Robert U. and Clarence C. Buel, eds. *Battles and Leaders of the Civil War*. (4 Vols.) New York, The Century Co., 1884-1887.

Kellogg, John A., *Capture and Escape: A Narrative of Army and Prison Life*. Madison, Wis., Wisconsin History Commission, 1908.

Klement, Frank L., *Wisconsin and the Civil War*. Madison, State Historical Society of Wisconsin, 1963. [Originally published in the *Blue Book of the State of Wisconsin*, 1961.]

Lassen, Coralou Peel, *Dear Sarah: Letters Home from a Soldier of the Iron Brigade*. Bloomington, Indiana, Indiana University Press, 1999.

Linderman, Gerald F., *Embattled Courage: The Experience of Combat in the American Civil War*. New York, The Free Press, 1987.

Long, E.B. [and] Barbara Long, *The Civil War Day by Day; An Almanac, 1861-1865*. Garden City, N.Y., Doubleday, 1971.

Love, William D., *Wisconsin in the War of the Rebellion*. Chicago, Church & Goodman, 1866.

McClellan, George B., *McClellan's Own Story*. Philadelphia, J.B. Lippincott & Co., 1887.

McPherson, James M., *Battle Cry of Freedom*. New York, Ballantine Books, 1989.

Mitchell, Reid, *Civil War Soldiers*. New York, Viking, 1988.

Nolan, Alan T., *The Iron Brigade*. New York, Macmillan, 1961.

Otis, George H., *The Second Wisconsin Infantry*, with letters and recollections by other members of the regiment, ed. by Alan D. Gaff. Dayton, Ohio, Morningside Press, 1984. [Originally serialized in *The Milwaukee Sunday Telegraph* in 11 parts between July-December, 1880.]

Quiner, E[dwin] B., *The Military History of Wisconsin*. Chicago, Clarke & Co., 1866.

Reid-Green, Marcia, ed., *Letters Home: Henry Matrau of the Iron Brigade*. Lincoln, Nebraska, University of Nebraska Press, 1993.

Smith, Donald, *The Twenty-fourth Michigan of the Iron Brigade.* Harrisburg, Pa., Stackpole Co., 1962.

Soldiers' and Citizens' Album of Biographical Record, 2 vols. Chicago, Grand Army Publishing Company, 1888.

Steensma, Robert C., ed., *Drifting Along to an Unknown Future: The Civil War Letters of James E. Northup and Samuel W. Northup.* Sioux Falls, S.D., The Center for Western Studies, Augustana College, 2000.

Still, Bayrd, *Milwaukee, The History of a City.* Madison, Wis., State Historical Society of Wisconsin, 1948.

Stine, J.H., *History of the Army of the Potomac.* Philadelphia, J.B. Rogers Printing Co., 1892.

Swinton, William, *Campaigns of the Army of the Potomac.* New York, Charles B. Richardson, 1866.

Vipound, Sharon Eggleston and Nolan, Alan T., eds., *Giants in Their Tall Black Hats: Essays on the Iron Brigade.* Bloomington, Indiana, Indiana University Press, 1998.

War of the Rebellion, Official Records of the Union and Confederate Armies. Washington, D.C., United States Government Printing Office, 1889-1900.

War Papers Read Before the Commandery of the State of Wisconsin, Military Order of the Loyal Legion of the United States, Vol. I., Milwaukee, 1896.

War Papers Read Before the Commandery of the State of Wisconsin, Military Order of the Loyal Legion of the United States, Vol. II., Milwaukee, 1896.

War Papers Read Before the Commandery of the State of Wisconsin, Military Order of the Loyal Legion of the United States, Vol. III., Milwaukee, 1903.

Warner, Ezra J., *Generals in Blue: Lives of Union Commanders.* Baton Rouge, 1964.

Washburn, William H., *Jerome A. Watrous: The Civil War Years.* Madison, Wis., Wisconsin Veterans Museum, Unpublished manuscript.

Watrous, J[erome] A., *Richard Epps and Other Stories.* Milwaukee, 1906.

Wert, Jeffry D., *A Brotherhood of Valor: The Common Soldiers of the Stonewall Brigade, C.S.A., and the Iron Brigade, U.S.A.* New York, Simon & Schuster, 1999.

Whitehouse, Hugh L., ed., *Letters from the Iron Brigade: George W. Partridge, Jr., 1839-1863.* Indianapolis, Guild Press of Indiana, 1994.

INDEX